ECONOMIC ISSUES, PROBLEMS AND PERSPECTIVES

THE FEDERAL BUDGET PROCESS

AN INTRODUCTION

ECONOMIC ISSUES, PROBLEMS AND PERSPECTIVES

Additional books in this series can be found on Nova's website under the Series tab.

Additional E-books in this series can be found on Nova's website under the E-book tab.

GOVERNMENT PROCEDURES AND OPERATIONS

Additional books in this series can be found on Nova's website under the Series tab.

Additional E-books in this series can be found on Nova's website under the E-book tab.

ECONOMIC ISSUES, PROBLEMS AND PERSPECTIVES

THE FEDERAL BUDGET PROCESS

AN INTRODUCTION

ADELE WILKINSON
EDITOR

NOVINKA

New York

For permission to use material from this book please contact us:
Telephone 631-231-7269; Fax 631-231-8175
Web Site: http://www.novapublishers.com

Additional color graphics may be available in the e-book version of this book.

Library of Congress Cataloging-in-Publication Data

ISBN: 978-1-62417-838-2

Published by Nova Science Publishers, Inc. † New York

CONTENTS

PREFACE

Budgeting for the federal government is an enormously complex process. It entails dozens of subprocesses, countless rules and procedures, the efforts of tens of thousands of staff persons in the executive and legislative branches, millions of work hours each year, and the active participation of the President and the congressional leaders, as well as other members of Congress and executive officials. This book provides an introduction to the federal budget process with a focus on the executive and congressional process; points of order in the congressional budget process; and issues for the fiscal year 2013 federal budget and beyond.

Chapter 1 – Budgeting for the federal government is an enormously complex process. It entails dozens of subprocesses, countless rules and procedures, the efforts of tens of thousands of staff persons in the executive and legislative branches, millions of work hours each year, and the active participation of the President and congressional leaders, as well as other members of Congress and executive officials.

The enforcement of budgetary decisions involves a complex web of procedures that encompasses both congressional and executive actions. In the last four decades or so, these procedures have been rooted principally in two statutes—the Congressional Budget Act of 1974 and the Balanced Budget and Emergency Deficit Control Act of 1985. The 1974 act established a congressional budget process in which budget policies are enforced by Congress during the consideration of individual measures. The 1985 act embodies additional statutory enforcement procedures, substantially modified in 1990 and 1997, that have been used by the executive to enforce budget policies after the end of a congressional session. The 1997 iteration of these enforcement procedures were set aside in the latter years of their existence and effectively expired toward the end of the 107th Congress. Efforts to renew them in the 108th through 110th Congresses were not successful. In the 111th Congress, the pay-as-you-go procedures affecting direct spending and revenue legislation were restored in a modified version by the Statutory Pay-As-You-Go Act of 2010.

More recently, in the 112th Congress, statutory limits on discretionary spending and a new automatic process to reduce spending were established by the Budget Control Act of 2011.

The President's budget is required by law to be submitted to Congress early in the legislative session. While the budget is only a request to Congress, the power to formulate and submit the budget is a vital tool in the President's direction of the executive branch and of national policy. The President's proposals often influence congressional revenue and spending decisions, though the extent of the influence varies from year to year and depends more on political and fiscal conditions than on the legal status of the budget.

The Congressional Budget Act of 1974 establishes the congressional budget process as the means by which Congress coordinates the various budget-related actions (such as the consideration of appropriations and revenue measures) taken by it during the course of the year. The process is centered on an annual concurrent resolution on the budget that sets aggregate budget policies and functional spending priorities for at least the next five fiscal years.

Because a concurrent resolution is not a law—it cannot be signed or vetoed by the President—the budget resolution does not have statutory effect; no money can be raised or spent pursuant to it. Revenue and spending amounts set in the budget resolution establish the basis for the enforcement of congressional budget policies through points of order.

Congress implements budget resolution policies through action on individual revenue and debt- limit measures, annual appropriations acts, and direct spending legislation.

In some years, Congress considers reconciliation legislation pursuant to reconciliation instructions in the budget resolution. Reconciliation legislation is used mainly to bring existing revenue and direct spending laws into conformity with budget resolution policies. Initially, reconciliation was a major tool for deficit reduction; in later years, reconciliation was used mainly to reduce revenues.

Chapter 2 – The U.S. Constitution vests Congress with the power to raise revenue and borrow money. Those funds may only be drawn from the Treasury in consequence of appropriations made by law. The Constitution, however, is largely silent with respect to the President's role in the budget process. Instead, the current executive budget process is largely the result of statutes enacted by Congress.

The executive budget process consists of three main phases: development of the President's budget proposal, submission and justification of the President's budget proposal, and execution of enacted appropriations and other budgetary legislation. The purpose of this report is to provide an introduction to many elements of the executive budget process, highlighting the roles of the President, the Office of Management and Budget (OMB), and executive agencies.

The Budget and Accounting Act of 1921 established the modern executive budget process. It created a legal framework for a federal budget proposal to be developed by the President and submitted to Congress prior to the start of each fiscal year. In practice, development of the President's budget proposal begins approximately 18 months prior to the start of the fiscal year to which it applies. Executive agencies submit their requests and justification materials to OMB for examination and review. After final decisions have been made by the President, the budget proposal is compiled by OMB. Under current law, the President must submit the budget proposal to Congress no later than the first Monday in February.

Once the President has submitted the budget, OMB and agency officials explain and justify the request to Congress. Early in the congressional budget process, often in the week following the submission of the President's budget, the OMB director and other cabinet officials typically provide testimony regarding the President's broad budgetary objectives before congressional committees. In addition, agencies typically submit written justifications of their budget requests to Congress and agency officials often will testify before the committees of jurisdiction.

The President's budget, though not legally binding, provides Congress with recommended spending levels for programs, projects, and activities that are funded through appropriations and other budgetary legislation. Funds provided in appropriations and other budgetary legislation are not immediately available for obligation or expenditure. With certain exceptions, the Antideficiency Act requires that funds be apportioned (or divided), often by fiscal quarter, prior to obligation or expenditure. Agencies then allocate those funds to programs, projects, and activities.

Congress has recognized the need to permit agencies some flexibility during budget execution, and it has provided agencies with limited authority to make spending adjustments.

For example, Congress may provide agencies with limited authority to reallocate funds from one appropriations account to another (i.e., transfers), or from one purpose to another within an appropriations account (i.e., reprogramming). Under the Impoundment Control Act (ICA) of 1974, the President may withhold appropriated funds temporarily (referred to as deferrals) or propose to Congress permanent cancellations of budget authority (referred to as rescissions).

Finally, certain executive budgetary procedures are triggered under limited, less common circumstances. For example, OMB and agencies have established procedures for implementing a shutdown of certain government operations in the event that their full-year or interim appropriations are not enacted by the start of the fiscal year. OMB and agencies may also be subject to additional procedures in the event of a statutorily prescribed sequestration.

Chapter 3 – The term "budget process," when applied to the federal government, actually refers to a number of processes that have evolved separately and that occur with varying degrees of coordination. This overview, and the accompanying flow chart, are intended to describe in brief each of the parts of the budget process that involve Congress, clarify the role played by each, and explain how they operate together. They include the President's budget submission, the budget resolution, reconciliation, sequestration, authorizations, and appropriations.

Chapter 4 – The Congressional Budget Act of 1974 (Titles I-IX of P.L. 93-344, as amended) created a process that Congress uses each year to establish and enforce the parameters for budgetary legislation. Enforcement of budgetary decisions is accomplished through the use of points of order, and through the reconciliation process. Points of order are prohibitions against certain types of legislation or congressional actions. These prohibitions are enforced when a Member raises a point of order against legislation that may violate these rules when it is considered by the House or Senate.

This report summarizes points of order under the Congressional Budget Act of 1974, as amended, and related points of order established in the budget resolutions adopted by Congress in 2007 (S.Con.Res. 21, 110th Congress), 2008 (S.Con.Res. 70, 110th Congress), and 2009 (S.Con.Res. 13, 111th Congress), as well as the Rules of the House for the 112th Congress, the Budget Enforcement Act of 1990 (P.L. 101-508), and the Statutory Pay-As-You-Go Act of 2010 (P.L. 111-139).

In addition, it describes how points of order are applied and the processes used for their waiver in the House and Senate.

Chapter 5 – The federal budget is central to Congress's ability to exercise its "power of the purse." Over the last several fiscal years the imbalance between spending and revenues has grown as a result of the economic downturn and policies enacted in response to financial turmoil. In FY2011, the U.S. government spent $3,598 billion (24.1% of GDP) and collected $2,302 billion in revenue (15.4% of GDP), resulting in a budget deficit of $1,296 billion (8.7% of GDP). The FY2012 deficit is currently estimated at $1,079 billion (7.0% of GDP).

The Obama Administration released its FY2013 budget on February 13, 2012. In FY2013, the President's budget projects that the deficit will reach $901 billion. Budget deficits are projected throughout the 10-year budget window. The President's budget proposes a variety of short-term tax and spending measures aimed at job creation, largely drawn from the American Jobs Act submitted to Congress in September 2011. These proposals amount to nearly $350 billion in additional spending and tax cuts, including immediate funding for roads, rails, and runways; aid to states and local governments for teachers and first responders; school modernization; and a full-year extension of the Social Security payroll tax reduction and unemployment benefits.

In August 2011, the Budget Control Act of 2011 (BCA) placed limits on spending via discretionary spending caps and included provisions for additional spending cuts in the amount of $1.2 trillion. In January 2013, the additional cuts are scheduled to take effect via an automatic process. In his FY2013 budget, President Obama proposes replacing the automatic cuts with prescribed spending cuts and tax increases. The largest of these proposals includes allowing the 2001/2003/2010 tax cuts for singles making over $200,000 and households making over $250,000 to expire; savings generated from changes to Medicare, Medicaid, agriculture, and other mandatory programs; and placing caps on spending on Overseas Contingency Operations (OCO).

The FY2013 budget also included other tax proposals including changes in the estate tax parameters, limits to the value of itemized deductions for married taxpayers with incomes over $250,000 and single taxpayers with incomes over $200,000, and eliminating various tax expenditures. The Administration also released a framework for corporate tax reform, which included a reduction in the corporate tax rate combined with an elimination of certain corporate tax expenditures. The Administration is committed to reform that would not add to the deficit.

On March 21, 2012, the House Budget Committee reported the budget resolution (H.Con.Res. 112, 112th Congress) by a vote of 19-18. It was agreed to by the House on March 29, 2012, by a vote of 228-191. The resolution provided for a FY2013 deficit of $797 billion, or approximately 5.0% of GDP, falling to $287 billion or 1.2% of GDP in FY2022. Like the President's budget proposal, the House budget resolution specifies a replacement of the BCA's automatic cuts. The budget resolution replaces the majority of the cuts in FY2013 with $261 billion in deficit reduction over 10 years to be achieved via reconciliation. In order to proceed with the consideration of FY2013 appropriations bills, both the House and the Senate took action to "deem" enforceable levels of discretionary spending for FY2013 because no agreement has been reached on the budget resolution. CBO, GAO, and the Administration agree that the current mix of federal fiscal policies is unsustainable in the long term. The nation's aging population, combined with rising health care costs per beneficiary, seems likely to keep federal health costs rising faster than per capita GDP.

In: The Federal Budget Process: An Introduction ISBN: 978-1-62417-838-2
Editor: Adele Wilkinson

Chapter 1

INTRODUCTION TO THE FEDERAL BUDGET PROCESS*

Bill Heniff, Megan Suzanne Lynch and Jessica Tollestrup

SUMMARY

Budgeting for the federal government is an enormously complex process. It entails dozens of subprocesses, countless rules and procedures, the efforts of tens of thousands of staff persons in the executive and legislative branches, millions of work hours each year, and the active participation of the President and congressional leaders, as well as other members of Congress and executive officials.

The enforcement of budgetary decisions involves a complex web of procedures that encompasses both congressional and executive actions. In the last four decades or so, these procedures have been rooted principally in two statutes—the Congressional Budget Act of 1974 and the Balanced Budget and Emergency Deficit Control Act of 1985. The 1974 act established a congressional budget process in which budget policies are enforced by Congress during the consideration of individual measures. The 1985 act embodies additional statutory enforcement procedures, substantially modified

---

* This is an edited, reformatted and augmented version of the Congressional Research Service Publication, CRS Report for Congress 98-721, dated December 3, 2012.

in 1990 and 1997, that have been used by the executive to enforce budget policies after the end of a congressional session. The 1997 iteration of these enforcement procedures were set aside in the latter years of their existence and effectively expired toward the end of the 107th Congress. Efforts to renew them in the 108th through 110th Congresses were not successful. In the 111th Congress, the pay-as-you-go procedures affecting direct spending and revenue legislation were restored in a modified version by the Statutory Pay-As-You-Go Act of 2010.

More recently, in the 112th Congress, statutory limits on discretionary spending and a new automatic process to reduce spending were established by the Budget Control Act of 2011.

The President's budget is required by law to be submitted to Congress early in the legislative session. While the budget is only a request to Congress, the power to formulate and submit the budget is a vital tool in the President's direction of the executive branch and of national policy. The President's proposals often influence congressional revenue and spending decisions, though the extent of the influence varies from year to year and depends more on political and fiscal conditions than on the legal status of the budget.

The Congressional Budget Act of 1974 establishes the congressional budget process as the means by which Congress coordinates the various budget-related actions (such as the consideration of appropriations and revenue measures) taken by it during the course of the year. The process is centered on an annual concurrent resolution on the budget that sets aggregate budget policies and functional spending priorities for at least the next five fiscal years.

Because a concurrent resolution is not a law—it cannot be signed or vetoed by the President—the budget resolution does not have statutory effect; no money can be raised or spent pursuant to it. Revenue and spending amounts set in the budget resolution establish the basis for the enforcement of congressional budget policies through points of order.

Congress implements budget resolution policies through action on individual revenue and debt- limit measures, annual appropriations acts, and direct spending legislation.

In some years, Congress considers reconciliation legislation pursuant to reconciliation instructions in the budget resolution. Reconciliation legislation is used mainly to bring existing revenue and direct spending laws into conformity with budget resolution policies. Initially, reconciliation was a major tool for deficit reduction; in later years, reconciliation was used mainly to reduce revenues.

THE EVOLUTION OF FEDERAL BUDGETING

The "power of the purse" is a legislative power. The Constitution lists the power to lay and collect taxes and the power to borrow as powers of Congress; further, it provides that funds may be drawn from the Treasury only pursuant to appropriations made by law. The Constitution does not state how these legislative powers are to be exercised, nor does it expressly provide for the President to have a role in the management of the nation's finances.

During the nation's early years, the House and Senate devised procedures for the enactment of spending and revenue legislation. As these procedures evolved during the 19th century and the first decades of the 20th century, they led to highly fragmented legislative actions. In the course of each session, Congress passed many separate appropriations bills and other measures affecting the financial condition of the federal government. Neither the Constitution nor the procedures adopted by the House and Senate provided for a budget system—that is, for a coordinated set of actions covering all federal spending and revenues. As long as the federal government was small and its spending and revenues were stable, such a budget system was not considered necessary.

Early in the 20th century, the incessant rise in federal spending and the recurrence of deficits (spending exceeded revenues in half of the 20 years preceding FY1920) led Congress to seek a more coordinated means of making financial decisions. The key legislation was the Budget and Accounting Act of 1921, which established the executive budget process.

The 1921 act did not directly alter the procedures by which Congress makes revenue and spending decisions. The main impact was in the executive branch. The President was required to submit his budget recommendations to Congress each year, and the Bureau of the Budget— renamed the Office of Management and Budget (OMB) in 1970—was created to assist him in carrying out his budgetary responsibilities. Congress, it was expected, would be able to coordinate its revenue and spending decisions if it received comprehensive budget recommendations from the President. In line with this expectation, the House and Senate changed their rules to consolidate the jurisdiction of the Appropriations Committees over spending. The 1921 act also established the General Accounting Office (GAO), headed by the Comptroller General, and made it the principal auditing arm of the federal government. (The GAO recently was renamed the Government Accountability Office.) The 1921 act, as amended, remains the statutory basis for the presidential budget system.

After World War II, the belief that the presidential budget sufficed to maintain fiscal control gave way to the view that Congress needed its own budget process. Some members of Congress feared that dependence on the executive budget had bolstered the President's fiscal powers at the expense of Congress's; others felt that as long as its financial decisions were fragmented, Congress could not effectively control expenditures.

The Congressional Budget and Impoundment Control Act of 1974 established a congressional budget process centered on a concurrent resolution on the budget, scheduled for adoption prior to legislative consideration of revenue or spending bills. The congressional budget process initiated in the 1970s did not replace the preexisting revenue and spending processes. Instead, it provided an overall legislative framework within which the many separate measures affecting the budget would be considered. The central purpose of the budget process established by the 1974 act is to coordinate the various revenue and spending decisions which are made in separate revenue, appropriations, and other budgetary measures. To assist Congress in making budget decisions, the 1974 act established the Congressional Budget Office (CBO) and directed it to provide data on and analyses of the federal budget.

During the years that the congressional budget process has been in operation, its procedures have been adapted by Congress to changing circumstances. Following a decade of experience with the 1974 Congressional Budget Act, Congress made further changes in the budget process by enacting the Balanced Budget and Emergency Deficit Control Act of 1985 (also known as the Gramm-Rudman-Hollings Act), the Budget Enforcement Act of 1990 (BEA), the Line Item Veto Act in 1996, the Budget Enforcement Act of 1997, the Statutory Pay-As-You-Go Act of 2010, and the Budget Control Act of 2011, among other laws.

The 1985 act prescribed declining deficit targets intended to achieve balance in FY1991; the targets were enforced by sequestration, a process involving automatic, across-the-board cuts in nonexempt spending programs if the targets were expected to be exceeded. The 1990 act replaced the deficit targets with caps on discretionary spending and a pay-as-you-go (PAYGO) requirement for revenue and direct spending legislation; sequestration was retained as the means of enforcing the two new mechanisms. The 1996 act authorized the President to cancel discretionary spending in appropriation acts, as well as new direct spending and limited tax benefits in other legislation, subject to expedited legislative procedures by which Congress could overturn the cancellations. (The Supreme Court struck down the Line Item Veto Act in June 1998 as unconstitutional.) The 1997 act extended the BEA procedures for several more years. Without a consensus on extending the control mechanisms under the BEA, however, they expired at the end of FY2002. The Statutory Pay-As-You-Go Act of 2010 restored a modified version of the PAYGO requirement for direct spending and revenue legislation. More recently, as part of an agreement to increase the statutory limit on the public debt, the Budget Control Act of 2011 restored statutory limits on discretionary spending for each fiscal year through FY2021 and established an automatic process to reduce spending if subsequent legislation reducing the deficit by at least $1.2 trillion was not enacted, with spending reductions beginning in January 2013.

Basic Concepts of Federal Budgeting

The federal budget is a compilation of numbers about the revenues, spending, and borrowing and debt of the government. Revenues come largely from taxes, but stem from other sources as well (such as duties, fines, licenses, and gifts). Spending involves such concepts as budget authority, obligations, outlays, and offsetting collections. The numbers are computed according to rules and conventions that have accumulated over the years; they do not always conform to the way revenues and spending are accounted for in other processes.

Budget Authority and Outlays

When Congress appropriates money, it provides *budget authority*, that is, authority to enter into obligations. Budget authority also may be provided in legislation that does not go through the appropriations process (*direct spending* legislation). The key congressional spending decisions relate to the obligations that agencies are authorized to incur during a fiscal year, not to the outlays made during the year. (*Obligations* occur when agencies enter into contracts, submit purchase orders, employ personnel, and so forth; *outlays* occur when obligations are liquidated, primarily through the issuance of checks, electronic fund transfers, or the disbursement of cash.)

The provision of budget authority is the key point at which Congress exercises control over federal spending, although the outlay level often receives greater public attention because of its bearing on the deficit. Congress does not directly control outlays; each year's outlays derive in part from new budget authority and in part from "carryover" budget authority provided in prior years. For example, President Barack Obama's initial budget submission for FY2013 estimated that outlays would total $3,803 billion for that year. Approximately $2,833 billion of this amount was estimated to come from new budget authority for the fiscal year, while the remainder ($970 billion) was estimated to come from budget authority enacted in prior years.

The relation of budget authority to outlays varies from program to program and depends on *spendout rates*, the rates at which funds provided by Congress are obligated and payments disbursed. In a program with a high spendout rate, most new budget authority is expended during the fiscal year; if the spendout rate is low, however, most of the outlays occur in later years. Regardless of the spendout rate, the outlays in the budget are merely estimates of the amounts that will be disbursed during the year. If payments turn out to be higher than the budget estimate, outlays will be above the budgeted level. The President and Congress control outlays indirectly by deciding on the amount of budget authority to be provided or by limiting the amount of obligations to be incurred.

Certain receipts of the federal government are accounted for as "offsets" against outlays rather than as revenues. Various fees collected by government agencies are deducted from outlays; similarly, income from the sale of certain assets are treated as *offsetting receipts*. Most such receipts are offsets against the outlays of the agencies that collect the money, but in the case of offshore oil leases and certain other activities, the revenues are deducted from the total outlays of the government.

Scope of the Budget

The budget consists of two main groups of funds: *federal funds and trust funds*. Federal funds— which comprise mainly the general fund—largely derive from the general exercise of the taxing power and general borrowing and for the most part are not earmarked by law to any specific program or agency. One component of federal funds, called special funds, is earmarked as to source and purpose. The use of federal funds is determined largely by appropriations acts.

Trust funds are established, under the terms of statutes that designate them as trust funds, to account for funds earmarked by specific sources and purposes. The Social Security funds are the largest of the trust funds; revenues are collected under a Social Security payroll tax and are used to pay for Social Security benefits and related purposes. The *unified budget* includes both the federal funds and the trust funds. The balances in the trust funds are borrowed by the federal government; they are counted, therefore, in the federal debt. Because these balances offset a budget deficit but are included in the federal debt, the annual increase in the debt invariably exceeds the amount of the budget deficit. For the same reason, it is possible for the federal debt to rise when the federal government has a budget surplus.

Capital and operating expenses are not segregated in the budget. Hence, monies paid for the operations of government agencies as well as for the acquisition of long-life assets (such as buildings, roads, and weapons systems) are reported as budget outlays. Proposals have been made from time to time to divide the budget into capital and operating accounts. While these proposals have not been adopted, the budget provides information showing the investment and operating outlays of the government.

The budget totals do not include all the financial transactions of the federal government. The main exclusions fall into two categories—off-budget entities and government-sponsored enterprises. In addition, the budget includes direct and guaranteed loans on the basis of the accounting rules established by the Federal Credit Reform Act of 1990, which are discussed below.

Off-budget entities are excluded by law from the budget totals. The receipts and disbursements of the Social Security trust funds (the Old-Age and Survivors Insurance Fund and the Disability Insurance Fund), as well as spending for the Postal Service Fund, are excluded from the budget totals. These transactions are shown separately in the budget. Thus, the budget now reports two deficit or surplus amounts—one excluding the Social Security trust funds and the Postal Service Fund, and the other (on a unified basis) including these entities. The latter is the main focus of discussion in both the President's budget and the congressional budget process.

The transactions of government-owned corporations (excluding the Postal Service), as well as revolving funds, are included in the budget on a net basis. That is, the amount shown in the budget is the difference between receipts and outlays, not the total activity of the enterprise or revolving fund. If, for example, a revolving fund has annual income of $150 million and disbursements of $200 million, the budget would report $50 million as net outlays.

Government-sponsored enterprises (GSEs) historically have been excluded from the budget because they were deemed to be private rather than public entities. The federal government did not own any equity in these enterprises, most of which received their financing from private sources.

Although they were established by the federal government, their budgets were not reviewed by the President or Congress in the same manner as other programs. Most of these enterprises engaged in credit activities. They borrowed funds in capital markets and lent money to homeowners, farmers, and others. In total, these enterprises had assets and liabilities measured in trillions of dollars. Financial statements of the government-sponsored enterprises were published in the President's budget.

Although some GSEs continue to operate on this basis, the economic downturn and credit instability that occurred in 2008 fundamentally changed the status of two GSEs that play a significant role in the home mortgage market, Fannie Mae and Freddie Mac. In September of 2008, the Federal Housing Finance Agency (FHFA) placed the two entities in conservatorship, thereby subjecting them to control by the Federal Government until the conservatorship eventually is brought to an end.

Deficit Reduction and the Rules of Congressional Budgeting

Between the early 1980s and the late 1990s, annual consideration of the budget was dominated by concern about the budget deficit. In the mid-1980s, the deficit exceeded $150 billion and amounted to about 6% of GDP at one point. In the early 1990s, the deficit approached the $300 billion level. Following four years of surpluses (FY1998-FY2001), the budget returned to deficit for FY2002. Current budget projections show sizeable deficits persisting over the coming years.

The size of the deficit depends on how it is measured. The unified budget deficit combines all on- budget federal funds and trust funds with the off-budget entities (the Social Security trust funds and the Postal Service Fund). The unified budget deficit generally is regarded as the most comprehensive measure of the impact of the budget on the economy. A narrower measure of the deficit is derived by excluding the Social Security trust funds from the totals. This exclusion is mandated by law, although Social Security is counted in the budget in reports on the deficit. Excluding Social Security from computations of the deficit or surplus results in higher deficit or lower surplus figures.

Regardless of the measure used, it is evident that the deficit was unusually high for an extended period of time. The chronic deficits of the 1980s prompted Congress to enact the Balanced Budget and Emergency Deficit Control Act of 1985. The 1985 act established deficit targets for each year through FY1991, when the budget was to be balanced, and a sequestration process under which budgetary resources would be canceled automatically (through largely across-the- board spending cuts) if the estimated deficit exceeded the amount allowed under the act.

Even with the targets, the actual deficit for the covered years was above the targeted level. Failure to achieve the deficit targets, and other problems, led Congress to revise the process in the Budget Enforcement Act (BEA) of 1990. Sequestration procedures were retained, but the fixed deficit targets were replaced by adjustable ones (which expired at the end of FY1995), adjustable limits were imposed on discretionary spending, and a pay-as-you-go (PAYGO) process was established for revenues and direct spending. The discretionary spending limits and PAYGO process were extended (through FY1998) by the Omnibus Budget Reconciliation of 1993 and again (through FY2002) by the BEA of 1997.

Under the discretionary spending limits, different categories of discretionary spending were used for different periods. Under the 1997 changes, discretionary spending limits applied separately to defense and nondefense spending for FY1998-FY1999 and to violent crime reduction spending for FY1998-FY2000; for the remaining fiscal years, the 1997 changes merged all discretionary spending into a single, general purpose category. In 1998, as part of the Transportation Equity Act for the 21st Century, Congress added separate categories for highway and mass transit spending. Finally, in 2000, Congress added a category for conservation spending; unlike the other categories, the conservation spending category had six subcategories.

The PAYGO process under the BEA required that the budgetary impact of revenue and direct spending legislation be recorded on a multiyear "PAYGO scorecard," and that in the net any such legislation not yield a negative balance for the upcoming fiscal year. Legislation reducing revenues or increasing direct spending for a fiscal year had to be offset (in the same or other legislation) by revenue increases or reductions in direct spending for that fiscal year so that the applicable balance on the PAYGO scorecard remained at or above zero.

Under the BEA procedures, violations of the discretionary spending limits or the PAYGO requirement were to be enforced by sequestration. However, sequestration was not used for more than a decade, either because Congress and the President enacted budgetary legislation consistent with the discretionary spending limits and PAYGO requirement, or, during the latter years under the BEA, effectively waived these enforcement requirements.

The BEA enforcement procedures effectively expired toward the end of the 107th Congress. As budget deficits persisted through the last decade, proposals to restore the BEA statutory procedures had been made from time to time by members of Congress and the President, but none of the proposals were enacted until 2010.

The Statutory Pay-As-You-Go Act of 2010 (P.L. 111-139) restored in statute a modified version of the PAYGO requirement for direct spending and revenue legislation.[1] Subsequently, in 2011, the Budget Control Act (P.L. 112-25) established statutory limits on discretionary spending for each year through FY2021.

Like the previous statutory PAYGO requirement under the BEA, the new statutory PAYGO requirement is intended to discourage or prevent Congress from taking certain legislative action that would increase the on-budget deficit. It generally requires that legislation affecting direct spending or revenues not increase the deficit over a six-year period and an 11-year period. Likewise, the current statutory discretionary caps established under the Budget Control Act are similar to those under the BEA.

The limits essentially cap the amount of spending provided and controlled through the annual appropriations process each year, with upward adjustments to these limits permitted for certain purposes, such as for Overseas Contingency Operations.

The statutory PAYGO requirement and the statutory discretionary spending limits are enforced by sequestration—the cancellation of budgetary resources provided by laws affecting direct spending. Further information on sequestration is provided in the "The Sequestration Process" section, below.

During the 1990s to the present, the Senate has supplemented the statutory PAYGO requirement with a special PAYGO rule included in annual budget resolutions; following the expiration of the BEA procedures, the Senate extended its PAYGO rule (currently through FY2017). The Senate PAYGO rule currently prohibits the consideration of any legislation that proposes changes in direct spending or revenue that increase the deficit over six-year and 11-year time periods (including the current fiscal year). The House adopted its own PAYGO rule for the first time at the beginning of the 110th Congress.

At the beginning of the 112th Congress, however, the House modified this rule, renaming it CutGo, or cut-as-you-go, to prohibit the consideration of any legislation that would have the net effect of increasing direct spending over the same two time periods.

BUDGETING FOR DISCRETIONARY AND DIRECT SPENDING

The distinction drawn by the BEA and the congressional budget process between discretionary spending (which is controlled through the annual appropriations process) and direct spending (which is provided outside of the annual appropriations process) recognized that the federal government has somewhat different, though overlapping, means of dealing with these two types of spending. One set of procedures pertained to discretionary spending, another to direct spending.

Most of the direct spending subject to the PAYGO process under the BEA involved entitlement programs; the rest consisted of other forms of mandatory spending provided through authorizing legislation and interest payments. In fact, entitlements now account for about half of total federal spending (all direct spending, including net interest, accounts for about 60% of the total). The impressive feature of this trend is that most of the growth in spending and in the number of recipients has been built into existing law; for the most part, it has not been the result of new legislation.

The procedures for discretionary and direct spending converge at two critical points in federal budgeting: formulation of the President's budget and formulation of the congressional budget resolution. Both of these policy statements encompass discretionary and direct spending, but the procedures used in budgeting for these types of expenditure differ greatly. The distinctions have some notable exceptions. Some procedures associated with direct spending are applied to particular types of discretionary programs, and vice versa. Nevertheless, the generalizations presented here help to explain the complications of the budget process and explain how decisions are made.

(1) *Budgetary Impact of Authorizing Legislation.* An authorization for a discretionary spending program is only a license to enact an appropriation. The amount of budgetary resources available for spending is determined in annual appropriations acts. For direct spending programs (principally entitlements), on the other hand, the authorizing legislation either provides, or effectively mandates the appropriation of, budget authority. In those entitlement programs that are subject to annual appropriation, the Appropriations Committees have little or no discretion as to the amounts they provide.

(2) *Committees That Provide or Mandate Budget Authority.* The Appropriations Committees have jurisdiction and effective control over discretionary spending programs, while authorizing committees

effectively control direct spending programs (including those funded in annual appropriations acts). In fact, committee jurisdiction determines whether a program is classified as discretionary or direct spending. All spending under the effective control of the Appropriations Committees is discretionary; everything else is direct spending. Accordingly, when legislation establishes a program as discretionary or direct spending, it not only determines the character of spending but the locus of congressional committee control as well.

(3) *Frequency of Decision-Making*. Discretionary appropriations are, with few exceptions, made annually for the current or next fiscal year. Direct spending programs typically are established in permanent law that continues in effect until such time as it is revised or terminated by another law. The fact that many entitlements have annual appropriations does not diminish the permanence of the laws governing the amounts spent. It should be noted, however, that some direct spending programs, such as Medicare, have been subject to frequent legislative changes. The purpose of such legislation has been to modify existing law, not to provide annual funding.

(4) *Means of Enforcing the Budget Resolution*. The procedures used by Congress to enforce the policies set forth in the annual budget resolution differ somewhat for discretionary and direct spending programs. For both types of spending, Congress relies on allocations made under Section 302 of the 1974 Congressional Budget Act to ensure that spending legislation reported by House and Senate committees conforms to established budget policies. But although this procedure is effective in controlling new legislation—both annual appropriations measures and new entitlement legislation—it is not an effective control on the spending that results from existing laws. Hence, Congress relies on reconciliation procedures to enforce budget policies with respect to existing spending and revenue laws. Reconciliation is not currently applied to discretionary programs funded in annual appropriations measures.

(5) *Statutory Controls*. Discretionary programs have been subject to the spending limits set in the BEA. Direct spending has not been capped, but has operated under the PAYGO process, which required that direct spending and revenue legislation enacted for a fiscal year not cause the deficit to rise or the surplus to decrease. The lack of caps was due to the fact that most direct spending programs are open-

ended, with spending determined by eligibility rules and payment formulas in existing law rather than by new legislation.

Budget enforcement depends on timely information concerning the status of federal revenues and spending. When it acts on legislation, Congress must be informed of the estimated impact on future budgets. Measuring these impacts often is referred to as "scoring" or "scorekeeping." Scoring discretionary spending measures is a much simpler task than scoring direct spending and revenue legislation. In the latter case, scoring always is done in reference to baseline projections of future revenues and spending.

Most appropriations are for a definite amount and the budget authority is provided for a single fiscal year. The main task is to estimate the outlays that will derive in the next year and beyond from the budget authority provided in the appropriations bill. CBO and the Appropriations Committees base these estimates on outlay (or spendout) rates—the percentage of budget authority that is spent in each year. These outlay rates vary by account and are based on historical records. For example, if $1 billion is appropriated to an account which has a spendout rate of 80% in the first fiscal year that funds become available, the outlay estimate for that fiscal year will be $800 million; the remaining $200 million will become outlays in one or more subsequent years.

Scorekeeping is much more complex in enforcing budget rules, such as the PAYGO requirements, relating to direct spending and revenues. For one thing, unlike appropriations, revenue and direct spending legislation usually is open-ended; it does not specify the amount by which revenue or spending will be changed. For another, the impact of this type of legislation continues in future years. In enforcing the PAYGO requirements, Congress had to estimate the revenue gain or loss for the ensuing five years under the BEA, and for 11 years under the more recent statutory and Senate PAYGO rules. Congress cannot develop the revenue estimates simply by referring to the text of the legislation being scored. It must also take into account the behavior of taxpayers, economic conditions, and other factors that affect revenue collection.

Congress scores revenue and direct spending legislation by reference to baseline projections issued by CBO, sometimes in cooperation with OMB. The baseline is an extrapolation of future budget conditions, typically for each of the next five years, based on the assumption that current policies will continue in effect. The baseline projections incorporate assumptions about future inflation and workload changes mandated by law. These projections are made for the budget aggregates as well as for individual programs and accounts.

When Congress considers revenue or direct spending legislation, CBO estimates the amount of revenues or outlays that would ensue if the measure were enacted; in the case of most revenue legislation, CBO uses estimates prepared by the Joint Tax Committee. It then compares this amount with the baseline projection to score the legislation. Thus, the score measures budgetary impact as the difference between the amount projected under current policies and the amount estimated if the legislation were enacted. A score is reported for each of the years and often for the sum of the years as well.

Congress usually relies on the CBO score while it is considering legislation. The BEA gave OMB the authority to determine whether offsets or a sequester were required under the PAYGO rules. The more recent Statutory Pay-As-You-Go Act of 2010 provides that the budgetary effects of individual direct spending and revenue legislation are to be determined either by a reference in the legislation to a statement of budgetary effects submitted for printing in the *Congressional Record* by the chair of the House or Senate Budget Committee prior to passage, or by OMB if no appropriate reference in the legislation or statement exists. The OMB and CBO scores on legislation sometimes differ.

In addition to enforcing PAYGO, baseline projections and scoring are used in computing the amount of deficit reduction agreed to in budget summit negotiations between the President and Congress and enacted in reconciliation acts.

BUDGETING FOR DIRECT AND GUARANTEED LOANS

The Federal Credit Reform Act of 1990 made fundamental changes in the budgetary treatment of direct loans and guaranteed loans. The reform, which first became effective for FY1992, shifted the accounting basis for federally provided or guaranteed credit from the amount of cash flowing into or out of the Treasury to the estimated subsidy cost of the loans. Credit reform entails complex procedures for estimating these subsidy costs and new accounting mechanisms for recording various loan transactions. The changes have had only a modest impact on budget totals but a substantial impact on budgeting for particular loan programs.

The new system requires that budget authority and outlays be budgeted for the estimated subsidy cost of direct and guaranteed loans. This cost is defined in the 1990 act as "the estimated long- term cost to the Government of a direct loan or a loan guarantee, calculated on a net present value basis, excluding administrative costs."

Under the new system, Congress appropriates budget authority or provides indefinite authority equal to the subsidy cost. This budget authority is placed in a program account from which funds are disbursed to a financing account.

THE BUDGET CYCLE

Federal budgeting is a cyclical activity that begins with the formulation of the President's annual budget and concludes with the audit and review of expenditures. The process spreads over a multi-year period. The main stages are formulation of the President's budget, congressional budget actions, implementation of the budget, and audit and review. While the basic steps continue from year to year, particular procedures often vary in accord with the style of the President, the economic and political considerations under which the budget is prepared and implemented, and other factors.

The activities related to a single fiscal year usually stretch over a period of two-and-a-half calendar years (or longer). As the budget is being considered, federal agencies must deal with three different fiscal years at the same time: implementing the budget for the current fiscal year; seeking funds from Congress for the next fiscal year; and planning for the fiscal year after that.

THE PRESIDENTIAL BUDGET PROCESS

The President's budget, officially referred to as the *Budget of the United States Government*, is required by law to be submitted to Congress early in the legislative session, no later than the first Monday in February. The budget consists of estimates of spending, revenues, borrowing, and debt; policy and legislative recommendations; detailed estimates of the financial operations of federal agencies and programs; data on the actual and projected performance of the economy; and other information supporting the President's recommendations.

The President's budget is only a request to Congress; Congress is not required to adopt his recommendations. Nevertheless, the power to formulate and submit the budget is a vital tool in the President's direction of the executive branch and of national policy. The President's proposals often influence congressional revenue and spending decisions, though the extent of the influence varies from year to year and depends more on political and fiscal conditions than on the legal status of the budget.

The Constitution does not provide for a budget, nor does it require the President to make recommendations concerning the revenues and spending of the federal government. Until 1921, the federal government operated without a comprehensive presidential budget process. The Budget and Accounting Act of 1921, as amended, provides for a national budget system. Its basic requirement is that the President should prepare and submit a budget to Congress each year. The 1921 act established the Bureau of the Budget, now named the Office of Management and Budget (OMB), to assist the President in preparing and implementing the executive budget. Although it has been amended many times, this statute provides the legal basis for the presidential budget, prescribes much of its content, and defines the roles of the President and the agencies in the process.

Formulation and Content of the President's Budget

Preparation of the President's budget typically begins in the spring (or earlier) each year, at least nine months before the budget is submitted to Congress, about 17 months before the start of the fiscal year to which it pertains, and about 29 months before the close of that fiscal year. The early stages of budget preparation occur in federal agencies. When they begin work on the budget for a fiscal year, agencies already are implementing the budget for the fiscal year in progress and awaiting final appropriations actions and other legislative decisions for the fiscal year after that. The long lead times and the fact that appropriations have not yet been made for the next year mean that the budget is prepared with a great deal of uncertainty about economic conditions, presidential policies, and congressional actions.

As agencies formulate their budgets, they maintain continuing contact with the OMB examiners assigned to them. These contacts provide agencies with guidance in preparing their budgets and also enable them to alert OMB to any needs or problems that may loom ahead. Agency requests are submitted to OMB in late summer or early fall; these are reviewed by OMB staff in consultation with the President and his aides. The 1921 Budget and Accounting Act bars agencies from submitting their budget requests directly to Congress. Moreover, OMB regulations provide for confidentiality in all budget requests and recommendations prior to the transmittal of the

President's budget to Congress. However, it is quite common for internal budget documents to become public while the budget is still being formulated.

The format and content of the budget are partly determined by law, but the 1921 act authorizes the President to set forth the budget "in such form and detail" as he may determine. Over the years, there has been an increase in the types of information and explanatory material presented in the budget documents.

In most years, the budget is submitted as a multi-volume set consisting of a main document setting forth the President's message to Congress and an analysis and justification of his major proposals (the Budget) and supplementary documents providing account and program level details, historical information, and special budgetary analyses (the *Budget Appendix, Historical Tables*, and *Analytical Perspectives*), among other things.

Much of the budget is an estimate of requirements under existing law rather than a request for congressional action (more than half of the budget authority in the budget becomes available without congressional action). The President is required to submit a budget update (reflecting changed economic conditions, congressional actions, and other factors), referred to as the *Mid-Session Review*, by July 15 each year. The President may revise his recommendations any time during the year.

Executive Interaction with Congress

The President and his budget office have an important role once the budget is submitted to Congress. OMB officials and other presidential advisors appear before congressional committees to discuss overall policy and economic issues, but they generally leave formal discussions of specific programs to the affected agencies. Agencies thus bear the principal responsibility for defending the President's program recommendations at congressional hearings.

Agencies are supposed to justify the President's recommendations, not their own. OMB maintains an elaborate legislative clearance process to ensure that agency budget justifications, testimony, and other submissions are consistent with presidential policy. As the session unfolds, the President may formally signal his position on pending legislation through the issuance of a Statement of Administration Policy (SAP). These statements, which are maintained by OMB on its website, are sometimes used to convey a veto threat against legislation the President feels requires modifications to meet his approval.

Increasingly in recent years, the President and his chief budgetary aides have engaged in extensive negotiations with Congress over major budgetary legislation. These negotiations sometimes have occurred as formal budget "summits" and at other times as less visible, behind- the-scenes activities.

THE CONGRESSIONAL BUDGET PROCESS

The Congressional Budget and Impoundment Control Act of 1974 establishes the congressional budget process as the means by which Congress coordinates the various budget-related actions (such as the consideration of appropriations and revenue measures) taken by it during the course of the year. The process is centered around an annual concurrent resolution on the budget that sets aggregate budget policies and functional priorities for at least the next five fiscal years.

Because a concurrent resolution is not a law—it cannot be signed or vetoed by the President—the budget resolution does not have statutory effect; no money can be raised or spent pursuant to it. The main purpose of the budget resolution is to establish the framework within which Congress considers separate revenue, spending, and other budget-related legislation. Revenue and spending amounts set in the budget resolution establish the basis for the enforcement of congressional budget policies through points of order. The budget resolution also initiates the reconciliation process for conforming existing revenue and spending laws to congressional budget policies.

Formulation and Content of the Budget Resolution

The congressional budget process begins upon the presentation of the President's budget in January or February (see **Table 1**). The timetable set forth in the 1974 Congressional Budget Act calls for the final adoption of the budget resolution by April 15, well before the beginning of the new fiscal year on October 1. Although the House and Senate often pass the budget resolution separately before April 15, they often do not reach final agreement on it until after the deadline— sometimes months later. The 1974 act bars consideration of revenue, spending, and debt-limit measures for the upcoming fiscal year until the budget resolution for that year has been adopted, but certain exceptions are provided (such as the exception that allows the House to consider the regular appropriations bills after May 15, even if the budget resolution has not been adopted by then).

The 1974 Congressional Budget Act requires the budget resolution, for each fiscal year covered, to set forth budget aggregates and spending levels for each functional category of the budget. The aggregates included in the budget resolution are as follows:

- total revenues (and the amount by which the total is to be changed by legislative action);
- total new budget authority and outlays;
- the surplus or deficit; and
- the debt limit.

With regard to each of the functional categories, the budget resolution must indicate for each fiscal year the amounts of new budget authority and outlays, and they must add up to the corresponding spending or aggregates.

Table 1. Congressional Budget Process Timetable

Deadline	**Action to be completed**
First Monday in February	President submits budget to Congress.
February 15	CBO submits report on economic and budget outlook to Budget committees.
Six weeks after President's budget is submitted	Committees submit reports on views and estimates to respective Budget Committee.
April 1	Senate Budget Committee reports budget resolution.
April 15	Congress completes action on budget resolution.
June 10	House Appropriations Committee reports last regular appropriations bill.
June 30	House completes action on regular appropriations bills and any required reconciliation legislation.
July 15	President submits mid-session review of his budget to Congress.
October 1	Fiscal year begins.

Source: Compiled by the Congressional Research Service.

Aggregate amounts in the budget resolution do not reflect the revenues or spending of the Social Security trust funds, although these amounts are set forth separately in the budget resolution for purposes of Senate enforcement procedures.

The budget resolution does not allocate funds among specific programs or accounts, but the major program assumptions underlying the functional amounts are often discussed in the reports accompanying each resolution. Some recent reports have contained detailed information on the program levels assumed in the resolution. These assumptions are not binding on the affected committees. Finally, the 1974 act allows certain additional matters to be included in the budget resolution. The most important optional feature of a budget resolution is reconciliation directives (discussed below).

The House and Senate Budget Committees are responsible for marking up and reporting the budget resolution. In the course of developing the budget resolution, the Budget Committees hold hearings, receive "views and estimates" reports from other committees, and obtain information from CBO. These "views and estimates" reports of House and Senate committees provide the Budget Committees with information on the preferences and legislative plans of congressional committees regarding budgetary matters within their jurisdiction.

CBO assists the Budget Committees in developing the budget resolution by issuing, early each year, a report on the economic and budget outlook that includes baseline budget projections. The baseline projections presented in the report are supported by more detailed projections for accounts and programs; CBO usually revises the baseline projections one or more times before the Budget Committees mark up the budget resolution. In addition, CBO issues a report analyzing the President's budgetary proposals in light of CBO's own economic and technical assumptions. In past years, CBO also issued an annual report on spending and revenue options for reducing the deficit or maintaining the surplus.

The extent to which the Budget Committees (and the House and Senate) consider particular programs when they act on the budget resolution varies from year to year. Specific program decisions are supposed to be left to the Appropriations Committees and other committees of jurisdiction, but there is a strong likelihood that major issues will be discussed in markup, in the Budget Committees' reports, and during floor consideration of the budget resolution. Although any programmatic assumptions generated in this process are not binding on the committees of jurisdiction, they often influence the final outcome.

Floor consideration of the budget resolution is guided by House and Senate rules and practices. In the House, the Rules Committee usually reports a *special rule* (a simple House resolution), which, once approved, establishes the terms and conditions under which the budget resolution is considered. This special rule typically specifies which amendments may be considered and the sequence in which they are to be offered and voted on. It has been the practice in recent years to allow consideration of a few amendments (as substitutes for the entire resolution) that present broad policy choices. In the Senate, the amendment process is less structured, relying on agreements reached by the leadership through a broad consultative process. The amendments offered in the Senate may entail major policy choices or may be focused on a single issue.

Achievement of the policies set forth in the annual budget resolution depends on the legislative actions taken by Congress (and their approval or disapproval by the President), the performance of the economy, and technical considerations. Many of the factors that determine whether budgetary goals will be met are beyond the direct control of Congress. If economic conditions—growth, employment levels, inflation, and so forth—vary significantly from projected levels, so too will actual levels of revenue and spending. Similarly, actual levels may differ substantially if the technical factors upon which estimates are based, such as the rate at which agencies spend their discretionary funds or participants become eligible for entitlement programs, prove faulty.

Budget Resolution Enforcement

Congress's regular tools for enforcing the budget resolution each year are overall spending ceilings and revenue floors and committee allocations and subdivisions of spending. In addition, the Senate in some years has enforced discretionary spending limits in the budget resolution, which paralleled the adjustable limits established in statute and enforced by the sequestration process, and both chambers have imposed additional rules on direct spending and revenue legislation. Finally, the House and Senate in recent years have included procedural features in budget resolutions to limit the use of advance appropriations.

In order for the enforcement procedures to work, Congress must have access to complete and up- to-date budgetary information so that it can relate individual measures to overall budget policies and determine whether adoption of a particular measure would be consistent with those policies. Substantive and procedural points of order are designed to obtain congressional compliance with budget rules. A point of order may bar House or Senate consideration of legislation that violates the spending ceilings and revenue floors in the budget resolution, committee subdivisions of spending, or congressional budget procedures.

Budget Resolution Aggregates

In the early years after the 1974 Congressional Budget Act, the principal enforcement mechanism was the ceiling on total budget authority and outlays and the floor under total revenues set forth in the budget resolution. The limitations inherent in this mechanism soon became apparent. For example, the issue of controlling breaches of the spending ceilings usually did not arise until Congress acted on supplemental appropriations acts, when the fiscal year was well underway. The emergency nature of the legislation often made it difficult to uphold the ceilings.

Changes sometimes are made in budget resolutions by virtue of the operation of reserve funds. Generally, reserve funds allow increases to be made in various spending levels associated with the budget resolution for legislation meeting criteria specified in the budget resolution, as long as any increases spending from the legislation is offset (e.g., by revenue increases) so as to be deficit neutral.

Allocations of Spending to Committees

In view of the inadequacies in the early years of congressional budgeting of relying on enforcement of the budget totals, Congress changed the focus of enforcement in the 1980s to the committee allocations and subdivisions of spending made pursuant to Section 302 of the act. The key to enforcing budget policy is to relate the budgetary impact of individual pieces of legislation to the overall budget policy. Because Congress operates through its committee system, an essential step in linking particular measures to the budget is to allocate the spending amounts set forth in the budget resolution among House and Senate committees.

Section 302(a) provides for allocations to committees to be made in the statement of managers accompanying the conference report on the budget resolution. A Section 302(a) allocation is made to each committee which has jurisdiction over spending, both for the budget year and the full period covered by the budget resolution—at least five fiscal years.

The committee allocations do not take into account jurisdiction over discretionary authorizations funded in annual appropriations acts. The amounts of new budget authority and outlays allocated to committees in the House or Senate may not exceed the aggregate amounts of budget authority and outlays set forth in the budget resolution. Although these allocations are made by the Budget Committees, they are not the unilateral preferences of these committees. They are based on assumptions and understandings developed in the course of formulating the budget resolution.

After the allocations are made under Section 302(a), the House and Senate Appropriations Committees subdivide the amounts they receive among their 12 subcommittees, as required by Section 302(b). The subcommittees' Section 302(b) subdivisions may not exceed the total amount allocated to the committee. Each Appropriations Committee reports its subdivisions to its respective chamber; the appropriations bills may not be considered until such a report has been filed.

Scoring and Cost Estimates

As mentioned previously, scoring (also called scorekeeping) is the process of measuring the budgetary effects of pending and enacted legislation and assessing its impact on a budget plan— in this case, the budget resolution. In the congressional budget process, scoring serves several broad purposes. First, scoring informs members of Congress and the public about the budgetary consequences of their actions. When a budgetary measure is under consideration, scoring information lets members know whether adopting the amendment or passing the bill at hand would breach the budget. Further, scoring information enables members to judge what must be done in upcoming legislative action to achieve the year's budgetary goals. Finally, scoring is designed to assist Congress in enforcing its budget plans. In this regard, scorekeeping is used largely to determine whether points of order under the 1974 act may be sustained against legislation violating budget resolution levels.

The principal scorekeepers for Congress are the House and Senate Budget Committees, which provide the presiding officers of their respective chambers with the estimates needed to determine if legislation violates the aggregate levels in the budget resolution or the committee subdivisions of spending. The Budget Committees make summary scoring reports available to members on a frequent basis, usually geared to the pace of legislative activity. CBO assists Congress in these activities by preparing cost estimates of legislation, which are included in committee reports, and scoring reports for the Budget committees. The Joint Committee on Taxation supports Congress by preparing estimates of the budgetary impact of revenue legislation.

Points of Order

The 1974 Congressional Budget Act provides for both substantive and procedural points of order to block violations of budget resolution policies and congressional budget procedures. One element of substantive enforcement is based on Section 311 of the act, which bars Congress from considering legislation that would cause total revenues to fall below the level set in the budget resolution or total new budget authority or total outlays to exceed the budgeted level. The House and Senate both enforce the spending ceilings for the first fiscal year only; the revenue floor, however, is enforced for the first fiscal year and the full number of fiscal years covered by the budget resolution.

In the House (but not the Senate), Section 311 does not apply to spending legislation if the committee reporting the measure has stayed within its allocation of new discretionary budget authority. Accordingly, the House may take up any spending measure that is within the appropriate committee allocations, even if it would cause total spending to be exceeded. Neither chamber bars spending legislation that would cause functional allocations in the budget resolution to be exceeded.

Section 302(f) of the 1974 act bars the House and Senate from considering any spending measure that would cause the relevant committee's spending allocations to be exceeded; in the House, the point of order applies only to violations of allocations of new discretionary budget authority. Further, the point of order also applies to suballocations of spending made by the Appropriations Committees.

In addition to points of order to enforce compliance with the budget resolution and the allocations and subdivisions made pursuant to it, the 1974 act contains points of order to ensure compliance with its procedures. Perhaps the most important of these is Section 303, which bars consideration of any revenue, spending, entitlement, or debt-limit measure prior to adoption of the budget resolution. However, the rules of the House permit it to consider regular appropriations bills after May 15, even if the budget resolution has not yet been adopted.

When the House or Senate considers a revenue or a spending measure, the chairman of the respective Budget Committee sometimes makes a statement advising the chamber as to whether the measure violates any of these points of order. If no point of order is made, or if the point of order is waived, the House or Senate may consider a measure despite any violations of the 1974 act. The House often waives points of order by adopting a special rule. The Senate may waive points of order by unanimous consent or by motion under Section 904 of the act. The Senate requires a three-fifths vote of the membership to waive certain provisions of the act.

In several past years, the House and Senate failed to reach agreement on a budget resolution. On these occasions, one or both houses agreed to their own "deeming resolutions," which established the basis for enforcing points of order under the 1974 act in that house only.

THE SEQUESTRATION PROCESS

Sequestration was the principle means used to enforce statutory budget enforcement policies in place from 1985 through 2002, and it is the principle means used to enforce the PAYGO requirement under the Statutory Pay-As-You-Go Act of 2010 and the statutory limits on discretionary spending under the Budget Control Act of 2011 (BCA). In addition, sequestration is used to achieve a portion of the spending reductions required as a result of the failure to enact deficit reduction legislation tied to the Joint Committee on Deficit Reduction, as provided by the BCA.[2]

Sequestration involves the issuance of a presidential order that permanently cancels budgetary resources (except for revolving funds, special funds, trust funds, and certain offsetting collections) for the purpose of achieving a required amount of outlay savings to reduce the deficit. Once sequestration is triggered by an executive determination, spending reductions are made automatically; this process, therefore, is regarded by many as providing a strong incentive for Congress and the President to reach agreement on legislation that would avoid a sequester.

From its inception in 1985 until its revision by the Budget Enforcement Act (BEA) in 1990, the process was tied solely to the enforcement of fixed deficit targets. The BEA changed the sequestration process substantially. First, it effectively eliminated the deficit targets as a factor in budget enforcement. Second, the BEA established adjustable limits on discretionary spending funded in the annual appropriations process. Third, the BEA created pay-as-you-go procedures to require that increases in direct spending (i.e., spending controlled outside of the annual appropriations process) or decreases in revenues due to legislative action were offset so that there was effectively no net increase in the deficit or reduction of the surplus.

The BEA established adjustable limits on discretionary spending for FY1991-FY1995. These limits were extended through FY1998 in 1993. The Budget Enforcement Act (BEA) of 1997 revised the limits for FY1998 and provided new limits through FY2002. The limits were established for the following categories of discretionary spending: defense and nondefense, for FY1998-FY1999; discretionary (a single, general purpose category), for FY2000-FY2002; and violent crime reduction, for FY1998-FY2000. In 1998, as part of the Transportation Equity Act for the 21st Century, separate categories were added for highway and mass transit spending. Finally, a spending conservation category was added in 2000. The limits expired at the end of FY2002. As noted above, the Budget Control Act of 2011 revived the statutory limits on discretionary spending by establishing them for each year through FY2021.

The original discretionary spending limits had to be adjusted periodically by the President for various factors, including (among others), changes in concepts and definitions, a special outlay allowance (to accommodate estimating differences between OMB and CBO), and the enactment of legislation providing emergency funding and funding for the International Monetary Fund, international arrearages, an earned income tax credit compliance initiative, and other specially designated purposes. The more recent limits, under the BCA, may be adjusted for spending designated for emergencies, Overseas Contingency Operations, and disaster relief, among other specified purposes.

Under the pay-as-you-go (PAYGO) process created by the BEA, legislation increasing direct spending or decreasing revenues for a fiscal year had to be offset so that the balance on the PAYGO scorecard for that year did not fall below zero. The PAYGO process did not require any offsetting action when the spending increase or revenue decrease was due to the operation of existing law, such as an increase in the number of persons participating in the Medicare program. Direct spending consists largely of spending for entitlement programs. Most direct spending and revenue programs are established under permanent law, so there is not necessarily any need for recurring legislative action on them (and the PAYGO process did not require such action).

The PAYGO process did not preclude Congress from enacting legislation to increase direct spending; it only required that the increase be offset by reductions in other direct spending programs (which could include increases in offsetting receipts), by increases in revenues, or by a combination of the two in order to avoid a sequester. If a sequester under this process was required, it process. Additional spending reductions are also scheduled to be achieved in direct spending in each year through FY2021.

SPENDING LEGISLATION

The spending policies of the budget resolution generally are implemented through two different types of spending legislation. Policies involving discretionary spending are implemented in the context of annual appropriations acts, whereas policies affecting direct or mandatory spending (which, for the most part, involves entitlement programs) are carried out in substantive legislation.

All discretionary spending is under the jurisdiction of the House and Senate Appropriations Committees. Direct spending is under the jurisdiction of the various legislative committees of the House and Senate; the House Ways and Means Committee and the Senate Finance Committee have the largest shares of direct spending jurisdiction. (Some entitlement programs, such as Medicaid, are funded in annual appropriations acts, but such spending is not considered to be discretionary.) The enforcement procedures under the congressional budget process, mentioned above, apply equally to discretionary and direct spending.

Authorizing Measures

The rules of the House and (to a lesser extent) the Senate require that agencies and programs be authorized in law before an appropriation is made for them. An authorizing act is a law that (1) establishes a program or agency and the terms and conditions under which it operates; and (2) authorizes the enactment of appropriations for that program or agency. Authorizing legislation may originate in either the House or the Senate and may be considered any time during the year. Many agencies and programs have temporary authorizations that have to be renewed annually or every few years.

Action on appropriations measures sometimes is delayed by the failure of Congress to enact necessary authorizing legislation. The House and Senate often waive or disregard their rules against unauthorized appropriations for ongoing programs that have not yet been reauthorized.

The budgetary impact of authorizing legislation depends on whether it contains only discretionary authorizations (for which funding is provided in annual appropriations acts) or direct spending, which itself enables an agency to enter into obligations.

The Annual Appropriations Process

An appropriations act is a law passed by Congress that provides federal agencies legal authority to incur obligations and the Treasury Department authority to make payments for designated purposes. The power of appropriation derives from the Constitution, which in Article I, Section 9, provides that "[n]o money shall be drawn from the Treasury but in consequence of appropriations made by law." The power to appropriate is exclusively a legislative power; it functions as a limitation on the executive branch. An agency may not spend more than the amount appropriated to it, and it may use available funds only for the purposes and according to the conditions provided by Congress.

The Constitution does not require annual appropriations, but since the First Congress the practice has been to make appropriations for a single fiscal year. Appropriations must be used (obligated) in the fiscal year for which they are provided, unless the law provides that they shall be available for a longer period of time. All provisions in an appropriations act, such as limitations on the use of funds, expire at the end of the fiscal year, unless the language of the act extends their period of effectiveness.

The President requests annual appropriations in his budget submitted each year. In support of the President's appropriations requests, agencies submit justification materials to the House and Senate Appropriations Committees. These materials provide considerably more detail than is contained in the President's budget and are used in support of agency testimony during Appropriations subcommittee hearings on the President's budget.

Congress passes three main types of appropriations measures. *Regular appropriations* acts provide budget authority to agencies for the next fiscal year. *Supplemental appropriations* acts provide additional budget authority during the current fiscal year when the regular appropriation is insufficient or to finance activities not provided for in the regular appropriation. *Continuing appropriations* acts provide stop-gap (or full-year) funding for agencies that have not received a regular appropriation.

In a typical session, Congress acts on 12 regular appropriations bills and at least two supplemental appropriations measures. Because of recurring delays in the appropriations process, Congress also typically passes one or more continuing appropriations each year. The scope and duration of these measures depend on the status of the regular appropriations bills and the degree of budgetary conflict between the President and Congress. In recent years, Congress has merged two or more of the regular appropriations acts for a fiscal year into a single, omnibus appropriations act.

By precedent, appropriations originate in the House of Representatives. In the House, appropriations measures are originated by the Appropriations Committee (when it marks up or reports the measure) rather than being introduced by a member beforehand. Before the full Committee acts on the bill, it is considered in the relevant Appropriations subcommittee (the House and Senate Appropriations Committees have 12 parallel subcommittees). The House subcommittees typically hold extensive hearings on appropriations requests shortly after the President's budget is submitted. In marking up their appropriations bills, the various subcommittees are guided by the discretionary spending limits and the allocations made to them under Section 302 of the 1974 Congressional Budget Act.

The Senate usually considers appropriations measures after they have been passed by the House. When House action on appropriations bills is delayed, however, the Senate sometimes expedites its actions by considering a Senate-numbered bill up to the stage of final passage. Upon receipt of the House-passed bill in the Senate, it is amended with the text that the Senate already has agreed to (as a single amendment) and then passed by the Senate. Hearings in the Senate Appropriations subcommittees generally are not as extensive as those held by counterpart subcommittees in the House.

The basic unit of an appropriation is an account. A single unnumbered paragraph in an appropriations act comprises one account and all provisions of that paragraph pertain to that account and to no other, unless the text expressly gives them broader scope. Any provision limiting the use of funds enacted in that paragraph is a restriction on that account alone.

Over the years, appropriations have been consolidated into a relatively small number of accounts. It is typical for a federal agency to have a single account for all its expenses of operation and additional accounts for other purposes such as construction. Accordingly, most appropriation accounts encompass a number of activities or projects. The appropriation sometimes earmarks specific amounts to particular activities within the account, but the more common practice is to provide detailed information on the amounts intended for each activity in other sources (principally, the committee reports accompanying the measures).

In addition to the substantive limitations (and other provisions) associated with each account, each appropriations act has "general provisions" that apply to all of the accounts in a title or in the whole act. These general provisions appear as numbered sections, usually at the end of the title or the act.

The standard appropriation is for a single fiscal year—the funds have to be obligated during the fiscal year for which they are provided; they lapse if not obligated by the end of that year. An appropriation that does not mention the period during which the funds are to be available is a one- year appropriation. Congress also makes no-year appropriations by specifying that the funds shall remain available until expended. No-year funds are carried over to future years, even if they have not been obligated. Congress sometimes makes multiyear appropriations, which provide for funds to be available for two or more fiscal years. Appropriations measures also contain other types of provisions that serve specialized purposes. These include provisions that liquidate (pay off) obligations made pursuant to certain contract authority; reappropriate funds provided in previous years; transfer funds from one account to another; rescind funds (or release deferred funds); or set ceilings on the amount of obligations that can be made under permanent appropriations, on the amount of direct or guaranteed loans that can be made, or on the amount of administrative expenses that can be incurred during the fiscal year. In addition to providing funds, appropriations acts often contain substantive limitations on government agencies. Detailed information on how funds are to be spent, along with other directives or guidance, is provided in the reports accompanying the various appropriations measures. Agencies ordinarily abide by report language in spending the funds appropriated by Congress.

The appropriations reports do not comment on every item of expenditure. Report language is most likely when the Appropriations Committee prefers to spend more or less on a particular item than the President has requested or when the committee wants to earmark funds for a particular project or activity. When a particular item is mentioned by the committee, there is a strong expectation that the agency will adhere to the instructions.

REVENUE LEGISLATION

Article I, Section 8 of the Constitution gives Congress the power to levy "taxes, duties, imposts, and excises." Section 7 of this article requires that all revenue measures originate in the House of Representatives.

In the House, revenue legislation is under the jurisdiction of the Ways and Means Committee; in the Senate, jurisdiction is held by the Finance Committee. While House rules bar other committees from reporting revenue legislation, sometimes another committee will report legislation levying user fees on a class that benefits from a particular service or program or that is being regulated by a federal agency. In many of these cases, the user fee legislation is referred subsequently to the Ways and Means Committee.

Most revenues derive from existing provisions of the tax code or Social Security law, which continue in effect from year to year unless changed by Congress. This tax structure can be expected to produce increasing amounts of revenue in future years as the economy expands and incomes rise. Nevertheless, Congress usually makes some changes in the tax laws each year, either to raise or lower revenues or to redistribute the tax burden.

Congress typically acts on revenue legislation pursuant to proposals in the President's budget. An early step in congressional work on revenue legislation is publication by CBO of its own estimates (developed in consultation with the Joint Tax Committee) of the revenue impact of the President's budget proposals. The congressional estimates often differ significantly from those presented in the President's budget.

The revenue totals in the budget resolution establish the framework for subsequent action on revenue measures. The budget resolution contains only revenue totals and total recommended changes; it does not allocate these totals among revenue sources (although it does set out Medicare receipts separately), nor does it specify which provisions of the tax code are to be changed.

The House and Senate often consider major revenue measures, such as the Tax Reform Act of 1986, under their regular legislative procedures. However, as has been the case with direct spending programs, many of the most significant changes in revenue policy in recent years have been made in the context of the reconciliation process. Although revenue changes are usually incorporated into omnibus budget reconciliation measures, along with spending changes (and sometimes debt-limit increases), revenue reconciliation legislation may be considered on a separate legislative track (e.g., the Tax Equity and Fiscal Responsibility Act of 1982).

When the reconciliation process is used to advance revenue reductions (or spending increases) that would lead to a deficit, or would enlarge an existing deficit, Section 313 of the 1974 Congressional Budget Act (referred to as the Senate's "Byrd rule") limits the legislative changes to the period covered by the reconciliation directives. Accordingly, some recent tax cuts have been subject to sunset dates.

In enacting revenue legislation, Congress often establishes or alters tax expenditures. The term "tax expenditures" is defined in the 1974 Congressional Budget Act to include revenue losses due to deductions, exemptions, credits, and other exceptions to the basic tax structure. Tax expenditures are a means by which the federal government pursues public policy objectives and can be regarded as alternatives to other policy instruments such as grants or loans. The Joint Tax Committee estimates the revenue effects of legislation changing tax expenditures, and it also publishes five-year projections of these provisions as an annual committee print.

DEBT-LIMIT LEGISLATION

When the revenues collected by the federal government are not sufficient to cover its expenditures, it must finance the shortfall through borrowing. Federal borrowing is subject to a public debt limit established by statute. When the federal government operates with a budget deficit, the public debt limit must be increased periodically. The frequency of congressional action to raise the debt limit has ranged in the past from several times in one year to once in several years. When the federal government incurred large and growing surpluses in recent years, Congress did not have to increase the debt limit, but the enactment of increases in the debt limit has again become necessary with the recurrence of deficits.

Legislation to raise the public debt limit falls under the jurisdiction of the House Ways and Means Committee and the Senate Finance Committee. Although consideration of such measures in the House usually is constrained through the use of special rules, Senate action sometimes is far- ranging with regard to the issues covered. In the past, the Senate has added many non-germane provisions to debt-limit measures, such as the 1985 Balanced Budget Act.

In 1979, the House amended its rules to provide for the automatic engrossment of a measure increasing the debt limit upon final adoption of the conference report on the budget resolution. The rule, House Rule XLIX (commonly referred to as the Gephardt rule), was intended to facilitate quick action on debt increases. However, the Senate had no comparable rule. For years, the House and Senate could enact debt-limit legislation originating under the Gephardt rule or arising under conventional legislative procedures. During the past decade, Congress has enacted debt-limit increases as part of omnibus budget reconciliation measures, continuing appropriations acts, and other legislation. The House recodified the Gephardt rule as House Rule XXIII at the beginning of the 106th Congress, repealed it at the beginning of the 107th Congress, and reinstated it, as new Rule XXVII, at the beginning of the 108th Congress. At the beginning of the 112th Congress, the House once again repealed the rule, thereby requiring the House to vote directly on any legislation that changes the statutory limit on the public debt.

RECONCILIATION LEGISLATION

Beginning in 1980, Congress has used reconciliation legislation to implement many of its most significant budget policies. Section 310 of the 1974 Congressional Budget Act sets forth a special procedure for the development and consideration of reconciliation legislation. Reconciliation legislation is used by Congress to bring existing revenue and spending law into conformity with the policies in the budget resolution. Reconciliation is an optional process, but Congress has used it more years than not; during the period covering 1980 through 2010, 20 reconciliation measures were enacted into law and three were vetoed.

The reconciliation process has two stages—the adoption of reconciliation instructions in the budget resolution and the enactment of reconciliation legislation that implements changes in revenue or spending laws. Although reconciliation has been used since 1980, specific procedures tend to vary from year to year.

Reconciliation is used to change the amount of revenues, budget authority, or outlays generated by existing law. In a few instances, reconciliation has been used to adjust the public debt limit. On the spending side, the process focuses on entitlement laws; it may not be used, however, to impel changes in Social Security law. Reconciliation sometimes has been applied to discretionary authorizations (which are funded in annual appropriations acts), but this is not the usual practice.

Reconciliation was used in the 1980s and into the 1990s as a deficit-reduction tool. Beginning in the latter part of the 1990s, some reconciliation measures were used principally to reduce revenues, thereby increasing the deficit. At the beginning of the 110th Congress, both chambers adopted rules requiring that reconciliation be used solely for deficit reduction.

Reconciliation Directives

Reconciliation begins with a directive in a budget resolution instructing designated committees to report legislation changing existing law or pending legislation. These instructions have three components: (1) they name the committee (or committees) that are directed to report legislation; (2) they specify the amounts by which existing laws are to be changed (but do not identify how these changes are to be made, which laws are to be altered, or the programs to be affected); and (3) they usually set a deadline by which the designated committees are to recommend the changes in law. The instructions typically cover the same fiscal years covered by the budget resolution. Sometimes, budget resolutions have provided for more than one reconciliation measure to be considered during a session. The dollar amounts are computed with reference to the CBO baseline. Thus, a change represents the amount by which revenues or spending would decrease or increase from baseline levels as a result of changes made in existing law. This computation is itself based on assumptions about the future level of revenues or spending under current law (or policy) and about the dollar changes that would ensue from new legislation. Hence, the savings associated with the reconciliation process are assumed savings. The actual changes in revenues or spending may differ from those estimated when the reconciliation instructions are formulated.

Although the instructions do not mention the programs to be changed, they are based on assumptions as to the savings or deficit reduction (or, in some cases, increases) that would result from particular changes in revenue provisions or spending programs. These program assumptions are sometimes printed in the reports on the budget resolution. Even when the assumptions are not published, committees and members usually have a good idea of the specific program changes contemplated by the reconciliation instructions.

A committee has discretion to decide on the legislative changes to be recommended. It is not bound by the program changes recommended or assumed by the Budget Committees in the reports accompanying the budget resolution. Further, a committee has to recommend legislation estimated to produce dollar changes for each category delineated in the instructions to it.

When a budget resolution containing a reconciliation instruction has been approved by Congress, the instruction has the status of an order by the House and Senate to designated committees to recommend legislation, usually by a date certain. It is expected that committees will carry out the instructions of their parent chamber, but the 1974 Congressional Budget Act does not provide any sanctions against committees that fail to do so.

Development and Consideration of Reconciliation Measures

When more than one committee in the House and Senate is subject to reconciliation directives, the proposed legislative changes usually are consolidated by the Budget Committees into an omnibus bill. The 1974 Congressional Budget Act does not permit the Budget Committees to revise substantively the legislation recommended by the committees of jurisdiction. This restriction pertains even when the Budget Committees estimate that the proposed legislation will fall short of the dollar changes called for in the instructions. Sometimes, the Budget Committees, working with the leadership, develop alternatives to the committee recommendations, to be offered as floor amendments, so as to achieve greater compliance with the reconciliation directives. The 1974 act requires that amendments offered to reconciliation legislation in either the House or the Senate be deficit neutral. To meet this requirement, an amendment reducing revenues or increasing spending must offset these deficit increases by equivalent revenue increases or spending cuts.

During the first several years' experience with reconciliation, the legislation contained many provisions that were extraneous to the purpose of reducing the deficit. The reconciliation submissions of committees included such things as provisions that had no budgetary effect, that increased spending or reduced revenues, or that violated another committee's jurisdiction. In 1985, the Senate adopted a rule (commonly referred to as the Byrd rule) on a temporary basis as a means of curbing these practices. The Byrd rule has been extended and modified several times over the years. In 1990, the Byrd rule was incorporated into the 1974 Congressional Budget Act as Section 313 and made permanent. Although the House has no rule comparable to the Senate's Byrd rule, it may use other devices to control the inclusion of extraneous matter in reconciliation legislation. In particular, the House may use special rules to make in order amendments that strike such matter.

HOUSE AND SENATE EARMARK DISCLOSURE RULES

In 2007, both the House and Senate adopted rules intended to bring more transparency to the process surrounding earmarks. Although the definitions vary, an earmark generally is considered to be an allocation of resources to specifically targeted beneficiaries, either through discretionary or direct spending, limited tax benefits, or limited tariff benefits.[5]

Concern about earmarking practices arose over such provisions being inserted into legislation or accompanying reports without any identification of the sponsor, and the belief that many earmarks were not subject to proper scrutiny and diverted resources to lesser-priority items or items without sufficient justification, thereby contributing to wasteful spending or revenue loss.

In response to this concern, earmark rules were adopted that vary by chamber, but include three main features. The first feature is a requirement that members requesting a congressional earmark provide a written statement to the chair and ranking minority member of the committee of jurisdiction that includes the member's name, the name and address of the intended earmark recipient, the purpose of the earmark, and a certification that the member or member's spouse has no financial interest in such an earmark. (The Senate rule applies not only to the spouse but the entire immediate family.)

The second feature is a general requirement that committees provide a list of all earmarks included in reported legislation. The third feature is a point of order against legislation that is not accompanied by a list of included earmarks. These vary by chamber.

House of Representatives

House Rule XXI, clause 9, generally requires that certain types of measures be accompanied by a list of earmarks or a statement that the measure contains no earmarks.[6] If the list of earmarks or the statement that no earmark exists in the measure is absent, a point of order may lie against the measure's floor consideration. The point of order applies to the absence of such a list or statement, and does not speak to the completeness or the accuracy of such document.

House earmark disclosure rules apply to any congressional earmark included in either the text of the measure or the committee report accompanying the measure, as well as the conference report and joint explanatory statement. The disclosure requirements apply to items in authorizing, appropriations, and revenue legislation. Furthermore, they apply not only to measures reported by committees, but also to unreported measures, "manager's amendments," Senate measures, and conference reports.

These earmark disclosure requirements, however, do not apply to all legislation at all times. Not subject to the rule are floor amendments (except a "manager's amendment"), amendments between the Houses, or amendments considered as adopted under a self-executing special rule, including a committee amendment in the nature of a substitute made in order as original text. The earmark rule, as with most House rules, is not self enforcing and relies instead on a member raising a point of order if the rule is violated. When a measure is considered under suspension of the rules, House rules are laid aside and earmark disclosure rules are, therefore, waived. It is not in order to consider a special rule that waives earmark requirements under the House rule.

The Senate

Senate Rule XLIV creates a point of order against a motion to proceed to consider a measure or a vote on adoption of a conference report, unless the chair of the committee or the Majority Leader (or designee) certifies that a complete list of earmarks and the name of each Senator requesting each earmark is available on a publicly accessible congressional website in a searchable form at least 48 hours before the vote. If a Senator proposes a floor amendment containing an earmark, those items must be printed in the *Congressional Record* as soon as "practicable."[7] If the earmark certification requirements have not been met, a point of order may lie against consideration of the measure or a vote on the conference report. The point of order applies only to the absence of such certification, and does not speak to its accuracy.

Senate earmark disclosure rules apply to any congressional earmark included in either the text of the bill or a committee report accompanying the bill, as well as a conference report and joint explanatory statement. The disclosure requirements apply to items in authorizing, appropriations, and revenue legislation. Furthermore, they apply not only to measures reported by committees, but also to unreported measures, amendments, House bills, and conference reports.

The earmark rule may be waived either by unanimous consent or by motion, which requires the affirmative vote of three-fifths of all Senators (60, if there are no vacancies).[8] The earmark rule, as with most Senate rules, is not self enforcing and relies instead on a Senator raising a point of order if the rule is violated.

While not embodied in either chamber's rules, an earmark "ban" or "moratorium" is currently in effect in both the House and Senate, enforced by committee and chamber leadership.[9]

IMPOUNDMENT AND LINE-ITEM VETO

Impoundment

Although an appropriation limits the amounts that can be spent, it also establishes the expectation that the available funds will be used to carry out authorized activities. Therefore, when an agency fails to use all or part of an appropriation, it deviates from the intentions of Congress. The Impoundment Control Act of 1974 prescribes rules and procedures for instances in which available funds are impounded.

An impoundment is an action or inaction by the President or a federal agency that delays or withholds the obligation or expenditure of budget authority provided in law. The 1974 Impoundment Control Act divides impoundments into two categories and establishes distinct procedures for each. A *deferral* delays the use of funds; a *rescission* is a presidential request that Congress rescind (cancel) an appropriation or other form of budget authority. Deferral and rescission are exclusive and comprehensive categories; an impoundment is either a rescission or a deferral—it cannot be both or something else.

Although impoundments are defined broadly by the 1974 act, in practice they are limited to major actions that affect the level or rate of expenditure. As a general practice, only deliberate curtailments of expenditure are reported as impoundments; actions having other purposes that incidently affect the rate of spending are not recorded as impoundments. For example, if an agency were to delay the award of a contract because of a dispute with a vendor, the delay would not be an impoundment; if the delay were for the purpose of reducing an expenditure, it would be an impoundment. The line between routine administrative actions and impoundments is not clear and controversy occasionally arises as to whether a particular action constitutes an impoundment.

Rescissions

To propose a rescission, the President must submit a message to Congress specifying the amount to be rescinded, the accounts and programs involved, the estimated fiscal and program effects, and the reasons for the rescission. Multiple rescissions can be grouped in a single message. After the message has been submitted to it, Congress has 45 days of "continuous session" (usually a larger number of calendar days) during which it can pass a rescission bill. Congress may rescind all, part, or none of the amount proposed by the President.

If Congress does not approve a rescission in legislation by the expiration of this period, the President must make the funds available for obligation and expenditure. If the President fails to release funds at the expiration of the 45-day period for proposed rescissions, the comptroller general may bring suit to compel their release. This has been a rare occurrence, however.

Deferrals

To defer funds, the President submits a message to Congress setting forth the amount, the affected account and program, the reasons for the deferral, the estimated fiscal and program effects, and the period of time during which the funds are to be deferred. The President may not propose a deferral for a period of time beyond the end of the fiscal year, nor may he propose a deferral that would cause the funds to lapse or otherwise prevent an agency from spending appropriated funds prudently. In accounts where unobligated funds remain available beyond the fiscal year, the President may defer the funds again in the next fiscal year.

At present, the President may defer only for the reasons set forth in the Antideficiency Act, including to provide for contingencies, to achieve savings made possible by or through changes in requirements or greater efficiency of operations, and as specifically provided by law. He may not defer funds for policy reasons (e.g., to curtail overall federal spending or because he is opposed to a particular program).

The comptroller general reviews all proposed rescissions and deferrals and advises Congress of their legality and possible budgetary and program effects. The comptroller general also notifies Congress of any rescission or deferral not reported by the President and may reclassify an improperly classified impoundment. In all cases, a notification to Congress by the comptroller general has the same legal effect as an impoundment message of the President.

The 1974 Impoundment Control Act provides for special types of legislation—rescission bills and deferral resolutions—for Congress to use in exercising its impoundment control powers. However, pursuant to court decisions that held the legislative veto to be unconstitutional, Congress may not use deferral resolutions to disapprove a deferral. Further, Congress has been reluctant to use rescission bills regularly. Congress, instead, usually acts on impoundment matters within the framework of the annual appropriations measures.

Line-Item Veto

During the 104th Congress, the Line Item Veto Act (P.L. 104-130) was enacted as an amendment to the 1974 Impoundment Control Act. The Supreme Court ruled the Line Item Veto Act unconstitutional in June 1998.

The authority granted to the President under the Line Item Veto Act differed markedly from the veto authority available to most chief executives at the state level. First, the President could not veto individual parts of legislation submitted for his approval. Under normal constitutional procedures, the President must approve or veto any measure in its entirety. His authority to use the line-item veto came into play only after a measure had been signed into law. Second, this authority applied not only to annual appropriations, but extended to new entitlement spending and targeted tax benefits as well. The line-item veto authority was intended to be in effect for eight years, from the beginning of 1997 through the end of 2004.

The Line Item Veto Act reversed the presumption underlying the process for the consideration of rescissions under the 1974 Impoundment Control Act. Under the Line Item Veto Act, presidential proposals would take effect unless overturned by legislative action. The act authorized the President to identify at enactment individual items in legislation that he proposed not go into effect. The identification was based not just upon the statutory language, but on the entire legislative history and documentation. The President had to notify Congress promptly of his proposals and provide supporting information. Congress had to respond within a limited period of time by enacting a law if it wanted to disapprove the President's proposals; otherwise, they would take effect permanently.

President Clinton exercised the line-item veto authority several times during the 1997 session before the act was declared unconstitutional.

End Notes

[1] For more detailed information on the statutory PAYGO requirement, see CRS Report R41157, *The Statutory Pay-As-You-Go Act of 2010: Summary and Legislative History*, by Bill Heniff Jr.

[2] For further information on the BCA, see CRS Report R41965, *The Budget Control Act of 2011*, by Bill Heniff Jr., Elizabeth Rybicki, and Shannon M. Mahan.

[3] The five-year period covers the budget year and four fiscal years thereafter, and the 10-year period covers the budget year and nine fiscal years thereafter. The statutory rule also requires that any budgetary effects for the current year must be added to the budgetary effects for the budget year.

[4] Most direct spending programs and activities, including Social Security benefits, veterans' programs, retirement and disability benefits, and low-income programs, among others, are exempt from any sequestration. In addition, the amount of any sequestration is limited to 4% for Medicare and 2% for certain health and medical care activities.

[5] For more information on House and Senate earmark rules, see CRS Report RL34462, *House and Senate Procedural Rules Concerning Earmark Disclosure*, by Sandy Streeter.

[6] Depending upon the type of measure, the list or statement is to be included either in the measure's accompanying report, or printed in the *Congressional Record.*

[7] The rule does not apply to all earmarks in floor amendments, only those "not included in the bill or joint resolution as placed on the calendar or as reported by any committee, in a committee report on such a bill or joint resolution, or a committee report of the Senate on a companion measure," as stated in Rule XLIV, paragraph 4(a).

[8] These points of order may also be waived if the Majority and Minority Leaders jointly agree that "such a waiver is necessary as a result of a significant disruption to Senate facilities or to the availability of the Internet." Senate Rule XLIV, paragraph 12.

[9] The House Republican Conference Rules include a standing order, adopted December 8, 2010, stating that "It is the policy of the House Republican Conference that no Member shall request a congressional earmark, limited tax benefit, or limited tariff benefit, as such terms have been described in the Rules of the House," available at http://www.gop.gov/about/rules?standing-orders-for-the-112th. In the Senate, the chair of the Committee on Appropriations announced in a press release on February 1, 2011, and again on February 2, 2012, that an earmark moratorium would be enforced on all FY2011, FY2012, and FY2013 appropriations bills, available at http://www.appropriations.senate.gov/news.cfm? method= news.view&id=188dc791-4b0d-459e-b8d9-4ede5ca299e7 and http://www.appropriations.senate.gov/news.cfm?method=news.view&id=3883059e-7a0c-496e-8d51-440aa7c2d57c.

In: The Federal Budget Process: An Introduction ISBN: 978-1-62417-838-2
Editor: Adele Wilkinson

Chapter 2

THE EXECUTIVE BUDGET PROCESS: AN OVERVIEW*

Michelle D. Christensen

SUMMARY

The U.S. Constitution vests Congress with the power to raise revenue and borrow money. Those funds may only be drawn from the Treasury in consequence of appropriations made by law. The Constitution, however, is largely silent with respect to the President's role in the budget process. Instead, the current executive budget process is largely the result of statutes enacted by Congress.

The executive budget process consists of three main phases: development of the President's budget proposal, submission and justification of the President's budget proposal, and execution of enacted appropriations and other budgetary legislation. The purpose of this report is to provide an introduction to many elements of the executive budget process, highlighting the roles of the President, the Office of Management and Budget (OMB), and executive agencies.

The Budget and Accounting Act of 1921 established the modern executive budget process. It created a legal framework for a federal budget proposal to be developed by the President and submitted to Congress prior to the start of each fiscal year. In practice, development of

---

* This is an edited, reformatted and augmented version of a Congressional Research Service publication, CRS Report for Congress R42633, from www.crs.gov, prepared for Members and Committees of Congress, dated July 27, 2012.

the President's budget proposal begins approximately 18 months prior to the start of the fiscal year to which it applies. Executive agencies submit their requests and justification materials to OMB for examination and review. After final decisions have been made by the President, the budget proposal is compiled by OMB. Under current law, the President must submit the budget proposal to Congress no later than the first Monday in February.

Once the President has submitted the budget, OMB and agency officials explain and justify the request to Congress. Early in the congressional budget process, often in the week following the submission of the President's budget, the OMB director and other cabinet officials typically provide testimony regarding the President's broad budgetary objectives before congressional committees. In addition, agencies typically submit written justifications of their budget requests to Congress and agency officials often will testify before the committees of jurisdiction.

The President's budget, though not legally binding, provides Congress with recommended spending levels for programs, projects, and activities that are funded through appropriations and other budgetary legislation. Funds provided in appropriations and other budgetary legislation are not immediately available for obligation or expenditure. With certain exceptions, the Antideficiency Act requires that funds be apportioned (or divided), often by fiscal quarter, prior to obligation or expenditure. Agencies then allocate those funds to programs, projects, and activities.

Congress has recognized the need to permit agencies some flexibility during budget execution, and it has provided agencies with limited authority to make spending adjustments.

For example, Congress may provide agencies with limited authority to reallocate funds from one appropriations account to another (i.e., transfers), or from one purpose to another within an appropriations account (i.e., reprogramming). Under the Impoundment Control Act (ICA) of 1974, the President may withhold appropriated funds temporarily (referred to as deferrals) or propose to Congress permanent cancellations of budget authority (referred to as rescissions).

Finally, certain executive budgetary procedures are triggered under limited, less common circumstances. For example, OMB and agencies have established procedures for implementing a shutdown of certain government operations in the event that their full-year or interim appropriations are not enacted by the start of the fiscal year. OMB and agencies may also be subject to additional procedures in the event of a statutorily prescribed sequestration.

INTRODUCTION

The U.S. Constitution vests Congress with the power to raise revenue and borrow money. Those funds may only by drawn from the Treasury in consequence of appropriations made by law. [1] The Constitution, however, is largely silent with respect to the President's role in the budget process. Instead, the executive budget process as it exists today is primarily the result of statutes enacted by Congress.

The Budget and Accounting Act of 1921 (P.L. 67-13; 42 Stat. 20-27) established the modern executive budget process. Prior to its enactment, executive budgeting was highly decentralized. At that time, agencies submitted their budget estimates to Congress individually, either directly or through the Secretary of the Treasury, with varying levels of involvement or direction by the President.[2] The Budget and Accounting Act altered this practice by establishing a legal framework for a consolidated federal budget proposal to be developed by the President and submitted to Congress prior to the start of each fiscal year.

This report outlines many of the budgetary procedures that are performed by the President, the Office of Management and Budget (OMB), and agencies. This report provides an overview of the development, submission, and justification of the President's budget proposal. This report also describes how the President, OMB, and agencies execute the federal budget following the enactment of appropriations and other budgetary legislation by Congress.[3]

DEVELOPMENT OF THE PRESIDENT'S BUDGET

The President's budget, or the *Budget of the United States Government* as it is referred to in 31 U.S.C. §1105(a), is a statement of the President's policy priorities and a unified plan for the allocation of federal budgetary resources. The President's budget is a set of recommendations. Congress is not required to adopt the recommendations contained within the President's budget. Nevertheless, the budget is one of the President's most important policy tools. Though it is not legally binding, the President's budget initiates the congressional budget process and provides Congress with recommended spending levels for agency programs, projects, and activities funded through the annual appropriations acts. The President's budget also includes budgetary projections based on existing law and provides Congress with estimations of the effects the President's revenue and direct spending proposals will have on those projections.

Under current law, the President is responsible for developing and submitting a consolidated budget to Congress no later than the first Monday in February prior to the start of the fiscal year.[4]

The development of the President's budget begins approximately 18 months prior to the start of the fiscal year that the budget will cover, which is about 10 months before the President must submit the proposal to Congress. To put this timeline in context, as Congress begins action on appropriations bills and other budgetary legislation for the upcoming fiscal year, OMB and agencies have already begun planning for the subsequent fiscal year.

Initial Preparation of Agency Budget Requests

In practice, the President has delegated to OMB certain budgetary tasks and authorities necessary for developing the budget. OMB coordinates the development of the President's budget proposal by issuing circulars, memoranda, and guidance documents to the heads of executive agencies. Executive agencies then prepare their budget requests in accordance with the instructions and guidance provided by OMB.

OMB Circular No. A-11 (hereafter Circular A-11) is an extensive document that contains instructions and schedules for agency submission of budget requests and justification materials to OMB.[5] Updated annually, Circular A-11 provides agencies with an overview of applicable budgetary laws, policies for the preparation and submission of budgetary estimates, and information on financial management and budget data systems. Circular A-11 also provides agencies with directions for budget execution and guidance regarding agency interaction with Congress and the public.

Early in the development phase, OMB issues a budget planning guidance memorandum, also referred to as the "Spring Guidance," which provides executive agencies with detailed instructions and deadlines for submitting their budget requests and supporting materials to OMB.[6] The guidance may also include specific instructions for how agency budget requests may help achieve the President's budgetary priorities and other policy goals. For example, the FY2013 Budget Guidance instructed,

> [u]nless your agency has been given explicit direction otherwise by OMB, your overall agency request for 2013 should be at least 5 percent

> below your 2011 enacted discretionary appropriation ... [and] should also identify additional discretionary funding reductions that would bring your request to a level that is at least 10 percent below your 2011 enacted discretionary appropriation.[7]

While the general contents and timeline for agency budget submissions are guided by OMB, agencies also have their own internal procedures for developing the requests they submit to OMB.

In practice, budget preparation is likely a time and data intensive process for agencies, involving detailed analysis and estimation of past and future budgetary resources.[8]

OMB Review of Agency Budget Requests

Agency budget requests are submitted to OMB in early fall, approximately four to five months before the President must submit the budget to Congress. OMB has been delegated the responsibility of reviewing executive agency requests and justification materials to ensure that they are consistent with the President's policy objectives.

Agency requests are first reviewed by the OMB program examiners who are responsible for the associated policy areas. Agency requests may also be reviewed by more senior OMB officials.

Prior to making a recommendation, OMB program examiners may ask for additional information from agencies, either informally or by conducting formal hearings. Examiners' recommendations are reviewed by more senior OMB officials, culminating in review and approval by the OMB Director and the President.[9]

Agencies are notified of the President's decisions through a process known as "passback." During passback, OMB officials notify agencies of their approved budgetary levels, which may differ from the agencies' budget requests.[10]

The passback process and the content of passback decisions has differed under each administration and each OMB Director.

For example, passback decisions may also include program policy changes or personnel ceilings.[11]

Agencies may appeal these decisions to the OMB Director, or in some cases, to the President directly, depending on the procedures established by the OMB Director.[12]

SUBMISSION AND JUSTIFICATION OF THE PRESIDENT'S BUDGET

The President's budget submission is a multi-volume set of documents, which may vary in size and composition from administration to administration. This section briefly discusses the components of the President's budget submission to Congress, and highlights some of the formal and informal interactions between Congress, the President, OMB, and agencies.[13]

Composition of the President's Budget Submission to Congress

Under 31 U.S.C. §1105, the President is required to provide certain information in the budget submission to Congress. The complete list of content the President is required to submit as part of the budget proposal is extensive, and includes (1) estimated receipts, expenditures, and proposed appropriations for the next five fiscal years; (2) actual receipts, expenditures, and appropriations for the previous fiscal year; (3) information on the public debt; and (4) separate statements of amounts for specified appropriations accounts and trust funds, among other things.[14]

The budget submissions of the past three Presidents have each included the following volumes:

- *Budget of the U.S. Government* - includes a short budget message summarizing the President's policy priorities, summary tables of budgetary aggregates, and a detailed narrative description of proposed government activities, organized by issue and agency;
- *Historical Tables* - provides a historical overview of federal government finances, including time series statistics on budget authority, government receipts, outlays, government employment, gross domestic product (GDP), and the federal debt going back several decades and in some cases as far back as 1789;[15]
- *Analytical Perspectives* - contains in-depth analysis of government programs, including credit and insurance programs, discussion of crosscut budgets that span two or more agencies, and technical explanation of the budget baselines used in the analyses and estimates contained in the President's budget proposal; and

- *Appendix* - includes detailed budget estimates and financial information on individual programs and appropriations accounts, proposed text of appropriations language, and information on the legislative and judicial branch appropriations that are not included in other volumes of the President's budget proposal.[16]

Presidents have also included supplemental materials, such as legislative proposals for budget process reform, a brief guide to the budget that is intended for members of the public, or a summary of proposed spending reductions or program consolidations.

Supplements and Revisions to the President's Budget Request

The President may also update the budget by submitting supplemental requests and revisions to Congress. Under current law, the President is required to submit a supplemental summary of the budget, commonly referred to as the Mid-Session Review (MSR), before July 16 of each year.

The MSR is required to include any substantial changes in estimates of expenditures, receipts, or substantial changes to obligations plus any changes in outlays or budget authority requested.[17] The MSR may reflect changes in economic conditions, budgetary actions taken by Congress, or other factors that have led the President to make adjustments to the initial budget submission.

Agency Budget Requests and Justifications

Once the President has submitted the budget, OMB and agency officials explain and justify the request to Congress. This frequently involves both formal and informal interactions. Early in the congressional budget process, often in the week following the submission of the President's budget, the OMB Director and other cabinet officials usually provide testimony regarding the President's broad budgetary objectives before congressional committees. For example, in February of 2012, acting OMB Director Jeffrey Zients and Treasury Secretary Timothy Geithner each testified before the House and Senate Budget Committees.

Agencies also submit written justification of their budget requests to the appropriations committee and subcommittees of jurisdiction in each chamber.[18] As budgetary legislation is being formulated by Congress, agency officials are often called before the appropriations subcommittees to justify and explain their budget requests to Congress. To ensure that all testimony and written justification materials are consistent with the President's policy objectives, OMB may review materials before agencies provide them to Congress.[19]

Agency testimony and written justification materials facilitate dialogue and information sharing between federal agencies and congressional committees.

Justification materials are often the starting point for language contained in the committee reports that accompany each appropriations bill. Agency justification materials also provide program details that Congress may use when determining the amounts to be appropriated and the language to be included in reports accompanying appropriations acts.

Finally, agencies and other administration officials may interact with Members of Congress informally. While the specifics of these informal communications are not public, committees may seek to develop ongoing relationships with the agencies within their jurisdiction.

Statements of Administration Policy and Other Presidential Actions

As Congress is considering budgetary legislation, formal and informal communications may be used to clarify and reiterate the President's policy positions. For example, OMB may formally communicate the President's position on proposed or pending legislation by issuing Statements of Administration Policy (SAPs), which are brief documents expressing support or opposition to pending legislation. The President and his or her administration may also negotiate with Congress informally at any time during the congressional budget process by holding summits or private meetings with Members of Congress. The President may also attempt to influence Congress indirectly by promoting his or her policy priorities through direct appeals to the public.[20]

Finally, the President may veto, or threaten to veto, any budgetary legislation passed by Congress. Between 1973 and 2012, for example, Presidents have successfully vetoed appropriations acts on at least 33 occasions.[21]

EXECUTION OF APPROPRIATIONS AND OTHER ENACTED BUDGETARY LEGISLATION

Once appropriations and other budgetary legislation have become law, federal agencies are responsible for executing the budget.[22] The President, OMB, and agencies execute the budget by collecting, obligating, and expending federal resources in accordance with the budgetary laws that have been enacted. The President, OMB, and agencies also possess limited authority to make spending adjustments after appropriations and other spending legislation have been enacted.

Apportionment and Allocation of Budget Authority

Appropriations and other budgetary legislation provide agencies with budget authority, which allows agencies to enter into obligations, such as contracts or employment of new personnel. The budget authority provided to agencies may not be automatically available for obligation or expenditure. With certain exceptions, the Antideficiency Act requires that appropriated funds be apportioned (or divided)—by time period, function, or program—in order to prevent agencies from exhausting their appropriated funds prematurely.[23]

Under the Antideficiency Act, funds appropriated for a definite period of time shall be apportioned "to prevent obligation or expenditure at a rate that would indicate a necessity for a deficiency or supplemental appropriation," while funds appropriated for an indefinite amount of time shall be apportioned "to achieve the most effective and economical use."[24] Appropriations must be apportioned no later than (1) 30 days prior to the start of the fiscal year for which the appropriations were provided, or (2) 30 days after the date of enactment of the appropriations act.[25]

Funds appropriated to executive agencies are apportioned by OMB.[26] Executive agencies must submit an apportionment request to OMB at least 40 days before the start of the fiscal year or within 15 days of the enactment of the appropriations act.[27] OMB then determines how executive agency funds will be apportioned, generally by fiscal quarter or by project.[28] OMB may also apportion multi-year and no-year funds for a period longer than one fiscal year, provided that an apportionment is made at the beginning of each fiscal year.[29]

Once funds are apportioned by OMB, executive agencies determine how to allocate and sub-allocate those funds amongst the programs, projects, and activities that fall within the scope of each apportionment. While executive agencies may have legal discretion to determine how to allocate the funds available to them, they are also legally obligated to execute spending legislation as enacted. In practice, executive agencies may come to informal arrangements with appropriations committees and subcommittees to ensure that they allocate funds in a manner consistent with both the text of appropriations and the details contained within reports accompanying appropriations acts.

Under the Antideficiency Act, executive agencies are responsible for ensuring that their obligations and expenditures stay within the allowable limits throughout the fiscal year. Agency heads must report any Antideficiency Act violations to the President (through the Director of OMB), to Congress, and to the Comptroller General. In the event that an agency's budgetary needs exceed their funding resources, the agency must request additional funding if it wants to spend more than it has available. OMB is responsible for reviewing requests for supplemental appropriations prior to the President's transmittal of those requests to Congress.

Reallocation of Budget Authority: Transfers and Reprogramming

Agencies may also possess limited authority to reallocate funds during budget execution, either by transfers or by reprogramming. Transfers typically involve a shift of budgetary resources from one appropriations account to another, while reprogramming involves a shift of budgetary resources from one project or purpose to another *within* an appropriations account.[30]

Transfers

There are two types of transfers: "expenditure" and "non-expenditure" transfers. Expenditure transfers occur when one agency or program "purchases" goods or services from another agency or program.[31] Non-expenditure transfers are all other transfers, including movement of funds from one account to another for the purpose of increasing the budgetary resources available to a specific program or activity. Both types require prior statutory authorization.

A general restriction against transfers may be found in 31 U.S.C. §1532, which reads, "An amount available under law may be withdrawn from one appropriation account and credited to another or to a working fund only when authorized by law."[32] There are statutory exceptions to this general restriction, and Congress may provide agencies with transfer authority either in authorizing statutes or within appropriations.

Appropriations or authorizing statutes that provide agencies with transfer authority will frequently include language establishing limitations on that authority.

For example, transfers may be limited to a specific dollar amount. Alternatively, transfers may be limited to a certain percentage of the total amount appropriated. In addition, statutes may include language limiting the use of the transferred funds to specific purposes. In many of these instances, such transfer authority is governed by provisions requiring notification to Congress, either prior to the transfer or within a certain time period following the transfer.[33]

Reprogramming[34]

Reprogramming is the use of funds for a project or purpose other than that for which they were originally provided.[35] An agency's authority to reprogram "is implicit in an agency's responsibility to manage its funds."[36] Though agencies are not statutorily prohibited from reprogramming funds, Congress may limit an agency's ability to reprogram by including limiting language within appropriations bills. Alternatively, Congress may require agencies to notify committees within a specific time frame either before or after they reprogram funds.

Reprogramming of funds may require an agency to adjust its apportionments. For executive agencies, reapportionments are generally prohibited without prior approval from OMB. Under Circular A-11, executive agencies are generally allowed to adjust apportioned amounts by up to $400,000 or 2% of their total budgetary resources, whichever is lower, without obtaining prior approval from OMB.[37]

In addition, agencies may have additional procedures governing the reprogramming of certain funds.

For example, executive agencies are required to submit a request to the Office of National Drug Control Policy prior to reprogramming any drug-related budgetary resources.[38]

Congressional Notification and Holds

Congress may exercise oversight over agency budget execution by requiring congressional notification before certain expenditures take place. For example, under certain provisions of the Foreign Assistance Act of 1961 and the International Development and Food Assistance Act of 1978 (22 U.S.C. §2151, et seq.) the Secretary of Defense, and in some cases the Secretary of State, is required to submit a congressional notification (CN) to specified congressional committees at least 15 days before the obligation or expenditure of select foreign aid funds.[39]

Similar notification requirements may also be included in appropriations and authorization acts. For example, the National Defense Authorization Act for Fiscal Year 2012 (P.L. 112-81) included multiple provisions requiring a CN at least 15 days prior to the obligation or expenditure of specified funds, including certain funds for the Commanders' Emergency Response Program in Afghanistan and the Global Security Contingency Fund.[40]

Following receipt of a CN, one or more of the committees may issue a hold instructing agencies not to obligate the specified funds until the hold is released by the issuing committee.

While the congressional notification requirement is statutory, the hold on the obligation or expenditure of funds is a non-statutory understanding between congressional committees and the agencies under their jurisdiction.[41]

Impoundment of Appropriated Funds: Rescissions and Deferrals

Impoundment is a process by which budgetary authority is reduced (either permanently or temporarily) subsequent to the enactment of appropriations and other budgetary legislation.[42]

Under the procedures established by the Impoundment Control Act (ICA) of 1974 (Title X of P.L. 93-344, 2 U.S.C. §681 et seq.), the President has limited authority to reduce or withhold agency funding by impoundment (i.e., an executive action or inaction that prevents the obligation and expenditure of budget authority).

The act distinguishes between two types of impoundments: rescissions, which permanently cancel budget authority, and deferrals, which temporarily delay the spending of funds.

Rescissions

Rescissions permanently cancel a specified portion of the budget authority available to an agency. The President may initiate rescissions by submitting a special message to Congress requesting that the specified budget authority be rescinded.[43]

Under the ICA, if the President determines that the total amount of budget authority is no longer required to carry out the objectives for which it was provided, he or she may submit one or more rescission requests to Congress.

If a President's rescission request is approved by Congress and enacted into law, the funds are no longer available for obligation and expenditure. However, if after 45 days Congress has not approved the rescission request, the funds must be reapportioned and made available for obligation and expenditure.

Deferrals

Deferrals are the temporary delay in the obligation or expenditure of appropriated funds, generally for no longer than 45 days. Deferrals allow agencies to adjust the timing of their obligations and expenditures in response to changing circumstances, such as a reduction or delay in expenses.

Under the ICA, funds may only be deferred (1) to provide for contingencies, (2) to achieve savings made possible by changes in requirements or greater efficiency of operations, or (3) as specifically provided by law.

Funds may also be deferred pending congressional action on a rescission request from the President, but must be released if that request is not approved.[44] Funds may be deferred without prior approval of Congress. However, the President must inform Congress and the Comptroller General of all deferrals, including those initiated by legislative and judicial branch agencies.[45]

OCCASIONAL PROCEDURES DURING BUDGET EXECUTION

The previous section provided an overview of the budget execution procedures that the President, OMB, and agencies utilize under normal conditions. Under existing law, there are additional executive budgetary procedures that are triggered under specific, less common circumstances.

Budget Execution During Federal Funding Gaps and Government Shutdowns

Under the Antideficiency Act, agencies are generally prohibited from obligating or spending funds prior to the enactment of their appropriations. A funding gap occurs when full-year or interim appropriations are not enacted by the start of the fiscal year.[46] A funding gap may also occur at other times during the fiscal year if an agency's interim appropriations (i.e., a continuing resolution or CR), expires and an additional CR is not subsequently enacted.[47] During a funding gap, the only budgetary resources that may be obligated or expended are those that will be used to provide for excepted activities, such as those involving "the safety of human life or the protection of property."[48]

During periods when enactment of full-year or interim appropriates seems uncertain, OMB may instruct executive agencies to prepare for funding gaps and government shutdowns.[49] Circular A11 provides general guidance on how executive agencies should proceed if their regular appropriations or CRs are not enacted or if their existing CRs have expired.[50] For example, Circular A-11 instructs agencies to develop shutdown plans that identify "excepted" activities which will continue and "non-excepted" activities which will be terminated in the event of a funding gap. In addition, the circular instructs agencies to determine which of their employees will be subject to furlough and which will be retained. If a funding gap is imminent, OMB may issue additional guidance to agency heads.[51]

Budget Execution in the Event of Sequestration

Sequestration involves the cancellation of budgetary resources under a statutorily prescribed presidential sequester order. A sequester order identifies the specific budgetary resources that can no longer be obligated or expended despite their being enacted into law. Under the provisions of the Balanced Budget and Emergency Deficit Control Act of 1985 (BBEDCA; P.L. 99-177), as amended by the Statutory Pay-As-You-Go Act of 2010 (Statutory PAYGO Act; P.L. 111-139), a sequestration of nonexempt direct spending may be triggered if the new revenue and new direct spending legislation enacted during a congressional session are not "deficit neutral."[52] Under the BBEDCA and Statutory PAYGO, OMB is responsible for tracking the cumulative deficit impact of enacted budgetary legislation. If a sequestration is triggered, OMB is responsible for calculating the uniform percentage by which the budgetary resources of nonexempt programs will be reduced.

Under the provisions of the Budget Control Act of 2011 (BCA; P.L. 112-25) automatic spending reductions, including sequestration of nonexempt discretionary and direct spending, are triggered if legislation to reduce the deficit by $1.2 trillion by the end of FY2021 is not enacted by January 15, 2012.[53] The BCA also includes provisions requiring sequestration in the event that the statutory discretionary spending caps established by the BCA are exceeded.[54] Under the BCA, OMB is responsible for calculating and preparing the sequestration order using the formula provided in the BCA and following the same procedures as those specified in the BBEDCA. Once prepared, the sequestration order is to be issued by the President.

Under both the BCA and the BBEDCA, once issued, the implementation of a sequestration (and execution of the resulting spending cuts) are the responsibility of OMB and each agency, respectively.[55] Circular A-11 summarizes the requirements of the BBEDCA and the Statutory PAYGO Act, and briefly discusses how agencies should manage and record sequestrations issued under those statutes, in order to avoid potential Antideficiency Act violations.[56] However, the circular does not specifically discuss how agencies might manage sequestrations that may be issued under the provisions of the BCA.[57]

End Notes

[1] U.S. Constitution, Article I, §9.

[2] Allen Schick, The Federal Budget: Politics, Policy, Process, 3rd ed. (Washington, D.C.: Brookings Institution Press, 2007), pp. 13-14.

[3] Appropriations legislation provides agencies with budget authority (i.e., the authority to enter into obligations such as contracts or the hiring of personnel) and the ability to make payments from the U.S. Treasury. Other budgetary legislation includes direct spending (i.e., budget authority provided outside the appropriations process, by authorizing statute, for example), as well as revenue and debt-limit legislation. For a broad overview of the federal budget process, see CRS Report 98-721, Introduction to the Federal Budget Process, coordinated by Bill Heniff Jr.

[4] 31 U.S.C. §1105. The President's budget includes budget requests for all executive departments and agencies, as well as budget requests for the legislative and judicial branches. Since the legislative and judicial branches are co-equal branches of government, the President and OMB play no role in the development of their requests. Instead, the legislative and judicial branches transmit their budget requests to the President, who then is required to include them in the budget submission to Congress without modification (31 U.S.C. §1105(b)).

[5] U.S. Office of Management and Budget, Circular No. A-11, "Preparation, Submission and Execution of the Budget," August 18, 2011, http://www.whitehouse.gov/omb/circulars_default.

[6] The budget planning guidance memorandum is usually issued in mid-to-late spring, nearly a year before the President submits the budget proposal to Congress. However, the memorandum has been issued as late as August.

[7] Memorandum from Jacob J. Lew, Director of OMB, M-11-30, "Fiscal Year 2013 Budget Guidance," August 17, 2011, http://www.whitehouse.gov/omb/memoranda_2011.

[8] Allen Schick, Federal Budget: Politics, Policy, and Process, 3rd ed. (Washington, D.C.: The Brookings Institution, 2007), pp. 92-93.

[9] Shelley Lynne Tomkin, Inside OMB: Politics and Process in the President's Budget Office (New York: M.E. Sharpe, 1998), pp. 120-130. For additional information, see http://www.whitehouse.gov/omb/program_examiner.

[10] Ibid., pp. 131.

[11] U.S. Government Accountability Office, A Glossary of Terms Used in the Federal Budget Process, GAO-05-734SP, September 2005, pp. 105, http://gao.gov/assets/80/76911.pdf.

[12] Shelley Lynne Tomkin, Inside OMB: Politics and Process in the President's Budget Office (New York: M.E. Sharpe, 1998), pp. 131-134.

[13] The details of the congressional budget process are outside the scope of this report. For discussion of congressional budgetary procedures, see CRS Report RS20095, The Congressional Budget Process: A Brief Overview, by James V. Saturno and CRS Report R42388, The Congressional Appropriations Process: An Introduction, by Jessica Tollestrup.

[14] 31 U.S.C. §1105.

[15] The time frame for the information contained in the Historical Tables volume varies from table to table, presumably due to the availability of data. For example, information on aggregate levels of receipts and outlays is provided for all years starting with 1789, while information on total levels of federal government employment is only provided as far back as 1962.

[16] CRS Report R42384, FY2013 Budget Documents: Internet and GPO Availability, by Jared Conrad Nagel.

[17] 31 U.S.C. §1106.

[18] Federal agencies also make their justification materials available electronically. For a list of links to the justification materials for all 15 executive branch departments and selected independent agencies, please see CRS Report R42453, Selected Agency Budget Justifications for FY2013, by Justin Murray.

[19] For example, Circular A-11 §22 establishes guidelines regarding agency conversations with Congress or the public and emphasizes statutory restrictions on attempts to influence legislation outside of official channels.

[20] Samuel Kernell, Going Public: New Strategies of Presidential Leadership, 4th ed. (Washington: CQ Press, 2006).

[21] CRS Report RS22188, Regular Vetoes and Pocket Vetoes: An Overview, by Kevin R. Kosar.

[22] In the event that an agency's regular appropriations act has not become law prior to the start of the fiscal year, a temporary continuing appropriations act (i.e., a continuing resolution or CR) may be enacted. This allows the agency to continue operating for the period of time covered by the CR. See CRS Report RL30343, Continuing Resolutions: Latest Action and Brief Overview of Recent Practices, by Sandy Streeter and CRS Report RL32614, Duration of Continuing Resolutions in Recent Years, by Jessica Tollestrup.

23 The collection of statutes commonly referred to as the Antideficiency Act have been codified in multiple sections of Title 31 (31 U.S.C. §§1341-1342, 1349-1350, 1511-1519). Select

government entities are exempted from the apportionment requirements of the Antideficiency Act, including the Senate, the House of Representatives, congressional committees, and the Office of the Architect of the Capitol (31 U.S.C. §1511 (b)(3)).

[24] 31 U.S.C. §1512(a).

[25] 31 U.S.C. §1513(a).

[26] Under 31 U.S.C. §1513(b)(1), the President is statutorily responsible for apportioning funds for executive branch agencies. This responsibility has been delegated to OMB. For the legislative and judicial branches, apportionments are made by the officials who maintain administrative control of each appropriations account. For example, the appropriations bill for the judicial branch is currently comprised of 12 accounts. According to an official at the Administrative Office of the U.S. Courts, eight of those accounts—including accounts that provide funds for federal court jurors, court security, federal judicial salaries (excluding salaries of the Supreme Court) and retirement funds— are administered by the Director of the Administrative Office of the U.S. Courts, who also serves as the Secretary of the U.S. Judicial Conference. The remaining four accounts provide funds for Supreme Court salaries and expenses and for judicial organizations such as the U.S. Sentencing Commission and the Court of International Trade. These accounts are administered by the organizations they fund. Each of those organizations is responsible for apportioning the funds that they have been appropriated. (Telephone and email conversations with an official at the Administrative Office of the U.S. Courts, May 17, 2012 and June 12, 2012).

[27] 31 U.S.C. §1513(b)(1) states that agencies must submit "information required for the apportionment" to the President. Circular A-11 §120.26 has further specified that agencies should submit their apportionment requests by August 21, or "within 10 calendar days after the approval of the appropriation or substantive acts providing new budget authority, whichever is later."

[28] Circular A-11 §120 defines an apportionment as "a plan, approved by OMB, to spend resources provided by one of the annual appropriations acts, a supplemental appropriations act, a continuing resolution, or a permanent law (mandatory appropriations)." OMB may also apportion non-financial resources, such as personnel and motor vehicles. In addition to apportioning appropriated funds, OMB may also provide agencies with guidance regarding the implementation of laws related to mandatory spending (i.e., spending provided in acts other than appropriations), such as laws authorizing certain entitlement programs. For additional information, see CRS Report R41375, OMB Controls on Agency Mandatory Spending Programs: "Administrative PAYGO" and Related Issues for Congress, by Clinton T. Brass and Jim Monke.

[29] Multi-year funds are appropriations that remain available for obligation for more than one year. No-year funds are appropriations that remain available until expended. Unobligated balances from each quarter remain available until the end of the fiscal year without reapportionment. U.S. Government Accountability Office, A Glossary of Terms Used in the Federal Budget Process, GAO-05-734SP, September 2005, http://gao.gov/assets/ 80/ 76911.pdf.

[30] An "appropriations account" is the basic unit of an appropriation. In the case of funds provided in appropriations acts, each "account" reflects an unnumbered paragraph in an appropriations act, which may encompass a number of related programs, projects, and activities.

[31] Such transfers are subject to the procedures established by the Economy Act (31 U.S.C. §1535). The act established guidelines and procedures allowing agencies to perform work and provide goods and services to one another. Transfers to and from federal funds, (e.g.,

revolving, trust, or other special funds) are also considered expenditure transfers as are transfers between budget accounts and off-budget deposit accounts. For discussion of Economy Act transactions and other interagency procurement, see CRS Report R40814, Interagency Contracting: An Overview of Federal Procurement and Appropriations Law, by Kate M. Manuel and Brian T. Yeh.

[32] 31 U.S.C. §1532.

[33] CRS Report RL33151, Committee Controls of Agency Decisions, by Louis Fisher.

[34] It should be noted that the Department of Defense uses the term "reprogramming" to refer to both reprogramming and transfers.

[35] U.S. Government Accountability Office, A Glossary of Terms Used in the Federal Budget Process, GAO-05-734SP, September 2005, http://gao.gov/assets/80/76911.pdf.

[36] U.S. Government Accountability Office (then the U.S. General Accounting Office), Principles of Federal Appropriations Law, Volume I, GAO-04-261SP, January 2004, p. 30, http://www.gao.gov/products/GAO-04-261SP.

[37] Circular A-11 §120.37.

[38] R. Gil Kerlikowske, Director of the Office of Drug Control Policy, Fiscal Year 2010 Accounting of Drug Control Funds, Executive Office of the President, Office of Drug Control Policy, June 13, 2011, http://www.whitehouse.gov/ sites/default/files/ondcp/Fact_ Sheets/fy2010_accounting_of_drug_control_funds_report_and_letters_june_2011.pdf.

[39] The specified committees include the House Committee on Foreign Affairs, the Senate Committee on Foreign Relations, and the House and Senate Appropriations Committees. In cases involving funds for military assistance, the Secretaries may also be required to submit CNs to the House and Senate Armed Services Committees.

[40] P.L. 112-81, §1201(g) and §1207 (l)(1).

[41] Agencies maintain the authority to obligate funds despite a congressional hold. For further discussion of non-statutory understandings, see CRS Report RL33151, Committee Controls of Agency Decisions, by Louis Fisher.

[42] Budget authority may also be reduced by sequestration. Sequestration involves the cancellation of budgetary authority after a statutorily prescribed sequester order.

[43] Rescissions may also be initiated by Congress by introducing legislation that would cancel budget authority previously enacted.

[44] 2 U.S.C. §684.

[45] 2 U.S.C. §684(a).

[46] 31 U.S.C. §1341(a)(1)(A).

[47] For historical information on previous federal funding gaps, see CRS Report RS20348, Federal Funding Gaps: A Brief Overview, by Jessica Tollestrup. For discussion of the potential impact of CRs, see CRS Report RL34700, Interim Continuing Resolutions (CRs): Potential Impacts on Agency Operations, by Clinton T. Brass.

[48] 31 U.S.C §1342.

[49] CRS Report RL34680, Shutdown of the Federal Government: Causes, Processes, and Effects, by Clinton T. Brass.

[50] Circular A-11 §124.

[51] For example, on December 15, 2011, one day prior to the expiration of the third FY2012 Continuing Resolution, OMB Director Jacob J. Lew issued a memorandum instructing agencies on how to prepare for operations in the event of a funding gap and subsequent shutdown of the federal government. Memorandum from Jacob J. Lew, Director of the Office of Management and Budget, M-12-03, "Planning for Agency Operations During a

Lapse in Government Funding," December 15, 2011, http://www.whitehouse. gov/sites /default/files/omb/memoranda/2012/m-12-03.pdf.

[52] For additional information on sequestration under the BBEDCA and the Statutory PAYGO Act, see CRS Report R41157, The Statutory Pay-As-You-Go Act of 2010: Summary and Legislative History, by Bill Heniff Jr.

[53] The necessary deficit reduction legislation was not enacted by the January 15, 2012, deadline. Consequently, the reductions, including sequestration, are scheduled to take effect in January 2013.

[54] For additional information on the BCA, see CRS Report R41965, The Budget Control Act of 2011, by Bill Heniff Jr., Elizabeth Rybicki, and Shannon M. Mahan and CRS Report R42050, Budget "Sequestration" and Selected Program Exemptions and Special Rules, coordinated by Karen Spar. For discussion of the potential impact of sequestration, see CRS Report R42506, The Budget Control Act of 2011: The Effects on Spending and the Budget Deficit When the Automatic Spending Cuts Are Implemented, by Mindy R. Levit and Marc Labonte and CRS Report R42051, Budget Control Act: Potential Impact of Automatic Spending Reduction Procedures on Health Reform Spending, by C. Stephen Redhead.

[55] According to GAO, under the BCA "the execution and impact of any spending reductions will depend on the legal interpretations and actions taken by the Office of Management and Budget, which is vested with implementing the Budget Control Act." See U.S. Government Accountability Office, The Budget Control Act and the Department of Veterans Affairs' Programs, B-323157, May 21, 2012, pp. 4-5, http://gao.gov/assets/600/591052.pdf.

[56] Circular A-11 §20 and §81. The Antideficiency Act prohibits agencies from obligating or expending funds required to be sequestered under the BBEDCA (31 U.S.C. §1341(a)(1)).

[57] Circular A-11, Appendix F. The circular does, however, provide agencies with guidance for reporting budgetary information in a manner consistent with the new discretionary spending subcategories established by the BCA. These reporting guidelines may help facilitate agency identification of accounts that would be subject to sequestration.

In: The Federal Budget Process: An Introduction ISBN: 978-1-62417-838-2
Editor: Adele Wilkinson

Chapter 3

THE CONGRESSIONAL BUDGET PROCESS: A BRIEF OVERVIEW*

James V. Saturno

SUMMARY

The term "budget process," when applied to the federal government, actually refers to a number of processes that have evolved separately and that occur with varying degrees of coordination. This overview, and the accompanying flow chart, are intended to describe in brief each of the parts of the budget process that involve Congress, clarify the role played by each, and explain how they operate together. They include the President's budget submission, the budget resolution, reconciliation, sequestration, authorizations, and appropriations.

THE BASIC FRAMEWORK

The Constitution grants the "power of the purse" to Congress,[1] but does not establish any specific procedure for the consideration of budgetary legislation. Instead, a number of laws and congressional rules contribute to the

---

* This is an edited, reformatted and augmented version of a Congressional Research Service publication, CRS Report for Congress RS20095, from www.crs.gov, prepared for Members and Committees of Congress, dated August 22, 2011.

federal budget process, with two statutes in particular forming the basic framework.[2]

The Budget and Accounting Act of 1921, as codified in Title 31 of the *United States Code*, established the statutory basis for an executive budget process by requiring the President to submit to Congress annually a proposed budget for the federal government. It also created the Bureau of the Budget (reorganized as the Office of Management and Budget (OMB) in 1970) to assist him in carrying out his responsibilities, and the General Accounting Office (GAO, renamed the Government Accountability Office in 2004) to assist Congress as the principal auditing agency of the federal government.

The Congressional Budget and Impoundment Control Act of 1974 (P.L. 93-344, 88 Stat. 297) established the statutory basis for a congressional budget process, and provided for the annual adoption of a concurrent resolution on the budget as a mechanism for facilitating congressional budgetary decision making. It also established the House and Senate Budget Committees, and created the Congressional Budget Office (CBO) to provide budgetary information to Congress independent of the executive branch.

THE BUDGET CYCLE

The President is required to submit to Congress a proposed budget by the first Monday in February. Although this budget does not have the force of law, it is a comprehensive examination of federal revenues and spending, including any initiatives recommended by the President, and is the start of extensive interaction with Congress.

Within six weeks of the President's budget submission, congressional committees are required to submit their "views and estimates" of spending and revenues within their respective jurisdictions to the House and Senate Budget Committees. These views and estimates, along with information from other sources, are then used by each Budget Committee in drafting and reporting a concurrent resolution on the budget to its respective house. Other information is gathered by the Budget Committees in reports and hearing testimony. That information includes budget and economic projections, programmatic information, and budget priorities, and comes from a variety of sources, such as CBO, OMB, the Federal Reserve, executive branch agencies, and congressional leadership.

Although it also does not have the force of law, the budget resolution is a central part of the budget process in Congress. As a concurrent resolution, it represents an agreement between the House and Senate that establishes budget priorities, and defines the parameters for all subsequent budgetary actions. The spending, revenue, and public debt legislation necessary to implement decisions agreed to in the budget resolution are subsequently enacted separately.

Discretionary spending,[3] in the form of appropriation bills, involves annual actions that must be completed before the beginning of a new fiscal year on October 1. Changes in direct spending[4] or revenue laws may also be a part of budgetary actions in any given year. When these changes are directly tied to implementing the fiscal policies in the budget resolution for that year, the reconciliation process may be used. Reconciliation typically follows a timetable established in the budget resolution. Other budgetary legislation, such as changes in direct spending or revenue laws separate from the reconciliation process, changes in the public debt limit, or authorizing legislation, are not tied directly to the annual budget cycle. However, such legislation may be a necessary part of budgetary actions in any given year.

THE BUDGET RESOLUTION AND RECONCILIATION

The budget resolution represents an agreement between the House and Senate concerning the overall size of the federal budget, and the general composition of the budget in terms of functional categories. The amounts in functional categories are translated into allocations to each committee with jurisdiction over spending in a process called "crosswalking" under Section 302(a) of the Congressional Budget Act. Legislation considered by the House and Senate must be consistent with these allocations, as well as with the aggregate levels of spending and revenues. Both the allocations and aggregates are enforceable through points of order that may be made during House or Senate floor consideration of such legislation. These allocations are supplemented by nonbinding assumptions concerning the substance of possible budgetary legislation that are included in the reports from the Budget Committees that accompany the budget resolution in each house.

In some years, the budget resolution includes reconciliation instructions. Reconciliation instructions identify the committees that must recommend changes in laws affecting revenues or direct spending programs within their jurisdiction in order to implement the priorities agreed to in the budget resolution.[5] All committees receiving such instructions must submit recommended legislative language to the Budget Committee in their respective chamber, which packages the recommended language as an omnibus measure and reports the measure without substantive revision. A reconciliation bill would then be considered, and possibly amended, by the full House or Senate. In the House, reconciliation bills are typically considered under the terms of a special rule.

In the Senate, reconciliation bills are considered under limitations imposed by Sections 305, 310, and 313 of the Congressional Budget Act. These sections limit debate on a reconciliation bill to 20 hours, and limit the types of amendments that may be considered.

The Appropriations Process

The annual appropriations process provides funding for discretionary spending programs through regular annual appropriations bills.[6] Congress must enact these measures prior to the beginning of each fiscal year (October 1) or provide interim funding for the affected programs through a "continuing resolution." By custom, appropriations bills originate in the House, but may be amended by the Senate, as other legislation.

The House and Senate Appropriations Committees are organized into subcommittees, each of which is responsible for developing an appropriations bill. Appropriations bills are constrained in terms of both their purpose and the amount of funding they provide. Appropriations are constrained in terms of purpose because the rules of both the House (Rule XXI) and the Senate (Rule XVI) generally require authorization prior to consideration of appropriations for an agency or program.[7]

Constraints in terms of the amount of funding exist on several levels. For individual items or programs, funding may be limited to the level recommended in authorizing legislation. The overall level of discretionary spending provided in appropriations acts is limited by the allocations from the budget resolution made to the Appropriations Committees under Section 302(a) of the Budget Act.

These allocations provide limits that may be enforced procedurally through points of order in the House and Senate during consideration of legislation. In the absence of a final agreement on a concurrent resolution on the budget, the House or Senate may adopt a "deeming resolution" to establish provisional enforcement levels.[8]

Section 302(b) of the Budget Act further requires the House and Senate Appropriations Committees to subdivide the amounts allocated to them under the budget resolution among their subcommittees. These suballocations are to be made "as soon as practicable after a concurrent resolution on the budget is agreed to."

Because each subcommittee is responsible for developing a single general appropriations bill, the process of making suballocations effectively determines the spending level for each of the regular annual appropriations bills.

Legislation (or amendments) that would cause the suballocations made under 302(b) to be exceeded is subject to a point of order. The Appropriations Committees can (and do) issue revised subdivisions over the course of appropriations actions to reflect changes in spending priorities effected during floor consideration or in conference.

Revenue and Public Debt Legislation

The budget resolution provides a guideline for the overall level of revenues, but not for their composition. Legislative language controlling revenues is reported by the committees of jurisdiction (the House Ways and Means Committee and the Senate Finance Committee). The revenue level agreed to in the budget resolution acts as a minimum, limiting consideration of revenue legislation that would decrease revenue below that level. In addition, Article I, Section 7 of the Constitution requires that all revenue measures originate in the House of Representatives, although the Senate may amend them, as other legislation.

Revenue legislation may be considered at any time, although revenue provisions are often included in reconciliation legislation.[9]

The budget resolution also specifies an appropriate level for the public debt that reflects the budgetary policies agreed to in the resolution. Any change in the authorized level of the public debt must be implemented through a statutory enactment.[10]

Budget Enforcement and Sequestration

The Balanced Budget and Emergency Deficit Control Act of 1985 (P.L. 99-177, 99 Stat. 1037) established the sequester[11] as a means to enforce statutory budget limits.

Amendments to this act were designed to use sequesters to control direct spending and revenues (through the pay-as-you-go, or PAYGO, process) and discretionary spending (through spending caps). Under these mechanisms, the budgetary impact of all legislation was scored by OMB, and reported three times each year (a preview with the President's budget submission, an update with the Mid-Session Review of the Budget, and a final report 15 days after Congress adjourned).

If the final report on either the PAYGO or spending caps mechanism indicated that the statutory limitations within that category had been violated, the President was required to issue an order making across-the-board cuts of nonexempt spending programs within that category. Those mechanisms expired October 1, 2002.[12]

Although formal enforcement of these mechanisms was through a presidential order, by enforcing the allocations and aggregates for spending and revenues provided in the budget resolution consistent with these limits, Congress was able to use points of order to enforce them as well. Although these statutory limits expired at the end of FY2002, Congress has continued to use the concurrent resolution on the budget and points of order to establish and enforce budgetary limits.[13]

More recently, new statutory control mechanisms have been established. The first was the Statutory PAYGO Act of 2010 to limit increases in the deficit caused by new direct spending or revenue legislation.[14] Like its predecessor, it uses sequestration as its enforcement mechanism.

On August 2, 2011, the Budget Control Act of 2011 was signed into law.[15] This law reestablished discretionary spending caps to apply to FY2012-FY2021 as well as parameters for further deficit reduction to be achieved over the same period. It includes two separate sequester mechanisms to enforce its requirements.

These sequesters would enforce (1) the discretionary spending limit and (2) any amounts of the additional deficit reduction required under the act not achieved through a privileged measure to be authored by a Joint Select Committee on Deficit Reduction.

Although the primary enforcement of these limits is through sequestration, the Budget Control Act also established a point of order against the consideration of legislation that would exceed the discretionary spending caps. In addition, by enforcing allocations and aggregates in the budget resolution consistent with these limits, Congress can enforce them through existing points of order as well.

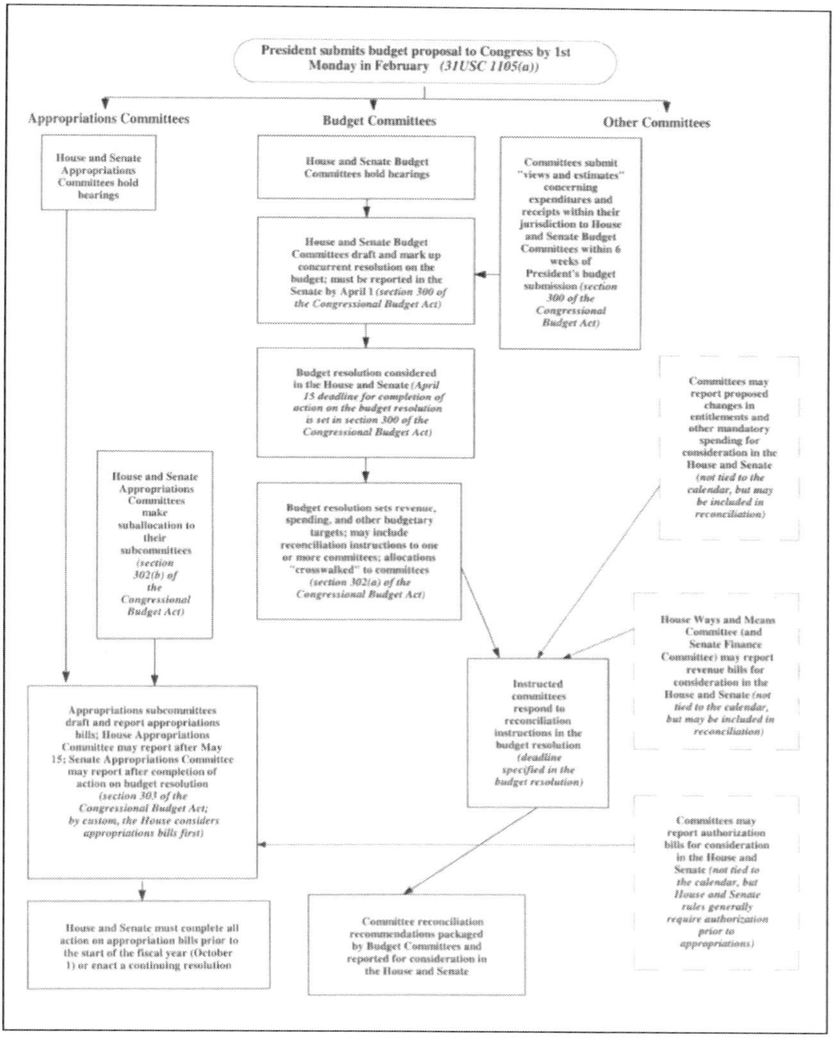

Figure 1. The Congressional Budget Process: Timetable for Annual Action.

End Notes

[1] Article I, Section 8 provides that "The Congress shall have Power To lay and collect Taxes, Duties, Imposts and Excises," and Section 9 provides that "No Money shall be drawn from the Treasury, but in Consequence of Appropriations made by Law."

[2] For a more extensive overview of the federal budget process, see CRS Report 98-721, Introduction to the Federal Budget Process, coordinated by Bill Heniff Jr.

[3] Discretionary spending is that spending not mandated by existing law, and therefore is made available in such amounts as Congress chooses through the appropriations process.

[4] Direct spending, also referred to as mandatory or entitlement spending, is that spending directly controlled through eligibility requirements and benefit payments mandated in laws other than appropriations.

[5] CRS Report R41186, Reconciliation Directives: Components and Enforcement, by Megan Suzanne Lynch.

[6] CRS Report 97-684, The Congressional Appropriations Process: An Introduction, by Sandy Streeter.

[7] Authorizations are legislation that establish, continue, or modify an agency or program, and authorize the enactment of appropriations to carry out such purposes. Authorizations may be temporary or permanent, and their provisions may be general or specific, but they do not themselves provide funding in the absence of appropriations actions. Although House and Senate rules generally prohibit unauthorized appropriations, both provide exceptions in their respective rules, and the prohibition itself may be waived.

[8] CRS Report RL31443, The "Deeming Resolution": A Budget Enforcement Tool, by Megan Suzanne Lynch.

[9] CRS Report R41408, Rules and Practices Governing Consideration of Revenue Legislation in the House and Senate, by Megan Suzanne Lynch.

[10] CRS Report RS21519, Legislative Procedures for Adjusting the Public Debt Limit: A Brief Overview, by Bill Heniff Jr.

[11] A sequester was an executive order canceling budgetary resources in accordance with the provisions of the Balanced Budget and Emergency Deficit Control Act of 1985, as amended.

[12] These mechanisms were first established under the Budget Enforcement Act of 1990 (Title XIII of P.L. 101-508, Omnibus Budget Reconciliation Act of 1990). Originally enacted with a sunset date of FY1995, they were extended twice, through FY1998 (Title XIV of P.L. 103-66, Omnibus Budget Reconciliation Act of 1993) and through FY2002 (Budget Enforcement Act of 1997, Title X of P.L. 105-33, Balanced Budget Act of 1997). See CRS Report R41005, The Statutory PAYGO Process for Budget Enforcement: 1991-2002, by Robert Keith.

[13] CRS Report 97-865, Points of Order in the Congressional Budget Process, by James V. Saturno.

[14] P.L. 111-139. For detailed information see CRS Report R41157, The Statutory Pay-As-You-Go Act of 2010: Summary and Legislative History, by Bill Heniff Jr.

[15] P.L. 112-25. For detailed information see CRS Report R41965, The Budget Control Act of 2011, by Bill Heniff Jr., Elizabeth Rybicki, and Shannon M. Mahan.

In: The Federal Budget Process: An Introduction ISBN: 978-1-62417-838-2
Editor: Adele Wilkinson

Chapter 4

POINTS OF ORDER IN THE CONGRESSIONAL BUDGET PROCESS*

James V. Saturno

SUMMARY

The Congressional Budget Act of 1974 (Titles I-IX of P.L. 93-344, as amended) created a process that Congress uses each year to establish and enforce the parameters for budgetary legislation. Enforcement of budgetary decisions is accomplished through the use of points of order, and through the reconciliation process. Points of order are prohibitions against certain types of legislation or congressional actions. These prohibitions are enforced when a Member raises a point of order against legislation that may violate these rules when it is considered by the House or Senate.

This report summarizes points of order under the Congressional Budget Act of 1974, as amended, and related points of order established in the budget resolutions adopted by Congress in 2007 (S.Con.Res. 21, 110th Congress), 2008 (S.Con.Res. 70, 110th Congress), and 2009 (S.Con.Res. 13, 111th Congress), as well as the Rules of the House for the 112th Congress, the Budget Enforcement Act of 1990 (P.L. 101-508), and the Statutory Pay-As-You-Go Act of 2010 (P.L. 111-139).

---

* This is an edited, reformatted and augmented version of a Congressional Research Service publication, CRS Report for Congress 97-865, from www.crs.gov, prepared for Members and Committees of Congress, dated August 12, 2011.

In addition, it describes how points of order are applied and the processes used for their waiver in the House and Senate.

INTRODUCTION

The Congressional Budget Act of 1974[1] established the basic framework that is used today for congressional consideration of budget and fiscal policy. The act provided for the adoption of a concurrent resolution on the budget (budget resolution) as a mechanism for coordinating congressional budgetary decision making. This process supplements other House and Senate procedures for considering spending and revenue legislation by allowing Congress to establish and enforce parameters with which those separate pieces of budgetary legislation must be consistent. The parameters are established each year when Congress adopts the budget resolution, setting forth overall levels for new budget authority, outlays, revenues, deficit, and debt.

These overall spending levels are then allocated to the various committees in the House and Senate responsible for spending legislation. The overall levels and allocations are then enforced through the use of points of order, and through implementing legislation, such as that enacted through the reconciliation process.[2] Points of order are prohibitions against certain types of legislation or congressional actions. These prohibitions are enforced when a Member raises a point of order against legislation that is alleged to violate these rules when it is considered by the House or Senate. Points of order are not self-enforcing. A point of order must be raised by a Member on the floor of the chamber before the presiding officer can rule on its application, and thus for its enforcement.

Although the congressional budget process encompasses myriad procedures dealing with spending, revenue, and debt legislation, this report focuses only on that portion of the process that stems from the Congressional Budget Act. The tables below list the points of order currently included in the Congressional Budget Act (*Table 1*), as well as related points of order established in other measures. These other measures include the FY2010 budget resolution (*Table 2*); FY2009 budget resolution (*Table 3);* the FY2008 budget resolution (*Table 4*); the Budget Enforcement Act of 1990 (*Table 5*); the rules and separate orders of the House as adopted under H.Res. 5, 112th Congress (*Table 6*); and the Statutory Pay-As-You-Go Act of 2010 (*Table 7*) that pertain to the consideration, contents, implementation, or enforcement of budgetary decisions.

Points of order are typically in the form of a provision stating that "it shall not be in order" for the House or Senate to take a specified action or consider certain legislation that is inconsistent with the requirements of the Budget Act. Other provisions of the act, formulated differently, establish various requirements or procedures, particularly concerning the contents and consideration of the budget resolution or reconciliation legislation. These provisions, however, are not typically enforced through points of order, and are not included here.[3]

As amended through the Balanced Budget Act of 1997, points of order in the Congressional Budget Act are permanent. None of the provisions listed in *Table 1* is scheduled to expire, although several points of order have limited applicability or have been rendered moot by the expiration of limits they were intended to enforce.[4] The freestanding point of order protecting the Social Security trust fund in the House established in the Budget Enforcement Act (see *Table 5*) is also permanent. However, other points of order established under recent budget resolutions have various sunset provisions or limited application (see *Table 3* and *Table 4* for examples).

APPLICATION OF POINTS OF ORDER

Most points of order in the Budget Act apply to measures as a whole, as well as to motions, amendments, or conference reports to those measures. When a point of order is sustained against consideration of some matter, the effect is that the matter in question falls.

The application of points of order in the House is clarified in Section 315 of the Budget Act. This provision states that for cases in which a reported measure is considered pursuant to a special rule, a point of order against a bill "as reported" would apply to the text made in order by the rule as original text for the purpose of amendment or to the text on which the previous question is ordered directly to passage. In this way, no point of order would be considered as applying (and no waiver would be required) if a substitute resolved the problem. In addition, the Rules of the House for the 111th Congress include a provision further specifying that for measures considered pursuant to a special rule, points of order under Title III of the Budget Act apply without regard to whether the measure considered is actually that reported from committee. Under Rule XXI, clause 8, points of order apply to the form of a measure recommended by the reporting committee where the statute uses the term "as reported" (in the case of a measure that has been reported), the form of the measure made in order as an original text for the purpose of amendment, or the form of the measure on which the previous question is ordered directly to passage.

The effect of a point of order in the Senate is clarified under Section 312(f), which provides that when a point of order against a measure is sustained, the measure is recommitted to the appropriate committee for any further consideration.

This allows the Senate an opportunity to remedy the problem that caused the point of order. Section 312(d) is also designed to provide the Senate with the opportunity to remedy a problem that would provoke a point of order. This provision states that a point of order may not be raised against a measure, amendment, motion, or conference report while an amendment or motion that would remedy the problem is pending.

Section 312(e) clarifies that any point of order that would apply in the Senate against an amendment also applies against amendments between the houses. Further, this section also states that the effect would "be the same as if the Senate had disagreed to the amendment." This would allow the Senate to keep the underlying measure pending, and thus retain the ability to resolve their differences with the House.

This provision therefore means that any resolution of the differences between the House- and Senate-passed versions of a measure, whether it is in the form of a conference report or not, must adhere to the provisions of the Budget Act.

There are exceptions to the general principle of applying points of order to a measure as a whole.

The most salient is probably Section 313, the so-called Byrd Rule. This section applies to matter "contained in any title or provision" in a reconciliation bill or resolution (or conference report thereon), as well as any amendment or motion.

If a point of order is sustained under this section, only the provision in question is stricken, or the amendment or motion falls.[5] Several of the points of order in the Senate established under recent budget resolutions have been written so that they apply to individual provisions rather than the measure as a whole, in the manner provided in Section 313(e) of the Budget Act.

The point of order against emergency spending designations (Section 403(e)(1) of S.Con.Res. 13 (111th Congress)) further provides that, if sustained, the effect of this point of order is that a provision making an emergency designation shall be stricken, and may not be offered as an amendment from the floor.

Procedures for Waiving Points of Order

The Congressional Budget Act sets forth certain procedures, under Section 904, for waiving points of order under the act. These waiver procedures apply in the Senate only. Under these procedures, a Senator may make a motion to waive the application of a point of order either preemptively before it can be raised, or after it is raised, but before the presiding officer rules on its merits.[6]

In the Senate, most points of order under the Budget Act may be waived by a vote of at least three-fifths of all Senators duly chosen and sworn (60 votes if there are no vacancies) (see *Table 1*). The three-fifths waiver requirement was first established for some points of order under the Balanced Budget and Emergency Deficit Control Act of 1985. Beginning with the Balanced Budget Act of 1997, this super-majority threshold was applied to several additional points of order on a temporary basis. These points of order are identified in Section 904(c)(2), and the three-fifths requirement is currently scheduled to expire September 30, 2017.[7] The three-fifths threshold has also been required for the Senate to waive the application of many of the points of order established in recent budget resolutions, such as the PAYGO point of order. As with other provisions of Senate rules, Budget Act points of order also may be waived by unanimous consent.

In the House, Budget Act points of order are typically waived by the adoption of special rules, although other means (such as unanimous consent or suspension of the rules) may also be used. A waiver may be used to protect a bill, specified provision(s) in a bill, or an amendment from a point of order that could be raised against it. Waivers may be granted for one or more amendments even if they are not granted for the underlying bill. The House may waive the application of one or more specific points of order, or they may include a "blanket waiver," that is, a waiver that would protect a bill, provision, or amendment from any point of order.

Table 1. Points of Order Under the Congressional Budget Act of 1974

Section	*Description*	*Application*	*Senate Waiver Vote*[a]
301(g)	In the Senate, prohibits consideration of a budget resolution using more than one set of economic assumptions	Budget resolution, amendment, or conference report	Simple majority
301(i)	In the Senate, prohibits consideration of a budget resolution that would decrease the Social Security surplus in any fiscal year	Budget resolution, amendment, motion, or	Three-fifths*

Table 1. (Continued)

Section	*Description*	*Application*	*Senate Waiver Vote*[a]
	covered by the resolution	conference report	
302(c)	Prohibits the consideration of any measure within the jurisdiction of the House or Senate Appropriations Committees that provides new budget authority for a fiscal year until the committee makes the suballocation required by Section 302(b).	Bill, joint resolution, amendment, motion, or conference report.	Three-fifths*
302(f)(1)	In the House, after action on a budget resolution is completed, prohibits consideration of legislation providing new budget authority for any fiscal year that would cause the applicable allocation of new budget authority made pursuant to Section 302(a) or (b) for the first fiscal year or for the total of all fiscal years to be exceeded[b,c]	Bill, joint resolution, amendment, or conference report	n/a
302(f)(2)(A)	In the Senate, after a budget resolution is agreed to, prohibits consideration of legislation (from any committee other than the Appropriations Committee) that would cause the applicable allocation of new budget authority or outlays made pursuant to Section 302(a) for the first fiscal year or for the total of all fiscal years to be exceeded	Bill, joint resolution, amendment, motion, or conference report	Three-fifths*
302(f)(2)(B)	In the Senate, after a budget resolution has been agreed to, prohibits consideration of legislation from the Appropriations Committee that would cause the applicable suballocation of new budget authority or outlays made pursuant to Section 302(b) to be exceeded	Bill, joint resolution, amendment, motion, or conference report	Three-fifths*
303(a)	Prohibits consideration of legislation providing new budget authority, an increase or decrease in revenues, an increase or decrease in the public debt limit, new entitlement authority (in the Senate only), or an increase or decrease in outlays (in the Senate only) for a fiscal year until a concurrent resolution for that fiscal year has been agreed to.[b,d]	Bill, joint resolution, amendment, motion, or conference report	Simple majoritye

Section	*Description*	*Application*	*Senate Waiver Vote*[a]
303(c)	In the Senate, prohibits consideration of any appropriations measure until a concurrent resolution for that fiscal year has been agreed to, and an allocation has been made to the Committee on Appropriations under Section 302(a).[d]	Bill, joint resolution, amendment or conference report.	Simple majoritye
305(b)(2)	In the Senate, prohibits consideration of nongermane amendments.[f]	Amendment.	Three-fifths
305(c)(4)	In the Senate, prohibits consideration of nongermane amendments to amendments in disagreement to a budget resolution (Section 310(e) applies this prohibition to amendments in disagreement to reconciliation legislation as well).	Amendment in disagreement to a budget resolution (or to reconciliation legislation).	Three-fifths
305(d)	In the Senate, prohibits a vote on a budget resolution unless the figures contained in the resolution are mathematically consistent.	Budget resolution or conference report.	Simple majority
306	Prohibits consideration of matters within the jurisdiction of the House or Senate Budget Committee except when it is a measure reported by the committee, or the committee is discharged from further consideration of the measure, or an amendment to such a measure.[g]	Bill, resolution, amendment, motion, or conference report	Three-fifths
309	In the House, prohibits consideration of an adjournment resolution for more than three calendar days during July until the House has approved all regular appropriations bills for the upcoming fiscal year.	Resolution	n/a
310(d)	Prohibits the consideration of amendments to reconciliation legislation that would increase the deficit either by increasing outlays or reducing revenues, except that in the Senate a motion to strike a provision shall always be in order.[h]	Amendment.	Three-fifths
310(e)	In the Senate, prohibits consideration of nongermane amendments to reconciliation legislation or to amendments in disagreement to reconciliation (by reference to Sections 305(b)(2) and 305(c)(4)).	Amendment.	Three-fifths
310(f)	In the House, prohibits consideration of an adjournment resolution of more than three	Resolution.	n/a

Table 1. (Continued)

Section	*Description*	*Application*	*Senate Waiver Vote*[a]
	calendar days during July until the House has completed action on any required reconciliation legislation.		
310(g)	Prohibits the consideration of reconciliation legislation that contains recommendations with respect to Social Security.	Bill, joint resolution, amendment, motion, or conference report	Three-fifths*
311(a)(1)	In the House, prohibits consideration of legislation that would cause new budget authority or outlays to exceed or revenues to fall below the levels set forth in the budget resolution for the first fiscal year or for the total of all fiscal years for which allocations are made pursuant to Section 302(a)b,[i]	Bill, joint resolution, amendment, motion, or conference report.	n/a
311(a)(2)	In the Senate, prohibits consideration of legislation that would cause new budget authority or outlays to exceed the levels set forth in the budget resolution for the first fiscal year, or revenues to fall below the levels set forth in the budget resolution for the first fiscal year or for the total of all fiscal years for which allocations are made pursuant to Section 302(a).	Bill, joint resolution, amendment, motion, or conference report.	Three-fifths*
311(a)(3)	In the Senate, prohibits consideration of legislation that would cause a decrease in Social Security surpluses or an increase in Social Security deficits relative to the level set forth in the budget resolution for the first fiscal year or for the total of all fiscal years for which allocations are made pursuant to Section 302(a).	Bill, joint resolution, amendment, motion, or conference report.	Three-fifths*
312(b)	In the Senate, prohibits the consideration of legislation that would cause any of the discretionary spending limits specified in Section 251(c) of the Balanced Budget and Emergency Deficit Control Act of 1985, as amended, to be exceeded.j	Bill, joint resolution, amendment, motion, or conference report.	Three-fifths*
312(c)	In the Senate, prohibits consideration of a budget resolution that provides for a deficit	Budget resolution, amendment, or	Three-fifths*

Section	*Description*	*Application*	*Senate Waiver Vote*[a]
	in excess of the maximum deficit amount specified in the Balanced Budget and Emergency Deficit Control Act of 1985, as amended, for the first fiscal year set forth in the resolution.[k]	conference report.	
313	In the Senate prohibits consideration of extraneous provisions in reconciliation legislation.[l]	Reconciliation bill or resolution (any title or provision), amendment, motion, or conference report.	Three-fifths
314(e)	Prohibits consideration in the House or Senate of legislation that would cause the discretionary spending limits set forth in Section 251(c) of the Balanced Budget and Emergency Deficit Control Act, as amended by the Budget Control Act of 2011 to be exceeded.[j]	Bill, joint resolution, amendment, motion, or conference report.	Three-fifths
401(a)	Prohibits consideration of legislation providing new contract authority, borrowing authority, or credit authority not limited to amounts provided in appropriations acts.[m]	Bill, joint resolution, amendment, motion, or conference report.	Simple majority
401(b)	Prohibits consideration of legislation providing new entitlement authority that is to become effective during the current fiscal year.[k]	Bill, joint resolution, amendment, motion, or conference report.	Simple majority
425(a)(1)	Prohibits consideration of legislation reported by a committee unless the committee has published a statement by CBO on the direct costs of federal mandates.	Bill or joint resolution.	Simple majority[e]
425(a)(2)	Prohibits consideration of legislation that would increase the direct costs of federal intergovernmental mandates by an amount greater than the thresholds specified in Section 424(a).	Bill, joint resolution, amendment, motion, or conference report.	Simple majoritye
426	In the House, prohibits consideration of a rule or order that would waive the application of Section 425.	Resolution, rule, or order.	n/a

Source: The Congressional Budget Act of 1974 (P.L. 93-344), as amended. U.S. Congress. House Committee on the Budget, Compilation of Laws and Rules

Relating to the Congressional Budget Process, 110th Congress, 2nd session, November 2008 (Washington: GPO, 2008), pp. 3-60, P.L. 112-25.

[a] This column indicates the type of Senate vote (as provided under Section 904 of the Congressional Budget Act) necessary to approve a motion to waive the point of order listed. The term "simple majority" means that the provision may be waived by a majority vote of the Members voting, a quorum being present. The term "three-fifths" means that a motion to waive the provision must be approved by three-fifths of the Members "duly chosen and sworn." For those provisions, which are marked with an asterisk (*), the threefifths requirement is scheduled to expire on September 30, 2017, (as identified under Section 904(e) and extended under S.Con.Res. 21 (110th Congress)), reverting to simple majority after that time. See footnote 7 in the text of this report for details on previous extensions. The same voting requirement (either simple majority or three-fifths) would also apply to a vote to appeal a ruling of the chair connected with a point of order. The term "n/a" is used for those provisions that apply in the House only.

[b] Section 302(g) of the Congressional Budget Act (known as the Pay-As-You-Go exception) provides that Sections 302(f)(1), 303(a) (after April 15), and 311(a), as it applies to revenues, shall not apply in the House to legislation (bill, joint resolution, amendment, or conference report) if for each fiscal year covered by the most recently agreed to budget resolution such legislation would not increase the deficit if added to other changes in revenues or direct spending provided in the budget resolution pursuant to pay-as-you-go procedures included under Section 301(b)(8).

[c] In the 109th Congress, the House adopted a provision in H.Res. 248 establishing that during the 109th Congress there would be a separate point of order in the Committee of the Whole against a motion to rise and report a general appropriations bill if that bill, as amended, were in a breach of the appropriate 302(b) allocation. This provision was subsequently readopted in the 110th -112th Congresses as a separate order of the House (see Section 3(a)(4) of H.Res. 5 (112th Congress)).

[d] Section 303(b) sets forth exceptions to the prohibitions under 303(a). In the House, the point of order does not apply to (1) advance discretionary new budget authority that first become available for the first or second fiscal year after the first fiscal year covered in a budget resolution; (2) revenue legislation that is to first become effective after the first fiscal year covered in a budget resolution; (3) general appropriations bills after May 15; or (4) any bill or joint resolution unless it is reported by a committee (see also table note b above for an additional exception to 303(a) provided under Section 302(g)). In the Senate, the point of order does not apply to advance appropriations for the first or second fiscal year after the first fiscal year covered in a budget resolution. The application of this point of order to appropriations bills in the Senate is provided specifically under Section 303(c), which requires an allocation be made to the Senate Appropriations Committee under Section 302(a) as well as agreement on a budget resolution.

[e] The points of order under Sections 303(a), 303(c), 425(a), and 425(b) were made subject to the three-fifths threshold under Section 403(b) of H.Con.Res. 95 (109th Congress). Section 205 of S.Con.Res. 21 (110th Congress) provides that Section 403 of H.Con.Res. 95 (109th Congress) shall no longer apply in the Senate.

[f] Section 204(g) of H.Con.Res. 290 (106th Congress) provided that for purposes of interpreting Section 305(b)(2) of the Budget Act, an amendment not be considered germane if it contains predominately precatory language (e.g., Sense of the Senate provisions), although this addition may not be enforceable.

[g] By standing order of the House, the application of this section to resolutions is construed in the House as a reference to a joint resolution (see Section 3(a)(1) of H.Res. 5 (112th Congress)).

[h] In the House, the impact of amendments is measured in relation to the levels in the reconciliation measure. In the Senate, the impact is measured in relation to the levels provided in the reconciliation instructions which relate to the measure.

[i] Section 311(c) provides that 311(a) shall not apply in the House to legislation that would not cause a committee's spending allocation under 302(a) to be exceeded.

[j] The point of order in Section 312(b) was written to apply to spending limits included in Section 251(c) of the Balanced Budget and Emergency Deficit Control Act of 1985 that expired at the end of FY2002. The point of order in Section 314(e) was written to apply to spending limits for FY2012-FY2021 included in Section 251(c) as amended by the Budget Control Act of 2011 (P.L. 112-25).

[k] Currently no maximum deficit amounts are specified under the Balanced Budget and Emergency Deficit Control Act of 1985, as amended.

[l] For more information on this provision (known as the "Byrd Rule"), see CRS Report RL30862, *The Budget Reconciliation Process: The Senate's "Byrd Rule"*, by Bill Heniff Jr.

[m] Section 401(d) provides that Sections 401(a) and 401(b) shall not apply to new spending authority described in those sections that flow from (1) a trust fund established under the Social Security Act or any other trust fund for which 90% or more of its expenditures are supported by dedicated revenues; (2) certain wholly owned or mixed ownership government corporations; or (3) gifts or bequests made to the United States for a specific purpose.

Table 2. Points of Order Under S.Con.Res. 13 (111th Congress) (Budget Resolution for FY2010)

Section	Description	Application	Senate Waiver Vote[a]
401(a)	In the Senate, prohibits the consideration of a measure or provisions that would exceed any of the discretionary limits for FY2009-FY2010 specified in Section 401(b), including any adjustments made	Bill, joint resolution, amendment, motion, or	Three-fifths

Table 2. (Continued)

Section	Description	Application	Senate Waiver Vote[a]
	under the provisions of Section 401(c).	conference report.	
402(a)	In the Senate, prohibits the consideration of advance appropriations, except as specified in this budget resolution.[b]	Bill, joint resolution, amendment, motion, or conference report.	Three-fifths
403(e)	In the Senate, provides for a point of order against the use of an emergency designation as allowed under Section 403(a) of this budget resolution to provide for exemption in the Senate from budget enforcement mechanisms specified in Section 403(b).[c]	Bill, resolution, amendment, motion, or conference report	Three-fifths
404(a)	In the Senate, prohibits the consideration of direct spending or revenue legislation that would cause a net increase in the deficit in excess of $10 billion in any fiscal year provided for in the most recently adopted budget resolution unless it is fully offset over the period of all fiscal years provided for in the most recently adopted budget resolution.[d]	Bill, joint resolution, amendment, motion, or conference report.	Three-fifths
405(a)	In the Senate, prohibits consideration of any measure or provision that extends or reauthorizes surface transportation programs that appropriates budget authority from sources other than the Highway Trust Fund.d	Bill, joint resolution, amendment, or conference report	Three-fifths
424(a)	In the House, prohibits the consideration of advance appropriations, except as provided in this budget resolution.[e]	Bill, joint resolution, amendment, or conference report.	n/a

Source: S.Con.Res. 13 (111th Congress).

[a]. This column indicates the type of Senate vote necessary to approve a motion to waive the point of orderlisted. The term "three-fifths" means that a motion to waive the provision must be approved by three-fifths of the Members "duly chosen and sworn." The same voting requirement would also apply to a vote to appeal a ruling of the chair connected with the point of order.

[b]. This section limits consideration in the Senate of advance appropriations, except that advance appropriations may be provided for FY2011-FY2012 for accounts

specified in the joint explanatory statement of the conference report for this budget resolution (H.Rept. 111-89) in an aggregate amount not to exceed $28.852 billion in each year. See also the point of order in the House under Section 424 of this budget resolution.

[c]. This section concerns the use of emergency designations, but does not establish a point of order against the spending or revenue itself. It also requires committees reporting legislation that include provisions designated as emergency to include in any accompanying written report a justification for the designation. The use of an emergency designation exempts resulting new budget authority, outlays or receipts for purposes of enforcing Sections 302 and 311 of the Budget Act, Sections 401 and 404 of this budget resolution, Section 311 of S.Con.Res. 70 (110th Congress) (see Table 3), and Section 201 of S.Con.Res. 21 (110th Congress) (see Table 4). This point of order supersedes earlier, similar points of order under H.Con.Res. 68 and H.Con.Res. 290 (both 106th Congress), H.Con.Res. 95 (108th Congress), Section 14007(b)(2) of P.L. 108-287, H.Con.Res. 95 (109th Congress), and S.Con.Res. 21 (110th Congress). No expiration date is provided for the current point of order. Note that while there is no similar point of order in the House, Section 423 of this budget resolution provides that appropriations for discretionary amounts designated as necessary to meet emergency needs shall not count for purposes of the Budget Act or this budget resolution.

[d]. This section is scheduled to expire on September 30, 2018.

[e]. This section limits the consideration in the House of advance appropriations, except that advance appropriations may be provided for FY2011-FY2012 for those accounts specified in the joint explanatory statement of the conference report for this budget resolution H.Rept. 111-89 in an aggregate amount not to exceed $28.852 billion. See also the point of order in the Senate as provided in Section 402 of this budget resolution.

Table 3. Points of Order Under S.Con.Res. 70 (110th Congress) (Budget Resolution for FY2009)

Section	Description	Application	Senate Waiver Vote[a]
311(b)	In the Senate, prohibits the consideration of a measure that would cause a net increase in deficits in excess of $5 billion in any of the four 10-year periods beginning in 2019 through 2058.[b]	Bill, joint resolution, amendment, motion, or conference report.	Three-fifths
314(a)	In the Senate, prohibits the consideration of appropriations legislation that includes a change in a mandatory program	Appropriations measure, amendment, motion, or conference report.	Three-fifths

Table 3. (Continued)

Section	Description	Application	Senate Waiver Vote[a]
	producing net costs as defined in Section 314(b).[c]		

Source: S.Con.Res. 70 (110th Congress).

[a] This column indicates the type of Senate vote necessary to approve a motion to waive the point of order listed. The term "three-fifths" means that a motion to waive the provision must be approved by three-fifths of the Members "duly chosen and sworn." The same voting requirement would also apply to a vote to appeal a ruling of the chair connected with the point of order.

[b] This point of order supersedes earlier, similar points of order provided in H.Con.Res. 95 (108th Congress) and S.Con.Res. 21 (110th Congress). This section is scheduled to expire on September 30, 2017.

[c] This point of order supersedes an earlier, similar point of order provided in S.Con.Res. 21 (110th Congress).

Table 4. Points of Order Under S.Con.Res. 21 (110th Congress) (Budget Resolution for FY2008)

Section	*Description*	*Application*	*Senate Waiver Vote*[a]
201(a)	In the Senate, prohibits consideration of any direct spending or revenue legislation that would increase or cause an on-budget deficit for the period of the current fiscal year and the five ensuing fiscal years or the period of the current fiscal year and the ten ensuing fiscal years.[b]	Bill, joint resolution, amendment, or conference report.	Three-fifths
202(a)	In the Senate, prohibits consideration of reconciliation legislation that would increase or cause a deficit (or decrease a surplus) for the period of the current fiscal year and the five ensuing fiscal years or the period of the current fiscal year and the ten ensuing fiscal years.	Bill, resolution, amendment, amendment between the houses, or conference report.	Three-fifths

Source: S.Con.Res. 21 (110th Congress)

[a] This column indicates the type of Senate vote necessary to approve a motion to waive the point of order listed. The term "three-fifths" means that a motion to waive the provision must be approved by three-fifths of the Members "duly chosen and sworn." The same voting requirement would also apply to a vote to appeal a ruling of the chair connected with the point of order.

[b] This point of order supersedes earlier, similar points of order provided in H.Con.Res. 67 (104th Congress), H.Con.Res. 68 (106th Congress), and H.Con.Res. 95 (108th Congress). This section is scheduled to expire on September 30, 2017. Paragraph 5 of this section specifically excludes the budget resolution or legislation that affects or continues the full funding of the deposit insurance guarantee commitment in effect on the date of enactment of the Budget Enforcement Act of 1990. Paragraph 6 of this section provides that the point of order would not apply in cases in which direct spending and revenue legislation when taken together with other direct spending and revenue legislation enacted since the beginning of the calendar year (and not accounted for in the baseline) result in a net decrease in the deficit (or increase in the surplus), although deficit reduction legislation enacted pursuant to reconciliation instructions may not be used in such calculations.

Table 5. Point of Order Under P.L. 101-508 (Budget Enforcement Act of 1990)

Section	Description	Application
13302(a)	In the House, prohibits consideration of legislation that would provide for a net increase in Social Security benefits or decrease in Social Security taxes in excess of 0.02% of the present value of future taxable payroll for a 75-year period, or in excess of $250,000,000 for the first five-year period after it becomes effective.[a]	Bill, joint resolution, amendment, or conference report.

Source: Subtitle C of the Budget Enforcement Act of 1990 (Title XIII of the Omnibus Budget Reconciliation Act of 1990).

[a] Section 13302(b) provides that the point of order would not apply to legislation that reduces Social Security taxes in excess of the threshold amounts if these reductions are offset by equivalent increases in Medicare taxes.

Table 6. Related Points of Order Under the Standing Rules of the House (112th Congress) and Separate Orders (as adopted under H.Res. 5, 112th Congress)

Rule and clause/ section	Description	Application
XXI, clause 7	In the House, prohibits consideration of a budget resolution that includes reconciliation instructions that would provide for an increase in net direct	Budget resolution, amendment, or conference report.

Table 6. (Continued)

Rule and clause/ section	Description	Application
	spending for the period covered by the resolution.[a]	
XXI, clause 10	In the House, prohibits consideration of legislation that would have the net effect of increasing mandatory spending for the period comprising the current fiscal year, the budget year, and the four fiscal years following that budget year, or the current fiscal year, the budget year, and the nine fiscal years following that budget year.[b]	Bill, joint resolution, amendment, or conference report.
Section 3(g)(1)	In the House, prohibits consideration of a measure reported by a committee (other than the Appropriations Committee) if the provisions of the measure have the net effect of increasing mandatory spending in excess of $5 billion for any of the first four consecutive 10-fiscal year periods following the period covered by the budget resolution.[c]	Bill, joint resolution, amendment, or conference report.

Source: H.Res. 5 (112th Congress).

[a] This point of order supersedes earlier points of order adopted by the House as part of the rules of the House for the 110th and 111th Congresses prohibiting reconciliation instructions that would increase the deficit (or decrease the surplus) for a period comprising the current fiscal year, the budget year, and the four fiscal years following that budget year, or the current fiscal year, the budget year, and the nine fiscal years following that budget year.

[b] Rule XXI, clause 10(b) provides that when a measure is considered by the House under the terms of a special order directing the Clerk to add at the end of the measure, the provisions of another measure previously passed by the House, those additional provisions are included in determining the application of this point of order. Rule XXI, clause 10(c) excludes provisions designated as an emergency for purposes of the Statutory PAYGO Act of 2010 from calculations to determine the application of this point of order. This point of order supersedes earlier point s of order adopted as part of the rules of the House for the 110th and 111th Congresses prohibiting the consideration of direct spending or revenue legislation that would have the net effect of increasing the deficit (or reducing the surplus) for similar periods. For more on the House Pay-As-You-Go rule in the 110th and 111th

Congresses, see CRS Report R41510, Budget Enforcement Procedures: House Pay-As-You-Go (PAYGO) Rule, by Bill Heniff Jr.

[c] Section 3(g)(2)(A) specifies the time periods as the four consecutive 10-fiscal year periods beginning with the first fiscal year following the last fiscal year for which the applicable budget resolution sets forth appropriate budget levels. Section 3(g)(2)(B) further specifies that the applicable budget resolution is the one most recently adopted.

Table 7. Point of Order Under P.L. 111-139 (Statutory Pay-As-You-Go Act of 2010)

Section	Description	Application	Senate Waiver Vote[a]
4(g)(3)	In the Senate, if a point of order is raised during consideration of legislation subject to PAYGO against an emergency designation in that measure, the provision making the designation shall be stricken.[b]	Bill, joint resolution, amendment, or conference report.	Three-fifths

Source: P.L. 111-139.

[a] This column indicates the type of Senate vote necessary to approve a motion to waive the point of order listed. The term "three-fifths" means that a motion to waive the provision must be approved by three-fifths of the Members "duly chosen and sworn." The same voting requirement would also apply to a vote toappeal a ruling of the chair connected with the point of order.

[b] For more information on the Statutory Pa-As-You-Go Act of 2010, see CRS Report R41157, The Statutory Pay-As-You-Go Act of 2010: Summary and Legislative History, by Bill Heniff Jr.

End Notes

[1] The Congressional Budget Act (Titles I-IX of P.L. 93-344) has been amended on a number of occasions since its enactment. The most salient of the modifications has been as a result of the Balanced Budget and Emergency Deficit Control Act of 1985 (P.L. 99-177, also known as Gramm-Rudman-Hollings or GRH); the Balanced Budget and Emergency Deficit Control Reaffirmation Act of 1987 (P.L. 100-119); the Budget Enforcement Act of 1990 (Title XIII of the Omnibus Budget Reconciliation Act of 1990, P.L. 101-508); Title XIV of the Omnibus Budget Reconciliation Act of 1993 (P.L. 103-66); and Title X of the Balanced Budget Act of 1997 (P.L. 105-33). For the text of the Budget Act, as amended, see U.S. Congress, House Committee on the Budget, Compilation of Laws and Rules Relating to the Congressional Budget Process, 110th Cong., 2nd sess., November 2008 (Washington: GPO, 2008), pp. 3-60.

[2] The reconciliation process is an optional procedure set forth in Section 310 of the Congressional Budget Act. First used in 1980, reconciliation is a two-step process triggered when the budget resolution includes instructions to one or more committee(s) directing them to recommend changes in revenue or spending laws necessary to achieve the overall levels agreed to. The recommendations are then considered in one or more reconciliation measures under expedited procedures. Certain features of the reconciliation process are enforced by points of order that are included in this report. For more on the reconciliation process generally, see CRS Report RL33030, The Budget Reconciliation Process: House and Senate Procedures, by Robert Keith and Bill Heniff Jr.

[3] For example, the prohibition against motions to recommit concurrent resolutions on the budget in the House under Section 305(a)(2) of the act is typically not counted as a separate point of order. Likewise, the requirement under Section 308(a) of the act for reports on legislation to include cost estimates is not formulated as a point of order, although the House has deemed it necessary to formally waive the provision on occasion.

[4] The expiration of the provisions of the Balanced Budget and Emergency Deficit Control Act at the end of FY2002 has rendered moot a number of points of order. For example, points of order provided in the Congressional Budget Act to allow the Senate to enforce discretionary spending limits (Section 312(b)) or maximum deficit amounts (Section 312(c)) have been rendered moot because no statute currently specifies such a limit or amount.

[5] Section 313(d) provides a special procedure for further consideration of a measure should a point of order under this section be sustained against a provision in a conference report.

[6] In the case of points of order under Section 313 of the Budget Act (and by extension, points of order under Sections 402 and 403 of S.Con.Res. 13 (111th Congress)), as well as points of order under Section 314 of S.Con.Res. 70 (110th Congress), a single point of order may be raised against several provisions. The Presiding Officer may sustain the point of order "as to some or all of the provisions," and a motion to waive the point of order may, likewise, be made concerning some or all of the provisions against which the point of order was raised.

[7] As originally provided in Title X of the Balanced Budget Act of 1997, the three-fifths requirement expired on September 30, 2002. The Senate subsequently adopted S.Res. 304 on October 16, 2002, renewing the three-fifths requirement for all of the points of order identified in Section 904(c)(2) (except for Section 302(f)(2)(B)) through April 15, 2003. The three-fifths requirement (including for Section 302(f)(2)(B)) was renewed through September 30, 2008, under Section 503 of H.Con.Res. 95 (108th Congress), extended through September 30, 2010, under Section 403 of H.Con.Res. 95 (109th Congress), and is currently extended through September 30, 2017, under Section 205 of S.Con.Res. 21 (110th Congress).

In: The Federal Budget Process: An Introduction ISBN: 978-1-62417-838-2
Editor: Adele Wilkinson

Chapter 5

THE FEDERAL BUDGET: ISSUES FOR FY2013 AND BEYOND*

Mindy R. Levit

SUMMARY

The federal budget is central to Congress's ability to exercise its "power of the purse." Over the last several fiscal years the imbalance between spending and revenues has grown as a result of the economic downturn and policies enacted in response to financial turmoil. In FY2011, the U.S. government spent $3,598 billion (24.1% of GDP) and collected $2,302 billion in revenue (15.4% of GDP), resulting in a budget deficit of $1,296 billion (8.7% of GDP). The FY2012 deficit is currently estimated at $1,079 billion (7.0% of GDP).

The Obama Administration released its FY2013 budget on February 13, 2012. In FY2013, the President's budget projects that the deficit will reach $901 billion. Budget deficits are projected throughout the 10-year budget window. The President's budget proposes a variety of short-term tax and spending measures aimed at job creation, largely drawn from the American Jobs Act submitted to Congress in September 2011. These proposals amount to nearly $350 billion in additional spending and tax cuts, including immediate funding for roads, rails, and runways; aid to states and local governments for teachers and first responders; school

* This is an edited, reformatted and augmented version of a Congressional Research Service publication, CRS Report for Congress R42362, from www.crs.gov, prepared for Members and Committees of Congress, dated May 1, 2012.

modernization; and a full-year extension of the Social Security payroll tax reduction and unemployment benefits.

In August 2011, the Budget Control Act of 2011 (BCA) placed limits on spending via discretionary spending caps and included provisions for additional spending cuts in the amount of $1.2 trillion. In January 2013, the additional cuts are scheduled to take effect via an automatic process. In his FY2013 budget, President Obama proposes replacing the automatic cuts with prescribed spending cuts and tax increases. The largest of these proposals includes allowing the 2001/2003/2010 tax cuts for singles making over $200,000 and households making over $250,000 to expire; savings generated from changes to Medicare, Medicaid, agriculture, and other mandatory programs; and placing caps on spending on Overseas Contingency Operations (OCO).

The FY2013 budget also included other tax proposals including changes in the estate tax parameters, limits to the value of itemized deductions for married taxpayers with incomes over $250,000 and single taxpayers with incomes over $200,000, and eliminating various tax expenditures. The Administration also released a framework for corporate tax reform, which included a reduction in the corporate tax rate combined with an elimination of certain corporate tax expenditures. The Administration is committed to reform that would not add to the deficit.

On March 21, 2012, the House Budget Committee reported the budget resolution (H.Con.Res. 112, 112th Congress) by a vote of 19-18. It was agreed to by the House on March 29, 2012, by a vote of 228-191. The resolution provided for a FY2013 deficit of $797 billion, or approximately 5.0% of GDP, falling to $287 billion or 1.2% of GDP in FY2022. Like the President's budget proposal, the House budget resolution specifies a replacement of the BCA's automatic cuts. The budget resolution replaces the majority of the cuts in FY2013 with $261 billion in deficit reduction over 10 years to be achieved via reconciliation. In order to proceed with the consideration of FY2013 appropriations bills, both the House and the Senate took action to "deem" enforceable levels of discretionary spending for FY2013 because no agreement has been reached on the budget resolution. CBO, GAO, and the Administration agree that the current mix of federal fiscal policies is unsustainable in the long term. The nation's aging population, combined with rising health care costs per beneficiary, seems likely to keep federal health costs rising faster than per capita GDP.

INTRODUCTION

The federal budget is central to Congress's ability to exercise its "power of the purse." Federal budget decisions also express Congress's priorities and reinforce Congress's influence on federal policies. Making budgetary decisions for the federal government is a complex process and requires balancing competing goals. Recent economic turmoil has strained the federal budget as a result of declining revenues and increasing spending levels. As the economic recovery continues, the budget process will allow the President and Congress to negotiate priorities and refine spending plans.[1]

The federal government faces very large budget deficits, rising costs of entitlement programs, significant spending on overseas military operations, and low revenue levels. The enactment of financial intervention and fiscal stimulus legislation in FY2008 and FY2009 may have helped to bolster the economy, though they increased the budget deficit.[2] While the economy is growing again, unemployment remains elevated and government spending on "automatic stabilizers," such as unemployment insurance and income security programs, remains higher than historical averages.[3]

This suggests that the recession's effects on the budget will likely remain for several more fiscal years. In addition to the current challenges, concerns remain about the federal government's long-term fiscal situation.

Work on improving the budget outlook resulted in the enactment of the Budget Control Act of 2011 (BCA; P.L. 112-25), which contained provisions to reduce the budget deficit by about $2 trillion over the next decade.[4] However, the rising costs of federal health care programs and the effects of the baby boom generation's retirement, which present serious challenges to future fiscal stability, have yet to be addressed.

Operating these programs in their current form may pass on substantial economic burdens to future generations. To avoid this would require additional government action and public sacrifice at levels greater than those needed to counteract the recent economic downturn.

OVERVIEW

Budget Cycle

A single year's budget cycle takes roughly three calendar years from initial formation by the Office of Management and Budget (OMB) until final audit.[5] The executive agencies begin the budget process by compiling detailed budget requests in the calendar year before the President's budget submission. Many agencies start working on their budgets during the spring and summer—about a year and a half before the fiscal year begins. OMB oversees the development of these agency requests. The President is required to submit a budget to Congress, which is based on OMB's work, by the first Monday in February or about 8 months before the fiscal year begins.[6]

Congress typically begins formal consideration of the budget resolution once the President submits his budget request. The budget resolution sets out a plan, agreed to by the House and Senate, that establishes the framework for subsequent budget legislation. Because the budget resolution is a concurrent resolution, it is not sent to the President for approval.[7]

House and Senate Appropriations Committees and their subcommittees typically begin reporting discretionary spending bills after the budget resolution is agreed upon. Appropriations Committees review agency funding requests and propose levels of budget authority (BA). Appropriations acts passed by Congress set the amount of BA available for specific programs and activities. Authorizing committees, which control mandatory spending, and committees with jurisdiction over revenues also play important roles in budget decision making.[8]

During the fiscal year, which begins on October 1, Congress and OMB oversee the execution of the budget. Once the fiscal year ends on the following September 30, the Treasury Department and the Government Accountability Office (GAO) begin year-end audits.

Budget Baseline Projections

Budget baseline projections are used to measure how future legislation would affect the budget picture. They are not meant to be predictions of the future budget outlook. Due to the nature of projections, slight changes in assumptions can lead to large effects in outyear totals. Therefore, it is important to understand what projections include and the assumptions on which they are based. Baseline projections are included in both the President's budget and the Congressional budget resolution.

The Congressional Budget Office (CBO) computes current law baseline projections using assumptions set out in budget enforcement legislation.[9] Forecasts based on these assumptions typically yield higher revenue estimates and may understate discretionary spending levels. More specifically, CBO baseline projections incorporate certain assumptions: that the 2001/2003/2010 tax cuts fully expire after 2012 (as current law specifies), that one-year "patches" to the alternative minimum tax (AMT) will lapse even though past Congresses have extended AMT patches year after year, that sharp reductions in Medicare's payment rates for physician services will take effect as scheduled, and that extensions of unemployment compensation and the payroll tax cut will expire per current law. Baseline discretionary spending levels are based on the caps currently in law, with adjustments for war funding and disaster spending. In addition to these current law assumptions, macroeconomic assumptions, specifically of GDP growth, inflation, and interest rates, will also affect the baseline estimates and projections, especially given the current economic climate. Baseline projections show substantial growth in receipts after 2012, when most of the tax cuts from 2001/2003/2010 expire. This results in budget deficits that would reduce the level of debt as a percentage of GDP, particularly after FY2013. In other words, these budget deficits would be fiscally sustainable. Under the baseline assumptions, budget deficits are projected to average 1.5% of GDP over the FY2013 to FY2022 period.

CBO also provided projections based on alternative policy assumptions, which illustrate the levels of spending and revenue if current laws continue, rather than expire as scheduled. If the 2001/2003/2010 tax cuts are extended, the AMT is indexed for inflation, Medicare payment rates for physician services remain the same, and the provisions of the Budget Control Act's automatic spending reduction process do not take effect, CBO projects budget deficits to average 5.4% of GDP over the FY2013 to FY2022 period. Cumulative budget deficits under the alternative fiscal scenario are projected to be $7.9 trillion higher over the next decade (totaling $11.0 trillion) than under the baseline scenario.

Beyond the 10-year forecast window, federal deficits are expected to grow rapidly unless major policy changes are made. This is a result of rapidly growing outlays largely attributable to health care costs and baby boomer retirements.

Spending and Revenue Trends

Over the last four decades, on average, federal spending accounted for approximately 21% of the economy (as measured by gross domestic product—GDP), while federal revenues averaged roughly 18% of GDP. Since FY2001, spending has exceeded revenues, resulting in budget deficits. Over the last several fiscal years the imbalance between spending and revenues has grown as a result of the economic downturn and policies enacted in response to financial turmoil. In FY2011, the most recently completed fiscal year, the U.S.

government spent $3.6 trillion and collected $2.3 trillion in revenue. Relative to FY2008, FY2011 outlays increased by $616 billion while revenues decreased by $222 billion (in nominal terms). The trends in revenues and outlays between FY1970 and FY2011 are shown in *Figure 1*.

(as a percentage of GDP)

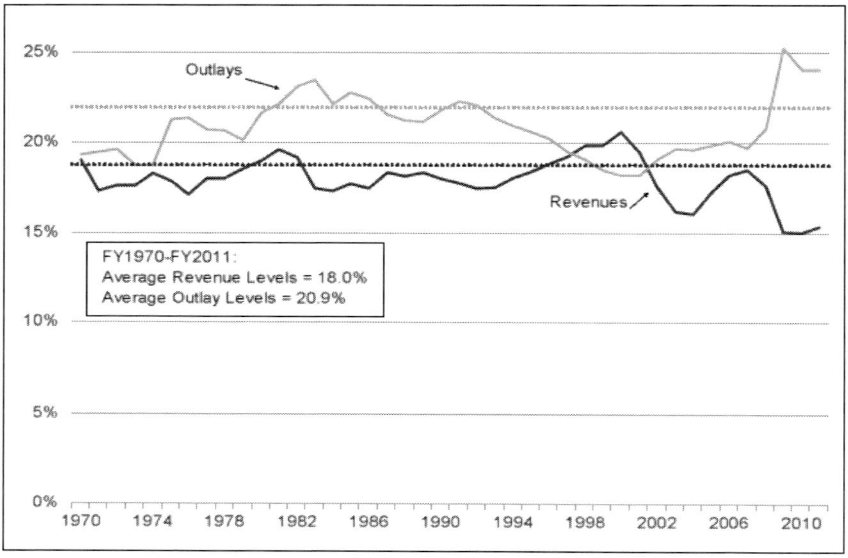

Source: CRS figure using data from CBO, Historical Tables, available at http://www.cbo.gov/doc.cfm?index= 12699.

Figure 1. Total Outlays and Revenues, FY1970-FY2011.

Federal Spending

Federal outlays are often divided into the broad categories of discretionary and mandatory spending, and net interest. Discretionary spending is controlled by annual congressional appropriations acts. Mandatory spending encompasses spending on entitlement programs and spending controlled by laws other than annual appropriation acts.[10] Entitlement programs such as Social Security, Medicare, and Medicaid make up the bulk of mandatory spending. Congress sets eligibility requirements and benefits for entitlement programs, rather than appropriating a fixed sum each year. Therefore, if the eligibility requirements are met for a specific mandatory program, outlays are made automatically. Net interest comprises the government's interest payments on the debt held by the public, offset by small amounts of interest income the government receives from certain loans and investments.[11]

In FY2000, total outlays equaled 18.2% of GDP. By FY2011, total outlays reached 24.1% of GDP.[12] Under the CBO baseline, total outlays are projected to be 22.4% of GDP in FY2022. Under CBO's alternative fiscal scenario, outlays are projected to total 24.4% of GDP in FY2022. *Figure 2* shows the level of federal spending as a percentage of GDP, broken into the discretionary, mandatory, and net interest categories, between FY2000 through FY2022, as projected in the CBO baseline.

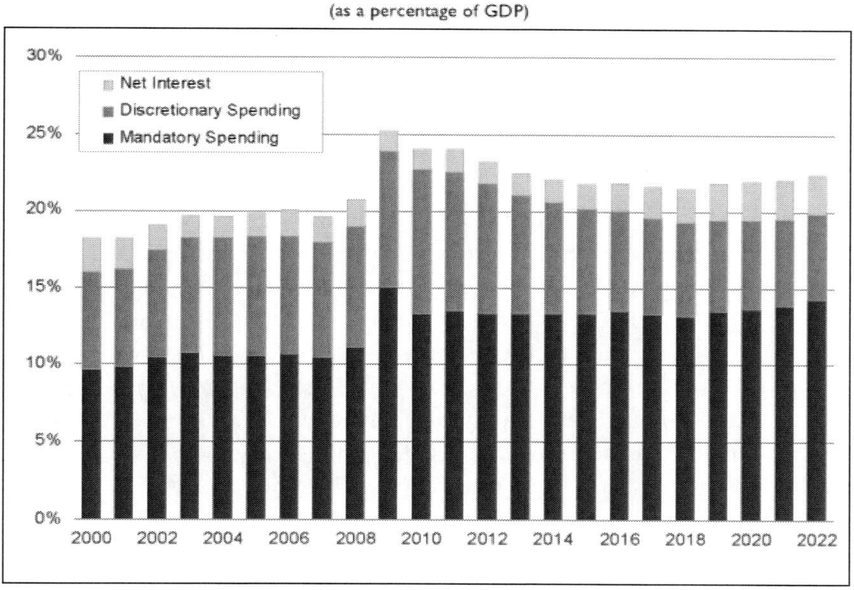

Source: CRS figure using data from CBO, Historical Tables, January 2012.
Notes: Data for FY2012 are estimates and data for FY2013-FY2022 are projections under the current law baseline.

Figure 2. Outlays by Type, FY2000-FY2022.

In FY2011, discretionary spending totaled 9.0% of GDP. Since FY2000, discretionary spending as a share of GDP has increased 7.4% a year, on average, in nominal terms. Increases in discretionary spending over this period have largely been a result of military operations in Iraq and Afghanistan and, more recently, the funding provided in the American Recovery and Reinvestment Act of 2009 (ARRA; P.L. 111-5). On average, from FY2000 to

FY2011, defense discretionary outlays grew 8.2% per year in nominal terms, while non-defense discretionary outlays grew 6.6% per year in nominal terms. By FY2022, according to CBO's baseline projections, discretionary spending will fall to 5.6% of GDP, its lowest level ever.[13]

Mandatory spending totaled 13.5% of GDP in FY2011, up from 9.7% of GDP in FY2000, as shown in *Figure 2*. Mandatory spending levels have been elevated mainly as a result of increases in outlays in income security programs.[14] Though the economic recovery is expected to lower mandatory spending on certain programs over the next few fiscal years, the growth in mandatory spending is projected to resume by the end of the decade due to increases in certain entitlement programs. As a result, under current law, CBO projects that FY2022 mandatory spending will total 14.3% of GDP, higher than the FY2011 level.

In FY2011, mandatory spending totaled 56.3% of total outlays, discretionary spending totaled 37.4% of total outlays, and net interest comprised 6.3% of total outlays. Social Security, Medicare, and the federal share of Medicaid alone constitute 43.4% of all federal spending. Because discretionary spending represents roughly one-third of total federal outlays, some budget experts contend that any significant reductions in federal spending must include mandatory spending cuts. Other budget and social policy experts contend that cuts in mandatory spending would cause substantial disruption to many households, because mandatory spending funds important parts of the social safety net.[15] Nevertheless, there is widespread agreement that action is needed to bring down anticipated high debt and deficit levels to restore long-term fiscal health.[16]

Federal Revenue

In FY2000, revenues equaled 20.6% of GDP. In FY2011, federal revenue collection totaled 15.4% of GDP, one of the lowest levels since FY1950.[17] Revenue collection has remained depressed over the last few fiscal years as the result of the economic downturn and several tax relief provisions. The longer term revenue outlook depends on the speed of economic recovery and the legislative actions of Congress on certain expiring tax provisions and potential tax reform. Under the CBO baseline, revenues are projected to total 21.0% of GDP in FY2022. The increase in revenue levels in the baseline is largely due to the assumptions that certain tax provisions expire as scheduled under current law, resulting in increases in tax rates and higher revenue collection.[18] Under CBO's alternative fiscal scenario, revenues are projected to total 18.3% of GDP in FY2022.

Individual income taxes have long been the largest source of federal revenues, followed by social insurance (payroll) and corporate income taxes.[19] In FY2011, individual income tax revenues totaled 7.3% of GDP. Payroll tax revenue accounted for 5.5% of GDP[20] and corporate income tax revenues equaled 1.2% of GDP in FY2011. Overall, federal revenues increased very slightly relative to their FY2009 levels. *Figure 3* shows revenue collections between FY2000 through FY2022, as projected in the CBO baseline.

(as a percentage of GDP)

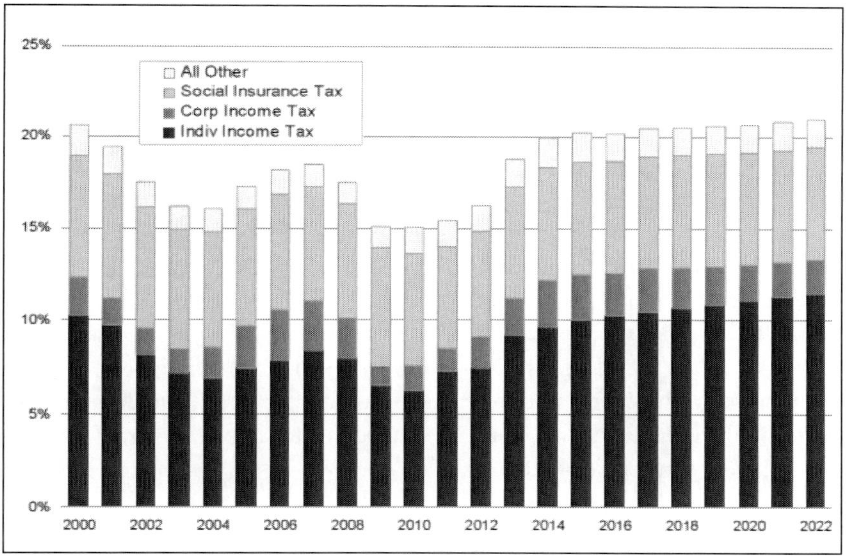

Source: CRS figure using data from CBO, Historical Tables, January 2012.

Notes: Data for FY2012 are estimates and data for FY2013-FY2022 are projections under the current law baseline.

Figure 3. Revenue by Type, FY2000-FY2022.

Deficits, Debt, and Interest

The annual differences between revenue (i.e., taxes and fees) that the government collects and outlays (i.e., spending) result in the budget deficit (or surplus).[21]

Annual budget deficits or surpluses determine, over time, the level of federal debt and affect the growth of interest payments to finance the debt.

Budget Deficits

Beginning with FY2009, annual budget deficits as a percentage of GDP have been sharply higher than deficits in any period since FY1945. The total deficit in FY2011 was $1,296 billion, or 8.7% of GDP. The total deficit, according to some budget experts, gives an incomplete view of the government's fiscal condition because it includes Social Security surpluses (which are held in Treasury trust funds until used to pay future benefits).[22] Excluding off-budget items (Social Security benefits paid net of Social Security payroll taxes collected and the U.S. Postal Service's net balance), the on-budget FY2011 federal deficit was $1,363 billion. The FY2011 total deficit was slightly lower as a percent of GDP than the FY2010 deficit ($1,293 billion or 9.0% of GDP) and lower than the FY2009 deficit ($1,413 billion and 10.1% of GDP).[23]

Occasional deficits, in and of themselves, are not necessarily problematic. Deficit spending can allow governments to smooth outlays and taxes to shield taxpayers and program beneficiaries from abrupt economic shocks in the short term, while also temporarily boosting GDP when the output gap is large. Persistent deficits, however, lead to growing levels of federal debt that may lead to higher interest payments and may also have adverse macroeconomic consequences in the long term, including slowing investment and lowering economic growth. Since the debt cannot grow faster than GDP forever, large deficits will eventually need to be reduced through increases in taxes, reductions in spending, or both.

Federal Debt and Debt Limit

Gross federal debt is composed of debt held by the public and intragovernmental debt.[24] Intragovernmental debt is the amount owed by the federal government to other federal agencies, to be paid by the Department of the Treasury. This amount largely consists of money contained in trust funds, such as Social Security, that has been invested in federal securities as required by law. Debt held by the public is the total amount the federal government has borrowed from the public and remains outstanding. This measure is generally considered to be the most relevant in macroeconomic terms because it is the debt sold in credit markets.

Changes in debt held by the public generally track the movements of the annual on-budget deficits and surpluses.[25] Whether or not the movements of gross federal debt will follow those of debt held by the public depends on how intragovernmental debt changes.

Congress sets a ceiling on federal debt through a legislatively established limit. The debt limit also imposes a form of fiscal accountability that compels Congress, in the form of a vote authorizing a debt limit increase, and the President, by signing the legislation, to take visible action to allow further federal borrowing when nearing the statutory limit. The debt limit, however, can hinder the Treasury's ability to manage the federal government's finances when the amount of federal debt approaches this ceiling. In those instances, the Treasury has had to take unusual and extraordinary measures to meet federal obligations, leading to inconvenience and uncertainty in Treasury operations at times.[26]

At the end of FY2011 (September 30, 2011), federal debt subject to limit was approximately $14,747 billion, of which $10,127 billion was held by the public.[27] The debt limit currently stands at $16,394 billion, as a result of the provisions of the Budget Control Act of 2011 (P.L. 112-25).[28]

Net Interest

In FY2011, the United States spent $227 billion or 1.5% of GDP on net interest payments on the debt. What the government pays in interest depends on market interest rates as well as on the size and composition of the federal debt. Currently, low interest rates have held net interest payments as a percentage of GDP below the historical average despite increases in borrowing to finance the deficit.[29] Some economists, however, have expressed concern that federal interest costs could rise sharply once the economy recovers, resulting in future strain on the budget.[30] Net interest payments, under the CBO baseline, are projected to rise to $624 billion or 2.5% of GDP in FY2022.

BUDGETING IN TOUGH ECONOMIC TIMES

The economic downturn increased the deficit as a result of elevated levels of spending related to "automatic stabilizers," like unemployment compensation and the Supplemental Nutrition Assistance Program (SNAP), and subsequent policy actions taken by the federal government to address the recession.

Federal spending tied to means-tested social programs has also been increasing due to persistently high levels of unemployment, while federal revenues have fallen as individuals' incomes and corporate profits dropped. The pace of the economic recovery could continue to affect deficit levels.

Federal Responses to the Economic Downturn

The federal government responded to financial turmoil with an extraordinary set of measures in 2008 and 2009, including two major economic stimulus measures and a variety of programs within the Federal Reserve, Treasury, and Federal Deposit Insurance Corporation (FDIC).

In February 2008, Congress enacted a $152 billion package (P.L. 110-185, Economic Stimulus Act of 2008) to stimulate consumption by sending refunds to taxpayers and letting firms depreciate capital investments more quickly. Another effort to jump-start economic growth came in the form of a second stimulus package signed into law by President Obama on February 17, 2009. The American Recovery and Reinvestment Act of 2009 (ARRA; P.L. 111-5) included provisions that are now estimated to total $831 billion in increased discretionary and mandatory spending and reduced tax revenue over the FY2009-FY2019 period.

CBO estimates that over 90% of ARRA's direct impact on the deficit will have occurred by the end of FY2011.[31] ARRA contains support for state and local governments in the form of increased transportation project, Medicaid, and school funding; funding for health care information technology; extended unemployment benefits; as well as tax cuts and rebates among other provisions.[32]

In addition to these stimulus efforts, various governmental bodies, through legislative and existing authority, engaged in numerous financial stability programs.

These programs included the conservatorship of government-sponsored enterprises Fannie Mae and Freddie Mac and the Emergency Economic Stabilization Act of 2008 (EESA; P.L. 110-343), which authorized the purchase of troubled assets through the Troubled Assets Relief Program (TARP).

The Federal Reserve created a variety of lending facilities to provide financial institutions with loans in exchange for various types of collateral. The FDIC used its standing authority to resolve failed banks and administer the federal guarantees on individual deposits, in addition to carrying out a broad guarantee program on debt issued by banks and supporting joint interventions in large banks.[33]

Though these financial interventions had significant budgetary impact particularly in FY2009 and FY2010, they are not projected to have a major impact on the budget deficit going forward.

Budget Deficit Estimates for FY2012

The January 2012 CBO baseline estimated the FY2012 budget deficit at $1,079 billion or 7.0% of GDP, lower than the FY2011 (8.7% of GDP) deficit. Spending, though lower than its FY2009 peak, remains several percentage points above the historical average, while receipts remain well below their historical average (see *Figure 1*). The decline in the estimated budget deficit for FY2012, relative to FY2011, is mainly due to increases in tax revenue expected under current law with the expiration of the payroll tax reduction on February 29, 2012 and the deceleration of business tax depreciation for new equipment.

Under the President's budget, deficit estimates for FY2012 amount to $1,327 billion or 8.5% of GDP. This is larger than CBO's baseline deficit estimate primarily due to the cost of short-term measures to stimulate job growth, including an extension of the payroll tax reduction for the entire calendar year, extending long-term unemployment benefits, extending the first-year depreciation deduction for certain property, and providing a temporary tax credit for new jobs.[34]

Budget for FY2013

The Obama Administration released its FY2013 budget on February 13, 2012. Congress has also begun its consideration of the FY2013 budget.

Obama Administration's FY2013 Budget

Consistent with the presentation of previous budgets, the Obama Administration provided three separate deficit projections.[35] First, OMB projected a Budget Enforcement Act (BEA) baseline, using methods that mirror those CBO uses to project its current-law baseline. The BEA baseline assumes that discretionary spending remains constant in real (i.e., inflation-adjusted) terms, the 2001/2003/2010 tax cuts expire at the end of calendar year 2012, and that the alternative minimum tax (AMT) will not be "patched."[36] Many budget analysts believe such projections offer an overly rosy scenario of the long-term budget picture. Under this scenario, the FY2013 deficit is projected to total $598 billion.

The Obama Administration also projected an Adjusted Baseline, which in its view, provides a more transparent and realistic reflection of the federal government's current fiscal situation.[37] They use this methodology as a basis for understanding how new policy choices would affect the fiscal outlook, essentially replacing the current BEA baseline. The Administration's Adjusted Baseline assumes that the 2001/2003/2010 tax cuts will be extended, that the alternative minimum tax (AMT) will be patched, effectively adjusting the exemption level for inflation, that the estate taxes will be extended at 2011 levels, and the spending limits set in the Budget Control Act are in place. This baseline also includes an adjustment for disaster costs. The deficit under this scenario is projected to reach $772 billion in FY2013.

The final deficit projection, the Proposed Budget, illustrates the impact on the budget outlook if all of the policies of the Obama Administration are implemented. In FY2013, the Administration projects that the deficit will reach $901 billion. Both the Adjusted Baseline and the Proposed Budget project deficits throughout the 10-year budget window. Under the Proposed Budget, the deficit would fall from 5.5% of GDP in FY2013 to 2.7% of GDP by FY2018, before rising to 2.8% of GDP from FY2019 to FY2022.[38]

Generally, the deficit levels in the Proposed Budget scenario fall between the lower BEA baseline and the higher Adjusted Baseline figures. Critics argue that the President's budget makes the deficit worse in the short-term and takes credit for deficit reduction over 10 years that would happen automatically under the baseline.

What Do These Baselines Reflect?

As stated above, the Adjusted Baseline assumes that certain policies due to expire will be continued. The President's budget views the Adjusted Baseline as the most realistic projection of the budget deficit and it is used as their benchmark to measure the impact of their budget proposals. The Proposed Budget, however, is the one that illustrates the resulting budget outlook if all of the policies proposed by the President were implemented. Whether or not a certain policy proposal increases or decreases the deficit depends on which baseline is being used as the starting point.

There are no real limits on what assumptions can be used to construct the Adjusted Baseline as opposed to the BEA baseline whose parameters were set by legislation. The Adjusted Baseline in the FY2013 budget assumes, for example, costly increases in the deficit to "patch" the AMT and continue the 2001/2003/2010 tax cuts. Because these policies serve to increase the deficit, the Administration can show decreases in the deficit by measuring its Proposed Budget against this constructed Adjusted Baseline, rather than against the BEA baseline. For example, because the Administration assumes a full continuation of the 2001/2003/2010 tax cuts in its Adjusted Baseline, at a cost of $2,173 billion between FY2013 and FY2022, their proposal included in the Proposed Budget to allow the tax cuts on top income earners to expire, results in a "savings" of $1,433 billion over the same period. However, relative to the BEA baseline, the extension of the tax cuts increases the deficit by $740 billion.[39]

A similar methodology can be used in understanding how the AMT patch is being accounted for in each baseline. The Adjusted Policy baseline incorporates an annual AMT patch at 2011 parameters, which increases the deficit by $1,898 billion over the FY2013-FY2022 period relative to the BEA Baseline. Because this proposal is already included in the Adjusted Baseline, it does not have any additional deficit impact in the Proposed Budget, which maintains the patch.

Major FY2013 Budget Proposals

In his budget for FY2013, President Obama presented his policy agenda, largely focused on providing additional stimulus to create jobs and bolster the economic recovery while operating within the discretionary spending limits currently in law. The main policy initiatives he emphasized include various spending and tax proposals, as well as longer term deficit reduction. The budget also emphasizes continued investment in and reform of education and job training programs as well as a continued push for research and development incentives and infrastructure improvements. Overall, the proposed budget cuts the deficit in half, in dollar terms (and as a percentage of GDP) by the middle part of the decade. However, the deficit begins to rise again in the second half of the decade.

The President's budget proposes a variety of tax and spending measures aimed at job creation, largely drawn from the American Jobs Act submitted to Congress in September 2011. These proposals amount to nearly $350 billion in additional spending and tax cuts, including immediate funding for roads, rails and runways, aid to states and local governments for teachers and first responders, school modernization and a full-year extension of the Social Security payroll tax reduction and unemployment benefits. Of this funding, approximately $178 billion is expected to be spent in FY2012 and $137 billion in FY2013, with smaller amounts in later years.

While the President proposes additional stimulus that increases the deficit in the short term, he also includes a package of spending cuts and revenue increases to reduce the deficit over the next 10-years. In August 2011, the Budget Control Act (BCA) placed limits on spending via discretionary spending caps and included provisions for additional spending cuts in the amount of $1.2 trillion (for more information see the section titled "Budget Control Act of 2011"). In January 2013, the additional cuts are scheduled to take effect via an automatic process. In his FY2013 budget, President Obama proposes replacing the automatic cuts with prescribed spending cuts and tax increases. The largest of these proposals include allowing the 2001/2003/2010 tax cuts for singles making over $200,000 and households making over $250,000 to expire, savings generated from changes to Medicare, Medicaid, agriculture, and other mandatory programs, and placing caps on spending on Overseas Contingency Operations (OCO).[40] Together, these deficit reduction proposals total $1,992 billion.[41]

The budget proposal also included other tax proposals changes in the estate tax parameters, limits the value of itemized deductions for married taxpayers with incomes over $250,000 and single taxpayers with incomes over $200,000, and eliminates various tax expenditures.[42] The Administration also released a framework for corporate tax reform, which included a reduction in the corporate tax rate combined with an elimination of certain corporate tax expenditures. The Administration is committed to reform that would not add to the deficit.[43]

Finally, the President's Budget also includes a *Cuts, Consolidations, and Savings* volume that contains proposed changes to 210 discretionary and mandatory programs, which could save approximately $24 billion in FY2013 if enacted.[44]

Longer term budgetary challenges remain the biggest driver of fiscal challenges. These challenges are partially addressed by a variety of budget proposals. However, further programmatic reforms, beyond those laid out in the budget proposal, will likely be needed to fully address these longterm deficit drivers.

Congressional Consideration of the FY2013 Budget Resolution

The House and Senate Budget Committees are responsible for formulating and reporting an annual budget resolution. The budget committees typically develop the budget resolution as they receive information and testimony from various sources, such as the Administration, CBO, and congressional committees with jurisdiction over spending and revenues. The timetable established in the Congressional Budget Act directs the Senate Budget Committee to report a budget resolution by April 1, and for the House and Senate to reach final agreement on a budget resolution by April 15.[45]

On March 21, 2012, the House Budget Committee reported the budget resolution (H.Con.Res. 112, 112th Congress) by a vote of 19-18. The resolution provided for revenue levels of $2,734 billion and outlays of $3,530 billion in FY2013 for a deficit of $797 billion, or approximately 5.0% of GDP. By FY2022, the deficit is projected to fall to $287 billion or 1.2% of GDP. Debt held by the public is projected to rise in nominal terms from $12,261 billion in FY2013 to $15,364 billion by FY2022.[46] The budget resolution was agreed to by the House on March 29, 2012, by a vote of 228-191.

The budget proposal contains changes to both spending and revenue. The Budget Control Act specified a statutory cap on discretionary spending of $1,047 billion for FY2013. Under the House budget resolution, top line discretionary spending for FY2013 would be further reduced to $1,028 billion. Like the President's budget proposal, the House budget resolution specifies a replacement of the Budget Control Act's automatic cuts, scheduled to take place in January 2013, with spending cuts to be achieved elsewhere. The budget resolution contains reconciliation instructions to six committees to find further deficit reduction of $261 billion over 10 years. Though the committee report accompanying the budget resolution does contain preferred policy options by which to achieve these savings, the committee has the authority to report whatever changes it wants within its jurisdiction in response to the reconciliation directive. Policy options from the budget committee include changes to federal health programs, the Supplemental Nutrition Assistance Program, job training and education programs, and the federal workforce. Under this proposal, overall government spending would be reduced to the historical average of roughly 20% of GDP by FY2015.

On the revenue side, the Budget Committee, in the report accompanying the budget resolution, suggests replacing the current system with two tax brackets of 10% and 25% and repealing the Alternative Minimum Tax. The corporate tax rate would also be reduced from 35% to 25%. To offset the reduction in tax rates, certain tax expenditures would be eliminated in order to broaden the base of taxable income. Revenue collection would average roughly 18% of GDP between FY2013 and FY2022 under this proposal.

Because the budget resolution does not become law, separate legislation would have to be enacted in order to make some of the policy changes that are relied upon in the proposal. The budget proposal does not contain specifics on how some of the revenue and spending proposals would be achieved. Therefore, if some of the policy proposals do not become law, the spending, revenue, and deficit projections could change significantly. Further affecting deficit levels are the economic assumptions used in making any budget projections. The House budget resolution uses CBO's January 2012 estimates, which are roughly in line with those in the President's budget.[47] If economic growth is higher or lower, the deficit levels and related components in the budget resolution would be affected.

The Senate Budget Committee has not yet reported a budget resolution for FY2013.

In order to proceed with the consideration of FY2013 appropriations bills, both the House and the Senate took action to "deem" enforceable levels of discretionary spending for FY2013 because no agreement has been reached on the budget resolution.[48] In the past, deeming resolutions have been used when the House and Senate are late in reaching final agreement on a budget resolution or fail to reach an agreement altogether.

CONSIDERATIONS FOR CONGRESS

Congress faces ongoing budgetary challenges in FY2013 with both short-run and long-run budget priorities that may conflict in critical ways. In the short term, economic issues may continue to dominate the policy debates. In addition, Congress will have to make decisions in several key policy areas. Over the long term, increasing federal health care costs are expected to keep mandatory spending rising, placing ever-increasing focus on how to achieve fiscal sustainability.

Addressing the Budget Deficit

Over the next several months, Congress is expected to discuss several revenue and spending policies that, if changed from current law, could have a large impact on the size of the budget deficit going forward.

Tax Provisions

On December 17, 2010, the Tax Relief, Unemployment Insurance Reauthorization, and Job Creation Act of 2010 (P.L. 111-312) was signed into law. This legislation had numerous provisions, including the extension of the 2001 and 2003 ("Bush") tax cuts until the end of 2012, reinstating the estate tax until the end of 2012, and "patching" the alternative minimum tax until the end of 2011. Under the law, long-term unemployment benefits were also extended and the employee portion of the Social Security payroll tax was cut by two percentage points until the end of 2011. Relative to current law, CBO estimated that the spending and revenue measures in the bill would increase the deficit by $390 billion in FY2011 and by $468 billion over the FY2012-FY2020 period, with nearly all the impact on the deficit occurring between FY2011 and FY2013.[49]

The payroll tax reduction, long-term unemployment benefit extension, and "doc fix" were extended for two months, through February 29, 2012, as part of Temporary Payroll Tax Cut Continuation Act of 2011 (P.L. 112-78). These measures were extended through the end of calendar year 2012 as part of Middle Class Tax Relief and Job Creation Act of 2012 (H.R. 3630). CBO estimates that this legislation, enacted as part of H.R. 3630, will increase the deficit by $89.3 billion over the FY2012-FY2022 period.[50]

Budget Control Act of 2011

On August 2, 2011, the President signed into law the Budget Control Act of 2011 (BCA; P.L. 112- 25).[51] The BCA contained a variety of measures intended to reduce the deficit by at least $2.1 trillion over the FY2012-FY2021 period, along with a mechanism to increase the debt limit. The deficit reduction provisions included $917 billion in savings from statutory caps on discretionary spending and the establishment of a Joint Select Committee on Deficit Reduction (Joint Committee) to identify further budgetary savings of at least $1.2 trillion over 10 years. On November 21, 2011, the co-chairs of the Joint Committee announced that they were unable to reach an agreement before the committee's deadline. As a result, a $1.2 trillion automatic spending reduction process has been triggered to begin in January 2013 unless Congress and the President act to eliminate or change the process before then. While the BCA is projected to reduce the deficit, it does not eliminate budget deficits or growth in the federal debt over the 10- year budget window.

Even with the deficit reduction contained in the BCA, many budget analysts believe that additional savings are required to put the budget on a sustainable path over the long-term, particularly if some of the policies set to expire under current law are, instead, continued. (See earlier discussion in the section "Budget Baseline Projections".) Even under the current law baseline, which includes the BCA's $2.1 trillion in deficit reduction, projected deficits of $3.1 trillion over 10 years remain.

Other Short-Term Considerations

The economy is still recovering from the most recent recession, which lasted from December 2007 to June 2009. Conditions remain weak, in part, due to budget challenges facing state and local governments, high levels of consumer debt, and continuing weakness in many real estate markets. Most economists expect unemployment rates to remain elevated for the medium term. During this period, the budget deficit grew largely as a result of government actions taken to combat the economic downturn as well as significantly lower revenue and higher spending levels directly attributable to the economic conditions.

As the economy continues to recover, revenue should increase as unemployment falls and spending should decrease due to less reliance on federal programs meant to provide assistance during economic downturns. This should lead to decreases in the budget deficit relative to current levels in the short term. Though many argue that fiscal stimulus and other actions were needed to help the economy recover, the resulting large budget deficits and high debt levels will have an effect for many years.

Many budget analysts are concerned about future levels of federal debt and acknowledge that the current spending and revenue collection cannot continue at current or projected future levels. However, making significant changes to spending or revenue policies at this time may be harmful to the ongoing economic recovery. On the other hand, the longer that the country continues without a plan to stabilize its fiscal future, the more costly reform may be. In addition, the likelihood of a severe fiscal crisis caused by an unwillingness of private investors to continue financing unsustainable deficits may increase, and if that occurs, reforms may be forced by events, rather than being well planned.[52]

General Budget Issues

Congress may wish to consider some general budgeting issues beyond these short-term considerations.

Budget Transparency

The budget, reflecting the size and complexity of the federal government, is complicated and detailed. The budget books that OMB compiles provide an enormous amount of information, and other budget data reported by federal agencies provide even more detail on federal spending plans. The Federal Funding Accountability and Transparency Act of 2006 (P.L. 109-282) included several measures to increase the accessibility of budget information. For example, as a result of that act, OMB now runs the USAspending.gov website, which provides detailed information on federal spending. Concerns have been raised about the quality of those data.[53] Moreover, it is not clear that those data are thoroughly coordinated with other federal budgeting data systems.

Congress and the President have undertaken additional efforts in an attempt to improve transparency in light of the large amounts of spending currently occurring as a result of economic stabilization efforts and federal financial interventions. For example, Recovery.gov was launched to track stimulus spending. The Congressional Oversight Panel was established in the Emergency Economic Stabilization Act to oversee TARP spending. Despite this, criticisms remain and requests for greater transparency continue.

In certain cases, despite the large amount of data provided by OMB and other government agencies, it can be difficult to answer relatively simple budget questions. Critics maintain that the federal government in general and OMB in particular should take steps to make data on federal spending even more transparent to taxpayers and more useful to policymakers. Even as the President's budget mentions "a new tracking tool" to provide daily updates on spending by agency, Congress may wish to consider requiring these changes to provide more organized and transparent budget data to citizens and to itself.[54]

Long-Term Considerations

Budget deficits or surpluses are not always the best indication of long-term fiscal stability. Most economists agree that, under certain conditions, running a budget deficit may be necessary to provide economic stimulus or pull an economy out of recession. A large budget deficit in a single year, in itself, does not necessarily indicate a longer term problem. The federal government, however, does face serious long-term budget challenges. Some measures of fiscal solvency in the long term indicate that, under current policy, the U.S. may face a major future crisis, specifically as it relates to rising health care costs and the likely impact on government-financed health care spending.

CBO, GAO, and the Administration agree that the current mix of federal fiscal policies is unsustainable in the long term. The nation's aging population, combined with rising health care costs per beneficiary, seems likely to keep federal health costs rising faster than per capita GDP. CBO projected in June 2011 that under current policy, federal spending on federal health programs (including Medicare, Medicaid, CHIP, and exchange subsidies) would grow from 5.6% of GDP today to 10.3% of GDP in 2035, and to nearly 20% by

2085.[55] The 2010 Economic Report of the President also called the trajectory of future federal spending on Medicare and Medicaid unsustainable.[56] GAO's recent long-term fiscal simulations, under an alternative policy scenario, projected debt held by the public as a share of GDP to exceed the post World War II historical high in about 15 years.[57]

Keeping future federal outlays at 20% of GDP, or approximately at its historical average, and leaving fiscal policies unchanged, according to CBO projections, would require drastic reductions in all spending other than that for Medicare, Social Security, and Medicaid, or reining in the costs of these programs.

Under the extension of current law, CBO estimates that the nation's current fiscal gap, a present-value measure of fiscal imbalance for a given time period, would reach 0.2% of GDP over the next 75 years.

This means that an immediate and permanent reduction in spending, increase in revenues, or a combination of spending cuts and revenue increases amounting to 0.2% of GDP would be needed to make the government's debt the same size (relative to the size of the economy) at the end of that period as it was at the beginning.

Under an alternative fiscal scenario, which incorporates policy changes that are widely expected to occur and that policymakers have regularly made in the past, the fiscal gap reaches 8.3% of GDP.[58] This indicates that an immediate and permanent reduction in spending, increase in revenues, or a combination of spending cuts and revenue increases amounting to 8.3% of GDP would be needed to make the government's debt the same size (relative to the size of the economy) at the end of that period as it was at the beginning.[59]

In other words, to ensure a sustainable fiscal path over the next 75-years where debt remains at the same level of GDP as it is currently, spending would have to be immediately and permanently cut by 31%, revenue would have to be increased by 44%, or some combination of the two.

As the economic recovery continues, Congress may focus more effort on balancing the budget and reining in the debt. This would require less spending, increases in revenue collections, fasterthan-average economic growth, or a combination of these things. Debt requires interest payments that can strain budgets if debt levels and interest rates are high. High debt levels could limit the government's flexibility in meeting its obligations or in responding to emerging needs of its citizens. Ultimately, failing to take action to reduce the projected growth in the debt potentially might lead to future insolvency or government default.[60]

APPENDIX. BUDGET DOCUMENTS

CBO Documents

The Congressional Budget Office (CBO) provides data and analysis to Congress throughout the budget and appropriations process. Each January, CBO issues a *Budget and Economic Outlook* that contains current-law baseline estimates of outlays and revenues. In March, CBO typically issues an analysis of the President's budget submission with revised baseline estimates and projections. In late summer, CBO issues an updated *Budget and Economic Outlook* with new baseline projections.

In these documents, CBO sets a current-law baseline as a benchmark to evaluate whether legislative proposals would increase or decrease outlays and revenue collection. Baseline estimates are not intended to predict likely future outcomes, but to show what spending and revenues would be if current law remained in effect. CBO typically evaluates the budgetary consequences of legislative proposals and the Joint Committee on Taxation (JCT) evaluates the consequences of revenue proposals.

CBO also releases other periodic publications focusing on the future fiscal health of the United States. In their publication, *The Long-Term Budget Outlook*, CBO makes projections on the state of the federal budget to FY2083. They discuss spending and revenue levels and the related issues that they expect will arise under different policy assumptions. In their *Budget Options* volumes, they provide specific policy options and the impact they will have on spending and revenues over a 10-year budget window. They also provide arguments for and against enacting each policy.

OMB Documents

The President's Budget typically contains six volumes: (1) *The Budget*; (2) *Historical Tables*; (3) *Analytical Perspectives*; (4) *Appendix*; (5) *Terminations, Reductions, and Savings*; and (6) *Supplemental Materials*.[61] These documents lay out the Administration's projections of the fiscal outlook for the country, along with spending levels proposed for each of the federal government's departments and programs. The *Historical Tables* volume also provides significant amounts of budget data, much of which extends back to 1962 or earlier. Along with the Administration's budget documents, the

Department of the Treasury also releases its *Green Book*, which provides further detail on the revenue proposals that are contained in the budget.[62]

End Notes

[1] For more information, see CRS Report 98-721, Introduction to the Federal Budget Process, coordinated by Bill Heniff Jr.

[2] Congressional Budget Office, Estimated Impact of the American Recovery and Reinvestment Act on Employment and Economic Output from July 2011 Through September 2011, November 2011, p. 2; U.S. Congress, U.S. House of Representatives Committee on Financial Services, Federal Reserve programs to strengthen credit markets and the economy, Testimony of Federal Reserve Chairman Ben S. Bernanke, February 10, 2009, available at http://www.federalreserve.gov/newsevents/testimony/bernanke20090210a.htm.

[3] Unless stated otherwise, data used in this report are from Congressional Budget Office, The Budget and Economic Outlook: Fiscal Years 2012 to 2022, January 2012, available at http://cbo.gov/publication/42905.

[4] For more information on the BCA, see CRS Report R41965, The Budget Control Act of 2011, by Bill Heniff Jr., Elizabeth Rybicki, and Shannon M. Mahan and CRS Report R42013, The Budget Control Act of 2011: How Do the Discretionary Caps and Automatic Spending Cuts Affect the Budget and the Economy?, by Marc Labonte and Mindy R. Levit.

[5] CRS Report 98-325, The Federal Fiscal Year, by Bill Heniff Jr.

[6] The contents of the Presidential budget submission are governed by 31 U.S.C. §1105. For reasons why the budget may be delayed, see CRS Report RS20179, The Role of the President in Budget Development, by Bill Heniff Jr.

[7] Congress does not always complete action on a budget resolution. In years when Congress is late in adopting, or does not adopt, a budget resolution, the House and Senate independently may adopt "deeming resolution" provisions for the purpose of enforcing certain budget levels. The last time Congress agreed to a budget resolution was for FY2010. The FY2010 budget resolution was agreed to on April 29, 2009. For more information, see CRS Report RL30297, Congressional Budget Resolutions: Historical Information, by Bill Heniff Jr. and Justin Murray and CRS Report RL31443, The "Deeming Resolution": A Budget Enforcement Tool, by Megan Suzanne Lynch.

[8] For more information on the appropriations and authorization process, see CRS Report R42388, The Congressional Appropriations Process: An Introduction, by Jessica Tollestrup.

[9] Many of the rules governing the baseline, contained in §257 of the Balanced Budget and Emergency Deficit Control Act, as amended, were extended or modified as part of the Budget Control Act of 2011 (P.L. 112-25).

[10] For more information on trends in discretionary and mandatory spending, see CRS Report RL34424, Trends in Discretionary Spending, by D. Andrew Austin and Mindy R. Levit and CRS Report RL33074, Mandatory Spending Since 1962, by D. Andrew Austin and Mindy R. Levit.

[11] Net interest is discussed in further detail below in the section "Deficits, Debt, and Interest."

[12] Total outlays peaked at 25.2% of GDP in FY2009.

[13] The division between discretionary and mandatory spending was first put into place in FY1962.

[14] Mandatory spending peaked in FY2009 at 15.0% of GDP.

[15] For more information, see CRS Report R41970, Addressing the Long-Run Budget Deficit: A Comparison of Approaches, by Jane G. Gravelle and CRS Report R41778, Reducing the Budget Deficit: Policy Issues, by Marc Labonte.

[16] In various reports, the Congressional Budget Office, the Government Accountability Office, and the Administration agree that the federal government's budget is on an unsustainable path. For more information, see the section of this report titled, "Long-Term Considerations."

[17] In FY2009 and FY2010, revenue collection totaled 15.1% of GDP.

[18] For more information, see CRS Report R41591, Tax Reform: An Overview of Proposals in the 112th Congress, by James M. Bickley.

[19] For more information, see CRS Report RL32808, Overview of the Federal Tax System, by Molly F. Sherlock and Donald J. Marples.

[20] Payroll tax revenue has declined over the last fiscal year largely due to a reduction in the employee payroll tax rate from 6.2% to 4.2%, which began on January 1, 2011.

[21] Most economists use data on federal outlays to track larger budget trends, while most program analysts use budget authority to track changes in specific program areas.

[22] From an overall budget perspective, these surpluses are used to offset other federal spending, thereby decreasing the current budget deficit while increasing the amount of Treasury securities held in the Trust Fund.

[23] U.S. Office of Management and Budget, Budget for Fiscal Year 2013, Historical Tables, Table 1-3, available at http://www.whitehouse.gov/omb/budget/Historicals/.

[24] Gross federal debt is also referred to as total debt or total public debt outstanding. Intragovernmental debt is also referred to as intragovernmental holdings or debt held by federal government accounts.

[25] In FY2009 and FY2010, the increase in the deficit was larger than that of debt held by the public due to the nature of the obligations incurred as a result of the government conservatorship of Fannie Mae and Freddie Mac and the TARP program.

[26] General Accountability Office, Delays Create Debt Management Challenges and Increase Uncertainty in the Treasury Market, GAO-11-203, February 2011.

[27] U.S. Office of Management and Budget, Budget for Fiscal Year 2012, Historical Tables, Tables 7-1 and 7-2.

[28] For further details, see CRS Report RL31967, The Debt Limit: History and Recent Increases, by D. Andrew Austin and Mindy R. Levit.

[29] Since FY1970, the U.S. spent an average of 2.2% of GDP on interest payments.

[30] Carmen M. Reinhart and Kenneth S. Rogoff, "The Aftermath of Financial Crises," American Economic Review, vol. 99 (2009), no. 2, p. 10; Alan Auerbach and William Gale, "The Economic Crisis and the Fiscal Crisis: 2009 and Beyond An Update," Tax Policy Center, September 2009, available at http://www.taxpolicycenter.org/UploadedPDF/ 1001284_ economic_crisis.pdf.

[31] The cost estimate for ARRA has changed since it was originally projected due to revised economic and technical assumptions and certain legislative changes. See source for additional notes. U.S. Congressional Budget Office, The Budget and Economic Outlook: Fiscal Years 2012 to 2022, January 2012, Box 1-1.

[32] For more information on the provisions of ARRA, see CRS Report R40537, American Recovery and Reinvestment Act of 2009 (P.L. 111-5): Summary and Legislative History, by Clinton T. Brass et al.

[33] For more information, see CRS Report R41073, Government Interventions in Response to Financial Turmoil, by Baird Webel and Marc Labonte.

[34] Office of Management and Budget, Budget for Fiscal Year 2013, The Budget, Tables S-2 and S-9.

[35] For details of these projections, see U.S. Office of Management and Budget, Budget for Fiscal Year 2012, The Budget, Tables S-1 (Proposed Budget) and S-7 (BEA Baseline and Adjusted Baseline).

[36] The tax cuts were enacted in the Economic Growth and Taxpayer Relief Act of 2001 (EGTRRA; P.L. 107-16) and the Jobs and Growth Tax Relief Reconciliation Act of 2003 (JGTRRA; P.L. 108-27) and extended as part of The Tax Relief, Unemployment Insurance Reauthorization, and Job Creation Act of 2010 (P.L. 111-312). For more information, see CRS Report R42020, The 2001 and 2003 Bush Tax Cuts and Deficit Reduction, by Thomas L. Hungerford.

[37] In prior years, this scenario had been known as the Current Policy Baseline.

[38] U.S. Office of Management and Budget, Budget for Fiscal Year 2013, The Budget, Tables S-4 and S-6. In March 2012, CBO estimated that the President's Proposed Budget would result in a deficit of $977 billion or 6.1% of GDP in FY2013. By FY2022, CBO projects a deficit of $728 billion or 3.0% of GDP based on the President's proposals. Congressional Budget Office, An Analysis of the President's 2013 Budget, Table 1.

[39] These figures do not include related debt service costs or savings.

[40] OCO spending is currently exempt from the BCA discretionary spending caps. Part of the savings would be used to invest in a six-year surface transportation reauthorization package. Whether or not savings can be generated by reducing OCO spending from current levels has been controversial. For CBO's take on the issue, see Congressional Budget Office, Director's Blog, Can Proposed Reductions in Future War-Related Spending Be Used To Offset Proposed Deficit Increases in Other Areas?, February 1, 2012.

[41] The deficit reduction proposed in the President's budget to replace the automatic spending reduction process total $3,187 billion. However, the budget also proposes to cancel the $1,195 billion automatic process cuts. Therefore, the cumulative effect of these reductions is $1,992 billion. CRS calculations based on Office of Management and Budget, Budget for Fiscal Year 2013, The Budget, Table S-2.

[42] For full detail on the revenue proposals included in the President's budget, see Department of the Treasury, General Explanations of the Administration's Revenue Proposals (Green Book), February 2012.

[43] The White House and the Department of the Treasury, The President's Framework for Business Tax Reform, p. 1, February 2012.

[44] Office of Management and Budget, Budget for Fiscal Year 2013, Cuts, Consolidations, and Savings, p. 1.

[45] For more information on the congressional budget process, see CRS Report RS20368, Overview of the Congressional Budget Process, by Bill Heniff Jr.

[46] U.S. House of Representatives, Committee on the Budget, The Path to Prosperity: A Blueprint for American Renewal, Table S-1.

[47] U.S. House of Representatives, Committee on the Budget, H.Rept. 112-421, p. 26 and Table 6.

[48] For more information, see CRS Report RL31443, The "Deeming Resolution": A Budget Enforcement Tool, by Megan Suzanne Lynch.

[49] Between FY2014 and FY2020, the legislation is estimated to reduce the deficit by $59 billion. Congressional Budget Office, The Budget and Economic Outlook: Fiscal Years 2011 to 2021, January 2011, Box 1-1.

50 Congressional Budget Office, Budgetary Effects of the Conference Agreement for H.R. 3630, the Middle Class Tax Relief and Job Creation Act of 2012, as Posted on the Web Site of the

House Committee on Rules on February 16, 2012. For more information, see CRS Report R42103, Extending the Temporary Payroll Tax Reduction: A Brief Description and Economic Analysis, by Donald J. Marples and Molly F. Sherlock and CRS Report RL33362, Unemployment Insurance: Programs and Benefits, by Julie M. Whittaker and Katelin P. Isaacs.

[51] For more information on the Budget Control Act of 2011, see CRS Report R41965, The Budget Control Act of 2011, by Bill Heniff Jr., Elizabeth Rybicki, and Shannon M. Mahan and CRS Report R42013, The Budget Control Act of 2011: How Do the Discretionary Caps and Automatic Spending Cuts Affect the Budget and the Economy?, by Marc Labonte and Mindy R. Levit.

[52] Congressional Budget Office, Federal Debt and the Risk of a Fiscal Crisis, July 27, 2010, p. 1.

[53] For more information, see CRS Report RL34718, The Federal Funding Accountability and Transparency Act: Implementation and Proposed Amendments, by Garrett Hatch.

[54] Office of Management and Budget, Budget for Fiscal Year 2011, The Budget, p. 44.

[55] Congressional Budget Office, The Long-Term Budget Outlook, June 2011, pp. 45-46 and "Supplemental Material."

[56] Council of Economic Advisors, Economic Report of the President, February 2010, p. 140.

[57] Government Accountability Office, The Federal Government's Long-Term Fiscal Outlook: Fall 2011 Update (GAO12-28SP), October 23, 2011, p. 1.

[58] The alternative fiscal scenario includes things like the extension of certain expiring tax provisions and the continued indexation of AMT to inflation through 2021 and Medicare physician payment rates are maintained at 2011 levels through 2021 and not restrained thereafter by policies in current law. For a complete description of the assumptions included in the extended baseline and alternative fiscal scenarios, see Congressional Budget Office, The Long-Term Budget Outlook, June 2011, Table 1-1.

[59] U.S. Congressional Budget Office, The Long-Term Budget Outlook, June 2011, Table 1-3.

[60] See Alan Auerbach and William Gale, "The Economic Crisis and the Fiscal Crisis: 2009 and Beyond: An Update," Tax Policy Center working paper, September 2009, available at http://www.brookings.edu/~/media/Files/rc/papers/ 2009/06_fiscal_crisis_gale/06_fiscal_crisis_gale_update.pdf.

[61] The President's budget proposals can be found on the OMB website at http://www.whitehouse. gov/omb/. The Supplemental Materials include the Federal Credit Supplement, the Object Class Analysis, the Balances of Budget Authority, and the Public Budget Database.

[62] The Green Book is available at http://www.treasury.gov/resource-center/tax-policy/Pages/ general_explanation.aspx.

INDEX

E

F

G

H

I

J

L

M

U

V

W

Y

LEGAL DESIGN

Legal design is a rapidly growing field that seeks to improve the legal system's accessibility, usability, and effectiveness through human-centered design methods and principles. This book provides a comprehensive introduction to legal design, covering fundamental concepts, definitions, and theories. Chapters explore the role of legal design in promoting dignity, equity, and justice in the legal system. Contributors present a range of community-driven projects and method-focused case studies that demonstrate the potential of legal design to transform how people experience the law. This book is an essential resource for anyone interested in the future of law and the intersection of design and justice.

Dr. Miso Kim is an Associate Professor of Experience Design at Northeastern University and the Design Director of the NuLawLab. She holds a PhD in Design, an MDes in Interaction Design, and an MDes in Communication Planning and Information Design from Carnegie Mellon University.

Dan Jackson is Executive Director of NuLawLab at Northeastern University School of Law. Jackson is also Chair of the American Bar Association Standing Committee on the Delivery of Legal Services and holds a JD from Northeastern University.

Jules Rochielle Sievert is pursuing an Interdisciplinary PhD at Northeastern University and has been with NuLawLab since 2013. Sievert was recently Ambassador for Health Equity at Policy Link and Creative Placemaking Policy Fellow at Arizona State University through the Herberger Institute for Design and the Arts.

Legal Design

DIGNIFYING PEOPLE IN LEGAL SYSTEMS

Edited by

MISO KIM
Northeastern University

DAN JACKSON
Northeastern University

JULES ROCHIELLE SIEVERT
Northeastern University

CAMBRIDGE
UNIVERSITY PRESS

CAMBRIDGE
UNIVERSITY PRESS

Shaftesbury Road, Cambridge CB2 8EA, United Kingdom

One Liberty Plaza, 20th Floor, New York, NY 10006, USA

477 Williamstown Road, Port Melbourne, VIC 3207, Australia

314–321, 3rd Floor, Plot 3, Splendor Forum, Jasola District Centre, New Delhi – 110025, India

103 Penang Road, #05-06/07, Visioncrest Commercial, Singapore 238467

Cambridge University Press is part of Cambridge University Press & Assessment, a department of the University of Cambridge.

We share the University's mission to contribute to society through the pursuit of education, learning and research at the highest international levels of excellence.

www.cambridge.org
Information on this title: www.cambridge.org/9781009437073

DOI: 10.1017/9781009437042

When citing this work, please include a reference to the DOI 10.1017/9781009437042

First published 2024

A catalogue record for this publication is available from the British Library.

A Cataloging-in-Publication data record for this book is available from the Library of Congress.

ISBN 978-1-009-43707-3 Hardback

The editors would like to dedicate this volume to our students, for whom we do this work, and to our community partners, with whom we share a vision of a universally just, peaceful, and equitable world.

Contents

Figures and Tables

FIGURES

TABLES

Contributors

Mirian Calvo's research challenges conventional architecture by demonstrating how communities transform urban environments. She leads research and consultancy projects, such as My Mainway, Placemaking-with-Young-Adults, and Mapping Values. She is a lecturer in participatory architecture at Lancaster University's School of Architecture, Architect ARB, ImaginationLancaster researcher, and ENSAP-BX guest lecturer.

Antonio M. Coronado (they/them/elle) is a professor of practice/community legal education lead at Innovation for Justice, jointly housed by the University of Arizona James E. Rogers College of Law and the David Eccles School of Business, University of Utah. In their work as an interdisciplinary storyteller and cross-jurisdictional advocate, Antonio seeks to build community legal power, center the experiences of multiply marginalized peoples, and honor the scholarships of fellow queer and trans* writers of color. As an abolitionist educator, they are dedicated to pedagogical practices of dreaming, disrupting, and radical reflection.

Leon Cruickshank is a founding member of ImaginationLancaster at Lancaster University. Collaborations ranging from the UN to communities in food poverty use co–design to establish a more equitable society. He leads the Beyond Imagination project and the Leapfrog project looking at new forms of working creatively outside academia.

Robert de Rooy is a South African attorney who developed the world's first illustrated legal contract, known as Comic Contracts. Recently he developed a digital audio-visual Comic Contract authoring and contracting tool to improve and scale the delivery of Comic Contracts. Apart from his legal practice, he is an adjunct associate professor of private law at the University of Cape Town and working on his doctorate in business law at the University of Vaasa, Finland.

Kanan Dhru is a senior lecturer of legal technology at The Hague University of Applied Sciences with a rich background in legal innovation, entrepreneurship, and legal design. Possessing a bachelors of law from London School of Economics and masters in public administration from Indira Gandhi National Open University, she is a cofounder of Lawtoons and has dedicated 18 years to the exploration of the areas at the intersection of law and technology.

Kelly Dhru researches in the areas of legal philosophy and neuro/bioethics. She has been a theatre artist and cofounder of Lawtoons. A lawyer from India, Kelly holds a BCL and MPhil from University College, Oxford and an LLM from Harvard Law School, and is currently a research associate at the law faculty, Hamburg University, Germany, where she is completing her PhD.

Michael Doherty is Associate Head of the Law School, Lancaster University, coauthor of *Public Law* (3rd edn, Routledge 2023), cofounder of the *Connecting Legal Education* online community, and former Chair of the Association of Law Teachers. His legal design work encompasses education, disciplinarity, and access to justice, and he is founding editor-in-chief of the *Legal Design Journal*.

Steven Geofrey is an associate teaching professor at Northeastern University, where they teach and conduct applied research in data visualization and creative coding. Steven also runs a freelance practice, *Fluid Encodings* (https://fluidencodings.com/), that uses the methods of data, computation, and information design in digital humanities.

Alana Greer is the Director and cofounder of the Community Justice Project in Miami, Florida. As a movement lawyer, she supports community-led campaigns for racial justice and human rights. Alana is passionate about supporting grassroots organizing seeking to dismantle structural racism and inequality.

Margaret Hagan directs the Legal Design Lab at Stanford University. She holds a JD from Stanford University, a DPhil from Queen's University Belfast, an MA from Central European University, and an AB from University of Chicago. She designs new ways to make the legal system more accessible, dignified, and just.

Dan Jackson has directed the NuLawLab at Northeastern University School of Law since 2013. Dan is a 1997 graduate of Northeastern Law and a 1990 graduate of Northwestern University. He currently serves as Chair of the American Bar Association Standing Committee on the Delivery of Legal Services.

Meena Jagannath is Director of Global Programs at Movement Law Lab and coordinates the Global Network of Movement Lawyers. She cofounded the Community Justice Project. She believes in multidisciplinarity and creative solutions to complex problems, and is passionate about forging bonds of solidarity across borders, languages, cultures, and species.

Renee Knake Jefferson is the Doherty Chair in Legal Ethics and Professor of Law at the University of Houston. She is an elected member of the American Law Institute and former Fulbright Distinguished Chair in Entrepreneurship and Innovation at Australia's RMIT University. She was named a "Legal Rebel" by the *ABA Journal* and received an Ewing Marion Kauffman Foundation grant for teaching and research on innovation in access to justice.

Joonas Keski-Rahkonen is a researcher and teaching fellow in the Department of Physics at Harvard University. His research in theoretical and computational physics comprises the study of classical and quantum nature of chaos, transport phenomena in nano- and mesoscopic structures, and the development of simulation techniques.

Dr. Miso Kim is an associate professor of experience design at Northeastern University. She holds a PhD in design, an MDes in interaction design, and an MDes in communication planning and information design from Carnegie Mellon University. She also holds a BS in architecture from Sungkyunkwan University in South Korea. She is the design director of the NuLawLab and the founding codirector of the Health and Wellness Design Lab at Northeastern University. Her research focuses on dignity, autonomy, and participation in service design.

Sanea Lamas graduated from Northeastern University School of Law in 2024. While at Northeastern University, she worked as a research assistant with the University's NuLawLab. During her time with the NuLawLab, she conducted literature reviews on the built environment and its impact on the design of courthouses.

Jennifer Leitch is a researcher in legal ethics and professionalism, access to justice, and dispute processes. She is a member of the Law Society of Ontario, the Director of the National Self-Represented Litigants Project, and the Associate Director in the Ethics, Society & Law program at Trinity College, University of Toronto.

Alexander Nally is a dynamic attorney and legal designer, specialized in bringing constituents and policymakers together to codesign policies that center dignity and human experiences within legal systems. Alex was selected as a Rappaport Law Fellow in 2017, held CIPP/US certification since 2019, and joined the Massachusetts Bar in 2021.

Dr. Katri L. Nousiainen is a lawyer and professional in legal and economics education. She is teaching faculty member in the management program at Harvard University and holds a Resident Research Fellow position at Harvard Law School in the Program on Negotiation (PON). In addition, she is affiliated with the University of Cambridge Law (the United Kingdom) and Hanken School of Economics (Finland). She is known for her articles, podcasts, and book chapters on legal design, negotiation, and contracting, and on law and emerging technologies, especially related to quantum technologies. In her work, she supports and assists companies and other operators in improving the quality and efficiency of their legal processes, products, and services. Presently she is pioneering research projects on law, emerging technologies, and legal design in negotiation and commercial contracting.

Kürşat Özenç is a design executive, educator, and an author. He teaches designing organizational culture at Stanford University; has written two books, *Rituals For Virtual Meetings* (2021, Wiley) and *Rituals For Work* (2019, Wiley), to help organizations; and holds a PhD in design from Carnegie Mellon, an MFA from Sabanci University, and BID from Middle East Technical University.

Amanda Perry-Kessaris is Professor of Law at the University of Kent and an elected fellow of the Academy of Social Sciences. She holds postgraduate qualifications in law and in design and is the author of *Doing Sociolegal Research in Design Mode* (2021) and co-editor with Emily Allbon of *Design in Legal Education* (2022).

Purvi Shah has spent decades lawyering for progressive social movements including the Movement for Black Lives; Right to the City Alliance; and taxi drivers, tenant unions, and immigrant rights groups. In 2018, she founded Movement Law Lab to organize more lawyers to work alongside movements to shift culture, systems, and power.

Jules Rochielle Sievert has been with NuLawLab since 2013. Jules is currently the primary research lead for the National Endowment for the Arts Research Lab known as the East Boston Spatial Justice Lab and currently pursuing an Interdisciplinary PhD at Northeastern University College of Art Media and Design. Jules was recently an ambassador for Health Equity at PolicyLink and a creative placemaking policy fellow at Arizona State University through the Herberger Institute for Design and the Arts.

Sofia Stolk is an assistant professor at Vrije Universiteit Amsterdam and associate fellow at the Asser Institute, The Hague. Her research focuses on international law's visual life. She has widely published on the intersection of art, architecture, culture and law, and is cofounder of the Legal Sightseeing platform.

Gabriel H. Teninbaum is the Assistant Dean for Innovation, Strategic Initiatives & Distance Education, as well as a tenured professor of legal writing at Suffolk University Law School. He is also a visiting fellow at Yale Law School's Information Society Project. He has been called "perhaps the most tech-savvy law professor in the nation" by the *American Bar Association Journal*.

Natalicia R. Tracy, PhD is a senior policy advisor at the United States Department of Labor, was Executive Director of Boston's Brazilian Worker Center (2010–21), and a lecturer in labor studies, sociology and human services and resident scholar at the Labor Resource Center at the University of Massachusetts Boston (2010–21).

Phoebe Walton is a designer and researcher working in the intersection of law, critical design, architecture, and filmmaking. Her research engages with critical legal design and examines the roles of performativity, speculation, and artificial intelligence within legal systems. She works as a researcher at Forensis e.V, using spatial investigations and counter-forensic methods for investigating human rights violations.

Morgan A. Wilson was the Interim Director of the Domestic Violence Institute at Northeastern Law School, where she ran the Domestic Violence Clinic. In 2021, she was recognized by the Institute for Nonprofit Practice as a changemaker for her work supporting survivors of dating, domestic, and sexual violence.

Dr. Tiana Yom is an assistant research professor and the Director of the Northeastern University Public Evaluation Lab. She is committed to building community–academic partnerships via culturally responsive evaluation and participatory action research. Her research areas are in adolescent health, youth development, school-based health promotion, school climate, and health and nutrition education.

Foreword

Martha F. Davis

This volume arises from an important, even revolutionary, insight: Both legal institutions and law itself are products of deliberate design decisions. If a courthouse feels cold and intimidating, or a legal document is unintelligible, that is by design. If housing law disempowers tenants, it is because it is designed to do so. If labeling laws confuse consumers, that is a reflection of deliberate design choices. Sometimes, well-meaning laws are designed to emphasize fairness in outcomes while neglecting the dignity of the participants. Very often, these design decisions have the effect of expanding the power of lawyers themselves, who have been trained to navigate the vagaries of laws that were designed (often by lawyers) to ensure full employment for members of the legal profession.

Critiquing law's design opens up the possibility of alternative approaches to problem-solving for individuals and communities. If legal institutions or laws have been poorly designed, they can be redesigned in collaboration with affected communities, in ways that shift unearned power away from lawyers. Lawyers may still employ their specialized training in drafting, negotiating, and problem-solving; there will always be a role for specialization. But as described by the contributors here, centering human dignity through legal design facilitates expanded opportunities for collaboration and codesign, resulting in more effective legal institutions and laws.

Because of its deep connection to individual humans and communities, the practice of legal design is necessarily experiential, context specific, and place based. Many of the examples explored in depth in this volume are case studies that can offer ideas, inspiration, and lessons, but they are not blueprints. In fact, more formulaic approaches to legal design would be antithetical to its essential goals of reinventing law and legal institutions as endeavors devoted to enhancing human dignity and empowerment. In the absence of rigid formulae, effective legal designers must remain flexible, nimble, and humble, retaining a constant posture of learning and exploration.

A particular strength of legal design as it stands today is its breadth, with relevance to every interaction with law and legal institutions. Legal design crosses boundaries of all sorts, from the international to the hyperlocal, constitutional to regulatory law, and litigation to drafting. It even offers opportunities to envision entirely new models for mediating between individuals and society that do not rely on existing conceptions of the rule of law. Again, in defying the current constraints of legally constructed boundaries, legal design can reposition human dignity at the center of every interaction and challenge the empty rationales that purport to justify too many existing legal frameworks.

Legal design also has revolutionary implications for legal education, promoting critical evaluation and experiential approaches over simple classroom reception and debate of legal norms. Law schools are already starting to respond to this challenge with more clinical offerings, community-based externships, law labs, codesign workshops, and interdisciplinary opportunities. As legal design continues to take hold, law students and communities will demand even more.

Finally, the open latticework of legal design methodologies particularly values direct engagement with the creative arts, which offer an especially effective portal for community exchanges across language, cultures, and experiences. Using the approach of legal design, lawyers can offer the whole of their experiences and talents, including their inherent human creativity, to the community. Allowing lawyers to leave behind the tight professional straitjackets that have constrained their contributions can only be good, for both the lawyers and their community partners.

The contributors to this pathbreaking, agenda-setting volume are the dreamers and doers of the legal design movement. Readers, you are in good hands as you join this journey. Welcome to the revolution!

***

Acknowledgments

The editors would like to acknowledge the dedication and support of the following individuals and organizations, without whom this volume would not be possible:

The NuLawLab founder and faculty director, Martha Davis, who had the vision and tenacity to get our legal design lab off the ground fifteen (or so) years ago.

Stephen Evans, our stalwart project manager, without whom this volume would have been unthinkable.

AJ Jarrett, our lead copyeditor with a saint's patience and a steel trap's skills.

All our chapter authors who have been doing remarkable work for years and who answered our call to action with the inspiring content you see in these pages.

Our research assistants, Erica Brangwynne, Sanea Lamas, and Ingrid Vianna Sydenstricker, who enthusiastically and ably supported the research that underpins a number of these chapters.

Our copyeditors, Max Bloodgood and Sara Conroy, who diligently helped us move the submissions from complete to final.

Students Arielle Behar and Danyah Alshebel, who ably assisted at the end of the process.

Our cover artist, Sunny Cheng, who created the evocative work that binds these pages.

Our extended NuLawLab team, both current and former, with a special thanks to our inaugural design director, Patricia Voorhies, who guided Dan and Jules in the first few years with care and persistence, and our advisory board, who have provided an indispensable sounding board for these creative ideas.

To Northeastern University, for creating the conditions for transdisciplinary education and engagement.

Finally, to Northeastern University School of Law, a fifty-five-year radical (and successful) experiment in legal education that provides us the platform to educate the legal inventors of the future.

Introduction

Miso Kim, Dan Jackson, and Jules Rochielle Sievert

This book is an introduction to the new field of legal design and a primer on both the application and theory of legal design that has developed so far in a decade of exploration and experimentation. We have assembled case studies of pioneering efforts from around the world, collected examples of methods and perspectives just now coming into focus, and offer a handful of proscriptions for the future. Bookending those three subject areas are both individual and collective articulations of these editors' frames of reference and influence in our work together – dignity, law, and radical imagination.

Our collective frame for this volume is relentlessly optimistic. We believe that the new field of legal design provides a promising intervention for challenging the harmful systems, structures, methodologies, and outcomes that currently define legal systems, and designing systems that actually embody and effectuate the full promise of the rule of law – a just, peaceful, and equitable world for everyone. Our optimism is fueled by a fierce urgency that derives from both our growing concern with large-scale threats to the rule of law and our growing frustration with a world stubbornly blind to the human pain and suffering caused by existing legal systems. This book therefore ends with a manifesto of sorts – a call to further and quickly unite the worlds of design, law, and radical imagination to collectivize as the inventors, ambassadors, revolutionaries, and foot soldiers in the work to come.

This brief introduction serves as your road map for accessing the ideas contained in *Legal Design: Dignifying People in Legal Systems*. We start with a summary description of legal design for the unfamiliar, followed by our articulation of what we think this book adds to the mix. We then summarize each substantive section and super-summarize the chapters therein.

I.1 WHAT IS LEGAL DESIGN?

Legal design is a burgeoning field that is already significantly impacting legal systems around the world. Practitioners in the space have spent the better part of the last ten years focusing ideas and human resources on radically improving what the design world calls the "user experience" for those navigating and operating our legal systems. (They are still working to unlock the financial resources that many in the field believe can accelerate the movement and multiply the outcomes.) Academics have established successful legal design outposts around the world in a variety of educational systems and a variety of forms such as laboratories, studios, and courses, and the papers, conferences, symposia, and books (like this one) are proliferating. Inspiringly, legal design has become a beacon, attracting a diverse range of professionals. Designers, lawyers, activists, and artists are finding common ground in the remaking of society's core structures. It's not just these sectors, however. Scholars from varied disciplines – such as sociology, anthropology, computer science, and more – are also being drawn to legal design. They're bringing their unique perspectives, methodologies, and insights to the table, providing an enriching cross-disciplinary approach.

Even more encouragingly, we're witnessing a cross-sector convergence around legal design. Corporate leaders, government officials, nonprofit advocates, and educators are all rallying around these ideas and organizations, seeing them as catalysts for change. They're showing up at conferences and meetings, eager to participate in the creative reinvention of societal norms. All these varied participants see in legal design a potent avenue for driving transformation in the world we inhabit. Why? They desire to creatively reimagine and reshape society's core architecture and, by extension, our collective future. Their involvement underscores the power and potential of this interdisciplinary and cross-sector collaboration in achieving meaningful change.

Legal design at its core involves applying various design principles to the rule of law, laws, and legal systems and institutions, with the goal of making them more accessible, affordable, understandable, human-centered, and user-friendly. Design, at its core, is an act of creation, manifested by a designer (person, people, collaborative), to accomplish a goal or goals, where the outcome enhances a certain aspect of human life, and the creation is subject to certain contexts or constraints. As a matter of both practice and theory then, legal design is about people using established humanistic approaches and creative methods such as user research, codesign, and visualization and modeling to develop innovative ways of delivering law to themselves and other people. At its most concrete, legal design happens when court staff and judges work with access-to-justice commissions and organizations to simplify court forms. At its most abstract, legal design can envision speculative environments that promote future change by critiquing current systems with daring alternatives that expose systemic flaws.

The most important thing to understand about legal design for purposes of the introduction to this volume is that it is incredibly new, having been preliminarily articulated as the specific thing it has become in only 2013. Those ten years have been productive years, however, and the trajectory for the field is promising in terms of outcomes so far. Legal design is ready for a more rigorous development of principle, method, and theory from the practices underway around the world as it begins to scale out beyond early proof of concept to tackle bigger and more complex justice system challenges.

I.2 WHAT THIS VOLUME CONTRIBUTES TO LEGAL DESIGN

Legal Design: Dignifying People in Legal Systems rests on the premise that law is one of the fundamental architectures of human society, and that legal design holds the promise of improving how people experience law and, by extension, society. We choose dignity as our benchmark frame for this volume because dignity as a concept has evolved to encompass the idea that all humans, simply by virtue of their humanity, are entitled to a certain measure of individual personal rights, group political rights, and the protection of shared common cultural bonds. Those core conditions for dignity overlap neatly with many of the outcomes promised by the rule of law. Because our evolving understanding of inalienable rights protected by the rule of law mirrors our conception of what a dignified society should be, it follows that enhanced human dignity can (and should) be a goal and a requirement of any legal design intervention. We therefore see one outcome of successful legal design interventions as the enhancement of dignity for people moving through a particular legal system or institution, and we offer this volume as a measuring stick of sorts for understanding legal design, its potential to unlock change, and one way to start to evaluate it.

In assembling this volume of legal design case studies and methods around the concept of human dignity, we seek to make a number of contributions to our shared nascent field. First, by intentionally decoupling the human dignity that legal design seeks to achieve from the concept's ancient Roman origins of social and political status (which served as one of the forces behind our legal system) we add legal design to the schools of thought that push for the continued evolution of dignity as something to which we are all entitled by mere virtue of our shared humanity. This aligns our corner of the legal design world with universalist principles of human dignity and seeks to include the rule of law as something, like dignity, to which we are all equally entitled. It also squarely engages the legal design movement with the rise of legal empowerment and movement lawyering.

Second, we seek to illuminate certain paradoxes of the legal system by viewing the system in tandem with the paradox of dignity. In this regard, we see legal design as an opportunity to critique our legal institutions and the power structures supporting them while at the same time building momentum for reform within those same power structures. We do so by restating the narrative of what law can and should be. Simple fairness – a touchstone of dignity – is our opening salvo. Law is ostensibly premised on the proposition that all people are entitled to equality of treatment, if not outcomes. Yet, more often than not, law has historically been deployed as a means of oppression – of asserting the will of certain political groups over others.

While capable by virtue of its structure and power of protecting human dignity, in reality law often creates conditions that de-dignify the human experience. Often intentionally.

In this regard, we are speaking directly to changemakers inside and outside of our legal systems and institutions, present and future. This call to action seeks to confront the injustice that has been historically embedded within our legal system. Legal design provides us with a unique vantage point, ready to address this complex challenge. It propels a more optimistic vision of justice, distinctly contrasting with the current reality many face today. Moreover, it requires the imaginative involvement of every stakeholder in the justice system – giving rise to a collective force for change. Importantly, this means even the most change-averse must actively contribute to the development and execution of the very reforms we urgently need.

Finally, and perhaps most importantly for legal design *as* legal design,[1] with this volume we are beginning to establish some core theoretical foundations for the field. As we do so, we have a handful of goals. First, we think it is time for more legal designers to spend more time thinking about and communicating those theoretical foundations if we expect the discipline to advance. Fortunately, the field has matured sufficiently that there is already a small cadre of legal design *elders* these days, so designated perhaps only by virtue of tenacity (or stubbornness). Regardless, this group can ramp up the work of pulling together conversations for developing, debating, deliberating over, and communicating foundational theories, values, and positions. Most of us olds would probably estimate that their initial legal design "think-and-do tanks" spent 10% of their time thinking and 90% doing. How exciting that there are now enough people, experience, ideas, initiatives, and institutional support to do a lot of both doing and thinking. This book helps get us going in one of the many directions that can and must manifest in the coming years.

Second, we underscore the importance of developing core theoretical foundations, values, and principles if we expect legal design to advance as a field of practice and thought. And here we want to swing for the fences (recall we are relentlessly optimistic on this subject). The intellectual, political, spiritual, and scientific movements that have transformed our world are those that developed and secured strong foundational ideas for themselves. Consider the centrality of "free and fair elections" to "representative democracy." Or early feminism without challenging gender stratification and sexual violence. We see legal design as holding the potential for as transformational a role in our world and collective humanity as those two sociopolitical movements. (No pressure, legal designers.) We therefore think we need to aim high as we identify and critique emerging ideas and modes of practice. It is

[1] In legal speak shorthand, "legal design as legal design" would be stated "legal design qua legal design." It means taking positions about legal design as the very thing we are trying to create with our creative energies: in other words, not legal design ideas applied onto a problem set that needs addressing, but legal design ideas applied to legal design as a discipline and community of practice.

therefore incumbent upon everyone who participates in legal design to spend some time and energy thinking about these core values.

It is also incumbent upon all of us that we continue to deploy radical kindness in the idea exchange that awaits us. Although the very early manifestations of legal design were perhaps centered around neoliberal objectives, more recently the field has moved toward such kindness as a distinguishing feature. We must preserve that value so that our collective grows under a larger and larger tent that incorporates more and more ideas, people, disciplines, and collectives. The changes we envision legal design effectuating will, in many instances, require popular action. Such things require political movements by people – lots of people. Such people need ideas to inspire and motivate them. That is the work ahead of all of us, and to which we hope this volume contributes.

Finally, an important note on what this volume is not, at least as it relates to dignity and how that term has been deployed in constitutional systems and examined by judges. While the concept of dignity has certainly played a significant role in constitutional law models globally, it has had limited success as a bedrock principle or as an interpretive guide for securing more specific rights and protections. While some countries such as Germany and South Africa have enshrined the idea and the word itself into their constitutions, the ambiguities of the meaning of "dignity" have left the concept vulnerable to its rejection by jurists and legal scholars as vague, which can be a death knell in constitutional analysis. This is certainly the case in the United States, where dignity's deployment as a framework for establishing or enhancing protections for marginalized groups has had limited success.

This book is therefore not about dignity as that term is applied or analyzed by systems of law and jurisprudence. This book is instead about deploying dignity as a central design choice as we remake the systems of law themselves. In this volume, dignity is not a position to take for purposes of arguing one's case, or a concept that is contained within a penumbra surrounding other core rights; it is what we propose designing the system for. Let's now turn to how we can do so and why we should.

I.3 THE CASE STUDIES, METHODS, AND FUTURES CONTAINED IN THIS VOLUME

The substance of this volume is divided into four sections: why legal design, what legal design can do, how legal design works, and where legal design goes. Part I, "Why Legal Design: A Theoretical Value Proposition," contains individual chapters from the three coeditors. Miso Kim frames dignity for us with "Dignifying Law in Design," which introduces philosophical conceptions of dignity as a framework for the interdisciplinary collaboration between design and law and as a way to promote human and social values in everyday lives. Dan Jackson follows with "Dignifying Design in Law," in which he argues that legal design fits squarely into the traditions and values of law and the rule of law, and makes the case for the further embrace of legal design by our social, political, and legal systems in order to advance desperately needed reforms. Jules Rochielle Sievert wraps up the section with "Dignifying Imagination in Legal Education," a call for new methods to develop students' imaginations in educational institutions and shift narratives and power structures in the legal system and beyond.

Part II offers "What Legal Design Can Do: Case Studies Across Sectors," and is clustered into two groups of studies. The first focuses on dignifying narratives of agency. Jennifer Leitch offers compelling observations and ideas from self-representation in Canada's civil justice system in "Dignity in the Courtroom: Judges and Self-Represented Litigants." Robert de Rooy thoughtfully challenges some traditional frames of the law of contracts with "Contracts for Dignity." Morgan A. Wilson then carefully details one law school clinic's experience in "Dignifying the Experience of Domestic Violence Survivors Seeking Legal Services," which is followed by Dan Jackson and Sanea Lamas's "More Than a Building," summarizing a successful 2018 intervention by local architecture and law students in Boston Housing Court that was led by architect Marilyn Moedinger.

Our second cluster of case studies focus on dignifying human experience in law and policymaking, kicked off by Purvi Shah, Meena Jagannath, and Alana Greer's inspiring "Movement Lawyering: Legal Strategies to Build People Power." It is followed by Natalicia R. Tracy's deep dive into "Deploying Art and Design to Highlight the Dignity of Domestic Workers in Their Struggle for Labor Rights." Alexander Nally then offers inspiration with "The Massachusetts Commission on LGBTQ Youth," an examination of how the design and evolution of the Massachusetts Commission on LGBTQ Youth elevated respect for the lived experience of queer youth in setting policies that impact their lives. This cluster, and all of Section Two, concludes with Leon Cruickshank and Mirian Calvo's "My Mainway: Designing in Dignity for Policy Making," which chronicles what happened when the Lancaster City Council, in the northwest of England, United Kingdom, set up an inclusive process to determine the future of a run-down housing estate known as "Mainway."

Part III pivots away from case studies to offer detail on "How Legal Design Works: Approaches, Methods, and Perspectives." Three concepts structure these chapters. We lead off with examinations of dignifying design in legal education, which first offers the perspective of this volume's three coeditors in "Designers, Lawyers, and Students: A Decade of NuLawLab Experience," which focuses on external project work, and "Teaching the Legal Inventors of the Future," which addresses our pedagogy. Margaret Hagan and Kürşat Özenç round out the grouping with the pioneering history and experience of "The Stanford Legal Design Lab." The next conceptual subgroup tackles dignifying experimentation in legal design. It commences with the position of Kanan Dhru and Kelly Dhru in "Graphically Novel: The Role of Visuals in the Legal Design Movement" – that legal design must retain the ability to visualize law in order to achieve the movement's goal of making law available at scale. Next up is Steven Geofrey's masterful rejection of an exclusively skills-forward approach to incorporating technology into law pedagogy and practice in "Building Technology With(out) People." Sofia Stolk then unpacks and repacks the opportunities, challenges, and alternatives to international law through a critique of the design of the International Criminal Court and the architecture's relationships with its surroundings and visitors in "International Courts and Design." We close this focus on experimentation with Phoebe Walton's powerful demonstration of why such an approach is essential in "*James v Birnmann*: The Potential of Critical Design for Examining Legal Issues."

Our final conceptual cluster of Section Three's musings on methods and approaches covers dignifying the field of legal design itself. Here we initially detail some personal reflections on two efforts that informed legal design's earliest days. Renee Knake Jefferson revisits her work establishing and running Michigan State University's ReInvent Law in "The ReInvent Law Archive." Margaret Hagan then offers us an insider's look at her personal journey to articulate the promise for design in the legal space with "The Open Law Lab Blog." We close this group and all of Section Three with Michael Doherty's skillful "Disciplinarity and the Modes of Legal Design," which examines the emerging field of legal design through a critical reflection on the literature on academic disciplines and disciplinarity and argues that legal design meets the criteria for recognition as an academic subdiscipline.

Having detailed what legal designers have done and how legal design works, Part IV focuses on the future. "Where Legal Design Goes: Building a Field Across Disciplines" contains five chapters intended to offer some guideposts for the next ten years of legal design's trajectory. Amanda Perry-Kessaris compellingly argues that "Legal Design Could and Should be More Sociolegal," pointing to the benefits that could flow to legal design, cross-disciplinary research, and to the wider world from such an approach. Katri Nousiainen and Joonas Keski-Rahkonen's "Navigating in a Post-Quantum Legal Design Landscape" ambitiously presents a pragmatic road map through an uncharted legal design landscape that will be transformed by quantum computing. Tiana Yom raises awareness for legal design evaluation and introduces existing theoretical evaluation frameworks that can be used in "Evaluation Capacity Building in Legal Design." Gabriel H. Teninbaum then helpfully provides some reflections and notes of caution for educators and professionals in "The Peril and Promise of Certificates and Degree Programs in Legal Design." We close this section on a high note for the future, with Antonio M. Coronado's passionate "Repair and Resistance: Law Students as Leaders of the Legal Design Movement."

This volume ends with a brief concluding chapter in which we attempt to synthesize the collective wisdom of these chapters, offer some reflections on how we are enacting that wisdom ourselves, and reiterate the fierce urgency we feel motivating many in the field. Thank you for reading some (or all) of this collection.

1

Why Legal Design

A Theoretical Value Proposition

1

Dignifying Law in Design

Miso Kim

1.1 DESIGN, LAW, AND DIGNITY

On the surface, law and design may seem unrelated, or even radically opposed to each other. Generally speaking, law may be considered the application of logical, fixed, and abstract ideas, whereas design may be perceived as the creation of aesthetic, expressive, and tangible materials. However, design philosopher Richard Buchanan argues that the subject of design has shifted from visual and tangible things to the exploration of holistic problems through the design of experiences, services, and systems that provide "vivid arguments about how we should live our lives" (Buchanan 2001a, 194). Buchanan argues that designers "organize conversations and debates about the values of a community and how those values may be implemented with productive results" (Buchanan 2001a, 202). Taking up his perspective, law and design are closer than they may seem. Both areas deal with how people perceive and use the web of systems comprising our sociopolitical environment and the rhetorical meanings structuring our everyday lives. In many cases, law and design are inextricably interrelated.

How does law inevitably influence design? One example is the City Geukdong Apartment, an eye-catching high-rise building on the southern side of Han River in Seoul, Korea. This building clearly stands out among many apartments surrounding the Han River because it features an asymmetrical pyramid shape, with one side slanted at a gradual 27-degree angle and the other close to vertical. This architectural form reflects local law protecting cultural heritage. The apartment building is located right next to the Pungnap Earthen Fortification of the Baekje Kingdom from the third century CE, and the cultural heritage law requires that the height of buildings within the protected area be within an invisible 27-degree line starting from the boundary of the cultural heritage (Lee 2021). The slanted side of City Geukdong Apartment follows this 27-degree standard exactly. As shown in this case, design sometimes materializes invisible laws in ways that people can perceive or apply in their everyday lives.

Conversely, design constantly influences law. For example, in 2016, Juul sensationalized the electronic cigarette market with its sleek, portable, and convenient cartridge design and fruity flavors. Juul's elevated brand image earned it the nickname "Apple of the vaping industry" (Robinson 2016). However, e-cigarettes soon became a social problem, as the smoking rate among high school students sharply increased from 11.7% in 2017 to 27.5% in 2019 (Kirkham and Banerjee 2021). Eventually, many local governments, including the State of New York, banned the sale of e-cigarettes entirely. In 2021, the US Food and Drug Administration followed suit and ordered the complete removal of flavored cartridge-based e-cigarettes, most notably Juul, from the market. As demonstrated in this case, design often leads to the creation of new products and services that influence society, and then laws are created to regulate the changes brought by them (Kirkham and Banerjee 2021).

We can also consider law itself as a product of design. Design can be defined as "devising courses of action aimed at changing existing situations into preferred ones" (Simon 1969, 111) and the "deliberate shaping of the environment in ways that satisfy individual and societal needs" (Norman 2009, 171). These definitions suggest that the legal system itself can also be understood as the outcome of creative design activities. For example, the eighteen roundtable discussions leading to the development of the United Nations Declaration of Human Rights, spearheaded by philosopher Richard McKeon (1990), resemble the process of collective codesign. Likewise, the legal process that plays out during a trial, the state and federal court systems, and judicial artifacts such as legal documents and modern digital tools that support legal processes can all be considered products of a design process instituted by multiple people over a long period of time – just as traditional crafts, such as wagon parts, were designed by trial and error over hundreds of years (Jones 1992).

All these associations – design shaping law, law shaping design, and law as design – are themselves interconnected and interwoven. Designed products and services that follow different regulations constantly impact how law manifests in our daily activities, how we make decisions about our actions and interactions with other citizens, how we consider the law when making decisions and taking actions, and how we appeal to the law in controversial situations. Design also translates technological and cultural changes in the world and crystalizes them into products and services, leading to the reconfiguration of the law in alignment with social changes and emerging needs. In these processes, legal systems are constantly designed and redesigned. These innate and dynamic connections between law and design can inspire us to deliberate on legal design.

As law significantly impacts billions of people's lives, there is a vital need to discuss the political and moral principles that should operate in the field of legal design. Without these, how can legal designers consider the power relationships between people in different positions to make the design equitable? What values should legal designers be guided by when considering people's diverse voices, defining problems, and ensuring that solutions result in the intended social impact? What aims should legal designers pursue, and what guidance should they follow when making key decisions about design processes? We can find the answers to these questions in the foundational legal documents that set out the principles determining how today's democratic society is organized. Many of these earliest declarations and fundamental laws mention the word "dignity" as the core of such principles:

> United Nations Charter: Preamble Line 1; June 26, 1945: "We the Peoples of the United Nations determined ... to reaffirm faith in fundamental human rights, in the dignity and worth of the human person..."
>
> Universal Declaration of Human Rights: Preamble Line 1; December 10, 1948: "Whereas recognition of the inherent dignity and of the equal and inalienable rights of all members of the human family..."
>
> Grundgesetz (Basic Law) of the Federal Republic of Germany (considered one of the foundational modern democratic legal systems): Article 1; May 23, 1949: "(1) The dignity of man is inviolable. To respect and protect it shall be the duty of all public authorities. (2)
>
> The German People therefore uphold human rights as inviolable and inalienable, and as the basis of every community of peace and justice in the world."

Additionally, many countries declare dignity as the first principle of law that defines their political systems. For example, South Africa's Constitution, which was written after government officials met to reflect on the country's legacy of racial inequality, begins with the founding provisions in Chapter 1: "The Republic of South Africa is one, sovereign, democratic state founded on the following values: a. Human dignity, the achievement of equality and the advancement of human rights and freedoms" (South African Constitution 1996, ch. 1). The Canadian Constitution Act declares dignity as a foundational principle: "The idea of human dignity finds expression in almost every right and freedom guaranteed in the Charter" (Canada Constitution Act 1982, part I). Peru's constitution also grounds itself in dignity in article 1: "The defense of the human person and respect for his dignity are the supreme purpose of the society and the State" (Peru Constitution 1993, ch. 1).

As such, the rules and norms of many modern democratic societies have been founded on dignity, thereby enabling discussions of diverse political and moral issues. As McKeon (1990) describes, "faith in freedom and democracy is founded on the faith in the inherent dignity of men and women" (McKeon 1990, 40). Dignity is also considered a basic good that justifies the value of our shared humanity, a principle of morality that establishes "a normative status and that many human rights may be understood as incidents of that status" as foundational given rights in comparison to goals or telos (Waldron 2012, 212). Thereby, dignity serves as a social norm from which individual action, a sense of value, or attempts to define the meaning of life emerges (Margalit 1998).

Dignity is also a key principle in design. For example, in his foundational article "Human Dignity and Human Rights: Thoughts on the Principles of Human-Centered Design," Buchanan starts by discussing what can happen if practices from design and law intersect but are not grounded in principles that provide ethical direction: "The Holocaust was one of the most thoroughly designed experiences of the twentieth century, with careful attention to every obscene detail" (Buchanan 2001b, 35). He argues that if designers do not understand the significance of what they create, design is merely a tool for implementing social constructs, some of which can be harmful. Buchanan proposes that designers should transition from the principle of methodology to that of design thinking. He further argues that in addition to the principles of economics, technology, and functionalism from the last century, there is a need to deliberate on first principles, such as dignity, on which human-centered design as a discipline is grounded. However, there is a dearth of studies that investigate the definitions and dimensions of this important concept: dignity.

Dignity is a complicated concept that has evolved to include many different nuances throughout human history, and this is evident in the area of law as well. For example, legal and bioethics scholar Leslie Melzer Henry (2011) conducted the first empirical study of US Supreme Court opinions about dignity and stated that while dignity has been a central concept in US constitutional law (cited in 900+ Supreme Court decisions), its meaning and function have not been clearly articulated, thus generating both confusion and disagreement. Henry argues that the invocation of dignity in Supreme Court decisions is increasing, and both conservative and liberal justices are invoking the term with equal frequency. However, there is confusion because dignity is not one concept, but a conflation of concepts including equality, liberty, a person's legal status, personal integrity, and collective virtue. Likewise, human rights law scholar Christopher McCrudden (2008) raises a concern that the meaning of dignity vastly varies from jurisdiction to jurisdiction, and therefore is subject to judicial manipulation. Political scientist Doron Shultziner (2017) also argues that while dignity as a concept is being used increasingly in judicial decisions, the vagueness of the term poses challenges for legal applications. Shultziner proposes the need to define the concept and explain its meaning within the legal system, as well as to maintain consistency in the use of the concept in current and future decisions in the courts.

In this chapter, I explore the different meanings and dimensions of dignity throughout human history and how they relate to law and design. In so doing, this study will contribute to the idea that the aim of legal design is to enhance dignity in people's everyday lives and to open up diverse directions for the creative collaboration of law and design. The dimensions of dignity that are introduced in this research include the following understandings of the concept: (1) dignity as merit, popularized in Antiquity and the Middle Ages, which defines dignity relative to a person's public rank; (2) dignity as autonomy, as conceptualized in the Renaissance and the Age of Enlightenment, with emphasis on the capacity for moral action that justifies the end value of the agent; (3) dignity as a universal and inviolable human right in contemporary democratic societies, which is considered innate to human nature and is granted through political processes; and (4) the recent focus on dignity as interpersonal care in everyday interactions – characterized by respect, care, and empathy – and bonding us as a society.

1.2 *DIGNITAS*: AN ANCIENT MERIT-BASED CONCEPTION OF DIGNITY

One of the most referenced books on dignity in the field of law is law philosopher Jeremy Waldron's (2012) *Dignity, Rank, and Rights*, in which he proposes that dignity is a key moral concept of legal ethics. He defines dignity as a legal concept regarding how individuals relate to the law according to their ability to use and respond to legal systems, and he argues that the law has evolved to protect dignity. Waldron also suggests that the concept of dignity is rooted in rank and status, in line with its historical origins. This historical origin, according to legal scholar Stéphanie Hennette-Vauchez (2011), goes back to ancient times. She argues that the contemporary principle of human dignity in some of its dignitarian uses does not have much in common with the contemporary conception of universal dignity, but rather originates from the ancient legal concept of *dignitas* as a ground for obligations rather than rights.

Today, the meaning of dignity generally indicates a fundamental and inviolable moral worth belonging to all humans, which is equally bestowed to everyone. Historically, however, it was only in the mid-twentieth century that the statement "All human beings are born free and equal in dignity and rights" formally appeared in the preamble of the United Nations Declaration of Human Rights (United Nations 1948). Philosophy scholars propose that for most of human history, dignity meant "high social status and rank" (Darwell 2017, 186) and "the honors and respectful treatment that are due to someone who occupied that position" (Rosen 2012a, 11). This might seem strange and even oppositional to the notion of dignity in today's democratic societies, yet in the ancient hierarchical world, dignity referred to a comparative value that had to be acquired or inherited; it was also one that could be lost if the individual could not prove they deserved it.

According to classics scholar Patrice Rankine (2017), the ancient Greek concept of *axios* (Greek ἄξιος, "worthy of") has the closest meaning to dignity, indicating relative value in comparison to others. He proposes that axios can be found in well-known examples of ancient Greek literature, such as when Homer (1260–1180 BCE) praised Hector for being worthy (axios) because he was braver than others and better represented the community values of loyalty to family and loyalty to the gods. In the Roman Republic, this comparative worth combined with class and rank, thus forming the concept of *dignitas*, referring to an honorable reputation (Griffin

2017). Dignitas, from the Latin word *dignus* ("worthy"), was a complicated concept. It was a combination of the achievements that a public figure had built up throughout their life, the social influence they acquired as a result of such achievements, and the personal manner and elegant style befitting the figure's social status.

In general, dignitas was earned, outward looking, and based on merit value. According to the scholar of Greek and Latin Literature Warren Stone Gordis (1905), because honor was considered a direct outcome of fulfilling one's societal duty, one could not obtain dignitas without the approval and support of the public. Official praise increased one's dignitas, whereas public blame decreased it. Thus, dignity was largely gained through duties such as serving in the military, holding a public office, or serving in the senate. A person honed their ethical reputation by carrying out such duties, as they involved dedicating oneself to the good of the country and were accompanied by a clear sense of rank. However, dignitas had a private dimension as well, referring to personal well-being and manner with gravitas: an aesthetic quality of demeanor. Gordis concluded that dignitas is a concept that merges social duty and personal expediency.

Gordis also explains that people with dignitas held political power, as dignitas was closely related to *auctoritas* ("authority"). If a person served in a position of authority, that person was seen as having more dignitas. Auctoritas was also a product of dignitas, as dignitas served as the rhetorical ethos through which participants in political debates could gain the approval of others. However, personal expediency does not explain everything about dignitas, as it is a practical yet ethical concept. For example, Roman statesman and stoic philosopher Cicero ([44 BC] 1991) argues that what is proper (*dignum*) for human beings is to control desire when it conflicts with reason. He considers this will to act reasonably and morally as evidence of dignity, which makes human beings superior to other animals. Cicero's theory of dignitas merges the concepts of practical expediency and ethical good by proposing that what is truly expedient is pursuing what is morally right for society.

This conception of dignity as merit continues throughout history, along with other major perspectives. For example, the dominant worldview of the Middle Ages was strictly hierarchical, as all earthly phenomena was under the supremacy of God. Angels were seen as more dignified than humans in the cosmic hierarchy, and animals were below humans. Humans were born depraved because of the fall of Adam; they had to regain dignity through penance and baptism, and they could lose it again through sin and anathema. The idea that dignity is associated with a hierarchical relationship to centralized authority can still be found in many societies today. Legal scholar Ann Althouse (2000) observes that jurists have advanced the idea of *states' rights* and the prioritization of their sovereignty by arguing that states have inherent dignity attributed exclusively to their status as ruling governments. In the seventeenth century, political philosopher Thomas Hobbes ([1651] 1904) argued that dignity is a public worth with a "market value" that is determined by the degree of public tribute a person receives, foreshadowing a certain nature of dignity in a capitalist society (Darwell 2017). Today, merit and rank remain important components of dignity, as evidenced in the word "dignitaries" or in one of the definitions of dignity: "high rank, office, or position" (Merriam Webster 2024).

An example in which the principle of dignity as autonomy manifests itself in the junction of law and design can be found in ancient architecture. Architectural design today is regulated by urban planning laws, such as a right to light, and diverse safety laws to secure the humane living conditions of residents and citizens in the neighborhood. However, in ancient societies, many architectural rules existed based purely on the principle of merit. Royal authorities across the world used architectural design, along with fashion and vehicles, as a way to highlight the sovereignty of authorities. The ruling classes used design to fortify the social strata. They persuaded the higher classes below them to accept the existing social structure of the feudal society by showcasing the comparative benefit that the higher class still had compared to the lower classes.

For example, traditional Korean houses served as symbols of the owner's social status through architectural regulation. A generally known rule was those who were not royalty could not construct houses or buildings that had more than 99 rooms. According to the *Encyclopedia of Korean Culture*, King Sejong the Great in the Joseon dynasty established the Regulation on Houses and Buildings, declaring not exhibiting social hierarchy as disorderly. The regulation designated that royal families could have houses with up to 50 rooms; the upper-class Yangban (gentry), 40 rooms; the middle-class Yangban, 30 rooms; and the commoners, up to 10 rooms. The sizes of columns and foundations, height and widths of rooms, and decoration of the columns and crossbeams were all regulated based on the social status of the owner. For example, the wings where slaves lived were required to have lower foundations and heights. While these regulations helped preserve traditional Korean architecture style, there is also a criticism that they limited individual design experiments, as architects had to stick to these regulations until the old laws were lifted in the Gabo Modern Reformation of 1894 (Chun 2018). Overall, the example of Korean architectural law shows how law and design can work together to reveal the social principle of merit as it applies to people's everyday lives.

1.3 RENAISSANCE AND THE AGE OF ENLIGHTENMENT: DIGNITY AS AUTONOMY

As we reviewed in the previous section, Roman dignitas was a social virtue encompassing public good, private manner, practical expediency, and innate moral value. Throughout the Middle Ages and the Enlightenment, the idea of dignity as moral value gained greater importance as people began to seek dignity via human reason. Indeed, this perspective was already part of dignitas, as the Roman Stoics emphasized the dignity of moral action. Individuals were expected to learn how to control their desires and consciously act in a way that fulfilled their duties to society. Even in ancient Greece, individuals with *hamartia* – a fatal pride leading to their tragic downfall – fighting against their fate were depicted as having the quality of dignity of free will. Another meaning of dignity emerges here: autonomous action.

In the Middle Ages, dignity is often discussed in relation to *imagio Dei*, which refers to a passage in the Bible that describes humans being created "in the image of God" (Genesis 1:26–27). According to theologists, imagio Dei does not necessarily refer to physical appearance; rather, it indicates the holy trinity of intellect, memory, and will, which are the key attributes of human reason. Gregorius of Nyssa explains this resemblance to God as proof of human value, although he compares human life and will to paintings by apprentices attempting to imitate the masterpiece of God (Balthasar 1995). Although the medieval worldview was hierarchical – humans were considered inferior to angels – the immortal human soul was believed to have the capacity for dignity. For example, St. Augustin and St. Thomas Aquinas suggest that virtuous Christian action leads to dignity. Humans can fall to the level of animals if they misuse their free will, but if they make the right choice to engage in moral action, they are elevated in the divine order (Kent 2017).

This perspective on choice and action led to philosophical discussions during the Renaissance, when humanists began to redefine dignitas as human value. As a concept of how the ideal and the worldly are unified in action, dignitas became one of the most commonly used words during the Renaissance to describe human capacity cultivated by pursuing *studia humanitatis*, or the secular study of the humanities (Trinkaus 1970). For example, politician and humanist scholar Giovanni Manetti wrote about the dignity of humans represented in Florence's artistic and literary achievements during the Renaissance. Manetti argues that the individual glory of the great figures of his era proves all humans' capacity for dignity (Copenhaver 2017).

Renaissance philosopher Giovanni Pico della Mirandola ([1486] 1996) wrote one of the most famous treatises on dignity, "Oration on the Dignity of Man." Mirandola argues that human dignity emerges from an individual's ability to decide to transform themselves. Human beings carry the seeds of angels and animals together, such that they may become whatever they want: plants, animals, angels, or even divine beings. Even angels have a predetermined nature, but only human beings are born with unlimited potential and freedom of choice. Mirandola explains that human beings have the ethical responsibility to cultivate themselves into godlike beings; however, human dignity lies not in the outcome but in the process. Humans have the autonomy to choose.

Throughout the Enlightenment, this conception of dignity originating from autonomy continued to develop especially via the emphasis on human reason, flourishing as a key concept of the philosophy of Emmanuel Kant. According to Kant ([1785] 1993), human dignity does not depend on external factors such as public recognition or social status. Humans have dignity because they are rational agents who have autonomy within themselves. Kant first describes the concept of dignity (*Würde*) by stating that everything in this world has either value or dignity, and things with measurable value can replace one another; however, things that have moral dimensions have absolute and incomparable value – that is, dignity.

Kant further argues that people are an "end in themselves," whose value cannot be measured or replaced, and can therefore be said to have dignity. According to Kant, "the basis of the dignity of human[s] and of every rational nature" is autonomy (Kant [1785] 1993, 52). Humans are "ends" because they are autonomous, which describes their ability to set up moral rules and act according to those rules. When individuals act in the service of externally imposed ends, such as regulations, desires, or necessity, they become not ends but means. However, when a human being acts autonomously by self-imposed rules grounded in reason, that person is an end and thus has dignity.

Throughout these periods, interpretations of dignity shifted from emphasizing individual social status to moral and autonomous action. One historical view is that the notion of dignity as autonomy later influenced the political processes of the Age of Revolution, which led to the birth of dignity as a universal human right. As a matter of fact, Kant was not a supporter of the Enlightenment concept of rights, as they are externally conditioned by nature or society. Regardless, along with the other dimensions of dignity, autonomy remains a theoretical foundation of ethics and guidelines to protect human dignity, especially in situations where humans may be treated as means rather than ends. The concept of moral and individual autonomy later served as the precedent for political autonomy and political rights.

The conception of dignity as autonomy also serves as the basis for interpretations of dignity in a legal context. Legal scholar Erin Daly (2020) conducted a comparative analysis of dignity in law, including the development of dignity jurisprudence, its aims, and the interpretations of dignity as a constitutional value rather than a constitutional right. Based on this study, she argues that dignity rights converge around three main values: (1) an individual's right to control their own life, (2) the material conditions allowing one to live with dignity, and (3) the rights of people who are dependent on others to live in dignity. She asserts that "If there is any coherence to dignity jurisprudence across the globe it may be encapsulated in the notion of autonomy – i.e. self-rule" (Daly 2013, 3). She further argues that autonomy is the reason that dignity rights are fundamental to other constitutional rights, as autonomy requires conditions such as fulfilling people's basic needs and protecting them from the state.

An example of how design and law influenced the development of citizens' individual autonomy can be found in the case of coffeehouses in seventeenth-century Europe. Muslims have had a long tradition of socializing around coffee, as alcoholic drinks were prohibited; the first coffeehouse opened in Istanbul in 1555. These coffeehouses were exported to London in 1652, and to Paris in 1672 (Debry 1994). These coffeehouses sold imported drinks such as coffee, chocolate, and tea, but people actually went there for services, such as conversations, sharing information, and political debates. As depicted by the historian Brian Cowan (2005), Button's Coffee House was known for its letterbox with a lion's head, where patrons dropped their written pieces for publication in the local newspaper *The Guardian*. Jonathan's Coffee House was a meeting place for stockbrokers, which later became the London Stock Exchange. The Grecian provided a venue for debates, as it was a popular gathering spot for people with legal professions. By 1683, there were approximately 2,000 coffeehouses in London. As the main product of these coffeehouses was information, Londoners dropped in at least once a day to exchange news. Coffeehouses did not discriminate based on the social status of their patrons, and thus nurtured liberal discussions among the diverse members of society (Cowan 2005).

Naturally, the states viewed these coffeehouses as a public nuisance and intended to control them via licensing laws, import duties, and even orders to close them. The history of coffeehouses is characterized by a continuous struggle between laws that protect the dignity and authority of the Crown and the emerging sense of citizen autonomy. According to Cowan (2005), in 1675, Charles II ordered the closure of coffeehouses, claiming that rumors circulating within them defamed the dignity of the Crown. However, he had to renounce this order in just one month because of nationwide demonstrations. Instead, Charles banned coffeehouses from publishing newspapers. Coffeehouse owners were required to demonstrate that they were loyal subjects; otherwise, their licenses could be suppressed by a review of councils. Infamous keepers, such as John Thomas and Peter Kidd, were imprisoned under the charge of being a public nuisance (Cowan 2005). However, coffeehouses in Paris eventually became the epicenter of the French Revolution. Coffeehouses in Boston, which first opened in 1689, also served as the birthplace of the American Revolution. As Habermas (1991) argues, coffeehouses were public spheres where citizens could grow their private autonomy, which led to citizen societies.

1.4 MODERN DEMOCRATIC SOCIETIES: DIGNITY AS A UNIVERSAL RIGHT

In addition to merit and autonomy, another view of dignity as construed through today's democratic lens is dignity as the equal, universal, and inviolable worth of any human. We are all born with dignity, which cannot be taken away; at the same time, we are all responsible for respecting others' dignity and treating them in a manner that befits such respect. This notion of inherent, unearned dignity is the foundation of universal human rights. For example, the United Nations Declaration of Human Rights (1984) states that human rights are those possessed equally by all people solely by virtue of their humanity. However, the gap between the ancient conception of dignity as comparative merit and today's conception of dignity as universal rights remains a popular topic in scholarly discussions.

One explanation for the difference between ancient and modern conceptions of dignity is that universal inborn dignity was already embedded in the concept of dignitas, although this was only retrospectively recognized by scholars; that is, the conception of human rights has always existed from ancient times but was only revealed as our civilizations developed. The Roman Stoics recognized the bond of universal human fellowship and discussed the superiority of human nature over animals, regardless of individual moral conduct. Catholic tradition similarly proposed the notion that dignity is at least somewhat universal to all humans. For example, in the speech of Leo the Great, a fifth-century pope, he stated, "Wake up, human being, and recognize the dignity of your nature. Recall that you have been made according to the image of God, which, although it has been corrupted in Adam, has nevertheless been reformed in Christ" (Kent 2017, 91). Today, the Roman Catholic Church considers itself the protector of universal dignity, which is the "absolute worth of each human life" (Waldron 2012, 28).

Other scholars posit that the meaning of dignity as merit has never been abandoned; rather, the scope has been expanded to include all humans under one high rank. For example, Waldron (2012) argues that the meaning of dignity today is essentially the same as that in ancient times; that is, it is based on comparative rank. The difference is that rank has since been expanded to include all humans, as the core value of dignity has shifted from individual honor to universal worth. Therefore, Waldron describes dignity as a "universalized high social rank" (Waldron 2012, 4) that is "assigned now to every human person, equally without discrimination: dignity as nobility for the common man" (Waldron 2012, 22). He further compares modern society to a kingdom in which everybody is a monarch, or a caste society in which there is only Brahmin.

Yet another perspective is that universal dignity is a new concept unique to our time, a perspective for which autonomy has served as the philosophical ground. Many scholars posit that the idea that humans have distinctive and intrinsic value is a legacy of the Enlightenment, especially of Kant. Enlightenment philosopher Jean-Jacques Rousseau argues that humans are obliged not to harm another being like themselves because they are rational (Debes 2017). Kant's ([1785] 1993) argument that dignity is an intrinsic value is also derived from the universality of reason. Autonomy, leading to the end value of dignity, requires two conditions: (1) our internal law should align with the universal moral law, and (2) we should treat other humans as ends because they have the capacity to follow universal moral law. Therefore, dignity as autonomy inevitably requires universality as its logical foundation. Moral philosopher James Griffin (2008) argues that human rights have been established to ensure that people exercise agency in a universal way. Philosopher Avishai Margalit (1998) suggests that today's notion of dignity requires environmental conditioning because "autonomy requires opportunity as well as capacity" (Margalit 1998, 23). Only a society with human rights – a minimal condition for autonomy – can support the concept of dignity.

Another view is that the meaning of dignity has evolved over time and is still in the process of developing, along with our political system. The concept of dignity may have progressed from rank to autonomy to human rights. Along with a philosophical redefinition of dignity, political processes, such as lawmaking, revolutions, and strikes, have expanded the application of this concept so that it better serves the changing cultural landscape. Waldron (2012) argues that the concept of dignity largely originated from the legal system because of its foundational and explicative function in society. He describes one of the key roles of law as the protection of dignity. Historically, laws were created to protect noble people from degrading in rank and were thus focused on protecting certain groups of people from violence or contempt. When dignity is situated in an egalitarian system, its legal meaning becomes the "high and equal rank of every human person" (Waldron 2012, 14). The history of human rights is the history of people fighting to expand the law so as to protect everybody, especially social minorities, from threats to their dignity.

Catholic philosopher Jacques Maritain suggests that dignity is the "right to be respected" (Maritain 1951, 65), and political philosopher Michael Rosen (2012b) further argues that dignity can be "respect-as-respectfulness" in comparison to "respect-as-observance." In this view, we respect the rights of others not because they have dignity but vice versa. Debes (2017) points to an example posed by political philosopher Hanna Arendt: Ancient Athens made equality a legal principle not because society was equal but because its political system could only work on that principle. Legal philosopher Joel Feinberg also proposes that dignity as universal rights may also manifest as a socially agreed-upon respect for the "recognizable capacity to assert claims" (Feinberg 1970, 252) about dignity. Philosopher Alan Gewirth states that the final purpose of legal rights is to secure individuals "a certain fundamental moral status: that of having rational autonomy and dignity in the sense of being a self-controlling, self-developing agent who can relate to other persons on a basis of mutual respect and cooperation" (Gewirth 1984, 743). Therefore, democratic societies have created a system that allows the concept of human rights to serve as the ground upon which citizens exercise dignity. Each citizen has the universal right to claim dignity while simultaneously acknowledging other human beings as equally worthy of respect. Together, individuals behave in a certain direction to protect the overall dignity of human society.

Through the revolutions and labor movements of the nineteenth century, as well as the world wars, the Cold War, and the civil rights movement of the twentieth century, dignity was established as universal human rights in politics and law: an evolution that is continuing today to account for the diversity of human needs and definitions of dignity. Part of this process can be found in McKeon's (1990) report on how the development of the United Nations Declaration of Human Rights started with political rights, expanded to include economic rights, and finally moved on to cultural rights, such as the right to inquiry, expression, and communication. McKeon posits that "[h]uman rights are natural, inborn, inalienable; yet they have a history, they are acquired, and they are increased and developed" (McKeon 1990, 37). He concludes that the history and philosophy of human rights must be continuously reformulated from the perspective of the problems and opportunities presented by modern-day situations, with unconditional universality yet enough flexibility to allow for numerous interpretations.

Today, the legal conception of dignity also generally refers to human rights or to the equal dignity of all members of human societies. For example, Connor Ewing (2018), a politics and law scholar, documents the development of the jurisprudence of equal dignity, in which there is a partial convergence of liberty and equality in American constitutional law. Ewing argues that the convergence of liberty and equality is both the cause and the effect of the increased salience of dignity and its emergence in American constitutional law. He argues that dignity played an important role in cases such as *Lawrence v. Texas*, *United States v. Windsor*, and the *Obergefell* decision, and that through these cases the concept of equal dignity evolved. He concludes that equal dignity will continue to be centralized in constitutional discourse as a fundamental constitutional value.

As an example of design's profound relationship with human rights and law, I introduce universal design and inclusive design. The universal design movement began in the 1950s and was later inspired by the civil rights movement and the subsequent development of the Americans with Disabilities Act (ADA), which specifies architecture guidelines that any member of society can access regardless of their disability status. Universal design aims to remove physical, environmental, and legal barriers so that anybody can access and use products, regardless of their gender, age, or disability status. For example, OXO's Good Grips series is often referenced as a successful case of a universal design because of its ergonomic design that is convenient for people of all ages and abilities (Johnson and Finn 2017). OXO's cooking tools feature large rubber handles and levers that require less grabbing power, with the aim of enabling diverse populations, including arthritis patients, to easily cook. Indeed, such a design is also more convenient for other populations. An interesting aspect of universal design in relation to law is that its design principles have evolved to address needs not covered by the limited accessibility guidelines provided by codes such as ADA, American National Standards Institute (ANSI), and International Standards Organization (ISO) (Story 2001).

While universal design has mostly been applied in the United States and focused on accessibility to products and architecture, inclusive design is a movement that began in the United Kingdom (Persson et al. 2015). It encompasses communication and service, aiming to enhance the inclusiveness of society. While universal design and inclusive design share the common goal of providing alternatives that consider the needs of less represented populations, inclusive design emphasizes the design process to understand diverse populations. Therefore, codesign and participatory design are often used as ways to reflect the needs of people of different ages, bodies, and sociocultural conditions. Legal support is necessary for expanding an inclusive design approach, such as the Disability Discrimination Act of 1995 and the Special Educational Needs and Disability Act of 2001. These legal interventions can nurture the inclusive design approach by helping designers persuade their clients, organizations, and communities to adopt designs that seek to remove barriers and help ameliorate discriminatory situations (Casserley and Ormerod 2013).

1.5 CONTEMPORARY DIGNITY AS INTERPERSONAL CARE

The three perspectives of dignity reviewed so far – merit, autonomy, and universal rights – commonly place the origin of human dignity in logos. The concepts of duty, autonomy, and rights emphasize the supremacy of a human being or the human race from an intellectualist point of view, especially compared with other, supposedly inferior beings such as animals. However, we should note that humans are passionate beings as well as rational beings, as observed by Enlightenment philosopher Denis Diderot (Debes 2017). While most Enlightenment philosophers focus on human reason, Diderot argues for the importance of empathetic and sympathetic awareness to foster "sensitivity to humankind" (Debes 2017, 225). He suggests that humans have a natural tendency to care for one another because emotion leads to empathy and moral imagination, which encourages human connection. In this sense, dignity is not in the nodes but in the connections; that is, the relationships between individuals.

Diderot was not the first to draw attention to the empathic nature of dignity. The benevolent action of helping strangers or burying an unknown person's body was a popular topic of discussion for the Roman Stoics. Both Cicero and Seneca conclude that people should care for others not because of duty or benefit but out of pity and for *humanus in publicum* ("humane and public reason"). Greek myths and epic poems also depict how compassion unites people in tragedy. This is another place where we find dignity: interpersonal care originating from emotion, empathy, benevolence, and hospitality. In this sense, people can be seen to have dignity regardless of rank, autonomous action, or political foundation.

Kant proposes many important aspects of dignity, and one is the link between dignity and humiliation. In his view, dignity originates from the inner morality of all humans, which leads to emotions, such as humiliation. Humiliation is a social emotion that is usually considered the opposite of dignity. Margalit (1998) defines humiliation as an existential threat to an individual's respect and the rejection of their humanness; therefore, humiliation is always caused by other humans. This treatment can include the following: (1) not being regarded as human, for example, as animals, tools, or subhuman beings; (2) being deprived of basic control or emphasizing such a condition; and (3) being rejected from humanity, or groups that are essential to individual identity.

Dignity is therefore a matter of identity, especially belonging. Margalit argues that a sense of belonging and connection allows people to have "an adverb for describing the way people act and live their lives" (Margalit 1998, 142). Humiliation is a form of rejection initiated by the group that one identifies with or has a legitimate right to belong to. Therefore, dignity is not only about extreme situations but also about everyday lives at our doorstep. Every individual, even a stranger, can influence whether another individual respects themselves as a human being because we see one another as members of a common humanity; therefore, as proposed by Margalit, the capacity to form caring relationships is one of the key conditions of a "decent society" that respects and exudes dignity.

Donna Hicks (2011), a conflict resolution specialist, also discusses dignity from this perspective, defining dignity as "the way we treat one another in everyday interactions" (Hicks 2011, 1). According to Hicks, dignity is a profoundly emotional issue because we are "feeling beings" (Hicks 2011, 5). Human beings exist in a network of relationships. The feeling of dignity is therefore crucial to human survival, as humans often equate dignity with worthiness, which can then translate to social acceptance within a group. Hicks further argues that this biological necessity has been hardwired into our brains, which is why our emotional responses to indignity are similar to our responses to physical threats.

The problem, then, is how dignity can be honored in everyday interactions. Hicks proposes a dignity model that she developed in workshops about mediating political conflicts. The ten elements of dignity, which she derived from her observations in these workshops, include acceptance of identity, inclusion, safety, acknowledgment, recognition, fairness, benefit of the doubt, understanding, independence, and accountability. Hicks argues that we must become more sensitive to the ways others perceive us in everyday interactions, thereby honoring dignity in a way that brings out the best in each of us. She concludes with Archbishop Tutu's comment: "A person is a person through another person . . . My humanity is caught up, bound up, inextricably, with yours. We can only be humans together" (Hicks 2011, 198).

In the legal world, this emphasis on emotion in the interpretation of dignity is fairly new given the tendency of legal workers to present their cases in a nonemotional manner. However, legal philosopher David Luban (2005) argues that the moral foundation of lawyering is to defend human dignity and that to do so requires preventing another person from humiliation. Legal and political philosophy scholar Emily Kidd White (2014) highlights the emotional potency of the concept of dignity in the law. She proposes that emotion has played a role in initiating legal interventions in human right issues and even promoted the development of constitutional laws to protect dignity. She argues that the emotional dimension of human dignity must be considered to fully understand the legal concept of dignity. She presents a typology for understanding how emotions impact the adjudication of dignity by categorizing emotions as fulfilling one of three roles: orientation, tracking, or service.

As an example that inspires us to think about dignity from the perspective of interpersonal care, I introduce a case of a controversial advertisement. In 2018, the luxury fashion house Dolce & Gabbana presented a series of video advertisements before their big fashion show in Shanghai, China. These advertisements featured a Chinese female model attempting to eat Italian foods, including pizza and spaghetti, by using chopsticks in a clumsy manner, while an unidentified voice instructed her in English. These advertisements resulted in heated discussions on social media. Chinese, Korean, and Japanese people on multiple social media platforms voiced concerns that these ads amounted to racial microaggressions. As a result, models and celebrities boycotted the Shanghai fashion show and it was canceled. Dolce & Gabbana apologized and explained that they have nothing but respect for China and its people (Chung and Holland 2018).

In 2021, it was reported that Dolce & Gabbana filed action suits against the bloggers who first raised concerns about the Shanghai advertisements (Garrison 2021; O'Connor 2021). According to the media, not only did the fashion house demand €3 million in damages for Dolce & Gabbana and €1 million for Stefano Gabbana himself after an Instagram message exchange with the bloggers, but the fashion house also sought €450 million to restore the brand's tarnished image since 2018. Dolce & Gabbana also claimed that the bloggers, by calling out its controversial campaign, caused the company to lose $89.6 million in revenue due to the cancelation of the Shanghai show and lost sales in Asia. This case shows there are gray areas in advertisement design. There have been many advertisements accused of humiliating and discriminating against certain populations. However, there is a lack of legal guidelines to advise or regulate the design of advertisements, despite the power imbalance lawsuits between large corporations and individuals who raise concerns.

1.6 DIGNITY AND THE FUTURE OF LEGAL DESIGN

In this chapter, we have examined diverse perspectives on dignity as this concept has evolved over human history. The classic conception of dignity as merit is defined by one's social rank. Dignity as autonomy originates from one's autonomous actions. Dignity as a universal right suggests that it is part of human nature and that everyone is equal in dignity. Finally, an ongoing interpretation of dignity positions it as the everyday practice of respectful treatment. The variety in how the meaning of dignity has been conceptualized reveals the significant role it has played throughout many human civilizations.

Dignity is a principle that has diverse meanings and is a paradox in itself. Contradictory conceptions of dignity still exist today, such as in the theoretical debates concerning equity and equality, universal rights and individual autonomy, as well as freedom and safety. To apply these diverse conceptions of dignity in a way that ensures the respectful treatment of others, individuals must consider the plurality of meanings ascribed to dignity and make a choice in each action they take. Sometimes certain cultures reach a consensus about how to correctly interpret dignity that trumps all others, and it influences the law and design of the era.

However, even the most accepted interpretations of dignity have shifted over time. Thus, the diversity in the interpretations of dignity may be what makes humans dignified; the process of contemplating the varied meanings of dignity to arrive at a choice, redefine its meaning, and expand its boundaries is an expression of dignity.

How, then, can we project the future research direction of legal design as it relates to the principle of dignity? First, we can consider the design of dignity; dignity can serve as the main topic or key perspective of a specific project. For example, the redesign of hospital gowns for patients (Reiblein 2015) or evidence collection toolkits for sexual violence victims (Ulluoa and Strømsnes 2012) is an example of creating experiences or products that focus on protecting the dignity of users. These projects proposed design solutions centered on the theme of dignity because dignity was identified in the research process as one of the most pressing needs of user groups, such as hospital patients or the victims of sexual violence.

Second, design *for* dignity is another potential approach, the goal of which is to create a better system to enhance dignity in legal design projects, regardless of subject area or user group. For example, the Morphology of Dignity project (Kim, Srinivasan, and Zhou 2019) aims to create a system of tools based on the key elements and patterns distilled from the participants' experiences of dignity in service. The research team conducted qualitative research in the areas of donation to distill the factors and patterns of dignity in service experiences. The team then applied Folklorist Vladimir Propp's ([1928] 2010) storytelling morphology to organize the research outcomes into actants and narratemes, before creating three kinds of design tools that can enhance dignity in design processes. These tools included an online archive that captures the common patterns of dignity and indignity, a virtual reality simulator for modeling and testing these patterns from multiple stakeholders' perspectives, and a participatory workshop to evaluate and codesign a service based on the dignity patterns. In so doing, this project explored how dignity can be applied as a general principle of design through the creation of systematic tools, regardless of the subject or user group.

A third approach is to design *with* dignity, which involves treating people who are engaged in the legal design process in a dignified way. For example, many user studies in the field of design undergo the approval process of an institutional review board (IRB) to ensure that they observe the proper training and protocols for interacting with human subjects in an ethical manner. This legitimate process and protocol become even more important in legal design, in which the impacts on the participants or vulnerable individuals, such as victims and formerly incarcerated people, can be significant. Therefore, legal design research should consider not only the dignity of users but also that of the diverse stakeholders who are directly or indirectly involved. There is also a need to include diverse perspectives in the design team or committee to reflect a broad range of voices, and special attention and care are needed when dealing with minority subjects. The dignity of the diverse workers who comprise the legal system should likewise be discussed. In the end, there is a need to develop legal design-specific methods, models, processes, and tools that reflect the unique dignity needs in the legal process, the legal profession, and the stakeholders in legal situations.

Finally, we can explore design *as* dignity in the law. Design is characteristic of humans; we collaborate to create an artificial world embedded with meanings, which becomes the environment that shapes our actions and thoughts. In a sense, design itself is an autonomous action that has been developed to enhance individual lives, humanity, and the whole world. Buchanan (2001b) argues that "design is fundamentally grounded in human dignity," describing how dignity is the beginning and end of design. Design starts from the pursuit of human values and the surrounding society's constitutional life, thus transforming the abstract principle of dignity into a concrete reality. Buchanan proposes that we are obliged to understand what we mean by dignity and how our creations foster or fail dignity. This view, in turn, inspires us to think about the dignity of design itself as a collective activity in recreating the legal system in a human-centered and humanizing way. The activity of design is not merely a decoration or method to supplement other fields; it has its own end value.

The study of legal design and dignity has just begun, and many issues remain for further discussion. For example, what about the dignity of nonhuman life? According to the traditions of the Middle Ages, every living being, including animals, plants, and the entire planet, has dignity. How, then, should legal design be positioned as the boundaries of dignity continue to expand? If dead bodies have dignity, do objects have dignity as well? Do things that humans anthropomorphize, empathize with, are emotionally attached to, or consider part of their identity have dignity? If artificial things have dignity, how about robots? During an era when service roles are increasingly mediated by robots, what forms of dignity should we consider when designing humanoids? How about artificial intelligence? With today's rapid changes in technology and the economy, design needs to be built on a stable foundation of dignity, encouraging designers, legal professionals, and the stakeholders we serve to deliberate legal design and beyond.

REFERENCES

Althouse, Ann. 2000. "On Dignity and Deference: The Supreme Court's New Federalism." *University of Cincinnati Law Review* 68, no. 2 (Spring): 245–68.

Buchanan, Richard. 2001a. "Design and the New Rhetoric: Productive Arts in the Philosophy of Culture." *Philosophy & Rhetoric* 34, no. 3 (August): 183–206.

2001b. "Human Dignity and Human Rights: Thoughts on the Principles of Human-Centered Design." *Design Issues* 17, no. 3 (Summer): 35–39.

Canada. Canadian Charter of Rights and Freedoms. 1982. *Canada Constitution Act*. https://lois-laws.justice.gc.ca/eng/Const/Const_index.html.

Casserley, Catherine, and Marcus Ormerod. 2013. "The Legal Argument for Inclusive Design." In *Inclusive Design: Design for the Whole Population*, edited by John

Clarkson, Roger Coleman, Simeon Keates, and Cherie Lebbon, 142–54. London: Springer.
Chun, Euyoung. 2018. "How the Social Hierarchy Discouraged New Experiments in Korean Architecture." *Maeil Economics*, May 11, 2018. www.mk.co.kr/news/business/view/2018/05/299311.
Chung, Stephy, and Oscar Holland. 2018. "Dolce & Gabbana Cancels China Show amid 'Racist' Ad Controversy." *CNN*, November 22. https://edition.cnn.com/style/article/dolce-gabbana-shanghai-controversy/index.html.
Cicero, Marcus Tullius. [44 BC] 1991. *On Duties (De Officiis)*. Edited by M. T. Griffin and E. M. Atkins. Translated by M. T. Griffin. Cambridge: Cambridge University Press.
Copenhaver, Brian. 2017. "Dignity, Vile Bodies, and Nakedness." In *Dignity: A History*, edited by Remy Debes, 127–74. Oxford: Oxford University Press.
Cowan, Brian William. 2005. *The Social Life of Coffee: The Emergence of the British Coffeehouse*. New Haven, CT: Yale University Press.
Daly, Erin. 2020. *Dignity Rights*. Philadelphia: University of Pennsylvania Press.
2013. "The Constitutional Right to Dignity." Accessed August 31, 2022. www.ialsnet.org/meetings/constit/papers/DalyErin%28USA%29.pdf.
Darwell, Stephen. 2017. "Equal Dignity and Rights." In *Dignity: A History*, edited by Remy Debes, 181–202. Oxford: Oxford University Press.
Debes, Remy. 2017. "Human Dignity before Kant: Denis Diderot's Passionate Person." In *Dignity: A History*, edited by Remy Debes, 203–36. Oxford: Oxford University Press.
Debry, Gérard. 1994. *Coffee and Health*. Eshre, UK: John Libbey Eurotext.
Ewing, Connor M. 2018. "With Dignity and Justice for All: The Jurisprudence of Equal Dignity and the Partial Convergence of Liberty and Equality in American Constitutional Law." *International Journal of Constitutional Law* 16, no. 3 (July): 753–75. https://doi.org/10.1093/icon/moy061.
The Federal Republic of Germany. Federal Ministry of Justice. *Grundgesetz (Basic Law) of the Federal Republic of Germany*. 1949. www.gesetze-im-internet.de/englisch_gg/englisch_gg.html.
Feinberg, Joel. 1970. The Nature and Value of Rights. *Journal of Value Inquiry*: 245–57. https://home.csulb.edu/~cwallis/382/readings/160/nature_and_value_of_rightsb.html
Garrison, Anna. 2021. "Dolce & Gabbana Is Trying to Sue Fashion Instagram Diet Prada for $600 Million." *Disractify*, September 19, 2021. www.distractify.com/p/diet-prada-lawsuit.
Gewirth, Alan. 1984. "Rights and Virtues." *Analyse & Kritik* 6, no. 1: 28–48. https://doi.org/10.1515/auk-1984-0103.
Gordis, Warren Stone. 1905. *The Estimates of Moral Values Expressed in Cicero's Letters: A Study of the Motives Professed or Approved*. Chicago: University of Chicago Press.
Griffin, James. 2008. *On Human Rights*. Oxford: Oxford University Press.
Griffin, Miriam. 2017. "Dignity in Roman and Stoic Thought." In *Dignity: A History*, edited by Remy Debes, 47–66. Oxford: Oxford University Press.
Habermas, Jurgen. 1991. *The Structural Transformation of the Public Sphere: An Inquiry into a Category of Bourgeois Society*. Cambridge, MA: MIT Press.
Hennette-Vauchez, Stéphanie. 2011. "A Human Dignitas? Remnants of the Ancient Legal Concept in Contemporary Dignity Jurisprudence." *International Journal of Constitutional Law* 9, no. 1 (January): 32–57. https://doi.org/10.1093/icon/mor031.
Henry, Leslie Meltzer. 2011. "The Jurisprudence of Dignity." *University of Pennsylvania Law Review* 160, no.1 (December): 169–233.
Hicks, Donna. 2011. *Dignity: The Essential Role It Plays in Resolving Conflict*. New Haven, CT: Yale University Press.

Hobbes, Thomas. [1651] 1904. *Leviathan: Or, The Matter, Forme and a Power of Commonwealth, Ecclesiasticall and Civil*. Cambridge: Cambridge University Press.
Johnson, Jeff, and Kate Finn. 2017. *Designing User Interfaces for an Aging Population: Towards Universal Design*. Burlington, MA: Morgan Kaufmann.
Jones, John Chris. 1992. *Design Methods*. Hoboken, NJ: John Wiley & Sons.
Kant, Immanuel. [1785] 1993. *Groundwork for the Metaphysics of Morals*. London: Hackett.
Kent, Bonnie. 2017. "In the Image of God: Human Dignity after the Fall." In *Dignity: A History*, edited by Remy Debes, 73–98. Oxford: Oxford University Press.
Kim, Miso, Divya Srinivasan, and Xing Zhou. 2019. "The Morphology of Dignity: Service Storytelling and Prototypes for a Service Design Tool." *The Design Journal* 22, no. 6 (Fall): 793–812. https://doi.org/10.1080/14606925.2019.1662633.
Kirkham, Chris, and Banerjee, Ankur. 2021. "U.S. FDA Says It Needs More Time to Decide on Juul, Other E-cigarettes." *Reuters*, September 10. www.reuters.com/business/healthcare-pharmaceuticals/us-fda-ask-more-time-before-deciding-juul-e-cigarettes-2021-09-09.
Lee, Sunmi. 2021. "The Traces of Baekje within Seoul." *City of Seoul News*, December 30. https://mediahub.seoul.go.kr/archives/2003475.
Luban, David. 2005. "Lawyers as Upholders of Human Dignity (When They Aren't Busy Assaulting It)." *University of Illinois Law Review* 2005, no. 3 (April): 815–45. https://doi.org/10.1017/CBO9780511487484.003.
Margalit, Avishai. 1998. *The Decent Society*. Cambridge, MA: Harvard University Press.
Maritain, Jacques. 1951. *Man and the State*. Essex Junction, VT: Phoenix Books.
McCrudden, Christopher. 2008. "Human Dignity and Judicial Interpretation of Human Rights." *European Journal of International Law* 19, no. 4 (September): 655–724. https://doi.org/10.1093/ejil/chn043.
McKeon, Richard. 1990. "Philosophy and History in the Development of Human Rights." In *Freedom and History and Other Essays: An Introduction to the Thought of Richard McKeon*, edited by Zahava K. McKeon, 37–61. Chicago: University of Chicago Press.
Merriam-Webster. (2019). Dignity. In Merriam-Webster.com dictionary. Retrieved February 22, 2024, from www.merriam-webster.com/dictionary/dignity.
Norman, Donald. 2009. *The Design of Future Things*. New York: Basic Books.
O'Connor, Maureen. 2021. "The Trials of Diet Prada." *Vanity Fair*, September 16. www.vanityfair.com/style/2021/09/diet-prada-roasting-the-runway.
Persson, Hans, Henrik Åhman, Alexander Arvei Yngling, and Jan Gulliksen. 2015. "Universal Design, Inclusive Design, Accessible Design, Design for All: Different Concepts—One Goal? On the Concept of Accessibility—Historical, Methodological and Philosophical Aspects." *Universal Access in the Information Society* 14, no. 4 (November): 505–26. https://doi.org/10.1007/s10209–014-0358-z.
Pico Della Mirandola, Giovanni. [1486] 1996. *Oration on the Dignity of Man*. Washington, DC: Regnery Publishing.
Propp, Vladimir. 2010. *Morphology of the Folktale*. Austin: University of Texas Press.
Rankine, Patrice. 2017. "Dignity in Homer and Classical Greece." In *Dignity: A History*, edited by Remy Debes, 19–46. Oxford: Oxford University Press.
Reiblein, Erik. 2015. "The Problem with Hospital Gowns." Master's thesis, Industrial and Interaction Design, Syracuse University.
República del Perú. 1993. "Peru Constitution." www.constituteproject.org/constitution/Peru_2021?lang=en.
The Republic of South Africa. 1996. "South African Constitution." www.gov.za/documents/constitution-republic-south-africa-1996.

Robinson, Milia. 2016. "The CEO of the 'Apple of Vaping' Explains Why the Comparison Makes Sense." *Business Insider*, August 25. www.businessinsider.com/pax-labs-apple-of-vaping-2016-8.

Rosen, Michael. 2012a. *Dignity: Its History and Meaning*. Cambridge, MA: Harvard University Press.

2012b. "Dignity Past and Present." In *Dignity, Rank, and Rights (The Berkeley Tanner Lectures)*, edited by Jeremy Waldron, 79–98. Oxford: Oxford University Press.

Shultziner, Doron. 2017. "Human Dignity in Judicial Decisions: Principles of Application and the Rule of Law." *New Europe Law Review* 25, no. 3 (Summer): 435–81.

Simon, Herbert A. 1969. *The Sciences of the Artificial*. Cambridge, MA: MIT Press.

Story, Molly Follette. 2001. "Principles of Universal Design." In *Universal Design Handbook*, edited by Dian Pratiwi, 58–67. New York: McGraw Hill.

Trinkaus, Charles Edward. 1970. *In Our Image and Likeness: Humanity and Divinity in Italian Humanist Thought*. Notre Dame, IN: University of Notre Dame Press.

Ulluoa, Manuela Aguirre, and Jan Kristian Strømsnes. 2012. "Design for Dignity in a Sexual Violence Response System." *Systems Oriented Design*. https://systemsorienteddesign.net/design-for-dignity-in-a-sexual-violence-response-system.

The United Nations International Court of Justice. 1945. "United Nations Charter." www.un.org/en/about-us/un-charter.

The United Nations General Assembly. 1948. "Universal Declaration of Human Rights." www.un.org/en/about-us/universal-declaration-of-human-rights.

Von Balthasar, Hans Urs. 1995. *Presence and Thought: Essay on the Religious Philosophy of Gregory of Nyssa*. San Francisco, CA: Ignatius Press.

Waldron, Jeremy. 2012. *Dignity, Rank, and Rights*. Oxford: Oxford University Press.

White, Emily Kidd. 2014. "Till Human Voices Wake Us: The Role of Emotions in the Adjudication of Dignity Claims." *Journal of Law, Religion and State* 3, no. 3 (August): 201–39. Social Science Research Network (SSRN).

2

Dignifying Design in Law

Dan Jackson

2.1 INTRODUCTION

Law and its application in our society as the rule of law[1] are among humankind's most creative ideas. It isn't just an idea, of course. It is one that has been put into practice in some form or another for at least 4,000 years, when the Code of Ur-Nammu, the world's earliest known legal text, was crafted in what is now modern-day southern Iraq (Kramer 1953). That is a very long time. That 4,000 years, of course, is only 2% of the 200,000 years modern humans have existed. Those 4,000 years have seen about 160 generations of up to 16 billion people (Kaneda and Haub 2011). If you believe, as I do, that law as a concept has been around much longer,[2] and likely predates all 200,000 years of modern human history, we are talking about at least 8,000 generations of 104 billion humans creating, applying, breaking, reimagining, and recreating the rule of law (Kaneda and Haub 2011). That's a lot of people and a lot of user testing. It is also a lot of experimentation and iteration, all of which has led to the legal systems and institutions we have today.

The rule of law has been applied to achieve great things and staggering evil. Compare Abraham Lincoln's Emancipation Proclamation, which in the United

[1] One of the questions that my colleague and book coeditor Jules Rochielle Sievert asks me whenever I start down this road is to define what I mean by the rule of law. My answer has evolved over time, but it usually boils down to a system of consistent rules enacted by some collection of people that apply equally to everyone within that collection of people, and includes the protection of some core human rights (Dicey 1885). I think that final component (the protection of core rights and liberties) is a good one, but not necessarily one that adheres to the concept of the rule of law automatically. It is instead a choice that much but not all of our modern society has decided is a good one to add and keep, at least for now (MacCormick 2008).

[2] It seems likely to me that humans and our ancestors started deriving rudimentary laws along with rudimentary hand tools. I can imagine that an early law might have been a common agreement that the person who *made* the hand tool is the only person who gets to *use* the hand tool. Or perhaps the exact opposite – all hand tools, whether found or created, are common property, which must not be used to kill other humans. You get the idea.

States freed slaves in rebellious states, with the Nuremberg Laws of 1935, which stripped Jews of their rights as German citizens (Lincoln 1863; Burleigh and Wippermann 1991). And the rule of law, of course, remains only an idea for much of humanity – past and present (Gowder 2016). It need not remain merely aspirational for the future, however. What is broken can be fixed.

Indeed, the history of the rule of law is characterized by repeated and regular creative reimaginings and refinements. Consider my country – the United States – and our ongoing experiment in democracy, imperfect, messy, and recent as it is (Hamilton et al. 1787–88). Or the concept of common law, where the nuances of the basic rules of engagement for humanity evolve over time based on how different judges interpret the law and apply them to different situations (Baker 2002). Law in concept and in practice is a human invention. And what humans invent can be rejected, reinvented, and refined. Most optimistically, human inventions such as law[3] can be improved over time based on what we learn as we use our invention by interacting with it.

This chapter argues legal design is the next significant iteration of law. I take this position first and foremost because I believe that the rule of law is worth improving, and that humanity can, with a great deal of hard work and perseverance, actually achieve it for everyone. I believe legal design is the best means to make all of that happen because it offers us a process by which we can undertake that improvement with the same deliberation, precision, and attention to detail for which the law is known, and the same creativity, speed, and structure for which design is known. A good case can be made that law and design are each separately responsible for how we have created the world we live in now. A good case can also be made that they are each separately capable of creating the world we want to live in in the future, subject of course to the laws of physics. But joined closely in careful balance with each other as legal design, they have the potential to do much more for each other and for that future world. Imagine then what we could do collectively with our world and our future in the next 200,000 years if everyone enjoyed the full promise of the rule of law – certainty, equality, and fundamental rights.

This chapter will stitch together my argument from a collection of divergent strands of thought and knowledge. I start with a quick sketch of the history of the development of the rule of law over the last 4,000 years, which sets the stage for an examination of that history as a design history – humanity's collective work over four millennia of ideating, prototyping, testing, and refining the systems of rules we use to live collectively. I'll then pivot to make a few points about the benefits of design as design – its relative speed, flexibility, and responsiveness to making things that are useful to people. I will then introduce the concept of "longtermerism," which refers to a concept or ideology that emphasizes the importance of long-term thinking and

[3] I'll be using "law" and "the rule of law" interchangeably throughout this chapter, except where discussing a specific law, in which case I will be referring to that law's name.

decision-making in various aspects of life. I'll wrap things up with a note of urgency and optimism based on my belief that no human should be denied the benefit of the rule of law.

2.2 THE HISTORY OF LAW IN 874 WORDS

The history of law is as complex and diverse as the cultures that have deployed it. What follows is a quick spin through six of the most prominent and influential examples, in as close to chronological order as the overlapping timelines of these examples permit.

First up are prehistoric cultural indigenous systems. Long before the advent of written legal codes, we know societies were governed by oral laws and customs that regulated social behavior and provided mechanisms for dispute resolution (Finnegan 1970). These oral traditions are still practiced in modified form in many indigenous communities around the world. These traditions embody complex systems of law that balance individual rights with communal responsibilities (Merry 1988). Such traditions are frankly deserving of an entire field of study within legal design for the remarkable insights that can be, and already are being, gleaned to inform where justice goes next in our society (Pranis 2003).

Next up is ancient Mesopotamia and Babylon. Recall the earliest known written legal code is the Code of Ur-Nammu from ancient Sumer in Mesopotamia, dating back to around 2100–2050 BCE (Kramer 1954). The Code, while not complete, is believed to have included provisions for both criminal offenses, such as theft and murder, and civil matters like divorce and property disputes. It also introduced the principle of proportionality in punishment, a precursor to the "eye for an eye" principle (Kramer 1954). A few centuries later, the Code of Hammurabi (1792–1750 BCE) emerged in ancient Babylon, a city within Mesopotamia, known for its detailed laws and punishments. This Code is famous for its principle of "lex talionis" or law of retaliation, though it also covered a wide range of civil matters such as trade, slavery, and property rights (Van De Mieroop 2007).

Predating both the Codes of Ur-Nammu and Hammurabi is ancient Egypt (circa 3000 BCE–30 BCE), in which law was intertwined with religion and morality. There was no comprehensive legal code, and precedent played an important role. Much of what we know about ancient Egyptian law comes from court documents, wisdom literature, and tales depicting legal cases (van Blerk 2018).

Ancient Chinese law, especially during the Qin (221–206 BCE) and Han (206 BCE–220 CE) dynasties, was influenced by a concept known as "Legalism," which emphasized strict enforcement of laws. However, it also incorporated elements of Confucianism, focusing on moral duties and social harmony (MacCormack 2001).

As we know from my coeditor Miso Kim's chapter (Chapter 1), Roman law (circa 753 BCE–476 CE) was one of the most sophisticated legal systems in the ancient world and has had a profound impact on the legal systems of many countries. The

Romans developed advanced legal principles and concepts, many of which – such as "innocent until proven guilty" – are foundational to modern Western legal systems. Roman law also produced the Corpus Juris Civilis, a comprehensive codification ordered by Emperor Justinian I, which has been influential in the civil law tradition (Dingledy 2016).

And last but certainly not least, the common law tradition, which began in England after the Norman Conquest (1066 CE), is distinguished by its reliance on judicial decisions to create law. These decisions serve as precedents to be followed in future similar cases decided (usually) by different judges. The common law system, with its adaptable and evolving nature, is the basis of legal systems in many countries, including the United States, Canada, and Australia (Baker 2002).

To any actual historian of law, the preceding short paragraphs do nothing more than place these moments in time and place and not extrapolate insights from such history into legal design. Such insights are not the focus of this chapter, however. I seek only to make the point that cultures and civilizations have been *experimenting* with law for millennia, and that the contours of each (re)invention of law is uniquely informed by, among other things, culture, time, and place. It is also sufficient to make a simplistic case that these experiments are connected to each other, if not in explicit knowledge or influence, then in purpose: Modern humans evolved in social groups that found ways to live together for the common good, those ways became (among other things) oral legal traditions (indigenous prehistory), which evolved into simple written legal codes (Mesopotamia), complex oral and cultural ones (Egypt), more complex written codes (Chinese and Roman), and interpretive systems (common law).

Today, our system of laws has grown so much in complexity and influence that the US federal tax code alone spans 70,000 pages (Internal Revenue Code of 1986), 27 countries have (partially) joined economically and legislatively into the European Union (European Union 2023), and nearly 8 billion people are alive today driving an $85 trillion global economy. The foundation for much of this growth in size and complexity is law. Law is therefore a very successful experiment in creating a system that supports a civilization and society. That system presently is not equitably designed or distributed, but that should not diminish the fact the system itself has stood the test of time (so far), and that one of its core defining features has been our ability to evolve, adjust, and reinvent it as our cultures, exigencies, economies, and evolution demand.

2.3 LAW AS DESIGN

Before making a few observations about law as design, it will help to have a baseline definition of design. This is especially helpful for legal types not engaged with a design or design-adjacent practice of some kind.

> As a verb, "design" connotes a process of creation. This may be how most lawyers not affiliated with traditional design professions have recently encountered the term; processes originally developed by, and for, product designers are increasingly

used for innovation in other professions. These design methods include developing empathy through observation, cyclical iteration of ideas, prototyping, beta testing, and so on.

[T]he term "design" [can also be understood] more formally as a noun. As such, "design" describes object creation, manifested by an agent, to accomplish a goal or goals, where the object satisfies a set of requirements, and its creation is subject to certain fixed constraints. Used in this traditional sense, the design "object" is a physical one, the agent is a human being (the "designer"), the goal is the purpose of the design exercise ("move this large object from here to there"), the set of requirements are materials specifications ("use only found objects"), and the constraints are things such as available found materials ("stone and wood"). Thus, the first rudimentary wheel was not invented, but "designed." (Lippe, Katz, and Jackson 2015)

In modern legal scholarship, the concept of law has long been recognized as an essential tool for shaping society (Hart 1961). In recent years, an emerging body of scholarship has reframed this perspective, arguing that law is not merely a tool but a form of design itself (Hagan n.d., Bhatnagar 2022). This perspective views the creation and implementation of laws as a process that involves designing our social, economic, and governmental institutions. The brief historical interlude in the previous section supports this view by surfacing law's inherent malleability and responsiveness to human reinvention.

The roots of this concept of law-as-design can be traced back to the works of legal scholars such as Roberto Unger, who in the 1970s proposed a view of law as a form of social theory that designs and redesigns institutions (Unger 1976). By defining law as a design activity, Unger provided a novel lens to view the law not just as rules and regulations but as a product of human imagination and creativity. Fast forward a few decades, and scholars like Herbert Simon (1996) advanced this view by arguing that law is a kind of "artifact," a product of human invention designed to achieve certain social, economic, and political goals. This perspective was influential in highlighting the "design" nature of law, suggesting law, like any designed object, can be improved, modified, and redesigned to better serve its purpose.

More recently, of course, legal design has emerged as a full-fledged subdiscipline of both design and law, which formalizes certain aspects of "law as design" while also expanding the contours of what is considered design. The rise of powerful and reasonably accessible digital technologies means there is more and more complexity and economy for us to regulate with law. Frank Pasquale (2020) rightly proposes that law is a design process of economic and governmental institutions. He emphasizes the role of law in designing algorithms and digital platforms that shape our economic and political systems. This perspective positions law (and legal design) as a key tool for designing our digital society, with vast implications for privacy, democracy, and equity. It is noteworthy in this regard that as this manuscript was finalized, those scientific, academic, and corporate leaders actively engaged with researching, developing, and launching artificial intelligence are almost begging legislators to enact some urgently needed policy guardrails (Center for AI Safety, n.d.).

Before moving on, let me summarize where I'm at. I've observed that one of law's core defining features has been our ability to evolve, adjust, and reinvent it as our cultures, exigencies, economies, and evolution demand. I've now added the point that, as a design activity, law can be understood as a human creation that has been manifested by an agent, to accomplish a goal or goals, and is subject to requirements and constraints. I'm now going to add a really obvious point to the mix – basically that humans are really good designers.

2.4 OUR ABILITY TO DESIGN IS REALLY USEFUL TO PEOPLE

The discipline of design has emerged as a vital tool in our ever-evolving society. Its utility lies not just in the important work of creating aesthetically pleasing products or structures but in its speed, flexibility, and responsiveness to human needs and experiences. Design's practical value is further heightened when considered through the lens of human-centered design (Norman and Stappers 2015), which emphasizes understanding users' needs and involving them in the design process.

The iPhone's evolution serves as a well-known and illustrative example of design's practical utility, marked by a rapid redesign and reengineering cycle based on extensive user data collection. This iterative process, embedded into the popular myth of the product, has propelled the iPhone's success by enabling Apple to respond swiftly to changing user needs and market trends. As a telecommunication device it is a far cry from the plastic rectangles that Ma Bell mounted to walls of homes in the United States, but as a design process it is a remarkable distillation of aspects of the operations of Bell Labs (Gertner 2013).

This human-centric approach to design echoes the arguments of scholars such as Bryan Lawson (2006), who emphasizes design's role as a problem-solving activity. Lawson's work highlights design's capacity to identify, analyze, and respond to human needs quickly and flexibly. Recent history also demonstrates how design's practical utility extends beyond physical products to societal systems and services. Buchanan (1992) argued that design can help solve complex problems in our rapidly changing world, with his concept of "wicked problems" in design thinking becoming a landmark in the field of design. His work underscored design's potential to respond to intricate issues that defy traditional problem-solving methods. In the context of public health crises, design methods have been instrumental. During the COVID-19 pandemic, design principles were used to rapidly develop and improve testing processes, information dissemination, and remote work solutions (Capolongo et al. 2020).

Everything we encounter in our world that has been created by people in this world is the product of a design process of some kind. The iPhones and the COVID-19 tests are obvious examples of design, but with very complex details. Simpler examples are all around us. The desk at which I am writing this paragraph has, among other things, a picture frame and a water glass on it. Both are things that people designed for human use in some way. Temporary creations are no less designed just because they are temporary or otherwise impermanent. An herb garden or a forest path are human creations that have been manifested by an agent, to accomplish a goal, and are subject to requirements and constraints. Nor does the creation need to be made for others – we all design things for our own exclusive use all the time.

Humans design; it is what we do. Indeed, many scholars acknowledge that humans' ability to drastically modify their environment is a distinctive part of human nature (Wilson 1978; Harari 2015). As a result of our exceptional design capabilities, our species has been able to not only thrive on this planet but so impact the physical corpus of the Earth that some scientists suggest we've reached a new geological age – the Anthropocene (Zalasiewicz 2019). That's a remarkable achievement. While recent attention has rightly focused on humans' abuse of our planet, the scale of our impact is also an indication of our power. By virtue of what we are, what we can do, and our sheer numbers we have the capacity to change our world, and to do so at a remarkable scale.

Where does that leave us in my argument? I've observed that one of law's core defining features is evolution, adjustment, and reinvention. I've also shown that, as a design activity, law can be understood as a human creation to accomplish, and is subject to requirements and constraints. I've now added the point that humans are really good at designing – so good, in fact, that it is one of our defining characteristics as a species. I'm now going to add some insights from a field of study that emphasizes the value of society prioritizing long-term goals.

2.5 LONGTERMERISM

I was introduced to the idea of longtermerism in a recent guest essay by William MacAskill in *The New York Times* (2022). His definition of the heart of the concept is better than anything I could come up with.

> Longtermism is about taking seriously just how big the future could be and how high the stakes are in shaping it. If humanity survives to even a fraction of its potential life span, then, strange as it may seem, [those of us alive today] are the ancients: we live at the very beginning of history, in its most distant past. What we do now will affect untold numbers of future people. We need to act wisely. (MacAskill 2022)

Longtermerism's roots lie in various philosophical, economic, and environmental movements. Its philosophical underpinnings can be traced back to utilitarianism, which advocates for actions that maximize overall happiness and well-being over time (Driver 2022). Economically, the idea of sustainable development, as outlined in the Brundtland Report (1987), shares parallels with longtermerism's emphasis on meeting present needs without compromising future generations.

The optimism inherent in longtermerism is what drew me to the concept as this book was taking shape. Thinking long term promotes stability, consensus, and collective action. By encouraging long-term thinking we pursue decisions that favor sustainability and the common good. This approach can bridge political and ideological divides, fostering consensus around shared long-term goals. Indeed, we are seeing some of these ideas manifest themselves most recently in the (still fledgling) global response to climate change. The Paris Agreement (2015) represents a global consensus to tackle climate change, a quintessential long-term issue.

In the context of law, longtermerism offers an interesting perspective. Recall I've made the point that law's been part of our social framework for a really long time, quite possibly from the very beginning of anything resembling a social framework. Law is designed intentionally as a long-term institution, providing a stable framework for social order (Fuller 1964). Recent legal scholarship has explored this connection. For instance, Martinez and Winter (2023) discuss how longtermerism can shape legal norms and institutions to better address long-term challenges. They argue that longtermerism encourages a precautionary approach, which prioritizes preventing harm to future generations.

My point with longtermerism and law is a little different. Recall MacAskill's (2022) observation that those of us alive today are living at the very beginning of human history – we are the ancients. Recall also my point that humanity has a very successful experiment underway with law. There is lots of work to be done on law, of course, but the experiment so far has shown law to be flexible and adaptive *in the long term*. Join these two ideas, and we see that the law itself is also in its infancy together with human history. This means we have both the time and space ahead of us to continue this experiment, and that the *design choices* we make today *must* be considered in the long term because they *will* impact the untold numbers of people who will live in the future. This perspective instills in me both a deep humility toward humanity's impact on our world and an abiding optimism toward what we can achieve.

So far, I've stitched together an argument that one of law's core defining features is its ability to evolve, adjust, and be reinvented, and that as a design activity, law can be understood as a goal-centered human creation responsive to requirements and constraints. We know from experience that humanity's design talent is quite impressive – we can create really useful things at a global scale. We see now our useful and flexible creation – law – is at the very beginning of its existence in the world. Our experiment is only now getting started.

2.6 THE SITUATION IS URGENT AND THE FUTURE IS BRIGHT

I'm now going to throw a bit of a curveball as this chapter wraps up. Despite my focus above on the long history behind us and the vast future in front of us, my concluding points are that we need to act quickly to reinvent law for today's world and we have the power and the ability to do so. One essential fact drives this conclusion: The vast majority of people alive on the planet today do not enjoy the full promise of the rule of law.

Five billion people alive today – fully two-thirds of the planet's current population – have unmet justice needs, including those who cannot obtain justice for everyday problems, those who are excluded from both the modest and remarkable opportunities the law provides, and those who live in extreme conditions of injustice (World Justice Project 2019). In my backyard, and in the legal space with which I am most familiar – the United States – 86% of civil legal problems faced by low-income Americans receive inadequate or no legal help (Legal Services Corporation 2017). This is an ongoing (and growing) crime against humanity. I use that term quite deliberately, but not in the international law context with which we most associate the term (Bassiouni 1992). I use it to describe the scale of real human suffering such an injustice exacts every single day. That is five billion people with current or very recently[4] unmet justice needs *every single day*. The scale of misery is staggering.

It is the scale of injustice that drives the argument for urgency. Although current political/global developments also compellingly support the need for urgent action, recall that longtermerism teaches us that humanity is at the very beginning of our history. Today's developments will be all but forgotten in the eons ahead.[5] The urgency derives instead from asking the question how we, as a society, can continue to perpetuate a world where five billion people have unmet justice needs but three billion people do not. Should not the very benefit being meted out so unevenly – justice – compel us toward a different outcome? The scale of the paradox is staggering.

Despite this miserable paradox, the very thing we've created so far – law – already possesses the characteristics and components it needs to adjust for this moment in history. Law features the ability to evolve, adjust, and be reinvented as our cultures, exigencies, economies, and evolution demand, and as a design activity, it responds well to human agency that seeks to accomplish goals within requirements and constraints. Because humans are good designers, our experiment of law has shown a tremendous amount of promise, at least based on very early prototypes and testing results. We can understand ourselves as now iterating the design for a very long future with more comprehensive, detailed, and voluminous global data about justice needs and the successes and failures of our prototypes to date in meeting them. The scale of opportunity is inspiring.

4 The many categories of measurement that the World Justice Project (2019) "Measuring the Justice Gap" reported ranged from ongoing justice deprivations such as modern slavery and statelessness to temporal deprivations such as unmet civil justice needs no further than two years prior.

5 This presumes that humanity survives past its infancy, and I believe that we will, provided the planet remains habitable long enough for us to be able to figure out how to live at scale off this planet.

2.7 CONCLUSION

This moment feels like a good time to reinvent law and our legal institutions. Much of what exists today has either long lost its practical utility or exists as seemingly antiquated performative gestures. Much of it is so weighted with the prejudices and errors of the past that it has rightly lost legitimacy within contemporary society. Yet many of the people who work within our justice systems are already motivated to rethink, recalibrate, and reform their institutions. These factors indicate a certain ripeness to this historical moment. Things are ready to change.

In that context, there is an inherent design function of law. As we face the increasingly glaring need for change, we must remember law is a human creation that has been manifested by agents, to accomplish our goals, and is subject to our requirements and constraints. History has shown that when the goals and requirements of society change, we change or evolve our law and legal systems. This capacity for redesign is embedded in the law. Let us make full use of that feature now.

REFERENCES

Baker, J. H. 2002. *An Introduction to English Legal History*. Oxford: Oxford University Press.

Bassiouni, M. Cherif. 1992. *Crimes against Humanity in International Criminal Law*. The Hague: Springer Netherlands.

Bhatnagar, Sankalp. 2022. "What Legal Design Is as Opposed to Could/Should Be." *Proceedings of DRS Biennial Conference Series, Design Research Society, Bilbao, Spain, June 25 – July 3, 2022*. London: Design Research Society.

Buchanan, Richard. 1992. "Wicked Problems in Design Thinking." *Design Issues* 8, no. 2 (Spring): 5–21. https://doi.org/10.2307/1511637.

Burleigh, Michael, and Wolfgang Wippermann. 1991. *The Racial State: Germany 1933-1945*. Cambridge, MA: Cambridge University Press.

Capolongo, S., Gola, M., Brambilla, A., Morganti, A., Mosca, E., & Barach, P. 2020. COVID-19 and Healthcare Facilities: A Decalogue of Design Strategies for Resilient Hospitals. *Acta Biomed.*, 91(9-S), 50–60.

Center for AI Safety. n.d. "Statement on AI Risk." Accessed June 11, 2023. www.safe.ai/statement-on-ai-risk.

Dicey, A. V. 1885. *Introduction to the Study of the Law of the Constitution*. London: Macmillan.

Dingledy, F. 2016. The Corpus Juris Civilis: A Guide to Its History and Use. *Legal Reference Services Quarterly*, 35, no. 4: 231–55.

Driver, Julia. 2022. The History of Utilitarianism. In Edward N. Zalta and Uri Nodelman (eds.), *The Stanford Encyclopedia of Philosophy* (Winter Edition). https://plato.stanford.edu/archives/win2022/entries/utilitarianism-history/.sophy.

European Union. "The European Union Consists of 27 Member Countries." Accessed June 11, 2023. https://europa.eu/european-union/about-eu/countries_en.

Finnegan, Ruth. 1970. A Note on Oral Tradition and Historical Evidence. *History and Theory* 9, no. 2: 195–201. doi.org/10.2307/2504126.

Fuller, L. 1964. *The Morality of Law*. New Haven, CT: Yale University Press.

Gertner, Jon. 2013. *The Idea Factory: Bell Labs and the Great Age of American Innovation*. New York: Penguin.

Gowder, Paul. 2016. *The Rule of Law in the Real World*. Cambridge, MA: Cambridge University Press.

Hagan, Margaret. n.d. "Law by Design." Accessed August 5, 2023. https://lawbydesign.co.

Hamilton, Alexander, James Madison, and John Jay. 1787–88. *The Federalist Papers*. New York: McLean.

Harari, Yuval N. 2015. *Sapiens: A Brief History of Humankind*. First U.S. edition. New York: Harper, an imprint of HarperCollinsPublishers.

Hart, H. L. A. 1961. *The Concept of Law*. Oxford: Oxford University Press.

Hassenzahl, Marc, and Noam Tractinsky. 2006. "User Experience – A Research Agenda." *Behaviour & Information Technology* 25, no. 2 (March): 91–97. https://doi.org/10.1080/01449290500330331.

Kaneda, Toshiko, and Carl Haub. 2011. "How Many People Have Ever Lived on Earth?" *Population Reference Bureau*, November 15, 2022. www.prb.org/howmanypeoplehaveeverlivedonearth/.

Kramer, Samuel Noah. 1953. "The Oldest Laws." *Scientific American* 188, no. 1 (January): 26–29. JSTOR.

Kramer, S. N. 1954. Ur-Nammu Law Code. *Orientalia* 23, no. 1: 40–51. www.jstor.org/stable/43073169.

Lawson, Bryan. 2006. *How Designers Think: The Design Process Demystified*. Oxford: Architectural Press.

Legal Services Corporation. 2017. "The Justice Gap: Measuring the Unmet Civil Legal Needs of Low-income Americans." *Legal Services Corporation*. Accessed June 1, 2023. www.lsc.gov/sites/default/files/images/TheJusticeGap-FullReport.pdf.

Lincoln, Abraham. 1863. "Emancipation Proclamation." Washington, DC, January 1. In *The U.S. National Archives and Records Administration*. Accessed August 5, 2023. www.archives.gov/exhibits/featured-documents/emancipation-proclamation.

Lippe, P., D. Martin Katz, and D. Jackson. 2015. "Legal by Design: A New Paradigm for Handling Complexity in Banking Regulation and Elsewhere in Law." *Oregon Law Review* 93, no. 4 (December): 833–43.

MacAskill, William. 2022. "The Case for Longtermism." *The New York Times*, August 5, 2022. www.nytimes.com/2022/08/05/opinion/the-case-for-longtermism.html.

MacCormack, Geoffrey. 2001. *Traditional Chinese Penal Law*. Edinburgh, UK: Edinburgh University Press.

MacCormick, N. 2008. *Law, Justice, and Power: Between Reason and Will*. Oxford: Hart Publishing.

Martínez, E., and C. Winter. 2023. Experimental Longtermist Jurisprudence. In K. Prochownik and S. Magen (Eds.), *Advances in Experimental Philosophy of Law*. Part III(10). Bloomsbury Academic. https://papers.ssrn.com/sol3/papers.cfm?abstract_id=3933618.

Merry, Sally Engle. 1988. "Legal Pluralism." *Law & Society Review* 22, no. 5: 869–96. https://doi.org/10.2307/3053638.

Norman, D., and P. Stappers. 2015. DesignX: Complex Sociotechnical Systems. *She Ji: The Journal of Design, Economics, and Innovation*, 1, no. 2: 83–106.

Ober, Josiah. 1989. *Mass and Elite in Democratic Athens: Rhetoric, Ideology, and the Power of the People*. Princeton, NJ: Princeton University Press.

Pasquale, Frank. 2020. *New Laws of Robotics: Defending Human Expertise in the Age of AI*. Cambridge, MA: Harvard University Press.

Pranis, Kay, Mark Wedge, and Barry Stuart. 2003. *Peacemaking Circles: From Conflict to Community*. St. Paul, MN: Living Justice Press.
Simon, Herbert A. 1996. *The Sciences of the Artificial*. Cambridge, MA: MIT Press.
Unger, Roberto Mangabeira. 1976. *Law in Modern Society: Toward a Criticism of Social Theory*. New York: Free Press.
United States of America Internal Revenue Service. 1986. "Internal Revenue Code of 1986." January 18, 2023. www.irs.gov/privacy-disclosure/tax-code-regulations-and-official-guidance.
van Blerk, N. 2018. The Emergence of Law in Ancient Egypt: The Role of Maat. *Fundamina*, 24, no. 1: 69–88.
Van De Mieroop, M. 2007. *A History of the Ancient Near East ca. 3000 – 323 BC* (2nd ed.). Oxford: Wiley-Blackwell.
Wilson, E. O. 1978. *On Human Nature*. Cambridge, MA: Harvard University Press.
World Justice Project. 2019. "Measuring the Justice Gap: A People-Centered Assessment of Unmet Justice Needs Around the World." https://worldjusticeproject.org/our-work/research-and-data/access-justice/measuring-justice-gap.
Zalasiewicz, Jan, Colin N. Waters, Mark Williams, and Colin P. Summerhayes, eds. 2019. *The Anthropocene as a Geological Time Unit: A Guide to the Scientific Evidence and Current Debate*. Cambridge: Cambridge University Press.

3

Dignifying Imagination in Legal Education

Jules Rochielle Sievert

3.1 UNVEILING URGENCY: RETHINKING SOCIAL-LEGAL SYSTEMS IN RESPONSE TO TURBULENT TIMES

The turbulent times we are experiencing have heightened the urgency to reimagine our social-legal systems. The prevalence of systemic racism, police violence, and post-truth trends have created a pressing need for solutions that shift power structures and narratives in the legal system and beyond. For instance, the violent demonstration of white supremacy in Charlottesville, Virginia, on August 12, 2017, left Heather Heyer dead and several others injured, representing a surge in public incidents of white supremacy and domestic terrorism (Barrón-López and Conciatori 2022).

During 2020, a series of distressing events in the United States set the stage for widespread discord and an insistent call for systemic overhaul. This tumultuous climate was stirred by the severe impact of COVID-19, episodes of police brutality, and protests against racial inequities, symbolized particularly by the sorrowful losses of Breonna Taylor, George Floyd, and countless others to law enforcement excesses. These incidents provoked a wave of anger, public demonstrations, and collective grief that echoed not just within the country but also on a global scale. Addressing these deep-seated issues goes beyond the realm of individual initiative. Instead, it requires a cooperative effort to join forces with leaders of movements, advocates, and diverse stakeholders to reshape narratives and disrupt entrenched power hierarchies in legal and wider societal structures. Concerning education and pedagogy, such revolutionary changes and approaches are instrumental in reimagining our social and legal systems within the ambit of educational institutions.

According to Mapping Police Violence data sets, between 2013 and 2019, police officers in the United States killed approximately 7,666 people. Additionally, Mapping Police Violence reports that Black people are "three times more likely to be killed by police than their White counterparts" (Mapping Police Violence 2022). Unfortunately, the ongoing narrative of excessive police brutality and violence repeated in January 2023. On January 3, 2023, Keenan Anderson was repeatedly tased and restrained by the police, resulting in his hospitalization and death from cardiac arrest. Keenan was the nephew of Patrisse Cullors, the influential cofounder of Black Lives Matter. *The Guardian* reported that Keenan got pulled over for a reported traffic accident at the intersection of Lincoln and Venice near Mar Vista in Los Angeles (Levin 2023).

In a distressing episode on January 8, 2023, Tyre Nichols, a 29-year-old Black man, met a tragic end following an intense confrontation with five Black police officers during a traffic stop in Memphis, Tennessee. This event spurred renewed focus on the ongoing issue of disproportionate force used against individuals, notably those who are young and Black, leading to a federal civil rights investigation into the circumstances surrounding Nichols's death (Cochrane and Jaglois 2023).

The backdrop of this event is characterized by an influx of legislative changes. As Adeel Hassan chronicled in the *New York Times* (2023), the ripple effects of George Floyd's May 2020 demise led to many cities and municipalities introducing legislative amendments aimed at altering the operations of police departments. These regulations encompass laws that call for de-escalation tactics, place restrictions on force utilization, and ban chokeholds. In Hassan's exposition, it is revealed that over 30 states have adopted over 140 new laws aimed at policing oversight and reform. These legislative efforts seek to revamp disciplinary systems, demand accountability in misconduct cases, and establish civilian oversight committees. At the same time, many police departments nationwide have adopted policies that curtail or outright forbid the use of chokeholds.

However, the progress at the federal level has been less consistent. The Justice in Policing Act, which was intended to create a universal standard for police use of force and significantly alter qualified immunity protections for law enforcement officers, received approval from the House but stumbled in the Senate (Hassan 2023). These incidents highlight the intricate and multidimensional nature of situations associated with chronic power misuse and institutional complicity, emphasizing the urgent necessity for comprehensive reforms in nationwide law enforcement practices (Hassan 2023).

The urgency to reevaluate our social-legal systems has never been more evident. From the alarming rise of white supremacy in Charlottesville to the tragic deaths that have ignited powerful protests against racial injustice, we are confronted with the stark reality of systemic racism, police violence, and the erosion of truth. These issues permeate every aspect of our society, underscoring the critical need for solutions that address power imbalances and reshape narratives within our legal system and beyond. How can we respond to these challenges and initiate transformative change within our social-legal systems?

3.2 EMBRACING RADICAL IMAGINATION: RETHINKING EDUCATION, DESIGN, AND LAW FOR TRANSFORMATION

Rittel and Webber (1973) defined "wicked problems" as intricate, multifaceted issues challenging to resolve, like climate change, pandemics, and species extinction.

These collectively constitute unsustainable practices occurring globally (Stony Brook University n.d.). In recent decades, universities have faced criticism for adopting a neoliberal approach to research and community engagement. Scholars are now actively exploring alternative methods to promote access and equality in marginalized communities. These approaches encompass establishing enduring partnerships, undertaking brief initiatives, and fostering interdisciplinary collaborations to address intricate problems with racial dimensions. Bridging the gap that exists between community and academic institutions remains challenging, but by embracing models such as Community Based Participatory Action Research (CBPAR), where research is collaboratively designed and implemented with community input, universities can make significant strides toward achieving inclusivity, social justice, and sustainable solutions for marginalized communities.

Take inspiration from Ananya Roy, Professor of Urban Planning, Social Welfare, and Geography at UCLA and affiliated with the UCLA Luskin Institute on Inequality and Democracy. Roy offers an optimistic perspective on the role of universities in unequal cities and their potential to foster connections between academia and social movements. Influenced by postcolonial studies, feminist theory, and the Black radical tradition, Roy critically examines the capacity of universities to challenge dispossession and displacement through interinstitutional spaces. She acknowledges the negative impact of universities on urban development and gentrification, often leading to the displacement of low-income communities due to physical expansion and real estate development (UCLA Luskin Institute on Inequality and Democracy n.d.). However, she also identifies universities as potential sites of resistance and transformation. Roy advocates for the establishment of "publicly engaged universities" that actively collaborate with community-based organizations and social movements to address inequality and injustice (UCLA Luskin Institute on Inequality and Democracy n.d.). Key to her vision is the concept of research justice, which underscores the importance of being accountable to communities directly affected by state-organized violence. Through her emphasis on teaching, public scholarship, and community engagement, Roy aims to bring about a transformative shift within the public university system and promote research justice.

Building upon a foundation of thoughtful ideas, adrienne maree brown, a renowned writer and activist, underscores the inescapable reality that our world has been marred by persistent issues such as homelessness, poverty, inequality, and a slew of systemic biases throughout history (Grandoit n.d.). Ananya Roy shares a similar viewpoint to adrienne maree brown, highlighting the unsettling reality that prevailing cultural narratives in the United States are deeply rooted in notions of supremacy, dominance, and triumph (Grandoit n.d.; UCLA Luskin Institute on Inequality and Democracy n.d.). These narratives, strongly influenced by white supremacist ideologies, uphold existing power structures dominated by white hegemony. Regrettably, these narratives continue to create harm and contribute to the marginalization of individuals who do not align with the white able-bodied paradigm, further reinforcing the power dynamics embedded within the current situation.

Transitioning to the concept of post-truth, we confront a complex tapestry of interconnected historical traumas that reverberate throughout society. *New Discourses* (n.d.) highlights the closely associated notion of "epistemic violence," which has been examined by renowned scholars including Michel Foucault, Gayatri Chakravorty Spivak, Miranda Fricker, and Kristine Dobson. Foucault argues that knowledge is not an independent entity but rather a socially constructed tool of power, often leading to politically influenced interpretations that obscure reality. Spivak sheds light on the oppressive side of epistemic violence, revealing how marginalized voices are systematically silenced and their knowledge systems, traditions, beliefs, and languages dismissed under colonial rule. This further perpetuates their confinement and marginalization. The critical works of adrienne maree brown, along with the insights of Foucault and Spivak, offer profound insights into the enduring scars of historical traumas and the intricate interplay between power, knowledge, and post-truth rhetoric.

Dean Spade's insightful analysis, "For Those Considering Law School" (2010), sheds light on the perpetuation of oppressive systems within law schools. Spade employs a thought-provoking analogy, likening the law school experience to a language immersion program, suggesting that these institutions effectively immerse students in the language of rationalizing oppressive structures such as white supremacy, settler colonialism, patriarchy, and capitalism (Spade 2010). Expanding on this perspective, Spade argues that the US legal system itself functions as a stronghold, upholding these oppressive structures and inherently lacking the ability to dismantle them (Spade 2010). This critical examination prompts us to reflect on the role of law schools in maintaining and reinforcing existing power dynamics. Spade's assertion challenges prevailing notions of legal education, prompting critical reflection on the role of law schools in perpetuating oppressive systems. By highlighting how legal education reinforces the language and frameworks that uphold these structures, Spade invites us to question the very foundations of the legal system. His proposition serves as a call to action, urging us to reimagine legal education and advocate for transformative change that dismantles oppressive systems instead of perpetuating them.

This perspective aligns with the broader discourse on decolonization, dismantling systemic racism, and challenging power dynamics within legal institutions. It compels us to critically examine how legal education can be transformed to foster social justice and liberation.

Dr. Foluke Ifejola Adebisi echoes Spade's viewpoint, emphasizing the law's complicity in perpetuating societal injustices. According to Foluke Adebisi's article, the process of decolonizing the law school involves examining the presences, absences, and silences within the curriculum. Adebisi highlights the need to confront the historical legacies that have shaped the law and enabled systemic oppression (Adebisi 2020). Through a discourse on decolonization, Adebisi underscores the importance of critically dissecting the far-reaching impacts of colonialism, empire, and racism on our contemporary world, offering alternative lenses through which to understand our present realities.

Within the academic sphere, discussions challenging systemic racism have ignited conversations aimed at reshaping education and dismantling structures that uphold white supremacy. The Radical Law Student Project (RLSP) emerges as a crucial voice in this discourse, exposing systems and frameworks that perpetuate elitism and conservatism in law schools and the legal system itself (Pasley and Yoder 2016). In line with this viewpoint, the project advocates for a transformative legal education achieved through collaborative efforts among students and their allies. Pasley and Yoder (2016) support this argument in the National Lawyers Guild Radical Law Student Manual by critiquing traditional Socratic and case law methodologies, which they argue offer limited perspectives in addressing deeply rooted issues of race, sexism, classism, and homophobia within the legal system. They emphasize the importance of expanding the case method and embracing unconventional pedagogical strategies to facilitate a comprehensive exploration of these systemic challenges.

Together, these perspectives challenge us to critically examine legal education, confront historical legacies, and actively work toward transformative change.

3.3 REIMAGINING LEGAL EDUCATION AND DESIGN FOR SOCIAL CHANGE

Around the turn of the decade in 2011, the legal education sphere began experimenting with design thinking, leading to the inception of "legal design." This emerging discipline applies design thinking methods to law, and it was first introduced at Stanford University through the establishment of the d.school and Stanford's Legal Design Lab. Presently, an array of law schools have incorporated legal design via courses, workshops, conferences, and labs, primarily aimed at enhancing existing legal services. Nonetheless, it is crucial to highlight that these endeavors continue to be rooted in a legal structure that was initially established on colonial ideologies.

Taking this narrative into account, we must critically reflect on our methods, tactics, and strategies. We must question whether these approaches effectively confront deeply ingrained issues of epistemic injustice and violence within the intersecting domains of design, law, and our educational frameworks. As educators, it is incumbent upon us to rise to the challenge and cultivate an educational environment that nurtures collective imagination to address the complex, so-called "wicked problems" of our era.

Daniel Farbman's work "A Commons in the Master's House" provides valuable insights for envisioning a path forward. Farbman argues that lawyers, law students, and law professors have the power to ignite radical imagination by creating pedagogical opportunities within institutional practices. By transcending the boundaries of whiteness and Eurocentric ideals, education can become a transformative force for the future (Farbman 2022). Building upon Farbman's ideas, Anna Akbar emphasizes the importance of a comprehensive analysis of histories such as colonialism, settler colonialism, the Atlantic slave trade, and mass incarceration within legal scholarship. By considering the critiques and transformative visions put forth by radical social movements, legal scholars can broaden their understanding and contribute to transformative change (Akbar 2018). Connecting these perspectives, Walidah Imarisha emphasizes the power of imagination in envisioning a world free from the constrictions of white supremacy, patriarchy, capitalism, and heterosexism. This act of imagination holds the potential to shape future decisions and actions, paving the way for a society that is free from oppressive systems such as prisons, police violence, scarcity, and inadequate education (Imarisha 2015).

These insights strongly emphasize the potential of education, legal scholarship, and the power of imagination to drive transformative change and challenge oppressive structures. Activist communities recognize the exceptional effectiveness of speculative design and speculative fiction as tools for transformation. These approaches can serve as catalysts for desired shifts in society while also illuminating the discrepancies between our current reality and the envisioned future. Throughout the course of history, Black women, queer individuals, trans individuals, and nonbinary individuals have consistently taken the lead in envisioning and reshaping the trajectory of Black futures, exemplifying the boundless potential for attaining liberation and freedom. Scholar Syd Thorne argues that speculative fiction engenders profound discussions about social justice, empowering students to articulate their visions of a more promising future and fostering a sense of critical hope (Thorne 2021). Collectively, these perspectives underscore the profound influence of imaginative practices and speculative thinking in envisioning and actively working toward a society that is more equitable and emancipated.

Karma Dabaghi, an architect and product designer, emphasizes the valuable role of fiction in enabling designers to critically analyze current conditions and envision future challenges (Dabaghi 2022). By engaging in imaginative thinking, designers can gain a deeper understanding of the root causes behind societal circumstances, thereby enabling them to propose more impactful solutions. Building upon this perspective, Hallie Jay Pope, an expert in legal design, underscores the importance of both dismantling oppressive systems and constructing innovative structures in driving social transformation. Pope advocates for the use of creative legal problem-solving and positions Liberatory Legal Design as a catalyst for radical imagination and substantial social change (Pope 2022).

Moreover, the concept of Liberatory Design, as outlined by the National Equity Project (n.d.), draws attention to the routines and practices that unintentionally perpetuate inequality. Its goal is to shift power dynamics between designers and those affected by their designs, working toward significant social change and the creation of a more equitable world.

3.4 STRATEGIES FOR TRANSFORMATIVE CHANGE

Expanding on this knowledge, the article "It's Critical: Legal Participatory Action Research" in the *Michigan Journal of Race & Law* delves deeper into the intersection of design and law. Authors Emily Houh and Kristin Kalsen shed light on Legal Participatory Action Research (LPAR) as a framework to examine the "fringe economy," which includes alternative lending services and products like pawnshops, payday lenders, direct deposit loans, refund anticipation loans, and car title loans. Their research positions LPAR as a critical race/feminist praxis that addresses the interconnected issues of race, gender, poverty, and widening economic disparities (Houh and Kalsen 2014).

Further elaborating on this theme, Legal Participatory Action Research (LPAR) can be viewed as a form of "action research," a design research approach aimed at unraveling the roots of inequality, epistemic violence, and suppression. Kurt Lewin, a prominent figure in the field, was associated with the scholarship and practice of action research, which is also known by various names such as practitioner research, self-study, action science, site-based inquiry, or emancipatory praxis. Lewin's work, including his article "Action Research" published in the *Journal of Social Issues* in 1946, laid the foundation for understanding the transformative potential of action research (Lewin 1946). Within the realm of action research, Participatory Action Research (PAR) takes center stage as a collaborative effort between researchers and participants, all working toward social justice. PAR fosters a dynamic exchange of research, action, and reflection, emphasizing a reciprocal process. The PAR framework values the experiential knowledge and lived experiences of those most affected by a particular issue, positioning them as crucial contributors in the design research process.

To encourage meaningful participation and agency among community members, the NuLawLab of Northeastern University's School of Law has adopted a specific method known as Community-Based Participatory Action Research (CBPAR). This approach actively engages all stakeholders in the research process, paying attention to community members. CBPAR seeks to foster partnerships between researchers and communities, generating learning opportunities that boost participant engagement and agency. The principal goal of CBPAR is to instigate change at the community level by leveraging research outcomes to drive policy reforms, alter narratives, and improve services. At the heart of CBPAR is the acknowledgment and application of the unique insights and lived experiences of community members, with the ultimate ambition of effecting societal change.

The NuLawLab applies CBPAR in a project called the East Boston Spatial Justice Lab (EBSJL). This recent initiative received funding from the National Endowment for the Arts for this project, which will allow for the study of the combined impact of art, advocacy, and cultural organizing in the space of housing justice. The project has an overarching objective aimed at enhancing the socioemotional well-being of residents, thereby contributing to holistic healing and a sense of belonging within the community. The leadership team comprises this author and Dan Jackson from NuLawLab. Their collaborative effort extends to Maverick Landing Community Services and the artist/community organizer Gabriela Cartagena. Further diversifying the project's multidisciplinary approach is Dr. Tiana Yom from Northeastern University's Public Evaluation Lab (NU-PEL), who brings her expertise in public evaluation, along with Dr. Miso Kim from Northeastern's College of Arts, Media and Design, who contributes insights from the arts and design perspective.

This synthesis of law, public evaluation, arts, and design knowledge forms a potent constructive collaboration, augmenting the potential impact of the project. This collaborative endeavor aspires to stimulate transformative change within the community, concentrating on social justice issues, primarily within housing, and works toward improving community well-being, agency, and belonging. This approach exemplifies the radical imagination at work in liberatory practices, offering a compelling model for how scholars and practitioners can engage with communities to address pressing social issues and contribute to the ongoing project of social transformation.

In our exploration of envisioning a reimagined future, there exists a practice of immense power that embodies the transformative essence of Afrofuturism. The visionary endeavors of the Black Quantum Futurism Collective and the Collective Futures Lab, cofounded by Rasheedah Phillips and Camae Ayewa, serve as a profound source of inspiration (A Blade of Grass 2018). Through their utilization of art, technology, and community organizing initiatives they delve into the intersections of race, space, and time, presenting alternative futures that empower marginalized communities.

The Black Quantum Futurism Collective functions as a multidisciplinary collaboration of creatives and activists based in Philadelphia. Their work amalgamates various forms of expression, including art, music, writing, and community engagement, to address issues such as displacement, gentrification, and historical erasure (Black Quantum Futurism n.d.a). By challenging oppressive systems and imagining new possibilities for marginalized communities, they foster critical dialogue and envision pathways toward liberation and agency.

Similarly, the Collective Futures Lab explores speculative futures as a catalyst for transformative change. It brings together artists, scholars, activists, and community members to envision and actively work toward alternative futures that prioritize justice, equity, and collective well-being. This imaginative and influential practice centers on the experiences and perspectives of Black individuals, providing a space for critical dialogue that challenges systemic injustices while nurturing community care, agency, and mobilization (Black Quantum Futurism n.d.b).

Rasheedah Phillips, in addition to her involvement with the collective and lab, currently holds the position of Director of Housing at PolicyLink. In this role, she spearheads national advocacy efforts in support of tenants' rights, housing, and land use movements. Combining her legal expertise with her passion for Afrofuturism, Phillips contributes to reshaping legal practice through her work (PolicyLink n.d.b). In a conversation with Angela Glover Blackwell, a prominent figure in the realms of social justice and equitable development, Phillips expounds on the transformative power of Afrofuturism in reshaping legal practice.

Angela Glover Blackwell is renowned for her advocacy work and leadership in advancing policies and strategies that address racial and economic inequalities. As the Founder in Residence at PolicyLink, a national research and action institute focused on promoting equity and creating sustainable communities, she has played a pivotal role in shaping the discourse around equity and social justice. Blackwell's advocacy for inclusive policies and practices that uplift marginalized communities aligns with her conversation with Phillips, where they collectively emphasize the significance of comprehending the dimension of time and its profound impact on the lives of Black and Brown individuals facing housing insecurity and other adversities (PolicyLink n.d.a).

For both Phillips and Blackwell, Afrofuturism transcends a mere conceptual framework. It serves as a dynamic mechanism, an empowering tool, and a community that centers the experiences of Black people, offering them access to a future teeming with boundless possibilities. Their conversation exemplifies the transformative potential of Afrofuturism in reshaping legal practice and propelling social justice efforts forward.

Like the work of Phillips and Ayewa, the Future IDs project employs storytelling, art, and collaboration to challenge stigmas and biases surrounding reentry after incarceration. Under the leadership of Gregory Sale, this project aims to collectively transform the reentry experience by amplifying the voices of formerly incarcerated individuals and those navigating their post-incarceration identities (Lee 2019). Future IDs provides an alternative framework that centers marginalized voices, promotes personal transformation, and facilitates community healing.

Through art, activism, and collaborative approaches, such as represented in Figure 3.1, the Future IDs project reimagines narratives, challenges oppressive systems, and creates spaces for marginalized communities to shape their own futures. By offering a pathway to collective liberation and inspiring transformative change, this endeavor fosters a narrative shift in the reentry process after incarceration (Future IDs n.d.a). It highlights the transformative journeys of individuals and empowers them to reshape their identities as they reintegrate into society, challenging traditional narratives. The project also aims to shift power dynamics and provide a platform for collective envisioning of a more inclusive and supportive world (Future IDs n.d.a).

FIGURE 3.1. Future IDs artists Candice Price and Emiliano Lopez in discussion with Roberto Bedoya (arts administrator/thought leader) during the Art and Justice Summit on Alcatraz.
(Photo credit: Peter Merts.)

To guide their collaborative efforts, the Future IDs team has developed a set of guiding considerations for engagement. These principles emphasize the importance of sharing control with collaborators, respecting diverse artistic approaches, and maintaining flexibility and openness to others' expertise (Future IDs, n.d.b). The guidelines also address ethical considerations, power dynamics, hospitality, deep listening, and the delicate balance between aesthetics and advocacy in project objectives (Future IDs, n.d.b).

By adhering to these considerations, artists and collaborators involved in art and design practices can cultivate meaningful and effective relationships. The Future IDs Guiding Considerations provide valuable insights for building equitable and respectful collaborations, fostering mutual respect, trust, and open dialogue. These guidelines serve as essential tools for creating an environment where all participants can contribute their unique strengths and perspectives, working together toward a shared vision of transformative change.

Shift attention now to the Design Justice Network, an influential organization in the field of design, that puts forth a powerful vision that emphasizes the potential of design practices and processes to foster care, healing, liberation, joy, and deep sustainability (Design Justice Network n.d.). By recognizing the profound impact that design choices can have on individuals, policies, and economies, they advocate for a design process that is guided by the experiences and embodied knowledge of marginalized communities who are affected by intersecting systems of oppression.

The Design Justice Network offers a practical framework rooted in design principles that seeks to address hidden biases, power structures, and systemic inequities that often go unnoticed in the design process. Their transformative approach challenges traditional notions of design and provides a compelling set of ethics for the design community (Design Justice Network n.d.). At its essence, their methodology employs liberatory experiences, practices, and tools that aim to empower marginalized voices and reshape the design landscape.

These approaches hold immense potential for informing the field of legal education, particularly as future generations call for tools, methods, and narratives to transform our justice system models. The strategies and principles espoused by the Design Justice Network can inspire the development of innovative approaches within legal education, promoting a more equitable and inclusive justice system (Design Justice Network n.d.). By incorporating these liberatory practices, the legal community can work toward dismantling oppressive structures and embracing a justice system that truly serves all individuals.

The field of legal design can benefit from studying and embracing the strategies and approaches employed by initiatives working within a community context through art and design for legal empowerment. These initiatives vividly highlight the transformative power of art, storytelling, collaboration, and community engagement in challenging oppressive systems, amplifying marginalized voices, and envisioning alternative futures rooted in justice, equity, and collective well-being.

The potential for artists and designers to significantly enhance legal design is evident through their diverse tactics, principles, methods, and strategies. By integrating these approaches, legal design can purposefully employ a cocreation process that effectively engages marginalized communities, challenges power dynamics, and fosters the development of more inclusive frameworks. This deliberate integration sets the stage for a participatory, accessible, and empathetic justice system. By embracing the transformative power of art and design, legal design not only drives social transformation and addresses systemic inequities but also meets the diverse needs and aspirations of marginalized individuals. To shape a truly inclusive legal framework that genuinely centers marginalized voices, it is crucial for legal design to meticulously study, explore, and wholeheartedly embrace the profound impact of this type of legal empowerment work.

3.5 INTEGRATING TRAUMA-INFORMED DESIGN AND LAW IN EDUCATION

To meet the call to action, legal education professionals must create educational spaces that inspire students to use their imaginations in addressing the concerns surrounding systems shaped by harmful legal norms. It is crucial for our collective methods, ideas, and techniques to expand across disciplines, seeking new ways of utilizing the law in both legal and design education to break the perpetual cycle of harm. Restorative justice and transformational justice offer design approaches rooted in repairing past harms, promoting healing, and transforming existing systems and structures.

Trauma-informed design serves as a catalyst for new approaches that bridge and strengthen connections between legal advocacy, legal education, and design. To confront the injustices within our fields, legal designers and design educators must integrate trauma-informed design and law into their pedagogy. By doing so, they can effectively address the repercussions of multiple marginalization, oppression, and unequal access to justice.

Acknowledging and understanding the profound influence of historical trauma is imperative in tackling the "wicked problems" present in our legal design work. Trauma-informed design creates the conditions necessary to approach design with a lens focused on healing and improving the well-being of individuals and communities. Purvi Shah, a founder of the Movement Lab, states that social unrest offers us an opportunity to reenvision what needs repair (Shah 2018). Rachael Dietkus, an expert in design research, social work, and trauma-responsive practices, emphasizes the importance of integrating trauma-informed approaches into our work.

Integrating trauma-informed approaches into our work, Dietkus states that this process requires understanding how our own experiences of trauma influence our design methodologies. This transformative shift calls for changes in education, training, and practice, encouraging a relational and ethical approach to designing with, by, and for others. It fosters a holistic understanding of people and their environments (Dietkus 2022).

Social movements act as catalysts, shedding light on the deep-rooted inequities and injustices within society. They offer pathways for potential transformation and reform. Social movements encourage the expression of alternative perspectives, fostering alignment, shared vision, and the creation of narratives that embody collective imagination. This process of reimagining society plays a pivotal role in community organizing, healing, and social transformation. Through these collective efforts, we can create educational spaces that promote healing, dignity, and social justice, breaking free from the cycle of harm perpetuated by harmful legal norms.

3.6 CONCLUSION

In conclusion, the integration of trauma-informed design and law holds immense potential for driving transformative change in education and practice. By creating educational spaces that foster imaginative thinking, we can effectively address harmful legal norms and promote social justice. Approaches such as restorative justice and transformational justice prioritize healing, repairing past harms, and transforming existing systems and structures.

This integration acts as a catalyst, forging connections between legal advocacy, legal education, creativity, and design. Through radical collaboration, individuals from diverse backgrounds can tackle complex societal challenges in law, legal education, and social justice. This interdisciplinary approach encourages innovative possibilities and initiates transformative shifts.

To confront injustices in our fields, we must actively incorporate trauma-informed design and law into pedagogy. This integration allows us to address the repercussions of marginalization, oppression, and unequal access to justice. Recognizing the profound influence of historical trauma is essential for effectively addressing the intricate problems inherent in legal design work.

Furthermore, social movements play a pivotal role as catalysts, drawing attention to societal inequities and providing avenues for transformation and reform. They foster alternative perspectives, shared visions, and narratives that embody collective imagination. Tangible examples and case studies demonstrate the impact of social movements in tackling complex challenges in law, legal education, and social justice.

To act, educators in design and law must actively engage in nurturing the imagination of students and collaborating with them to envision a world beyond the limitations of the current legal framework. This involves advocating for trauma-informed design in educational institutions, supporting social movements, and fostering interdisciplinary collaboration between legal and design professionals.

Looking ahead, actively reimagining our social-legal systems becomes our collective responsibility. By teaching new strategies in legal education and codesigning solutions with movement leaders and advocates, we can work toward shifting narratives and power structures in the legal system. Together, we can create a world that prioritizes health, dignity, equity, healing, human rights, and transformative justice.

However, achieving this transformation is not an effortless task. It demands a shift away from traditional pedagogical approaches that have long dominated our educational institutions. It requires intentionally nurturing a collaborative and participatory ethos within and beyond the classroom. Fostering imagination and critical consciousness among students is crucial, as it enables them to recognize their roles as agents of change in society.

Throughout this chapter, I explored various dimensions of this effort, ranging from the nuances of Community-Based Participatory Action Research (CBPAR) employed by NuLawLab to the Afrofuturist explorations of the Black Quantum Futurism Collective. These examples offer valuable lessons and models for educators and students, emphasizing the transformative potential of combining interdisciplinary practices with community-based action and advocacy.

Initiatives such as the East Boston Spatial Justice Lab, the Future IDs project, and the radical potential of trauma-informed design and law underscore the power of art, creativity, and collective action in addressing deep-rooted systemic inequities. They emphasize the importance of honoring and integrating the lived experiences, narratives, and perspectives of marginalized communities in the pursuit of social justice and transformative change.

The guiding principles of the Design Justice Network provide an ethical framework that recognizes and challenges power structures and biases within design practices. It emphasizes the need for equitable and respectful collaborations, grounding the design process in the embodied experiences of those marginalized by interlocking systems of oppression. This approach invites us to reimagine design and law as tools for liberation and healing rather than instruments of harm (Design Justice Network 2018).

The call for a trauma-informed approach in design and law underscores the crucial need to acknowledge and address the impacts of historical and ongoing trauma within our legal and educational systems. This necessitates a transformative shift in our pedagogical approaches, encouraging a relational and ethical engagement with a design centered on the well-being and healing of individuals and communities.

REFERENCES

Adebisi, Foluke. 2020. "Decolonising the Law School: Presences, Absences, Silences... and Hope." *The Law Teacher* 54, no. 4 (November): 471–74. https://doi:10.1080/03069400.2020.1827774.

Akbar, Amna. 2018. "Toward a Radical Imagination of Law." *New York University Law Review* 93, no. 3 (June): 405–79. http://dx.doi.org/10.2139/ssrn.3061917.

Barrón-López, Laura, and Tess Conciatori. 2022. "Charlottesville Reckons with Trauma 5 Years after a Deadly White Supremacist Rally." *PBS News Hour*, August 12. www.pbs.org/newshour/show/charlottesville-reckons-with-trauma-5-years-after-a-deadly-white-supremacist-rally.

Black Quantum Futurism. n.d.a. "About." Accessed May 28, 2023. www.blackquantumfuturism.com/about.

n.d.b. "Community Futurisms." www.blackquantumfuturism.com/community-futurisms.

A Blade of Grass. 2018. "Black Quantum Futurism." https://abladeofgrass.org/fellows/black-quantum-futurism/.

Cochrane, Emily, and Jessica Jaglois. 2023. "Autopsy Shows Tyre Nichols Died of Head Injuries from Police Beating." *The New York Times*, May 4. www.nytimes.com/2023/05/04/us/politics/tyre-nichols-autopsy.html.

Dabaghi, Karma. 2022. "Beyond Design Thinking and into Speculative Futures in Legal Design." *Proceedings of DRS Biennial Conference Series, Design Research Society, Bilbao, Spain, June 25 – July 3, 2022*. London: Design Research Society.

Design Justice Network. n.d. "Read the Principles." Last modified 2018. Accessed May 28, 2023. https://designjustice.org/read-the-principles.

Dietkus, Rachael. 2022. "The Call for Trauma-Informed Design Research and Practice." *Design Management Review* 33, no. 2 (June): 26–31.

Farbman, Daniel. 2022. "A Commons in the Master's House." *Fordham Law Review* 90, no. 5 (April): 2061–87. https://ir.lawnet.fordham.edu/flr/vol90/iss5/8.

Future IDs. n.d.a. "About Future IDs." Accessed March 27, 2023. https://futureids.com/info/about/.

n.d.b. "Future IDs Guiding Considerations." Accessed January 28, 2023. https://futureids.com/info/future-ids-guiding-considerations/.

Grandoit, Alice. n.d. "Adrienne Maree Brown on Creating the Future." *Deem Journal*, n.d. www.deemjournal.com/stories/amb.

Hassan, Adeel. 2023. "When Are the Police Allowed to Use Deadly Force?" *The New York Times*, January 26. www.nytimes.com/2023/01/26/us/police-deadly-excessive-force.html.

Houh, Emily M., and Kristin Kalsen. 2014. "It's Critical: Legal Participatory Action Research." *Michigan Journal of Race & Law* 19, no. 2 (October): 287–347. https://repository.law.umich.edu/mjrl/vol19/iss2/3.

Imarisha, Walidah. 2015. "How Science Fiction Can Re-envision Justice." *Bitch Media*, February 11. Accessed May 28, 2023. www.bitchmedia.org/article/rewriting-the-future-prison-abolition-science-fiction.

Lee, Lloyd. 2019. "Future IDs at Alcatraz Reveals a Road to Reintegration." *San Francisco Examiner*, July 25. www.sfexaminer.com/culture/future-ids-at-alcatraz-reveals-a-road-to-reintegration/article_cf942f03-a7c3-5f34-b6a5-57da93e1cfbd.html.

Levin, Sam. 2023. "Teacher and Cousin of Black Lives Matter Founder 'Tased to Death' by LAPD." *The Guardian*, January 12. www.theguardian.com/us-news/2023/jan/11/black-lives-matter-co-founder-cousin-killed-los-angeles-police.

Lewin, Kurt. 1946. "Action Research." *Journal of Social Issues* 2, no. 4 (November): 34–46. https://doi.org/10.1111/j.1540-4560.1946.tb02295.x.

Lindsay, James. n.d. "Epistemic Violence." *New Discourses*. Last modified July 13, 2020. Accessed May 28, 2023. https://newdiscourses.com/tftw-epistemic-oppression/.

"Mapping Police Violence." Last modified 2023. https://mappingpoliceviolence.org.

National Equity Project. n.d. "Liberatory Design." Accessed May 28, 2023. www.nationalequityproject.org/frameworks/liberatory-design.

Pasley, Will, and Traci Yoder. 2016. "Changing Legal Pedagogy." www.nlg.org/wp-content/uploads/2016/03/Changing-Legal-Pedagogy.pdf.

PolicyLink. n.d.a. "Angela Glover Blackwell." Last modified 2023. www.policylink.org/aboutUs/staff/angela-glover-blackwell.

n.d.b. "Rasheedah Phillips: Director of Housing." Last modified 2023. www.policylink.org/aboutUs/staff/rasheedah-phillips.

Rittel, H. W. J., and M. M. Webber. 1973. "Dilemmas in a General Theory of Planning." *Policy Science* 4: 155–169. https://doi.org/10.1007/BF01405730.

Shah, Purvi. 2018. "Rebuilding the Ethical Compass of Law." *Hofstra Law Review* 47, no. 1, Article 4 (Fall): 11–18. https://scholarlycommons.law.hofstra.edu/cgi/viewcontent.cgi?article=3039&context=hlr.

Spade, Dean. 2010. "For Those Considering Law School." www.deanspade.net/wp-content/uploads/2010/10/For-Those-Considering-Law-School.pdf.

Stony Brook University. n.d. "What's a Wicked Problem?" Accessed 2023. www.stonybrook.edu/commcms/wicked-problem/about/What-is-a-wicked-problem.php.

Thorne, Syd. 2021. "Through Critique and Beyond: Speculative Fiction as a Tool of Critical Pedagogy." M.A. capstone, University of San Francisco, USFCA Repository Master's Projects and Capstones (1288). https://repository.usfca.edu/capstone/1288.

UCLA Luskin Institute on Inequality and Democracy. n.d. "Ananya Roy." Accessed August 5, 2023. https://challengeinequality.luskin.ucla.edu/ananya-roy/.

II

What Legal Design Can Do

Case Studies across Sectors

4

Dignity in the Courtroom

Judges and Self-Represented Litigants

Jennifer Leitch

4.1 INTRODUCTION

For the self-represented litigant (SRL), entering the courtroom can be a daunting experience. The setting is intimidating, the personnel speak a language all their own, and the processes are unfamiliar; there is an alienating ambience of formality and gravity. The consequence for many SRLs is an inability to participate in the process in a meaningful way. This results in and is precipitated by a loss of dignity that is associated with the belief that they are not welcome in that process. Rather they are considered a peculiarity or, worse, a problem to be contained. This has lasting consequences for the individual's ability to participate in the adjudicative process as well as their perceptions of the fairness and justness of the adversarial process.

However, this does not need to be the case. Crucial to SRLs' experiences in the courtroom is the role played by the judge. Empirical research has demonstrated that the judge may have a negative or positive impact on the SRL's experience in the courtroom. Key to the SRL's evaluation of their experience is the extent to which they were accepted as a critical part of the process and thereby treated with respect and dignity. Given this relationship between the SRL's perception of their treatment by the judge and their overall evaluation of the process and their role within it, this chapter will examine ideas of dignity in the context of proceedings in the civil justice system with a focus on the role judges can and do play in furthering or degrading notions of dignity in the courtroom. This examination is based on qualitative research involving SRLs in adjudicative processes. However, it is not sufficient to simply report on qualitative observations; it is also important to examine the ways in which changes in judicial attitudes, approaches, and practices might improve and positively enhance SRL's experiences in the courtroom.

Section 4.2 will explore the particular situation of self-representation in the civil justice system. Section 4.3 will consider some different aspects of dignity that arise within the context of a proceeding in the civil justice system. In considering how dignity is either fostered or deflated in the courtroom, it is important to consider the role of the judge as well as judicial perceptions of and attitudes toward SRLs. Section 4.4 supports these accounts with research that has explored SRLs' experiences in the courtroom. Finally, this chapter will canvass different approaches that seek to foster SRLs' sense of dignity in the courtroom. Underlying such a shift in judicial approaches is the belief that fostering dignity encourages and promotes meaningful participation by those entering the justice system, and in turn, providing opportunities for meaningful participation enhances an individual's sense of personal dignity. Together, meaningful participation in decision-making processes and enhanced dignity promote the administration of justice more broadly.

4.2 THE RISE OF SELF-REPRESENTATION

There is a fundamental shift occurring in the composition of the justice system. In some legal settings, SRLs comprise the overwhelming majority of litigants. For example, in the civil justice system, SRLs currently make up approximately 50% of litigants. And in some urban centres, up to 80% of family law litigants are unrepresented.[1] The reality is, therefore, that self-representation is becoming as much the norm as the exception. In terms of the reasons for a sharp rise in self-representation,[2] most individuals represent themselves in civil or family court because they cannot afford legal services. Statistical data also show that a significant number of SRLs may start with legal counsel, but as their matter drags on and/or becomes more complicated, the clients run out of money and are left to represent themselves. In fact, one recent statistic indicated that approximately 68% of a sample of SRLs had started with counsel (Sullivan and Macfarlane 2021).

For most litigants entering the civil justice system without legal training, the organization and operation of the legal process are, at best, stressful to navigate and, at worst, paralyzingly indecipherable and inaccessible. Furthermore, SRLs are thrust into the "deep end of the pool" of litigation when their counsel withdraws services for the client's lack of payment partway through the case. Consequently, the reality is that without counsel, SRLs are less likely to be successful in their legal matter

[1] See https://representingyourselfcanada.com for statistics on self-representation in Canada. In the US context, Deborah L. Rhode suggests that "[A]n estimated four-fifths of the individual legal needs of the poor, and a majority of the needs of middle-income Americans, remain unmet" (Rhode 2009). A 2001 article suggested that the number of SRLs in Ontario's Family Court rose by 500% between 1995 and 1999 (Cohen 2001, 40). Recent statistics in the United States suggest that 76% of litigants in non-family civil courts are unrepresented, and the vast majority of these litigants are defendants. In the family law context, the number is closer to 80–90% of litigants being unrepresented (Carpenter 2017).

[2] In the US context, some of the earliest statistics suggest that the increase in self-representation over the past fifty years is dramatic. For example, in 1971, only 1% of California's family litigants were self-represented; by 2004, 80% of family cases included at least one SRL by the time a case was adjudicated (Judicial Council of California 2004).

(Macfarlane, Trask, and Chesney 2015). In conjunction with this lack of success, SRLs also experience a sense of disempowerment and disengagement that is reflective of being compelled to participate in a process for which they are untrained and inexperienced. Given SRLs' alienating experiences in the civil justice system, it is not difficult to see the correlation between these experiences and SRLs' sense of dignity (Felstiner, Abel, and Sarat 1981; Macfarlane 2013).

For the individual obligated to represent themselves in the civil justice system, there are a multitude of challenges. In fact, the very organization and operation of the adversarial model are problematic for SRLs; it is a procedural system that was built exclusively by and for lawyers and judges whereby two represented parties bring their case before an impartial third-party adjudicator. The principles of party autonomy and party prosecution result in the parties being held responsible for the preparation and presentation of their case. Consistent with this structure is the underlying assumption that the parties are self-motivated to present their strongest case (and strongest challenge of their opponent's case) and are equally resourced in this undertaking. Traditionally, this task is undertaken by the parties' legally trained representatives who were trained in the rules of courts, the relevant substantive law, as well as the presentation of cases (Brooks 2010). This arrangement allows the adjudicator to play a passive role as the recipient of the legal information and arguments presented by the parties' legal representatives (Brooks 2010). However, the introduction of SRLs into the adversarial process has challenged the workability of this process, particularly where one party has access to trained and knowledgeable counsel and the opposing party is unrepresented. In such a case, the SRLs has been likened to a novice boxer being forced into the ring, with one arm tied behind their back, against a seasoned and stronger opponent.[3]

Regarding dignity, SRLs' challenges can be broadly divided into procedural and substantive categories. With respect to the latter, SRLs must "learn" the substantive law relevant to their legal issues; this engages a need for legal research and access to public legal education resources that help break down some of the more complicated legal principles at play in their legal issues. From an access to justice perspective, much work remains to be done in assisting SRLs prior to their attendance in court and to support their substantive positions.

However, the focus in this chapter will be on the challenges (and possible reforms) associated with the procedural and practical aspects of self-representation before an adjudicator. For the SRL who has never been in a courtroom before, it is not difficult to appreciate how daunting an experience this might be. This is particularly true given the overwhelming number of rules and customs that a SRL must learn and navigate in the civil justice system. For instance, even appreciating when to and when not to speak in court must be learned. Added to this are the challenges associated with understanding the relevant procedural rules that include issues of timing,

[3] *Girao v. Cunningham*, 2020 ONCA 260 (April 20, 2021).

organization, and submission of relevant materials, order of presentations, and rules of evidence. All these elements of the process are learned by lawyers through training, often watching more senior lawyers and amassing courtroom experience. By contrast, the SRL is often learning as they go, with significant and negative implications for their case. Moreover, unlike the trained lawyer representing a client, the SRL is personally impacted by the outcomes of the matter. Essentially, it is their lives that are directly affected by the decision, potentially affecting their employment, housing, or family relationships. The pressure of this ought not to be underestimated. Added to all these challenges is also the represented party's willingness to take strategic advantage of the SRL's lack of knowledge and experience (Leitch 2017b).

For the SRL, the consequences associated with these challenges are significant. First, there is, of course, the impact on legal outcomes; if you are unable to make use of the relevant procedure and rules of evidence that may assist your case (or that you must respond to defend your case), you are less likely to succeed. However, even when the SRL can familiarize themselves with the right information, there are the additional challenges associated with the effective deployment of that knowledge in the decision-making process (Greiner, Jimenez, and Lupica 2017, 1124). For the SRL, there are a multitude of steps that they must undertake, including initiating or responding to a legal problem, rearranging their schedule and other life responsibilities to participate in hearings, collecting and presenting evidence, and navigating through an alienating court system. The failure to deploy learned knowledge is linked to effects that include feeling a lack of agency and the presence of debilitating emotions such as fear, shame, guilt, or hopelessness. These emotions may be compounded by the sense of anxiety that many SRLs have about presenting their case in open court (Macfarlane 2013, 98). As noted, the ambience of formality and gravity reinforce a sense of anxiety that likely prevents an individual from effective self-representation (Steinberg 2015, 755; Greiner, Jimenez, and Lupica 2017, 1124).[4] Recent research in the field of effective self-help legal resources suggests that those attempting to handle their own legal case may suffer from an overtaxed mental and cognitive bandwidth associated with having to contend with various debilitating emotions. Moreover, SRLs expend an inordinate amount of energy to manage their case (Greiner, Jimenez, and Lupica 2017, 1128). Together all these challenges contribute to and reinforce feelings of frustration and disempowerment—a SRL's sense of dignity is reduced or even occluded.

4.3 SOME THOUGHTS ON DIGNITY IN THE CONTEXT OF THE CIVIL JUSTICE SYSTEM

Dignity may have different meanings depending on the context in which the concept is deployed. For instance, dignity in medically assisted suicide may engage

4 Nowhere is this more evident than in family law where self-represented litigants are addressing intensely personal and financial crisis.

ideas of bodily integrity and autonomy, as well as the right to make decisions about one's own medical care and life.[5] However, dignity in the context of the provision of public services may engage ideas of equality of treatment, respect, privacy, and meaningful access (Kim 2021, 93). In the context of SRLs, the idea of dignity engages a consideration of human worth. An evaluation of a person's worth often considers how she or he is treated by other individuals, in institutional settings or in society more broadly. Systems of organization in society (including systems of laws) work more effectively and fairly when there is mutual respect between individuals (Fuller 1965, 665; Luban 2010). Mutual respect requires that we think about how we treat others and how we expect others to treat us. However, within the context of the justice system, perceptions of mutual respect and, by association, dignity are often positional. There is often no question of the respect expected by and afforded to the adjudicator. However, the respect given to other participants may be less clear. Specifically, the presence of SRLs in the justice system raises difficult questions about who is afforded dignity, on what basis, and how dignity may be fostered or denied. The implications of these questions are that perceptions of dignity (or the lack of dignity) further engage questions of fairness, meaningful participation, and justice in the justice system.

In considering the nature of dignity within the context of a courtroom, it is important to remember that SRLs base their assessment of the process on their treatment in court. The SRL (unlike the represented party) does not have a lawyer who can explain the process and/or the meaning or reasons behind the judge's interactions with the party. Thus, the SRLs' experiences in court have a profound impact on their perceptions about the respect they were afforded (or not) and their ability (or lack thereof) to participate in the system. Considerations such as whether the individual felt they were listened to, treated kindly, or, alternatively, ignored, overlooked, or dismissed play a significant role in their assessment. Thus, whether SRLs felt that they had been listened to and heard becomes significant (Leitch 2016). Collectively, these considerations inform the individual's sense of self-worth, their views about their place within the process, and their perceptions about the overall legitimacy of the process.

More specifically, the evidence gathered from qualitative interviews with SRLs suggests that the way in which the SRL was treated by a judge directly impacted their sense of being taken seriously and their corresponding sense of dignity and self-worth. Additionally, empirical research shows that the politeness and honesty exhibited by adjudicators were factors that impact the individual's assessment of fairness (Tyler 1988, 128). Thus, there are important links between dignity, respect, and the SRL's broader views about their ability to participate in decision-making processes as well as the overall fairness of that process. However, what is also

5 *Carter v. Canada (Attorney General)*, 2015 SCC 5 (February 6, 2015).

interesting about this correlation is that it may be relatively small positive (or negative) acts that ultimately sway the individual's feeling of dignity (Leitch 2016).[6]

Finally, within the context of civil proceedings, there is a link between dignity and empowerment. When individuals are treated with respect and able to develop feelings of self-worth, there is a corresponding sense of empowerment inculcated in the individual (Leitch 2016). Individuals who are treated with respect and who believe that they have been (and will be) heard within a process are likely to feel empowered by such experiences. Where such empowerment is encouraged, there is likely to be a strengthening of broader and stronger participation (Leitch 2016). By contrast, disregarding SRLs' dignity negatively impacts open debate as well as discourse and dissemination of information and ideas, all of which are crucial to legal empowerment as a necessary component of decision-making processes (United Nations 2008, 3–4). The question that flows from this link between dignity and empowerment is how legal processes might be rejigged or reimagined such that dignity is encouraged. Again, within the context of the civil justice system, the role of the judge is a key factor in answering this question. As such, the following section will consider judicial views about self-representation as well as how judicial conduct affects SRL's experiences.

4.4 THE ROLE OF THE JUDGE AND THE IMPACT ON SELF-REPRESENTED LITIGANTS

In the adversarial system, judges are expected to reflect impartiality and neutrality in their decision-making. Impartiality serves to promote confidence by others in judicial decisions as well as respect for the overall administration of justice. Maintaining impartiality and, to a lesser extent, neutrality is an important principle of procedural justice. In practical terms, this commitment to impartiality and neutrality is affected by the stance judges adopt within a hearing; they are supposed to represent the "neutral umpire" who passively receives the information, arguments, and evidence presented to them by the parties in an action (Brooks 2010; Leitch 2017). However, a more critical evaluation of "fairness" within the decision-making process questions this commitment to passivity.

As previously noted, the rationale for passivity assumes that cases involve a contest between lawyers who are equally well resourced and versed in both the procedural and substantive law. However, in many cases, this assumption is a fiction (Brooks 2010). The reality is that a significant portion of civil litigation encompasses unequally resourced parties. In cases involving individuals versus institutions, government, or

6 In one empirical example, a judge overseeing a self-represented litigant's hearing moved her matter to the end of the day when the court was less busy (and therefore less of an audience of lawyers and clients), and as a result, the self-represented litigant felt less intimidated or nervous speaking in court.

corporations and even in the context of family law, where the parties are both private individuals, there is usually a power imbalance between the two parties (Rosen-Zvi and Fisher 2013; Sabbeth 2015). The consequence is that inequality between the parties results in the judicial process being manipulated by the stronger party, often through the weaponization of procedures and resources. In the context of self-representation (especially when pitted against represented parties), this consequence is both exacerbated and more prevalent. Given the presence of this inequality in both process and outcome, SRLs are disproportionately impacted by the judge's passivity.

Moreover, for SRLs, the judge's passive role is often viewed through a different lens, which takes judicial passivity as disinterest in their plight or an unwillingness to assist them. This perception is further complicated by the fact that SRLs remain outsiders when it comes to the language and operation of law in the courtroom, while judges and lawyers are privy to an insider's view of the law. Thus, SRLs view judicial passivity toward them in light of an ongoing dialogue between the judge and the lawyers in the courtroom, in which they are not included. This further reinforces the SRLs' perceptions that they are extraneous to or unwelcome in the process. Further complicating this dynamic is the fact that asymmetrical litigation (including a represented and an unrepresented party) raises a tension for lawyers as well. Namely, that represented parties expect their counsel to act as their zealous advocates who do not assist unrepresented opponents. In addressing this tension, the adjudicator may be inclined to rely on the tried-and-tested method of the adjudicator serving as the neutral umpire.

Finally, it is also important to remember that judges are imbued with a high degree of respect and authority within their own courtroom. This viewpoint is particularly true for SRLs whose perceptions of judges are infused with mystique and notions of power. Moreover, many SRLs see the judge as belonging to a particular socioeconomic class that is far removed from the socioeconomic circumstances of the SRL's life (Leitch 2016). For these reasons, the sitting judge represents a very powerful and often alienating figure to the SRL.

As previously noted, empirical research has examined SRLs' experiences in the courtroom and suggests that SRLs interaction with adjudicators has a serious impact on the SRL's perceptions about their ability to be heard, and their corresponding perceptions of self-worth (Macfarlane 2013, 98; Leitch 2017a, 322–23).[7] For example, some SRLs describe experiences in court that left them feeling embarrassed or ineffectual in representing themself. SRLs have described being in court like being in the "hot seat" where SRLs may be scolded for not knowing when to speak, the proper formatting of their materials, or generally how to conduct themselves in court. This experience is compounded by the fact that a reprimand from the adjudicator often takes place in a crowded courtroom populated with a variety of

[7] In one account, a SRL with a brain injury was told to stop writing when the judge was talking to her.

lawyers and clients, which further diminishes the SRL's perception of their value or ability to participate. Even without admonishment, SRLs report that they often experience hostility, rudeness, eye-rolling, and impatience from adjudicators as they attempt to make their case. While SRLs may be dismissed and/or their submissions downplayed, they also express concern over the way in which adjudicators may have particular conversations with the lawyers representing an opposing party (Leitch 2016, 257).[8] This is also problematic in situations where the adjudicator advises that they "do not have to hear from the self-represented party."[9] For the SRL who is new to court proceedings this has a very different implication than for the experienced litigator. The experienced litigator may recognize that the judge does not need to hear from the SRL because they understand and accept their submissions. However, from the SRL's perspective, the judge is either ignoring or dismissing them. The result is that the SRL feels isolated within the hearing – unable to understand what is happening and unable to contribute to the conversation.

Unfortunately, some SRLs' experiences in court are reflective of lingering attitudes toward the presence of SRL in the civil justice system. It is often assumed that SRLs choose to represent themselves and/or cannot keep a lawyer on retainer because they are difficult to deal with. However, the reality is that the overwhelming number of individuals who represent themselves do so because they have no choice; they cannot afford to hire or continue to retain a lawyer. Additionally, SRLs are often viewed as vexatious litigants who want to take on the system and tie up court resources with frivolous legal claims. Linked to these attitudes and grounded in traditional notions of the adversarial system are assumptions about how an adjudicator ought to interact with a SRL in the courtroom. Assuming incorrectly that the SRL either chooses to be there or is raising frivolous claims, SRLs are advised by the adjudicator that the individual will receive "no leniency" or special treatment from the court and will be expected to perform like legal counsel (Macfarlane 2013).[10] This type of commentary reflects a serious disconnect between lingering perceptions of SRLs and the realities of obtaining counsel in the civil justice system. Moreover, these continuing attitudes serve to negatively impact the SRLs' experiences in the court and further contribute to the individual's belief that they do not belong in the process.

[8] In one example, a self-represented litigant reported that the judges repeatedly referred to the Latin legal term *nunc pro tunc* without every stopping to ask if the SRL was familiar with that term; in another example, the SRL was asked to explain their case in one or two sentences: a challenging task even for an experienced litigator.

[9] *Grand River Conservation Authority v. Ramdas*, 2021 ONCA 815.

[10] This is despite the Canadian Judicial Council's *Statement of Principles on Self Represented Litigants and Accused Persons* (September 2006) and the decision of *Pintea v. Johns* [2017] 1SCR 470. A recent articulation of such a position was outlined in a letter from the Canadian Judicial Council (CJC) responding to a complaint from a SRL. In that correspondence, the CJC advised the SRL that the individual is expected to know and follow the rules of court and that the role of the judge is to remind the individual that they would be better served by retaining counsel.

4.5 A DIFFERENT APPROACH

The growth of self-representation and SRLs' negative experiences in the courtroom signal that a different approach to adjudication is needed. Starting from the premise that most self-represented litigants do not choose to participate without counsel, it is incumbent on those working within the justice system to think about how the system might be reorganized to better account for the influx of SRLs. Crucial to this undertaking is the role of the judge. Within their individual courtrooms, judges have significant power in setting the tone of the proceeding, organizing the order of the process, and ensuring that the parties are treated with dignity and fairness. Therefore, if we want to ensure that nonrepresented parties are treated with dignity, the judge has a vital role to play in facilitating meaningful participation within their courtroom.

A critical first step in undertaking such an evaluation involves engaging those who have historically been excluded from the conversation. In designing more inclusive courtrooms for all participants, the architects engaged in a project in New South Wales, Australia stated that, "seeking the input of people beyond those with the power to authorize construction offers opportunities to subvert elite/traditional conventions about courtroom conduct" (Rowden and Jones 2018, 326; see also Sangiorgi and Clark 2004). While we are addressing attitudes and process design rather than physical design, the sentiment remains. The lived experiences of those engaged in civil court proceedings can provide important insights into how the process is experienced by those who otherwise feel like outsiders. In addition to engaging with SRLs regarding their experiences using the system, it is important that more efforts are put into dialogue with members of the bench. What are their experiences? Where do they see SRLs struggling the most? How do they think about addressing some of these challenges? Early research sometimes placed an exclusive focus on lawyers and judges, but the goals of future research should be for the views of the judiciary to compliment, rather than overshadow, the views and experiences of the SRLs. Instead, the purpose is to encourage a dialogue in which various stakeholders are engaged in problem-solving. Importantly, in undertaking this research, researchers need to draw on additional fields of study such as sociology, anthropology, and psychology. These added perspectives can assist researchers in better understanding the dynamics of human interaction, communication, and dispute resolution and then applying these understandings to the context of the civil justice courtroom (Greiner, Jimenez, and Lupica 2017, 1124).

In addition to engaging in a sustained research agenda, there are also more immediate and essential changes that might ensure more meaningful participation by SRLs and, by extension, a commitment to mutual respect and dignity. Many of these reforms anticipate a different attitude and role for the adjudicator. First, there is a need for a conscious shift in how adjudicators treat SRLs in the courtroom. At its most basic, this shift contemplates treating SRLs with empathy. While SRLs are often concerned about making mistakes or making an incorrect statement, some patience from the adjudicator can go a long way in signalling to SRLs that their voice is heard and listened to. In exhibiting empathy, an adjudicator may adopt an approach that includes allowing the individual an opportunity to tell their story in their own words, reflecting to the individual what the adjudicator believes the individual to be saying, and inquiring as to whether there were any missed points or clarifications required when the SRL completes a submission. Consistent with principles of active listening, these are some of the ways an adjudicator might demonstrate that the individual is being listened to and heard.

Related to adopting a more empathetic approach is the deployment of stress reduction strategies. Again, if we understand that heightened levels of anxiety are likely to interfere with an individual's cognitive performance, then taking steps to reduce the SRL's anxiety is likely to positively impact a proceeding. While this does not automatically assume that, with lowered stress levels, the SRL will obtain a different outcome in the proceeding, it does reflect a different approach to the process that encourages meaningful participation (Tyler 1988).[11]

The empirical research also suggests that where adjudicators engaged with SRLs, the SRLs had more positive perceptions of the process. A key indication of the adjudicator's engagement with the parties is the degree to which the adjudicator took steps to ensure that the process is understood by all the participants. In cases involving SRLs, ensuring that the process is understood may require that, at the outset of the proceeding, the adjudicator explains the different aspects of the proceedings. This may include the order of the proceeding, when a party may speak, and what different documents might be required at different stages of the proceeding. Adjudicators may also articulate the decision-making steps that they anticipate engaging in to make a decision, including the elements of the *prima facie* case and the defences that may be raised (Zorza 2002). Once the proceeding has commenced, the adjudicator may also stop along the way to add more detail as the hearing proceeds and ensure that the participants continue to understand what is happening and why. Explaining the steps as well as the basic expectations of courtroom protocol will serve to alleviate some of the "unknowns" for SRLs that take up much-needed cognitive bandwidth. In short, such steps will reduce alienation and enhance dignity.

On a more systemic level, the redesign of the adjudicator's role requires a critical evaluation of what procedural reform in the field of evidence-gathering is likely to facilitate the SRL's participation but not undermine the overall legitimacy of the hearing. In this regard, systemic reform engages principles of active adjudication in which the adjudicator takes on a more active role in the presentation of the parties'

[11] Tyler's research on procedural fairness suggests that, independent of the outcomes reached, individuals assess the fairness of a proceeding (as well as legitimacy of outcomes) on their ability to be heard and participate in the decision-making.

evidence (Flaherty 2015, 119). Reforms may span conduct that ranges from adjudicators posing more questions of the parties when they present their evidence to adjudicators being involved in the ordering of evidence before a hearing and engaging in discussions of what evidence would be required by a specific party (Flaherty 2015, 119). A further reform contemplates more single-judge case management where a judge is assigned to a case involving a SRL at the outset of the matter and maintains oversight through to the end of trial (Superior Court of Justice 2019). Among others, the strength of this is that SRLs are not required to constantly restart the presentation of their case at each hearing, and judges avoid the recurring problem of seeking clarification on the status of a case from a represented party. Finally, a more radical course of reform involves the designing of SRL courtrooms where specially trained judges oversee hearings with SRLs. These courts may include some elements of traditional civil proceedings (i.e., presentation of evidence) but also considers the unique nonlegal position of the SRLs appearing before them. While this represents a more comprehensive overhaul of certain civil justice proceedings, it offers the potential of ensuring that as SRLs continue to enter the civil justice system, there is a process that legitimately allows for their meaningful engagement.

4.6 CONCLUSION

For the self-represented litigant, there is an undeniable link between the ability to participate in the decisions being made about them and their sense of individual dignity. Very simply, those who feel that they are heard are more likely to believe they are valued and legitimately part of the process. As it currently stands, the courtroom is an alienating process that is neither designed nor operated with SRLs in mind. It is urgent that this change from both a fairness perspective and a broader administration of justice perspective. Key to any response is the role of the decision-maker. Some reform will require structural reorganization of adversarial processes that must take account of often competing interests and considerations. However, there are also more immediate shifts in judicial attitudes and approaches that could serve to encourage and support SRLs' participation and, by extension, their sense of dignity.

REFERENCES

Brooks, Neil. 2010. "The Judge and the Adversary System." In *The Civil Litigation Process*, edited by Janet Walker, 89–119. Toronto, ON: Emond Montgomery Publications.

Carpenter, Anna E. 2017. "Active Judging and Access to Justice." (unpublished manuscript, February 3, 2017).

Cohen, Lynne. 2001. "Unrepresented Litigants." As cited in MacFarlane, Julie. 2003. "The NSRLP: Identifying & Meeting the Needs of SRL Final Report." https://scholar.uwindsor.ca/lawnsrlppubs/22.

Felstiner, William LF, Richard L. Abel, and Austin Sarat. 1981. "The Emergence and Transformation of Disputes - Naming, Blaming, Claiming." *Law & Society Review* 15, no. 3–4: 631–54. https://doi.org/10.2307/3053505.

Flaherty, Michelle. 2015. "Self-Represented Litigants, Active Adjudication and the Perception of Bias: Issues in Administrative Law." *Dalhousie Law Journal* 38, no. 1 (March): 120–46. Social Science Research Network (SSRN).

Fuller, Lon L. 1965. "A Reply to Professors Cohen and Dworkin." *Villanova Law Review* 10, no. 5 (Summer): 655–66.

Greiner, David J., Dalie Jimenez, and Lois Lupica. 2017. "Self-Help, Reimagined." *Indiana Law Journal* 92, no. 3 (Summer): 1119–73.

Judicial Council of California. 2004. "Statewide Action Plan for Serving Self-Represented Litigants." www.courts.ca.gov/documents/selfreplitsrept.pdf.

Kim, Miso. 2021. "A Study of Dignity as a Principle of Service Design." *International Journal of Design* 15, no. 3 (December): 87–100.

Leitch, Jennifer. 2016. "Having a Say: Democracy, Access to Justice and Self-Represented Litigants." Ph.D. diss., Osgoode Hall Law School of York University.

2017a. "Coming off the Bench: Self-Represented Litigants, Judges and the Adversarial Process." *The Advocate's Quarterly* 47 (April): 309–43.

2017b. "Lawyers and Self-Represented Litigants: An Ethical Change of Role?" *Canadian Bar Review* 95, no. 3: 669–705.

Luban, David. 2010. "The Rule of Law and Human Dignity: Re-examining Fuller's Canons." *Hague Journal on the Rule of Law* 2, no. 1 (May): 29–47. https://doi.org/10.1017/S1876404510100025.

Macfarlane, Julie. 2013. "The National Self-Represented Litigants Project: Identifying and Meeting the Needs of Self-Represented Litigants." *National Self-Represented Litigants Project*. www.lsuc.on.ca/uploadedFiles/For_the_Public/About_the_Law_Society/Convocation_Decisions/2014/Self-represented_project.pdf.

Macfarlane, Julie, Katrina Trask, and Erin Chesney. 2015. "The Use of Summary Judgment Procedures against Self-Represented Litigants: Efficient Case Management or Denial of Access to Justice?" *National Self-Represented Litigants Project*. https://representingyourselfcanada.com/nsrlp-research/page/2/.

National Center for State Courts and State Justice Institute. 2015. *The Landscape of Civil Litigation in State Courts*. Williamsburg, VA: National Center for State Courts. www.ncsc.org/~/media/Files/PDF/Research/CivilJusticeReport-2015.ashx.

Rhode, Deborah L. 2009. "Whatever Happened to Access to Justice?" *Loyola of Los Angeles Law Review* 42, no. 4 (June): 869–911.

Rosen-Zvi, Issachar, and Talia Fisher. 2013. "Overcoming Procedural Boundaries." *Virginia Law Review* 94, no. 1 (March): 79–155. JSTOR.

Rowden, Emma, and Diane Jones. 2018. "Design, Dignity and Due Process: The Construction of the Coffs Harbour Courthouse." *Law, Culture and the Humanities* 14, no. 2 (June): 317–36. https://doi.org/10.1177/1743872115612954.

Sabbeth, Kathryn. 2015. "The Prioritization of Criminal and Civil Cases and the Discounted Danger of Private Power." *Florida State University Law Review* 42, no. 4 (December): 889–936. Social Science Research Network (SSRN).

Sangiorgi, Daniela, and Brendon Clark. 2004. "Toward a Participatory Design Approach to Service Design." In *Proceedings of the Eighth Conference on Participatory Design*, 148–51. Toronto, ON: ACM Press.

Steinberg, Jessica K. 2015. "Demand Side Reform in the Poor People's Court." *Connecticut Law Review* 47, no. 3 (February): 741–805.

Sullivan, Charlotte, and Julie Macfarlane. 2021. "Tracking the Trends of the Self-Represented Litigant Phenomenon: Data from the National Self-Represented Litigants Project, 2019-2021." *National Self-Represented Litigants Project*. https://representingyourselfcanada.com/nsrlp-research/.

Superior Court of Justice. 2019. "Practice Advisory Concerning the Provincial Civil Case Management – One Judge Model." *Superior Court of Justice*, February 1. www.ontariocourts.ca/scj/practice/civil-case-management-pilot.

Tyler, Tom R. 1988. "What Is Procedural Justice? Criteria Used by Citizens to Assess the Fairness of Legal Procedures." *Law & Society Review* 22, no 1: 103–35. https://doi.org/10.2307/3053563.

United Nations. 2008. "Making the Law Work for Everyone: Report of the Commission on Legal Empowerment of the Poor." https://ycsg.yale.edu/sites/default/files/files/making_the_law_work.pdf.

Zorza, Richard. 2002. *The Self-Help Friendly Court: Designed from the Ground Up to Work for People Without Lawyers*. Williamsburg, VA: National Center for State Courts. www.srln.org/system/files/atachments/Zorza%20SRL%20Friendly%20Court.pdf.

5

Contracts for Dignity

Robert de Rooy

How wonderful it would be if we all, everyone of us, became agents of dignity.

—Archbishop Emeritus Desmond Tutu[1]

5.1 PEOPLE'S EXPERIENCE OF THE LEGAL SYSTEM

One of the first people to mention design as a science is Herbert Simon. He said: "Everyone designs who devises courses of action aimed at changing existing situations into preferred ones" (Simon 2008). Flowing from this idea, legal design aims to change suboptimal legal experiences into preferred ones. The key consideration of legal design is the experience of people in the system and how to improve it. This chapter will thus start with two short vignettes[2] bringing to the fore the legal experiences of people who have very basic reading and writing skills. Their experience matters, as they represent more than 14% of the worldwide population (UNESCO 2020).

Nonkululeko lives in a very modest house with her two young daughters. She works as a fruit picker from March to September and for the rest of the year survives on a government grant and by selling craftwork. In early March, the farms send word about where and when they hire pickers. Nonku goes early in the day to get as close to the farmgate as possible as the small crowd of job seekers swells behind her. Finally, the farm's HR manager arrives, and as she hands out contracts to the first 300 people, everyone is pushing to reach for a contract.

Nonku is lucky to grab one and stands in a queue at a table where there are pens to sign the contracts. When Nonku gets to the front of the line, a supervisor asks her if she has read and understood the contract. Nonku speaks fluent isiXhosa and good

[1] In 1984, Archbishop Emeritus Desmond Tutu received the Nobel Prize for Peace for his role in the opposition to apartheid in South Africa. The quote is from the preface, written by Archbishop Emeritus Desmond Tutu, of the book *Dignity: Its Essential Role in Resolving Conflict*, by Dana Hicks (Tutu 2013).

[2] These vignettes are fictionalised accounts of people who shared their stories with the author. Names and circumstances have been changed to prevent identification.

English and Afrikaans, but her reading and writing skills are rudimentary. Although she looked at the contract while waiting in the queue and noticed this year's rate per picked crate, she could not understand much else. Aware of the crowd behind her, she did not want to risk getting the job, and, like everyone else, she nodded and signed her name.

Three months later, Nonku is up all night with her youngest daughter, who is ill. She is distraught, and at dawn, she and her daughter take a taxi to the local clinic. They wait until the early afternoon to get attended to by the nurse. When she arrives at work the next day, the supervisor hands her a written warning for having been absent. He expresses sympathy but explains that this is what the contract says must happen if she is absent, and if it happens again, she will lose her job. He explains that he is under pressure to get the fruit off the trees and that if he does not know who is working or not, he cannot plan each day's work properly. While her co-workers all offer different advice, she is left feeling ashamed, anxious, and confused. What happens if her daughter has a relapse? Will she lose her job?

David works as a gardener. Hardworking, affable, and reliable, he earns double the minimum wage. He speaks fluent isiZulu and good English, but his reading and writing skills are basic. He lives in a modest house with his wife and four children. He saved about half of his monthly salary to buy a small colour TV. He goes to the nearest furniture store, a national brand. When he left the store, he had been sold a TV and cabinet at a total cost of two months' salary, on credit. He had tried hard to pay the installments, but he had missed some payments and the amount kept going up. Four years later, the furniture store is sending demands for payment that exceeds the original total purchase price and claims the items will be repossessed if not paid for.

David was unaware he had been sold insurance on the items and an extended warranty as part of the contract and that his numerous late payments accumulated fees and penalties, and that compound interest accumulated on everything at the maximum permissible rate. The credit agreement formally complied with the applicable regulations.

A reconciliation showed that all payments already made totalled nearly six times his monthly salary. Moreover, David ended up paying sixteen times what he had set out to pay when he went to the store that day simply because he signed a contract he could not read and the implications of which he could not understand. While the company made a profit, David feels anxious, ashamed, and confused. His only options to settle the balance are to go to a money lender who will charge abusive interests or to move his children from a higher-quality fee-paying school to a lower-quality free school, stunting their education and their prospects.

5.2 CONTRACTS AS SOCIETY'S ORGANISING PRINCIPLE

Although there is no settled definition of a contract, for present purposes contracts are defined as "legally valid agreements between two or more parties embracing some promise" (Morawetz 1925, 1). Contract law, which evolved to regulate when and how contracts are legally binding and enforceable by the state, is based on the principle that agreements that are freely entered into must be honoured. To express this principle, lawyers refer to the Latin expression *pacta sunt servanda* (Christie and McFarlane 2006). The moral authority of this principle is based on the concept of freedom of contract, which assumes that every person with legal capacity[3] has the autonomy to choose whether, with whom, and on what terms to contract.

The fundamental and pervasive role of contracts in our modern world cannot be overestimated. In his seminal work, *Capitalism and Freedom*, Milton Friedman held that there are two ways society can be organised: through coercion by a totalitarian state or cooperation through the market (Friedman 2020). While the reality is seldom this binary, following the fall of the Berlin Wall in 1989, the market economy has emerged as the world's dominant organising principle, and the dominant institutional foundation of a market economy is contracting (Foka-Kavalieraki and Hatzis 2009). Moreover, contract theory[4] holds that there is no essential difference between a firm and a market; they are both contracts (Smith 2004). Hence the statement by the Nobel Prize committee that "Modern economies are held together and governed by innumerable contracts" when introducing the relevance of awarding the Nobel Prize in Economic Sciences in 2016 to Oliver Hart and Bengt Holmström for their work as "valuable to the understanding of real-life contracts and institutions, as well as potential pitfalls in contract design" (The Royal Swedish Academy of Sciences 2016).

While Milton Friedman saw human relations through the lens of competition and conceptualised citizens as consumers (Monbiot 2016), he nevertheless recognised the conditions on which the market economy and contracts rest: "The possibility of co-ordination through voluntary cooperation rests on the elementary – yet frequently denied – proposition that *both parties to an economic transaction benefits from it*, provided the transaction *is bi-laterally voluntary and informed*" (Friedman 2020, 13; emphasis added).

Elementary logic teaches us that any principle, such as *pacta sunt servanda*, can only be valid if the underlying assumptions are true. If we rely on contracts and contract law to advance core socioeconomic goals, like autonomy, trust, ability to plan, utility maximization, etc., awareness of the contractual arrangements is vital (Becher and Benoliel 2021). Yet, for many people like Nonku and David, the assumptions on which the market economy, contracts, and contract law rest are not only unrealistic in general

[3] "[C]apacity is defined negatively, that is to say, by its absence: the very young, very old or very ill are deemed, to varying degrees according to particular contexts, to lack the ability to make legally enforceable contracts" (Deakin, 2006, 1).

[4] Contract theory studies contracts from a legal point of view, as an institutional arrangement for the way in which resources flow, which defines the various relationships between the parties to a transaction or limits the rights and obligations of the parties, and from an economic perspective, how economic actors can and do construct contractual arrangements, generally in the presence of information asymmetry.

but patently false (Louw 2014). Choosing between signing a contract you cannot understand or feeding your children is not a choice; it's an institutional failure.

This failure should not be a surprise if we consider that despite the enormous socioeconomic responsibility of contracts, there are no indicators around their effectiveness to achieving its stated purpose of generating mutual value (Cummins 2009). Apart from the very narrow focus of contract theory on transaction costs and incentives, research into how contracts actually serve the interests of the parties and society is still a relatively recent field of study, emerging with work on relational contracting, proactive contracting, and integrative law.

This institutional failure is important to consider in a world that is increasingly unequal. Recent numbers show that 71% of people live in countries where inequality has grown over the last 25 years (United Nations 2020). Rising inequality drives more people into a cycle of poverty, where self-reinforcing mechanisms of unemployment, homelessness, and bad health trap people into lives of perpetual vulnerability. My beautiful country, South Africa, has the shameful distinction as the most unequal in the world (Sulla, Zikhali, and Facundo 2022). The institutions therefore persist with false assumptions while, in countries like South Africa, sometimes deigning to temper the worst failures with convoluted legal exceptions and (unreadable) consumer legislation (Davis 2011; Bauling and Nagtegaal 2015).

We must remember that institutions are shaped by the views and needs of privileged actors in society who define what is just and what is not, often to their benefit (Samuels 1973; Kennedy 1991; DiMatteo 1995). Privileged actors are those who have access to resources, whether financial, social, or educational, to influence, promote, and enforce their rights (Feront 2021). They are contractually literate, can afford a good lawyer, and are less likely to suffer legal injustices. Vulnerable individuals, on the other hand, have limited access to resources, whether financial, social, or educational, to protect let alone promote their rights. They are not contractually literate, cannot afford a good lawyer, and are more likely to suffer injustices. While in most legal systems we are all supposed to be equal before the law, this is rarely the case in practice, and the interests of vulnerable individuals tend to be subordinated to those of more privileged and powerful parties.

Reinforcing this unequal dynamic, contracts have become increasingly opaque, "walls of text" that are "written by lawyers for lawyers" (Berger-Walliser, Bird, and Haapio 2011; Passera 2017). Most people – even privileged individuals – don't like to read their contracts, and if they do, few understand them adequately (Barton, Berger-Walliser, and Haapio 2013). Most people do not like to engage with contracts, read them, or comprehend much of them (Keating and Baasch Andersen 2016). Research from World Commerce & Contracting[5] shows that 88% of contract users find contracts "difficult or impossible to understand." Aggravating further this

[5] World Commerce & Contracting is an organisation with over 65,000 members, including 90% of Global 500, an annual ranking of the top 500 corporations worldwide as measured by revenue.

situation, recent years have seen an increase in practices that some have called "dark contracts" (Becher and Benoliel 2021). Although such practices have mainly been analysed in the context of consumer contracts, many of the various non-transparent mechanisms and instruments they exposed are pervasive in all contracts between more powerful parties and vulnerable individuals.

Yet, legal institutions impose on the more vulnerable members of society, like Nonku and David, the responsibility to navigate a complex legal process if they signed a contract that they cannot understand or under unfair conditions. The onus is on them, with their limited resources, to prove why the state should not hold them to contracts they do not understand.

When it comes to vulnerable people, it is fair to say that the practice of contracts does not meet the fundamental preconditions on which the market economy and contract law rest for their authority. Whether or not the individuals maintaining those practices have oppressive intentions, when vulnerable people are made to sign contracts that they cannot understand or under coercive conditions, these practices serve to perpetuate the oppression of vulnerable people (Seabrook and Wyatt-Nichol 2016; Kelly and Varghese 2018).

5.3 DIGNITY IN THE CONTEXT OF CONTRACTS

Few terms have the intuitive power of the word "dignity" (Sperling 2022). Following the Enlightenment, and more recently after the Second World War, many declarations and constitutions proclaimed human dignity as the pre-eminent fundamental and inviolable inherent right that must be respected and protected. Like the definition of a contract, dignity is a contested concept for which there is no agreed definition (O'Mahony 2012; Bal 2017; Kim 2021). In some countries, such as South Africa and Germany, dignity is a constitutional right that must be respected and protected (Ackermann 2012). In others, it is a normative principle or natural law from which rights flow (Gilabert 2015; Riley 2015). Is dignity status or equality? Does dignity flow from autonomy (O'Mahony 2012)? Debates and variations in the concept abound. Just like it is easier to identify and get consensus about what constitutes an injustice than to measure a situation against the transcendental concept of justice (Deakin 2006; Sen 2009), it is easier to identify when someone's dignity is violated than to define someone's dignity (Ackermann 2012).

In this chapter, we will adhere to Immanuel Kant's conceptualisation of dignity: "that every human being should never be treated as a means, but always as an end in itself" (Bal 2017; Sperling 2022). Apart from it being the most famous and well-known definition of dignity, Kant's definition exposes how no one should be treated as mere means to an end, or as stated by Professor Tjakie Naude, "as objects of economic gratification" (Louw 2014, 104).

However, the institutions which predate the Second World War, such as law, education, government, and criminal justice, did not develop with the express purpose of respecting or protecting the dignity of vulnerable people. And as a result, they often don't.

Moreover, it has become the norm in contracts to refer to people as anything except a person with inherent dignity. For example, a person is referred to as a consumer, a lessee, an insured, a tenant, an employee, a mortgagee, a surety, a worker, a debtor, etc. And when it comes to enforcing contracts, it's much easier to treat "an employee" or "a debtor" with complete indifference than having to think about forcing Nonku or David to suffer the consequences of contracts that they may not understand. In other words, it is the practice of the institution to refer to real people, even vulnerable people, as faceless objects of an economic transaction, as mere means to someone else's economic gratification.

Yet, this outcome of legal institutions is not inevitable. Dignity does not have to be an incidental and intermittent by-product of dominant practices. On the contrary, we can achieve dignity for all only if we define it as the purpose of the law, the purpose of the law of contracts, and the purpose of contracts.

Serving the dignity of vulnerable people is not only an act of charity by the more privileged. As pointed out by Albert Camus, serving the dignity of the vulnerable can serve the dignity of the privileged (Camus 1992). It was this liberating insight that led to agreement on the pre-eminence of dignity in South Africa's new constitution (Surty 2019).

Whereas inclusivity is often presented as the answer to inequality and discrimination, true inclusivity requires alleviation of the indignities suffered by vulnerable people within the law in general and contracts specifically. The question is then: What would a legal system look like that is designed to enhance human dignity and, therefore, justice? More specifically, what would contracts designed to enhance human dignity and, therefore, justice look like? I argue that we can also serve the dignity of vulnerable people by applying legal design principles to contracts and contracting processes.

5.4 WHERE CONTRACTS, LEGAL DESIGN, AND DIGNITY MEET

First named and advocated by Colette Brunschwig with a focus on visual law and visual legal communication generally, the concept of legal design has expanded to include a human-centred design approach to bring systemic changes to legal systems, including the design of documents, products, services, spaces, policies, and laws (Brunschwig 2001; Hagan 2020).

The human-centred approach of legal design overlaps with design for dignity, a field of design that seeks to help people that live with disabilities to enjoy autonomy and dignity in the built and medical environments (Institute for Human Rights and Business Ltd. 2019; Seshadri et al. 2019). Some have also shown that we can serve various aspects of dignity through better legal service design (Hagan and Kim 2018; Hagan 2020; Kim 2021).

In the context of vulnerable and marginalised people, legal design's human-centred approach aims to prevent or solve legal problems by prioritising the point of view of the "users" of the law, and it aligns directly with Kant's definition of dignity, namely that we treat people as ends in themselves, and never as mere means to an end (Hagan and Kim 2018; Rossi et al. 2019; Kim 2021). Using design in contracts can help to alleviate the inequality of dignity (Ackermann 2012) that so many people in the world experience.

The legal design approach is also atuned to the risks of designing for people instead of with people (Hagan 2020; Kim 2021). Participatory design is especially important to avoid privileged people determining vulnerable people's needs and priorities without involving them in those determinations. Participatory design serves to alleviate well-intended kindness that ends up denying vulnerable people's autonomy and dignity in overcoming their challenges.

Just as it has become the norm to design buildings and products that people living with physical disabilities can access autonomously (for example, by using ramp access in a building for people who need to use wheelchairs), legal documents, and specifically contracts, should also be designed so that they are accessible to vulnerable people so that they can autonomously access the information that affects and binds them, whenever they need to (Barclay 2018; Institute for Human Rights and Business Ltd. 2019).

I am advocating for dignity to be the purpose, the lodestar, of contracting. By considering contracts through the lens of dignity, lawyers and designers can help to prevent injustice and the indignity of what happened to Nonku and David. Designing contracts for dignity is about enhancing the capacity and capability of the weaker, subordinate, or vulnerable party to autonomously understand their rights and obligations (Deakin 2006; Bal 2017). Autonomy is an essential element common to contracts and dignity. By enhancing the autonomy of vulnerable parties, the dignity of those vulnerable people is better served, and the assumptions that underpin the law of contracting are validated.

Systems thinking teaches us that if you want to change the output of a system, you can either try to change the parts or the interactions or relationships between them (Hoebeke 1994; Senge 2006). As contracts serve to define the interactions or relationships in the legal and free market–based economic systems, they hold responsibility for the current outputs of poor access to justice and rising inequality. By improving how we contract, and specifically by using design to create contracts that serve the autonomy and dignity of vulnerable people, we can produce an exponential impact to improve economic inclusivity and reduce the systemic forces that keep millions of people trapped in vulnerability. This approach aligns with legal design's vision where cascading layers of efforts are necessary for transformative impact (Hagan 2020).

5.5 CONTRACT VISUALISATION

The International Labour Organisation (ILO) promotes the adoption and enforcement of model employment contracts in agriculture, construction, domestic work, and the garment industry – sectors in which low- and middle-skilled migrants are particularly vulnerable to exploitative working conditions (Artiles 2008). But as I have argued, having a contract is not a panacea. Contracts can be good or bad; they can enhance or oppress a vulnerable person. A contract can improve a person's position (medical insurance); or it can exploit a person, as we saw with David's installment payment plan; or it can fail to achieve its purpose, as we saw with Nonku's employment contract. And what is the purpose of a contract when vulnerable people cannot read what they sign and, more importantly, are not able to access it when they need to rely on the contract? Put differently, "You can't fight for your rights if you don't know what they are" (Longley, n.d.). All too often companies treat contracts as an item on a compliance or audit list.

If we know that businesspeople who can read well don't like to read contracts and find them hard to understand, what is the user experience of people that struggle to read even plain language? Among farm workers in South Africa, the illiteracy rate is 40% (Visser and Ferrer 2015), and among women in Afghanistan, it is 77.4% (Central Intelligence Agency 2021). And it's not just the developing world problem. In the Netherlands, 1.3 million people are functionally illiterate, and in the United States, approximately 32 million are (Strauss 2016; Van Vugt 2016).

Illiteracy goes unnoticed because vulnerable and illiterate people often hide it, afraid to admit to it, as it may expose them to exploitation or feeling shame. So, people with low literacy skills, like Nonku and David, have developed coping mechanisms, like not telling anyone they cannot read the document and just doing what everyone does: signing documents without even pretending to read them.

It means that each time we bind a vulnerable person to a contract that they cannot reasonably and autonomously understand, we are treating vulnerable people as an object of economic gratification, as mere means to an end, and thereby denigrating their dignity, and ours. This is not a remote issue. Sometimes it is the people who clean our offices or people who work in our shops and restaurants to prepare the products and services we consume who are treated as a means to an end. This practice is too often at the heart of the global value chains of so many of the products and services that we consume, whether they come from the garment industry, the agricultural industry, the mining sector – the list goes on (Snyder, Maslow, and Dadusch 2022).

Touched by the experiences of people like Nonku and David, and inspired by the work of Helena Haapio, Colette Brunschwig, and Marietjie Botes, I explored over several years whether it is possible to create a visual contract for vulnerable people. The use of visualisation in contracts was predominantly advocated by the proactive contracting movement, which advocates for contracts to be designed to achieve the intended success of the agreement it captures (Berger-Walliser, Bird, and Haapio 2011; Barton, Berger-Walliser, and Haapio 2013; Haapio 2013; Passera 2017). The movement includes scholars of design, who thought the theories and practice of information design actualised and systematised the use of visualisation in contracts (Passera 2017; Waller 2020). Within this movement, the use of visualisation in the

FIGURE 5.1. Example of the power of images to transcend language barriers.
(Image owned by Creative Contracts: Founder – Robert de Rooy.)

context of contracts has developed to include: (1) visualisation in contracts, (2) visualisation about contracts, (3) visualisation for contracts; and (4) visualisation as contracts (Haapio, Plewe, and de Rooy 2016).

Visualisation offers many advantages over text to convey information within the context of a contract. Education research has shown that using pictures to illustrate a text strongly improves comprehension. Pictures make the text more focused (to direct a reader's attention), concise/compact ("a picture is worth a thousand words"), concrete (due to its representation function), coherent (organising information), comprehensible (facilitating interpretation), correspondent (relating the unfamiliar text to a reader's prior knowledge), and easy to remember (assisting the mnemonic function) (Levin and Mayer 1993). The medium of visualisation is in many ways much better than conventional text for achieving at least one of the underlying assumptions of the role of contracts and contract law, specifically to be informed and understand whether to contract and on what terms.

While the above is true for commercial contracts, what about contracts with vulnerable people, people who may have low literacy capabilities, or people who are asked to sign a contract in a language they are not proficient in? As demonstrated in Figure 5.1, "Drawing is a kind of Universal Language, understood by all Nations. A Man may often express his Ideas, even to his own Countrymen, more clearly with a Lead Pencil, or Bit of Chalk, than with his Tongue. And many can understand a Figure, that do not comprehend a Description in Words, tho' ever so properly chosen" (Franklin 1749).

As illustrated in Figure 5.2, our brains process images much faster than text, and we follow visual instructions much better than we do text instructions.

Pictures are also a medium through which important relational concepts can be subtly conveyed, such as care, respect, trust, and kindness. Complex ideas can be easily conveyed with visual images, and it is easy for people to absorb and remember large amounts of information. While some images may be 'subjective', like abstract art, pictures in the context of health and safety, instruction manuals, patent

FIGURE 5.2. Depiction of value of visual instruction over text instruction for tent assembly.
(Image owned by Creative Contracts: Founder – Robert de Rooy.)

descriptions, and safety cards in the back of airline seats are preferred ways in which to describe what to do and how things work, a way of understanding that limits the risks of translation into a language or between languages. And in the meantime, scholars are developing a body of knowledge on using visuals in contracts (Annola, Haapio, and Koskela 2022).

5.6 COMIC CONTRACTS

Ultimately, it was reading the works of Scott McCloud, *Understanding Comics*, that concretised for me a path towards alleviating the injustice of vulnerable people having to sign contracts they can hardly read. In his book, the author used comics to explain and show the power of comics, the art that merges visuals and stories, complementary mediums which create connections between people and ideas, illustrate relationships better than factual statements, and are also easy to remember.

With a transdisciplinary team made up of a lawyer, an illustrator, a designer, and a writer, and using an iterative process of development and user testing, we finally implemented our first comic contract in May 2016, with 250 seasonal farmworkers on a ClemenGold citrus farm in Letsitele in South Africa. We called it a Comic Contract, which we define as legally binding contracts where the parties are represented as characters, the terms are written in pictures, whether independently (i.e., instead of any text) or complemented by text or in the context of text, and the parties sign the comic as the contract. In other words, the comic is the contract, an example of which is Figure 5.3.

Working iteratively, we had first feared that the workers would feel patronized by the pictures in a contract. Yet, to the contrary, they engaged with the contract and felt empowered to ask questions. We also made mistakes that needed to be adjusted. For instance, most of the workers that were contracted were women, and they felt that we should have offered them a contract with female characters, and they also asked for the headings and other text elements to be in their local language. It made us realise that apart from the power of pictures and stories, there were many ways to

FIGURE 5.3. Example of a comic contract.
(Image owned by Creative Contracts: Founder – Robert de Rooy.)

make contracts more relevant and easier to understand. Despite early mistakes, our first trial was successful, and the employer reported that using comic contracts had reduced their typical induction time from 3 hours to 45 minutes overall.

In a subsequent project, we created a contract between a creche in an economically depressed area and the parents of the young children attending the creche. We learned two important lessons from this project. The first lesson was that parents understood better what was expected of them and how they could be involved in the education of their young children owing to the contract. The second lesson was that teachers found it easier to have something in their hands both parties could understand, and it helped the teachers to engage with the parents around all the issues.

This experience has been consistent in other areas too: for example, we developed new ways to communicate informed consent for medical research, where the barriers to contracting include comprehension of what medical research people are consenting to, the process, and risks, among other elements. Additionally, one of the big advantages of using visualisation in informed consent is that nurses who normally spend copious time explaining the same things to each new patient can use the contract as a teaching aide and boundary object to communicate the information easily and quickly.

We are continuing to discover the advantages of comic contracts. Professor Camilla Andersen at the University of Western Australia contemporaneously developed a comic book contract for an engineering firm, which, their research showed, outperformed text agreements in terms of engagement, comprehension, and perception (Keating and Baasch Andersen 2016). Moreover, some research suggests that comics help with the perception and usability of complex policy text, which can lead to increased uptake of the insurance product (Harcourt-Cooke, Els, and van Rensburg 2022).

Overall, it has been our experience that making important information available to vulnerable and illiterate people in an engaging, clear, relevant, and non-threatening way makes them feel empowered and respected, as illustrated by the following feedback sourced by an independent third-party organisation: "I have more faith in the picture contract. People who cannot read are able to see and also understand it better" (English translation of Agatha Le Fleur). "They showed us that we are valued as human beings. In other jobs[,] they just give you orders to work, and they don't care about you. So, I like the fact that my manager shows us that he cares about us. That is what makes me happy" (English translation of Nonzwakazi Nowata). "I am also illiterate. There are words that I don't understand well but if I look at this [contract], I can understand. And it gives me [the] power to do my work" (English translation of Dineo Cuphe).

This feedback opened my eyes to the fact that what we are doing is not just about making information easier to understand but is also about the dignity of vulnerable people and treating them with the dignity they deserve. While my early motivation was to alleviate the injustice of vulnerable people suffering from having signed contracts they could not understand under unfair conditions, the insight into the impact on people's dignity came later. And it's been enormously motivating to comprehend our work through this lens. It gives a lot of meaning to the days, months, and years we have done this work. It's a privilege to be in a position to help companies show vulnerable people that it matters that they understand their contracts, that it matters that they don't feel embarrassment or shame, and that it matters that they are empowered to know what was agreed to so they can choose what they want to do and to be able to conduct themselves according to the terms of their agreements with confidence.

Alleviating the risks of institutional oppression suffered by vulnerable people when they sign a contract is within our reach. Companies only need to spend but a small percentage of their marketing budgets or their legal retainers on making important information in their contracts more engaging and easier to understand to the people they want to work with or sell their products or services.

5.7 CONCLUSION

In a world characterised by both an extreme amount of wealth and growing inequality, it is time we turn our efforts to serving the dignity of vulnerable people. Legal design offers rich potential to help discover and develop ways to afford people more dignity. With dignity as the lodestar, there are exciting opportunities for people of all disciplines, like information designers, plain language practitioners, UX practitioners, illustrators, designers, lawyers, artists, scholars, developers, and many others, to work together with a clear and meaningful purpose. There are more than enough people already spending their lives trying to increase sales, clicks, convenience, efficiencies – you name it. Legal design offers an opportunity to contribute to people's autonomy, people's dignity, a better life, and a better society. Let every one of us become agents of dignity.

REFERENCES

Ackermann, Laurie. 2012. *Human Dignity: Lodestar for Equality in South Africa*. Cape Town, South Africa: Juta.

Annola, Vesa, Helena Haapio, and Merja Koskela. 2022. "Interpreting Images in Contracts." In *Research Handbook on Contract Design*, edited by Marcelo Corrales Helena Haapio, and Mark Fenwick, 365–81. Cheltenham: Edward Elgar Publishing.

Artiles, Antonio Martín. 2008. "Towards a Fair Deal for Migrant Workers in the Global Economy." *Transfer: European Review of Labour and Research* 14, no. 4 (Winter): 706–09. https://doi.org/10.1177/102425890801400417.

Bal, Matthijs. 2017. *Dignity in the Workplace*. Cham, Switzerland: Springer International Publishing.

Barclay, Linda. 2018. *Disability with Dignity: Justice, Human Rights and Equal Status*. New York: Routledge.

Barton, Thomas D., Gerlinde Berger-Walliser, and Helena Haapio. 2013. "Visualization: Seeing Contracts for What They are, and What They Could Become." *Journal of Law, Business & Ethics* 19 (February): 47–64.

Bauling, Andrea, and Annelize Nagtegaal. 2015. "Bread as Dignity: The Constitution and the Consumer Protection Act 68 of 2008." *De Jure* 48, no. 1 (January): 149–71. http://dx.doi.org/10.17159/2225-7160/2015/v48n1a9.

Becher, Samuel, and Uri Benoliel. 2021. "Dark Contracts." *Boston College Law Review* 64 (August): 55–117. https://doi.org/10.2139/ssrn.3911528.

Berger-Walliser, Gerlinde, Robert C. Bird, and Helena Haapio. 2011. "Promoting Business Success Through Contract Visualization." *Journal of Law, Business and Ethics* 17, 1–20. Social Science Research Network (SSRN).

Brunschwig, Colette. 2001. *Visualisierung von Rechtsnormen: Legal Design*. Zurich, Switzerland: Schulthess.

Camus, Albert. 1992. *The Rebel: An Essay on Man in Revolt*. 1st Vintage International ed. New York: Vintage Books.

Central Intelligence Agency. 2021. "The World Factbook: Afghanistan." Last modified August 1, 2023. www.cia.gov/the-world-factbook/countries/afghanistan/.

Christie, R. H., and Victoria McFarlane. 2006. *The Law of Contract in South Africa*. 5th ed. Durban, South Africa: LexisNexis Butterworths.

Cummins, Tim. 2009. "The Purpose of a Contract." Commitment Matters (blog), November 18. https://commitmentmatters.com/2009/11/18/the-purpose-of-a-contract/.

Davis, D. M. 2011. "Developing the Common Law of Contract in the Light of Poverty and Illiteracy: The Challenge of the Constitution." *Stellenbosch Law Review* 22, no. 3 (January): 845–64.

Deakin, Simon. 2006. "'Capacitas': Contract Law and the Institutional Preconditions of a Market Economy." *European Review of Contract Law* 2, no. 3 (July): 1–25. http://dx.doi.org/10.1515/ERCL.2006.025.

DiMatteo, Larry A. 1995. "The Norms of Contract: The Fairness Inquiry and the 'Law of Satisfaction' – A Nonunified Theory." *Hofstra Law Review* 24, no. 2: 349–454.

Feront, Cecile. 2021. "How Do Privileged Insiders Become Change Agents? A Study of Institutional Volition." Doctor of Philosophy dissertation. Cape Town: University of Cape Town.

Foka-Kavalieraki, Yulie, and Aristides N. Hatzis. 2009. "The Foundations of a Market Economy: Contract, Consent, Coercion." *European View* 8, no. 1: 29–37. https://doi.org/10.1007/s12290–009-0081-y.

Franklin, Benjamin. 1749. "Proposals Relating to the Education of Youth in Pennsylvania, [October 1749]." *Founders Online*, National Archives, https://founders.archives.gov/documents/Franklin/01-03-02-0166.

Friedman, Milton. 2020. *Capitalism and Freedom*. Chicago: University of Chicago Press.

Gilabert, Pablo. 2015. "Human Rights, Human Dignity, and Power." In *Philosophical Foundations of Human Rights*, edited by Rowan Cruft, S. Matthew Liao, and Massimo Renzo, 196–213. Oxford: Oxford University Press. https://doi.org/10.1093/acprof:oso/9780199688623.003.0011.

Haapio, Helena. 2013. *Next Generation Contracts: A Paradigm Shift*. Helsinki, Finland: Lexpert.

Haapio, Helena, Daniela Alina Plewe, and Robert de Rooy. 2016. 'Next Generation Deal Design: Comics and Visual Platforms for Contracting'. In *Networks. Proceedings of the 19th International Legal Informatics Symposium IRIS 2016*, 373–80. Vienna.

Hagan, Margaret. 2020. "Legal Design as a Thing: A Theory of Change and a Set of Methods to Craft a Human-Centered Legal System." *Design Issues* 36, no. 3 (Summer): 3–15. https://doi.org/10.1162/desi_a_00600.

Hagan, Margaret, and Miso Kim. 2018. "Design for Dignity and Procedural Justice." *Advances in Intelligent Systems and Computing* 585: 135–45. https://doi.org/10.1007/978-3-319-60495-4_15.

Harcourt-Cooke, Claire, Gideon Els, and Eugene van Rensburg. 2022. "Using Comics to Improve Financial Behaviour." *Journal of Behavioral and Experimental Finance* 33 (March): 100614. https://doi.org/10.1016/j.jbef.2021.100614.

Hoebeke, Luc. 1994. *Making Work Systems Better: A Practitioner's Reflections*. New York: Wiley.

Institute for Human Rights and Business Ltd. 2019. "Dignity by Design – Human Rights and the Built Environment Lifecycle." www.ihrb.org/focus-areas/built-environment/report-dignity-by-design-human-rights-and-the-built-environment-lifecycle.

Keating, Adrian, and Camilla Baasch Andersen. 2016. "A Graphic Contract: Taking Visualisation in Contracting a Step Further." *Journal of Strategic Contracting and Negotiation* 2, no. 1–2 (December): 10–18. https://doi.org/10.1177/2055563616672375.

Kelly, Diann Cameron, and Rani Varghese. 2018. "Four Contexts of Institutional Oppression: Examining the Experiences of Blacks in Education, Criminal Justice and Child Welfare." *Journal of Human Behavior in the Social Environment* 28, no. 7 (June): 874–88. https://doi.org/10.1080/10911359.2018.1466751.

Kennedy, Duncan. 1991. "The Stakes of Law, or Hale and Foucault." *The Legal Studies Forum* 15, no. 4: 327–65.

Kim, Miso. 2021. "A Study of Dignity as a Principle of Service Design." *International Journal of Design* 15, no. 3 (December): 87–100.

Levin, Joel R., and Richard E. Mayer. 1993. "Understanding Illustrations in Text." In *Learning from Textbooks Theory and Practice*, edited by B. K. Britton, A. Woodward, and M. R. Binkley, 95–113. Hillsdale, NJ: Lawrence Erlbaum Associates, Inc.

Longley, Robert. n.d. "John G. Roberts, Supreme Court Chief Justice." *ThoughtCo*. Last modified April 3, 2021. www.thoughtco.com/john-g-roberts-biography-3322403.

Louw, A. M. 2014. "Yet Another Call for a Greater Role for Good Faith in the South African Law of Contract: Can We Banish the Law of the Jungle, While Avoiding the Elephant in the Room?" *Potchefstroom Electronic Law Journal/Potchefstroomse Elektroniese Regsblad* 16, no. 5: 44–120. https://doi.org/10.4314/pelj.v16i5.2.

Monbiot, George. 2016. "Neoliberalism – the Ideology at the Root of All Our Problems." *The Guardian*, April 15. www.theguardian.com/books/2016/apr/15/neoliberalism-ideology-problem-george-monbiot.

Morawetz, Victor. 1925. "The Elements of a Contract." *American Bar Association Journal* 11, no. 2: 87–90.

O'Mahony, C. 2012. "There Is No Such Thing as a Right to Dignity." *International Journal of Constitutional Law* 10, no. 2: 551–74. https://doi.org/10.1093/icon/mos010.

Passera, Stefania. 2017. "Beyond the Wall of Contract Text: Visualizing Contracts to Foster Understanding and Collaboration within and across Organizations." Ph.D. diss., Aalto University. http://urn.fi/URN:ISBN:978-952-60-7528-0.

Riley, Stephen. 2015. "Human Dignity and the Rule of Law." *Utrecht Law Review* 11, no. 2: 91–105. https://doi.org/10.18352/ulr.320.

Rossi, Arianna, Rossana Ducato, Helena Haapio, and Stefania Passera. 2019. "When Design Met Law: Design Patterns for Information Transparency." https://orbilu.uni.lu/bitstream/10993/40116/1/A.%20Rossi,%20R.%20Ducato,%20H.%20Haapio%20et%20S.%20Passera.pdf.

The Royal Swedish Academy of Sciences. 2016. "Press Release: The Prize in Economic Sciences 2016." www.nobelprize.org/prizes/economic-sciences/2016/press-release/.

Samuels, Warren J. 1973. "The Economy as a System of Power and Its Legal Bases: The Legal Economics of Robert Lee Hale." *University of Miami Law Review* 27, no. 3 (July): 261–371.

Seabrook, Renita, and Heather Wyatt-Nichol. 2016. "The Ugly Side of America: Institutional Oppression and Race." *Journal of Public Management & Social Policy* 23, no. 1: 20–46. https://digitalscholarship.tsu.edu/jpmsp/vol23/iss1/3.

Sen, Amartya. 2009. *The Idea of Justice*. London: Penguin Books.

Senge, Peter M. 2006. *The Fifth Discipline: The Art and Practice of the Learning Organization*. Revised and updated. New York: Currency Doubleday.

Seshadri, Priya, Cole Hatfield Joslyn, Morgan M. Hynes, and Tahira Reid. 2019. "Compassionate Design: Considerations That Impact the Users' Dignity, Empowerment and Sense of Security." *Design Science* 5 (May): 1–21. https://doi.org/10.1017/dsj.2019.18.

Simon, Herbert Alexander. 2008. *The Sciences of the Artificial*. 3rd ed. Cambridge, MA: MIT Press.

Smith, Stephen A. 2004. "What Is Contract Theory?" In *Contract Theory*, edited by Stephen A. Smith. Oxford: Oxford University Press.

Snyder, David V., Susan A. Maslow, and Sarah Dadusch. 2022. "Model Contract Clauses to Protect Workers in International Supply Chains, Version 2.0." *American Bar Association, Business Law Today*. Last modified September 26, 2022. https://businesslawtoday.org/tool/model-contract-clauses-protect-workers-international-supply-chains/.

Sperling, Gene. 2022. *Economic Dignity*. New York: Penguin Press.

Strauss, Valerie. 2016. "Hiding in Plain Sight: The Adult Literacy Crisis." *Washington Post*, November 1. www.washingtonpost.com/news/answer-sheet/wp/2016/11/01/hiding-in-plain-sight-the-adult-literacy-crisis/.

Sulla, Victor, Precious Zikhali, and Pablo Facundo Cuevas. 2022. *Inequality in Southern Africa: An Assessment of the Southern African Customs Union*. Washington, DC: World Bank Group. https://documents.worldbank.org/en/publication/documents-reports/documentdetail/099125303072236903/P1649270c02a1f06b0a3ae02e57eadd7a82.

Surty, Mohamed Enver. 2019. *In Pursuit of Dignity*. Johannesburg: Awqaf.

Tutu, Desmond. 2013. "Foreword by Archbishop Emeritus Desmond Tutu." In *Dignity: Its Essential Role in Resolving Conflict*, by Donna Hicks, ix–xi. New Haven, CT: Yale University Press.

UNESCO. 2020. *Global Education Monitoring Report 2020: Inclusion and Education: All Means All*. Paris: UNESCO. https://en.unesco.org/gem-report/report/2020/inclusion.

United Nations. 2020. "Inequality – Bridging the Divide." www.un.org/sites/un2.un.org/files/2020/02/un75_inequality.pdf.

Van Vugt, Gaby. 2016. "On the Relationship Between Functional Illiteracy and Poverty." *Electronic Platform for Adult Learning in Europe*, July 25. https://epale.ec.europa.eu/en/resource-centre/content/relationship-between-functional-illiteracy-and-poverty#:~:text=In%20the%20Netherlands%2C%201.3%20million,similar%20relationship%20in%20the%20Netherlands%3F.

Visser, Margareet, and Stuart Ferrer. 2015. "Farm Workers' Living and Working Conditions in South Africa: Key Trends, Emergent Issues, and Underlying and Structural Problems." *The Pretoria Office of the International Labour Organization*. www.ilo.org/wcmsp5/groups/public/—africa/documents/publication/wcms_385959.pdf.

Waller, Rob. 2020. "Contract Design for Humans: Preventing Cognitive Accidents." *Simplification Centre*. https://uploads-ssl.webflow.com/5c06fb475dbf1265069aba1e/5f69de7c9248fa58b79ad3c9_SC16HumanContracts.pdf.

6

Dignifying the Experience of Domestic Violence Survivors Seeking Legal Services

Morgan A. Wilson

6.1 INTRODUCTION

The law and legal systems in the United States are violent. The police, courts and court staff, and attorneys maintain and perpetuate this violence in their everyday interactions with those around them, particularly people seeking legal services. Mapping Police Violence estimates that 1,134 people were killed by police in 2021, more than almost any other year in recent history, and that "most killings began with police responding to suspected non-violent offenses or cases where no crime was reported" (Mapping Police Violence, Inc. 2021C, 8). Judges and court staff can be dismissive and rude to unrepresented litigants, and the police are known to arrest and detain survivors simply for seeking safety and assistance. Similarly, legal services geared toward survivors that do not center their experiences or build a legal strategy around their desired outcome further entrench the violence of legal systems and the law. However, there is possibility (and hope!) in the human-centered approach of legal service design methodologies, which focus on quality of service, customer experience, and satisfaction. Using the Domestic Violence Institute's (DVI) virtual clinic as a case study, I contend that legal service design can address systemic and pernicious access to justice issues that have a chilling effect on survivors seeking legal services.

6.2 BRIDGING THE GAP: THE APPLICATION OF SERVICE DESIGN TO CLINICAL LEGAL EDUCATION

6.2.1 *The Domestic Violence Institute Pre-Covid Clinical Operations: Who We Are, What We Do, Who We Serve*

The Northeastern School of Law Domestic Violence Institute (DVI) is a clinical legal program in which attorneys, student attorneys, and advocates offer free legal and social services to survivors of dating, domestic, and sexual violence. The institutional ethos is driven by a model of trauma-informed lawyering that looks holistically at and centers the experiences, needs, and desires of survivors. By allowing survivors, who know their needs and safety interests best, to have decision-making autonomy, the DVI offers appropriate wraparound services and support to clients, their families, and communities.

Before the World Health Organization declared COVID-19 a global pandemic on March 11, 2020, the DVI was composed of two programs: (1) the Legal Assistance to Victims (LAV) Program and (2) the Domestic Violence Clinic (DV Clinic). The first-year LAV Program provides referrals to legal and social services programs and offers housing support, safety planning, case management, and other services as needed, while second- and third-year law students in the upper-level DV Clinic represent survivors in restraining and harassment prevention order hearings in the Greater Boston trial courts.

In both programs, students and attorneys met their clients in places the clients first turned to for help. For student advocates in the LAV Program this meant community health clinics, hospitals, churches, and community centers. Conversely, student attorneys in the upper-level DV Clinic often met their clients for the first time in court. Meeting survivors at court or in community has many benefits. For example, it is easier to confirm a client's identity in person when you can verify their likeness against a valid form of identification. Meeting clients at a health clinic leverages a preexisting doctor's visit to provide services to a parent or child being abused. The doctor's visit may not arouse the abuser's suspicion, and the office provides a confidential space to conduct an intake and needs assessment to ensure appropriate referrals and support. Further, it is much easier to identify and document bruising, scrapes, cuts, discoloration, and other injuries that may have occurred during an abusive incident. The same is true for physical disabilities that may otherwise go unnoticed during video or teleconferencing calls. For non-English and limited English proficiency speakers, in-person interpretation often ensures a smoother conversational experience. Most importantly, for purposes of safety, in-person meetings help identify and sometimes mitigate the immediate risk of harm (e.g., should an abusive party be present). As evidenced above, the importance of being in person *and* in community with survivors is not only critical to their safety and dignity but also pivotal to the provision of services for a high-risk population.

With a mandate to provide high-caliber, free legal services to indigent survivors in Boston, the DVI primarily operated in the Dorchester, Roxbury, and Mattapan neighborhoods and the municipal courts serving those areas, with a few cases and clients in the Greater Boston area. Data compiled from the 2015–2019 United States Census Bureau American Community Survey (ACS) by the Boston Planning & Development Agency Research Division (2021) revealed the aforementioned communities had some of the lowest educational attainment levels and per capita income across all Boston neighborhoods. For example, Mattapan had the lowest percentage of residents with a bachelor's degree (11.7%), followed by Roxbury (15%), with Dorchester (18.7%) ranking fourth lowest after Hyde Park by less than 0.3%. Looking at the median household income by neighborhood and income range, 18.2% of households in Dorchester made $14,999 or less each year during this five-year period. In Roxbury, that number jumped to 31.9%, correlating to some of the highest poverty rates in Boston. Specifically, Dorchester had the fifth highest neighborhood poverty rate in Boston at 22.2%, though it had the highest percentage of Boston's total impoverished residents at 23.1%, with the next highest percentage in Roxbury at 13.3%. Roxbury also had a neighborhood poverty rate of 31.7%. These numbers reflect data collected by students and attorneys during client intakes and assessments over the course of the same period.

Consistent with Boston rental trends, neighborhoods in the DVI's catchment area had a high percentage of renters; however, they also held the top three spots for highest female-owned or -rented property where no spouse was present. With pathways to homeownership increasingly more difficult due to low income and high rents (NLIHC 2022), individuals and families in these areas face significant housing instability and homelessness. According to the United States Department of Housing and Urban Development, Office of Community Planning and Development 2019 Annual Homeless Assessment Report (AHAR) to Congress, "Between 2007 and 2019, the number of people experiencing homelessness in families with children increased in four states … Massachusetts had the largest percentage increase, with 79 percent more people in families with children experiencing homelessness (or 5,377 more people)" (Henry et al. 2020, 38). Indeed, the estimated total homeless population in Massachusetts in 2019 according to the AHAR Report was 18,471 with 12,212 of that number reflecting homeless people in families with children (Henry et al. 2020). It's no wonder that Massachusetts had one of the highest total homelessness estimates in 2019 (Henry et al. 2020).

Intensifying these socioeconomic problems are issues of systematic and pernicious racism, xenophobia, and generalized class discrimination. The DVI's catchment area is diverse, and clients often report experiencing a myriad of challenges based on their intersectional identities (e.g., lack of culturally competent services, lack of language access, discrimination in housing). According to the ACS study, Dorchester is 77% Black, Hispanic, Asian, and other races, Roxbury is 89%, and Mattapan is 94% (Boston Planning & Development Agency Research Division 2021). A 2019 data mapping project by Data USA made clear that in Suffolk County, where these cities are located, 29.3% of the residents identified as foreign-born and another 39.3% identified as non-English speakers, with the top three languages identified as Spanish, Chinese (collectively Mandarin and Cantonese), and Haitian Creole (Deloitte, Datawheel, and Hidalgo n.d.). This is consistent with data compiled by the Boston Planning and Development Agency in 2015, which revealed that the top five languages spoken in Boston, generally, were Spanish, Chinese, Haitian Creole, Portuguese and Cape Verdean Creole, and Vietnamese (2017).

Ultimately, understanding the experience of survivors from intentionally under-resourced, underserved, and exploited communities and the barriers they face accessing care and services ensures that students and attorneys see clients as more than their legal issue but as *people* wrestling with a myriad of overlapping challenges, many of which are life-generated risks that impact their safety. Humanizing survivors offers a pathway to holistic care, rooted in dignity, with the aim of providing culturally competent, trauma-informed, client-centered services.

6.2.2 *COVID-19 Exposed More than Germs: Abusers and Courts Put Survivors at Risk*

Although the global pandemic was beginning to change how we engaged with the people and places around us, its impact was yet to be fully realized. With concern for the health and well-being of Massachusetts residents, Governor Charles Baker issued a series of orders mandating closures and implementing social distancing protocols in hopes of decreasing rising COVID-19 numbers. However, the combination of three such orders proved devastating to survivors, having the unintended consequence of putting them at higher risk of abuse. Specifically, on March 15, 2020, Governor Baker issued COVID-19 Order 3 closing public and private elementary and secondary schools (Office of the Governor 2020a). Shortly thereafter, on March 18, 2020, he issued COVID-19 Order 10 closing all childcare programs (Office of the Governor 2020b). Then, on March 23, 2020, Governor Baker issued COVID-19 Order 13, restricting "all non-essential person-to-person contact and movement outside the home" (Office of the Governonr 2020c). Order 13 also mandated the temporary closing of all nonessential businesses and organizations, though restaurants and bars were designated essential and "encouraged to offer food and beverages for take out and delivery" (2020c). Simply put: (1) survivors and their children were stuck at home with abusers; (2) school and childcare facilities that may have been safe havens to children experiencing or witnessing abuse were closed for in-person services; (3) key community organizations to which survivors turned for help were also closed for in-person services; and (4) bars and restaurants that sold alcohol were considered essential businesses. As Andrew Campbell (2020, 1) notes, "alcohol abuse, a commonly reported risk factor for family violence, has been linked to an accumulation of stressful events and a lack of social support." He goes on: "With bars and restaurants being limited to take-out service only in many communities, family violence perpetrators who abuse alcohol may be even more likely to do so in the home, likely increasing risk for the entire household" (Campbell 2020, 1). As the pandemic continued, many employers reduced hours, laid off workers, or closed altogether (Ansell 2021). Thus the "associated risk factors for family violence such as unemployment, reduced income, limited resources, and limited social support" (Campbell 2020, 1; see also Fana, Torrejón Pérez, and Fernández-Macías 2020, 4) compounded emotional stress and social isolation (Dooling 2020).

Domestic violence shelters were not immune to de-densifying measures. On April 23, 2020, the Massachusetts Department of Public Health (DPH) updated their interim guidance for sexual and domestic violence programs operating residential and congregate care facilities (Massachusetts Department of Public Health 2020). While acknowledging “the already insufficient capacity of the shelter system as a whole” (Massachusetts Department of Public Health, 2020, 10), the guidance required that “all program participants and their families have a private bedroom and access to a bathroom” to mitigate the risk of spreading COVID-19 (Massachusetts Department of Public Health, 2020, 8). Although local, state, and federal aid programs helped defray rising program costs (Massachusetts Department of Public Health, 2020, 21), much of the funding was short-lived. Moreover, it took shelter programs time to implement the required changes to ensure compliance with the Governor’s orders and the DPH guidance. During that time, attorneys, advocates, and survivors reported that some judges were disinclined to grant motions to vacate the marital home because of limited alternative housing options (Mineo 2022). Failure to remove an abuser from the home, particularly after a survivor testified in court about the abuse, very likely placed the survivor and anyone else in the home in immediate risk of harm. In this and so many other ways, gaps in service design made survivors less safe, especially during the pandemic.

On March 13, 2020, the Supreme Judicial Court (SJC) of Massachusetts issued its first order restricting access to state courthouses and court facilities (oE–144a). In its next order, on March 17, 2022, the SJC limited in-person proceedings to emergency matters that could not be resolved by telephonic or videoconferencing (oE–144b). The SJC also required that *each* trial court department issue standing orders outlining what constitutes an emergency matter for purposes of their courthouse (oE–144b). the trial courts followed suit.[1] The Boston Municipal Court issued Standing Order 3–20 on March 17, 2020, confirming court closures and defining applications for abuse prevention orders pursuant to G.L. c. 209A and harassment prevention orders pursuant to G.L. c. 258E as emergency matters (Ronquillo 2020a, 1, 2). A few weeks later on April 3, 2020, the Boston Municipal Court issued Standing Order 4–20, adding the requirement that each clerk’s office “implement a protocol for handling the in-person filings of pleadings and other documents in Emergency Matters” where “the filing of pleadings and other documents in emergency matters cannot be accomplished virtually” (Ronquillo 2020b, 3). At the same time, Order 4–20 required “First Justices, Clerk-Magistrates, and Chief Probation Officers . . . to designate a reduced schedule of the necessary personnel needed on site to accomplish the administrative tasks and to be available to answer telephone calls from the public” (Ronquillo 2020b, 3). The reduced schedule meant insufficient staffing to

[1] In addition to the Boston municipal courts, the district courts and probate and family courts issued a series of standing orders outlining their COVID-19 court operations policy (Casey 2020).

adequately respond to increased demand for legal services and support from the court. Attorneys, advocates, and survivors reported difficulty speaking to anyone on the phone, little or no ability to leave a message, in addition to ineffective and poor communication regarding critical information like hours of operation and alternative filing procedures for restraining order applications, which had to be printed and filed with the court. Without digitized restraining order forms or an electronic filing system for affidavits, evidence, and notices of appearance, the only remote filing option necessitated expensive software like Adobe (to create fillable forms) or a printer and fax machine – items indigent survivors rarely have in-home access to. Consequently, survivors often drove to court only to find a piece of paper taped to the door with a number to call and some very brief information on services. These ad hoc notices were only helpful if a survivor was able to leave the house, had access to personal or public transport, and could read and understand English. For non-English speakers, blind or visually impaired people, and for people who have not learned to read, these notices did little to allay confusion about court closures or where and how to file for a restraining order. Searching the information for court updates was not always feasible. Some survivors do not have internet access; others had their online activity monitored by their abuser. Even with creative workarounds, like clearing cookies and browsing history, the stay-at-home orders severely curtailed time away from watchful eyes. For survivors who were able to research online, knowing where to look for court updates was not intuitive, and most survivors would not have known to read and review the standing orders for their respective court.

As outlined above, gaps in the court's systems created and exacerbated by COVID-19 led to significant barriers accessing legal services. Although some delays and oversights are understandable, they nonetheless had a chilling effect on survivors seeking services at a time when incidents of domestic abuse were on the rise.[2]

6.2.3 *Leveraging Legal Service Design: Dignity in Action*

In light of and in addition to the aforementioned closures, social distancing protocols, and limited or otherwise inaccessible information regarding the availability of court facilities and services, survivors faced a daunting task: juggling multiple, compounding impediments to their safety and overall well-being while simultaneously dealing with the socioeconomic instability of the pandemic. For these reasons, not long after the March 17, 2020 SJC order effectively closing court

[2] Initial reports indicate that incidents of domestic abuse declined at the outset of COVID-19, based on the decrease in calls to domestic and sexual violence hotlines. However, the decline can and should be attributed to a lack of safe and confidential spaces, in person or by phone, where survivors could access help and not because incidents of abuse actually decreased. In fact, a report by the National Commission on COVID-19 and Criminal Justice shows an 8.1% increase in reported domestic violence across the United States during the pandemic (Fana, Torrejón Pérez, and Fernández-Macías 2020, 3, 10).

facilities to the public, the DVI, NuLawLab, and College of Arts, Media and Design (CAMD) at Northeastern University collaborated to address gaps in services both created and exacerbated by COVID-19 using legal service design approaches as applied to a virtual clinic model. Namely, the collaborative focused on increasing access to the DVI's programs by creating web-based and other technological interventions, fundraising, starting a short-stay shelter service, and digitizing paper court forms for faster completion and filing. Design components such as the Hero's Journey, Storyboards, and Service Blueprints provided visual representations of diverse user experiences to anticipate engagement with remote court and clinical operations. This allowed the collaborative to address gaps and challenges resulting from COVID-19 and identify potential issues in pivoting to a remote clinical model.

To begin, the Hero's Journey is a storytelling framework that "can help organizations better understand how to address the wants and needs of a user" (Zaidi 2018). More specifically,

> by exploring their stories, we seek to understand how [users] interact with us, our designs, and/or the world at large. This often includes examining users' actions, emotions, thoughts, and the challenges they face. By doing so, we attempt to identify design opportunities and interventions that create new value for our user, but also for our organization, client, etc. (Zaidi 2018)

Mapping the hero's transformation and growth throughout their journey (i.e., use of the service) provides a useful metaphor for the scope and propriety of the service itself (Goldstein 2005, 8). As such, the collaborative constructed three Hero's Journeys based on anonymized, aggregate data from 2017–2020 about DVI clients. As composites, the hero-survivors included: (1) Survivor 1 – a single mom with limited access to technology whose relationship status and abusive partner are intentionally ambiguous; (2) Survivor 2 – a non-citizen immigrant mother with limited English proficiency, whose abusive partner threatens to deport her and their shared son; (3) and Survivor 3 – an unmarried, employed woman with no children whose live-in boyfriend physically abuses her and threatens her parents.[3] Each hero-survivor engaged with some or all of the proposed remote services (e.g., shelter, digitized court forms, web- and tech-based support). Moreover, because the DVI provides holistic care in partnership with other legal and social services organizations, it was equally important to construct Hero's Journeys for service providers in

[3] These composites are largely focused on cisgendered, heterosexual (cis-het) relationships, because the 2017–2020 data subset confirmed the DVI's largest client base are cis-het women in relationships with cis-het men. In further analyzing the client data from 2017–2022, cis-het female survivors have been and remain the DVI's largest client base. The DVI recognizes that dating, domestic, and sexual violence happens across gender expressions, sexual identities, relationship formations, and other intersectional identities. We strive to serve all clients and tailor our services as best we can to meet their specific needs.

symbiotic relationships with the DVI (e.g., hotel staff, student attorneys, and case managers). This ensured effective service for survivors and efficiency for providers (Frauendorf 2007, 47).

Once the collaborative addressed potential challenges and gaps in the service experience and had a sense of how survivors and service providers would engage with the remote clinic, the next step was to create a storyboard. A storyboard captures the front-stage service experience from the point of view of the end user (Miller and Flowers 2017). Put differently, it is a "visual representation of what you expect might happen from moment to moment in a service encounter ... allow[ing] us to 'see' the service before it's made and spot potential issues tied to use, resources, interactions, and possible touch-points" (Cense 2021). For these reasons, storyboarding is empathy in action (Miller & Flowers 2017). Breaking down each touchpoint (i.e., each contact, interaction, or encounter an end user has with a business, organization, or service provider) into its most basic elements helps identify and rethink assumptions built into the service plan (Cense 2021), and target infrastructural deficiencies that might otherwise be overlooked. Taking it a step further, storyboarding offers a medium through which service designers can ideate on future end user experiences (Miller and Flowers 2017). Moving through the remote clinical and shelter operations as a survivor utilizing these services, the collaborative immediately became aware of holes in our shelter plan, which leveraged use of empty long-term stay hotels across Massachusetts. Historically, the DVI worked closely with the shelter providers across the state to safely and anonymously house survivors; however, running a shelter was never part of the DVI's organizational or operational framework pre COVID-19. As such, the initial draft of the shelter program was flawed. Attorneys at the DVI did not consider survivors fleeing abuse (1) may not have identification to complete the hotel check-in process; (2) may need food, diapers, personal protective equipment (PPE), and other such resources upon arrival; and (3) need hotels located near public transport due to limited or no vehicle access. Storyboarding helped identify and rectify these oversights before rolling the program out to survivors.

For a comprehensive overview of the DVI's remote operations and services, the collaborative made service blueprints. A service blueprint charts "the relationships between different service components – people, props (physical or digital evidence), and processes – that are directly tied to touchpoints in a specific customer journey" (Gibbons 2017). Creating a service blueprint provides three main benefits: (1) a bird's eye view of multiple end user experiences to identify systemic issues; (2) opportunities for optimization, specifically eliminating redundancy and reducing risk of inconsistent or missing data; (3) and the visualization of front- and back-stage interactions that add cohesiveness to the end user experience (Frauendorf 2007, 47; Gibbons 2017). Using three service blueprints, the collaborative depicted how differently situated survivors, based on the hero-survivors outlined above, would (1) learn about the remote clinic; (2) use the new website and other newly designed technology to facilitate interaction with the DVI; (3) and be connected to DVI funded shelter services. Combining the people, props, and processes into an end-to-end, survivor-centered blueprint improved the support structures of the survivor experience by "creating process transparency at all stages of the service process" (Frauendorf 2007, 45).

Ultimately, an interdisciplinary collaboration among the DVI, NuLawLab, and CAMD applying legal service design approaches provided a multifaceted, survivor-centered solution to a complex socioeconomic and legal problem. Within the span of three and a half months, the DVI launched its website, DVILegal.org, and began accepting clients into its shelter program.

6.3 AN ENHANCED MODEL OF CLINICAL LEGAL EDUCATION: PIVOTING TO REMOTE OPERATIONS

6.3.1 *DVILegal.org: A New Place to Turn for Help*

On July 1, 2020, the DVI launched DVILegal.org, its virtual clinic. Leveraging legal service design approaches allowed the DVI to achieve three vital objectives for website users: (1) privacy and safety, (2) convenience, and (3) information and referrals.

To begin, the website includes a "Quick Escape" button. Once pressed, the website user is directed to an innocuous search engine like Google or Microsoft Bing, with no ability to use the back button on their browser to return to the DVI's web page. For users unfamiliar with the Quick Escape feature, the homepage includes a pop-up explaining its use and instructions to clear computer cookies so that information about online activity is not stored on the server or browser. Once appropriate safety measures were in place, the DVI turned its attention to language access. Given the DVI's pre-COVID-19 catchment area, client data from 2017–2019 about language needs, and census data outlining the most spoken languages in Boston, the website was translated into English, Spanish, Haitian Creole, and Portuguese. Language access decreases barriers to critical information and makes the experience more convenient and user friendly. Finally, the website includes a concise list of resources for state and national crisis, domestic, and sexual violence hotlines; legal services and court advocacy programs; community resources and social services; and abuse prevention, education, and support programs. This information allows website users time and capacity to find appropriate services tailored to their particular needs. Website users also have the option of completing the quick referral form for services and support from the DVI, which are received by DVI attorneys. Specifically, with the exception of three short-answer questions (e.g., name, contact information, safe contact times), the referral form is predominately in a yes/no drop-down format. With survivors and stay-at-home orders in mind, the quick referral form was created to maximize access to services while simultaneously decreasing the amount of time on the website so as not to raise flags for abusive partners.

The creation of DVILegal.org empowered the DVI to expand its catchment area and respond to increased demand by survivors for legal services. Attorneys and student attorneys represented survivors across the Commonwealth at virtual restraining order hearings in courts that historically were inaccessible to the DVI due to geographic restrictions.

6.3.2 *Digitally Automated Court Forms and Electronic Filing*

In late March 2020, the NuLawLab, in partnership with Suffolk Law School's Legal Innovation and Technology (LIT) Lab, began digitally automating court forms for which there were no electronic filing options. The MassAccess Document Assembly Line Project, spearheaded by the LIT Lab, allowed users to complete and file most court forms online (n.d.b). Law students in the NuLawLab seminar converted the abuse prevention order application and other forms, giving survivors the option to read or hear step-by-step instructions to complete the application and other documents (Suffolk Law School Legal Innovation and Technology Lab n.d.a). On May 20, 2020, the DVI was asked to review the first draft of the project. In response, the DVI provided suggestions to improve the MassAccess project based on data collected between March and May 2020 from survivors about challenges they faced accessing court services and filing their restraining order applications. Thereafter on June 3, 2020, the DVI had the opportunity to beta test the project with clients. In so doing, students and attorneys could keep track of errors the users encountered and their general impressions, thoughts, or suggestions to improve the end user experience. More importantly, firsthand impressions from survivors about areas of confusion and oversight in the design made the tool more user friendly for advocates and survivors alike. By July 21, 2020, a few short weeks after the DVI launched DVILegal.org, the LIT Lab made its MassAccess project publicly available, and the DVI used this tool to aid survivors applying for restraining orders. The intersection of law, service design, and digital technology through collaboration with the NuLawLab and LIT Lab gave the DVI's clients *more* access to legal services centered around their needs while also responding to service gaps by the court system.

6.3.3 *Safety Planning: Technology-Facilitated Abuse and Virtual Court*

To address safety concerns and update survivors on when and how to access their virtual hearings, the DVI implemented four action items: (1) an update to the client intake and risk assessment questionnaire with more robust information about technology, online activity, and technology-facilitated abuse (TFA)[4]; (2) research

[4] Technology is a tool that abusers use to facilitate harassment, control, and abuse. In the context of domestic violence and sexual assault, online harassment and crimes are part of a larger system of abuse (Lee 2016).

technology and online safety planning tools; (3) train survivors, community partners, student groups, and the public on TFA as well as online and technology safety; and (4) create Zoom and telephone safety guides for survivors attending court virtually.

The updated intake and risk assessment included, for example, questions about what types of devices were in the home or in survivors' possession, if the children owned devices, who purchased the devices, who has administrator access to devices and associated accounts (e.g., internet and phone), and if the devices are on a shared cloud or family plan. With this information, students and attorneys are better able to incorporate more robust technology and online safety planning in conversations with their clients. Furthermore, these questions give the DVI a clearer sense of which clients need more support and training to safely use their phones, tablets, and computers, as well as safeguard their online presence. For example, the DVI created targeted training and support materials to address safety and privacy concerns expressed by survivors regarding virtual hearings. Offering advice and concrete steps about masking IP addresses, blocking phone numbers, and the benefits of Zoom backgrounds validated survivors' concerns for their safety and, when properly implemented, kept them safe during virtual hearings when the abuser was present. These are just a few examples of safety strategies addressed by legal service design approaches.

6.3.4 *Making a Dollar Out of Fifteen Cents: Fundraising, Shelter, and Wraparound Services*

To address the increased demand in shelter and other services, the DVI put into motion a long-term fundraising campaign, developed partnerships with hotel chains, and joined a newly organized housing collaborative with shelter providers across the Commonwealth to create and share resources. Donations supported such wraparound services as rides to shelter programs (including hotels) and food, clothing, personal protective equipment, and cleaning supplies for families in shelter. The funding also covered rental and utility arrearages, home and car safety equipment and technology, as well as storage and moving costs. Costs associated with these items can make leaving an abusive situation more difficult. A timely partnership with a local ad hoc shelter collaborative gave the DVI points of contact for the Commonwealth's domestic violence shelters, a place to brainstorm best practices for running a shelter program, and access to local, state, and federal shelter funding through Casa Myrna (a Boston domestic violence services organization). The DVI's shelter program opened on July 1, 2020, the same day DVILegal.org went public. As of the time of this writing, forty individuals, including twenty-five children, have received shelter, with stays ranging from one to eight months, though most participants stay about three months. Further, Casa Myrna gave the DVI gift cards to local grocery and chain stores (like Target), and new computers to ease a survivor's transition into shelter. When given a choice about a welcome basket or gift cards to large retail stores, survivors chose the gift cards, which gave them freedom to make appropriate decisions for themselves and their children. The computers were given to clients with children, clients who did not own a computer, and clients who had their computers broken during an abusive incident. Survivors were free to complete online intakes for legal and other services, as well as fill out applications for jobs, housing, school, and benefit programs without concern that their online activity was being monitored.

In the end, incorporating service design components in the DVI's systems created a survivor-centered framework that tackled systemic and pernicious access to justice issues that have a chilling effect on survivors seeking legal redress, while simultaneously amplifying the voices, experiences, and needs of survivors.

6.4 THE HYBRID APPROACH: AN ENHANCED MODEL OF CLINICAL LEGAL EDUCATION

The past two and a half years have given the DVI new insight on best practices for the provision of survivor-centered services. Although COVID-19 rages on and has found a boon companion in monkeypox, stay-at-home orders are no longer in effect and community centers, courts, health clinics, hospitals, and schools have reopened for in-person services. In response, the DVI has once again restructured, fusing its virtual clinic with its in-person / in-community pre-COVID-19 operations. Not only will survivors have numerous options and opportunities for how, when, and where to seek services, but also legal service design will continue to inform the DVI's work benefiting survivors, students, attorneys, and community partners alike.

REFERENCES

Ansell, Ryan, and John P. Mullins. 2021. "COVID-19 Ends Longest Employment Expansion in CES History, Causing Unprecedented Job Losses in 2020." *Monthly Labor Review*, June 16. https://doi.org/10.21916/mlr.2021.13.

Baker, Charles. 2020. "COVID-19 State of Emergency." *Commonwealth of Massachusetts*. Last modified June 15, 2021. www.mass.gov/info-details/covid-19-state-of-emergency#limits-on-gatherings-(archive)-.

Boston Planning & Development Agency. 2017. "Boston's Top 5 Foreign Languages Spoken at Home, 2015." *Boston: Norman B. Leventhal Map & Education Center*. Last modified 2017. https://collections.leventhalmap.org/search/commonwealth:h989r7038.

Boston Planning & Development Agency Research Division. 2021. "Boston in Context: Neighborhoods 2015-2019 American Community Survey." *Boston Planning & Development Agency Research Division*. Last modified 2021. www.bostonplans.org/getattachment/e2eb8432-ac72-4a7e-8909-57aafdfbecd9.

Campbell, Andrew M. 2020. "An Increasing Risk of Family Violence during the Covid-19 Pandemic: Strengthening Community Collaborations to Save Lives." *Forensic Science International: Reports* 2 (April): 100089. https://doi.org/10.1016/j.fsir.2020.100089.

Carey, Paula M. Chief Justice of the Trial Court. 2020. *Trial Court Emergency Administrative Order 20-8: Trial Court Order Supplementing the Supreme Judicial Court Order*

Regarding Court Operations Under the Exigent Circumstances Created by the COVID-19 (Coronavirus) Pandemic. https://archives.lib.state.ma.us/bitstream/handle/2452/826494/on1153169107.pdf.

Casey, John D. 2020. "Probate and Family Court Standing Order 2-20, as Amended Effective April 6, 2020." *State Library of Massachusetts. Probate and Family Court.* Last modified April 6, 2020. https://archives.lib.state.ma.us/bitstream/handle/2452/825963/on1151409488.pdf?sequence=2&isAllowed=y.

Cense. 2021. "Concept Scenarios + Storyboards for Service Design." *Cense Ltd.* (blog), October 19. www.cense.ca/storyboards-for-service-design/.

Centers for Disease Control and Prevention. 2022. "CDC Museum COVID-19 Timeline." *David J. Spencer CDC Museum.* Last modified March 15, 2023. www.cdc.gov/museum/timeline/covid19.html.

Deloitte, Datawheel, and Cesar Hidalgo. n.d. "Data USA: Boston, MA Census Place." *Data USA.* Accessed August 22, 2022. https://datausa.io/profile/geo/suffolk-county-ma.

Dooling, Shannon. 2020. "Advocates Fear Domestic Abuse Survivors Are 'Trapped with Their Abusers' during Pandemic." *WBUR*, April 13. www.wbur.org/news/2020/04/13/coronavirus-domestic-abuse-violence-survivors-boston.

Fana, Marta, Sergio Torrejón Pérez, and Enrique Fernández-Macías. 2020. "Employment Impact of Covid-19 Crisis: From Short Term Effects to Long Terms Prospects." *Journal of Industrial and Business Economics* 47, no. 3 (July): 391–410. https://doi.org/10.1007/s40812–020-00168-5.

Frauendorf, Janine. 2007. *Customer Processes in Business-to-Business Service Transactions.* Berlin, Germany: Springer Science & Business Media.

Gibbons, Sarah. 2017. "Service Blueprints: Definition." *Nielsen Norman Group.* Last modified August 27, 2017. www.nngroup.com/articles/service-blueprints-definition/.

Goldstein, Lisa S. 2005. "Becoming a Teacher as a Hero's Journey: Using Metaphor in Preservice Teacher Education." *Teacher Education Quarterly* 32, no. 1 (Winter): 7–24.

Henry, Meghan, Rian Watt, Anna Mahathey, Jillian Ouellette, Aubrey Sitler, Abt Associates, and The U.S. Department of Housing and Urban Development. 2020. *The 2019 Annual Homeless Assessment Report (AHAR) to Congress, Part 1: Point-in-Time Estimates of Homelessness.* www.huduser.gov/portal/sites/default/files/pdf/2019-AHAR-Part-1.pdf.

Kim, Miso. 2021. "A Study of Dignity as a Principle of Service Design." *International Journal of Design* 15, no. 3 (December): 87–100.

Lee, Kaofeng. 2016. "Technology Abuse: It's Still About Power & Control." *Women's Media Center*, February 10. https://womensmediacenter.com/speech-project/technology-abuse-its-still-about-power-control.

Mapping Police Violence, Inc. 2021. "2021 Police Violence Report." *The Official Mapping Police Violence Database.* Edited by Samuel Sinyangwe. www.google.com/url?sa=t&rct=j&q=&esrc=s&source=web&cd=&ved=
2ahUKEwjn772modOAAxUUrYkEHQizCvgQjBB6BAgREAE&url=https%3A%2F%2Fpoliceviolencereport.org%2Fpoliceviolencereport2021.pdf%3Fo&usg=
AOvVaw3TSCh1fjlT2WfSuH9M1wm4&opi=89978449.

Massachusetts Department of Public Health. 2020. "Sexual and Domestic Violence Programs 2019 Novel Coronavirus (COVID-19) Guidance." *Mass.Gov. Commonwealth of Massachusetts.* Last modified April 23, 2020. www.mass.gov/lists/april-2020-massachusetts-official-state-agency-resources-related-to-covid-19.

Miller, Megan Erin, and Erik Flowers. 2017. "The Difference between a Journey Map and a Service Blueprint." *Practical by Design (blog)*, October 16. https://blog.practicalservicedesign.com/the-difference-between-a-journey-map-and-a-service-blueprint-31a6e24c4a6c.

Mineo, Liz. 2022. "'Shadow Pandemic' of Domestic Violence." *Harvard Gazette*, June 29. https://news.harvard.edu/gazette/story/2022/06/shadow-pandemic-of-domestic-violence/.

National Low Income Housing Coalition. 2022. "Housing Needs by State: Massachusetts." *National Low Income Housing Coalition*. Last modified 2022. https://nlihc.org/housing-needs-by-state/massachusetts.

Office of the Governor. 2020a. COVID-19 Order (2020-03-15): Order Temporarily Closing All Public and Private Elementary and Secondary Schools, March 15, 2020, State Library of Massachusetts Digital Collections, COVID-19 Orders, available at https://archives.lib.state.ma.us/items/2e09e942-3873-4842-a413-cae622c5b5fb (last visited March 19, 2024).

2020b. COVID-19 Order (2020-03-18): COVID-19 Order (2020-03-18): Order Temporarily Closing All Child Care Programs and Authorizing the Temporary Creation and Operation of Emergency Child Care Programs, March 18, 2020, State Library of Massachusetts Digital Collections, COVID-19 Orders, available at https://archives.lib.state.ma.us/items/dacc1d21-29e6-44b2-b9cd-e9cb3d21b43c (last visited March 19, 2024).

2020c. COVID-19 Order (2020-03-23): COVID-19 Order (2020-03-23): Order Assuring Continued Operation of Essential Services in the Commonwealth, Closing Certain Workplaces, and Prohibiting Gatherings of More Than 10 People, March 23, 2020, State Library of Massachusetts Digital Collections, COVID-19 Orders, available at https://archives.lib.state.ma.us/items/79553984-91bb-4576-82c5-3e4d9c3b87ce (last visited March 19, 2024).

Pickens, Josie. 2020. "Kassandra Jackson Was Seeking a Protection Order, Judge Assaulted Her Instead." *Essence Magazine*, October 23. www.essence.com/news/kassandra-jackson-michael-bachman/.

Ronquillo, Roberto Jr. 2020a. Commonwealth of Massachusetts. Boston Municipal Court. *Boston Municipal Court Standing Order 3-20: Limiting In-Person Appearances in Boston Municipal Courthouses to Emergency Matters*. www.mass.gov/boston-municipal-court-standing-orders/boston-municipal-court-standing-order-3-20-limiting-in-person-appearances-in-boston-municipal-courthouses-to-emergency-matters.

2020b. State Library of Massachusetts. Boston Municipal Court. *Boston Municipal Court Standing Order 4-20: Limiting In-Person Appearances in Boston Municipal Courthouses to Emergency Matters*. https://archives.lib.state.ma.us/bitstream/handle/2452/825659/on1150889493.pdf.

Suffolk Law School Legal Innovation and Technology Lab. n.d.a. "Court Forms Online (MassAccess)." Accessed August 24, 2022. https://courtformsonline.org/.

n.d.b. "The Document Assembly Line." Accessed August 24, 2022. https://suffolklitlab.org/docassemble-AssemblyLine-documentation/docs/.

Zaidi, Leah. 2018. "How to Use the Hero's Journey as a Design-Thinking + Foresight Tool." *NYC Design*, October 28. https://medium.com/nyc-design/how-to-use-the-heros-journey-as-a-design-thinking-tool-c4901be5ce.

7

More Than a Building

The Architecture of Fairness and Dignity

*Dan Jackson and Sanea Lamas**

7.1 INTRODUCTION

When you walk into a courtroom, what is the first thing you notice? Perhaps it is the elevated dais where the judge sits. Perhaps it is the box on the side where members of the jury sit. Or perhaps it is the tables directly across from the judge where the parties and their lawyers sit. How about the low bar or barrier between all those institutional legal folks and everyone else? Your answer to this question is going to depend very much on your perspective and whether you interact much with formal court processes. Judges, attorneys, and court personnel will navigate these spaces with the secondhand familiarity we all bring to physical spaces we exist in for any significant amount of time and routine.

A person who is coming to a courthouse for the first time, however, will by the very virtue of necessity take a closer look at the space as they figure out how to navigate it. They will look for things like signs to guide them to the right courtroom, or at least the place they've been told to show up. They are likely arriving at a foreign location and a foreign experience with a lot of anxiety, frustration, and fear. If they are fortunate enough to be accompanied by a friend, witness, or lawyer, they may be surprised by the lack of private space for conversations with confidants. They are likely to encounter the person or entity with whom they are in litigation. Conversations between the parties can ensue, and they aren't pleasant.

A courthouse is a unique part of our built environment: the places where we live, work, and interact with others. Our built environment has a defining influence over our ability to experience healthy, fulfilling, and dignified interactions with the spaces around us (Institute for Human Rights and Business 2019). Because court is the place where we go to settle disputes both small (traffic tickets) and large (child custody and evictions), its design has a big influence on the experiences of those

* With contributions from Marilyn Moedinger.

using it. Courthouse design has been shown to have the power to enhance or detract from human dignity, and poorly designed courthouses and courtrooms can create heightened apprehension and anxiety for people (Jandura 2018). Yet every detail of the building is decided by someone or some group of people – from the large gestures (the buildings' facades) to the small details (the languages, font, and size of wayfinding signage). Nothing is inadvertent. Some less permanent details emerge through use, such as the tables and chairs and their placements in waiting areas and other parts of the building. But each such decision is a design decision by *someone*, and each decision can either enhance or degrade the dignity of the people moving through each space.

This chapter argues that prioritizing dignity for everyone in the design of courthouses and courtrooms makes them operate better by making them less harrowing and easier to navigate for those unfamiliar with them. We start with a modest examination of the relatively recent history of the architecture of adjudication generally and courthouses in the United States in particular, which includes some details on how courthouses are generally conceived, funded, and designed. Our argument then pivots to a detailed case study of a spatial and pedagogical collaboration among Wentworth architecture faculty and students, Northeastern Law faculty and students, and a Massachusetts court.[1]

7.2 A BRIEF HISTORY OF COURTHOUSES

Adjudication and dispute resolution have a long history, dating back thousands of years. In ancient times, judges announced verdicts and rulers administered penalties as part of quasi-religious rituals. Today, courts are recognized as public institutions that provide essential services, and it is essential that they are accessible to all. As Resnik and Curtis (2011) note, courts must be both physically and substantively accessible to the public.

When the legal institutions and traditions that undergird today's US systems formed in feudal England and Britain, judges were appointed based on their loyalty to the sovereign or the state, among other qualifications (Baker 2002). In countries like the United States and many other western nations that draw on this history, the courts and judges are now quasi-independent, with the unique power to invalidate executive and legislative actions. In modern times, anyone can ostensibly participate in the court process. Almost anyone can be called as a witness, and almost anyone can serve on a jury. Moreover, everyone can end up in a courtroom as a litigant whether they want to or not.

[1] Our focus is on legal institutions in the United States, and we direct readers interested in an international perspective to Sofia Stolk's analysis of international courts and design in Chapter 17 of this volume.

Over time, the buildings that housed courts have undergone significant transformations. Initially in the United States, state court functions were situated in versatile town halls and administrative buildings that were shared by different public officials and offices (Resnik and Curtis 2011). For instance, in the 1800s, state courts were widespread in the United States while the federal government owned very few buildings. None of those buildings with the state courts functioning within them were specifically designated as "courthouses" until the 1850s. By the close of the twentieth century, however, the federal government had constructed over 550 specialized courthouses for its cases and judges (Resnik, Curtis, and Tait 2013). These structures were purposely built to meet the unique needs of the judiciary and the judicial branch of the growing federal government. That exclusive designation is now an overwhelming feature of state courts as well.

Courthouse building design variations have most recently been propelled by a marketplace of lawyers, judges, architects, and court administrators who cross national boundaries and shape construction plans at the regional, national, and international levels (Stolk 2024). When we think about court design in the United States, we tend to think about the neoclassical style of the Supreme Court building (built in 1935) with its formal entrance to the "temple of justice" and the marble white stairs. The style of the Supreme Court building was chosen to reflect democratic ideals as expressed in the classical architecture of Ancient Greece (Craven 2018). Its sculptures inside the building and outside depict narratives of mercy and classical symbols of justice. Of course, the ideals being spatialized in the architecture were not available, or even applicable, to entire swaths of Americans at the time the building was built. To this day, the architecture's messaging is aspirational, and still not representative of reality. Yet the building holds as a dominant symbol of justice in the United States.

By 1991, the federal judiciary had secured $868 million in new construction funds in sixteen years (McCarthy and Treacy 2000). In the decade that followed, plans were made for 160 courthouse constructions or renovations to be supported by $8 billion. Ten federal courthouse projects represented the federal government's largest customer for building constructions from 1995 to 2005 (Resnik, Curtis, and Tait 2013). At the same time, the American with Disabilities Act (ADA) legislated equal access for people of various disabilities in these new structures (Jandura 2018).

Thanks to the ADA and state analogs, new courthouses around the country now must have doors wide enough for wheelchairs, and majestic stone staircases cannot be the only means of entering and leaving a courthouse. This is important to underline for our purposes. Significant architectural transformation can be achieved at scale in society, even when it looks like – and is – a monumental task. For most Americans, we don't notice the impact the ADA had on architecture because we don't require those modifications to access and occupy the spaces. For the mobility-impaired, those changes affect a radically different, and more dignified, experience with built space.

7.3 RECENT EVOLUTIONS

Other enlightenments are beginning to crawl into the built justice environment beyond the requirements of the ADA. One recent contemporary design issue that a few actors are pursuing is creating trauma-informed courthouses and courtrooms. "A trauma-informed courthouse creates a safer environment for traumatized individuals" (Jandura 2018). One could argue that some of these interventions are ostensibly already required under the law, given that trauma-related conditions can qualify as disabilities under the ADA and the law's broad mandate. Regardless, individuals who come to court often have experienced trauma in various forms and degrees, which can be triggered or exacerbated by elements in their surrounding environment. Indeed, certain physical elements in a building design can trigger traumatic episodes for some individuals. For instance, congested waiting spaces, dimly lit rooms, and a lack of signage can contribute to feelings of anxiety and distress (Evans 2003). There is movement in this regard as new courthouse buildings are contemplated, planned, and built. The National Center for State Courts (NCSC), for example, devotes considerable resources to the development of court design guides, principles, and critical thought pieces that touch on the need for space design informed by a variety of factors not previously contemplated (McKenzie and Matthias 2020). And the National Child Traumatic Stress Network (NCTSN) produces guides for judges and court administrators on how to be aware of the impact of trauma on individuals and how to take steps to create a safe and supportive environment, including within the built environment (National Child Traumatic Stress Network 2015). Guides and thought pieces are not legally binding, of course, but they do provide some frameworks for courts to think about in creating more thoughtfully designed spaces.

One challenge regarding how courthouse designs happen is that the people designing courtrooms and courthouse spaces have little to no knowledge of what kind of spaces are actually needed in order to provide a comfortable experience to everyone within the general public (Duncanson and Henderson 2022). This is not to say that the architects, engineers, and court personnel dedicating time (and careers) to the work are not experts or are somehow approaching the task with bad motives. But by tradition and design, courthouse creation has had relatively little input from the general public.

None of this is to suggest that the entire enterprise has been stuck in Ancient Greece for the last 2,500-plus years. Like the aforementioned NTCSN and NCSC initiatives, efforts to reimagine the American courthouse have been plentiful over the years, extending a grand tradition of at least *trying* to perfect self-government. One such design exercise took place in New York when the Center for Court Innovation (CCI) worked with the strategy and graphic design studio Zago to test improvements to a Manhattan Criminal Court building, which had been designed in the 1940s and handled over 100,000 filings a year at the time of the work in 2007

(Gold-LaGratta 2018). They had two goals: (1) make the court processes that exist clearer, and (2) make transparent and explain the processes court users cannot see but that would be helpful for users to see in order for them to understand things that impact them. With a comprehensive and inclusive design process and a clear understanding of the design constraints, their intervention was simple but powerful: improve and add signage throughout the court. Additional interventions were tested in two select courtrooms, including signs outlining the courtroom rules and a name placard for the judge. Seems pretty straightforward, doesn't it?

Our pedagogical and practical mashup among Wentworth Institute of Technology, Northeastern University School of Law's NuLawLab, and the Massachusetts Housing Court is of a similar vein.

7.4 MORE THAN BUILDINGS

We now turn to that project as a case study in designing for dignity. The effort was centered on Wentworth adjunct professor Marilyn Moedinger's graduate architecture course "More Than Buildings" at Wentworth Institute of Technology in 2018.[2] Her course was an iteration of a graduate-level architectural design seminar in advanced topics but offered with a significant twist. It was held in tandem with the NuLawLab's first iteration of its "Master Class in Legal Design" at Northeastern University School of Law, a course envisioned to embed law students into graduate design courses, which was led by chapter coauthor Dan Jackson. Our external partner for key experiential components was the Massachusetts Housing Court, which was gracious enough to invite the seminar students and faculty into the Edward W. Brooke Courthouse in Boston and enthusiastically agreed to allow the students to install and test a number of temporary interventions in the building atrium, hallway outside the courtrooms, and clerk's office. For the balance of this chapter, we shall refer to the entire project and both classes combined as "More Than Buildings."

The individuals working on this project included thirteen graduate architecture students from Wentworth Institute of Technology and one law student from Northeastern University School of Law.[3] Our partners at the Massachusetts

[2] Marilyn Moedinger is better known as the founder and principal of Runcible Studios, which for ten years has "executed projects ranging from ground-up residential to extensive renovations of residences to commercial and industrial spaces, from high-concept feasibility studies for developers to graphics and social media management and everything in between" (Runcible Studios, n.d.). Marilyn also served as the chair of the NuLawLab advisory board for five years and has contributed to a number of NuLawLab projects over the years. This chapter is dedicated to Marilyn's unyielding belief in the power of design.

[3] We expected a low number of law students for the first iteration of the Master Class in Legal Design but did not anticipate it would be quite this low (the enrollment for the Master Class is capped at eight). Nevertheless, we found a workable solution. Rather than embed one or two law students in each one of four teams of architecture students, we had the single law student

Housing Court were The Honorable Timothy Sullivan, Chief Justice of the Housing Court, Paul Burke, Housing Court Clerk, and Benjamin Adeyenko, Housing Court Deputy Clerk. Because the two academic calendars between Wentworth and Northeastern did not align perfectly, the architecture course ran for a good month before the law school course joined, which then ran a couple of weeks longer than the architecture class.

Marilyn's vision for the course was for the students to work together to research, identify, frame, and propose solutions to issues they uncover in the processes surrounding housing court and in the physical space of the court itself. Students were to carefully consider the diverse users of the space and legal system, the financial implications of their ideas, and the logistical nature of making physical and/or logistical interventions in the highly regulated, and possibly contentious, spaces found in court buildings. The course was designed to be highly interactive, combining lecture, workshop, and field-learning formats, and was tailored on the architecture side for students interested in the impact of design thinking and training outside the bounds of traditional practice, design-build, and community engagement. The entirety of the student experience was chronicled in a blog, which at the time of the publication of this volume remains available at www.morethanbuildings .blogspot.com, and from which some of the observations and insights summarized below are derived.

Texts assigned included *Evicted* by Matthew Desmond and The 2017 Greater Boston Housing Report Card by The Boston Foundation. Twice a week, faculty and students convened on Wentworth's campus for two hours, engaging in rounds of conversation, creation, teaming, ideating, critiquing, and visiting Housing Court on "eviction days" (Thursdays). By the mid-point of the course, four teams of students had formed to generate, build, install, and test ideas in two discrete areas: wayfinding/signage and separation/privacy. Out of class work included additional observational field research, design/build activities to create the specific installations, on-site installation, and observations of actual litigants in Boston Housing Court using the spaces with the temporary installations over the course of one full day.

The balance of this chapter section focuses on outcomes from the four student teams in the following order: Wayfinding, Signage, Separation, and Privacy, as detailed in the four teams' final project reports and informed by the reflections and learning documented in the seminar blog, to which we direct readers who would like to explore the student learning experience and reflections in greater detail. Each subsection details select insights that the team derived from observational field research at the courthouse (informed by the course material and

circulate among the four architecture teams. Shoutout here to Mark Costas, NUSL '2018, for being that first brave Master Class student. We've solved the low enrollment issue, with our most recent offering of the Master Class in 2022 filling all eight slots.

FIGURE 7.1. Brooke Courthouse Atrium schematic as proposed by Team Wayfinding and Brooke Courthouse signage as installed.
(Image and photo credit: Sarah Edwards, Sachia Chin Loy, and Omar Malkawi)

activities), the interventions proposed and built, and the observations of public use of the interventions on "eviction day."[4]

7.4.1 *Wentworth Team Wayfinding*[5]

Team Wayfinding's courthouse observations initially revealed what was surprising to them: the dedication of court staff and judges to *preventing* evictions rather than simply processing them.[6] Observing judges actively engaging with tenants and landlords to mediate disputes and prevent forced departures motivated this team to extend that ethos to the court's architectural design, with a particular focus on wayfinding in the entrance atrium and hallways along the perimeter of the atrium.

By focusing design interventions on user awareness of space, this team sought to assist visitors in navigating the building by reducing confusion in the expansive atrium space. Because the overall space design was identical on each floor, and the central atrium and hallways generally lacked large signs to reference in navigating the space, Team Wayfinding found themselves disoriented upon visiting the courthouse. Their solution was specific to the atrium: large, bold color coding of the architectural elements of the atrium itself to guide unfamiliar visitors to the locations they needed to go to at a glance (Figure 7.1).[7]

[4] For purposes of conciseness, not every idea and intervention are detailed in this chapter.

[5] Team Wayfinding was composed of Wentworth students Sarah Edwards, Sachia Chin Loy, and Omar Malkawi.

[6] This is a testament to the hard work and dedication of the judges and staff of the Massachusetts courts. A special note of recognition is extended to Trial Court Chief Justice Paula M. Carey, Housing Court Chief Justice Timothy Sullivan, Court Clerk Paul Burke, and Deputy Clerk Benjamin Adeyenko, who set the bar high for the institutional commitment toward effective dispute resolution.

[7] Because the Brooke Courthouse serves other business beyond Housing Court, a permanent installation would need to accommodate others as well.

The color-coded outlines were developed to point to specific locations key for every visit: the Court Service Center, Housing Court Information Desk, Housing Court Clerk's Office, and the Housing Court Courtrooms. Visitors could then see exactly where they needed to go just by standing in the atrium and looking up and around.

Implementation involved the planned installation of numerous printouts of varying sizes. On site it became clear the original plan of applying the printouts around the architectural elements was not practical, primarily for installation safety reasons coupled with the short amount of time available to install. Eventually, team members placed the signage along the atrium's existing railing. While this solution lacked the visual punch of using the architectural elements of pillars and floors to convey location, the observations of the public in the atrium after installation showed that those who were unfamiliar with the building found their necessary location by looking at the signs up on the railings. Because the signs were visible from all points around the atrium (other than immediately behind the sign placement), the students observed that they became reference points throughout the day for those visiting the Brooke Courthouse.

7.4.2 *Wentworth Team Signage*[8]

The second team to tackle location markers and spatial directions was Team Signage. Their initial courthouse observations homed in on the existing signage for building information, largely contained on wall-mounted computer screens, which cycled through names and locations for the day's hearings, and the small and unobtrusive bronze room markers outside locations such as the clerk's office and the numbered courtrooms. Their design intervention consisted of a cohesive, easily identifiable signage system for the Housing Court, with placements at the courthouse entrance, the elevator banks, the entrances to all circulation areas on all floors, and door tags at the entrances of the Housing Court–related spaces. The signs were color coded, branded, and plentiful, directing users through the courthouse to their specific destination (Figure 7.2).[9]

Evaluating the effectiveness of the signage proved challenging for this team. Despite observing people looking at the signs, discerning whether they were genuinely using them for guidance was difficult. Encouragingly, court staff noticed and appreciated the signs, sparking discussions about comprehensive wayfinding within the courthouse. Both the color-coding program and the location tags were well received by staff (including non–Housing Court employees), indicating a

[8] Team Signage was composed of Wentworth students Gizelle Hourani, Brian Sanford, and Katya Stassen.

[9] Teams Wayfinding and Signage coordinated on the color scheme and fonts for installation.

FIGURE 7.2. Wentworth Team Signage results.
(Image credit: Gizelle Hourani, Brian Sanford, and Katya Stassen.)

receptiveness among the building personnel to scaling out the signage program to the entire courthouse.

7.4.3 *Wentworth Team Separation*[10]

We now turn to the two teams that tackled issues of interpersonal space needs and privacy. Team Separation focused attention on an overlooked issue: the desire for separation among the litigants going through the eviction process from the landlords evicting them (recall that tensions run high on eviction day). This team identified the lack of privacy and space for legal consultations as intensifying already tense landlord–tenant relations, and thus overall discomfort for both parties.

To address the issue, Team Separation proposed a remarkably simple intervention in the Clerk's Office waiting room: a wooden partition wall, splitting the generously sized waiting area into two sections. No labels or signs were introduced (Figure 7.3). This allowed individuals to easily separate themselves from the opposing party or anyone else with whom they did not want to interact, decreasing unwanted interactions and increasing overall comfort.

Post-installation observations showed the divider acting precisely as intended. While students were not able to identify who was avoiding whom in the waiting

[10] Team Separation was composed of students Brody Walsh, Mykaela Scarpace, and Victoria Deveau.

FIGURE 7.3. Wentworth Team Separation illustration of Clerk Office waiting area divider as installed.
(Image credit: Brody Walsh, Mykaela Scarpace, and Victoria Deveau.)

area, they did observe people customizing their spaces within the divided areas by moving and grouping chairs. This behavior was different than what the students had observed before the divider was installed, when all the chairs faced in one direction and were not generally moved around by the people sitting in the waiting area. Students and faculty concluded that this demonstrated promising comfort levels in that space on that particular day by those particular people.

7.4.4 *Wentworth Team Privacy*[11]

The final team tackled privacy, with initial observations revealing a notable lack of private spaces for confidential conversations between litigants and witnesses as well as lawyers and clients. This included those participating in the Lawyer for a Day program run by the Boston Bar Association that pairs unrepresented tenants with volunteer attorneys for just that one day in court. Lacking the privacy necessary for sensitive and rushed discussions, attorney–client conversations were seen to occur in public hallways and other open areas throughout the building.

Team Privacy installed booths in the generous hallways directly outside the main Housing Courtrooms. With these corridors open to the atrium below, they exploited the white noise from the atrium as a natural sound barrier, providing an additional layer of privacy. The design consisted of two 5' x 5' portable booths, specifically intended for the Lawyer of the Day volunteers to have private conversations. These booths, collapsible and mobile, were built with 1′ × 3′ wood frames, braced for stability, and wrapped in white vinyl printed with a graphic outline of people seated in conversation on the outside, which was reflected in reality with each booth equipped with two chairs and a folding table (Figure 7.4).

[11] Team Privacy was composed of students Ben Gilbert, Mackenzie Kane, Tyler Winslow, and Craig Johnson.

FIGURE 7.4. Wentworth Team Privacy illustration of portable privacy booths as built. (Image credit: Ben Gilbert, Mackenzie Kane, Tyler Winslow, and Craig Johnson.)

Installation was directly outside the courtrooms for easy access by the volunteer lawyers and litigants. Observations during public use showed the booths providing adequate room for conversations and the vinyl covering offering a good balance between visual/sound privacy and aesthetics. It was clear, however, that some courthouse users were uncertain about the booths' purpose, suggesting a need for better signage. In addition, few of the volunteer lawyers made use of the booths, significantly limiting the number of observed uses. This revealed the importance of more effective cultivation of stakeholder groups in the design process.

7.5 REFLECTIONS AND CONCLUSION

As we were preparing to strike the installations at the close of the day, the Housing Court Clerk Paul Burke surprised us all: he asked if the Housing Court could keep all of them in place to continue to use another day, until such time as they wore out or were no longer desired. The students were happy to donate their creations to our Massachusetts courts. While we obviously can't assess from a single day of installation and observation whether interventions like these impact the dignity of the many tenants moving through the space while they are being evicted, we do know that the Housing Court employees found the interventions useful to the operation of the court. This supports a finding that our courts consider interventions like better signage and more sensitive space arrangements to be something that enhances the litigants' experience in a way that advances dispute resolution.

Our reasoning is as follows. Recall that Housing Court Clerk Burke and Deputy Clerk Adeyenko were among the leaders seeking to make the experience of the Housing Court more emotionally conducive to dispute resolution. Recall also that handing over the built interventions was never in the cards when planning this project with them. It was quite a surprise to all of us when Paul requested the Housing Court keep the artifacts. The fact that they wanted to keep them all is a data point supporting the observation that the decisions architects, space planners, and designers make in designing courthouses impact the both the emotional experience of litigants (part of Burke and Adeyenko's motivation) and the efficient operation of the court (which is the biggest part of their job). All of which brings us back to Marilyn's vision for the course: for the students to propose solutions to issues they uncover in the processes surrounding the Housing Court and in the physical space of the court itself by carefully considering the diverse users of the space within the legal system and the logistical nature of making physical interventions in the highly regulated, and possibly contentious, spaces found in court buildings.

What of that student experience at the time, and what was learned? The course blog offers plenty to digest regarding what the students were experiencing in their learning and journeys through the course, but we are not going to analyze and summarize that here. We thought it would be more interesting to examine one student's journey as reported on the blog, and then catch up with that same student five years later, to explore what was remembered from the course and is being applied today.

Omar Malkawi is that student. He was a member of Wentworth Team Wayfinding, three students who proposed the architectural coding of atrium structures to guide new visitors to the correct spaces for the Housing Court. Omar obtained his Bachelor of Science and master's degree, both in architecture, from Wentworth. He now works as a project manager for Terva Project Management (TERVA Corporation, n.d.). There are only three direct entries from Omar on the blog, but a few insights stand out: one from the very beginning of the course, and one as the course wrapped up and the installation and testing were over. They are quoted below (Malkawi 2018a, Malkawi 2018b):

> *Evicted,* by Matthew Desmond, has been an eye-opening introduction to [the] complex world of housing and evictions that has helped me better humanize people's personal stories and struggles. With housing, many parties are involved, each with their own goals and challenges. Housing is more than a roof and utilities; it shapes the lives of people and can greatly affect their quality of life.
>
> [T]he process of design for public spaces is a complex and risky [one] . . . . The parameters for our interventions were very strictly guided by the court staff and the installations had to meet a rigorous set of guidelines. Throughout the term, we came to understand that legally, it takes a very (very very) long time and much effort to change anything in the court[s] . . . . I now fully understand why it is such a complex process. The government is trusted by the public to represent all its constituents, therefore, any change that will affect[] the public has to go through a rigorous analysis and be scrutinized down to a T.

Speaking with Omar five years later, it was striking how his learning in the course is firmly baked into his career building spaces for people. Some of that comes from the law of ADA compliance with which Omar is exceptionally facile, and some from the experience in the course. We will let Omar speak for himself:

> There's multiple different clients for almost every project ... and everybody has different priorities. [We] find ourselves sometimes educating clients about why the

> hallway can't be [only] two feet wide because you want this office to be a little bigger . . . things that are basic for people who work in this world [of building] often, but not for people that are [approaching the project] from whatever their priorities [are]. Reduce the cost as much as possible, yes, but at what point will it start pushing some people out? On the other end, sometimes there's the unfortunate reality [that t]he budget constraints and schedule still exist. So, you do get to a point where there is one "want to have" that you can't get to. There [are] certainly things [in] the case of cost or security that you [must do, and those] limit certain accessibility items. It's always a balancing game. *But as a society, we can probably lean a little bit further towards making things more accessible. I'll tell you that much.*[12]

"More Than Buildings" was not a course that focused specifically on dignity *as* dignity. Nevertheless, these interventions and the reception they received from users and observers reveal some interesting things about how dignity for the people navigating courts can be enhanced by deploying intensive human centered design in the design of the architecture and the space itself. Consider again the experience of the people who were using the newly divided Clerk's Office waiting area. They became secure enough in the space that they moved and grouped chairs to facilitate the very kind of experience that the architecture students had hoped to facilitate: a more comfortable one for the people going to court.

To close, we harken back to our observations regarding the very real impact that the ADA has effectuated on the built environment over the past thirty years in the United States, and how that has dignified the experience of people who, for example, use wheelchairs. Consider also how the details of ADA compliance are baked into what our former student Omar is doing professionally today building public spaces. Imagine now if we were to undertake a similarly ambitious effort to elevate human dignity in our courthouse designs as a specific priority design choice. What a remarkably different justice system we could have in thirty more years.

REFERENCES

Baker, John. 2018. *An Introduction to English Legal History*. 5th ed. Oxford: Oxford University Press.

Craven, Jackie. 2018. "About the U.S. Supreme Court Building: Architecture and Symbolic Sculpture at the Highest Court, 1935," *ThoughtCo*. Last modified December 28, 2018. www.thoughtco.com/us-supreme-court-building-by-cass-gilbert-177925.

Duncanson, Kirsty, and Emma Henderson. 2022. *Courthouse Architecture, Design, and Social Justice*. New York: Routledge.

Evans, Gary W. 2003. "The Built Environment and Mental Health." *Journal of Urban Health* 80, no. 4 (December): 536–55. https://doi:10.1093/jurban/jtg063.

[12] NuLawLab interview with Omar Malkawi, May 19, 2023, transcript on file with author Dan Jackson.

Gold-LaGratta, Emily, Justin Barry, and Manuel Toscano. 2018. "Retrofit for Fairness." *Urban Omnibus*, February 7. https://urbanomnibus.net/2018/02/retrofit-for-fairness/?print page=true.

Institute for Human Rights and Business. 2019. "Dignity by Design: Human Rights and the Built Environment Lifecycle." www.ihrb.org/uploads/reports/Dignity_by_Design_-_Human_Rights_and_the_Built_Environment_Lifecycle_IHRB_-_updated.pdf.

Jandura, Ken. 2018. "Trauma-Informed Courthouse Design." *NACM Court Manager*, March. https://thecourtmanager.org/articles/trauma-informed-courthouse-design-33-1/.

Malkawi, Omar. 2018a. "Omar Malkawi – Blog Post 1." *More Than Buildings* (blog), January 25. https://morethanbuildings.blogspot.com/2018/01/.

2018b. "Blog Post #4 (Omar Malkawi)." *More Than Buildings* (blog), April 4. https://morethanbuildings.blogspot.com/2018/04/.

McCarthy, Cathy A., and Tara Treacy, eds. 2000. *History of the Administrative Office of the United States: Sixty Years of Service to the Federal Judiciary*. Washington, DC: Administrative Office of the United States Courts.

McKenzie, Allison and Matthias, John T. 2020. "What Will Shape the Future of Courthouse Design?" www.ncsc.org/__data/assets/pdf_file/0020/42158/what_will_shape_the_future_McKenzie-Matthias.pdf

National Center for State Courts. n.d. "Public Information and Wayfinding." *The Courthouse: A Guide to Planning and Design*. Accessed May 30, 2023 www.ncsc.org/courthouseplanning.

National Child Traumatic Stress Network. 2015. "Essential Elements of a Trauma-Informed Juvenile Justice System." www.nctsn.org/resources/essential-elements-trauma-informed-juvenile-justice-system.

Resnik, Judith, and Dennis E. Curtis. 2011. *Representing Justice: Invention, Controversy, and Rights in City-States and Democratic Courtrooms*. New Haven, CT: Yale University Press.

Resnik, Judith, Dennis E. Curtis, and Allison Anna Tait. 2013. "Constructing Courts: Architecture, the Ideology of Judging, and the Public Sphere." *Law, Culture, and Visual Studies* 2013 (Spring): 515–45. http://dx.doi.org/10.2139/ssrn.2447895.

Runcible Studios. n.d. "About Us." Accessed August 12, 2023. www.runciblestudios.com/about-us/.

Stolk, Sofia. 2024. "International Courts and Design." In *Legal Design: Dignifying People in Legal Systems*, 380–94. Cambridge: Cambridge University Press.

TERVA Corporation. n.d. "Discover Our Family of Companies." Accessed May 25, 2023. www.tervacorp.com/.

8

Movement Lawyering

Legal Strategies to Build People Power

Purvi Shah, Meena Jagannath, and Alana Greer

8.1 INTRODUCTION

As South Asian and Latina lawyers who have spent our careers at the intersection of law, social movements, and power, we began our careers away from our desks to go to taxi stands, tent camps, restaurant kitchens, community meetings, rural villages, and housing projects to have candid conversations with clients and organizers. We learned how to weave litigation, education, media, policy, and protest into coordinated campaigns alongside organizers and accomplished far more than we could have ever achieved in the courtroom alone.

We call this approach "movement lawyering." Rather than simply aiming to win cases in the traditional sense, movement lawyers work on behalf of base-building organizations to deploy law strategically to change culture, systems, and power. We see ourselves as long-term partners to grassroots leaders and broader movements for change. We embed ourselves in these movements and use legal tools creatively to win material change in peoples' lives, shift power relationships in society, and change people's sense of their own individual power. This approach has helped us better diagnose issues, see how they are connected, and identify strategic opportunities for solutions.

There has long existed a global lineage of lawyers who are primarily concerned with a critical practice of the law in service of organized communities. The three of us – along with numerous peers and mentors – have spent fifteen years building on that legacy to expand and deepen the field of movement lawyering.

As agitators trying to shift our profession, we kept contending with the barriers to change in the legal sector. The law in the United States is built on the concept of precedent. Legal education acculturates lawyers to look backward, but often fails to inspire and encourage us to look forward. Virtually every other field – science, technology, labor, art, journalism, media – has seen widespread innovation during the last fifty years. When we interacted with these other disciplines, we sensed the generative possibility in their intersection with our profession. This was particularly true of working with organizers and community leaders, who pushed to envision a world beyond what was possible today. Partnering with other changemakers helped us dream. It helped us think bigger. Yet, legal organizations remained mostly stagnant, undisturbed by the creative disruptions revolutionizing so many other industries. This seemed doubly true for public interest law, in which change has been constantly thwarted by overwhelm, crisis, and disinvestment.

Where we participated in the earliest iterations of legal design workshops nearly ten years ago, our experiences were mixed. These workshops seemed geared toward fixing the delivery of legal services but lacked awareness of directly impacted communities' perspectives on their problems with the legal system. Nonprofit managers and design-thinking experts led and designed sessions targeted for staff at legal organizations. Their combined elite perspectives created significant blind spots in identifying challenges or solutions that got to the heart of the problem. Without a shared analysis or alignment on a broader theory of social change, these innovation spaces did not go deep enough. Some solved for problems that were not at the heart of communities' concerns, such as improving "access to justice" instead of solving for the root causes of injustice. And yet, the numbers made it such that there would never be enough lawyers to represent everyone suffering. While the groups we worked with excelled at maneuvering through challenges and centering impacted people, design thinking and innovation were tricky tools to bring into the legal world. Without grounding in real movements, the methodology can easily become an exercise that looks and feels good but lacks substance and impact.

As we learned more about the roots and practice of design thinking, we were struck by the similarities to practices that organizers and community groups had long cultivated and mastered. Questioning the status quo, unapologetically and continuously centering those with firsthand experience, envisioning and winning things that previously felt impossible: these daily practices and goals of organizing seemed to be exactly what some of the more corporate models of design thinking sought to recapture. As curious students of change, interdisciplinary thinkers hungry to become skilled at the project of societal transformation, we sought to find ways to apply design thinking on our terms and the terms of the communities with which we worked. We decided to run our own experiments on legal design.

In this chapter, we share our experiences and experiments blending design-thinking principles, as we interpreted them, in our work as movement lawyers. Specifically, this chapter argues that legal design is a versatile and valuable tool to increase dignity but is most impactful when used to deepen the self-determination of impacted communities and grounded in an astute understanding of power. When combined with movement lawyering, legal design can lead to the following powerful outcomes:

- It can help level the playing field and elevate the expertise and stories of those often left out of conversations that shape the society we live in.
- It can help communities expand our imagination and our sense of possibility.
- It can transform people's sense of their own power and dignity along the way.
- It can enlist a broader cross-section of the public in the work of collectively solving the issues of our neighbors: not in a paternalistic manner, but rather in a manner that centers the experiences of those directly impacted such that the solutions truly meet their needs.

To make this case, we first introduce the movement lawyering approach more deeply and delineate the unique values, analyses, and historical traditions from which it comes. We then share some short, detailed examples of how we deployed legal design in our movement lawyering work. Next, we offer some wisdom and reflections on what legal designers can learn from movement lawyering, and conversely what movement lawyers can learn from legal design to share our thoughts on the challenges and limitations of using legal design to build people power. Finally, we end with some open questions for all lawyers of conscience concerned with the struggle for human dignity.

8.2 OUR JOURNEY TOWARD MOVEMENT LAWYERING

Legal work always takes place in a particular political context. In recent times in the United States, the context is one in which the flaws and cracks in the structures, systems, and ideas that have undergirded contemporary society are being exposed. A racist, misogynistic, homophobic, and xenophobic backlash is gaining momentum. The crises of economy, democracy, and climate play out in fierce and inexorable interconnection, and, as always, Black and Brown working-class communities have borne the brunt of the pain.

In moments of crisis, lawyers are often looked to as a first line of defense to protect rights and expand protections for the most vulnerable. Yet, in our analysis, the law was designed to build the power of the white, male, wealthy, and powerful. Law has been used to justify war, internment, slavery, and more. One of the earliest lessons we learned as young attorneys was that many of the horrors our clients were facing were perfectly legal.

As such, early in our careers, we began the process of distinguishing ourselves from more traditional legal services and impact lawyers. These predominant tools and legal approaches were limited in addressing the root causes of injustice because most lawyers focus on winning remedies for individuals caught in larger systems of oppression, not changing policies or systems themselves. It seemed most lawyers were being trained to use their skills to patch up clients stuck in a revolving door of crisis.

We found ourselves on the cutting edge of a new flank of lawyers who were militantly committed to using law to build collective power and facilitate systems change. We knew that our practice had to move beyond court victories that changed little in people's lives. We had deep respect for lawyers doing this kind of work day in and day out – we started out as those lawyers – but we aspired to be something different. As we watched the burgeoning crises of the times escalate, we pulled our heads up and asked hard questions about how law could facilitate deep transformation of deeply exploitative and entrenched political and economic systems.

Along with escalating crisis and unrest, the past decade has also been marked by a resurgence of bold, creative, and visionary social movements. All around the United States, we see organized groups of people – workers, students, women, youth, indigenous, poor – joining together and fighting to transform the trajectory of their lives and of the planet. From the Movement for Black Lives, organizing among the largest protests in US history, organic rebellions on the streets of Minneapolis and Ferguson, workers unionizing at Amazon warehouses and Starbucks, the Land Back movement, and young people seeking transformative change to avoid climate catastrophe, social movements in the United States have continued to organize and resist.

8.3 MOVEMENT LAWYERING'S UNIQUE THEORY OF CHANGE

"Movement lawyering" is a methodology for working alongside these social movements, centering the community's expertise and displacing the lawyer's traditionally elite status, using strategies for collective action and systemic change (even when working with individuals). As movement lawyers, a theory of change focused on building collective power guides all of our work. We see the law as one tool among many, a means to achieve the objectives of the communities with which we work, versus seeing the use of law as a strategy in itself. We ground our thinking about the law in a study of history, social change, and political theory to decipher how to change some of the hardest challenges in our society. Our theory of change gives us a distinct starting point for our experiments in legal design:

- **Social change requires shifting power, culture, and systems.** Social change involves more than tinkering on the margins of systems, mitigating immediate harms, or even changing laws. It requires redesigning the underlying systems and structures of society, shifting norms and culture, and, most importantly, changing who has economic and political power.

- **Social movements create social change.** Throughout history, from the labor and civil rights movements of the past to the climate justice and Movement for Black Lives of the present, social movements have been the engine of social change. When directly affected people take collective action, lead their own struggles, and build power to change the root causes of oppression, social change results.
- **Social movements are powered by visionary activists, organizers, and community organizations fighting for a world that is better for people and the planet.** Grassroots groups such as those fighting for climate justice, disability justice, indigenous communities, and queer communities are the driving force behind movements to *dismantle* existing systems of oppression in our society while *building* alternative institutions to take their place. Their approach is moral, unifying, and sustained through powerful leadership.
- **Law and lawyers have a role to play in social change.** We are frequently reminded by the Supreme Court and legal jurisprudence that law is neither objective nor neutral; law is not ethical or moral on its own. However, throughout history, lawyers have worked alongside social movements to use law to codify social justice wins, defend leaders, and transform our collective sense of what is possible. When put in the hands of the people, law can be both a sword and a shield for advancing the causes of the most marginalized in our society.
- **Law is an important arena of struggle, but it has its limits.** Movement lawyers walk the tightrope of engaging in zealous advocacy, bringing the fight to the courts while acknowledging that law alone will not solve community challenges. Managing this careful balance is what it means to be a movement lawyer.

Investing in movement lawyers and driving the legal sector toward more movement-aligned practice is vital because legal work is ultimately about governance and democratic expression. When we help marginalized people wield law to defend community interests and fight oppressive systems, it strengthens the fabric of democracy.

There is a growing sector of lawyers and legal organizations that are deeply invested in questions of justice and are using their skills in this way. These movement lawyers see their role as that of conscious tacticians – not saviors – in support of historically marginalized people seeking to transform the conditions of their lives. In this way, legal tools are used to build the power of, make space for, validate, bolster, defend, and protect social movements and the activists and communities in them.

By pairing legal assistance with organized constituencies, movement lawyers avoid the pitfalls of traditional public interest lawyers who are constrained by structures in which they work to provide legal assistance in an atomized and reactive fashion. We treat the root causes of injustice by supporting our clients to become leaders in their own communities who create systemic change and shift power such that their community is not exploited time and time again. This model is not only strategic but more transparent and accountable, as it allows clients to weigh in about where scarce legal resources are spent. By treating clients as partners, lawyers can help clients regain control over their lives and their communities. The urgency of varying crises mandates that lawyers work directly with impacted communities to transfer skills, capacity, and leadership.

8.4 OUR EXPERIMENTS IN LEGAL DESIGN IN MIAMI

Our experiments in this respect have taken many forms – from designing a hackathon-style workshop to hosting a poetry collective and artist residency program – but we focus on two of our projects in Miami for the sake of this chapter: the JusticeHack and Salon Juste.

To set the stage, legal advocacy is desperately needed in a city like Miami where glitzy beaches and a fast-paced nightlife hide its reality of concentrated and persistent poverty and exploitation. Miami is the least affordable city in the United States, and more than 20% of its residents currently live below the poverty level with little hope of advancement. Miami's main industries – tourism, construction, services, and retail – generate a disproportionate number of dead-end, low-paying jobs with no benefits. The rise of the gig economy and the pandemic have only deepened these inequities. Wage theft, especially in the undocumented immigrant community, is rampant. More than 90% of welfare recipients are women, and nearly 50% of recipients are African American. Even worse, Miami is currently experiencing an affordable-housing crisis. The process of gentrification, under tremendous pressure from market forces and climate change, is displacing entire communities. As luxury towers continue to rise, more and more Miami families are caught in a downward spiral of missed meals, disconnected utilities, evictions, and homelessness.

Our experiments with legal design began as much as a product of the emerging arts, tech, and design zeitgeist in Miami as of the tough political and social conditions for progressive change that have marked the city for decades. The 2010s spelled the growth of an "entrepreneurship ecosystem" characterized by the multiplication of tech startups, design-thinking workshops, and innumerable meet and greets. But for all the excited talk about the investment, growth, and prosperity this would bring to Miami's residents, it was clear from our work at Community Justice Project (CJP) that much of that frothy optimism – and the supposed resources that accompanied it – was neither intended for nor reaching the community organizations we had been accompanying. Often, these same forces laid the groundwork for gentrification and displacement. We thus sought to leverage the moment to draw attention to the need for these resources to flow to those communities left out of this new wave of activity in Miami.

At the same time, we found we were hitting a wall in terms of fulfilling some of the advocacy goals of our community groups. The prevailing narratives about taxi drivers, farmworkers, youth of color, and public housing tenants were disparaging and dismissive, making it harder for the broader public to rally behind the policy shifts and programs community groups representing these populations were fighting for. Relationships between these community groups and those seemingly crafting this "new" Miami were virtually nonexistent. From our unique vantage point working across these seemingly disparate issue areas, it was clear that the problems were consequences of a fundamental imbalance of power against the communities we represented. For many of the campaigns we were involved in, we would look across the table and see the same faces or interests standing in opposition to our partners' demands. With that being the case, we knew that we needed to engage a larger cross-section of the population in paying attention to and understanding the needs of these communities to be able to take significant steps forward. The idea was that if we could help create a space where community members could connect with others more proximate to power and resources in Miami in a nonhierarchical manner, we could help our partner groups access and leverage the power of those new relationships. Simultaneously, those wielding these resources and power had much to learn from the expertise of these long-time, but often overlooked, community leaders and become resource allies to them.

8.5 CASE STUDY: JUSTICEHACK

In 2014, we had the opportunity to design and host a conference in Miami. While it is not always evident that conferences can result in material gains, we had already experienced the transformative potential of such gathering spaces in other convenings we had designed (the list to follow). Thus, equipped with the resources and freedom to develop a convening space oriented toward advancing the campaigns in which we were already engaged, we began thinking of how to remix the conference form to actually meet the challenges we were facing at the time: apathy or lack of awareness of the issues faced by low-income communities of color in Miami; lack of connection between grassroots communities and new resources flowing into Miami; and the need for creative solutions to entrenched systemic problems. We took the opportunity to not only design substantive content but also tinker with the form and process of presenting information such that we reached a broader Miami audience and also engaged participants in consuming the content more actively. The result was the JusticeHack, a hackathon-inspired convening that had three main goals: educating the Miami public about issues impacting the communities organized by our partners; connecting our partners and community members to multidisciplinary resources and people whom they might not otherwise interact with; and surfacing creative solutions to the issues presented.

We considered the last goal to be of tertiary significance; more important to the ongoing campaigns of our partners were the goals of raising awareness and helping our partners build stronger connections with a bigger cross-section of the Miami public across disciplines.

The event consisted of four main parts: an opening storytelling night, in which representatives of each of the partner communities (taxi drivers, plant-nursery workers, youth of color, and public housing residents) grounded our event in their lived experiences; a morning of learning through reviewing preassembled information packets ("hack packs") and meeting with representatives of the communities who were both the "users" and the experts on the issue; an ideation and prototyping session; and a gallery/idea presentation stage where participants shared prototypes and selected the ideas that most resonated with them.

Given the novelty of the format of the conference, we held numerous meetings with our partners representing the different communities: New Vision Drivers Association of Florida (taxi drivers), WeCount! (plant-nursery workers), Power U Center for Social Change and Dream Defenders (youth of color), and Miami Workers Center (public housing residents). Existing relationships of trust made it such that the organizations readily accepted the invitation to collaborate, but we had to hold several workshops with the organizations to explain the format and collectively define the question we were going to present at the JusticeHack as the subjects for ideation. Though we had some initial thoughts on the desired outcomes and the methodology for the conference, it was important to us to ensure that our partners codesigned and guided the substantive content. Interestingly, while our partners addressed diverse issues that did not overtly overlap, the bilateral workshops revealed a common thread for all issues: a lack of respect and the failure to recognize the dignity of the community members most directly impacted. We ultimately landed on the following questions:

- How might we preserve and strengthen the community networks of families in low-income housing?
- How might we make schools supportive environments for youth of color?
- How might we align the needs of riders and drivers?
- How might consumers or employees be advocates of plant nursery workers' rights?

We designed each question to orient participants toward a spirit of joint problem-solving and collaboration, and communicated the fundamental value of dignity and respect for the communities we were serving. The corresponding information provided in the "hack packs" also drew from historical and current campaigns driven by our partner organizations, further valorizing their expertise and drawing upon their long-standing work on the different issues.

There were two elements on which the success of the event hinged: outreach and publicization to attendees beyond those who were already in our network; and facilitation, since we had never designed or hosted a hackathon-type event before.

With respect to outreach and publicity to specific sectors that we did not interact with on a regular basis, we had to be creative. We identified leaders in the design and ideation space; attended numerous public events for technology, social enterprise, and start-up audiences; organized one-on-one meetings with key actors in the civic engagement, tech activism, and coding sector; and spoke at events where we could inform people about the event. We publicized the event widely through social media and independent news media channels and deputized people to spread the word to their networks. With respect to facilitation, we identified and worked with a local group that experimented with holding human-centered design events to generate civic participation in Miami and had experience with the hackathon model. To deepen that local experience, we also recruited an international partner that dedicated several designers to the facilitation team so that we could run two ideation and prototyping groups for each of the four issues. In the lead-up to the event, we held several meetings with the facilitators so that we – new to this facilitation style – could learn new methodologies we were putting into practice, and they – new to the activism, law, and organizing space – could understand our goals for the event and work to meet them.

Ultimately, we assembled a team of 10 facilitators, and over 130 people attended the event, representing a wide array of disciplines: design, art, law, activism, technology, and social enterprise. The event also resulted in fifteen ideas, but more importantly, we laid the roots for future collaborations between the community groups and resource allies. While the ideas were not fully executed as presented at the JusticeHack, the relationships our community partners could make with a broader cross-section of Miami continued to bear fruit, as we came to recognize in the years since the event in which we watched new projects and collaborations blossom from those connections. Another key outcome from the JusticeHack was that it provided our partner groups with an experience of how a conference that convened diverse participants (as opposed to the converted choir) can serve to enhance their campaigns in an innovative and engaging manner. The JusticeHack also provided us with rich observations that we could draw on for later iterations and experiments we would design, including a salon series called Salon Juste, and numerous other spaces, as we describe in the next section.

8.6 CASE STUDY: THE SALON JUSTE SERIES

Building off of the success and lessons we learned from the JusticeHack, as well as our participation in a wave of racial justice activism from the Ferguson uprising in 2014 after the police killing of Mike Brown Jr. and subsequent street protests in Baltimore, Baton Rouge, Cleveland, Minneapolis, Miami, and elsewhere, we delved further into the idea that connection and storytelling in intentionally designed spaces were key strategies to generate support and awareness of the campaigns our partners were leading. We understood our work could not simply stop at our advocacy in legal or quasi-legal forums; we needed additionally to design our own complementary and auxiliary spaces to bolster and echo the demands of community organizations while lifting up their leadership and stories in a personal way. At the same time, we were taking inspiration from Ella Baker and generative moments of history like the Harlem Renaissance to explore what could come of spaces designed to encourage cross-pollination, debate, and reflection on one's own proximity or relationship to a given issue. The result was an event format loosely based off the salons that took place in Harlem in the 1920s and 1930s that we called Salon Juste (The Just Salon) and launched in 2016.

The JusticeHack provided the confirmation that Miami desperately needed a space that brought people together across sectors, disciplines, communities, and income levels to talk about pressing issues. But we needed a format that could allow us to address the granularity and human impact of the issues in a less resource-intensive way. Further, we observed that the organizers and community groups we worked with were interacting with potential allies primarily at the height of their campaigns, in moments of conflict and agitation, and did not have access to these constituencies to do the foundational relational work to convert them to allies before those pivotal moments. The Salon Juste provided such an opportunity with ample space to play with various variables (such as number of participants, participant-driven conversations vs. structured prompts, number of speakers, length of panel, use of art and interactive elements, curated guest list versus open guest list, and more), and iterate based on the goals for the event. Our goals for these spaces were to:

- remove barriers of hierarchy or power differentials for people to connect across communities and sectors;
- raise awareness of the issue through direct engagement with those most impacted by it;
- valorize community leaders as experts and important sources of knowledge on key Miami issues;
- advance conversations related to the ongoing campaigns of our community partners; and
- help members of the broader public recognize that they are also impacted by the injustices experienced by other members of the Miami community.

Unlike the JusticeHack, there was no "ideation" portion of these events. The most important elements were learning, connecting, and reflecting. We always began the event with a 20- to 30-minute panel of experts – intentionally not professors or technocrats but primarily members of the partner organization and those most affected by the issue at hand – moderated by someone with a journalism background to get at questions that the public tends to want to know. For example, at the salon on taxi drivers' issues as ride-sharing apps entered the system, we had a panel of taxi drivers and the head of New Vision Drivers Association moderated by a writer at

The New Tropic (Miami's independent online newsletter). Rather than simply concentrate on facts and figures, we facilitated conversations that were rooted in the lived experience of these experts and fostered deeper relationship building. Community members and potential allies were encouraged to share personal experiences where common ground could be found. In doing so, foundations for relationships that could weather the storms of future campaigns were built. Once the panel concluded, the panelists would join the audience at their tables to discuss the subject of the salon: sometimes with guidance, sometimes without. Crafting a warm, relaxed atmosphere was a key element in the design of these events. We made food and drink available and partnered with a designer to create event-specific art pieces and installations to transform the space we were occupying into one conducive to conversation and connection. We also did not force the conversations to have a defined outcome or overly curate what people had to talk about. The result was that people would often come back to subsequent salons and bring others along. We also had the ability to recruit journalists and participants due to the rich, welcoming, inclusive, and reflective space we created.

The pandemic interrupted what had become a generative and versatile tactic we could put at the disposal of our partner community organizations to be able to move through difficult conversations and draw new supporters to the table. However, we have learned a great deal from our experiments with salons and intend to continue iterating on this form for the sake of building power of the communities with which we work.

8.7 BRIEF NOTES ON OTHER EXPERIMENTS

8.7.1 *Using Arts and Culture to Sharpen Our Collective Analysis and Build Stronger Relationships*

Freedom Flicks was a community-rooted film series that sought to drive critical conversation among movement partners while building trust and relationships in a reemerging ecosystem. The series was put together in a period when organizers and many long-time leaders had left Miami or moved on from their respective organizations, creating a void where political education spaces and institutional memory were once held. The films chosen offered lessons on movement victories and struggles from across the globe, sparking reflection and creating opportunities for a new generation of movement leaders to build with each other socially. These shared moments of political education and connection fostered a sense of shared possibility.

The series cultivated an audience of organizers, members, leaders, and partners in the movement-building ecosystem. The films screened, most often documentaries made by both US and global filmmakers, provided deeper insight into struggles across the globe and successful models of resistance and change-making.

8.7.2 *Integrating the Medium of Poetry into a Law and Organizing Campaign*

Voices: Poetry for the People, a poetry collective, emerged under the leadership of poet Aja Monet, after Community Justice Project first worked with her to host poetry workshops for residents facing displacement and closure of their Miami area mobile home park. The workshops took place alongside litigation meetings the residents held with CJP and partner lawyers to fight the displacement and created a much-needed counterbalance to the draining processes of litigation, allowing participants to recharge and bring their whole selves to the fight.

Later, we hosted writing workshops with a broader cohort of community members, including organizers from Dream Defenders. This project tackled the concepts of displacement, climate catastrophe, and state violence by providing space where those who find themselves silenced, stripped of their voice, or ignored can reclaim their narratives in poetry. It sought to build a community of trust among workshop participants who engage with each other not just as "lawyer," "client," or "organizer" but as fellow learners, writers, and friends. Over and over again, we saw participants in these workshops emerging as stronger leaders, sharper advocates, and more engaged litigants. These workshops eventually built toward a larger collective and transformational event: the 2018 **Maroon Poetry Festival**. The collective continued to build on this historic event by creating more spaces where people could feel something akin to freedom and love in their bodies so as to create an associative embodied experience of the demands we express rhetorically but that at times can seem abstract.

8.7.3 *Embedding Artists in Campaigns for Social Change*

Seeing the transformational power of embedding poetry into our collective work and hearing more from artists hungry for a more meaningful role in community-led campaigns, we next asked how we could integrate artists more deeply into the work to simultaneously transform the artist and the audience, as well as those within CJP itself. Through a first-of-its-kind **Artist Residency** program launched in 2020, we hosted a musical artist who curated virtual "rent parties" – reminiscent of those held during the Harlem Renaissance – to create a "community collection plate" in service of specifically excluded tenants in the early days of the pandemic, such as undocumented workers and transgender women of color, that incorporated tenants' rights education. We then hosted a visual artist who highlighted the cruelty of the eviction process in Florida that denied people a bit of time to come up with the funds needed to keep their homes. They each spent time with our staff and organizing partners, building understanding of the issues and tactics we each had at our disposal. More than the final projects they produced, the process of relationship building throughout the residencies provided opportunities for transformation on the personal and systemic levels. Together, we continue to ask: How might we better wield the power of art in service of social change? How can we facilitate the translation of the artist's critique into changes in the material conditions of the folks with whom we work and the policies that shape those conditions? We have continued and expanded the residency program to include partnerships with local filmmakers.

8.7.4 *Pushing Lawyers to Imagine a World beyond the Confines of the Status Quo*

The law and its constituent systems are an inherently confining field that often strips participants (both lawyer and client) of their full dignity. If those in this profession wish to counteract that reality, they must first be able to restore their own ability to see a work beyond those confines. **Are There Courts in Wakanda?** was a facilitated world-building workshop at the Allied Media Conference that sought to create space for movement lawyers to imagine what the law, the legal system, and lawyers would do in the fictional world of Wakanda, or if they would even exist. The session cultivated creativity, in a profession stripped of it, by encouraging participants to design a legal system for a world without saddles of oppression. What purpose would it serve? How would it treat those that passed through it? What would that mean for the society it served?

Surfacing the deeper challenges and insights of long-time movement lawyers and organizers, **RadTalks** and **RealTalks** within the Law for Black Lives convenings provided additional agitation for this audience. We also sought to expose more movement lawyers to the language and tools of design thinking. Throughout the **Legal Innovators Fellowship**, we modeled how one might break through the confines of legal thinking using tools such as SCAMPER and user profiling.

8.7.5 *Lessons and Reflections from Blending Movement Lawyering and Legal Design*

This ensemble of experiments and multidisciplinary forays has left us with a growing body of reflections and observations that we will continue to fold into new iterations to advance our work alongside movements for equity, dignity, and justice. Here, we highlight some of the key insights we have gathered.

- **We Must Set Our Sights on Transformation, Not Tinkering.** Making oppressive systems more "user friendly" is not a worthy enough challenge for our creative disruptions in the law. While we understand the short-term value of finding interim solutions that improve and humanize the legal system, we think it would be a missed opportunity to stop here. Can we set our sights higher? How might we transform law from a building block of oppression into a tool of progress and liberation? Change for the sake of change does not always result in qualitative improvements. We need change that solves for the enduring challenges in our field.

- **A Solution without the Power to Implement It Is Not a Real Solution.** In our experience, oftentimes the people closest to problems have brilliant solutions but just lack the power to implement them. As such, we think more legal design spaces should be solving for how to increase community power or reduce the power of decision-makers to ensure community-designed and -vetted solutions are implemented. Therefore, the success of our work as legal designers and movement lawyers should be measured by how much power we have built, shifted, or transferred. Have we expanded a person's sense of their individual power? Have we nurtured processes of collective power-building? Have we shifted power relationships in society? Did we gain enough power to change the material conditions of people's lives? Do people in power listen to communities more? Coming up with brilliant solutions is exciting, but more than the solution, changing who has power to implement solutions is what creates more long-term change.
- **Communities Are More than Users.** Beyond users, outreach strategies, and focus groups, it is important to involve the community as co-facilitators, co-sponsors, and co-leaders in legal design efforts. Taking time to map out the deliberate steps and providing the preparation necessary for community members to take advantage of design spaces that are meant for broad democratic participation represent a key role we as movement lawyers have played in ensuring that the exciting language of design thinking does not in fact mask elite and exclusive spaces.
- **Grassroots Organizers Are the Original Human-Centered Designers.** Though there exists a whole vocabulary to describe the work of centering a user in design – design thinking, human-centered design, and equity-centered design – we found that the methodologies of design thinking were actually quite similar to grassroots organizing. In fact, organizers could be even better at it because the concept of centering the most impacted and building leadership is a necessary, core principle of successful organizing. Whereas designers may feel more comfortable with a solitary creative process and consider centering users in the design process an innovation on more traditional design thinking, this is actually the sweet spot for organizers even if they might not have mastery over all the design lingo. This makes a designer–organizer duo a potentially powerful combination for achieving community-focused ends.
- **Going Slowly Is the Fastest Way to Build Trust.** While the values of user-focused and human-centered design are motivated by the values of inclusion and equity, they do not always result in inclusive and equitable spaces. Many communities are highly distrustful of elite people (lawyers

and designers) who have consistently benefited from fields of practice tied to their oppression. Overcoming this understandable distrust requires slowing down considerably and being intentional to connect and draw in directly impacted, low-income communities that are often left out of spaces that tend to target a hip, youthful creative class of people.

- **People Over Products.** By liberating ourselves from the burden of coming out with a material product from our workshops and instead focusing on enhancing the experience and the benefits that can arise from connections and understanding, we can create more generative, authentic spaces that leave room for organic relationship building (which, in turn, can translate into more sustainable solutions going forward).
- **How We Define the Problem Shapes Everything.** Tailoring the "how might we. . ." question to the needs of the community really matters. In the JusticeHack, we had numerous conversations and consultations to make sure that we were asking the right questions that were getting at the core of what was troubling the community organizations we were accompanying. Though it seems like such a minor part of building an agenda for a legal design workshop, these questions really direct the decisions on what information is most important to provide to participants and to know, who should be in the room, and what the community is prioritizing for the purpose of the workshop.
- **Self-Determination Is the North Star.** Those who are most directly impacted by an issue are the best experts to speak on the issue and must always be centered. We must be deliberate in providing platforms for these leaders to tell their stories and share what they know for the sake of arriving at better solutions. Legal design spaces can thus serve as a way of intentionally breaking down relations of hierarchy and power differentials, but we must design for that.
- **Hypothesis, Prototype, Iterate, Test, Iterate.** Design thinking taught us that the road map for iteration is key. We almost never get anything right the first time, and there is always room for improvement. Taking an experimental approach that allows us to make observations based on a range of variables can then help us tweak those variables for the next iteration. It is important to set goals and understand the variables we are playing with (i.e., number of issues being addressed, number of attendees, number of disciplines, amount of time, etc.) so that we can make more accurate observations about what may have led to different outcomes. It is critical to be adaptive, responsive, and willing to let the work shift our thinking and practice as we do it. We cannot predict the outcomes of our work with any certainty, and unexpected things often arise. It is important to be able to

make rapid assessments about whether we are moving on track with our goals and to pivot quickly if and as necessary.

- **Evolution Is Constant.** Legal designers and movement lawyers are a part of an actively evolving discipline and discourse. As movement lawyering is a practitioner-driven approach, it evolves over time and changes shape as more practitioners coming from diverse issue/practice areas contribute to the discourse. It is important to be in conversation with peers and scholars developing and contributing to theoretical frameworks to be able to work through difficult questions, learn new tactics, and evolve our own practice.
- **Blend and Borrow Methods and Tools.** Legal design, like other legal tactics, is just a tool: it is not the end in itself. As such, it is important to situate legal design alongside other tactics for it to be effective. It can be included as one tool in a movement lawyer's toolbelt that can come in handy at the right social or political moment in a campaign.

8.8 CONCLUSION

Throughout history, the process of organizing has been about harnessing collective power and fostering a collective hope that our world can be different, that our world can be one in which the dignity of all lies at the center of all policymaking and institution building. In this sense, we have found that legal design can be an important tool in the hands of movement lawyers and communities. The power of putting legal design at the disposal of organizers is that it helps us keep imagining that it is possible for the legal system to look different.

We still have many open questions that we can only begin to answer as we iterate and apply these lessons to further experiments and shifting contexts. In an increasingly tough environment, it is necessary to stay grounded in the values that have guided us to this point, and we only hope that we can continue to work with the humility, creativity, and openness to evolution that the moment demands.

But perhaps our biggest lesson in all of this is that hope is a collective process. If we cannot imagine it and cannot believe it is possible, we will not be able to build it. We must keep imagining that it is possible for our world – the legal system – to look different. We must build spaces that nurture collective and community imagination in our attempts to redesign and reimagine legal systems that yield more dignity. We need spaces for bold ideas to pierce through the cynicism and routine of legal work, recentering us on what is possible when we find the courage to dream. What gives us hope is the courage of everyday people. Every single day marginalized folks challenge the hardest things in their lives, and that takes tremendous courage. The job of the movement lawyer and the legal designer is to walk alongside them.

9

Deploying Art and Design to Highlight the Dignity of Domestic Workers in Their Struggle for Labor Rights

Natalicia R. Tracy

9.1 EMPOWERMENT, VOICE, AND DIGNITY AS CORE THEMES IN MOVEMENT BUILDING FOR DOMESTIC WORKERS

Most meaningful broad-based popular movements for social transformation require empowerment and participation from the intended beneficiaries of the sought-for change. Where domestic workers have been concerned, and despite the important work they do – no matter how much others have depended on it, and notwithstanding that it is the work that makes all other work possible – they have been accorded little dignity by our legal system and culture. The immigrant women of color who make up most of today's national domestic labor workforce of 2.5 million (NDWA 2022), many of whom also have uncertain immigration status, typically cope with this marginalization by keeping their heads down and working hard at their assigned tasks. They keep a low profile socially and politically to avoid retaliation for any complaints they might have, trying their best to avoid damage to their already precarious individual and family situations in the community.

This is why the contemporary movement for domestic worker rights over the last decade, both at the national and at so many linked state-level contexts, has been centered on building a sense of empowerment and dignity among workers. It's clear this has been effective in engaging them in the struggle for rights and justice. Their own strong voices have been important in advocating for their more just treatment as workers, and in calling out our culture and our legal system for their unconscionably racist and sexist exclusion from standard labor rights enjoyed by other workers. Standing up in this way, and publicly naming their mistreatment, for the workers themselves are important steps toward not only empowerment and dignity but also healing. The following account of movement building for domestic worker rights profiles the actions of several nonprofit organizations who productively joined together in the early 2010s in order to change labor law in Massachusetts through the passage of a state-level Domestic Worker Bill of Rights. Most of our work organizing and movement-building centered on bolstering and giving supportive opportunities for domestic workers to claim and to feel a sense of their own dignity in the contributions they make to sustaining millions of American families. Beginning in 2010 and culminating in 2015, a state-level campaign in Massachusetts won implementation of a new Bill of Rights for these workers, led by the Brazilian Worker Center (BWC) and allies, including Northeastern University's NuLawLab and Studio Rev- of New York City.

The years of work entailed mobilizing domestic workers and labor allies, organizing a broad grassroots coalition for change, mounting legislative and media campaigns, and designing education for workers and employers for the final implementation stage. Organized labor, especially the state-wide AFL-CIO, and a range of faith-based social justice groups were also key to this broad-based effort. Throughout the movement's narratives and advocacy, raising the dignity and voice of workers was a key ingredient. A variety of arts projects created to advance these efforts, including building the esteem and voice of workers, yielded many spaces and opportunities for public recognition of these workers' humanity, as well as their need for a legal system that defended their dignity as workers.

9.2 DOMESTIC WORKERS AND THEIR HISTORIC CHALLENGES: ROOTS OF THEIR MARGINALIZATION

Domestic work is one of the most common paid jobs for women. There are an estimated 75.6 million female domestic workers worldwide (ILO 2022), while domestic work comprises 4.5% of all human employment. One out of every thirteen women globally work for pay in this industry. Domestic workers, by definition, work inside the private, domestic sphere, performing a variety of household services from caring for children, the elderly, and those with special needs to taking actions that maintain the family's everyday functioning such as cleaning, cooking, or household maintenance. Two and one-half million now work in the United States, and in our aging society, that number is expected to grow to more than four million by 2035, according to the National Domestic Workers Alliance (Sieber and Tracy 2020, 81).

In the Global North today, in both the United States and Europe, most domestic workers – up to 80% in many places – are international migrants. These migrant women have histories of traveling north to more affluent countries in what has been called by Rhacel Salazar Parreñas a global "chain of care." The migrant workers give care to more affluent families and send remittances home that allow their own children to have a better life back in the Global South, where they are cared for by kin or local domestic workers (Parreñas 2015). Though these employers are obligated to follow US labor laws in compensation and working conditions of these domestic workers, many do not.

Egregious exploitative working conditions and labor trafficking of domestic workers from poorer, more vulnerable countries also continues to be a hidden problem. Many of them are forced into domestic servitude where they are compelled to work ten to sixteen hours a day with little or no pay (Tracy 2018). These victims of domestic servitude in the United States are often foreign national women with or without documentation living in the home of their employer. Many also arrive with US visas granted to them as household employees accompanying elite visiting sojourners, especially diplomats and corporate executives for whom special visas are available (such as A-3, G-5, NATO-7, or B-1) (Human Trafficking Hotline 2022).

The domestic labor industry has always been mired in the informal economy because workers labor in isolation from one another in private spaces and their labor has always been considered women's work akin to wifely and motherly duties or those of servants. Eighty-one percent of all domestic workers work in the informal sector (ILO 2022). Because it takes place in the private sphere and mimics much of the work of traditional female family members, it has long been considered by many as "not real work." This work situation has always presented many obstacles to organizing the workers as a labor force and to gaining protections for domestic workers under standard labor laws applying to other workers.

More than sexism, of course, has shaped the exclusion of domestic workers from respect and recognition as real workers who deserve to enjoy the same rights as others who labor. Domestic workers' exclusion also draws deeply from roots in racism, classism, and xenophobia. In the United States, for the first centuries of the nation's history, only people with less than full citizenship – slaves, indentured servants, disenfranchised minorities, impoverished rural migrants to cities, and poor and recently arrived immigrants – furnished the people, always mostly women, who did domestic work. More than we like to admit, this remains true today. This deeply institutionalized, structural classism and especially racism still existing today likely explains our slowness to change the labor standards that still prevail for domestic workers, over eight decades after their enshrinement in Depression-era foundational US labor laws. Labor rights defended by most US workers today originate in 1930s New Deal labor legislation, especially the 1933 National Labor Relations Act (NLRA) and the 1938 Fair Labor Standards Act (FLSA). Domestic workers – including African American women throughout the southern states and more widely as well as landless African American tenant farmers still toiling on their former plantations – were excluded from the new, emerging New Deal labor legislation. This exclusion was the result of the infamous "Devil's Bargain" that northern labor-friendly politicians made with Southern Democrats to help the South maintain severe Jim Crow labor market segregation in their region in exchange for labor rights for white northern industrial workers.

For all the same reasons, the exclusion of domestic workers continued in the succeeding decades: they were later excluded from the Social Security Act of 1935 (until 1950), the Occupational Safety and Health Act of 1970, and the Family Medical Leave Act of 1993. Except for social security eligibility and extension of minimum wage protections, all of these exclusions – including FLSA's fundamental exclusion – remain today for domestic workers.

It has been a slow process to reverse these exclusions and to begin to grant domestic workers the same legal protections as other kinds of labor. Domestic workers themselves have been organizing and fighting for improved labor rights since the nineteenth century, mostly led by Black workers under the mantle of various phases of the US civil rights movement (Tracy, Sieber, and Moir 2014, 3–5). Only since 2010 has significant progress occurred, through the passage of a state-level Domestic Worker Bill of Rights (DWBoR) in ten US states (as of 2022) and a few fragile executive orders dating from the Obama Administration. This progress has mainly happened due to the grassroots organizing and legislative campaigns promoted by the National Domestic Workers Alliance – initially formed at the first US Social Forum held in Atlanta in 2007 – and especially by its affiliate organizations, who represent more than 20,000 nannies, housekeepers, and caregivers for the elderly. Today these seventy affiliates and seven regional chapters do the grassroots organizing and movement building for the NDWA in twenty-one states and the District of Columbia.

The national effort in the United States is closely linked, of course, to a worldwide movement for domestic workers' rights occurring on a global level. This movement recently led the International Labor Organization (ILO) to pass Convention 189, *Concerning Decent Work for Domestic Workers*, and the related Recommendation 201 in 2011. By October 2022, this convention had been endorsed by thirty-five nations globally (though the United States has not yet endorsed) (The General Conference of the International Labour Organization 2011).

In the United States, most of NDWA's efforts have focused on supporting campaigns for state-level DWBoRs. New York was the first to pass one in 2010, joined later by Hawaii (2013), California (2013), Massachusetts (2014), Connecticut (2015), Oregon (2015), Illinois (2016), Nevada (2017), New Mexico (2019), and Virginia (2021) (National Domestic Workers Alliance 2019; Virginia Legislative Information System 2021).[1] The bills all represent steps forward, though they vary considerably in the scope and coverage of their provisions and the strength of their enforcement components. The Massachusetts campaign in the early 2010s brought together the BWC, Northeastern University School of Law and its NuLawLab, and Studio REV- of New York City, who proved to be central partners in our campaign efforts.

9.3 THE DOMESTIC WORKER MOVEMENT IN MASSACHUSETTS

Massachusetts efforts to organize the state's 110,000 domestic workers began in the summer of 2010 with the visit of BWC staff to Domestic Workers United in New

[1] The Biden–Harris administration is currently backing in 2022 a "National Domestic Workers Bill of Rights," co-sponsored by Rep. Pramila Jayapal (WA) and Senators Kirsten Gillibrand (NY) and Ben Roy Lujan (NM), introduced to the House Education and Labor Committee as H.R. 4826. Before her election as vice-president in 2020, Senator Kamala Harris (CA) was one of the original co-sponsors when the bill was first introduced in its first iteration.

York, seeking guidance in the wake of their fresh DWBoR win there. At the BWC, there had been many conversations and meetings among domestic workers to make sense of the issues that were plaguing them in Massachusetts. The BWC in that year also became women-led, with an all-female staff, including me, Natalicia Tracy – a former domestic worker for fifteen years – becoming the executive director. The engagement with domestic worker rights widened in December 2010 with the formation of the Massachusetts Coalition for Domestic Workers, established by the Brazilian Worker Center, Dominican Development Center, Brazilian Women's Group–Vida Verde Cooperative, Matahari Eye of the Day, and Women's Institute for Leadership Development. The coalition also retained Greater Boston Legal Services as legal counsel and began benefiting from legal advice and education from Northeastern University School of Law and its NuLawLab.

BWC and the Coalition resolved to follow the model set earlier by New York's Domestic Workers United in forging our own campaign. The first step was significant outreach to all the involved organizations to assemble a statewide Congress of Domestic Workers to dialogue and debate over what legal protections were most important and lacking for their workers in Massachusetts. The Congress, which took place in 2012, included 150 workers present and defined the key issues for a new draft of the Domestic Worker Bill of Rights submitted to the Massachusetts Legislature in January 2013.

9.3.1 *Knowing Your Rights Is a Key First Step to Dignity as a Person and a Worker*

Knowing and claiming your rights is a first step toward any informed advocacy to improve your work situation. We in the movement have found that, despite the restrictions on their labor rights, workers are also denied many other rights that current laws afford them. Examples include the right to receive minimum wage, not to be overcharged for food and lodging costs if you are a live-in household worker, and not to have to accept sexual and other forms of abuse from employers. In order to bring domestic workers into parity with other workers, education on both limited existing rights and new rights being sought is a necessary first step in organizing and movement-building. In our campaign, there were several different channels through which workers' critical understandings of their rights were shared and nurtured.

9.3.2 *Organizing, Education, and Solidarity-Building*

Meetings among workers were organized on a regular basis. This effort overcame the isolation that domestic workers typically feel working alone in their employer's home, out of touch with other workers. The meetings allowed domestic workers to discuss their working conditions and strategies for legal change, and to see how much they had in common in terms of shared injustices and prideful accomplishments in their work to support US families. These meetings took place at the BWC's offices. "Know Your Rights" trainings were always a key part of these facilitated meetings.

9.3.3 *Domestic Worker Legal Manual*

Our efforts to define and convey understandings of labor rights were greatly facilitated by Northeastern University's School of Law's Legal Skills in Social Context (LSSC) program. Through this program, groups of Northeastern law students twice worked closely with our staff to develop and produce versions of the *Domestic Worker Legal Manual*, which summarized all relevant Massachusetts legislative, regulatory, and case law regarding domestic work. In 2012, we translated this manual into both Spanish and Portuguese so that Massachusetts' mostly immigrant domestic workers could more easily use it. During our multiyear efforts, succeeding cohorts of law students working through the LSSC program updated the manual in 2014. This manual was important not only in shaping trainings that we prepared for workers but also in assisting staff at our organization to advocate effectively with employers or higher authorities on behalf of workers who were being abused or mistreated at their workplaces.[2]

9.3.4 *The Northeastern University School of Law's NuLawLab as an Engaged, Valuable, and Consistent Ally in Our Movement*

Students, staff, and faculty affiliated with the NuLawLab were consistent, dependable, and valuable allies in our organizing efforts. They were immersed in and active participants and supporters at many gatherings that brought together advocates, workers, our staff, and other partner organizations for discussions of campaign strategy. We understood this as part of a strategy that benefited the students engaged in the legal assessment of our situation and in preparing manuals for us.

[2] From the Acknowledgments section: "Who Created This Manual? This manual is the product of collaboration between Northeastern University School of Law (NUSL) and the Brazilian Immigrant Center (BIC). Specifically, Lydia Edwards, Director of Legal Services and head of the Domestic Worker Law and Policy Clinic at BIC partnered with NUSL Class of 2014's Law Office 10 to help produce the manual. Under the guidance of NUSL's Social Justice Program, Law Office 10, supervised by Professor Peter Enrich and lawyering fellows Shaun Robinson and Lisa Swanson, was comprised of first-year law students Jessica Arthur, Lucas Blackadar, Alexis Burns, Nicole Costanzo, Ryan Deck, Jenna Fegreus, Maggie Hamlin, Natalie Higgins, Tiffany Ko, Oren Nimni, Matthew Stieglitz and Andrew Walsh. NUSL Librarian Jootaek Lee provided research assistance. NUSL Dean Emily Spieler also provided helpful input and Audrey Richardson of Greater Boston Legal Services provided legal guidance and final review and editing." [Note: In 2015, the Brazilian Immigrant Center was legally renamed the Brazilian Worker Center.]

The NuLawLab made sure to insert students and their staff into these situations, taking advantage of opportunities to engage directly on a face-to-face, human level with domestic workers at all kinds of campaign events. Through these personal relationships, the students were able to see how the DWBoR connected with workers' aspirations, daily struggles at the worksite, in the community, and to learn how to speak and write clearly and respectfully to workers and to us their advocates. This personalized immersion in the campaign was a means of supporting and honoring the dignity of domestic workers and our cause.

The NuLawLab was always available to support us with any legal requests needed to advance the bill, make better arguments for its passage, and draw from progressive legislation already enacted in other states. Once our own bill passed in 2014 and became effective in Massachusetts in 2015, the NuLawLab engaged with our next DWBoR organizing project in Connecticut, where they were even more instrumental in drafting legislation and a legal rationale for the measure that was under consideration there during the 2014–2016 period.

9.3.5 *Storytelling*

In this movement-building, it was critical to build the capacity of the domestic workers to tell their own true stories about unjust job conditions, their experiences resisting mistreatment, how they persisted in their work despite these obstacles, and what changes they believed were needed in the laws in order to protect them. Ai-Jen Poo, long-time leader of the National Domestic Workers Alliance, has spoken of the great potential of what she calls "narrative power," a power that the excluded always have in their struggle for equal rights (Poo 2011). Through telling and sharing their personal stories, domestic workers – like so many others – can help break down isolation and validate one another's experiences. Those experiences also gain new meaning; they are no longer just unique misfortunes happening to individuals. Instead, they are revealed to be common experiences across the group, shaped by shared structural disadvantages under economics and the law – it is here that solidarity can be built, and collective resilience recognized and nurtured.

Already knowing what your rights are supposed to be, or need to become, of course, always must be the foundation for building this capacity. BWC set aside separate sessions at regular domestic worker meetings for workers to receive coaching and encouragement in practicing exchanging their personal stories. Occasionally, larger and longer facilitated sessions focused solely on storytelling.

9.3.6 *Legislative Education: Giving Testimony to Lawmakers through Storytelling*

Lessons from these practice storytelling sessions were critical to take away from internal meetings for use in different kinds of practical settings where the compelling voices of domestic workers have all too often been missing. The principal setting for these was in what we and others have called "legislative education," that is, in visits to legislators' offices at the capitol building (referred to in Massachusetts as "the State House") in order to advocate for their support in deciding to co-sponsor the proposed Domestic Worker Bill of Rights, then under active consideration by the Joint Labor & Workforce Development Committee, the Ways & Means Committee, and ultimately by both full houses of the legislature. Hundreds of visits of this sort to legislators occurred between 2013 and 2014. This whole process for us took a year and a half, time for hundreds of small group visits to the 200 elected Senators and Representatives who make up the Massachusetts Legislature. More than one person's story would be told at these meetings.

9.3.7 *Testifying at Legislative Hearings*

In the context of legislative politics, many domestic workers who had previously never had any or much public speaking experience were tapped to testify individually in panels in support of the DWBoR during public legislative hearings held before the Joint Labor & Workforce Development Committee. They received workshops in public speaking and were very effective in conveying the human benefits of having the new legislation in force. This was accompanied by training focused, of course, on educating workers on how to understand and speak about the larger legal and historical context of their workplace struggles and to see their struggles as part of a wider domestic worker rights movement at state, national, and global levels.

9.3.8 *Storytelling as Advocacy at Public Arts Events, Designed to Influence Legislators and Build the Movement*

One other final important context for telling one's own story or testifying about the need for the DWBoR to provide for dignified, decent working conditions also took place at large public "in-district meetings" that were held in the home districts – typically urban agglomerations – of legislators who were critical to the bill's success. A program of speakers typically included stories or testimonies from domestic workers and other advocates for the Bill of Rights.

These meetings, however, were not ostensibly political meetings: instead, they were couched as community arts events, typically held in public libraries or other public buildings, and attracted anywhere from 25 to 200 attendees. While these events showed local legislators – very specifically invited – the large and diverse community of voters in their own districts that supported the DWBoR, the events (sometimes informally called "in-district meetings" by our team) took place ostensibly as openings for photo exhibitions honoring domestic workers.

These meetings were also attended by representatives of the campaign's large group of more than 300 allied organizations who lived or worked in that particular legislative district, including labor unions, faith groups, and nonprofit organizations, all of whom had been carefully and deliberately recruited by our team. These were meetings of such size and importance that local legislators – who were always given a chance to speak – did not want to miss them. In fact, they were invited to and usually were happy to give some kind of speech, typically to announce their support or appreciation for the bill. In the space of two years, exhibit openings took place throughout the state at public libraries in Quincy, Newton, Everett, Framingham, Brighton, Chelsea, Hyannis, Somerville, Lawrence, Burlington, Lowell, and Brookline.

9.3.9 *The Dignified Portraits Set a Respectful Tone for These Gatherings*

The tone of most of these "in-district meetings" was also strongly marked by the presence of the encircling set of dignified portraits of the faces of domestic workers involved in our organizing groups. The purpose of this moving exhibit – originally entitled "Domestic Workers: The Invisible Wheels that Empower our Economy" before the passage of the DWBoR in June 2014, and later entitled "Invisible No More: Domestic Workers, New Labor Laws & A Changing Culture" after its passage – was stated on the program brochure: "This portrait exhibit highlights the priceless contributions that caretakers make to our communities in supporting many New England families and their homes, children and their seniors. The project is an artistic element in the effort to create public awareness of the dignity of household workers whose labors make all other work possible."

The display of the dignified portraits at what was officially billed as an exhibit "opening" and "reception" lent an air of seriousness to these meetings, at which many voices were heard in a chorus of support for the workers. Local domestic workers, organizers, town or neighborhood civic leaders from the area, representatives of local labor unions, and political leaders joined for an evening program on the perspectives and problems of doing domestic work in Massachusetts and advocacy for passage of a Massachusetts' Bill of Rights, with a strong overall display of community support for the legislation. The discussion occurred under the watchful gaze of these impressive women, so present in the room and looking out from their framed portraits, calling out for respect (Figure 9.1).

FIGURE 9.1. Portraits of Angela Sena, Sonia Felix, and Fatima Chraska. (Photo credit: Mario Quiroz-Servellón.)

The event's program brochure explicitly advanced the purpose of the exhibit and its dignified portraits, which usually circled the meeting room and numbered up to as many as twenty-five: "This portrait exhibit highlights the priceless contributions that caretakers make to our communities in supporting many New England families and their homes, children and their seniors. The project is an artistic element in the effort to create public awareness of the dignity of household workers whose labors make all other work possible." All the portraits were professionally done by famed documentary photographer Mario Quiroz-Servellón, who has a long history of completing photo projects dignifying US immigrants, including earlier collections he completed on the elderly in US Chinatowns and on Mexican farmworker families.

For the workers themselves, the rotating portrait exhibit of a collection of over 150 images was deeply appreciated, gratifying, and validating. Far from being invisible and isolated in their jobs inside other people's homes, and from being seen (or not seen) in public places as a nondescript "just any person" that might hold any kind of job, their individual characters, their seriousness, and their dignity as immigrant women came through. The pride that domestic workers normally feel about themselves, their work, and its meaning for improving the quality of life for others was also evident in the dignified portraits of these amazing women.

9.3.10 *Studio REV- of New York City: An Artistic and Strategic Partner in Movement-Building for Domestic Worker Rights*

Studio REV- is a nonprofit arts organization that creates public art and creative media to impact the lives of low-wage workers, immigrants, youth, and women. From the beginning it has been led by visionary multimedia artist Marisa Morán Jahn. Jahn and Studio REV- joined our campaign early on to secure and implement new rights for domestic workers and developed several different projects in collaboration with NDWA and related state-level initiatives like our Massachusetts Bill of Rights campaign. We were fortunate as well to have Studio REV- and Northeastern University's NuLawLab within our broader coalition of key movement supporters to collaborate with one another in creative ways to use the arts and design to promote social justice in the law.

Studio REV- developed several notable projects, each of which involved extensive participation from domestic workers in project conception, design, and execution. Their projects were also typically celebrated in group situations and worked to build joy and solidarity among activists engaged with the campaign. All of Studio REV-'s projects used humor, satire, irony, and often parody to lighten their messages for public consumption and to help domestic workers and the public face up to important issues of injustice and struggle in their movement to gain parity in labor rights with other workers.

The underlay of humor in their projects gave a less confrontative presentation to difficult messages about injustice for the workers, eased domestic workers' taking voice about their working conditions and challenges, and made it easier for outsiders to understand clear accounts of the unfairness of their work situations. Finally, all of

Studio REV-'s projects emphasized the dignity, power, vigor, and everyday heroism of domestic workers – often simply disarmingly presented as superheroes – once again drawing in actual grassroots movement leaders as characters and participants to celebrate.

9.3.11 *The Nanny Van and Careforce One*

The Nanny Van, a refurbished 1976 Chevy van, crossed the United States many times as a mobile information and advocacy unit, typically stopping at parks, playgrounds, transit hubs, crossroads, worker centers, and other locations where activists would likely encounter domestic workers and the public. There they could hold rallies and distribute literature, publicity, and educational materials on issues like worker's rights and safety and health to passersby (Figure 9.2). When the van eventually broke down, it was replaced by a 1967 Mercury Station Wagon, "Careforce One," which also embarked on a never-ending journey of education and movement-building (Figure 9.3).

The theming of the domestic worker movement as a celebration of the "Careforce," where workers were really superheroes, proved powerful. It led to a series of independent television programs featuring Marisa Jahn, her son, and a family friend traveling all over North America, to museum exhibits on the project in

FIGURE 9.2. Crowds gathered around the Nanny Van to rally for expansion of domestic workers' rights, as it moved from city to city.
(Photo owned by Studio REV-.)

FIGURE 9.3. Careforce One, the Vehicle, with Marisa Jahn, her son, and friend Anjum Asharia.
(Photo owned by Studio REV-.)

the United States and abroad, and to the production of a series of trading cards modeled after cards of sports figures but featuring domestic worker heroes instead (Figures 9.4, 9.5).

9.4 CONCLUSION

As indicated in the profiles of campaign activities described in the preceding sections, today's advancement of domestic worker labor rights is an especially important frontier in the movement to dignify all forms of work and to humanize and dignify all working people. It represents, as well, an important front in the extension of democracy within the wider US economic and political project. This front is especially important for women workers of color, who have been doubly depreciated and excluded for centuries from dignity and equity in our labor laws and our culture's estimation of the value and difficulty of their labor.

It is no surprise that the fight for domestic workers' dignity, in order to attack these inequities at their roots, must be intimately connected to the struggle to win legal parity in the protections they are accorded as workers. This fight for dignity implies dismantling and replacing many legal and regulatory structures that reflect long-

FIGURE 9.4. Examples of trading cards for domestic worker superheroes. In Boston, these were released at a special event organized by the NuLawLab at Northeastern University School of Law.
(Design credit: Marisa Jahn.)

standing racial and gender discrimination, such as in the Jim Crow–era FLSA exclusions that have long disadvantaged domestic workers. Despite the essential work domestic workers do to support families and individuals in need of loving care, the fight for equal rights for domestic workers is far from over in the United States. So far, domestic workers have achieved some parity in their labor rights in only ten of fifty states.

Our Massachusetts strategies focusing on domestic worker education, empowerment, and dignity appear to have been quite effective so far and resulted in 2014 in the passage of perhaps the strongest state-level domestic worker bills of rights in the nation. This is true even if implementation and enforcement are not complete and of necessity must continue to be a work in progress.

What allowed these organizing efforts to gain so much ground? The work of Hagan and Kim (2017) offers some clues. They argue that for organizations designed to improve access to justice within the legal system it is crucial to first recognize and enhance "the dignity of the individual person." This goal is furthered when the worker's "autonomy and agency" are enhanced, as in the Massachusetts example, through carefully educating workers on their rights – what they already have and

FIGURE 9.5. Brazilian Worker Center domestic workers and organizers with special Careforce/Superhero eyeglasses worn during many public events, 2016.
(Photo credit: Marisa Jahn.)

what they might achieve through further collective struggle. Being conscious of one's rights, in their words, fosters for the workers a sense of "perceived control within the system" (Hagan and Kim 2017, 5).

Through education on the dignity of their work, we have seen that Massachusetts domestic workers learned to value and tell their own stories and used this capacity for truthful, compelling testimony to powerful effect in interaction with lawmakers and within legislative processes. The reality is that an informed, organized public with a just cause can affect genuine legal change. Even if they are leading these change efforts, worker advocacy organizations such as the Brazilian Worker Center, or the wider Massachusetts Coalition of Domestic Workers, however, do not always have the resources and especially expertise to nurture this capacity alone. In generating this kind of powerful grassroots movement, legal service organizations with compelling social justice missions, such as Northeastern University's NuLawLab and Studio REV-, and photographer-activists such as Mario Quiroz-Servellón can and did play essential supportive roles in recognizing and enhancing the dignity of women workers of color in a depreciated industry, and cultivating informed, conscious grassroots leadership embarking on a trajectory toward hopeful, genuine change.

REFERENCES

The General Conference of the International Labour Organization. 2011. "R201 – Domestic Workers Recommendation, 2011 (No. 201)." www.ilo.org/dyn/normlex/en/f?p=NORMLEXPUB:55:0::NO::P55_TYPE,P55_LANG,P55_DOCUMENT,P55_NODE:REC,en,R201,/Document.

Hagan, Margaret, and Miso Kim. 2017. "Design for Dignity and Procedural Justice." *Advances in Intelligent Systems and Computing, Proceedings of the Applied Human Factors and Ergonomics International Conference, 2017*. New York: Springer Press.

Human Trafficking Hotline. 2022. "Labor Trafficking Venues & Industries – Domestic Work." Accessed August 28, 2022. https://humantraffickinghotline.org/labor-trafficking-venuesindustries/domestic-work.

International Labor Organization. 2022. "Who Are Domestic Workers?" Accessed August 31, 2022. www.ilo.org/global/topics/domestic-workers/who/lang–en/index.htm.

National Domestic Workers Alliance. 2019. "Philadelphia DWBOR Summary." https://domesticemployers.org/wp-content/uploads/2019/12/Philadelphia-DWBOR-Summary-Comms-Briefing.pdf.

2022. "About Domestic Workers." Accessed September 1, 2022. www.domesticworkers.org/about-domestic-work/.

Parreñas, Rhacel Salazar. 2015. *Servants of Globalization: Migration and Domestic Work*. 2nd ed. Redwood City, CA: Stanford University Press.

Poo, Ai-Jen. 2011. "A Twenty-First Century Organizing Model: Lessons from the New York Domestic Workers Bill of Rights Campaign." *New Labor Forum* 20, no. 1(Winter): 51–55. https://doi.org/10.4179/NLF.201.0000008.

Sieber, Tim, and Natalicia Tracy. 2020. "Worker-Led Research Makes the Case for Labor Justice for Massachusetts Domestic Workers: Social Research and Social Change at the Grassroots." In *Collaborating for Change: A Participatory Action Research Casebook*, edited by Susan D. Greenbaum, Glenn Jacobs, and Prentice Zinn, 80–94. New Brunswick, NJ: Rutgers University Press.

Tracy, Natalicia R. 2018. "I am a Survivor of Human Trafficking: Natalicia's Story." *The Atlantic*, March 12. www.theatlantic.com/business/archive/2018/03/human-traffickingnatalicia/553100/.

Tracy, Natalicia R., Tim Sieber, and Susan Moir. 2014. "INVISIBLE NO MORE: Domestic Workers Organizing in Massachusetts and Beyond." *University of Massachusetts Boston Labor Studies Faculty Publication Series* 2014 (October): Paper 1. http://scholarworks.umb.edu/laborstudies_faculty_pubs/1.

Virginia's Legislative Information System. 2021. "2021 Session." https://lis.virginia.gov/cgi-bin/legp604.exe?211+sum+SB1310.

10

The Massachusetts Commission on LGBTQ Youth

Alexander Nally

10.1 INTRODUCTION

Established in 1992 initially as the Commission on Gay & Lesbian Youth, the Massachusetts Commission on LGBTQ Youth was the first state agency established in the United States dedicated solely to improving the lives of LGBTQ youth. Although the Commission's continued existence and level of funding embody the Massachusetts legislature's dedication to LGBTQ youth in Massachusetts, it does so in duality with the sobering reality that LGBTQ youth continue to experience disparate health, social, and economic outcomes compared to their non-LGBTQ peers. Yet, the Commission's composition and posture within a state government, along with its youth-centered mission and dedication to centering the experiences of queer, transgender, black, indigenous, young people of color (QTBIPOC), offer a compelling model of successful policy codesign methods that center human dignity.

In this chapter, I discuss the historical and political context and composition of the Commission, summarize the key tenets of the Commission's codesign methods for dignity-centered policymaking, share one of the Commission's policy interventions in action, and conclude with considerations for developing public policy codesign structures that center human dignity.

10.2 HISTORICAL CONTEXT AND COMPOSITION

The Commission was first established as the Governor's Commission on Gay and Lesbian Youth by Governor William Weld in 1992 pursuant to Executive Order 325. Among the reasons for the establishment of the Commission was the 1989 report published by the United States Health and Human Services agency acknowledging the suicide epidemic among gay and lesbian youth. At that time, an estimated 30% of all suicides in the United States were among gay and lesbian youth (Gibson 1989).

In the 1992 executive order that first established the Commission, Governor Weld contemplated a gay and lesbian youth-centric public policy codesign framework in acknowledging that "many of the problems facing gay and lesbian youth are within the purview of state government and can be corrected by promulgation of information, training and the implementation and diffusion of formal guidelines and state policy," and by appointing directly impacted stakeholders to lead the Commission, specifically "at least one parent of a gay or lesbian person; one high school student; one college student; one representative from an educational institution; and one representative of the mental health profession." Although the lived experiences of LGBTQ youth vary across race, gender identity, and sexual orientation among other intersectional demographics, the direct appointment and inclusion of these initial representative members on the Commission placed those at the heart of the LGBTQ youth suicide epidemic at the policymaking table. Further empowering the LGBTQ community and education advocates to recommend policy interventions to improve the lives of LGBTQ youth, the Commission's mission in its inception and today continues to revolve specifically around the lived experiences and life outcomes of the Commonwealth's LGBTQ youth population.

During its initial period of existence, the Commission's Safe Schools Program established "a national model for creating a safe school environment for gay and lesbian students best practices," as acknowledged in Acting Governor Cellucci's Executive Order 407 in 1998, which amended the Commission's mission to include within its purview the obligation to "make recommendations about policies and programs supporting gay and lesbian youth on an ongoing basis to the Massachusetts Department of Education, the Massachusetts Department of Public Health and the Executive Office of Health and Human Services (Celluci 1998)." In this iteration of the Commission's charge, the foundation was laid for the Commission's statewide policy recommendations. The Commission, however, has not always benefited from full support over its thirty-year history. Its initial existence as a Governor's Commission left the Commission vulnerable to compositional or funding changes at the whim of the governor. In 2006, the Commission escaped a terminal fate promised by Governor Romney after the Commission sought to include bisexual and transgender youth in a communication regarding the Commonwealth's annual Youth Pride Parade (Gray 2019). Although the Romney administration sought to initially dissolve the Commission or severely curtail its mission, the Massachusetts legislature acted to establish a new iteration of the Commission as a legislative commission. Bringing the Commission under the legislative branch instead of the executive branch would ensure that the Commission's existence and important policy work would continue regardless of any changes in administration in the future.

Pursuant to a legislative override after Governor Romney's initial veto, the legislature established the permanent legislative commission on gay and lesbian youth with an expanded composition of members drawn from diverse racial, ethnic, religious, age, sexual orientation, and socioeconomic backgrounds from throughout the Commonwealth (2006 Mass. Acts 815–817). This iteration of the Commission, slightly modified since, continues today (M.G.L. ch.3 §67). The history, composition, and mission of the Commission are as important as the actual human-centered policy it has promulgated in its history, because the Commission's existence is a product of a codesign process (the legislative process) and demonstrates one example of how state governments can utilize existing policy structures to promulgate human-centered policies. Especially important is that the Commission's membership directly involves those whose lives are impacted by state agency policies: for example, LGBTQ youth who have experienced violence and representatives of organizations dedicated to reducing that violence and supporting youth.

10.3 KEY TENETS OF CODESIGN FOR DIGNITY-CENTERED POLICYMAKING

The Commission's ability to employ human-centered design approaches in implementing policy interventions benefits greatly from the Commission's LGBTQ youth-centered mission, compositional structure, and posture within state government. Human-centered design necessarily requires an unwavering commitment to improving the lives of the people who will be impacted by policy innovations. Although the names of agencies often resemble an alphabet soup of bureaucratic functions that stem from federal and state political frameworks, the Commission's name specifically centers the Commission's work to serve lesbian, gay, bisexual, transgender, queer, and questioning youth. The name of the Commission has evolved since its original namesake in 1992 to acknowledge the differences and varying experiences of LGBTQ youth. The Commission's inclusion of transgender, queer, and questioning youth is especially important because it enables the Commission to advocate not only for LGBTQ youth whose gender identity or sexual orientation align with increasingly recognized identities (lesbian, gay, bisexual, and transgender) but also for LGBTQ youth whose gender identity, sexual orientation, or human identities extend beyond current social or societal recognition (2014 Mass. Acts 712). Too often, LGBTQ resources and policies are developed for heteronormative or popular portrayals of LGBTQ experiences that, despite providing critical lifelines of support for cisgender lesbian and gay youth, do so at the exclusion of bisexual, transgender, queer, and questioning youth who have unique experiences from those of cisgender lesbian and gay youth.

Yet, although the Commission's name and central population are more inclusive than in prior years, they still do not include other key populations that are often considered within the broader LGBTQ+ umbrella, such as individuals who identify as intersex or asexual. Whether these identities will be added to the Commission's name in the future is an open question, but the work of the Commission in its history has sought and likely will continue to include an ever-expanding umbrella of LGBTQ youth identities. The identities of the LGBTQ youth the Commission is empowered by law to serve matter because of the unique experiences that are had by youth of these varying identities. As this relates to human-centered design, the Commission's composition and policy strategies over time have necessarily evolved to align with the experiences of youth who share these identities, as well as to ensure that the Commission's composition could genuinely serve and support these populations.

Another integral component to human-centered design is the consideration of who is working to serve the target population. Though it seldom may be the experience that legal designers employing a human-centered design approach to policy interventions share in identity with the population that stands to benefit most from the policy interventions, the Commission's composition uniquely aspires to mirror these identities to the extent possible. The Commission's current composition includes the following twenty-seven persons (M.G.L. ch. 3 §67(a)):

- three persons appointed by the Massachusetts chapter of the National Association of Social Workers;
- three persons appointed by the Massachusetts Coalition for Suicide Prevention;
- two persons appointed by the Fenway Community Health Center;
- four persons appointed by the Greater Boston Parents, Families and Friends of Lesbians and Gays;
- two persons appointed by the Massachusetts Gay and Lesbian Political Caucus;
- one person appointed by MassEquality;
- one persons appointed by the Massachusetts Teachers Association;
- one persons appointed by AFT Massachusetts;
- three persons appointed by the Massachusetts Chapter of the American Academy of Pediatrics;
- two persons appointed by the Gay, Lesbian and Straight Education Network of Boston;
- two persons appointed by the Massachusetts Public Health Association; and
- three persons appointed by the Massachusetts Association of School Superintendents.

In addition, the remaining twenty-three general members of the commission shall include, from diverse racial, ethnic, religious, age, sexual orientation, and socio-economic backgrounds from throughout the Commonwealth, at least:

- one parent of a gay or lesbian person;
- one high school student;
- one college student;
- one representative from an educational institution; and
- one representative of the mental health professions.

Commission members serve for a term of two years, renewable upon expiration (M.G.L. ch. 3 §67(b)). Such cadence allows for each member to meaningfully engage in providing direction and policy support to the Commission while also allowing flexibility for members to serve longer to support key projects, or to rotate out in order to bring in new voices and perspectives to the Commission. By virtue of the Commission's composition, the Commission often convenes additional community, education, and government stakeholders to provide further direction and support to the Commission's objectives.

Finally, the Commission's posture within the state government enables it to command a high degree of attention and support for its mission to ensure the Commonwealth is a place where all youth thrive. The policy recommendations it publishes further that mission. As an independent state agency, it is empowered by the legislature to annually make recommendations to the legislature and executive branch agencies on how to better serve LGBTQ youth in the Commonwealth (M.G.L. ch. 3 §67(c)). In addition, the Commission also receives funding each year from the state general appropriations act to implement the Commonwealth's Anti-Bullying Law enacted in 2010 (2022 Mass. Acts 188, 466), (2010 Mass. Acts 224–233), (M.G.L. ch. 71 §37O). The posture of the Commission elevates its policy recommendations to the legislature and executive branch agencies.

There are and will always be organizations and stakeholders outside the realm of government seeking to encourage and direct the legislature and state agencies to better serve the public. However, because the Commission exists as an independent state agency, the recommendations it provides receive heightened attention. Within the state government of Massachusetts there is a level of deference and respect among state agencies as they execute their individual missions. What is unique about the Commission is that its approach to developing policy recommendations provides an additional layer of vetting and process that, combined with the Commission's ongoing outreach and engagement with the legislature and executive branch agencies throughout the year, provides a more streamlined development pipeline for human-centered policy interventions. Unlike state agencies that must prioritize staff and resources for internal mission-critical objectives, the value of the Commission's posture within state government is that its mission-critical work is to seek where policy interventions could be employed in state government to better serve LGBTQ youth. At best, this is a luxury of time many state agencies cannot afford to expend in lieu of meeting more pressing legislative mandates, and at worst, agencies may not always have the leadership, expertise, or internal buy-in to explore such policy interventions. In contrast, the Commission's ability to dedicate time and resources to meeting, partnering, and at times providing technical support to state agencies enables it to employ codesign approaches in developing policy interventions that will efficiently leverage state resources throughout from design to implementation to ensure the best impacts for LGBTQ youth.

10.4 COMMISSION POLICY WORK IN ACTION

In carrying out its mission, the Commission engages in a major annual effort as required by the legislature to issue an annual report and policy recommendations to document its ongoing development and progress in implementing its LGBTQ youth-centered policy interventions. The Commission's annual report and policy recommendations serve as an annual snapshot of both new and carried-over policy recommendations. It has also included key resources such as terminology, current demographic and outcome data for LGBTQ youth nationally and in the Commonwealth, as well as detailed substantive and research reports regarding the evolving landscape for LGBTQ youth: both victories and new challenges that impact LGBTQ youth.

During my tenure on the Commission, we centered the development of policy interventions in three key areas: ending youth homelessness, reforming juvenile justice, and improving health outcomes. We aligned our committee structure to organize the Commission's membership into three working groups centered around community relations, government relations, and the safe schools program. By employing substantive areas of focus across the Commission, each working group then engaged their respective, extended constituencies outside of the Commission to convene and recommend policy interventions and programs to help achieve the Commission's objectives and, ultimately, ensure better outcomes for LGBTQ youth. Although the composition and governance structure of the Commission and its subdivisions are a topic that has been explored here in detail, its main purpose is to re-iterate the inherent dignity of each individual person that is involved in the Commission's work, and this recognition is necessary in order for the Commission to appropriately serve the population of LGBTQ youth, a population that we know and understand to have infinitely varied experiences of personal identity and life within the Commonwealth. This foundational network of Commission members and extended stakeholders outside of the Commission serves as the key building block for implementing policy interventions that center the lives of LGBTQ youth: not only by informing the Commission of what is needed on the ground in real time but also by ensuring that at any point in time, the Commission's extended composition includes sufficiently diverse LGBTQ youth and advocates capable of building appropriate interventions.

However, not all policy interventions necessarily require policymaking to improve a person's experience of government systems and programs. One particularly novel and relevant example of a policy intervention the Commission designed that did not actually involve policymaking so much as years of dedication and strategic convening of stakeholders was its development of the LGBTQ Resource Map (The Commonwealth of Massachusetts Commission on LGBTQ Youth, n.d.).

In its early phases of inception, the "geomapping project," first referenced in the Commission's FY15 Annual Policy Recommendations, was conceived as a statewide resource that state agencies could submit data to regarding available services and supports for LGBTQ youth (Massachusetts Commission on Lesbian, Gay, Bisexual, Transgender, Queer, and Questioning Youth 2014). Over time, the scope of the geomapping project broadened to include even more resources, programs, and services across the entire Commonwealth available to LGBTQ youth, including Gay-Straight Alliances and Gender and Sexuality Alliances (GSAs), education and employment services, health and awareness services, legal services, anonymous meetings, community groups and resources, hotline services, and faith-based organizations. The challenge for many years, however, was finding the funding, developers, and technical infrastructure required to evolve the geomapping project from an unwieldy spreadsheet of directory information into a free, vetted, interactive, and mobile-friendly tool that could be easily accessed by LGBTQ youth and advocates online at any time. Although an initial group of developers were able to volunteer time and resources to establish a first iteration of the geomapping project, due to turnover and insufficient resources to sustainably support it, the geomapping project's transformation from a mere database to a web app stalled until 2017.

In May 2017, however, the Commission struck gold. As previously mentioned, the Commission's compositional structure is key to its success in identifying and advancing policy interventions that center the lived experiences of LGBTQ youth. Commission leadership at the time sought to revive the geomapping project. Serendipitously, through a family connection, a Commission member shared some information about the organization Out in Tech and its Digital Corps program with Commission leadership, in case the Commission might have any tech projects that could benefit from becoming a project at Out in Tech's 2017 NYC hackathon. Over the next four weeks, I worked with Out in Tech's Program Director Gary Goldman to frame the geomapping project as a hackathon prompt and worked with the developers assigned to our project to develop the initial prototype for what evolved into the LGBTQ Resource Map.

The goal for this project was to create an online tool for LGBTQ youth to access resources across the Commonwealth, with careful attention to design for LGBTQ youth, social workers, nurses and primary care physicians, as well as school personnel. Our feature wishlist was broad and included the following: user friendliness; mobile friendliness; being able to receive feedback from the community about a resource or the website, including an option to sort resources by category; ease of maintenance by Commission staff or members without computer science backgrounds; a geolocator for users to find out which resources they are nearest to; a registered user database for users to create a login and password to "star" or "favorite" certain resources they might want to return to later; email or SMS reminders to notify the user when a place or resource next opens; the ability for organizations or agencies to submit notifications to registered users; and social media share buttons.

Miraculously, the team assigned to our project delivered an exceptional product that the Commission was able to launch publicly in 2018. At the closing reception for the hackathon, I stressed the importance of this project and noted that not all policy interventions require policymaking in the traditional sense to have a substantial impact in the civic realm. The beauty of the geomapping project was in its embrace of the dignity of LGBTQ youth: the fundamental and core belief that LGBTQ youth have inherent value as human beings as their identities and lives unfold and, most importantly, that they know not only who they are as human beings but also what they need to thrive. Service design often presumes an ineptitude of the populations the service is designed for. This inherent assumption that populations are helpless and that legal design and policy interventions are required to help those populations is a peril to progress. The geomapping project, in contrast, never entertained this notion. Rather, the underlying concept behind the geomapping project acknowledged that LGBTQ youth know who they are and what they need to succeed. This has never been nor will ever be a problem. Rather, the key problem the geomapping project sought to solve was one of access to information, and through years of codevelopment with state agencies and advocates, and with support from Out in Tech, Commission leadership, and continued funding and support, the LGBTQ Resource Map honors the dignity in LGBTQ youth and enables them to access the resources they identify as helpful to their ongoing growth and development as young adults.

10.5 CONCLUSION

Intentionality is essential to centering dignity in legal design. A team's mission or design challenge, how the design question is framed, who the effort is intended to help, and, most importantly, why that particular team is exploring the design question are important questions to explore before, during, and after any legal design process. It may not always be feasible to mirror a design team's composition with that of the intended beneficiary population. However, through intentionality and the process of inquiry, design teams can better equip themselves for the candid communication and authenticity necessary in deploying a human-centered legal design process that celebrates the dignity of people who are accessing legal services.

A design team might also consider how it centers dignity in project proposals, communications, and project management timelines. Relevant to these considerations also are the cadence of the project, the frequency at which internal or external stakeholders and end users are engaged, as well as any timing constraints. Whether the composition of the design team itself or the project's stakeholders reflect the diversity and lived experiences of the population to be engaged is particularly important, as well as how often the design team engages these stakeholders. There may be some projects that could benefit from a richer engagement with fewer stakeholders over a sustained period of time, while others may benefit from more concise engagement with a rotation of different stakeholders. Depending on the nature of the project and the design questions to be explored, ideally project proposals and communications center the voices of the beneficiary population in their own words, and project management timelines are built around the unique schedules and needs of the beneficiary population.

Design teams also must leverage appropriately skilled collaborators and resources to ensure that legal design processes, and the ultimate policy interventions, are intentionally accessible and in the same human language used by the target population. Bringing more people to the table, rather than developing a policy intervention that will serve the few over the many, will ensure the dignity of people on either side of the table is honored. To minimize or diminish in any way a person's unique experience denies them validity of their existence. This is true both for design team members as well as stakeholders and the intended beneficiary population, as a design team cannot equitably serve others to its own detriment. In addition, there is often more flexibility to timelines and scopes of work than we are willing to accept. Flexibility is key in fully realizing human-centered design interventions, even if more time is needed to bring additional skills and perspectives to the table to accomplish the task at hand.

The Commission's inherent value lies in its mission, its composition, and its posture within a state government. To date, it remains the first and only independent state agency of its kind in the United States. Although the Commission's structure is unique, especially for a state agency, the Commission offers a compelling model for public policy codesign structures that center human dignity. In leveraging its statutory mandate, skilled personnel and resources, stakeholders who share in identity and diversity with LGBTQ and QTBIPOC youth, and its continuous rotation of leadership and membership, the Commission enables LGBTQ and QTBIPOC youth to continuously codesign a Commonwealth where all youth can thrive.

REFERENCES

Act Making Appropriations for the Fiscal Year 2023 for the Maintenance of the Departments, Boards, Commissions, Institutions and Certain Activities of the Commonwealth, for Interest, Sinking Fund and Serial Bond Requirements and for Certain Permanent Improvements, ch. 126 §2, 2022 Mass. Acts 188, 466. https://malegislature.gov/Laws/SessionLaws/Acts/2022/Chapter126

Act Making Appropriations for the Fiscal Year 2015 for the Maintenance of the Departments, Boards, Commissions, Institutions and Certain Activities of the Commonwealth, for Interest, Sinking Fund and Serial Bond Requirements and for Certain Permanent Improvements, ch. 165 §5, 2014 Mass. Acts 712. https://malegislature.gov/Laws/SessionLaws/Acts/2014/Chapter165

Act Making Appropriations for the Fiscal Year 2007 for the Maintenance of the Departments, Boards, Commissions, Institutions and Certain Activities of the Commonwealth, for Interest, Sinking Fund and Serial Bond Requirements and for Certain Permanent Improvements, ch.139 §4, 2006 Mass. Acts 815–817. https://malegislature.gov/Laws/SessionLaws/Acts/2006/Chapter139

Act Relative to Bullying in Schools, ch. 92, 2010 Mass. Acts 224–233.
The Commonwealth of Massachusetts Commission on LGBTQ Youth. n.d. "LGBTQ Resource Map." Accessed October 4, 2022. https://ma-lgbtq.org.
Celluci, Argeo Paul. 1998. "Executive Order 407: Governor's Commission on Gay and Lesbian Youth." Accessed May 16, 2024. www.mass.gov/executive-orders/no-407-governors-commission-on-gay-and-lesbian-youth.
Gibson, Paul. 1989. "Gay Male and Lesbian Youth Suicide." In *Report of the Secretary's Task Force on Youth Suicide. Volume 3: Prevention and Interventions in Youth Suicide*, edited by Marcia R. Feinleib, 115–42. Washington, DC: U.S. Department of Health and Human Services.
Gray, Arielle. 2019. "How LGBTQ+ Youth Gained Protection in Massachusetts." *WBUR*, June 24. www.wbur.org/news/2019/06/24/lgbtq-youth-commission-massachusetts.
Massachusetts Commission on Lesbian, Gay, Bisexual, Transgender, Queer, and Questioning Youth. 2014. "Massachusetts Commission on LGBTQ Youth: Annual Policy Recommendations for FY15." https://archives.lib.state.ma.us/handle/2452/208066.
M.G.L. ch. 3 §67 (Official set).
M.G.L. ch. 3 §67(a) (Official set).
M.G.L. ch. 3 §67(b) (Official set).
M.G.L. ch. 3 §67(c) (Official set).
M.G.L. ch. 71 §37O (Official set).
Weld, William. 1992. "Executive Order 325: Governor's Commission on Gay and Lesbian Youth." Accessed October 4, 2022. www.mass.gov/executive-orders/no-325-governors-commission-on-gay-and-lesbian-youth.

11

My Mainway

Designing in Dignity for Policymaking

Leon Cruickshank and Mirian Calvo

11.1 INTRODUCTION

In this chapter, we describe how we sought to build community agency in a public sector–led development process. This empowered a community in a run-down residential estate to contribute to decisions about the further development of their council-owned homes. The estate, Mainway, in Lancaster in the north-west of the United Kingdom, has a crumbling housing stock that will be uninhabitable in the next four to five years. We describe below how members of the design research group ImaginationLancaster built dignity into this creative engagement process by designing interventions and activities to build an open, trusting space for dialogue between policymakers, housing officers, and the residents of Mainway. We are also presenting a *real* process, where the City Councillors are faced with making the biggest single financial decision in their history. The decision to demolish or rebuild the Mainway estate will cost approximately £35 million. Either option will involve eight years of building and residents moving out for three or so years in phases while the buildings are renovated and/or retrofitted.

This real context includes delays, politics, and bureaucracy. Even with the uniformly good intentions of the professional actors in the process, this has not been a "smooth" project. In light of this experience, we are also asking questions about the literature around design and dignity. We argue that dignity can be preserved and grown through good, meaningful dialogue, where interactions support and advocate for those not voicing an opinion and hearing the voices of the seldom heard. We contest that control and autonomy by proving participation is not the only route to dignity. This is important if we are to build models of dignified contributions and dignity of participants in areas such as policy design, where control is mediated across multiple stakeholders at local, regional, and national levels in addition to community involvement. We advocate for the public to play an active role in policy development with realistic expectations of control as well as dignity building through a real contribution to making better policy.

11.2 DIGNITY

Dignity is an idea with deep historical roots stretching back at least as far as Cicero in the first century BCE. In antiquity, dignity has been described as a respectful treatment due to positions of power, as well as something achieved or bestowed on those that fulfill public duty or service (Kim et al. 2019). Mirandola in the book *Oration on the Dignity of Man* (1996) describes dignity in terms of the freedom of individuals to make decisions about what they want to be as individuals, and by extension, the freedom to change what they want to be. This right to self-determination as a notion of freedom or autonomy is extended in some of the contemporary literature. Often dignity is described as an overall autonomy, as the agency to make changes in the world rather than the self. "People find dignity when they act as autonomous agents of their own doing and being. Dignity is in action" (Kim 2018). This is taken further in the thinking of radical groups directly engaging and working with community groups. For example, in collaboration with the Colombian community activist group "Saber y Vida," Grisales-Bohórquez et al. (2021) declare that "'Saber y Vida' equates dignity with power, an attribute of the model that helps mediate the intricacies of having influence, as opposed to power, within participatory processes, or what Palacin et al. (2020) call 'pseudo-participation'" (Grisales-Bohórquez et al. 2021).

The direct equation of dignity with power is challenging in a context beyond the hyper-local where power may always fundamentally be distributed amongst a range of actors, and we will be exploring this directly in our case study that follows. It is also worth noting, though, that there is also an interpretation that is focused on "increasing users' perceived control within a system" (Hagan 2017) rather than actual power. There are examples, especially in health care, where co-design projects have engaged with communities and not considered power structures sufficiently, giving communities only the *illusion* of power and agency, resulting in community disillusionment when expectations were not managed (Donetto 2015). As co-designers, we are acutely aware that empowering communities is quite different, and much more challenging, than giving the *appearance* of power.

In this chapter, we present a project that offers an alternative to the "strong" definition of dignity as requiring control, power, and autonomy. We propose that participants (all participants from lay members to policymakers and others) can retain and enhance their dignity without one group having power over the others. Genuine, mutually respectful, and honest dialogue and exchange recognising the aptitudes, abilities, and contributions of all participants can enhance dignity while presenting a collaborative process. This is critically important in areas such as policy design, urban development, and almost any large-scale intervention. Here information can be technical, obscure, and inaccessible to the lay population, with long timescales and the interplay of national, regional, and local legislation making it impractical for lay participants to be in a strong power position.

To explore how we designed a creative engagement process that supported dignified participation, we draw here on ideas from procedural justice. Hagan et al. (2017) describe the key characteristics of this as being a sense for participants of:

- their voice in expressing their views;
- the feeling of neutral application of law;
- individual's sense of respect; and
- their trust that authorities are sincerely trying to help them.

We use these four categories as a lens to describe the design and delivery of the My Mainway project, reflecting in the conclusion on the achievements and deficiencies of this process and its ongoing progress in the future.

11.3 DESIGN AND DIGNITY

Design and dignity are two terms which have been intrinsically linked at least since the Universal Declaration of Human Rights in 1948 (McKeon 1990). The nature of this link is supported by the definition of design as a process "fundamentally grounded in human dignity and human rights" (Buchanan 2001, 36). Equally, design is a key feature to embody dignity and transform our environment in a dignified way (Kim 2021; Grisales-Bohorquez et al. 2021). This places people at the centre of the binomial motivation-purpose of design and as its subject (Bason 2010). However, it also highlights the ethical and moral challenges (Buchanan, 2001) associated with diversity, equity, inclusion, distribution of power, social justice of the design process, and the way in which the design outcomes may differently affect diverse groups of people and contexts (Kim 2021). These foundational/ontological challenges of design are also associated with the notion of dignity. Kim (2021) unfolds its complexity by defining dignity as a multidimensional and subjective concept, with indivisible components: (1) the personal component that considers the absolute value or worth of the self (Waldron and Dan-Cohen 2012), self-autonomy, freedom of choice, self-determination, and interpersonal care (Kim 2021); and (2) the social or collective component, of a more subjective nature, since the value of the self is dependent on the community to which he/she belongs (Kim 2021). For instance, the merit of a person is based on the appreciation that the community has of them, by agglutinating economic value or power and/or by their social status.

The principle of human rights expands the notion of dignity to everyone, a collective right inherited in peaceful, just communities and societies (Rosen 2012). This collective spirit of peace, social justice, cultural inclusion, and human dignity has influenced design theory and practice. In this sense, design research has taken a new road map, moving away from top-down approaches (Head 2007) and increasingly drawing in local and national governments (Kimbell 2015) who are investing resources to build and revitalise bridges between their institutional leaders and community members (Forss et al. 2011), utilising design as an instrument to engender social innovations inside and outside of public institutions. This trend leans on participation and public engagement and aims to respond to the cultural demands of an emerging society, eager to engage socially and culturally in upcoming challenges (Smith, Bossen, and Kanstrup 2017). Some of these challenges are associated with intensifying ecological changes which impact places and their communities unequally. Design also plays a key role in the process of rethinking a society that will be "increasingly designed" (Kaptelinin and Nardi 2006, 10), and which will need to agilely adjust to drastic social and environmental changes.

Participatory design processes play (and will play) a fundamental role in generating long-term resilient communities, capable of finding design solutions based on resources and knowledge rooted in those local areas. From a legal point of view, in recent decades, participatory and community empowerment policies have emerged at international and national levels: for example, in the United Kingdom, the Localism Act (2011), Royal Institute of British Architects (2020) and Sustainable Outcomes and Social Value in the UK; the United Nations (2015) Agenda for Sustainable Development, through its Goal 11, "sustainable cities and communities," advocates for participatory planning and architecture, among other initiatives. These empowerment policies have opened opportunities to change societies' commitment to the urban landscape by legitimising participation as an "ongoing interaction between those involved in emergent processes of relating" (Said Mosleh and Larsen 2020). Moreover, this emergence of policies advocates for a greater emphasis on human dignity by expanding citizens' rights in decision-making processes (Calvo et al. 2022) and joint policy development. According to Grisales-Bohórquez et al. (2021), participation can lead to unblocking and/or activating collective and personal dignities through setting up multi-voiced engagement processes, particularly by including those unheard and unseen. This is not an easy task. As we experienced in the Mainway estate, socioeconomic constraints and sociocultural dynamics embedded in the neighbourhood operated simultaneously during the participatory process. For example, antisocial behaviour, delinquency, drug use, and high tenant turnover were behaviours that hampered interactions and design activities at specific times. Additionally, we faced COVID-19-related restrictions, and the reality that residents had very different, almost polarised views on the City Council's intentions about the future of the neighbourhood, and about our real reason (as a design research team) to develop a participatory process.

In scenarios of medium- to large-scale participation, the divergence of actors can bring novel and holistic visions (Bason 2010), but the facilitation and design tactics can only set the conditions to support and nurture dignified dialogues "rather than control outcomes, placing participation as a phenomenon requiring continuous investigation" (Grisales-Bohórquez et al. 2021, 79; see also Andersen et al. 2015). There is still a long way to go to establish dignified participatory processes which are constituent parts of the communities' and public authorities' present and not temporary and inclusive processes for imagining speculative future scenarios.

In the following sections, we present the context of the My Mainway project, explore the implementation of the creative engagement process, and outline key moments where dignified participation was brought to the forefront through active listening, fairness, respectfulness, and advocacy.

11.3.1 *Context*

The My Mainway project was initiated by Lancaster City Council (LCC) in May 2020. Lancaster is a small city close to the north-west coast of England in the United Kingdom. Mainway is a City Council–owned housing estate in the centre of the city – a mix of high-rise and low-rise flats with 257 dwellings in total. It is a "sink" estate where people go because there is no other option in the region for them. Mainway is regarded as being the poorest council housing in the city and has significant problems with endemic substance abuse and antisocial behaviour. This results in high tenant turnover, with many residents not staying in Mainway for long. There is a significant core of residents who are committed to living in Mainway in its current form. These may be people who happen to have excellent views of the highly picturesque River Lune that runs alongside the estate, or who chose to stay almost perpetually behind their heavily locked doors for reasons of poor physical or mental health (Figure 11.1).

Mainway presents another challenge for the Council and residents. The fabric of these concrete buildings from the 1960s is crumbling. Within a few years, the buildings will be unsafe to live in. Building on an ongoing ten-year collaboration with the Council, the design research lab, ImaginationLancaster, at Lancaster University, was invited to undertake a project on the Mainway estate to help build a stronger relationship between residents and the city planners. Specifically, the aims of the project were:

1. to begin building trust and mutual understanding with the dwellers;
2. to explore the benefits and disadvantages of two ways of redeveloping the social housing estate: (1) the refurbishment option (renovation) of the existing buildings in Mainway and (2) the regeneration option (rebuilding), which contemplated the demolition of all residential buildings; and
3. to explore which of the options is preferred by residents, and identify general space layouts and outcomes, for example, clustering, customisation within limits, and acknowledging the implications of these choices in terms of disruption.

11.3.2 *Programme of Engagement in Mainway*

The My Mainway project was originally proposed as a way of bringing together dwellers and locals from different buildings and backgrounds to explore prime social

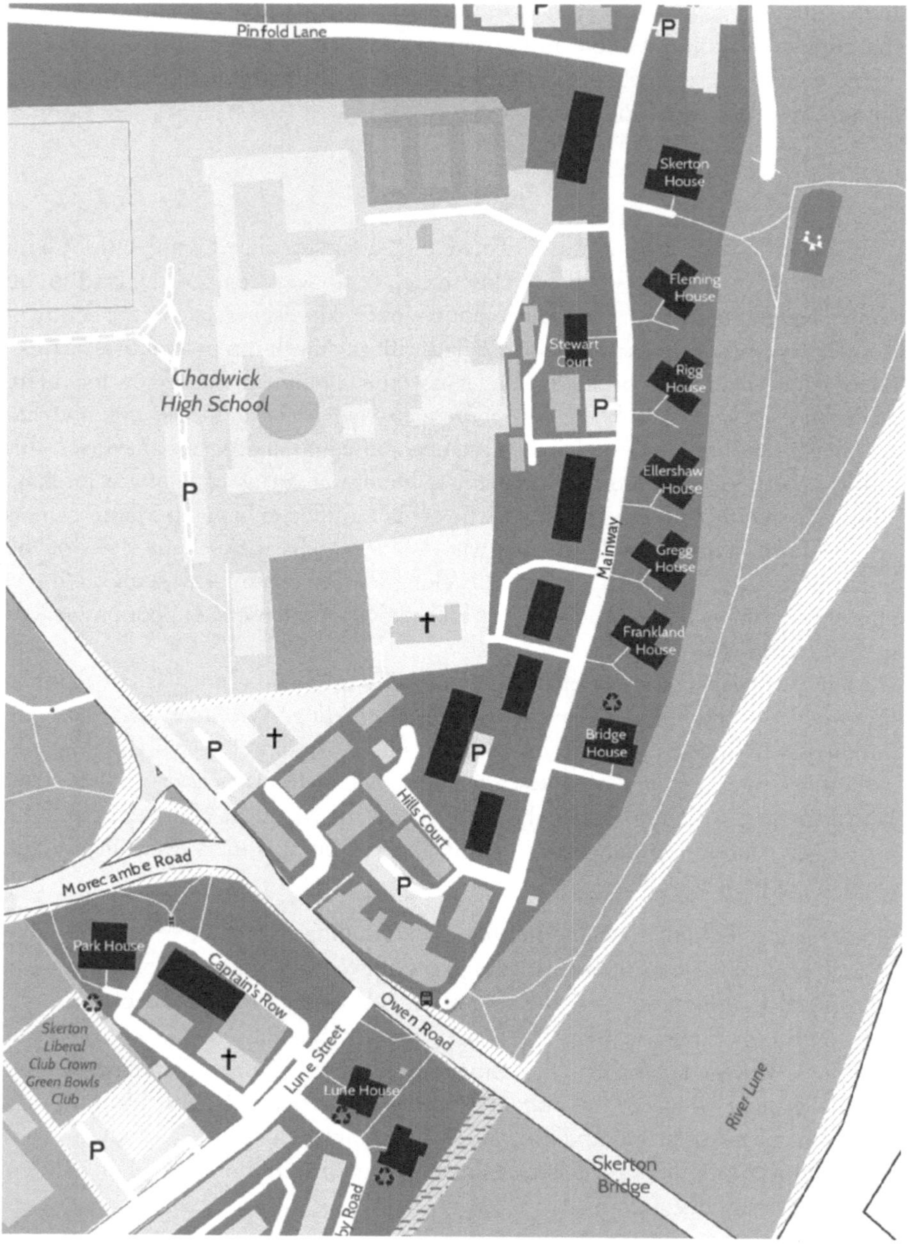

FIGURE 11.1. A map showing the Mainway site and how it relates to the River Lune and the busy main road running through the site.

issues and experiences of living in the estate and elicit conversations with essential information to illustrate an overview of resident views. Thinking that COVID-19-related restrictions would ease, allowing for more conventional participatory design methodologies, we designed a programme of engagement based on two strategies: (1) building a resilient community behind the estate's transformation (whatever outcome this would be) and (2) understanding participation as a structural component geared through planned participatory events.

We divided the events into five engagement blocks over six months (July 2020–January 2021) combining four participatory design methods: designing touring walks, public engagement events, mock-ups (prototype-tests of ideas on the neighbourhood), and thematic encounters (i.e., expert conversations, creative guest workshops, etc.).

We facilitated the first events, consisting of touring walks around Mainway estate with its dwellers (Figure 11.2). We took inspiration from "transect walks" (Narayanasamy 2009) and from Lynch's (1960) investigation on mental images of the city, which are prominent methods in participatory rural appraisal and urban planning, well used in the early stages of research to enter the field (Kanstrup et al. 2014). The walks enabled us to gain access to first-hand insights and build trust and rapport by inviting the dwellers to express their views and unfolding place-related affective values (Ehrström 2016). We achieved this by endowing the dwellers with the power to decide and guide the walking routes, stopping us to share their memories, unearthing "concrete" bad and good experiences, highlighting things they would like to see changed, and bringing them into discussions. Soon enough the residents let us know that the area suffers a host of antisocial behaviour, crime, and drug use and that they had to share communal spaces and/or live door-to-door with dangerous people. They were living in a continuous state of stress because of this proximity to danger. We also discovered the open public areas and green spaces have a lack of public life, without amenities, facilities, and shops that could bring cultural and vibrant activities to the area. Another revelation was that there was a substantial number of dwellers who did not come out at all from their households due to poor physical and mental health, with some not having access to the internet.

Considering these findings, coupled with the increasing trend of COVID-19 case spikes in 2020, we decided it was imperative to reconsider the previous programme of engagement and reorient our methodology to respond to global and local realities. Thus, we redesigned a new programme based on four strategies: (1) bringing the needs of the residents to the forefront of the project, promoting mutual understanding and sincere interactions; (2) establishing various routes for engagement that would adjust to the heterogeneity of the dwellers; (3) visiting all households in the development and meeting with each resident separately; and (4) incorporating a neighbourhood engagement centre, which was called "the Hub" and is described in more detail below.

The program of engagement activities was grouped into two engagement blocks spread over two to three months with activities designed flexibly, which would allow

FIGURE 11.2. One of the touring walks with City Councillors at the Mainway estate. (Photo credit: My Mainway Project Team.)

for agile adaptation to the possible convulsive changes the COVID-19 pandemic could cause. The time frame was illustrative and reviewed weekly by the management team to assess the social conditions and determine how to design and deploy the next event, or whether to stop the programme. The first block was oriented towards gathering the neighbourhood's feelings about the options for regeneration versus renovation, with attention to the neighbourhood scale, whilst the second block was devised to dig down into the detail of how that transformation would be, exploring the human scale.

We facilitated walking events with City Councillors and conducted online expert workshops. In addition, we designed two main participatory design methods tailored to the best of our understanding of Mainway's personal and social conditions: (1) an engagement combo of "creative activities" at the doorstep of all the residents, which we called door-to-door engagement and (2) thematic drop-in sessions at the Hub, such as refurbishing-versus-regeneration scenarios, new visions from Mainway, customisation of households, and so on. These design methods adjusted easily to the changing situation of the pandemic, alongside enabling us to align with our strategies and, to a great extent, to articulate an inclusive and transparent participatory process that brought to the forefront the undignified situations that dwellers experienced in their everyday life, which went beyond the spatial dimensions, turning them into dignified opportunities. In total, the programme facilitated eleven engagement events and weekly drop-in sessions over three months, engaged with 50% of the total households, captured more than 3,500 meaningful statements from dwellers and locals, and generated more than 260 participatory interactions. In the next sections, we explore how these interactions were natural consequences of embedding dignified attitudes in the programme of engagement.

11.3.3 *Dignity through Active Listening to Those Seldom Heard*

The My Mainway project faced a challenge when it came to listening. We had to address the prevalent attitude that "at the end of the day the Council are gonna do what they are gonna do" (Mainway resident). We sought to change this dynamic by changing the way they felt about Mainway and becoming active in improving their living space and, with it, their way of living. With this, the participatory process aspired to regenerate a sense of community action based on a strong understanding of their perspectives. Some residents expressed their scepticism about the whole engagement process. One of them shared a belief that Lancaster City Council already has a redevelopment plan with fewer social homes and an increase in the number of private houses. We addressed these assumptions in three key ways.

Firstly, going to the residents: we proactively sought out and listened to residents, especially those who might be less likely to come to events or activities. This involved the design of a COVID-19-safe, sterile doorstep activity tool to help residents open up about their hopes and fears for the future of Mainway. Working in pairs, a team of Council workers and design researchers visited each dwelling in Mainway, with repeat visits to those where there was no response. This led to detailed and sometimes extensive conversations which were recorded and analysed. This formed a key evidence base for the project, which served to create stronger bonds with some of the residents who respected the efforts we were going to and welcomed the chance to contribute to the dialogue.

Secondly, events and activities: as mentioned in the previous section, we created a series of interventions, workshops, and drop-in sessions at the Hub, often with a

FIGURE 11.3. The launch of the My Mainway Hub under strict COVID-19-related restrictions.
(Photo credit: My Mainway Project Team.)

theme to help residents not only have their voice heard but also build a common understanding of the possibilities of the future development of Mainway.

Thirdly, the Hub: following our strategies, in tandem with LCC, we opened a neighbourhood engagement centre by transforming a shop unit in the Mainway estate into our headquarters, drop-in centre, and information source for the project. This was a venue to share ideas and insights, exchange information, or just have a coffee and chat. The Hub was open five days a week 10:00 to 16:00. It was staffed by members of the Council's housing team with a range of seniority and experience, and by members of the design team (Figure 11.3).

These three types of activity are relevant to aspects of building participants' dignity. In terms of active listening, we devoted time and resources to make space for unhurried, deep listening, respecting the choice of residents to not come to special events. We also designed activities to act as boundary objects, helping bridge the gap between perceptions or disciplines by setting up a common "neutral space or activity" (Reily 2021). These activities helped make conversations more fun, engaging, and "fluid," resulting in longer, more revealing exchanges and a strong sense that the residents' views were taken seriously.

11.3.4 *Dignity through Fairness*

Another relevant aspect to build dignity in our participants was to embed, within our resources and possibilities, the principle of fairness. Fairness, understood within the context of human rights, comprises equal treatment of individuals within a community and/or society, and is closely related to legitimacy and the feeling of neutral application of law. In a process of this magnitude, it was a challenge to set the conditions for fairness because it was difficult to reach all the dwellers and let them know we were there and convey clearly the purpose of it, hence building trust and rapport. Also, in such a heterogeneous context, there were all kinds of attitudes and a wide variety of problems at personal and collective levels. Even so, we designed a responsive process that emphasised the emergence of spaces worthy of conversation and creative exchange, exercised from the attitude of recognising the significance of each resident who decided to engage in each activity. Fairness was particularly enacted through two types of events.

Firstly, through recommendation and feedback events: we aimed at connecting the agency of the inhabitants with the process and expanding their perspectives by endowing them with spaces to express their visions. This also included drop-in sessions dedicated to feedback to the dwellers on our ongoing analysis and sharing the status of our recommendations before being sent to The Council's Cabinet (the main decision-making body of the council), allowing a two-way feedback process where the data and interpretations were validated by the residents. These sessions also helped build transparency and gain trust by explicitly explaining the analysis process. We presented a summary of the key themes and subthemes found in the analysis, and displayed the data gathered to illustrate how the data were analysed and processed. Then, we invited the participants to reflect on the subthemes identified and prioritise their top five, as well as to corroborate statements and question others. Our findings were reinforced regarding, for example, the community request to include a community and/or health centre, enhance the walkability of the area, and the request for residential parking. The feedback-loop created was an essential aspect to build trust and gain access to the dwellers' real views, who felt free and safe to speak up and express their fears and desires.

Secondly, through children and young people's events: usually, children and young people are left out of the policymaking process. They are also demographic groups that are hard to reach through traditional engagement processes. So, we crafted two events dedicated to them, one using graffiti techniques and another based on a game-based theory applied to children's activities with guest experts. The events assisted in eliciting their views and prompting spaces, through the games and creative activities, which supported them in contributing their visions in similar conditions. The children's event, for instance, brought visions and insights not captured before. They expressed their desire for more outdoor activities and safe spaces. Safety was one of the issues they mentioned the most. They would like safer places to play with others without feeling exposed or in danger (Figure 11.4).

FIGURE 11.4. Children writing and drawing the activities they liked on the pavement, children drop-in session.
(Photo credit: My Mainway Project Team.)

11.3.5 *Dignity through Being Respectful*

One key to providing a dignified contribution for participants was to respect their views and agendas. Rather than turning this into a referendum on whether to knock down or renovate the Council estate, together we explored the issues that the residents thought were important and tailored how we engaged with them accordingly. Following a series of designed tours (described above), we realised that a significant proportion of the estate's population was unlikely to attend a meeting or activity. It was clear that there were high levels of isolation among community members. Given this and the limitations imposed on us by COVID-19, where mass events were prohibited for an unknown length of time, we changed tack. It became clear that we had to visit every household in Mainway, 257 households, investing an average of 30 minutes on each household, doing a series of creative activities "on the doorstep," capturing their views and concerns about the redevelopment. Before the five-day door-to-door engagements, we delivered an online training session with the engagement team members to illustrate the proposed engagement activities, clarify roles, explain data capturing, and cover health and safety protocols. Going to find the residents separately in their territories where they felt safe allowed us to show we were willing to make the effort to talk to them directly. It also helped us understand how people would like to contribute and communicate on their terms. This could be via email or social media but also through an interactive platform called Engagement HQ and/or through posters and physical newsletters. This allowed us to tailor an approach to fit each resident's personal agenda and situation rather than expecting them to change for us.

We also engaged with residents through physical and digital means about the issues they wanted action on, set up discussions, and signposted people to help address these issues. For example, we requested the help of translators to engage with several residents who did not speak English fluently yet wanted to contribute and understand what would happen to them in the upcoming transformation of the estate. Residents were most concerned with security and antisocial behaviour. A resident expressed this in an exchange between a senior housing officer and the budgetary authority.

> "Door being broken all the time, people coming in, homeless people sitting on the stairs shooting up all the time, yeah, people in Derby House screaming, yeah, I'm not being funny, I am going to speak my mind [to anonymised council officer], I want to speak my mind because I am sick and tired of it." (Mainway resident)

Our engagement methods resulted in a set of recommendations that not only addressed the overall aims of the project described above but also raised serious issues around safety, security, amenities, and community building. The recommendations were shared with residents for comment and, if necessary, modified *before* they went to the central Council cabinet meeting for discussion and approval or not. This was the residents' report, which highlighted their contribution on how best for the council to address this £35 million challenge.

11.3.6 *Dignity through Advocacy to Those in Need*

The engagement programme turned to the task of restoring dignity to the dwellers and locals, particularly those who suffered and still suffer the consequences of antisocial dynamics and delinquency; those who have not left their homes in more than seven years for health reasons, yet opened their homes to us and invested their time by contributing to the project; and those who explained to us in detail their problems associated with housing designs that exclude the vulnerable.

To reconstruct communication between LCC and the dwellers, and to reinvigorate the residents with their sense of agency, we articulated diverse engagement channels, ranging from light engagement (e.g., Engagement HQ, social media, physical posters, and newsletters delivery) to deep engagement (e.g., door-to-door activities, in-person drop-in sessions). Most people we engaged with were stressed and emotionally tired of being in a continuous state of alert, a state which was exacerbated by the COVID-19 pandemic. So, a key to reconstructing dignity was also adopting an attitude of advocacy. The programme of engagements and the analysis from these explicitly translate the residents' claims to have access to a dignified everyday life, away from dangers and unsafe situations. We became advocates for incorporating social and cultural facilities that the dwellers felt they needed during future redevelopment to nurture and give them back their right to the city.

We also drew City Councillors into the programme by inviting them to walk the neighbourhood with us and draw their attention to the social and cultural issues we discovered through the engagements. These walks helped them empathise with the communities' issues in Mainway whilst enabling us to gather their insights and views:

> "We want to find out what the residents want so this estate can be reutilised as they please. For instance, the bin areas do not serve their purpose and they have been used to dumping other stuff." (Councillor 1)

> "At the moment it is called Mainway, that is a road, and it doesn't seem to me to be very attractive. I would move people closer together, so they could see each other, talk to each other." (Councillor 2)

This advocacy attitude was crafted in the recommendations and explicitly advised the local authority to keep building a responsive approach over the ten years that it may take for the regeneration of Mainway. We recommended developing a long-term plan of engagement, using some of the means we employed and adopting others if necessary, and taking actions and measurements to respond to some of the prime claims and needs of the dwellers.

We also structured the analysis giving the participants a real, measured, and rigorously organised say in the decision to renovate or demolish. We used narrative inquiry as the analytical method to garner the residents' views about their preferences between the two options because it enabled us to look at the data through an introspective lens, where the narrative becomes a vessel for understanding people's opinions and their perspectives. This was aligned with the creative engagement activities we designed, meaning we elicited dwellers' real opinions rather than, as sometimes can occur during consultations or surveys/questionnaires, simplistic participant answers which tend to be framed according to what they think the interviewer is expecting to receive.

11.3.7 *Real-Life Complexities*

We believe we have identified, fostered, and amplified dignity in this phase of the ongoing My Mainway project. In this section, we talk about some of the practical realities of working on a complex, large public sector–led project. These realities affected, even disrupted at times, our plans to build a groundswell of activated community members ready to enter dialogue with the City Council's housing team and policymakers. We stress here that all the individuals in the process, especially in the public sector, were positive, proactively helpful, and accommodating. However, the My Mainway project revealed the contrasting perspectives and expectations of these two groups. This led to frustrations for the residents that in turn led to stress and difficult conversations for our public sector partners, who should also have dignity and respect. The housing team worked hard to explain these changes in plans through activity at the Hub and digital and print communication. Delays were caused by:

- The need to do the groundwork with politicians in the City Council to approve this major financial commitment for the council. This need might result in a decision being deferred from one monthly meeting to the next or the one after that, causing a three-month delay on a decision. Additionally, that decision could be that more information was needed on the technicalities leading to further delays and the need to re-present the updated proposal. These steps are important due diligence, but it is hard to communicate these intricacies to residents, especially when some aspects of the process need to be confidential.
- With a change of political control in the local government, environmental issues became more important for any new development. There was a desire for highly energy-efficient homes, which changed the financial models for the development.
- Late in this first phase of the My Mainway project, a large section of land adjacent to the Mainway estate became part of the potential plans for development. This was a very positive turn of events, but emergent plans and costs had to be completely redone.
- The COVID-19 pandemic gave us a seemingly constant change of regulations that affected the opening of the Hub, particularly in terms of the number of people who could gather both inside it and outside on the estate.

11.4 THE FUTURE

As design researchers, we can explore how to accommodate the inevitable frictions and turbulence of projects where communities and the public sector work together in a mutually respectful way. This could, for example, focus on managing expectations or designing "pop-up" events to explain changes of plans more effectively, to strengthen relationships between public sector staff and residents. One proposal, still under discussion with the Council, is to create a cohort of housing staff and members of the newly formed Residents' Committee. Treating them as members of a common cohort, we propose to run a series of creative engagement training sessions in a neutral location. The thinking behind these training sessions is that sharing a common new experience focusing on a topic useful to all of them will help knit housing staff and residents together as a team with the deep mutual respect grown from a common challenging experience.

There are a multitude of possibilities to help design the scaffolding or supports to help ensure both residents and the public sector participants in My Mainway have a dignified positive dialogue to shape the future of the site. Thinking about the dimensions of hearing those seldom heard, fairness, mutual respect, and advocacy will help shape this ongoing design research.

REFERENCES

Andersen, Lars Bo, Peter Danholt, Kim Halskov, Nicolai Brodersen Hansen, and Peter Lauritsen. 2015. "Participation as a Matter of Concern in Participatory Design." *CoDesign* 11, no. 3–4 (October): 250–61. http://dx.doi.org/10.1080/15710882.2015.1081246.

Arnstein, Sherry R. 1969. "A Ladder of Citizen Participation." *Journal of the American Institute of Planners* 35, no. 4 (November): 216–24. https://doi:10.1080/01944366908977225.

Bason, Christian. 2010. *Leading Public Sector Innovation*. Bristol, UK: Policy Press.

Buchanan, Richard. 2001. "Human Dignity and Human Rights: Thoughts on the Principles of Human-Centered Design." *Design Issues* 17, no. 3 (Summer): 35–39. JSTOR.

Calvo, Mirian, Rosendy Galabo, Violet Owen, Leon Cruickshank, and Rachel Sara. 2022. "Strategies and Tactics of Participatory Architecture." *Proceedings of DRS Biennial Conference Series, Design Research Society, Bilbao, Spain, June 25 – July 3, 2022*. London: Design Research Society.

Donetto, Sara, Paola Pierri, Vicki Tsianakas, and Glenn Robert. 2015. "Experience-Based Co-Design and Healthcare Improvement: Realizing Participatory Design in The Public Sector." *The Design Journal* 18, no. 2 (May): 227–48. https://doi:10.2752/175630615x14212498964312.

Ehrström, Peter. 2016. "Reflections on Deliberative Walks – A Participatory Method and Learning Process." *Proceedings of Standing Conference on University Teaching and Research in the Education of Adults, July 4-6, 2017*. Edinburgh, UK: University of Edinburgh Centre for Research in Education Inclusion & Diversity.

Forss, Kim, Mita Marra, and Robert Schwartz. 2011. *Evaluating the Complex: Attribution, Contribution and Beyond*. Comparative Policy Evaluation Volume 18. Piscataway, NJ: Transaction Publishers.

Grisales-Bohórquez, Claudia, Pedro Reynolds-Cuéllar, Gloria Inés Muñoz Martinez, and Andrés Sicard Currea. 2021. "Participation Reimagined: Co-Design of the Self through Territory, Memory, and Dignity." *CoDesign* 18, no. 1 (Fall): 78–94. https://doi:10.1080/15710882.2021.2016849.

Hagan, Margaret, and Miso Kim. 2017. "Design for Dignity and Procedural Justice." *Proceedings of the Applied Human Factors and Ergonomics International Conference, 2017*. New York: Springer Press.

Head, B. W. 2007. "Community Engagement: Participation on Whose Terms?" *Australian Journal of Political Science* 42, no. 3 (Summer): 441–54. http://dx.doi.org/10.1080/10361140701513570.

Kanstrup, Anne Marie, Pernille Bertelsen, and Jacob Østergaard Madsen. 2014. "Design with the Feet: Walking Methods and Participatory Design." *Proceedings of the 13th Participatory Design Conference, October 2014*. New York: Springer Press.

Kaptelinin, Victor, and Bonnie A. Nardi. 2006. *Acting with Technology: Activity Theory and Interaction Design*. Cambridge, MA: MIT Press.

Kim, Miso. 2018. "Designing for Participation: Dignity and Autonomy of Service (Part 2)." *Design Issues* 34, no. 3 (Summer): 89–102. https://doi.org/10.1162/desi_a_00499.

2021. "A Study of Dignity as a Principle of Service Design." *International Journal of Design* 15, no. 3 (December): 87–100.
Kim, Miso, Divya Srinivasan, and Xing Zhou. 2019. "The Morphology of Dignity: Service Storytelling and Prototypes or a Service Design Tool." *The Design Journal* 22, no. 6 (Fall): 793–812. https://doi:10.1080/14606925.2019.1662633.
Kimbell, Lucy. 2015. *Applying Design Approaches to Policy Making: Discovering Policy Lab*. Brighton, UK: University of Brighton.
Lynch, Kevin. 1960. *The Image of the City*. Cambridge, MA: MIT Press.
McKeon, Richard. 1990. "Philosophy and History in the Development of Human Rights." In *Freedom and History and Other Essays: An Introduction to the Thought of Richard McKeon*, edited by Zahava K. McKeon, 37–61. Chicago: University of Chicago Press.
Mirandola, Giovani Pico. 1996. *Oration on the Dignity of Man*. Washington, DC: Regnery Publishing.
Narayanasamy, N. 2009. *Participatory Rural Appraisal: Principles, Methods and Application*. Thousand Oaks, CA: SAGE Publications Ltd.
Palacin, Victoria, Matti Nelimarkka, Pedro Reynolds-Cuéllar, and Christoph Becker. 2020. "The Design of Pseudo-Participation." *Proceedings of the 16th Participatory Design Conference, June 2020*. New York: Association for Computing Machinery.
Reilly, A. C., R. L. Dillon, and S. D. Guikema. 2021. "Agent-Based Models as an Integrating Boundary Object for Interdisciplinary Research." *Risk Analysis* 41, no. 7 (July): 1087–92. https://doi.org/10.1111/risa.13134.
Rosen, M. 2012. *Dignity: Its History and Meaning*. Cambridge, MA: Harvard University Press.
Said Mosleh, Wafa, and Henry Larsen. 2020. "Exploring the Complexity of Participation." *CoDesign* 17, no. 4 (Winter): 454–72. https://doi:10.1080/15710882.2020.1789172.
Smith, Rachel Charlotte, Claus Bossen, and Anne Marie Kanstrup. 2017. "Participatory Design in an Era of Participation." *CoDesign* 13, no. 2 (April): 65–69. https://doi.org/10.1080/15710882.2017.1310466.
United Nations Department of Economic and Social Affairs: Sustainable Development. 2015. "Transforming Our World: The 2030 Agenda for Sustainable Development." https://sdgs.un.org/sites/default/files/publications/21252030%20Agenda%20for%20Sustainable%20Development%20web.pdf.
Waldron, Jeremy, and M. Dan-Cohen. 2012. *Dignity, Rank, and Rights*. Oxford: Oxford University Press.

III

How Legal Design Works

Approaches, Methods, and Perspectives

12

Designers, Lawyers, and Students

A Decade of NuLawLab Experience

Dan Jackson, Jules Rochielle Sievert, and Miso Kim

12.1 INTRODUCTION – THE NULAWLAB: WHY

The NuLawLab is the first staffed legal design and innovation lab at a US law school, established by our faculty directors in 2011–2012 within Northeastern University School of Law (NUSL), and staffed in 2013. There are now twelve to fifteen such legal design and innovation initiatives at US law schools (depending on how you define the terms), many of which have adopted the model initially deployed by the NuLawLab. This chapter is intended to give the reader an overview of the history of the NuLawLab and what we have learned exploring design and other structured creative processes through our pedagogy, projects, and in partnership with local communities. These learnings are not necessarily earth-shattering, but they deserve to be aired. Our targeted goal in this chapter is to describe our project work with an eye toward articulating the methods and tools we have used so that other legal designers can benefit from what we've learned.

Some background is in order before jumping into the weeds. Our current law school pedagogy includes coursework, legal design internships (called "co-ops" at NUSL), independent studies, and practical legal design capstone projects, all of which are intended to prepare law students to expertly apply legal design methods as innovation in the legal profession accelerates, and all of which are now bundled into a new Graduate Certificate in Legal Design. Much of this work is informed by and engages with our external projects, which are typically in partnership with external community and/or legal services organizations that are pursuing legal empowerment[1] ideas.

Since our launch, we've certainly been proud to describe ourselves as the "first staffed legal design lab" in the United States, but let's be clear about something up

[1] *Legal empowerment* generally refers to providing people with resources that allow them to access and assert their legal rights without the help of a lawyer. Over time, we have gravitated toward the term *legal agency*, which does not presuppose the intervention of others as *empowerment* does.

front. There is no shortage of innovative and design efforts in legal and design education and the professions that well precede us, often by decades. Early in our existence, on the legal side, we benefited from initiatives such as Chicago-Kent's Computer Aided Legal Instruction (CALI), Edgar Stuart Cahn and Jean Camper Cahn's Antioch School of Law, and Margaret Hagan's Open Law Lab blog. On the design side, we found the work of Stanford's d.school and the proselytizing of "design thinking" to be of initial interest, and the work of social practice artists such as Rick Lowe and Gregory Sale to be of significant inspiration. Perhaps most significantly as a precursor to our work, however, was the importance of our home. Northeastern University School of Law (NUSL) reopened in 1968 as a direct response to the dominant hegemony of American legal education. NUSL's core innovations – experiential learning, public interest lawyering, and a collaborative learning environment for students – ultimately informed our initial mission and vision, which we articulated at the time as:

- partnering with individuals and communities to identify unmet legal needs and design responsive solutions;
- cultivating knowledge and experiences from multiple disciplines and social perspectives to shed new insight on barriers to legal empowerment; and
- transforming legal education to create new means of connecting people to law, legal information, and legal services.

We emerged from the clinical movement in legal and experiential education, drawing specifically from the ethos of NUSL's status as the leading experiential and a premier public interest law school in the United States and from our initial faculty directors' positions as Associate Dean for Experiential Education. We draw from traditions in clinical pedagogy because those are sites where law school clinics place students in legal practice, usually with a focus on access to justice. You won't find, for example, any law clinics serving large multinational corporations. They can afford to hire lawyers, charging upward of $1,000 per hour for their time. Instead, we have seen that the ongoing access to justice crisis in the United State provides the material around which a clinical legal design curriculum can be built for educating and empowering future lawyer-inventors committed to full access for all.

Very early in that founding period, we embraced a deliberately expansive application of design and other creative methods to address issues in the justice system. Our decade of experience now affirms the fit between the fields of law and design, both in terms of process and productivity. We think that legal design labs such as the NuLawLab are a natural extension of this pedagogical framework. In this regard, we have found remarkable uptake of legal design ideas (if not results) within our state court systems, including our 2016 launch of an effort to completely redesign Massachusetts Housing Court for the age of self-representation. That proposal, which was in partnership with the design consultancy IDEO, had the enthusiastic support of the Chief Justices of the Massachusetts Supreme Judicial Court, Trial

Court, and Housing Court. It failed to launch only because we were unable to secure any foundation funding to get the project off the ground.

We have had more concretely successful outcomes in the classroom and in partnership with community organizations. In legal education, even within the relatively tight confines of the American Bar Association's law school accreditation standards, there is valuable, albeit little, room for experimentation in legal pedagogy. As one clinical law professor recognized, at "the margins of the field, a growing number of law school clinics and innovative legal advocacy organizations have played a key role in developing a new public interest practice. These lawyers and law students support and stimulate radical democratic resistance to market forces by developing litigation, legislative, and community education methods aimed at advancing collective mobilization" (Ashar 2008). This approach envisions the law school environment as a more transformational space than typically articulated, or experienced, in which "the clinic would become a center of activity in the community, a place where organizers and collective members interact with each other, build alliances, or mediate disputes (that seem inevitably to arise in progressive work)" (Ashar 2008). Seen this way, legal education offers tremendous promise as a site of creativity. And as more traditional law school clinics morph into innovation labs, we think they can start to "reinvent law and law practice in positive ways that could simply not be envisioned without the freedom provided by the 'change lab' methodology—developing new modes of legal outreach and education, and even redesigning law itself" (Davis 2018).

We find all of this is exciting (Doherty 2022) because legal design rests on, among other things, the premise that law is one of the most fundamental architectures of human society, and that design holds the promise of improving how people experience law and, by extension, society (Kim et al. 2022; Perry-Kessaris 2022). To date, however, much of the work in this space has tended to rely on commercial methods, often developed in corporate contexts where designers are focused on solving problems rather than posing them, and answering rather than asking questions. This is understandable – indeed desirable – as a practical and strategic matter. It has, for example, been crucial to the successful introduction of design to legal professionals that the proposed methods are tested and proven. It is also necessary to aggressively continue those efforts in our front-line sociolegal institutions (schools, courts, digital everything) in order to continue to improve any number of functions and steadily increase the number of professions with positive experiences with "legal design."

In this chapter, therefore, we will introduce a few projects of our NuLawLab, with a specific focus on extracting from the narrative the methods that we have used to achieve successful outcomes in nurturing the dignity of our community partners, students, and clients, by empowering them to claim their own agency in this space. In doing so, we hope to expand the universe of creative methods beyond design that can be considered "tested and proven" such that those methods are more readily available to legal professionals, designers, community organizations, and just about any person or organization seeking to make the law more accessible to more people.

Articulating actionable methods is important at this stage of the development of the "discipline" of legal design (Doherty 2022) because there are increasing opportunities to engage in meaningful change within our legal institutions. By distilling the method out of the madness of most of our project work, we can articulate mindsets (e.g., "design thinking"), principles (e.g., "designing for dignity"), and concrete actions (e.g., "design research hunt statements" and "critical design swap meets") that can be duplicated by others. We consider our methods to be a way of both conveying and shaping our thoughts as legal designers. Moreover, we will reflect on how these approaches and methods are in fact firmly based on the core value of dignity the NuLawLab upholds, further expanding the significance of methods to a systematized embodiment of the idea by itself.

For most of our history, we have considered ourselves to be "building the plane while flying it." While this sensation was initially quite uncomfortable for most of us, we now embrace the analogy as a distillation of the reflective practice that we bring to all that we do. Such a practice is quite different from what most American law students and faculty experience both long term and in the day-to-day experience of law school. For us, the approach enables us to change course – sometimes radically – as any circumstances warrant. With that in mind, here is what we have learned.

12.2 INTERDISCIPLINARY COLLABORATION

12.2.1 *The Early Development of Our Approach*

In early 2013, Dan Jackson and Jules Rochielle Sievert were hired to further develop, implement, and manage the NuLawLab full time. Dan Jackson came from a pre–law school background in theater design and a post–law degree career in employment law and talent development at a large law firm. Jules Rochielle Sievert came from the realm of socially engaged art practice. The first several months of their time together were spent in an intense period of collaboration meant to foster and develop a shared language and a set of common goals. They were guided by a very active faculty director team, including a faculty director (Luke Bierman; now Martha Davis), a creative director (Martha Davis; now Jules), and a design director (Pat Voorhies; now Miso Kim). Soon thereafter, a team of advisory board members (chaired by James Hackney, who is now NUSL's dean as of this publication date) were invited to foster and support the growth of the lab.

From the outset, our lab quickly shifted from "design thinking" to working directly with designers. This was a critical step for the NuLawLab, as we felt confined by the commercial focus of "design thinking" and the overarching message that design was a matter of mindset as opposed to expertise. The first external designer we collaborated with on a project was Marisa Jahn of Studio REV-, who was also an early member of our advisory board. That collaboration was an early risk that informed our direction and thinking about how to develop the Lab and our methods of practice and teaching. At the time, Marisa was developing tools and resources for domestic workers in New York following the passage of the New York Domestic Workers Bill of Rights. With a similar bill on the horizon in Massachusetts, our engagement with Marisa allowed us to pursue both an external project and a law school seminar that engaged law students in the project. This allowed us to incorporate codesign as a method in teaching legal innovation to law students by using Marisa's design process to collaborate with policymakers, domestic workers, law students, and a team of designers. The experience with Marisa also expanded the way we started to think about outreach to potential future codesigners among those who are underserved by existing legal institutions and systems. Although the model of practice that started to emerge from the NuLawLab can historically be rooted in movement lawyering and clinical practices in American legal education, what felt different to us was the egalitarian nature of the codesign process and the utilization of socially engaged art to collaborate with domestic workers to develop not just tools and resources but a narrative of transformational change.

During this same first year the team was also introduced to Casper Harteveld, at the time an assistant professor of game design at Northeastern's College of Art, Media and Design. Casper's work on articulating a three-part method for designing serious games[2] offered the NuLawLab an opportunity to experiment with how a serious game could be used to assist people who are going to civil court without a lawyer by their side. The result was *RePresent*, the first digital game intended to aid such self-represented (or *pro se*) litigants, cocreated with Statewide Legal Services of Connecticut and funded by the Legal Services Corporation's Technology Initiative Grant Program. The project idea resulted in our selection as one of three finalists for a 2014 Innovative Idea Award from the Hague Institute for Innovation in Law, allowing us to tap into a global network of like-minded collaborators very early in our existence.

By 2015, we were actively seeking substantial funding for a large-scale project addressing the housing crisis in Boston. That materialized with a generous grant from The Kresge Foundation's Arts & Culture program. The funding, which was renewed two years later, kicked off what we now see as the second phase of the NuLawLab's evolution.

12.2.2 *Interdisciplinary Collaboration Case Study: Stable Ground*

It is safe to say that our interdisciplinarity and intersectionality seek out radical differences.[3] We have found that the greater the distance among the various

[2] "Serious games" are those that use the fun world of game play to tackle serious topics (Harteveld 2010).

[3] We refer to interdisciplinarity as the work of multiple professional and/or academic disciplines coming together for collaborative problem solving and cocreation. We refer to intersectionality as the work of multiple, disparate lived experiences or personal and/or group identities coming together for the same purpose. We try to establish both methods in all our external projects.

disciplines and lived experiences, the greater the potential for a significant breakthrough on sticky problems. It is important to note here that we are not averse to collaboration with fields closely related or adjacent to the law. Those efforts, while similarly generative for us, are the exception rather than the rule at the NuLawLab.

The project we will use here to describe our interdisciplinary/intersectional approach is called Stable Ground, which initially (and successfully) leveraged arts-and-culture programming as a means of ensuring that the psychologically traumatic impact of housing instability was reflected in Boston's municipal housing policy. The first iteration of Stable Ground focused near-exclusively on housing instability in the Dorchester neighborhood of Boston. The second phase was a focused collaboration with local artist Anthony Romero, which allowed our students to contribute to a piece he created for an exhibition at Boston's Institute of Contemporary Art (ICA), and resulted in the development of a trivia board game called "Fight Displacement!" The third phase of Stable Ground was significantly impacted by the COVID-19 pandemic and resulted in a major pivot to focus on the more traditional work of housing rights lawyering and community organizing in the East Boston community. Throughout all three phases, we collaborated with artists, students, local residents, activists, municipal leaders, community organizations, museum professionals, legal designers, and other experts. All three iterations of the project resulted in a rich and resilient network of community assets and anchor institutions into which we are now tapping for empirical research on the impact of the cultural organizing we deploy.

The first iteration of Stable Ground ran from 2017 to 2018 and was funded by The Kresge Foundation's Arts & Culture program. It was centered around three artists-in-residence who were already working on creative responses to housing and discrimination, primarily in the Dorchester neighborhood of Boston, and the work of Violence Transformed, which uses creative art making as a means of helping individuals process and move through trauma caused by violence (Figure 12.1). The Kresge funding allowed us to bring the City of Boston's new Office of Housing Stability into the creative arts programming underway, thus informing their program and policy development with trauma recovery principles and methods. The full evaluation report of phase one can be found on our website (Sherman 2019), and we need not summarize any of it here beyond the core findings, that:

> Stable Ground moved the needle with respect to its goals of informing and impacting the city's housing policy to be more trauma-informed, supporting under-resourced community-based cultural organizing around affordable housing that is already happening in Dorchester and surrounding neighborhoods, and learning how to support a lawyer's approach to working with and alongside impacted communities. (Sherman 2019)

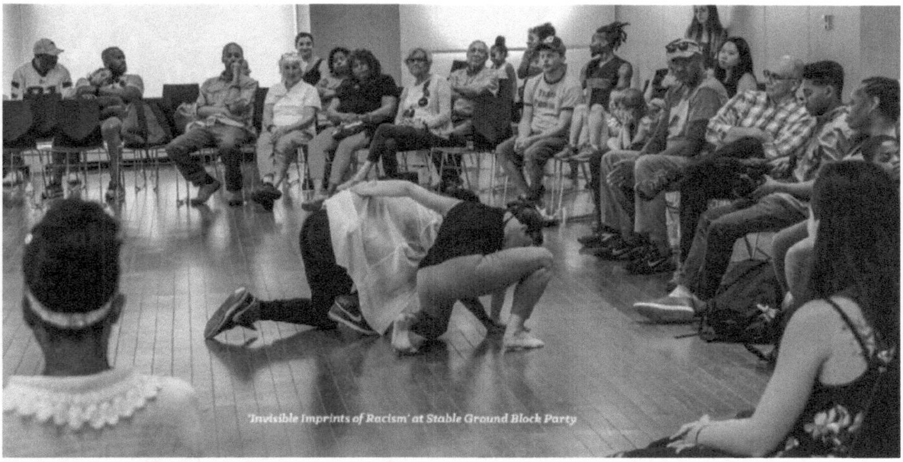

FIGURE 12.1. Dance performance "Invisible Imprints of Racism," Anna Myer/beheard. world choreography, at Stable Ground Block Party.
(Photo credit: Hakim Raquib.)

A second phase of Stable Ground, also funded by The Kresge Foundation during 2018–2019, expanded on creative housing justice work and deepened partnerships with local artists and institutions. This middle phase (phase 2.0, if you will) focused primarily on anti-displacement organizing in the East Boston neighborhood through creative means and partnerships with local artist, organizer, and educator Anthony Romero, the Institute of Contemporary Art Boston (ICA), and Our Home: An Eastie Community Archiving Project. This second version of the program included the creation of "Fight Displacement!," a trivia board game designed to educate local Bostonians on how to fight housing displacement and influence development, which was taught and featured at various local events (Figure 12.2). Additionally, Anthony Romero included Northeastern Law School students and NuLawLab in the creation of his work, ". . .first in thought, then in action" for the ICA exhibition "When Home Won't Let you Stay: Migration through Contemporary Art." Stable Ground also provided partnerships and support for the ICA's public relations with East Boston residents and created a model for how similar initiatives could meaningfully support local residents while also creating new, innovative contemporary art. Of benefit to the ICA, the program brought in and engaged new, local audiences with exhibitions and educational programming, and planted seeds for long-term partnerships with local organizations.

Stable Ground 3.0, funded by a renewal grant from The Kresge Foundation, was significantly impacted by the COVID-19 pandemic. While we originally envisioned it as an expansion of the original artists-in-residence program to cover more Boston neighborhoods, we had to completely reframe the purpose and goals of the work given the complete lack of in-person events over the entirety of the grant period. Our

FIGURE 12.2. Fight Displacement! Playtesting session at The Institute of Contemporary Art, Boston, Massachusetts.
(Photo credit: Donis Perkins.)

engagements with the three resident artists continued, but we backed off any specific outcome requirement for their effort, allowing them to use their grant-funded stipends to respond locally to the housing crisis brought about by the pandemic as they saw fit. But with in-person arts and culture programming suspended, we redirected the remaining funds toward a new eviction response and rental relief collaboration in East Boston with Maverick Landing Community Services (MLCS). We had begun working with MLCS through our work with Anthony, so the pivot was both welcomed by MLCS and easy to achieve.

At the outset of the crisis, our team began to prepare to respond to the coming wave of mass evictions and COVID-19 economic instability by providing residents experiencing housing insecurity with the technological access and legal knowledge to defend themselves against eviction. It was not long before it was apparent that most, if not all, of the residents seeking housing help were not facing eviction. Instead, they needed access to federal, state, and municipal rental relief that became available as the pandemic crisis worsened. This aspect of our pandemic response to the emerging crisis became known as the Boston Housing Support Station Coalition (BHSSC). Our BHSSC teamwork has included organizing neighbors, direct action, and supporting tenants at Maverick Landing affordable housing development (which is where MLCS is based). We trained teams of law students and neighborhood residents to assist residents by filling out pandemic rental relief applications and providing access to food by delivering bags of groceries every week. As the effort was fully implemented, it became a larger collaboration among the NuLawLab, Maverick Landing Community Services, the City of Boston Artist-in-Residence program and Office of Housing Stability, artists Anthony Romero and Pat Falco, City Life Vida Urbana, Tufts University/School of the Museum of Fine Arts, Suffolk University Legal Innovation & Technology Lab, Ropes & Gray, Runcible Studios, and Harvard Law School's Alianza student group.

Our unique position as an arts-forward legal empowerment laboratory embedded in a leading US public interest law school thus resulted in the Stable Ground project establishing a number of unique cross-sector partnerships. These include our engagement with artist and educator Anthony Romero and the Institute of Contemporary Art, our recent interdisciplinary pedagogical engagements with NU's College of Arts, Media and Design (with Professor Sarah Kanouse), and our long-standing partnership with the City of Boston Office of Housing Stability. Most tellingly, the COVID-19 pivot we steered brought us into a very deep partnership with MLCS and City Life / Vida Urbana, which is now resulting in our embedment in East Boston as one part of our new East Boston Spatial Justice Lab. We have learned, over the ten years of our existence, and with the benefit of all three iterations of Stable Ground, that we excel at establishing meaningful partnerships with nonlegal organizations and disciplines seeking meaningful change. Mindful of our privilege as a leading law school laboratory, we see our role as supporting existing grassroots efforts by bringing to bear the resources available from a large research university into the community work that has been underway for decades.

Outcomes to date from the BHSSC were favorable. On a macro level, we were able to support Boston residents and community organizations in their struggle against rent arrearage, eviction, and displacement during the pandemic; provide NUSL (and other local law school) students with experience in housing and public service law; effectively make the case for exploratory, interventional, radically interdisciplinary approaches to legal education and interventions; make the case that art and design are powerful tools against societal injustice; and promote positive and innovative change to the cultures of academic institutions.

Closer to the ground in East Boston, we submitted a total of 96 pandemic rental relief applications on behalf of families experiencing severe housing insecurity, provided legal help[4] to 23 individuals and/or families, and supported MLCS' distribution of 687,500 pounds of healthy uncut fruit and vegetables to over 1,000 East Boston families. A total of eleven organizations worked together for two years to accomplish these outcomes. Our coalition recently received a grant from the New

[4] The BHSSC did not provide legal representation or advice, but rather focused on help and assistance that falls short of that threshold.

England Foundation for the Arts (NEFA) that we used to engage local youth in the work, resulting in a podcast series that highlights the impacts of housing insecurity on young people. To this end, the coalition is revisiting our past success with using arts and games to engage youth and other community members. A coalition member shared that, "We are thinking about games as a popular education tool around housing rights, and we're thinking about how we can develop other kinds of games and interactive fun ways to educate young folks and their parents about their rights and other related issues" (Bruck Bennouna and Sherman 2022).

Most recently, the coalition received funding from The Kresge Foundation's Arts & Cuture Program and the National Endowment for the Arts Research Lab Program to implement the East Boston Spatial Justice Lab. Through this next iteration we will develop the new Spatial Justice Lab in East Boston to examine the intersection of public art, the housing crisis, and the well-being of ethnically diverse immigrant residents impacted by the housing crisis. We will organize a series of art and advocacy events around the concept of belonging and social cohesion and evaluate how these events impact residents' social/emotional well-being and whether they contribute to healing, the sense of belonging, and social cohesion. In addition, we will utilize participatory action research methods and cultural programming with residents to unpack the impact of redevelopment, gentrification, and displacement in East Boston. Such learning is intended to, among other things, form the foundation of future work for our coalition and all partners.

As you can see, little of the Stable Ground work looks like traditional design methods or even the predominant methods of legal design. This is intentional on our part. As explained in our introduction, we usually strive in our interdisciplinary collaborations to mine the potential in creative methods beyond product design. The outcomes we've seen in Stable Ground confirm the value of this approach.

12.3 PARTICIPATORY COLLABORATIVE DESIGN

12.3.1 *The Early Development of Our Approach*

It is safe to say that participatory or collaborative design – codesign for short – is at the very foundation of our Lab. The Lab's founding faculty directors staffed the NuLawLab in a way that is now reflected in how we approach codesign in our projects. Dan and Jules were hired at the same time and came from very different disciplinary backgrounds: Dan with fifteen years of employment law and talent development expertise, and Jules with the same number of years as a social practice artist and designer. We spent a fair amount of time in the first two years just developing a shared language, both for the immediate practical purpose of understanding each other's ideas and for the longer-term goal of designing justice solutions that were deeply *trans*disciplinary, meaning they could not exist absent an intentional fusing of ostensibly unrelated disciplines. We decided very early on, meaning within the first few weeks of working together, that the NuLawLab would experiment with and deploy collaborative design, or codesign, as one means of pursuing those solutions.

For those unfamiliar with the term, "codesign" is a process that involves the participation of various stakeholders in the design of products, services, or systems. It is an approach that values the collective knowledge, skills, and experiences of all participants, aiming to create solutions that reflect that diversity of experience in the ultimate outcome. The origins of collaborative design can be traced back to the 1960s and 1970s, when a wave of social movements and community activism emerged demanding greater participation and empowerment of marginalized groups. This gave rise to participatory design, a field involving users in the design of technology and systems that would meet their needs and aspirations. Participatory design was influenced by the work of political philosopher Paulo Freire, who emphasized the importance of dialogue and collaboration in achieving social change (Ehn and Kyng 1991).

Since its origins, collaborative design has evolved and expanded, incorporating new tools, methods, and approaches. In the 1990s, the concept of user-centered design emerged, which placed greater emphasis on the needs and preferences of users in the design process (Norman and Draper 1986). User-centered design involved methods such as ethnography, prototyping, and usability testing, which aimed to better understand user needs and preferences and to create designs that would meet them. This is how our early game design project deployed codesign as we created the first digital game to teach people how to represent themselves in court.

12.3.2 *Case: What We Did in* RePresent

Before we dig into the *RePresent* codesign details, some context is in order. Although there were plenty of legal games when we first started standing up the project, efforts to date had largely focused on educating lawyers and nonlawyers alike on more substantive areas of law. None focused on providing people without lawyers with the generally applicable skills and tasks required for adjudicatory proceedings, such as how to address the judge, how to cross-examine a witness, or the pragmatic details of navigating a given judicial system. Our project sought to change that. Broadly stated, the idea furthered two goals unique in the legal space in the United States. First, we pursued a digital game that provides *pro se* litigants with some foundational advocacy experience before doing it for real. Second, we used the highly collaborative design process to maximize the value of the game to the intended end-user, as well as contribute to building a community of support around the needs of those navigating the court system without lawyers. The project itself was the brainchild of Kate Frank, the tech guru at Statewide Legal Services of Connecticut, which

FIGURE 12.3. The *RePresent* team at the 2014 Innovating Justice Forum, convened by The Hague Institute for the Internationalisation of Law. From left to right: Kathy Daniels, Susan Nofi, Kate Frank, Dan Jackson, Jules Rochielle Sievert, and Martha Davis.

became our primary partner. The effort was funded by a 205 Technology Initiative ("TIG") grant from the Legal Services Corporation ("LSC") as a result of some helpful matchmaking by David Bonebrake, the LSC-TIG grant officer for the New England region.

We kicked off the game design process in November 2014 at the 2014 Innovating Justice Forum, convened by The Hague Institute for the Internationalisation of Law, where the project was one of three finalists for the Innovative Idea award (Figure 12.3). Although our game idea did not ultimately win the top prize, we were able to workshop the idea with a global gathering of justice sector innovators, including the Chief Justice of the Supreme Court of Kenya and the former Justice Minister of Rwanda. We left the forum bursting with ideas for the game, but resisted becoming overly invested in potential features until we had our Connecticut stakeholders at the table. That process began in earnest in January 2015. Funded as it was under an LSC-TIG grant to Connecticut legal services organizations, the initial iteration of the game was designed around that state's court system. Wherever possible, we generalized the game details so that only minimal modifications would be required to make the game relevant to other jurisdictions.

Our Connecticut codesign efforts began with a meeting of potential project stakeholders on January 7, 2015. At the table were representatives from all the major legal aid providers in the state, state court service centers, state court law libraries, public library system, bar associations and foundations, and a number of public service organizations working directly with our targeted population of *pro se* litigants. That meeting was followed immediately by in-depth end-user research conducted by NUSL students enrolled in our standing Laboratory Seminar in Applied Design & Legal Empowerment (Jackson 2016). By mid-January, our game design faculty colleagues had opened their Game Design Studio, where they employed an interdisciplinary mix of graduate and undergraduate students (e.g., psychology, digital art, cognitive science, programming) working to realize a number of projects, including ours.

The month of February was devoted to three structured codesign sessions, held in Hartford and New Haven, Connecticut. Relying on our growing network of stakeholders, we convened front-line court service center staff, legal aid lawyers, and current and former *pro se* litigants to collectively brainstorm the features and focus of the game. We started with a truly blank slate, limited only by the expected technical specifications of the Mad Science (now called StudyCrafter[5]) platform on which we were building the game. Although each codesign session was structured slightly differently to account for differences in participants, each roughly followed the game design methodology that Dr. Harteveld proposed in Triadic Game Design (Harteveld 2010). That methodology guides small groups through three spaces of exploration: Reality, Meaning, and Play. Reality asks participants to imagine the problem state to be tackled, the factors involved in that problem state, and the process to be followed in moving from problem state to desired state. Meaning explores the intention for designing the game and the strategy for achieving that purpose. Finally, Play interjects the gamification elements of a genre, a title, a goal, and the mechanics of game play. In using the Triadic approach, we were able to focus participants on the very serious reality and meaning of the *pro se* experience before turning our collective energies toward the fun (but foreign for lawyers) process of gamifying the experience. By moving from abstract notions of "problem state," "intention," and "strategy" to the mechanics of, say, fantasy role-play games, we were able in a very brief period of time to develop dozens of ideas for consideration and further development. By our second and third sessions, we began to focus participants on specific spaces and concepts, such as the hallway outside the courtroom and court hearing advance preparations ranging from weeks to hours.

Two months into the project, we had collected all the raw creative material we needed to begin to articulate the structure and features of the game. By early March, we had settled on a modular game that would move through the following five spaces/time frames: (1) home preparation weeks before a hearing; (2) the court service center and clerk's office; (3) home preparation the morning of the hearing; (4) the hallway outside the courtroom; and (5) the courtroom and hearing itself.

[5] https://studycrafter.com/, last accessed April 12, 2023.

The next two months were dedicated to development of digital art assets and the outlines of each of the scenario scripts, all in preparation for testing our ideas with our codesign participants.

That testing took place on April 30 and May 1, when we returned to Hartford and New Haven with paper prototypes of the game. By now, the group of core codesigners had grown beyond the numbers we first convened in January and February – a good sign for the project overall. At each session, we shared "visual decoys" of the game that provided a rough sketch of the digital art for each module, together with a ten-frame storyboard of the script for each. We specifically sought feedback on the look and feel of the game and the basic contours of the game play. Using paper cutouts of the characters-in-development, we brainstormed more nuanced gameplay within each scenario and came up with additional game features. For example, at the New Haven paper prototype testing session, participants came up with the idea for a "confidence meter" that would measure a player's progress across the game in a way that also tracked the extent to which they were making the right choices.

Early summer was dedicated to generating detailed branched scripts of the game, coding them into the underlying game framework, refining the art assets, and internal testing of digital prototypes. We next convened our codesign participants in early August for two sessions of digital prototype testing. Those sessions were held at a nearby ice cream parlor with a good-sized event space for rental in the rear. Again, the group had grown from our last convening. As an indication of growing local interest in the project, we were joined at one of the sessions by a local NBC television news crew, who produced a segment on the project for the local evening news. Our task for these two sessions was to observe participants playing two scenarios – the courtroom hearing and preparing at home – and obtain detailed group feedback from codesigners/testers. With observational results and comprehensive feedback, we returned to Boston for an autumn sprint to the finish line. This included settling on a name for the game, which had a working title at the time of *RePresent*. That name stuck.

Following the ice cream codesign and testing session, the game modules were stitched together and refined in preparation for beta-testing, which commenced in mid-October and ran for a couple months thereafter, with more than fifty individuals who had completed their *pro se* experience testing the game. The web browser game (*RePresent 1.0*) was released in January 2016. Another round of grant funding saw us expand the game to a mobile version for smartphones (*RePresent 2.0*), as well as a second game focused on defending against evictions (*RePresent Renter*).[6]

So, what end product has emerged as a result of this process? The game starts with a brief automated sequence, showing the player's avatar having a disastrous experience in court (while at the same time educating the player on the basic game mechanics). Fortunately for the player, the opening sequence is just a dream, and

6 www.representgames.org/, last accessed April 12, 2023.

they now have the opportunity to prepare properly for the court hearing. The first game module walks the player through preparing for court several weeks in advance and covers specifics that range from gathering relevant documents and arranging for the participation of necessary witnesses to lining up childcare (and backup childcare). From there, the player moves to the courthouse, where they interact with staff at the clerk's office and court service center, learning as a result the role of each department and the appropriate place to turn for help, depending on the need. Then it is back to home for preparations the morning of the player's hearing, including pragmatic details such as the importance of eating a good breakfast. The penultimate module takes place in the hallway outside the courtroom where, among other things, the player learns how to navigate a confrontation with the opposing party's attorney and how to respond to well-meaning strangers who want to share some advice. The game concludes in the courtroom and covers practicalities such as where to stand and how to address the judge, as well as some of the basics of trial advocacy, including offering documents into evidence and conducting direct and cross-examination. At the conclusion of the game, the player is presented with some basic analytics on how they performed navigating the various modules, areas for improvement, and resources to assist them with the same (Figure 12.4).

Readers from the legal profession or academy may be struck by how much of the gameplay focuses on decidedly nonlegal subjects like the value of a healthy breakfast and the importance of lining up backup childcare. These subjects were identified as crucial by people who had been through the self-representation experience themselves in every codesign session we held. As one of the participants noted, without that practical foundation, *pro se* litigants would stand little chance of navigating more complex trial mechanics. The elevation of pragmatic guidance in *RePresent* is also a testament to the value of collaborative end-user design methodologies when developing resources for *pro se* litigants. For those of us with a legal education and practice expertise, it is exceptionally difficult to put ourselves in the mindset of those navigating the judicial system without that background or the assistance of someone with it. In this regard, we think every individual and organization working to develop self-help resources or any justice system intervention should engage potential end-users in a robust codesign process, the better to meet the actual needs of the people who seek justice. Imagine that!

In recent years, collaborative design has become more interdisciplinary, incorporating insights and methods from fields such as social science, anthropology, and psychology. It has also expanded beyond the realm of technology and product design to encompass service design, social innovation, and community development. This is where (and when) the NuLawLab fits, and to which we have contributed. Our work fits well with the current state of the art of collaborative design, which is characterized by a diverse and dynamic landscape of practices and approaches. Collaborative design is now applied in a wide range of contexts, from urban planning and public policy to health care, education, and the field of design itself (Costanza-Chock 2020).

FIGURE 12.4. A screenshot of the web browser game *RePresent* 1.0, showing the beginning of the courtroom scenario, the basic structure of questions and answer options, and the confidence meter.
(Photo courtesy ofStatewide Legal Services of Connecticut, theNuLawLab, and NU Game Design Studio.)

12.4 SERVICE DESIGN FOR COMMUNITY MEMBERS

12.4.1 *What We Did in General*

The third and final example of our application of creative methods focuses on service design and how we deployed the approach in another recent COVID-19 rapid response project. The pandemic, lockdown, and decreased opportunities for public services exacerbated existing social issues while making it difficult for the affected people to access legal help. This is in addition to the new problems caused by the pandemic such as job loss and housing insecurities. At the same time, new remote solutions were required to keep social distancing requirements met that continued for multiple years, calling for the intervention of technology and design in the area of legal services. In other words, the pandemic created a situation that legal design was urgently needed by many of our communities and partnering organizations.

However, the pandemic also made it extremely difficult for us to conduct the participatory methods that we had been using. The pandemic itself, and the limitations on our ability to pursue more traditional means of discovery and design research, brought significant challenges to the participatory approach the lab had been utilizing. For example, we had to refrain from conducting in-person brainstorming workshops with partners, students, and community members to follow the social distancing guidelines. Virtual means of participation were not effective in achieving the dialectic impact of bringing the participants together to a shared understanding and creating a feeling of connections. Importantly, technological limitations and accessibility raised the issue of who could be included in the virtual conversations utilizing online tools such as Zoom and Mural and those who were excluded due to a low-bandwidth WiFi connection, assuming everybody even had expensive digital devices and big screens to join the virtual meetings.

To address the challenges we faced, we utilized the systematic tools and methods of service design, which take a holistic approach and focus on the interactions of multiple stakeholders and touchpoints. Service design was first proposed by marketing scholars (Levitt 1972; Shostack 1982) and includes methods like the service blueprint (Bitner, Ostrom, and Morgan 2008). Initially, service design aimed to increase the efficiency and effectiveness of intangible services by giving them a tangible form. However, service-dominant logic in the early 2000s proposed that service is the substance of the transaction rather than a counterpart to products (Vargo and Lusch 2008). With the influence of interaction design and the experiential economy, service design has evolved to include an experiential perspective and unique characteristics such as humanizing, holistic, participatory, tangible, procedural, and transformative (Karpen et al. 2017). Service design models such as service blueprints, customer journeys, and storyboard scenarios enable designers to consider multiple perspectives and organize them into a service system that supports the holistic experiences of stakeholders.

We utilized the holistic approaches and systematized models of service design as a way to fill in the gap of not being able to directly interact with the end-users of our legal design: community members. At the same time, these methods enabled us to consider the coordinated experiences of different stakeholders, nurturing a human-centered perspective in designing legal systems and empowering the people we aimed to help. In this section, we will showcase how we utilized service design in one of our pandemic-era projects: the Domestic Violence Institute at NUSL.

12.4.2 *What We Did with DVI Legal during COVID-19*

The COVID-19 pandemic has exacerbated the conditions that lead to intimate partner abuse, as evidenced by the sharp increase in reported cases of domestic violence in the United States during the COVID-19 lockdown. Between March and May 2020, during the time of the national stay-at-home order, reported cases of domestic violence increased by 7.5% to 20% (Boserup, McKenney, and Elkbuli 2020; Leslie and Wilson 2020). Unfortunately, survivors who sought help from domestic violence hotlines during the lockdown reported that their abusers were using pandemic health requirements to limit their access to support resources (Anurudran et al. 2020). Survivors faced a difficult choice between protecting themselves from violence or from the virus, as they were forced to spend 24 hours at home with their abusers without privacy, and their chances of being alone outside were reduced due to public health guidelines that limited access to public spaces and transportation. Community organizations, courts, and churches also had to reduce opportunities for legal help due to the pandemic, and many shelters reduced their numbers to comply with social distancing protocols. In summary, the pandemic made it more difficult for survivors of intimate partner abuse to access support resources and protect themselves from violence.

An interdisciplinary team at Northeastern University, consisting of lawyers and designers, collaborated to provide support to the Domestic Violence Institute (DVI) in the School of Law at Northeastern University in response to this pressing issue. The DVI functions both as a research institution and a legal clinic where free basic abuse prevention services are offered to individual clients and community-based advocacy groups. However, in the spring of 2020, immediately after the US lockdown order, DVI experienced a 66% decrease in calls for help. The lawyers at the clinic were concerned that this drop did not reflect an actual decrease in cases, but rather a lack of opportunities for clients to access the clinic. Prior to the COVID-19 lockdown, almost all of the DVI's work was conducted in-person. To support their clients during the pandemic, they reached out to NuLawLab to develop a remote service model.

However, the COVID-19 pandemic created significant obstacles for the NuLawLab's design research, which has utilized interdisciplinary and participatory approaches to engage with the communities. This was due to several unique challenges. First, social distancing guidelines limited the possibility of conducting in-person research. Second, domestic violence survivors were confined to their homes with their abusers, with limited privacy and access to communication devices, making it difficult to engage in alternative research methods like phone interviews, Zoom meetings, or Jamboard workshop participation. Third, we prioritized survivors' immediate needs over conducting human subject research, recognizing the added mental burden this could place on already strained individuals. Our priority was to provide urgent help to survivors to protect them from dangerous situations.

As a result of these obstacles, the NuLawLab was unable to employ its traditional codesign workshops. Instead, we adopted holistic service design approaches that incorporated the perspectives of various stakeholders, including information gathered from clinic lawyers with years of experience supporting survivors. The research was conducted between April 2020, shortly after the governor of Massachusetts declared a state of emergency, and December 2020, when the vaccine began to be distributed. This COVID-19 rapid response project encountered numerous pandemic-related challenges. Nevertheless, the NuLawLab and the DVI collaborated to develop a service aimed at addressing the reported increase in domestic violence cases following the outbreak of COVID-19. Our goal was to provide the survivors of intimate partner abuse in Boston with (1) remote law student assistance consistent with law clinic operations; (2) a novel, secure means of video-documenting client information and evidence using an app;[7] and (3) digitally automated court form generation and filing.[8] As the design director of the NuLawLab, Miso Kim led the service design effort to examine the journeys of diverse stakeholders before, during, and after the legal consultations at the DVI to effectively overcome the contact obstacles that the pandemic regulations posed. In addition to the three systems above, we designed (4) multiple channels that the survivors could use to learn about the DVI service and contact the clinic safely and securely. Lastly, (5) we detailed the experience following the legal consult, which included finding a safe shelter and helping survivors create action plans to follow after they leave the shelter.

Taking a service design approach to this project allowed the team to view the process holistically, identifying diverse needs at various touchpoints that needed to be coordinated and discovering problems from multiple stakeholders' perspectives. By prioritizing the principle of autonomy, we saw those we serve as active "survivors" rather than passive "victims." This compelled us to design the entire system to support their decision-making, planning, and action, empowering them to take control of their situation. We created two-stage major consulting channels: a website for information and digital intake,[9] and a specialized and generally available app to collect and report the abuse details and other information. Additionally, our service design approach enabled us to examine the journeys of diverse stakeholders before and after the legal consults at the DVI and to create touchpoint materials to support the holistic experience. We designed multiple channels that the survivors could use to learn about the DVI service and contact the clinic safely and securely. We also detailed the experience following the legal consult, which included finding a safe shelter and planning for a life after the sheltering.

To capture the comprehensive experiences of a law student, case manager, supervisor, shelter staff member, and three survivor personas, we employed a cyclic version of Joseph Campbell's Hero's Journey. We chose the Hero's Journey for several reasons. First, it is a classic storytelling model that portrays a hero's growth in courage and autonomy through mentorship and structured experiences (Campbell [1949] 2008). We saw our service as providing such mentorship and experiences. Second, storytelling is an essential practice in law and oral advocacy. Campbell's model provided a persuasive framing to create an argument that supports our users. By utilizing a storytelling model, we integrated service experience and legal design

7 This component was developed and operated by the social good app developer Quadrant 2. See www.quadrant2.us/ (last accessed April 12, 2023).

8 For this component we joined an effort already underway at Suffolk Law School's Legal Innovation and Technology Lab, the Document Assembly Line. See https://suffolklitlab.org/docassemble-AssemblyLine-documentation/docs/ (last accessed April 12, 2023) and https://courtformsonline.org/ (last accessed April 12, 2023).

9 See https://dvilegal.org/ (last accessed April 12, 2023).

into one flow, aimed at nurturing our users' autonomy and dignity in confronting and overcoming their situations. The high-level service storytelling models continued to serve as guiding principles to ensure that the team members remained focused on promoting the autonomous participation of all stakeholders.

In the following stage, the team employed various service design tools, including service blueprints involving multiple players (Figure 12.5) and experience prototyping through scenarios (Figure 12.6) to develop the DVI service in greater detail. The creation of these maps, coupled with the cocreation process, allowed the team to consider the service experience from various stakeholder perspectives, thereby optimizing the service as a whole. Additionally, the maps revealed challenges both preceding and following the consultation stage, emphasizing the importance of engaging with existing community networks beyond technological means for survivor consultation. To achieve this, we proposed collaborating with apartment managers, grocery store workers, and bank employees who regularly interact with those in need, creating contact points for survivors who are often unable to leave their homes. We also suggested repurposing vacant hotel chains and university dorms, which were empty during the pandemic's peak, as temporary shelters for domestic violence survivors, where they could establish plans for preparing for a life after sheltering. Approaching this project from a service design perspective helped the team examine the process holistically to identify diverse needs at different touchpoints that had to be coordinated together, and to discover problems from multiple stakeholders' points of view.

After mapping out the service experience, the team identified user needs and crucial touchpoints that required assistance, leading to the development of various touchpoint materials (Figure 12.7). These materials include a digital promotion piece for social media as well as a postcard and tear-off flier that could be placed in essential businesses to initiate the survivor's journey. To ensure the survivors' safety, we designed these materials to be portable and minimal in information. We also created process maps using universal visuals that could be understood across different languages, literacy levels, and cultures. These maps were placed on the website to serve as a systematic guide for the holistic process and improve communication between the survivors and lawyers. Furthermore, these maps are used to educate new volunteer attorneys and advocates who join the DVI.

We also began to develop the digital touchpoints necessary for DVI's lawyers, advocates, and law students to communicate with survivors remotely, building on the insights gained from the service design process. The website was launched on July 1, 2020, recognizing that the lockdown order was likely to be in place for some time. The website (Figure 12.8) features essential information about the services provided by DVI, a brief online intake form powered by Formstack, and a resources page detailing local social services available to survivors. Additionally, the website includes an "Escape Site" button, which leads survivors to the msn.com search engine, allowing them to quickly exit the site in case they are interrupted by abusive parties.

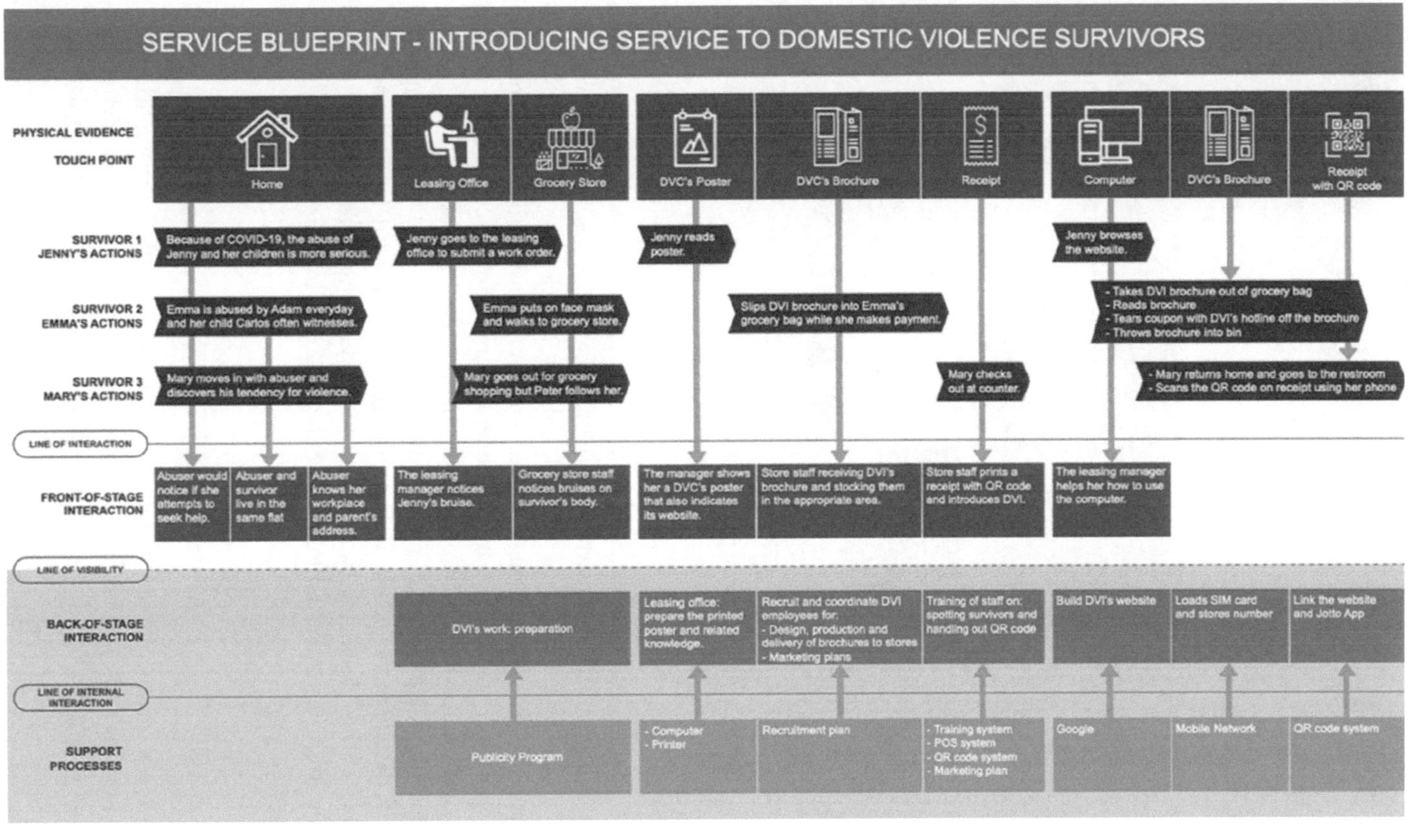

FIGURE 12.5. Service blueprint.
(Image credit: Fonnis Choo, Mingmei Yang, and Mavis Yu.)

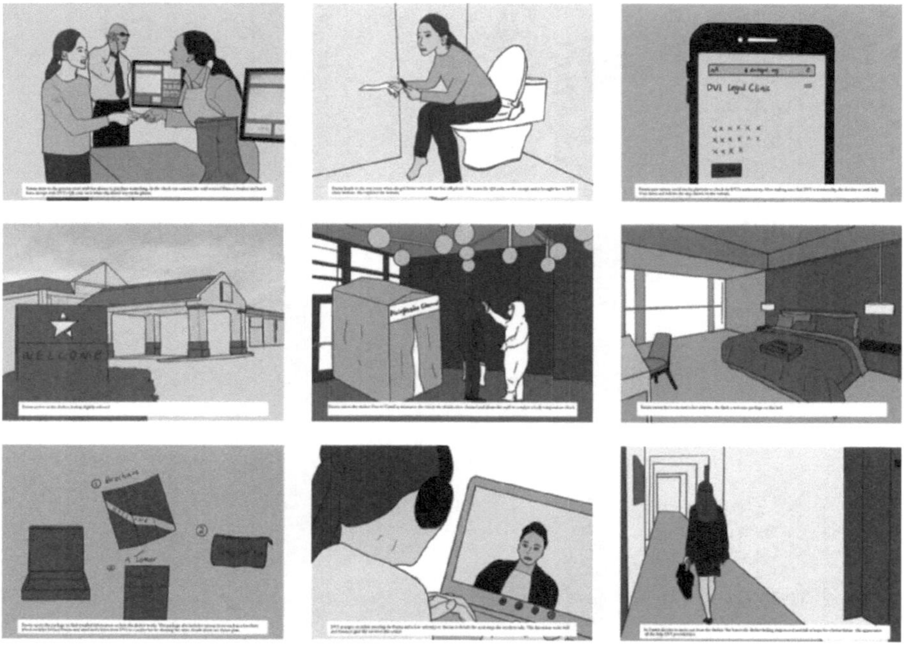

FIGURE 12.6. Experience prototype.
(Image credit: Fonnis Choo, Mingmei Yang, and Mavis Yu.)

Given the forced isolation caused by the pandemic, secure communication between survivors and lawyers was a top priority. Two strategies were implemented: the first was to leverage the existing text and chat functions of off-the-shelf smartphone apps like Signal and Google Voice. The second was to utilize the remote app Jotto (created by Quadrant 2) to transmit client information and evidence securely to lawyers, without leaving a trace on clients' smartphones, in situations where off-the-shelf apps were not preferred by clients. Finally, we collaborated with and supported the rapid development of new online emergency order court forms,[10] under the leadership of the Massachusetts Access to Justice Commission's COVID-19 Rapid Response Task Force and Suffolk Law School's Legal Innovation & Technology (LIT) Lab.

12.5 DISCUSSION

As we wrote at the outset, our experiences have not been earth-shattering. More and more universities, law schools, and organizations are investing in legal design labs, and more and more people of multiple disciplines are practicing "legal design"

[10] The emergency court order forms can be found at www.courtformsonline.org.

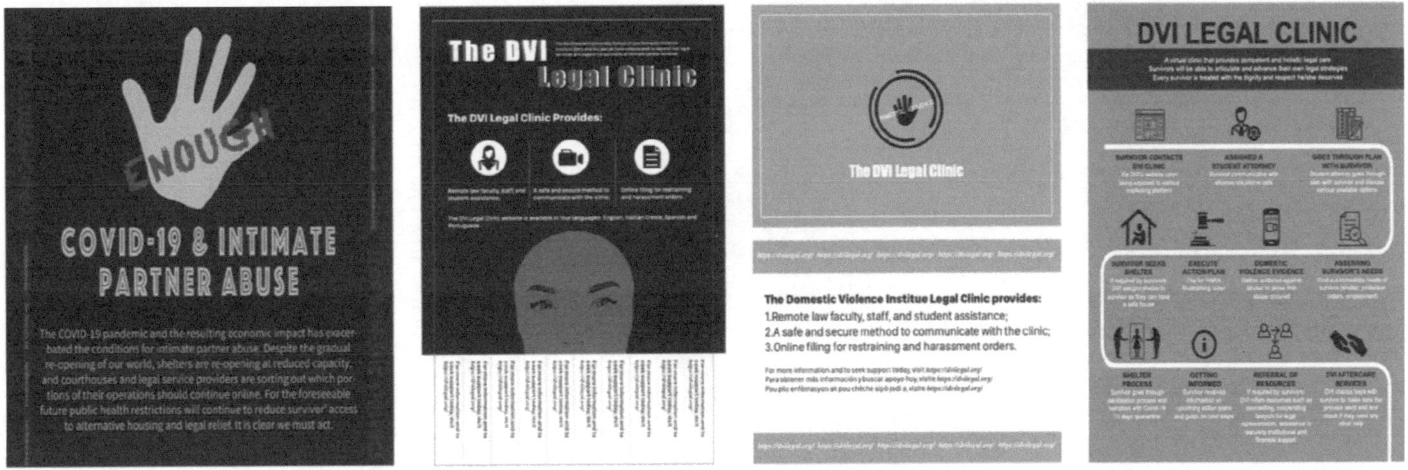

FIGURE 12.7. Social media promotion, tear-off flier, postcard (front and back), and consulting process map sample.
(Image credit: Fonnis Choo, Mingmei Yang, and Mavis Yu.)

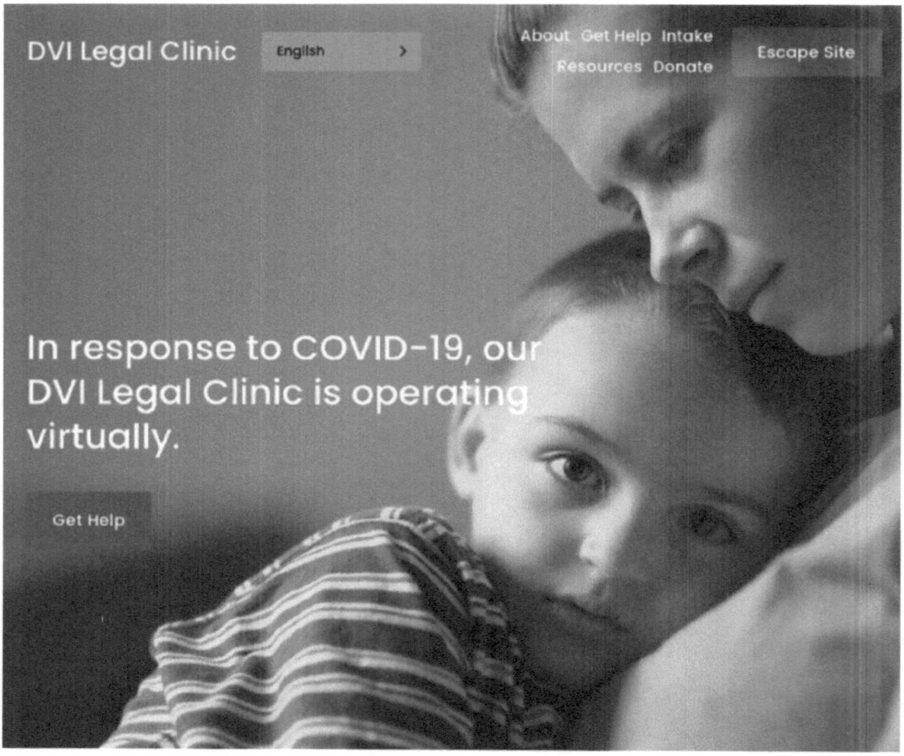

FIGURE 12.8. DVI legal website (https://dvilegal.org).
(Website design credit: Kyle Lasky.)

broadly defined. We therefore want to use this closing section to boil down what we've learned about interdisciplinary project collaboration, participatory design, and service design in our first decade. It is our hope future nascent interdisciplinarity legal innovation labs that stumble across this chapter will get a leap on creating lasting change.

12.5.1 *Interdisciplinarity*

Find interdisciplinary people. Much is made of the importance of reaching across disciplines, but precious little is said about the people with whom we are going to collaborate. If you want to have a successful interdisciplinary experience, find individuals with whom to work who already straddle two disciplines. Let's face it, we are still working with people. We've found that someone who has already made a significant disciplinary pivot in their lived experience is going to be much more comfortable with crossing other disciplinary lines. They've done it before in the most important project of all: their own lives. We think this matters because, in the end, it is a group of people working together to solve a problem. If you really want to execute on a truly interdisciplinary idea, staff the project with folks who already have the deepest experience one can get in that regard.

Take the time to develop a shared vocabulary. Dan and Jules spent a solid year developing a shared vocabulary between them as they began their shared journey. Blessed with a shared workspace, they were able to take advantage of the stretches of downtime one finds when launching a new academic initiative to talk and challenge each other on unfamiliar terms. They actively worked together to come up with terminology that better described what the NuLawLab was. A simple example is our movement over ten years from "access to justice" to "legal empowerment" to "legal agency." The investment is worth it. More focused projects that will be accomplished in a few years obviously don't need the time the NuLawLab needed, but build that step in at the outset. Your interdisciplinarity will function more efficiently and more genuinely.

Let the right people lead the way. Much has been written about how poorly lawyers' inherent personality traits and training equip them for letting others take the lead on collaborations. The same can often be said, frankly, for just about any discipline participating in collaborative work when that work turns toward that particular subject matter expert's wheelhouse. This problem – and it is a problem – can silence voices and experiences and perspectives that would be very advantageous to the effort's goals. In every collective problem-solving exercise, the participants should stay attuned to who should lead and when. The spotlight should shift regularly. Sometimes the right people will need some help getting their value acknowledged, respected, and integrated. But make sure it happens. Otherwise your outcomes will miss the mark.

Partnerships supported by projects. Much of the applied work in the legal design space is currently being done through projects (in academia and nonprofits) and focused engagements (in the commercial space). In our experience, projects are also what is demanded of most funders before an organization that relies on soft money gains admittance to the hallowed land of "operational" funding. In our first years, "projects" were how we envisioned and communicated our externally focused efforts. We've learned a more promising approach, for both funding and outcomes, is to seek partnerships supported by projects. We used projects to explore around Boston and New England with our various interventions, before finding ourselves deeply engaged in a long-term partnership in East Boston that has been supported by three projects (and counting). With the partnership well established, we have found greater funding success, and a much more resilient and creative team of collaborators. It takes work (for example, a one-hour weekly standing team meeting that has been running since September 2020), but it is worth it. The first thing community organizations will ask creative interventionists such as the NuLawLab is: "How long are you sticking around?" Devote the resources and build capacity to stick around. It's worth it in the long run.

12.5.2 *Participatory Design*

Lawyers can be codesigners. From the outset of our time working with lawyers on design projects, we faced tremendous skepticism from the lawyers themselves whether they had the "design skills" or knowledge to meaningfully participate in the effort. Early in each codesign effort, we always undertook to demonstrate why such skepticism was unwarranted. That usually involved some playful warmup activities allowing everyone at the table to experience their own inherent creativity in collaboration with others. In the realm of participatory design, the best tool for persuasion is an experience. While we still always start any formal codesign session with a playful exercise to get the creative juices flowing, fewer and fewer lawyers these days need to be convinced they have the chops to be codesigners. Whether this is on account of the uptake of design ideas in the law within the last ten years, the fierce urgency of the moment when it comes to contemporary problems, or any other number of factors in isolation or combined, we cannot say. We can say this development is a welcome one and bodes well for the future.

Legal procedures and substance are part of the design. In the early days of our involvement in legal design, we noted a somewhat artificial distinction between law and design. In our *RePresent* example, law was perceived as fixed, unchangeable, and fairly inaccessible, and the game design process was a way to make that inscrutable thing easier for people to understand and navigate. That was certainly true of that discreet project: our work together was not going to change the procedures and underlying laws folks in Connecticut had to navigate. But the distinction is an artificial one. The existing legal requirements we were working with were but one design constraint with which to work, just like the functionality of the StudyCrafter platform. When zooming out to look at participatory design generally in the larger context of legal design, there is no reason for the distinction. Design methods can be used to innovate the actual legal substantive law, and participatory design is already a part of many legislative and policymaking bodies and processes. It is called things like "legislative testimony" and "hearings," but it can serve a similar if not identical purpose: ensuring that the outcome reflects the needs and interests of a wide range of stakeholders.

Keep collaborative design fun. As we've said many times already in this book, we prioritize fun. But not just for fun's sake (well, sometimes it is just for that). In our experience to date, keeping things fun keeps our codesigners interested in what they are doing with us, and motivated to continue providing their ideas and insights. Without that investment over time, a participatory design process hollows out pretty quickly. Our ice cream parlor game-testing session was a particular hit, as one might expect for a convening in August in the US Northeast. It also serves as a model of sorts for how we approach such things in other projects. Keeping things fun takes more work, but the value always manifests right away.

12.5.3 *Service Design*

Storytelling methods can be used for practical application. There is a natural fit between law and storytelling, with the most obvious example being the lawyer making a summation or closing argument before a jury. But the tool can also be used to create legal services and law itself. For our DVI project, use of storytelling methods was in part borne of necessity on account of pandemic restrictions. But we advocate for using storytelling regardless of external factors such as the restrictions we faced. Storytelling allowed us to tap the complex emotional state of domestic violence survivors without subjecting a vulnerable population to an intrusive design process. With enough imagination and access to secondary sources such as clinic lawyers, oral histories, and documentaries, storytelling can get you pretty far.

Service design maintains the focus on dignity and autonomy. Service design methods, while incorporating and seeking to align disparate stakeholder viewpoints, ultimately prioritizes the dignity and autonomy of the individual accessing the service being designed. Any number of component parts of our justice system are, properly understood, a service. In many legal contexts, such services and operations were designed decades before the field of service design arose. These methods are now readily available for justice sector innovators, and our experience with them has been uniquely generative. The DVI Legal website remains a core component of the services that DVI's law clinic provides, fully three years after launch and with much of the worst of the pandemic behind us. That longevity suggests the methods worked in this instance. We, for one, will continue to use them and learn from them.

Service design allows for understanding and aligning diverse stakeholders perspectives. There are many design methods that can be used to align diverse stakeholder perspectives. Service design methods do a particularly good job of doing so but keeping the service seeker as the primary focus. Consider the service blueprint at Figure 12.5, which is only a portion of the entire blueprint. The three survivors' experiences and needs span the entirety of the map, given that their experience continues throughout. The three component parts of what the project was trying to do are then mapped out: one above the line of visibility to the survivor, and two out of her view. By mapping each component part out in horizontal chronological alignment, we could see conflicts where they would actually arise, allowing for a more targeted solution.

12.6 CONCLUSION

Three project examples, three to four insights articulated from each. Let's recap. Our Stable Ground project taught us to seek out already interdisciplinary collaborators to achieve the next result, and to take the time to develop a shared vocabulary. Both learnings allowed us to identify the right people to lead the way. Those three insights instilled in us a dedication to long-term partnerships over short-term projects. Our *RePresent* project gave us a chance to convince the lawyers that they too were designers, and had something to offer to a codesign process. This was in part because it was clear to all that the legal procedures and substance were part of the design, and not something that stood apart from it. By keeping the collaboration fun, we kept the participants engaged and active throughout a long codesign process. The exigencies of the COVID-19 pandemic taught us the value of storytelling not just for making sense of law but for creating access points into it. Because the service design methods we deployed maintains the focus on the dignity and autonomy of the service seeker, we were able to understand and align diverse stakeholder perspectives while keeping domestic violence survivors front of mind. A good collection of insights from our first ten years of project work. Here's to at least ten more years and many more insights.

REFERENCES

Anurudran, Ashri, Leah Yared, Cameron Comrie, Katherine Harrison, and Thomas Burke. 2020. "Domestic Violence Amid COVID-19." *International Journal of Gynecology & Obstetrics* 150, no. 2 (May): 255–56. https://doi.org/10.1002/ijgo.13247.

Ashar, Sameer M. 2008. "Law Clinics and Collective Mobilization." *Clinical Law Review* 14, no. 2 (October): 355–414. Social Science Research Network (SSRN).

Bitner, Mary Jo, Amy L. Ostrom, and Felicia N. Morgan. 2008. "Service Blueprinting: A Practical Technique for Service Innovation." *California Management Review* 50, no. 3 (Spring): 66–94. https://doi.org/10.2307/41166446.

Boserup, Brad, Mark McKenney, and Adel Elkbuli. 2020. "Alarming Trends in US Domestic Violence during the COVID-19 Pandemic." *The American Journal of Emergency Medicine* 38, no. 12 (December): 2753–55. https://doi.org/10.1016/j.ajem.2020.04.077.

Bruck Bennouna, Chelsea, and Danya Sherman. 2022. "The Boston Housing Support Station: Exploring the Impacts of an Arts-Engaged Coalition's Legal Response to Housing Crisis." https://drive.google.com/file/d/1785Gozw4-Jvos5fLjkgbnW9RDigF-tQK/view.

Campbell, Joseph. [1949] 2008. *The Hero with a Thousand Faces*. 3rd ed. San Francisco, CA: New World Library.

Costanza-Chock, Sasha. 2020. *Design Justice: Community-Led Practices to Build the Worlds We Need*. Cambridge, MA: MIT Press.

Davis, Martha F. 2021. "What Is Essential: Legal Design and Client Stories." *Elon Law Review* 13, no. 1 (February): 39–74. Social Science Research Network (SSRN).

Doherty, Michael. 2022. "Disciplinarity and the Modes of Legal Design." *Proceedings of DRS Biennial Conference Series, Design Research Society, Bilbao, Spain, June 25 – July 3, 2022*. London: Design Research Society.

Ehn, Pelle, and Morten Kyng. 1991. "Cardboard Computers: Mocking-It-Up or Hands-On the Future." In *Design at Work*, edited by Joan Greenbaum and Morton Kyng, 169–95. Boca Raton, FL: CRC Press.

Harteveld, Casper. 2010. *Triadic Game Design*. London: Springer Press.

Jackson, Dan. 2016. "Human-Centered Legal Tech: Integrating Design in Legal Education." *Law Teacher* 50, no. 1 (April): 82–97. https://doi.org/10.1080/03069400.2016.1146468.

Karpen, Ingo Oswald, Gerda Gemser, and Giulia Calabretta. 2017. "A Multilevel Consideration of Service Design Conditions: Towards a Portfolio of Organisational

Capabilities, Interactive Practices and Individual Abilities." *Journal of Service Theory and Practice* 27, no. 2 (March): 384–407. https://doi.org/10.1108/JSTP-05-2015-0121.

Kim, Miso, Dan Jackson, Jules Sievert, and Morgan Wilson. 2022. "Locked Down with Abusers: Designing for the Dignity and Autonomy of Domestic Violence Survivors during the Covid-19 Pandemic." *Proceedings of DRS Biennial Conference Series, Design Research Society, Bilbao, Spain, June 25 – July 3, 2022*. London: Design Research Society.

Leslie, Emily, and Riley Wilson. 2020. "Sheltering in Place and Domestic Violence: Evidence from Calls for Service during COVID-19." *Journal of Public Economics* 189 (September): 104241. https://doi.org/10.1016/j.jpubeco.2020.104241.

Levitt, Theodore. 1972. "Production-Line Approach to Service." *Harvard Business Review*, September. https://hbr.org/1972/09/production-line-approach-to-service.

Norman, Donald A., and Stephen W. Draper. 1986. *User-Centered System Design: New Perspectives on Human-Computer Interaction*. Boca Raton, FL: CRC Press.

Perry-Kessaris, Amanda. 2022. "Legal Design Could and Should Be More Sociolegal." *Proceedings of DRS Biennial Conference Series, Design Research Society, Bilbao, Spain, June 25 – July 3, 2022*. London: Design Research Society.

Sherman, Danya. 2019. "Building Stable Ground: An Evaluation Report." https://static1.squarespace.com/static/5e449744f09c237b23b1c5d3/t/5e4d480a73b13a2db328510e/1582123064441/SGFinal_Oct2019.pdf.

Shostack, G. Lynn. 1982. "How to Design a Service." *European Journal of Marketing* 16, no. 1 (January): 49–63. https://doi.org/10.1108/EUM0000000004799.

Vargo, Stephen L., and Robert F. Lusch. 2008. "Service-Dominant Logic: Continuing the Evolution." *Journal of the Academy of Marketing Science* 36, no. 1 (August): 1–10. https://doi.org/10.1007/s11747–007-0069-6.

13

Teaching the Legal Inventors of the Future

Jules Rochielle Sievert, Miso Kim, and Dan Jackson

13.1 INTRODUCTION

Northeastern University School of Law (NUSL)'s mission is to be a global leader in experiential legal education, providing students with the knowledge, skills, and ethical and social values essential to serving clients, citizens, and the public interest now and in the future. Through teaching, scholarship, and public service, NUSL works to promote dignity and justice as well as to enhance understanding of law's impact on individuals, enterprises, and communities here in the United States and around the world. The role of the laboratory model in making the connection between real-world problems and legal education (Davis 2015), and the NuLawLab's application of that concept focuses on actively and explicitly making connections among scholarship, community projects, and classrooms.

Pedagogical activities have been one of the founding visions of the NuLawLab. Despite having an enrollment of more than 2,400 in the mid-1920s and anchoring the formation of Northeastern University, by 1956, resources were scarce, and NUSL had to close its doors. Our graduates, however, fought for a revival. Finally, in the 1968–1969 school year, their efforts paid off, and the School of Law reopened. In keeping with the tradition of innovation, we made cooperative legal education the cornerstone of our program – a unique approach to educating lawyers that recognizes the independence of theory and practice.

By building on this deeply rooted history in experiential learning, public interest law, and the clinical movement in legal education, the NuLawLab was well positioned to pioneer a collaborative zone for interdisciplinary research and design in the context of legal education. In our ten-plus years of experience, we have discovered many overlapping pedagogical methods that connect design and law. This chapter focuses on how we teach law students art and design, and how we teach other graduate students law and activism. We will start this chapter with some foundation on our approach before turning to some explication of each aspect of our teaching.

Our engagement with both law and other graduate students at the School of Law typically begins with their enrollment in our upper-level Laboratory Seminar in Applied and Critical Legal Design, which is taught nearly every semester. We also offer the Master Class in Legal Design, which is often offered in collaboration with courses from other disciplines to provide an interdisciplinary perspective. Additionally, we sponsor both project-based and student-led independent study and work-study opportunities. We also host residencies and fellowship opportunities for individuals who propose an idea that is potentially generative for both the individual and the NuLawLab. Finally, we regularly host a paid co-op placement for NUSL students. To say we pull every possible lever at a large research university and experiential law school to pursue our teaching approaches is an understatement. All this work is folded into a new Graduate Certificate in Legal Design, which launched in Fall 2022.

13.2 LABORATORY SEMINAR AND CREATIVE PROBLEM-SOLVING APPROACH

The Laboratory Seminar in Applied and Critical Legal Design is a dynamic, four-credit course that encourages students to critically engage with design methods and principles to develop innovative solutions for legal systems, institutions, and problems. This course has evolved significantly since its inception in Summer 2013. It started as a three-person independent study, with each student earning two credits. Shortly after we started to prototype how this course could work, we introduced the Laboratory Seminar in Applied Design and Legal Empowerment, a six-week intensive course worth two credits. This course aimed to give students a rapid introduction to design methods for legal empowerment outcomes, either through a partnership with an outside organization or as a simulation without an outside partner. In part, the success of this course was due to a number of students who became early adopters of our methods and ideas.

The Laboratory Seminar in Applied and Critical Legal Design has a rich history of innovation and experimentation. The course has evolved significantly since its inception, with a strong focus on providing students with an immersive and engaging learning experience. The seminar fosters innovation and experimentation while preparing students to tackle the complex challenges of the legal system through creative problem-solving approaches. After a few years of iterating the course in the classroom, we expanded the academic credit to three and extended the course length to a full twelve-week quarter. Recently, in line with NUSL's transition to a fifteen-week semester, we further expanded the course to four credits, providing students with more time and opportunities to explore critical legal design methods.

The laboratory seminar course requires students to critically engage with various forms of design and legal research methodologies, emphasizing hands-on student engagement with structured creative processes, field observations, prototyping, and other methods derived from various creative disciplines. Students begin the process by conducting field observations, including ethnographic research, stakeholder interviews, surveys or focus groups, and other methods to gain insights into user needs and experiences. We then encourage them to utilize structured creative processes such as brainstorming sessions, mind mapping, concept mapping, and other methods to generate ideas and explore possibilities.

For example, in the lab seminar, one law student utilized an empathy map to gain a deeper understanding of the journey experienced by a *pro se* litigant. Drawing inspiration from principles of empathy and legal comprehension, this technique aimed to create a comprehensive visual representation of the *pro se* litigant's perspective. By delving into their experiences, challenges, and aspirations, the empathy map provided valuable insights for the law student to better comprehend and empathize with the complexities faced by individuals representing themselves in court.

The law student's empathy map revealed a range of emotions commonly experienced by *pro se* litigants throughout their legal journey, including anxiety, frustration, and determination. It became apparent that the litigant's primary need was to seek justice and protect their rights without the aid of legal representation. The map highlighted the litigant's desire for their voice to be heard, to navigate the legal system effectively, and to have a fair and unbiased legal proceeding (Figure 13.1).

Challenges identified within the empathy map encompassed understanding and applying complex legal procedures, grappling with legal terminology, and facing well-prepared opposing parties with legal expertise. Additionally, the map shed light on the emotional toll of the litigation process, including the strain on personal relationships, the financial burden of navigating the legal system alone, and the overall disruption to their daily life. With an enlightened understanding of the *pro se* litigant's perspective, the empathy map provided valuable insights for the law student to develop a more empathetic approach to their legal studies and future legal practice. It guided the student in gaining a deeper understanding of the unique challenges faced by individuals representing themselves, and it prompted them to consider ways to improve access to justice and provide resources to support *pro se* litigants. Ultimately, the empathy map served as a powerful tool for the law student, fostering a heightened sense of empathy and understanding for *pro se* litigants. By actively engaging with their experiences, challenges, and aspirations, the empathy map facilitated a more compassionate and informed approach to the study and practice of law, encouraging the law student to advocate for equitable access to justice and explore avenues to support individuals navigating the legal system without legal representation.

The next step typically involves building visual, physical, or digital prototypes to create mockups and test designs through simulations or other methods to evaluate their effectiveness. For example, journey maps visually depict how users interact with a product, service, or organization, providing insight into their emotions and pain points to generate a better understanding of lived experience. Persona,

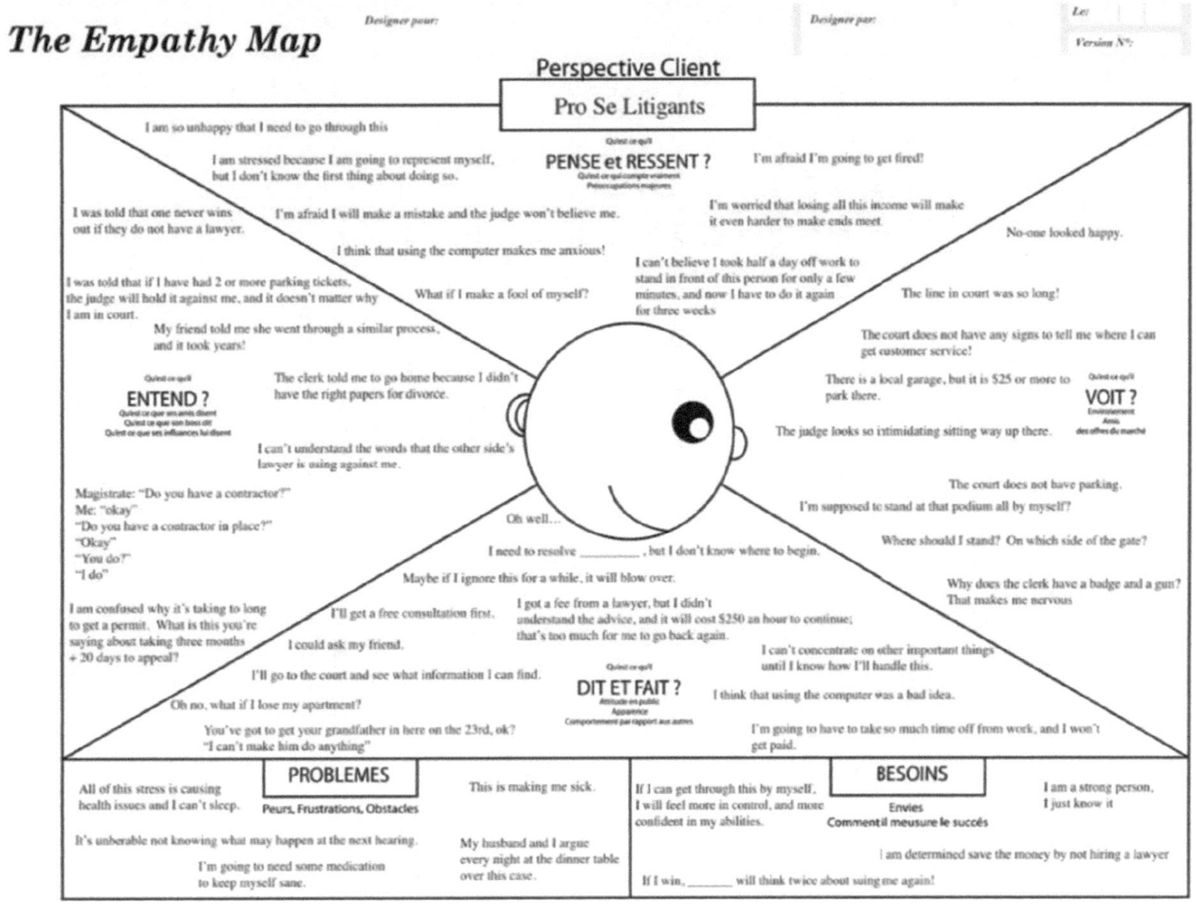

FIGURE 13.1. Example from student work that represents the structured creative process above (empathy mapping). (Image credit Madeline Lafitte.)

timeline, emotions, pain points, and opportunities for improvement are key elements of these maps. By utilizing journey maps, legal designers can better empathize with their users, identify areas for improvement, and create more user-centered products or services (Figure 13.2).

Journey mapping involves the creation of a visual depiction illustrating the unique experiences of a particular student within the foster care system. This mapping aimed to shed light on various stages, interactions, emotions, and challenges encountered throughout the journey. Specifically, the student focused on mapping the experiences of a youth as they navigated the complexities of the foster care system. Key stages were identified, which encompassed entering the system, living within it, and the arduous transition of aging out.

Throughout the mapping process, the student diligently documented the emotions experienced by these youths at each stage. This encompassed a broad spectrum of feelings, ranging from confusion and fear to loneliness and despair. In addition, the student identified significant pain points inherent within the foster care system. These included the lack of stability resulting from frequent relocations between homes, the bureaucratic obstacles impeding access to necessary services, the isolation and social stigma endured by these young individuals, and the formidable challenges faced upon aging out of the system with minimal support or resources.

By visually presenting the journey in this manner, the student effectively showcased the systemic issues deeply embedded within the foster care system. This presentation formed a compelling case for the urgent need for reform. Moreover, the journey map served as a powerful visual tool, aiding the student in envisioning and designing enhanced experiences and outcomes for youths in foster care. To address the identified pain points, the student proposed various solutions, including the establishment of improved support systems, enhanced allocation of resources, and policy changes to foster a more stable and nurturing environment for young individuals transitioning in and out of foster care.

Storytelling in design research is a powerful qualitative tool wielded by designers to unearth meaningful insights about individual experiences and needs. This method hinges on the dissection of personal narratives tied to a design issue, fostering the development of solutions deeply attuned to human contexts. It's an approach that inspires students to venture into unexplored territories, nurturing fresh solutions, concepts, and paths for our legal systems and institutional challenges. In addressing contemporary design questions, students exercise these methods and skills, with critical design structured to promote envisioning a future where everyone is empowered to activate and utilize the law.

Consider the example of a lab seminar student who chose to navigate the labyrinthine nature of whistleblowing, adopting the unique storytelling strategy of a comic book. This medium, chosen for more than its mere appeal, offered a potent mechanism for deconstructing complex ideas into understandable narratives and captivating visuals (Figure 13.3).

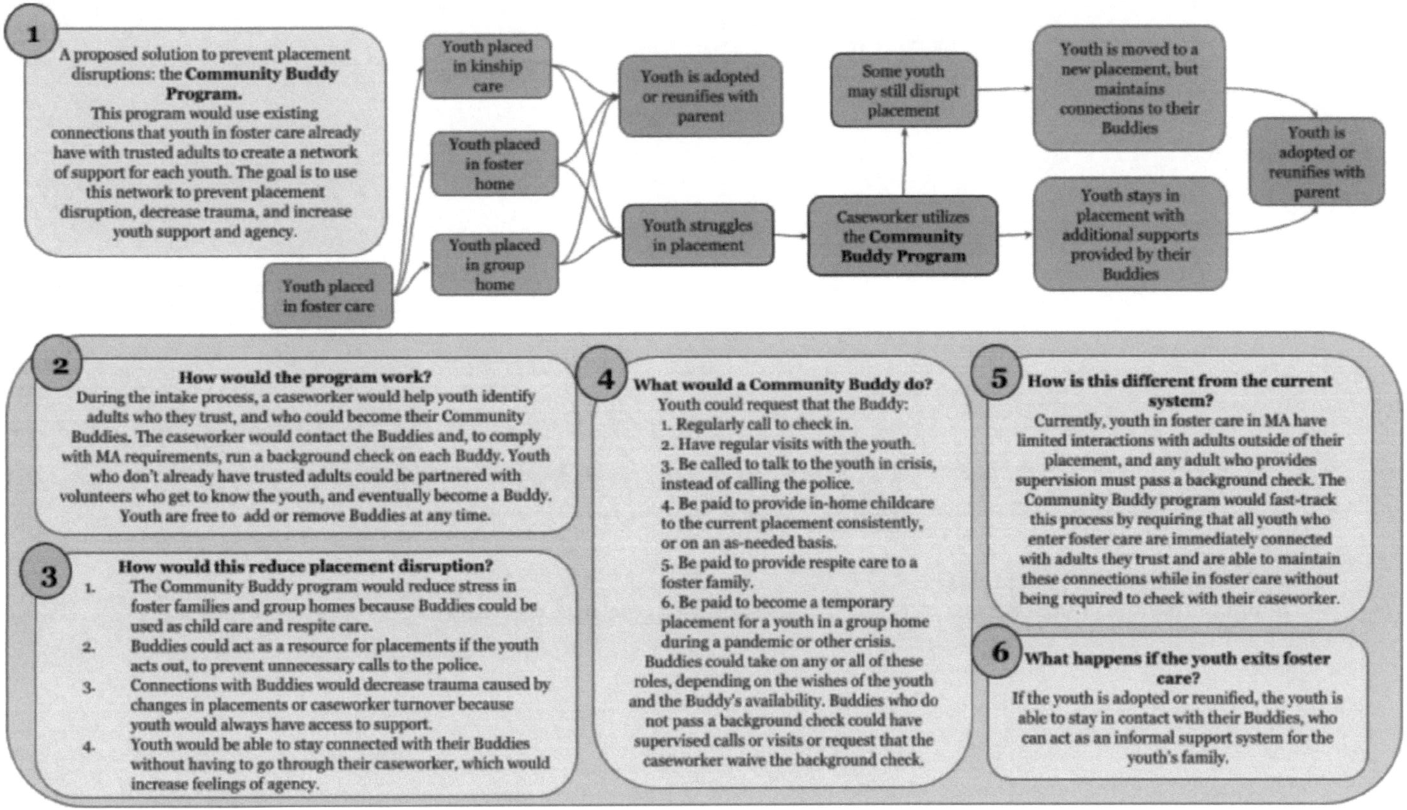

FIGURE 13.2. Example of youth in foster care journey map from lab seminar student work.
(Image credit: Maya Brown.)

FIGURE 13.3. Examples of storytelling from student work.
(Image credit: Madeline Lafitte.)

The student's journey commenced with an exhaustive exploration of whistleblowing. They delved into its multifaceted dynamics, potential hazards, and the protective measures in place. This broad investigation aimed to cultivate a fundamental understanding of whistleblowing from a spectrum of perspectives, acknowledging variations in backgrounds and privileges.

Progressing from there, they devised a "hunt statement" to provide sharper focus to their exploration. This pivotal research question sought to uncover overlooked specifics in a broad study, steering the research toward practical and theoretical solutions capable of assisting whistleblowers.

The culmination of this intricate research was its translation into a comic book storyboard. The student strove to condense complex findings into a compelling narrative. The storyboard enabled a vivid representation of the diverse experiences and trials whistleblowers confront, making them more relatable and easily digestible. This inventive tactic was designed to augment the reach and impact of the research, serving as a practical guide to help whistleblowers from all backgrounds navigate the legal and extra-legal challenges they might face in their brave journeys.

To enhance the learning experience, the Lab Seminar often invites guest lecturers and speakers from diverse fields, such as law, design, technology, and social sciences, exposing students to interdisciplinary perspectives and problem-solving approaches. Often the course partners with legal organizations, nongovernmental organizations, nonprofit organizations, or government agencies to provide students with real-world projects, helping them gain practical experience and build a professional network.

Recently, the course has incorporated methods from the field of critical (or speculative) design, which involves challenging established norms and assumptions while exploring alternative futures and possibilities. By integrating critical and speculative design approaches, the course encourages students to think critically about the role of design in society and how it can address complex legal and sociolegal challenges and opportunities. This innovative and forward-thinking approach helps students develop the creative, critical, and analytical skills necessary to succeed in today's rapidly changing world. However, it must also be stated that many activists and community organizers have used speculative fiction to aid people in the process of reimagining society as a collective strategy and response to systemic oppression, racism, homophobia, sexism, and classism.

13.3 CRITICAL LEGAL DESIGN IN THE CLASSROOM

Throughout its existence, the seminar has focused on introducing practical product design methods in response to specific design questions, often aligned with ongoing work at the NuLawLab. Recently, one of the most recent ambitious additions to our pedagogy has been the introduction of critical (or speculative) design into our curriculum and mindset. We consider critical design to be an opportunity for interested parties to convene creative minds and consider how this emerging discipline might inspire itself (Santuber and Edelman 2022; Doherty 2022) to best achieve what often feels tantalizingly close and excruciatingly far away – a lasting reorganization of law itself in order that it might fulfill its baseline promise of justice for all. This perspective encourages students to challenge established norms and explore alternative futures and possibilities.

Under the leadership of senior researcher Sankalp Bhatnagar, we explored the concepts of critical design in the classroom and in Sankalp's research projects for two years, culminating in our sponsoring the theme track "What Legal Design Could Be: Towards and Expanded Practice of Inquiry, Critique, and Action" in the 2022 Design Research Society Conference. That theme track (and the work that is following) is an opportunity for legal design to dream (Pope 2022). To dream about what could be, what should be, and what we hope will be (Dunne and Raby 2013). And to dream free of the restrictions of the existing disciplines of law and design, free even of the emerging norms of legal design (Bhatnagar 2022).

Much of the work in legal design has developed in quasi-corporate and commercial contexts where designers are focused on solving problems and answering questions rather than proposing problems to solve and questions to ask. Continuing exclusively in this vein at this point, however, leaves too much potential untapped. Because existing approaches to legal design remain largely affirmative, they maintain the status quo with efforts that are too narrow in scope, reductive in nature, or constrained in capacity to bring about critical reflection about, and action on, what exactly legal design should be designing. We have found critical design, which takes a discursive approach to design and works to prompt critical reflection upon our everyday beliefs, values, and worldviews through speculative proposals (Dunne and Raby 2013; Tharp and Tharp 2018), offers one potential to challenge fundamental issues at play in our existing systems, thereby assisting in setting the conditions for meaningful and lasting change in law and our legal systems and institutions (Walton 2022).

Incorporating critical design into legal education is important because it encourages students to think outside of established norms and assumptions about the role of design in society and its impact on the legal system. Critical design, as articulated by Anthony Dunne and Fiona Raby, diverges from traditional design practices by shifting focus from problem-solving to stimulating thought-provoking discourse on the cultural, societal, and political implications of technology (Dunne and Raby 2013). Instead of merely fulfilling user needs, critical design adopts a lens that challenges underlying assumptions, societal norms, and conventions associated with the roles products play in daily life (Bardzell and Bardzell 2013).

Through this approach, products are seen as a medium for debate, aiming to prompt individuals to critically assess the world around them and envision alternative futures (Dunne and Raby 2013). Critical design serves as a form of speculation, questioning current trends and raising awareness of the potential implications and unanticipated consequences of technology (Malpass 2017). By employing a speculative narrative, it allows users to consider different possibilities beyond the prevailing status quo.

NuLawLab believes that exposure to critical design can help students develop the creative and analytical skills necessary to navigate these challenges and propose innovative solutions that address the diverse needs and perspectives of stakeholders in the legal system. The Laboratory Seminar in Applied and Critical Legal Design fosters a dynamic culture of critique and collaboration, which are fundamental aspects of the course's learning experience. The course values a flexible and adaptive approach to learning, and more recently, the syllabus and design questions have been revised to align with students' interests and research.

Critique and collaboration are essential elements in both design and legal education. In the field of design, critique refers to the process of offering feedback on an ongoing project with the aim of enhancing its quality. Collaboration, on the other hand, involves individuals working together toward a shared objective. Similarly, within legal education, critique enables a thorough examination and assessment of legal ideas, concepts, and arguments, while collaboration allows students to cooperate and learn from each other's strengths and perspectives. In design education, critique is imperative for the development of critical thinking and problem-solving abilities among students. It provides students with constructive feedback on their work and helps them identify areas that require improvement. Likewise, in legal education, critique holds equal importance in honing students' analytical skills and facilitating an in-depth evaluation of legal concepts and theories.

In the lab we try to create a learning culture that values both group and individual reflection. We also value the learning that can happen from the facilitation of critique. Critique is the process of providing specific, well-reasoned reflective feedback aimed at helping an individual or a group improve their performance, skills, or work quality. It emphasizes strengths and areas of improvement while offering specific suggestions for development. Critique in the seminar maintains a positive and respectful tone, ensuring that the person receiving the feedback is supported, encouraged, and actively engaged in the discussion and group reflection (Figure 13.4).

The lab seminar's focus on critique ensures that students develop a critical mindset, challenging established assumptions and norms. By critiquing existing legal systems and institutions, students learn to identify and address complex legal issues, developing creative and innovative solutions. Overall, the Laboratory Seminar in Applied and Critical Legal Design provides students with a unique learning experience that emphasizes collaboration, critique, and innovation. The course's dynamic and flexible approach to learning is essential to prepare students to thrive in the ever-changing legal landscape. By exposing students to various design methods and principles and encouraging them to think critically and develop innovative solutions, the course equips students with the necessary tools to approach

FIGURE 13.4. Lab seminar students working as a team on an idea for an app related to child support.
(Photo credit: Dan Jackson.)

legal problems differently. This approach fosters a mindset of creativity and adaptability, allowing students to innovate solutions that address the diverse needs and perspectives of various stakeholders in the legal system and beyond.

The pedagogical evolution of the Laboratory Seminar in Applied and Critical Legal Design is a testament to the commitment of the NuLawLab to praxis and reflective action. This emphasis on continuous learning and experimentation inspires students to approach their work with the same level of passion and dedication, empowering them to make a meaningful impact on the legal system and society as a whole.

13.4 MASTER CLASS IN LEGAL DESIGN AND EXPERIENCE DESIGN STUDIO 2

The Master Class in Legal Design is an interdisciplinary course that pairs law students with graduate students from a design discipline such as architecture, experience design, or game design to reimagine aspects of our legal system for the age of self-representation. Law students join interdisciplinary student teams to apply advanced discipline-specific design methodologies and frameworks in response to a specific system design challenge. Our two most recent iterations of the course were taught in conjunction with Experience Design (XD) Studio 2: Group and Interpersonal, a core course for Experience Design MFA/MS students in the

Department of Art + Design. Our first iteration of the Master Class was paired with a graduate architecture course at Wentworth Institute of Technology, and is the subject of Chapter 7 in this volume.

This portion of the chapter will focus on our Spring 2022 version of the course, showcasing the unique interdisciplinary design education opportunity that NUSL and the College of Arts, Media and Design (CAMD) offer. In this joint class, experience design graduate students (twenty-one of them) and law graduate students (eight of them) worked together in four teams to resolve community controversies. As we teach this course, the three directors of the NuLawLab (and three coauthors of this chapter) drew upon our expertise in service design, legal design, and the art of rhetoric to encourage students to examine collective human experience through the lens of dignity and to enhance citizen autonomy.

Rhetoric is the art of devising and delivering an argument as a holistic form of communication. Aristotle ([4th century BCE] 1992) and Cicero ([2nd Century BCE] 1949) both describe rhetoric as a branch of politics because it deals with social communication and, in particular, controversial situations. While Cicero described persuasion as a combination of wisdom and eloquence and emphasized its essential role in conflict resolution, Aristotle highlighted how persuasion contributes to the community's decision-making.

Among the three kinds of rhetoric that Aristotle describes, judicial rhetoric, which aims to determine the just or unjust nature of past action, is the most common in legal contexts. It is notable, however, that Aristotle also introduces deliberative rhetoric, which aims to determine whether a certain future action would be useful or harmful in civic contexts. In the case of deliberative rhetoric, persuasion serves the substance in public discussions. While rhetoric is often misunderstood as manipulation, the end goal of persuasion in the context of deliberative rhetoric is to provide information to people so that they can make autonomous, informed decisions (Jackson, Kim, and Sievert 2020). In our class, we sought to lay the groundwork for the shared commonality of law and design – that both disciplines are arts of persuasion, embodied by words, visual means, material means, or service systems.

The class comprised two parts: seminar and projects. In the seminar part, students read and discussed rhetorical theories to understand how persuasion can serve as the principle of community deliberation, and therefore as the ground for collaboration between service design and law. In their in-class project 2, "Mediating a Conflict," students were asked to find a service controversy and apply rhetorical strategies to mediate conflict among the stakeholders. For example, "Team Flyers" conducted ethnographic research on dog parks and discovered from their interviews and observations that there are conflicting understandings of the conventions and etiquette that regulate social interactions in the local dog parks. They also surveyed related law and regulations while learning dog park users were either unaware of or confused about laws and regulations unless they were written on the dog park signs (Figure 13.5).

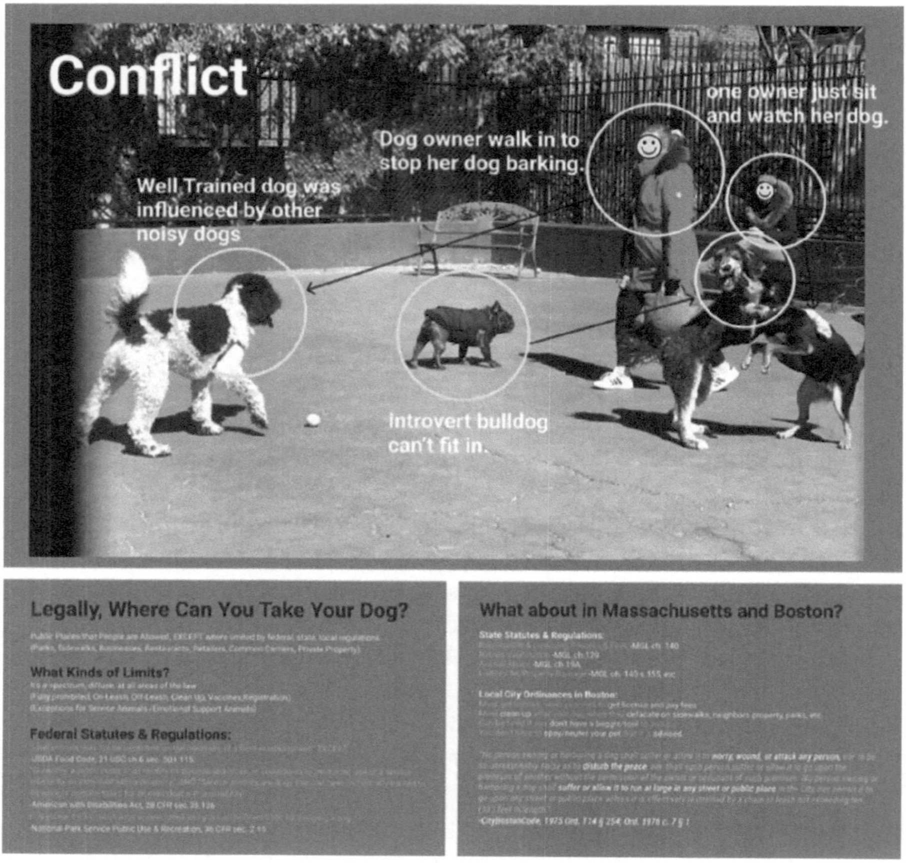

FIGURE 13.5. Conflict description based on observation research and research on regulations from student work.
(Image credit: Sky Olander, Zhiman Bai, Yue Yu, Xuhui Zhang.)

In the design process, the student teams utilized various models that would help them apply rhetorical frameworks to propose service design solutions to legal problems. These models enabled the students to effectively work in teams, to learn by doing, and to reflect through making. One of the models that students used was the rhetorical triangle consisting of the three modes of persuasion: pathos (stirring the emotion of the audience/user), ethos (communicating the credibility of the speaker/designer/service provider), and logos (logic and function of the service). For example, "Team Flyers" analyzed the nature of the key conflict they intended to address by presenting dogs and owners as the audience, the city (public safety) as the speaker, and the lack of communication among these stakeholders as the message (Figure 13.6).

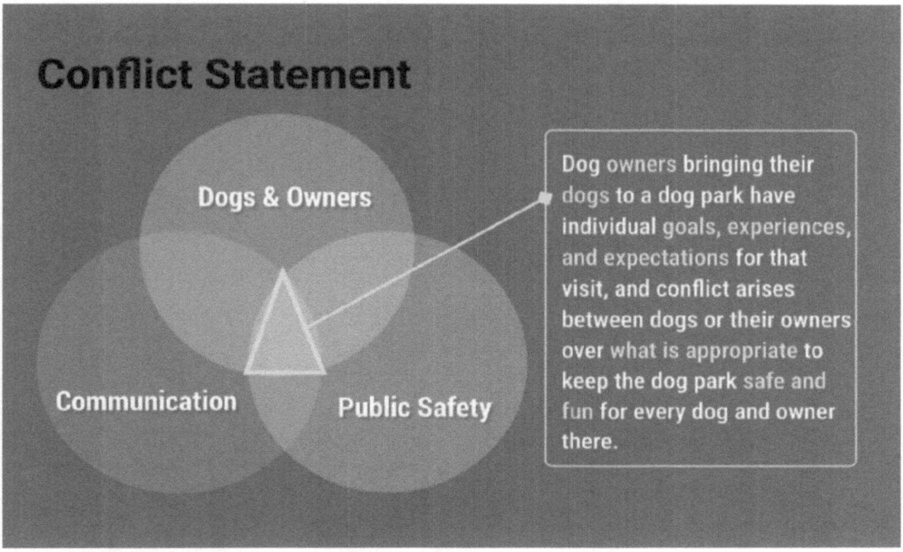

FIGURE 13.6. An example of rhetorical triangle used for analyzing the problem. (Image credit: Sky Olander, Zhiman Bai, Yue Yu, Xuhui Zhang.)

The rhetorical triangle approach helped the team analyze the gap in perceptions among the participants to define the opportunity area. We asked the students to compare and contrast pathos (customer expectation of the service) and ethos (organizational perception of the service) and then propose a redesigned concept of core competency. Specifically, "Team Flyers" identified a gap between the ethos (local government's perception that the playground does not need to be managed, as individual owners would educate their dogs) and pathos (the dog owners' perception that it is a battleground of conflicting attitudes and lack of shared guidelines). The designers proposed that the logos (core competency of the new service) should be aimed at persuading the stakeholders to form a community that can provide guidance and connection to its members. The team eventually developed the core competency perception into a more detailed service concept, which served as the argument that gave identity to the whole service and provides consistency across the touchpoints and products comprising the service (Figure 13.7).

By going through this rhetorical design process, the team designed an app-based service to help new residents become familiar with the community. Their app included information about available resources for dogs in the area as well as an action guide that lays out the procedures pet owners can follow to assist getting along with other animals and human residents. This was in addition to creating manuals and tools to help the communities manage their dog park guidelines via various community meetings and connections to local services to help the dogs

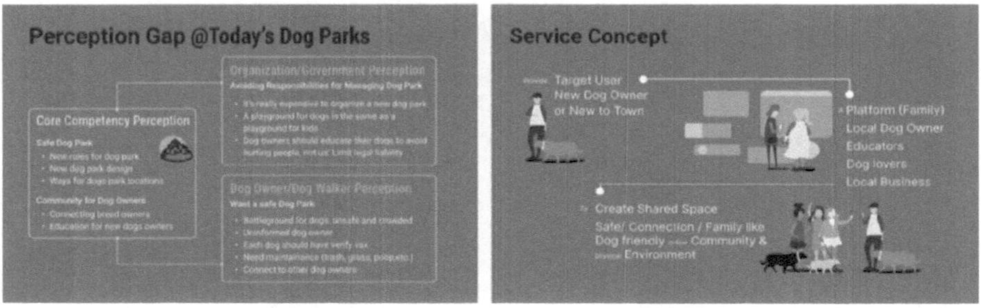

FIGURE 13.7. An example of a perception gap analysis map and a service concept map. (Image credit: Sky Olander, Zhiman Bai, Yue Yu, Xuhui Zhang.)

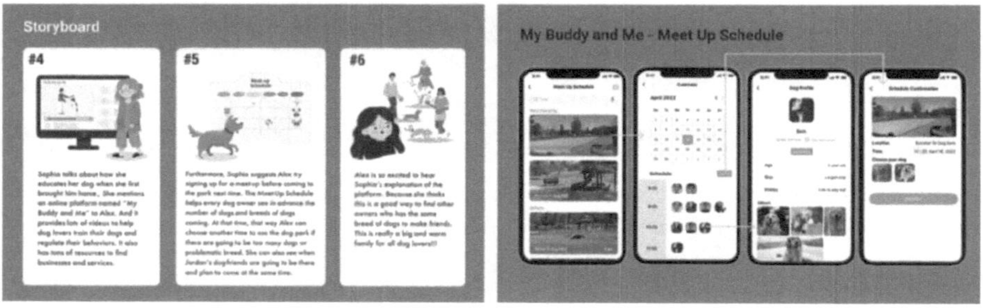

FIGURE 13.8. An example of an experience prototype and a product prototype produced by the 2022 Master Class students.

(Figure 13.8). The app and toolkits together contribute to a holistic service system that supports and welcomes novice members.

The pedagogical model implemented in the 2022 class stands as a testament to Northeastern's dedication to fostering interdisciplinary research and education, cultivating innovative teaching methodologies, and pushing the boundaries of design research. Notably, this course underscores the potential of rhetoric as a unifying principle that bridges the realms of law and design. By doing so, the course presents prospects for the development of distinctive processes, methods, and tools in the realm of legal design in the years to come.

13.5 GRADUATE CERTIFICATE IN LEGAL DESIGN

Both of these courses are part of our Graduate Certificate in Legal Design, launched in Fall 2022, which includes a practice requirement and a capstone project. The certificate is an effort to, in part, bring together all the components of NUSL's legal design program and to provide law students the opportunity for graduate courses in CAMD to count toward their law degree. Examples of such courses are Prototyping for Experience Design, Art, Context, and Action, Game Design Fundamentals,

Psychology of Play, Designing Infographics, and Web Creation Boot Camp. We see the interdisciplinary field of legal design taking hold in both professions, with its influence and reach expanding.

This is resulting in a concomitant rise in the number of job openings seeking legal design expertise. Many more such jobs see legal design experience as a plus, if not a requirement. The required courses of the certificate provide an opportunity for in-depth study and practice of legal design and its application in specific contexts. This certificate is a logical next step in NUSL's field building efforts. The training provided through this certificate, including coursework, a legal design co-op, and a practical legal design capstone project or paper, will prepare law students to expertly apply legal design methods as innovation in the legal profession accelerates, and position NUSL graduates for the increasing number of postgraduate jobs in the field.

The practice component must be accomplished by doing a co-op at an organization that is engaged with legal design, and where the co-op position is primarily focused on legal design work. The capstone requires substantial work on a project or a substantial piece of writing with a clear connection to the Legal Design Certificate. If project-based, the student must significantly advance a legal innovation project using legal design methods. If a paper, it must meet the requirements of Northeastern Law's Rigorous Writing Requirement. To ease the burden on students, the project or paper may be associated with a course, clinic, moot court, independent study, or a co-op.

13.6 INFLUENCING OTHER LAW SCHOOLS

From the outset of our launch, we have considered ourselves to be in the business of not only educating the legal inventors of the future or crafting legal agency solutions in community but helping build the field in the legal academy and beyond. We therefore have never shied away from engaging with other institutions and individuals who seek to launch their own legal design and/or innovation labs. Examples of such work include early and informal (lunch) conversations with the folks who launched Suffolk Law School's Legal Innovation and Technology Lab (LITLab) and more in-depth early advice to the Innovation for Justice (i4j)[1] program that is housed jointly at the University of Arizona and University of Utah. We have also had ongoing dialogue with the University of Amsterdam's Amsterdam Law Hub and, more recently, The University of Turku's School of Law. Most recently, we have been engaged by Seton Hall School of Law to advise them on their new legal design lab. We consider this work to be vital to the long-term efforts of ensuring recent law graduates from all law schools have a thriving legal design ecosystem in which to engage and create the conditions for the long-overdue work of overhauling

[1] As of the date of this publication, coauthor Dan Jackson sits on the advisory board of i4j.

our legal institutions to be fully responsible to the needs and rights of the people moving through them. We encourage as much of this cross-advising and consultation as possible.

13.7 REFLECTIONS ON PEDAGOGICAL LEARNINGS

Our work on teaching and incorporating design principles to law students and law principles to art students is ongoing and constantly evolving. Through our experiences, we have learned several critical pedagogical techniques that continue to shape our approach to teaching. One such key perspective we have gained is the importance of reflection in the practice of teaching. In education, valuing and incorporating student feedback is widely acknowledged as an effective approach that enhances teaching and learning outcomes. When teachers actively seek feedback from students and adjust their teaching accordingly, it cultivates higher levels of engagement and motivation among students. Student feedback provides valuable insights into effective classroom practices and areas that require improvement. Moreover, integrating student feedback into the reflective process of teachers is essential for the ongoing development and refinement of their teaching methods. Through reflection, teachers can critically evaluate their teaching strategies and identify specific areas for improvement based on the feedback received from students. This reflective practice also deepens teachers' understanding of students' perspectives on the learning environment, enabling them to create a more positive and efficient learning experience.

In summary, incorporating student feedback and engaging in reflective practices are crucial components for teachers to enhance their teaching approach and foster a positive and collaborative learning atmosphere.

We have learned much from opening up the transformative potential of integrating insights from various disciplines into our creative endeavors, resulting in innovative approaches to legal design. By drawing inspiration from fields such as art, technology, and social sciences, we have addressed legal design challenges with refreshed perspectives, ultimately generating distinctive solutions. This dynamic methodology revitalizes our pedagogical techniques, captivates students, and bolsters their motivation.

Additionally, we understand the importance of nurturing students' interests. Our students come to class with concerns and issues they've encountered through their cooperative learning environments, appointments, and past workplace settings. They're eager to transform how legal systems and services function. Encouraging them to explore their passions within the legal design context sparks their creativity and involvement and cultivates a diverse range of perspectives in our classrooms. This teaching approach creates a vibrant and inclusive learning atmosphere, empowering students to passionately pursue their interests.

Furthermore, we've realized that encouraging imagination within traditional law school education is crucial for addressing our students' needs and avoiding situations where innovation comes to a halt due to adherence to established norms or a lack of fresh ideas. By challenging these norms and envisioning new possibilities, students can push legal design boundaries and create inventive solutions. This approach fosters a forward-thinking and resourceful mindset in our students, which is essential for preparing them to tackle the complex challenges present within the legal system.

Collaboration has been a vital component of our teaching approach. By cocreating with students, colleagues, and community partners in the classroom, we've established a rich and diverse learning environment that offers students valuable real-world experiences. This has enabled us to foster a more cooperative and inventive learning atmosphere, where students gain knowledge not only from instructors but also from their peers and the community.

We've recognized the importance of documenting, presenting, and reflecting on our hands-on experiences. By sharing our expertise and insights, we contribute to the larger legal design community and inspire others to innovate in their teaching methods. This not only has let us aid in the growth of the legal design community but also ensures we remain up to date with the latest trends and innovations in the field.

To further our work in teaching legal design, we've set several key objectives. First, we strive to keep our teaching strategies straightforward and accessible, making legal design available to a broader range of students. Second, we're determined to explore every avenue to expand legal design's reach and integration into legal education. Lastly, we aim to collaborate across institutions to elevate the entire field and establish a more innovative legal design community. These goals align with our commitment to fostering a more inclusive, diverse, and inventive legal design community that empowers students to address the intricate challenges of the legal system.

13.8 CONCLUSION

Law schools and students are amid a rapidly evolving legal landscape. The concept of the rule of law itself has faced repeated crises, and it is imperative that legal education addresses these issues head-on. The pedagogy that we have introduced in this chapter taps into both doctrinal learning and movement lawyering, recognizing the need to adapt and respond to the changing nature of law. The flaws and deficiencies in the current law school curriculum are deeply understood, and legal design as an educational approach is undeniably radical. It involves recognizing the structures and limitations of the "master's house," as Audre Lorde (2003) eloquently articulated. The goal is to rebuild that structure, to reimagine legal education in a way that addresses the crises faced by students during periods of significant sociolegal change.

At the same time, the future of legal design education holds immense promise. By incorporating systematic and generative design processes, human-centered design methods, and technology with humanities such as rhetoric, we can empower each generation of legal students to better confront the complex challenges that lie ahead. The integration of legal design into education and practice has the potential to revolutionize the legal field, fostering greater access to justice and transforming the delivery and meaning of legal services in peoples' lives. It can also improve legal outcomes and equip legal professionals to navigate the complexities of the future.

Throughout this transformative process, it is crucial for educators to be mindful of the impact our work and methods have on the members of partnering communities, diverse stakeholders, codesigners, and society as whole. Inclusivity and justice must be central principles guiding the development of a legal system that benefits all individuals. Engaging communities in deliberative rhetoric, speculative design, and futures thinking can yield tangible benefits in the present, as it opens up new pathways for problem-solving and meaningful discussions.

Above all, the principle of dignity must be at the forefront of legal design education. Recognizing the inherent worth and value of each individual is of critical importance for fundamental change to legal education and transformation of the legal system. It is our hope this chapter and book contribute to the ongoing dialogue about dignity as a guiding principle for designing and integrating creativity in legal education and clarify its social purpose. It is crucial that legal education promotes human rights, inclusivity, and justice via design approaches, ultimately striving for a legal system that upholds dignity and serves individuals equitably.

REFERENCES

Aristotle. [4th century BCE] 1992. *Rhetoric*. Edited by George A. Kennedy. Oxford: Oxford University Press.

Bardzell, Jeffrey, and Shaowen Bardzell. 2013. "What Is 'Critical' About Critical Design?" In *Proceedings of the SIGCHI Conference on Human Factors in Computing Systems, Paris, France, April 27 – May 2, 2013*, 3297–306. New York: Association for Computing Machinery.

Bhatnagar, Sankalp. 2022. "What Legal Design Is as Opposed to Could/Should Be." *Proceedings of DRS Biennial Conference Series, Design Research Society, Bilbao, Spain, June 25 – July 3, 2022*. London: Design Research Society.

Cicero, Marcus Tullius. [2nd Century BCE] 1949. *On Invention*. Edited by H. M. Hubbel. Translated by De Inventione. Cambridge, MA: Harvard University Press.

Davis, Martha F. 2015. "Institutionalizing Legal Innovation: The (Re)Emergence of the Law Lab." *Journal of Legal Education* 65, no. 1 (June): 190–206. Social Science Research Network (SSRN).

Doherty, M. 2022. "Disciplinarity and the Modes of Legal Design." *Proceedings of DRS Biennial Conference Series, Design Research Society, Bilbao, Spain, June 25 – July 3, 2022*. London: Design Research Society.

Dunne, Anthony, and Fiona Raby. 2013. *Speculative Everything: Design, Fiction, and Social Dreaming*. Cambridge, MA: MIT Press.

Jackson, Dan, Miso Kim, and Jules Rochielle Sievert. 2020. "The Rapid Embrace of Legal Design and the Use of Co-Design to Avoid Enshrining Systemic Bias." *Design Issues* 36, no. 3 (June): 16–30. https://doi:10.1162/desi_a_00601.

Lorde, Audre. 2003. "The Master's Tools Will Never Dismantle the Master's House." In *Feminist Postcolonial Theory: A Reader*, edited by Reina Lewis and Sara Mills, 25–28. Edinburgh, UK: Edinburgh University Press.

Malpass, M. 2017. *Critical Design in Context: History, Theory, and Practices*. New York: Bloomsbury Publishing.

Pope, H. J. 2022. "Liberatory Legal Design and Radical Imagination." *Proceedings of DRS Biennial Conference Series, Design Research Society, Bilbao, Spain, June 25 – July 3, 2022*. London: Design Research Society.

Santuber, J., and J. A. Edelman. 2022. "Designing with Theories: Producing Legal Design Diffractively in Courts of Justice." *Proceedings of DRS Biennial Conference Series, Design Research Society, Bilbao, Spain, June 25 – July 3, 2022*. London: Design Research Society.

Tharp, Bruce M., and Stephanie M. Tharp. 2018. *Discursive Design: Critical, Speculative, and Alternative Things*. Cambridge, MA: MIT Press.

Walton, P. 2022. "James v Birnmann: The Potential of Critical Design for Examining Legal Issues." *Proceedings of DRS Biennial Conference Series, Design Research Society, Bilbao, Spain, June 25 – July 3, 2022*. London: Design Research Society.

14

The Stanford Legal Design Lab

Margaret Hagan and Kürşat Özenç

14.1 INTRODUCTION

The Stanford Legal Design Lab began in 2013 as a new kind of university organization to advance human-centered innovation in the legal system. It grew out of an idea that there must be a better way for universities – including their students, staff, and faculty – to engage in legal service provision, creation, and reform. In the 2013–14 school year, Margaret Hagan had just graduated from law school and received a one-year fellowship at the Stanford Institute of Design to explore a new venture for legal innovation. She began the prototype of the Lab, then called the "Program for Legal Tech and Design," with her colleague Ron Dolin, as that exploratory new venture. This program held design workshops with the California courts on how to serve self-represented litigants. It organized a design class with Fidelity Investments to redesign estate planning. It cohosted a legal design jam with Wikimedia on how to communicate trademark rules. And it wrote and published materials about how design methods could be used to develop new legal services and organizational change.

After this first "prototype" year, Stanford Law School's Center on the Legal Profession hired Margaret to continue work on this program, and gradually it grew into its own organization within the school, changed its name to the Legal Design Lab, and spun out of the Center to become its own institution within the Law School.

This chapter tells the story of the Legal Design Lab's founding and initial vision. It also reflects on how its mission and methods have evolved over the past decade as our team learned more about our limits and reset our expectations around what impact is possible. We intend this piece to help other academic and practitioner leaders see the opportunity of labs and centers that can be a home for public interest innovation, both for the legal sector and other systems facing wicked challenges. The chapter discusses the role of a university lab for the legal system in depth, but readers coming from other spaces – like systems of health, finances, environment, or otherwise – may consider how a design lab may become a home for public interest work to drive new solutions in their sector.

14.2 WHAT IS A DESIGN LAB DOING AT THE LAW SCHOOL?

The initial vision in 2013 – which remains largely intact a decade on – was that a lab within the university could be a new kind of academic institution that combined education of students, academic research, and engagement with practitioners and policymakers (Katz 2014; Davis 2015; Quintanilla et al. 2019). The lab's mission was threefold: (1) to generate new possible interventions for an improved legal system, (2) to do research about what is needed and what works to improve the system, and (3) to educate students to be leaders who could drive forward access to justice and improved legal organizations.

On the first theme, the lab was inspired by design classes and groups that the team experienced before. In these design or computer science classes, the teams worked to not just draft proposals but to prototype them and make them "real." As opposed to a traditional law school center, a lab would produce things beyond reports, white papers, and events. It would use the design process and an interdisciplinary group to produce new products, services, policies, and other "interventions" in the legal system. The lab would be generative, building new possible solutions.

The lab was to be a dedicated, institutional home to public interest innovation. It would identify key, meaningful wicked problems in the legal system (Buchanan 1992).[1] The lab would have the luxury of being at a university, enabling it to take a long-term, big-picture vision. Rather than having to deal with immediate challenges or launch a new product, the law school lab could work with partners to identify core policy and service challenges in the legal system. Then it could use design methods, legal research, policy work, and other interdisciplinary methods to create new and promising proposals to address these challenges.

On the second theme of evaluation, the lab could also conduct user research, prototype testing, and evaluation that could vet proposals for front-line partners. The lab would not produce white papers that listed off a laundry list of possible solutions. Instead, it would prototype these solutions and put them to the test, to see where resources should be invested. The lab would have a research mission: to evaluate the core needs in a challenge, the performance of different possible interventions, and the outcomes of pilots. The design lab would put innovation processes into action, but with the goal to find "what works" in a given legal system challenge. The university design lab would be a home for public interest innovation rather than commercial innovation that was already happening in start-ups and firms.

[1] Kürşat's doctoral research under Richard Buchanan at Carnegie Mellon University's School of Design was formative in this vision for the lab, particularly this notion of "wicked problems" and how design approaches could resolve them.

The third theme of education was overlaid on top of the design, research, and evaluation "innovation" work. The journey of doing user and policy research, convening stakeholders, drafting new designs, refining them into proposals for a pilot, and evaluating them along the way would be an educational one as well as a practical one. The design process would have educational benefits for the students, for their future careers in legal services, policy, and innovation. It would also be a practical benefit to the practitioners in this space and the members of the public involved in the legal system. The lab would provide a new kind of education to law students (and other undergraduates and graduates interested in the justice system, public interest technology, and legal services). The research, design, and evaluation work would be part of the traditional structures of law school courses, design school courses, and research assistantships for students, but would involve new kinds of educational experiences and outcomes.

The lab is hands-on and practical like a clinic, but it is not about training in traditional legal practice. The practical work in a lab might involve some discussions of legal service provision, like conducting legal research, authoring briefs and letters, or representing clients in court. But most of the lab classes' practical work would be from the position of an "innovator": a professional in a strategic position vis-à-vis the legal organization, who is tasked with analyzing the current services and policies, identifying opportunities, and piloting new solutions. Students in the lab class would learn some of the traditional law school skills of research, writing, and service provision, but they would also learn other skills to become a better leader within the legal system. This new layer of skills involved how to scope out new reform and improvement projects, how to build and lead interdisciplinary teams, and how to develop support, funding, and scale for innovation and reform efforts.

14.3 THE THIRD TRACK FOR LAW STUDENTS

The lab's vision was built around a vision (particularly of the mid-2010s) of a "new" law student. Many other law school technology and innovation ventures also were growing at the time (Hagan, n.d.), with the idea of developing a third pathway in law schools apart from training students aimed toward the first path of corporate legal work or the second path of traditional public interest legal work in government agencies or nonprofits. This new third pathway was discussed in the early 2010s in terms of legal entrepreneurship and technology leadership. How could law schools encourage more of their graduates to explore new business models and ventures? How could schools help them jump-start start-ups to develop new kinds of legal service offerings, or create more jobs in the legal sector?

The Legal Design Lab also was interested in developing new opportunities for law students, especially for those who wanted more control in their careers while still working in the legal system. This mission for a "third track" was born in part out of the lab team's experiences in law school, and the discussions with many of the lawyers who came to the lab's sessions in its formative years. A common theme was around the hope at the start of law school – that a person had worked so hard to enter this graduate program and had chosen this professional path because of a hope to have a positive impact on society and leadership in getting things done at the heart of systems. But the tracks available at law school seemed to channel these people into "the status quo" rather than encouraging them to question how legal organizations operate, how they offer services, and how (or if) they measured their impact on society. The lab became looped into this network of dissatisfied, creative, and visionary lawyers who wanted to spot new ways to "be a lawyer" and to serve those who needed legal services.

The first vision of the lab was to attract more of these students and young professionals early in their careers. If we could have them participate in our workshops, learn in our classes, and take ongoing research assistant positions in our lab, we could help them create a career in the legal system that would give them higher-quality career choices, the ability to create new solutions, and the opportunity to lead organizations that were responsive, innovative, and impactful. They wouldn't have to go work in a legal job where they would feel uncreative and stuck. As part of the lab, they would build a portfolio of innovation work in which they could show that they are capable of facilitating an innovation process, working with engineers, data scientists, and designers, creating and piloting new solutions, and determining which solutions work. As part of the lab work, students were given a privileged place to work with legal organizational leaders and asked to propose new strategies and visions. The goal was to have more of these students then build the skills to play these leadership roles after they graduated, with a portfolio, skills, and connections that could help them jump-start a new career path for themselves.

14.4 THE VISION IN PRACTICE

With this three-themed vision of generating new solutions, evaluating what works, and educating students in new roles and skillsets, the lab set out in the mid-2010s to tackle wicked problems in the legal system. In practice, this meant building partnerships with different kinds of legal organizations. Our strategy was to try out different kinds of relationships with nonprofit, for-profit, and government organizations through short-term workshops. These relationships lasted for approximately three to six weeks, in which our lab team could meet various organizational leaders, hear about their problems and goals, and scope out an initial workshop to go through a design cycle with them. This workshop-based relationship then let our lab see if the organization could demonstrate enough commitment, flexibility, and openness to build a more long-term relationship with. If we found an organization had enough leaders or groups that were committed to piloting new ideas, then we could see that they were aligned with our commitment to impact and not merely trying to use the lab to perform "innovation theater." Through the workshop, we could also see if a partner was open to sharing research findings, ideas, and methodologies with a larger community. Our lab was committed to sharing the best methods and ideas as widely as possible and not trying to make proprietary or exclusive projects for our partners. As an academic institution, we wanted to ensure our partnership would allow students to learn from a committed partner, that our design cycles would lead to impact, and that the lessons learned could be shared widely with an open community of practice.

In our first five years, the lab explored different wicked challenges with initial workshops and then more substantial courses and post-course development cycles. This included extensive work with state courts on improving services for self-help centers and legal aid groups serving litigants without attorneys in family, housing, and debt matters. Other partners included corporate legal teams interested in improving contracting experiences, privacy policy interfaces, and organizational culture. In these various challenges, our team did user research on-site at courts, clinics, firms, and legal aid groups and proposed new communications, services, tech, and policies that could enhance people's sense of dignity, procedural justice, and legal capability (Hagan 2018). Outside of the self-help space, the end-goal also included greater efficiency and predictability of legal processes, improved performance and satisfaction within legal organizations, and stronger ability for people to understand and use legal instruments such as contracts and privacy agreements.

Student and lab staff would dive into specific zones of the legal system, such as guardianships, evictions, debt collection cases, or plea agreement zones. Expert stakeholders would explain how the system currently works, and we would do on-site visits to experience the system, services, and environment firsthand. Students would learn about the legal challenge through some amount of reading, but mostly through stakeholder interviews, observations, empathy sessions, and service and journey mapping. Then the students, guided by the lab staff and the teaching team, would lead the stakeholders through synthesis, brainstorming, idea selection, and prototyping phases.

14.5 ADAPTING THE DESIGN CYCLE TO WORK FOR LEGAL

Each design cycle would build off of previous ones, with lab teams carrying through specific methods, principles, and learnings about how to design legal communications, services, and technology in better ways. In this way, the design cycles gradually began to become more "legal design" cycles than generic design cycles because they incorporated more best practices around solutions for these specific zones of people in a legal system, juggling high-stakes choices, with a large amount of regulation, and difficult legal concepts and processes to navigate (Hagan, n.d.). This was one of the most surprising and satisfying early signs of progress of the lab. Our organization was not just spreading established innovation methods and mindsets into the legal sector (which had been our initial way of working in the first year).

Rather, we were adjusting these methods and creating new ones to work in this specific sector – and even for specific challenge areas within law and government. For example, we started to create specific design principles and patterns for specific legal challenges we would teach and follow alongside the basic design process (Hagan and Kursat 2020).

We also recognized typical design methodologies did not easily adapt to the creation of new laws, policies, and regulation, so we began to develop new methods for policy prototyping along with other leaders in civic innovation (Hagan 2021a). This involved bridging from just those working on courts and legal organizations to partnerships with other innovation teams working for government agencies, nonprofits, and public policy. In the late 2010s, this meant our work began to go beyond developing better communications and websites or apps toward the design of new regulatory structures, policies, and systems. This was in part because of our team's recognition that our interdisciplinary working groups had competencies in policies and laws, but the design cycle still pushed them toward service and communication designs because of how much easier it is to prototype tangible things.

The lab team also focused in on participatory and community-driven design processes to ensure various community stakeholders were prioritized in the redesign of public institutions (Hagan 2019). This commitment to participatory design grew out of a realization that many of our partners were the "leaders" of the legal institutions, and our reflection that legal design should not just consult the "users" of the institutions at certain moments of the design cycle but should empower them to be part of the work and central to key decisions about agenda-setting and pilot selection. Our classes began to try out new lightweight ways to hold pop-up design sessions with legal system users who otherwise wouldn't necessarily sign up to participate in design workshops (Aldunate et al. 2018), and build new partnerships with community organizations to involve more people with lived experience in the design work and decision-making.

14.6 REDIRECTING TO THE NEXT VERSION OF A LAB: GETTING SPECIFIC, SCALED, AND STRUCTURED

After about five years of work in our lab, we reflected on what impact we were having and what kind of work we enjoyed doing. This led us to a few key redirections in our work as a lab, primarily focusing on narrowing our broad vision of work and impact to more specific goals. In particular, we chose to set constraints on all the possible challenges, solutions, and research that we might possibly work on. In the first generation of the lab, we were largely reactive to the organizations interested in partnering. By the five-year mark, we had enough of a reputation and set of relationships that we could be more deliberate in who we worked with and what kinds of projects and pilots we worked on.

One decision was to narrow our thread of legal work to a specific policy area. Rather than jump among many kinds of civil, criminal, and administrative justice matters, we chose to make eviction prevention and housing stability an ongoing theme of our lab's work. The goal here was to build upon our learnings from different design cycles, to gradually home in on an agenda of best practices for legal and government institutions across the country – this is the set of promising practices that can achieve the policy outcomes of reducing eviction rates, increasing people's legal capability in housing issues, and improving people's ability to have stable and safe housing.

In part, this choice to focus on a particular legal challenge was to achieve greater impact. In previous design cycles and coursework, we had created solutions according to our initial theory of change. We made partnerships, we did user research, we found promising solutions (like the design of a new website, or an improved court summons), and we refined them to pilot and evaluate them. But the problem was in scale. Doing one pilot of one idea with one jurisdiction was not enough to create change at large enough scale locally. One pilot is not enough to solve a wicked legal challenge. We realized that it would take a continuum of better communications, services, technologies, and policies. We also found that one part of our theory of change was broken. Just because one jurisdiction would pilot a design successfully did not mean that other jurisdictions would replicate it, even if there were studies, documentation, and evidence of impact. As such, we shifted our design work to focus on developing a "blueprint" of the continuum of the many promising practices that would be needed to make a significant impact on this specific policy goal of eviction prevention.[2]

The other lesson we learned about impact was about scaling partnerships. We enjoyed working with our "early adopter" courts, legal aid groups, and legal organizations. But we wanted to spread the promising pilots to more organizations. And we wanted to develop more leaders in more organizations, who would feel capable of innovation, trying out new pilots, and embracing a designer's sense of user-centered research and design. To this end, we moved away from single partnerships and toward developing communities of practice. For example, we began leading, alongside the National League of Cities, a cohort of multiple courts and regional governments in the Eviction Prevention Learning Lab (National League of Cities & Stanford Legal Design Lab 2021). This cohort approach let us do design work at scale, with multiple organizations going through similar problems. It also let us spread the research findings and promising ideas to pilot with multiple partners at once, so that we were building in the "scale" from the start. We found that more jurisdictions were willing to pilot new service and policy designs if they were part of

[2] See the design work of collecting and spreading new interventions for a specific policy space at our site Eviction Innovation, https://evictioninnovation.org/.

the community of practice rather than an "audience" that was reading about another jurisdiction's efforts after the fact.

A final redirection has been about the pilots the lab works on. In the first version of the lab, we chose specific projects for the lab staff and assistants to see to pilot, and often they were websites, apps, and communication designs. We still do some amount of these kinds of design pilots, but we have found "infrastructure" design projects to be more impactful. University teams are uniquely placed to develop infrastructure, such as data standards, taxonomies, and technical protocols. They are neutral, public interest, and able to work without profit motives or short-term horizons. In many of our projects, our partners were not able to deploy or scale pilots successfully because of the lack of good data and system standards. As such, our lab has taken the design of good common infrastructure as one of its primary goals, with the hope it can provide the base for a better ecosystem of justice innovation by other labs, nonprofits, agencies, and start-ups. For example, we have developed a list of legal problems in the Legal Issues Taxonomy (LIST) project (Hagan 2018), standard Schema markup for website encoding (Hagan 2021b), and e-filing form standards (Stanford Law School 2022). After seeing good ideas fail because of lack of infrastructure, we realized a law school lab could play a key role in building this better foundation for future innovation.

14.7 THE NEXT TEN YEARS

Coming toward a decade of work, the lab will continue to evolve. One possible evolution is to partner with other university labs on research and evaluation work in particular. A lab that is staffed toward generating solutions, managing partnerships, and educating students does not always have the capacity to establish extensive evaluation research designs, such as randomized control trials and extensive data analysis. Other engineering, data science, and policy labs that have grown across campuses do specialize in exactly this work – data-driven, empirical research about what policies and programs work. Our lab hopes to develop ongoing relationships with these evaluation-focused labs, to develop evaluation methods that can work with legal organizations that are piloting our designs (many of them right now do not have capacity or willingness to engage with the standard kinds of randomized control trials). This might involve developing standardized instruments and measures by which to evaluate "what works" in justice innovation, and also designing research protocols organizations feel comfortable with, are ethical, and low-burden enough to deploy regularly.

Another theme for our continuing work is designing national solutions. Based on our previous work in designing with cross-jurisdiction cohorts, we are now focused on finding national leaders that can implement and spread good legal innovations at scale. Making impact on large systemic challenges like "access to justice" requires finding new ways to scale and spread effective ideas, because the model of one judge borrowing an idea from another one does not work efficiently or predictably. Our lab will focus on strategic design, to find or elevate partners that can work at a national level to provide better services, communications, technology, and policies to reach more of the public. As our community of law school labs develops more knowledge about what works, what people need, and how to successfully roll out new designs, we hope to see more national leadership, laws, and incentives to get these innovative services out to serve the public at a large, meaningful scale.

REFERENCES

Aldunate, Guillermo, Margaret Hagan, Jorge Gabriel Jimenez, Janet Martinez, and Jane Wong. 2018. "Doing User Research in the Courts on the Future of Access to Justice." *Legal Design and Innovation*, July 5. https://medium.com/legal-design-and-innovation/doing-user-research-in-the-courts-on-the-future-of-access-to-justice-cb7a75dc3a4b.

Buchanan, Richard. 1992. "Wicked Problems in Design Thinking." *Design Issues* 8, no. 2 (Spring): 5–21. https://doi.org/10.2307/1511637.

Davis, Martha F. 2015. "Institutionalizing Legal Innovation: The (Re)Emergence of the Law Lab." *Journal of Legal Education* 65, no. 1 (June): 190–206. Social Science Research Network (SSRN).

Hagan, Margaret. n.d. "Legal Design Mechanics." *Law By Design*. Accessed August 5, 2023. https://lawbydesign.co/design-mechanics/.

2018a. "Every Legal Problem That Exists: The Legal Help Taxonomy for Machine Learning." *Legal Design and Innovation*, September 4. https://medium.com/legal-design-and-innovation/every-legal-problem-that-exists-the-legal-help-taxonomy-for-machine-learning-3c9f2f75460.

2018b. "Justice Innovation with Law School Design Labs." *ABA Dialogue*, June 15. www.americanbar.org/groups/legal_services/publications/dialogue/volume/21/spring-2018/iolta-design-labs/.

2019. "Participatory Design for Innovation in Access to Justice." *Daedalus* 148, no. 1 (Winter): 120–27. https://doi.org/10.1162/daed_a_00544.

2021a. "Prototyping for Policy." In *Legal Design: Integrating Business, Design and Legal Thinking with Technology*, edited by Marcelo Corrales Compagnucci, Helen Haapio, Margaret Hagan, and Michael Doherty, 9–31. Cheltenham, UK: Elgar Publishing Limited.

2021b. "Standards, Standards, Standards to Advance Justice Innovation." *Legal Design and Innovation*, July 9. https://medium.com/legal-design-and-innovation/standards-standards-standards-to-advance-justice-innovation-31f8fe0ad61e.

Hagan, Margaret, and F. Kursat Ozenc. 2020. "A Design Space for Legal and Systems Capability." *Design Issues* 36, no. 3 (Summer): 61–81. https://doi.org/10.1162/desi_a_00604.

Katz, Daniel M. 2014. "The MIT School of Law? A Perspective on Legal Education in the 21st Century." *University of Illinois Law Review*, no. 5 (October): 101–42. Social Science Research Network (SSRN).

National League of Cities & Stanford Legal Design Lab. 2021. "2021 Eviction Prevention Learning Lab." www.nlc.org/initiative/2021-eviction-prevention-learning-lab/.

Quintanilla, Victor D., Joan Middendorf, Francesca Hoffmann, Emily Kile, Danielle M. Sweet, and Kaelyne Yumul Wietelman. 2019. "Experiential Education and Access-to-Justice within U.S. Law Schools: Designing and Evaluating an Access-to-Justice Service

Learning Program within the First-Year Curriculum." *Indiana Journal of Law and Social Equality* 7, no. 1 (Winter): 88–140. www.repository.law.indiana.edu/ijlse/vol7/iss1/3.

Quintanilla, Victoria D., John Middendorf, Francesca Hoffmann, Emily Kile-Maxwell, Danielle Sweet, and Margaret D. Hagan. 2018. "A Human-Centered Design Approach to Access to Justice Generating New Prototypes and Hypotheses for Intervention to Make Courts User-Friendly." *Indiana Journal of Law and Social Equality* 6, no. 2 (Spring): 199–239. www.repository.law.indiana.edu/ijlse/vol6/iss2/2.

Stanford Law School. 2022. "Filing Fairness Project." Accessed Aug 9, 2022. https://law.stanford.edu/filing-fairness-project/.

15

Graphically Novel

The Role of Visuals in the Legal Design Movement

Kanan Dhru and Kelly Dhru

15.1 INTRODUCTION

"A picture is worth a thousand words." Graphics are the oldest forms of storytelling known to humankind. In terms of communication, visuals have always been more powerful than words. Yet, it has the potential for harnessing complexity, and that has its own advantages. The written word dominates most official legal communication (which, by the way, Socrates had warned us against). The law is not just any written word: it is pages and pages of material that carry legal information in forms which cannot be understood by citizens for whom, ironically, the laws are written. The inaccessibility of rights and obligations buried in black-on-white text silently creates an "access to justice" gap, which is an opportunity for the field of legal design to explore.

The field of legal design, with its commitment to autonomy and dignity, has the potential to transform access to justice gaps by simplifying the law for those for whom it is ultimately written. The significance of this is not to be downplayed. Globally, even prior to the pandemic, 1.5 billion people had unresolved justice problems, as improved data about the size of the global justice gap have revealed (Pathfinders for Peaceful, Just and Inclusive Societies 2021). According to a survey by the World Justice Project, 5.1 billion people – two-thirds of the world population – lack meaningful access to justice (World Justice Project and Pathfinders for Peaceful, Just and Inclusive Societies 2021). Data also show that some groups – for instance, women, children, and youth – are more likely than others to suffer injustice (World Justice Project and Pathfinders for Peaceful, Just and Inclusive Societies 2021). Keeping this in mind, we bring forward the case study of Lawtoons (Figure 15.1), an initiative the authors of this chapter cofounded, which aims to educate children about laws and rights (Lawtoons, n.d.a).[1]

[1] Lawtoons is a pioneering comic book series simplifying laws for children in India. The comic book series has been successfully crowdfunded twice and has been featured across prominent

FIGURE 15.1. "A comic is as a comic does." Image from *Lawtoons 1*.

Legal systems continue to fall short in addressing basic justice issues, and newer thinking and innovation in this space are severely lacking. Existing power dynamics and deeply entrenched incentive structures serve as perfect barriers to change. Sadly, this results in perpetuating strained relationships at various societal levels, erodes trust in public institutions, and exacerbates inequalities. Barriers to accessing legal information also create a burden on resources and people's mental and physical well-being.

Many of these problems can be addressed adequately if relevant legal information is made easily accessible and understandable. Most people hesitate to interact with complex legal texts and the complicated corridors of the justice delivery system. Due to suboptimal ways of communicating legal information to the general population, people feel vulnerable when they need legal support and end up trusting unreliable legal sources.

This chapter focuses on a specific understanding of legal design, namely visual depiction of the law. We argue that while legal design has become a buzzword, there is a need for better clarity in existing discussions about what legal design means. We propose that the legal design community must have, at its very core, the ability to visualise law and make legal information available at scale. Action and tangible tools that operationalise the discipline are needed to promote legal design and increase its impact.

This chapter begins with the prevailing definitions of legal design and sketches out our focus: visual depictions of law through comics supported with storytelling. We also look at the conceptual foundation of legal visualisation and how that breaks away from the traditional "black and white" model of law. We then explore some of

publications and legal design conversations. The books are available in Hindi and English on Amazon for worldwide delivery and have sold thousands of copies to date. The work on Lawtoons started as part of our work at Research Foundation for Governance: in India (RFGI) (Lawtoons, n.d.a; Research Foundation for Governance in India, n.d.).

FIGURE 15.2. Image from *Sentinels of Democracy* showing the importance of every vote based on a real-life story.

the international initiatives within this field and give an overview of the existing state of work in this area. Finally, we focus on Lawtoons as an example of how visual law can further the aims of autonomy and dignity, particularly among populations such as children, making them legal participants through changing the medium of interaction about the law.

What do we think of when we think of law? Usually, it is a bunch of black text on a white background. But a different question is whether words are the best or even the most effective way of communicating what law is and what it means for people.

15.2 LEGAL DESIGN: DEFINITIONAL INCONSISTENCIES OR A WIDENING SCOPE?

The field of legal design has been gaining steady momentum. Global conversations surrounding innovation in the access to and delivery of legal services more actively pay attention to possibilities which legal design offer. Various initiatives – including ones that pertain to simplifying legal language, processes of legal service delivery, or using different visual tools, among others – have been spurring excitement in those who believe the currently available law processes must change. These initiatives also subject themselves to the urgency of those who seek to create more accessible legal services to meet the growing access to the justice gap.

Enthusiasm for these initiatives is what actually lies in the scope of legal design and what forms this emerging discipline. At the outset, the terms *legal* and *design* taken together may seem self-explanatory. The combined term has been formally defined in several different ways. In fact, different organisations and individuals have put forward their own definitions for this term. While there are obvious overlaps, there are also, at times, definitional inconsistencies.

A popular definition of legal design is "the application of human-centered design to the world of law, to make legal systems and services more human-centered, usable, and satisfying" (Hagan n.d.). Legal design is also understood as "a methodology that allows to prioritize legal information and make it more accessible through a visual reading grid" (Remtoulah 2021) or "visual communication from a cognitive perspective" (Deloitte 2021). Additionally, the main goal of legal design is understood to be "restoring the Law to its true strategic and its performative functions in society" (The White Paper n.d.a).

These definitions suggest that understanding what legal design truly is or can be ranges broadly. The scope includes legal systems in their entirety, how a communication is understood, or even a potential expansion towards what functions the law plays in the society. While a vast canvas for legal design has been charted out over time, a growing space of ambiguity is also taking shape on the question of what is or is not legal design. This unfortunately creates room for ideas and initiatives that dilute the focus on what constitutes the very essence of legal design, namely simplification and ease of access. Considering the need for and challenge of scaling legal design endeavours, outlining a consistent definition and scope is important.

15.3 PUTTING STORIES BACK INTO LEGAL DESIGN

It is uncontroversial that law should be clearly communicated for there to be rule of law (Fuller 1969). Insofar as the law presupposes a certain legal knowledge from its participants, one may say there is good in making law known, particularly regarding claims and entitlements that may advance people's welfare. One may even extend this thinking to legal responsibilities, but let us leave that aside for the moment. In a similar vein, ignorance of law is not an excuse for non-compliance.

Significant populations of people are unaware of their legal rights and obligations, let alone understand the nuances of interpretation of complex legal concepts and language. While a central source of law might be a statute passed by the parliament or a decision of the court of law, it is not doubted that not all law is written, and most of law is about social behaviour and norms of legal participants. In fact, one may argue that much of law finds its basis in social practices. If that is the case, then the means to guide behaviour become important. While it is true that some law remains unclear and uncertain, much of the law can be simplified or at least sufficiently accessible to ensure it is fulfilling one of its key functions: guiding conduct (Raz 1979; Endicott 2000). In this context, the role of storytelling that can guide conduct becomes important.

In this respect, one can argue that legal design is a broader term under which one could put "legal visualisation." Within legal visualisation, one may distinguish between designs that aim to represent the legal texts merely visually, compared to stories that aim to guide human conduct or spread awareness about legal principles of fundamental rights.

This essential emphasis on storytelling, which the current range of definitions and initiatives lack, creates a scalable change initiative. In our opinion and experience, this focus is needed to ensure inclusion of examples that provide legal information to those at the margins of society and enhance the idea of dignity as currently understood by most academics researching the field of legal design.

15.4 LEGAL VISUALISATION DESIGN

For the purpose of this chapter, our central case of legal design means visualisation of law (hereinafter "legal visualisation design"), especially through elements of design such as comics, graphics, and storytelling. We specifically focus on these aspects owing to our own experience of starting and running a successful visual law initiative in India, Lawtoons (Lawtoons n.d.a).

The work of legal visualisation design is taking shape in different parts of the world and serves distinct purposes and aims. Efforts are being made to include them as part of the larger umbrella of legal design initiatives (The White Paper n.d.b; Perry Peterson n.d.; The Hague Institute for Innovation of Law [HiiL] n.d.; World Commerce and Contracting n.d.).

Insofar as the aims of existing visual depictions of law go, we find an overwhelming focus on creating visualised (read: simplified) contracts. Innovation labs on legal design across law schools and other private initiatives have created somewhat of a movement to bring visual contracts into the mainstream. We must take a step back and ask: Why is the focus only on private law and contracts? Which contracts are really being visualised here? And how does their simplification aid access to justice and help in advocating for ensuring dignity and rights?

In this light, some examples of legal visualisation design stand out more prominently than others. Creative Contracts from South Africa breaks down contracts in the form of visuals (Creative Contracts n.d.). This is especially effective in countries with low literacy rates and lack of adequate access to formal education, technology, or legal aid centres. Netherlands-based Visual Contracts offers custom legal design to clients and is also developing a platform to make visual contracts at scale (Visual Contracts n.d.).

These two initiatives are worth a mention, especially because they are founder-run enterprises offering legal visualisation design. They are different from other examples of legal visualisation design that provide consultancy services or are projects-based initiatives taking place in an academic or research organisation.

Legal visualisation design initiatives by civil society organisations all over the world have often used visual tools to reach populations that otherwise do not have access to technology or formal education (World Comics India n.d.). Such tools have remained a part of larger awareness campaigns and do not stem from standalone organisations or initiatives that provide visual law as their central offering. Furthermore, many of such examples are created by organisations or are supported by donor agencies based in the Global North for the consumption of those in the Global South. These tools fundamentally rest on assumptions *about* a certain population whose understanding and identification with dignity has a specific context when the *tool* of visualisation of law can have a much broader meaning and scope. While these initiatives are helpful in bridging the access to justice gap, they do not necessarily aid the conversation on reimagining different ways of expressing and understanding the law.

Hundreds of day-to-day laws still need to be simplified and made more easily accessible. While the case to be made for visual tools is an easy one, the scale and proliferation of these initiatives still leave much to be desired. This remains true across most legal jurisdictions. Unfortunately, while the domain of legal design or legal innovation continues to be dominated by the voices from the Global North, especially on social media, important strides are being taken in the other parts of the world. Our initiative, Lawtoons, can be considered one example.

15.5 LAWTOONS: VISUALISING THROUGH COMICS

Can the visual representation of law replace the black-and-white legal language, or can it (merely) substitute it? In the case of public law and fundamental rights, even providing education on certain concepts on which concrete legal provisions are based is useful. The purpose of visualisation of law may differ based on the context. There may be situations, particularly in the case of vulnerable groups, where the significance of visualisation as a medium may be greater. An interesting case study is the role of legal comics for children, who are not otherwise considered legal subjects in the sense of legal participants. While they are beneficiaries of legal rights, the fact they are already aware of their rights gives them more agency than they can otherwise have. This is increasingly important in the context of cyberspace and children's rights more generally, such as prevention from sexual abuse.

And if it is the black-and-white law that is being translated into legal visuals, there is already an interpretative step before law can be visualised, and whether it even has the status of law if it is not in a black-and-white language. In a similar vein, can the law be made so simple that even a ten-year-old child can understand? Perhaps the better question to ask would be: *Should* the law be made so simple that even a ten-year-old child can understand?

15.5.1 *History of Lawtoons*

In India, children study several aspects of legal information as part of the civics education between fifth to tenth standards, corresponding to ages ten to fourteen. Having closely observed varying degrees of engagement of students in civics classes at school, as part of the Research Foundation for Governance in India, we took up outreach activities. During our interactive sessions using storytelling and games on legal education for children, we saw a significant increase in and levels of engagement. We continued to receive requests to organise the sessions from teachers, parents, and largely from the children themselves. One of the ways to meet the overwhelming demand was to create a uniform tool which could reach a large number of kids even without our presence. After some thinking, we thought of creating a comic book on law for the kids. This helped us to transcend the medium of text alone, and we embraced visualisation of law.

> Law and Design are not often brought up in conversation with each other. This is a loss to both fields. Superficially, design and law could not be more different. Law is text-heavy and often quite abstract. Design implies visualization and emphasizes human elements of any situation. But Design and Law share a fundamental purpose — to shape how humans act and interact with each other. (Hagan n.d.)

Executing the idea of bringing law and design together had a steep learning curve. We had to throw ourselves in the deep end of comic design and the use of visualisations to express an idea, and we had to familiarise ourselves with the working methodology of the artists. The final product has been well received and has included positive media reviews (Lawtoons n.d.b). Most importantly, when we showcased the Lawtoons to the children in schools, all of the students preferred reading about law in the Lawtoons comic book compared to their textbook lesson (Figure 15.3). Additionally, 70% of the kids surveyed retained the legal information mentioned in the comic.[2] Through these reviews and word of mouth, we were able to collaborate with a publisher, Vani Prakashans, based in New Delhi.

One important aspect in the general discussion around legal visualisation design is the opportunity to target vulnerable populations through this medium. Children, who have a special interaction with the legal system as beneficiaries of legal protections, can be even more closely included through such a form of communication about the laws and rights that affect them. The benefits of comics extend to other vulnerable groups including young adults and new voters. The purpose of creating Lawtoons was to ensure that people, especially children, could understand and interact with the law consistent with what is considered permissible by the law. Working with children gives an opportunity to engage with the young minds towards developing an interest to understand and interact with law from a young age.

For example, the United Nations Convention on the Rights of the Child regards children as right-holders, and there is a case to be made for the importance of legal literacy among children as legal participants (United Nations 1989). The same could be true of other vulnerable groups that require more agency and accessibility in legal participation.

One crucial dimension in the context of Lawtoons is that the target audience has been minors between the ages of ten and fourteen. While traditionally whether children can be legal right-holders or indeed responsibility-bearers has been

[2] We surveyed a total of 250 students across three different schools in Ahmedabad.

FIGURE 15.3. Cover of the book *Lawtoons*, the first compendium on Fundamental Rights under the Indian Constitution.

controversial (MacCormick 1976). The fact is, children are already exposed to a wide variety of civic issues, and their interaction in society, especially in a technologically rapidly developing society, requires they understand their rights and obligations.

15.5.2 *Scaling Lawtoons: The Election Commission Project*

It has been observed over time that new ideas and initiatives that attempt to make legal information accessible and simple for people to understand do not scale (Dhru 2021). Oftentimes, new ideas find themselves fighting strong power holders and are ultimately nipped in the bud or are not supported so they may flourish.

However, our experience with Lawtoons has shown interesting results. The project allowed us to engage with public- and private-sector entities that were interested in simplifying specific laws with the use of visualisation. This included the Canadian Embassy, Swapath Trust – a civil society organisation working on children's rights – and even the Election Commission of India (ECI). The ECI especially wanted to educate new voters and those from remote areas about the possibilities of voter registration. Lawtoons was commissioned to create stories to make the electoral registration–related laws more accessible.

The project *Sentinels of Democracy* was created by the partnership of the Election Commission of India and Lawtoons to empower first-time and remote voters in India, the world's largest democracy (Dhru and Dhru 2017; see also Nair 2017). The

FIGURE 15.4. Cover of *Sentinels of Democracy*, a comic book simplifying election-related laws for citizens of India.

comic book reached millions of users in its very first print run (Figure 15.4). In terms of scale, we were able to tap into the gigantic reach of the public sector. For example, 1.5 million copies of Lawtoons were distributed in the first print run of the Election Commission project. This result made a strong case for how a multi-stakeholder collaboration can bring an innovation by a small creative team to a large number of people.

15.6 LEGAL DESIGN: UNITED BY THE COMMON CHALLENGES AND BARRIERS TO GROWTH

Definitional inconsistencies apart, the overall uptake of legal design as such remains low. Even the most well-funded and popularised examples have, at the very best, remained at the level of pilots or consulting projects. Legal information across the world continues to style itself in bulky cumbersome text, desperately seeking simplification and yet, sadly, failing the scale its needs or deserves.

Legal design services mainly are either provided by academic institutions or take the form of consulting organisations as a tool or service, or are at times offered even by start-ups or civil society organisations. The interest of private investors has not yet been significant, and government interventions so far have been minimal.

Lately, the consulting on legal design services is generating much-needed hope for a transformation. The advantage of these interventions is that there is a dedicated clientele to which a clear value proposition is offered. There are also several institutional entities that are actively looking to better design their legal documents. However, the conversion of entities to the discipline of legal design is steady but slow at best, especially compared to some of the other areas where legal services are being innovated and reimagined (Metinko 2021).

Over time, initiatives to bring legal design into courtrooms and efforts to make a more user-friendly legal experience have generated much-needed movement. Sadly, many such initiatives have stagnated at the pilot stage. Perhaps these interventions miss the relevant buy-in from the public sector and lack enactment of policies that can make these efforts sustainable and scalable.

We also see that, in the last few years, there has been a growing number of labs and conversations focusing on legal design (Hagan 2018). While a majority are at universities situated in the Global North, this is a welcome addition to the movement. Of course, a more concrete focus is needed to develop legal visualisation design initiatives in parts of the world with high illiteracy rates, which prevents a large number of people from affording legal dignity.

Through conversations and owing to our own work at Lawtoons, we have come to understand the following broad reasons behind the limited prevalence of this discipline.

15.6.1 *Lack of Formal Enforceability or Measurability*

Most of the legal visualisation design initiatives are still in nascent stages. While the community of practitioners and believers in principles of legal design is growing, a persisting challenge is that since the field reimagines the very fabric of the written law, practitioners are often met with questions around legal tenability and formal enforceability. For example, the question "Would a court of law accept the legal document that has been converted into visual form?" remains pressing. There are still those who doubt the validity of legal information that has been visualised, and ideas of comics and graphics may trivialise the complexities that are at times needed to allow for required nuance. Different analyses that observe the journey of an organisation working toward justice innovation show the legal lobby with strong connections to bar associations make it difficult for the status quo to change.

Additionally, visualisation of law raises exciting challenges for the legal system, such as what kind of legal interpretation might be required in such contexts. However, a silver lining is that, over time, the legal validation has been gaining momentum for legal documents represented visually. For example, Robert French, the former Chief Justice of Australia, clarified the question around legal enforceability of visual and plain-language contracts, wherein he stated how user-friendly contracts can help to bring the necessary validity and formal sanction for easier adoption (French 2017).

15.6.2 *Absence of a Strong Business Model*

The field of legal design struggles with finding a revenue model that works. Visualisation is an expensive proposition, and the business can only work if a certain scale of operations is achieved. However, the current initiatives that operate as businesses providing legal visualisation design are still in their nascent stages. This is also supported by our own experience of founding and running Lawtoons, where we experienced and have seen funding challenges as being one of the key barriers to growth and stability for legal visualisation design. Limited uptake by private entities, including law firms, makes donor dependencies quite high to meet the visualisation expenses. The entity offering the visualisation services also affects the duration and scale of the service offered. For example, those running the initiatives through donor funding (or start-ups that begin with grants or winning competitions) also suffer owing to the irregularities of such funding. This does not help to create a stable organisation. In turn, this prevents initiatives from scaling up to provide their products and services to a larger number of people. Over time, many initiatives have ended up closing or pivoting to providing visualisation of other information, not legal information, to stay afloat.[3]

3 Names are purposely withheld. This phenomenon merits more research to understand why legal visualisation design, or legal design in general, has not yet achieved the desired scale.

15.6.3 *Interdisciplinarity*

For legal visualisation design to be successful, it needs to work in an interdisciplinary manner across the fields of law and design. The disciplines of law and design operate differently and require different methods and forms of communication. Combining these two disciplines makes legal visualisation design difficult to achieve. There are many interpretive steps between how lawyers understand the law and what the illustrators end up visualising. It is not always easy to find visualisation experts who can understand the task of decoding complex legal information to present it in ways that can be palatable to audiences. Lawyers who can successfully simplify the relevant legal information effectively are also rare. A lot gets lost in translation, and this does not result in good final outcomes. The not-so-straightforward relationship between lawyers and designers is one of the central challenges for the initiators of legal design projects. And, truth being told, well-meaning intentions of the founders are not sufficient to help deliver quality products that can have a mass appeal. To understand the impact and palatability of the legal visualisation design outcomes, it is important to examine how different initiatives work across sectors.

15.7 CONCLUSION

In this chapter, we analysed the concept of legal design, focused on visual law through comics, and distinguished the different ways in which legal design may be understood. We argued that the scope can go far beyond the visual depiction of contracts and into the field of storytelling. We analysed the challenges inherent in going beyond private law and particularly focused on our experience with Lawtoons.

We have shown that some of the initiatives that often go unnoticed in usual conversations have actually been able to provide visual legal information to the people on the last mile. These initiatives include examples of successful public–private partnerships, which bring to the table the innovative and creative thinking of private individuals and provide it with scale and impact that only the public sector can bring. Additionally, we have also presented some of the barriers which limit the scale of the existing legal visualisation design initiatives.

REFERENCES

Creative Contracts. N.d. "Homepage." Accessed January 10, 2023. https://creative-contracts.com.

Deloitte. 2021. "Legal Design: The Science Behind Visual Design." www2.deloitte.com/content/dam/Deloitte/nl/Documents/legal/deloitte-nl-deloitte-legal-design-offering.pdf.

Dhru, Kanan. 2021. "Use of Digital Technologies in Judicial Reform and Access to Justice Cooperation." *The Hague Institute for Innovation of Law (HiiL)*. www.hiil.org/projects/digital-technology-and-judicial-reform/.

Dhru, Kanan, and Kelly Dhru. 2017. "Sentinels of Democracy." https://ceodelhi.gov.in/eLearningv2/admin/EnglishPDF/1.-Sentinels-of-Democracy.pdf.

Endicott, Timothy Andrew Orville. 2000. *Vagueness in Law*. Oxford: Oxford University Press.

French, Robert. 2017. "Closing Address: Comic Book Contracts Conference." Paper presented at Comic Book Contracts Conference, University of Western Australia, December 8, 2017. www.law.uwa.edu.au/__data/assets/pdf_file/0011/3442655/8.-French-Closing-Address.pdf.

Fuller, Lon L. 1969. *The Morality of Law*. New Haven, CT: Yale University Press.

Hagan, Margaret. n.d. "Legal Design." *Law By Design*. Accessed August 5, 2023. https://lawbydesign.co/legal-design.

2018. "Justice Innovation with Law School Design Labs." *ABA Dialogue*, June 15. www.americanbar.org/groups/legal_services/publications/dialogue/volume/21/spring-2018/iolta-design-labs/.

The Hague Institute for Innovation of Law (HiiL). n.d. "Innovating Justice." Accessed February 10, 2023. www.hiil.org/programmes/the-justice-accelerator/.

Lawtoons. n.d.a. "Lawtoons: Making Laws Simple." Homepage. Accessed January 10, 2023. www.lawtoons.in.

n.d.b. "Lawtoons in Press." Accessed February 10, 2023. www.lawtoons.in/press/.

MacCormick, Neil. 1976. "Children's Rights: A Test-Case for Theories of Right." *Archives for Philosophy of Law and Social Philosophy* 63, no. 3: 305–17. JSTOR.

Metinko, Chris. 2021. "Legal Tech Makes Its Case with Venture Capitalists, Tops $1B in Funding This Year." *Crunchbase*, September 23. https://news.crunchbase.com/venture/legal-tech-venture-investment/.

Nair, Avinash. 2017. "EC Comic on Poll Process Draws Out Lone Voter in Gir Forest, Other Tales." *Indian Express*, June 20. https://indianexpress.com/article/india/ec-comic-on-poll-process-draws-out-lone-voter-in-gir-forest-other-tales-4712639.

Nair, Rahul. 2017. "Watch: Law Can Be Confusing, but These Comic Books May Help." *The Quint*, December 11. www.ceodelhi.nic.in/eLearningv2/admin/EnglishPDF/1.-Sentinels-of-Democracy.pdf.

Pathfinders for Peaceful, Just and Inclusive Societies. 2021. "Reimagining Social Contracts: A Call to Put People at the Center of Justice." *Joint Letter to the UN Secretary-General*, April 14. www.justice.sdg16.plus/ministerial.

Perry Peterson, Andrea. n.d. "Podcast." Accessed January 9, 2023. www.andreaperrypetersen.com.au/podcast/.

Raz, Joseph. 1979. *The Authority of Law: Essays on Law and Morality*. Oxford: Clarendon Press.

Remtoulah, Shayan. 2021. "What Is Legal Design? Definition and Application Examples." *Your-Comics*, January 25. https://your-comics.com/en/article/definition-legal-design-14.html.

Research Foundation for Governance in India (RFGI). n.d. "Homepage." Accessed January 10, 2023. http://rfgindia.org/.

United Nations. 1989. "Convention on the Rights of the Child." Treaty Series 1577 (November): 3. www.ohchr.org/en/instruments-mechanisms/instruments/convention-rights-child.

Visual Contracts. n.d. "Homepage." Accessed January 10, 2023. https://visualcontracts.eu.

The White Paper. n.d. "Legal Design." Accessed January 10, 2023. https://legaldesign-community.com/definition?lang=en.

World Commerce and Contracting. n.d. "Homepage." Accessed January 10, 2023. www.worldcc.com.

World Comics India. n.d. "Homepage." Accessed February 10, 2023. www.worldcomicsindia.com/.

World Justice Project and Pathfinders for Peaceful, Just and Inclusive Societies. 2021. "Grasping the Justice Gap: Opportunities and Challenges for People-Centered Justice Data." Working paper. https://worldjusticeproject.org/our-work/publications/working-papers/grasping-justice-gap.

16

Building Technology with(out) People

Steven Geofrey

16.1 INTRODUCTION

The future of higher education is, unavoidably, defined in technological terms. Once limited to computer science alone, technology-based skills are now found widely across the curricula of disciplines well outside of the sciences and engineering, motivated by a push to infuse traditionally nontechnical disciplines with new computing literacies for the digital age (Kafka 2020). Variably advertised through interdisciplinary monikers like "digital humanities," "data journalism," "digital art and media," and other domains, these hybridized offerings reflect the nimbleness with which such disciplines have welcomed the adoption of digital methods, opening new directions for practice and research. But they also point to a collectively experienced anxiety: that technology is rapidly changing, and professions must keep up with the pace. Pushing these professional practices into new technological directions becomes not just an opportunity to reap the benefits of digitization but ultimately a summoning to modernize and future-proof. Otherwise, the messaging proclaims, professions risk being rendered irrelevant or even obsolete in a future where their work can be replicated quickly and cheaply by machines (Aoun 2017).

This push toward technological skills has also extended to the legal profession. In the past decade, courses dedicated to teaching computational methods and technical skills to practitioners of law have spread across colleges and universities throughout the United States. Many of these courses have a skills-based focus and emphasize learning the basics of programming, frequently proffered in the name of helping lawyers become more efficient, technologically literate, and simply "better" practitioners. One example of this, from a course named "Computer Programming for Lawyers" at Georgetown University, captures the central argument about why the legal profession should care about programming:

> The argument, I explain, is that every single lawyer – regardless of area of substantive speciality [*sic*] or style of practice – could become a more efficient lawyer if they

> learned some rudimentary computer programming skills. The argument builds on the observation that every lawyer processes information as a part of their job . . . Yet lawyers use an impoverished set of tools for obtaining, cleaning, and organizing all of this information: primarily word processors and search engines (Westlaw, Lexis, and Google). Sophisticated lawyers – including those at high-paying law firms – might supplement these tools and skills with spreadsheets and document management systems. But few lawyers use anything more powerful or sophisticated than these. (Ohm 2018)

The argument is predicated upon the observation that the conventional practices of law are impoverished by the use of antiquated, and thus inadequate, tools. If only those tools were modernized, then legal practice could be made more efficient and therefore more effective. Across other courses that similarly train future lawyers in digital skills, this argument is echoed in different words: in one course, programming is lauded in economic terms as "a good way to automate tedious or repetitive work, which can save you days or weeks of time" (Winge 2022); in another, programming has professional development value as a skill that "helps you understand and advise clients involved in the creation or use of technology," because the experience of learning such skills "helps you understand the technical culture, and removes a great deal of the mystery that can otherwise surround technological issues by opening the black box" ("Programming" 2016). In many of these courses, the tools of the trade become Python, R, regular expressions, and APIs, applied to common tasks like "caselaw and docket searching, data analysis of government websites, and statutory interpretation based on complex damage calculations" ("Computer Science for Lawyers" 2022). In the process, prospective graduates of these law programs become equipped to leverage technology to better their practice, giving them a competitive edge in an already competitive profession.

There is no question that technical skills have their place – an essential one that is both practical and economic – in a profession such as law that continues to evolve in parallel with the technologies that serve it. The utility of such skills is indisputable as the systems, institutions, and practices of law, like many other domains of professional practice, grapple with a rapidly transforming technological landscape. Technical skills and digital tools can and do improve the quality of research and practice of many disciplines and professional practices besides law, demonstrated by the popularity of cross-disciplinary training courses in digital methods like Software Carpentry, which has the mission of "teaching researchers the computing skills they need to get more done in less time and with less pain" (Software Carpentry, n.d.). Digital transformation is understood as pervasive and inevitable, regardless of disciplinary or technical background.

But without critical examination, this skills-forward approach to introducing technology to professions, legal and otherwise alike, runs the risk of becoming normative, prescriptive, and guided by a system of values that may be in tension with the values of the profession itself. It becomes premised upon the triumph of new over old, and of powerful over impoverished, characterized by the same colonialist and technologically deterministic episteme from which such skills are derived (Chun 2021). In law practice, the consequences of such risks cannot be understated. In getting tangled up in what technology can do for the profession here and now, technical pedagogy in law risks succumbing to a slippage within the proclaimed allure of technical skills to propel the profession into the digital age. The reality is that instrumentalizing those skills also carries the potential to subvert the values of the profession itself, if the values appropriated from technological contexts are not called out. Ultimately, when the value of teaching "technology" in a nontechnology profession becomes discursively constituted in that profession in the same techno-solutionist terms from which it has been adopted, any discussion of which values get imported along the way gets displaced by an overemphasis on skills-building, assuming that any discussion of values comes later.

Leaving the discussion of values for later is dangerous; it loses sight of a future in which the free rein of such technology has the potential to compromise the fundamental values of legal practice. Many disciplines that have already taken the leap into technology-based methods have thoroughly documented the tensions that arise when the adoption of those methods, and the values attached to them, collide with the traditional methods of the discipline. These caveats range from ethical considerations that call into question the nature of a practice itself to full-blown identity crises that destabilize a domain's sense of self. In data journalism, for example, the adoption of digital forms of storytelling and data-driven reporting has raised questions about what happens when the competencies required for quality data-driven storytelling – rigorous statistical reasoning and data analysis – are under-developed in newsrooms under the pressure to get stories out quickly, compromising the core values of integrity that are foundational to the profession (Cairo 2014). In digital humanities, debates abound about whether there is even a viable place for digital methods in humanities disciplines, creating a sharp divide between digital and analog methods that is rendered especially visible in spaces where the definition of *data* is contentiously debated ("Debates in the Digital Humanities" 2022). In one critique, a clarion call proclaims the fundamental tension at play in the datafication of humanities methods: "*Data are capta*, taken not given, constructed as an interpretation of the phenomenal world, not inherent in it," writes Johanna Drucker. Any assumption that data – and the digital conceptualizations of the world that accompany them – do represent objective fact, Drucker asserts, would be in violation of the hermeneutical orientation of humanities methods (Drucker 2011).

These conflicts arise because of what happens when technology, data, and digital methods are imported into spaces that predate the digital turn: the values that are embedded in the technology that is imported operate in tension with the fundamental values of the practice seeking to adopt them. These, too, are warning signs for the practice of law, as the adoption of technology is certain to continue. As technology becomes more deeply integrated into law curricula, it is not enough for curricula to teach tools purely for the sake of making the work of law more efficient, or to modernize the profession by equating the word "digital" with sophistication. Rather, what is needed is an equally prioritized self-awareness of how even seemingly benign technology can complicate the identity of the profession itself. In law, this self-awareness takes the form of a dispositional sensitivity toward the values attached to technology and technical approaches. It requires a critical, inquiry-driven orientation to how technology is designed, employed, and shaped by institutions that historically have been rooted in values that are antithetical to legal values of autonomy, agency, self-determination, and dignity. And given the proximity of law practitioners to the key legal and social issues of modern technology – privacy, surveillance, and extractive data practices, to name only a few – lawyers are perhaps uniquely poised to respond in radical ways to such value tensions, designing precisely the kinds of interventions required to transform technology in support of legal values outside the entanglements of corporate, commercial, and Silicon Valley interests (Chang 2019; Waldman 2021).

When questions of values become implicated in encounters with technology in the context of the legal profession, being literate practitioners of that technology is not only an epistemic imperative but also an ethical one. Technology, and the systems of practice in which we encounter it, co-constitute one another. As new stewards of technology-based practice, how can the legal profession reclaim the agency to command its own encounters with technology and interact with this intrinsic complexity, when that technology has been designed outside the values of law? To answer this question, we need to understand that the path leading to this point is situated in a longer epistemological arc that privileges digital values of order, simplicity, and objectivity over disorder, complexity, and subjectivity (Daston and Galison 2010).

16.2 VALUE TENSIONS

The word "digital," as part of our daily vernacular, denotes anything related to computers or machine-based technology. But the meaning of this word predates the modern sense of digital technology, in which digital systems are built upon exchanges of bits on engineered hardware. Instead, it points to a deeper epistemological shift around sense-making, one that prioritizes division and partitioning, whereby continuous and complex phenomena are decomposed into well-defined units of meaning that can be related to one another by consistent ratios. In *The Design Way*, Erik Nelson and Harold Stolterman offer an immediate example by considering our orientation to time and space: we divide days into hours, minutes, and seconds, and we divide land into grids. Both forms of subdivision take the continuous world and break it down into units of functional value that are indifferent to social habitation or natural terrain. In turn, these are digital approaches to organizing the living world that assume continuous and messy dimensions of human experience can be controlled and stabilized by discretizing them (Nelson and Stolterman 2012).

Nelson and Stolterman summarize this approach in terms of its emphasis on separation: "The digital approach divides information into packets that are stable and congruent but detached from the qualities of the substance or event itself" (Nelson and Stolterman 2012, 18). Importantly, it has been a pervasive force in the design of technology, often becoming a principle of design itself. To find examples of this, consider two often cited and desirable qualities in the design of technological systems: scalability and efficiency. Designing technology to be scalable and efficient optimizes performance of that technology while minimizing cost (in time, energy, resources, or money). But while these values are intrinsic to the world of machines, they operate less neutrally in the world of human experience. In *On Nonscalability: The Living World Is Not Amenable to Precision-Nested Scales*, Anna Tsing offers a critique of what happens when this same technological value of scalability is recycled in our relationship to the natural world and to social and political institutions of authority, arguing that ontological incompatibility between the domains of humans and machines produces dangerous epistemological slippages. Tsing defines a system that is *scalable* as one that is capable of growing in geometric ways, without distorting the framework in which it is designed. According to Tsing, the goal of scalability is to organize phenomena into *precision-nested scales*, which presumes cleanly hierarchical relationships between phenomena that are exhaustively representative of the total range of experience. "Because computers zoom across magnifications," Tsing writes, "it is easy to conclude that both knowledge and things exist by nature in precision-nested scales." But coercing the living world into scalable terms sacrifices indeterminate heterogeneity for precision, leaving the complexity of human experience by the wayside. Tsing writes, "Scalability is, indeed, a triumph of precision design, not just in computers but in business, development, the 'conquest of nature' and, more generally, world making." Scalability does not operate in the world of manufactured experience alone; it reflects a general attachment to coercing the living world into units of value that are measured in scalable ways (Tsing 2012).

In short, discretizing the complexity of human experience into scalable terms is not a philosophy constrained to business or computers. It is an entire orientation to world-making that is glamorized – perhaps even fetishized – by technologies that privilege forms of knowledge that are representationalist, assuming there is a world "out there" that can be captured in an exhaustively descriptive representation. But, as Tsing alludes, human experience is not clean, orderly, or entirely rational. The assumptions that get built into a digital orientation to the world get translated into the design of technologies that enable that orientation, having a hegemonic influence over technology's way of ordering and categorizing human experience.

The practice of law is concerned precisely with this world of human experience; it is not concerned with the world of computers. And yet because of the blurring of lines between them as technology increasingly defines the world of human experience, key values of legal practice – including self-determination, autonomy, and agency – are threatened by the assumptions of digital forms of representation. When this epistemological orientation toward representation is reified through the same technologies that are reshaping the practice of law, it seems only prudent to question whether those technologies support the values of the profession itself.

If this sounds alarmist, consider the basis of the legal profession. The law is intended to be impartial, just, and neutral, guided by the pursuit of equity and justice: properties that extend to the systems and institutions through which we encounter the law. But there are examples throughout history of the law being designed in ways that are not fundamentally neutral or objective; the law, having been designed by human hands, embeds the values of the social and political contexts in which it arises. Interactions with technology, much like law in this way, are thus interactions with a form of world-making. As Melvin Kranzberg posits, "Technology is neither good nor bad; nor is it neutral" (Kranzberg 1986). Having been designed by human hands, technology can tell us much about the norms, values, and philosophies of who or what created it.

This interactional stance, one in which technological design and use co-constitute one another, is well defined in recent design frameworks and theorizations. One such example is value-sensitive design. "Unlike approaches that lean toward technological determinism or social determinism," Batya Friedman and David Hendry write, "interactional theories such as value sensitive design posit that human beings acting as individuals, organizations, or societies shape the tools and technologies they design and implement; in turn, those tools and technologies shape human experience and society" (Friedman and Hendry 2019). The authors articulate that one implication of the interactional stance is that the design of technology matters as much as technology itself. "That is, values can be embodied, at least to some extent, within the features of a tool or technology" (Friedman and Hendry 2019).

When we recognize that our encounters with technology are embodied in systems, epistemologies, and values that privilege certain forms of encounters over others, being technology-literate demands something deeper than the skills requisite to write code, analyze data, or interact with APIs. Rather, it requires that we ask hard questions about the value tensions that emerge in those encounters. It demands a sensitive awareness of how the application of such technical skills represents more than a utilitarian execution of a task, but rather – and more importantly – a reflexive interaction between technology and practitioner. And this locus of reflexivity – where technology and practitioner are transformed and constituted in tandem – is precisely the powerful starting point for law practitioners to critique the cultural and epistemological values attached to these methods, and to design interventions that reimagine the use of technology in law in human-centered ways.

16.3 BUILDING TECHNOLOGY, WITH AND WITHOUT PEOPLE

Critiques of the ways in which technology capitalizes upon, reinforces, and reproduces exploitative and techno-solutionist values abound, and more have begun to enter mainstream public awareness. Grounding these critiques in more concrete terms in the context of legal practice requires considering what happens in learning technical skills. Often, technical skills are presented pedagogically as being inherently value-free and neutral. But as Hendry notes, such assumptions elide responsibility for how technology informs human experience:

> In technical education, students might pursue design and engineering projects in a largely value-neutral manner. However, technical projects, along with the tools and technologies they produce, are not value-neutral. To the contrary, tools and technologies make some goals easier to obtain and others harder, support some human experiences and values but not others, lead to unanticipated value tensions, and so forth. Thus, in general, tools and technologies unavoidably shape human experience. At the same time, when a technology is introduced into society, people and institutions adapt, leading to new practices, norms, and policies. (Hendry 2020)

The law profession, principally concerned with human agency and dignity, should be seriously concerned with this relationship. If technology plays some role in shaping human behavior, then instruction in technical skills by itself fails to acknowledge the potential harms those skills can have on shaping human dignity itself. To counteract this effect, law schools should move away from instruction that is constrained solely to teaching technical skills and toward instruction that situates those skills in larger social, political, cultural, and epistemological contexts.

A useful starting point for this shift is the acknowledgment that there is an important difference between skills that are purely *technical* and skills that are *technologically situated*. Technical skills prioritize solving problems, in a techno-solutionist sense; they see the world as a collection of problems that can and should be solved through code or data, encouraging a mindset of *computation for the sake of computation* and a "build fast and break things" mentality. As Wendy Hui Kyong Chun describes in *Discriminating Data*, one of the enduring aspects of this conceptualization of technology is its disembodied nature; it collapses diverse identities, needs, and experiences into discrete, categorizable personas (Chun 2021). In this way, privileging technical skills emphasizes the value of building technology *without* people: without factoring in human bodies, and without factoring in human needs.

But as many revelatory accounts of the failures of technology have illuminated, building technology without people produces downstream problems that conflict with human agency and dignity. For example, *Design from the Margins* articulates what happens when technology built without people must be retrofitted in its design to meet the needs of populations characterized as "extra needs" that are not factored into the original design. As a framework, designing from the margins privileges the consideration of decentered populations in the design of technology, designing from the outside and moving inward to ensure more inclusive and equitable aims. "The decentered include subpopulations who are the most impacted and least supported; they are often those that face highest marginalization in society, without legal, social or political support structures," Afsaneh Rigot writes. "In turn, they are often the most criminalized and at risk of having technology weaponized against them." This approach to designing technology is not only about ensuring justice and equity but also about reducing the risk of harm. "Still today," Rigot notes, "many technologies are built and then scaled in contexts they were not designed for; they are creating large-scale harms as they expand" (Rigot 2022).

In contrast, technologically situated skills prioritize systems thinking, encouraging inquiry into the value embeddings of technology and of the contexts in which it is designed and used. This shift toward a systems-based understanding of technology naturally invites design into the discussion of technology, and there are many design frameworks from which the practice of law can adopt strategies to critique the role technology plays in specifically legal contexts. For example, the civic technology sector's mantra of "design with, not for" offers a participatory design framework that centers human experience and the effects technology has on communities, folding an ethos of *building with* into technological design that is often absent from standard technology design culture (Ward and Bruce 2022). Meanwhile, the framework of design justice, offered by Sasha Costanza-Chock, provides a basis for deconstructing the ways that design "reproduces and/or challenges...white supremacy, heteropatriarchy, capitalism, ableism, settler colonialism, and other forms of structural inequality," values which themselves get embedded in technological design (Costanza-Chock 2020). Costanza-Chock takes it as given that reimagining design requires retooling, as the existing tools of design will only reproduce existing ways of being and systems of values. The practice of law, too, can consider its own retooling in this way, examining whether the standard tools and methods taught through technical skill instruction adequately afford the design of technology in pursuit of human dignity, or if they reproduce the same values that legal practice fights against.

The frameworks of design for transitions and autonomous design take this ethos a step further by reimagining what it means to be human, and how design, as world-making, participates in that reimagining. In *Designs for the Pluriverse*, Arturo Escobar situates the discussion of these frameworks by articulating a new conceptualization of design practice – *ontological* design practice – as a radical alternative to and critique of the unsustainable and de-futuring practices of modernist approaches to design. Taking ontology (world-making), design (ethical praxis of world-making), and politics (individual autonomy) as the starting point for this reimagined practice, Escobar argues that the intersection of these three axes yields a framework for designing for human experience that reclaims radical interdependence and relational values as central (Escobar 2018). Technology, too, has much to learn from this recentering, and practitioners of law are positioned to reimagine how technology can be designed to support human flourishing and agency in radically capacious ways.

Shifting from a techno-solutionist framing of *building technology without people* to a technological values orientation of *building technology with people* affords many opportunities to redesign technology in ways that break the status quo values dominantly prescribed by the tech industry. And the legal profession is well poised to leverage these affordances to redesign such technology in support of human agency and dignity. Preparing lawyers to operate generatively in this space of possibility, then, requires a reimagining of what technology instruction can look like in legal curricula.

16.4 ENCOURAGING TECHNOLOGICALLY SITUATED SKILLS

When defined in arguments of efficiency, power, and modernization, technical instruction in law encourages an orientation of building technology without people. But this orientation renders invisible key value tensions that exist between technological design and law practice, tensions that pose a reflexive threat to legal practice if left unchecked. To avoid this, law curricula that teach technical skills can move toward nourishing a mindset that privileges building technology with people, by designing pedagogy that leans into an awareness of the situatedness of technological skills. The following are strategies that law schools can consider to couple instruction in technical skills with the development of a critically reflective practice around those skills that reveals, and intervenes in, the value tensions hidden by skills-forward approaches.

Be careful of unnecessarily privileging technical skills as advanced replacements for other skills in the legal profession. As Amy Sample Ward and Afua Bruce argue in *The Tech that Comes Next*, using technology in ways that generatively support work in the social impact sector, such as the practice of law, does not mean that *everyone* in the profession needs to become technologists. Instead, taking the time to align the design and use of new technology with the values of the work being done ensures long-term sustainability. The authors write,

> Ultimately, the fetishization and veneration of technology, especially the newest and shiniest of technologies, isn't sustainable – or even accessible – for many people. What is sustainable is values alignment, deep investment, and thoughtful planning. If we can commit to the work of realigning these values in ourselves, our organizations, and the world around us as part of the work toward any other social mission or cause, we could more readily build new, different, and equitable technology. (Ward and Bruce 2022, 20)

One way to avoid the pitfalls of technological fetishization is to be selective about what technology is used, and when, to do the work of the profession. In many cases, advanced technical skills are unnecessary, and even overpowered, to perform the task at hand. Sometimes, simpler solutions to common tasks – such as organizing data in a spreadsheet – perform the work just as effectively as more technical approaches thrown at a problem, avoiding the unnecessary entanglements that come with those technical approaches. This philosophy is shared by *minimal computing*, which is a practice that aims to use technical solutions to problems in the most minimal capacity possible. Minimal computing acknowledges that techno-solutionist orientations are mired in privilege, as not everyone has access to more advanced technical capabilities, nor are such capabilities often designed with every population's best interests in mind. In the practice of law, applying the principles of minimal computing means reflecting on when and how existing tools may not be impoverished for the task at hand, and avoiding the application of advanced technical skills when it is not needed (Radio 2020).

In technical instruction, recenter the discussion of values, aims, and motivation over the compulsion to solve technical problems simply for the sake of solving problems. On engineering teams, developers often get caught up in the technical challenge of hard problems, overemphasizing the technical challenge aspect over the values and purpose of solving the problem. A straightforward way to counter this tendency and recenter the discussion of values in law is to take advantage of the client-facing nature of legal practice and leverage that as an interface in which to diminish the gap between technology and end user. Folding the people-oriented focus of legal practice into technology design and use can take many forms. From a practitioner perspective, one must be aware of the anxieties that clients might have toward technology, and the implicit harms one may be causing in the use of technology. These anxieties can come from feelings of not understanding how to use technology, but they can also come from systemic harms caused by technology that has not been designed for their well-being (Khanna 2022). Examples of such harm are well documented in such wide-ranging technologies as credit scoring, facial recognition, and web searching (Noble 2018; Benjamin 2019). Make visible these kinds of complex socioeconomic, cultural, and political histories and contexts lawyers interact with when using technology, such as the history of racial and gender inequality and lack of representation in technology (Khanna 2022).

From a user perspective, recenter marginalized voices in the technology design and use process. As previously discussed, the Design from the Margins framework uses as its starting point the premise that design should begin from the perspective of marginalized and decentered populations rather than a technology's prototypical user identity (Rigot 2022). Another helpful framework that encourages recentering of marginalized populations in concrete terms is offered by data feminism, which aims to interrogate the power structures at play in the creation and consumption of data (D'Ignazio and Klein 2020). Data feminism critiques the ways that datafication and technologies that intersect with such datafication interact with and even reinforce unequal power balances in the matrix of domination. As a profession that works with large amounts of data and information that represent and shape the lives of real people, law can learn a lot from a data feminist framework about how to recognize and intervene when such power imbalances may be instrumentalized by the very technologies employed by the profession, if they are made visible in the first place.

Collectively, these approaches challenge law practitioners to reorient themselves toward critical perspectives on the relationship between law, technology, and design, recognizing that the ability to design and use technology is not merely a technical act but also an exercise mired in privilege. Such privilege can be interrogated by asking questions about how it is embedded into the design of technologies that are often the focus of technical instruction in law curricula. For example, as a starting point, we can ask questions of authority – *Who has the power to decide how this technology is designed?* – that re-localize the power to design back in the hands of individual consumers rather than in the hands of specific people, identities, cultures, or hegemonic systems of existing power or precedence. Once that authority has been allocated, there are questions of selection: *Of the many possible ways to design this technology, which has been chosen?* Among these many possible choices, some are deemed more valuable than others; these are the ones that rise to dominance because they enable us to interact with the world in predictable, scalable, and measurable ways, often with the objective of perpetuating existing value systems and structures of authority. And whenever we make such choices about value, we also make choices about visibility: who gets included, what is left out, and where we point our attention. Educators can do more to encourage practices that interrogate the provenance of technology in this way, focusing on the contexts and systems of meaning-making in which that technology is situated.

Lastly, curricula can more intentionally integrate education on the various literacies required to use technical skills and design technology. Being proficient in interpreting the design of technology requires a holistic and integrative orientation to statistical literacy, design literacy, and historical development. A technology designed for human use has textual qualities much like a written text; it is composed and situated in systems of meaning-making. This means that we can read the design of technology as a text, too, that makes visible how technology, design, and human flourishing are fundamentally interactional. This requires a shift in orientation away from ingesting design as a consumable resource and toward a dispositional sensitivity that emphasizes how the value of information can be modulated by our interaction with that design. There is tremendous opportunity to fold design pedagogy directly into law curricula, and such inclusion would provide the necessary framework to interrogate critical literacy as an essential extension of training in technical skills, not just a supplementary offering (Jackson 2016).

These kinds of shifts do not happen overnight; they cannot be reduced to a single point-by-point procedure. Instead, they develop over the course of continuous critique, investigation, and self-reflection. There is no prescriptive measure of success in this work because the end point is an orientation, not a collection of skills and proficiencies. But if the way that technology is designed is wrapped up in questions of power and visibility, then it is time to acknowledge we as practitioners of that technology hold epistemic and political power as well. And through every interaction, we are implicated in its hegemony.

But there is hope. As *The Oracle for Transfeminist Technologies* proclaims, "Not all tech shall exist" (Transfeminist Technologies, Coding Rights, and Design Justice Network 2022). More than an incisive prognostication against the bludgeoning force of technological determinism, this invocation is a reminder of a fact that is often concealed in the technologies we interact with each day: that technology and the world it is designed into are co-constituted and tangled up in one another. In many ways, technology is itself world-building, and if we do not intervene in its assumptions, we run the risk of building a world we never wanted.

REFERENCES

Aoun, Joseph E. 2017. *Robot-Proof: Higher Education in the Age of Artificial Intelligence*. Cambridge, MA: The MIT Press.

Benjamin, Ruha. 2019. *Race After Technology: Abolitionist Tools for the New Jim Code*. Cambridge: Polity Press.

Cairo, Alberto. 2014. "Data Journalism Needs to up Its Own Standards." *NiemanLab* (blog), July 9. www.niemanlab.org/2014/07/alberto-cairo-data-journalism-needs-to-up-its-own-standards/.

Chang, Emily. 2019. *Brotopia: Breaking Up the Boys' Club of Silicon Valley*. New York: Portfolio/Penguin.

Chun, Wendy Hui Kyong. 2021. *Discriminating Data: Correlation, Neighborhoods, and the New Politics of Recognition*. Cambridge, MA: The MIT Press.

"Computer Science for Lawyers." 2022. *Harvard Law School*. https://hls.harvard.edu/courses/computer-science-for-lawyers-cs50-for-lawyers/.

Costanza-Chock, Sasha. 2020. *Design Justice: Community-Led Practices to Build the Worlds We Need*. Cambridge, MA: The MIT Press.

Daston, Lorraine, and Peter Galison. 2010. *Objectivity*. New York: Zone Books.

"Debates in the Digital Humanities." n.d. https://dhdebates.gc.cuny.edu/.

D'Ignazio, Catherine, and Lauren F. Klein. 2020. *Data Feminism*. Cambridge, MA: The MIT Press.

Drucker, Johanna. 2011. "Humanities Approaches to Graphical Display." *Digital Humanities Quarterly* 5, no. 1. www.digitalhumanities.org/dhq/vol/5/1/000091/000091.html.

Escobar, Arturo. 2018. *Designs for the Pluriverse: Radical Interdependence, Autonomy, and the Making of Worlds*. Durham, NC: Duke University Press.

Friedman, Batya, and David G. Hendry. 2019. *Value Sensitive Design: Shaping Technology with Moral Imagination*. Cambridge, MA: The MIT Press.

Hendry, David G. 2020. "Designing Tech Policy: Instructional Case Studies for Technologists and Policymakers." *Tech Policy Lab, University of Washington*. https://techpolicylab.uw.edu/wp-content/uploads/2020/08/TPL-Instructional-Case-Studies-08-05-2020a.pdf.

Illinois Tech Chicago-Kent School of Law. 2017. "LAW 496: Programming for Lawyers." Last modified Spring 2023. https://web.archive.org/web/20171009202052/https://www.kentlaw.iit.edu/courses/law-496-programming-for-lawyers.

Jackson, Dan. 2016. "Human-Centered Legal Tech: Integrating Design in Legal Education." *The Law Teacher* 50, no. 1 (April): 82–97. https://doi.org/10.1080/03069400.2016.1146468.
Kafka, Alexander C. 2020. "The Discipline That Is Transforming Higher Ed." *The Chronicle of Higher Education*, April 15. www.chronicle-com.ezp-prod1.hul.harvard.edu/article/the-discipline-that-is-transforming-higher-ed/.
Khanna, Ro. 2022. *Dignity in a Digital Age: Making Tech Work for All of Us*. New York: Simon & Schuster.
Kranzberg, Melvin. 1986. "Kranzberg's Laws." *Technology and Culture* 27, no. 3 (July): 544–60. https://doi.org/10.2307/3105385.
Noble, Safiya Umoja. 2018. *Algorithms of Oppression: How Search Engines Reinforce Racism*. New York: NYU Press.
Ohm, Paul. 2018. "The Philosophy of the Course." *Computer Programming for Lawyers* (blog), January 6. www.cp4l.org/post/philosophy/.
Chicago-Kent School of Law. 2016. "Programming for Lawyers." https://web.archive.org/web/20171009202052/https://www.kentlaw.iit.edu/courses/law-496-programming-for-lawyers.
Radio, Erik. 2020. "Minimal Computing and Ontologies." *Minimal Computing*, July 21. https://go-dh.github.io/mincomp/thoughts/2020/07/21/minimal-ontology/.
Rigot, Afsaneh. 2022. "Design from the Margins: Centering the Most Marginalized and Impacted in Design Processes – from Ideation to Production." *Belfer Center for Science and International Affairs, Harvard University*. www.belfercenter.org/publication/design-margins.
Software Carpentry. n.d. "Homepage." Accessed 2022. https://software-carpentry.org/.
Stolterman, Erik, and Harold G. Nelson. 2012. *The Design Way: Intentional Change in an Unpredictable World*. 2nd ed. Cambridge, MA: The MIT Press.
Transfeminist Technologies, Coding Rights, and Design Justice Network. 2022. "The Oracle for Transfeminist Technologies." Last modified 2023. www.transfeministech.codingrights.org/.
Tsing, Anna Lowenhaupt. 2012. "On Nonscalability: The Living World Is Not Amenable to Precision-Nested Scales." *Common Knowledge* 18, no. 3 (Fall): 505–24. https://doi.org/10.1215/0961754X-1630424.
Waldman, Ari Ezra. 2021. *Industry Unbound: The Inside Story of Privacy, Data, and Corporate Power*. Cambridge: Cambridge University Press.
Ward, Amy Sample, and Afua Bruce. 2022. *The Tech That Comes Next*. Hoboken, NJ: John Wiley & Sons, Inc.
Winge, Erik. 2022. "An Introduction to Programming for Lawyers." *University of Oslo*. Last modified 2022. https://uio-cell.github.io/programming-for-lawyers/docs/index.html.

17

International Courts and Design

Sofia Stolk

17.1 INTRODUCTION

Human dignity has a central place in international law. It features prominently in one of the key international legal documents, the UN Charter. The Charter's preamble states:

> [T]o save succeeding generations from the scourge of war, which twice in our lifetime has brought untold sorrow to mankind, and to reaffirm faith in fundamental human rights, in *the dignity and worth of the human person*, in the equal rights of men and women and of nations large and small, and to establish conditions under which justice and respect for the obligations arising from treaties and other sources of international law can be maintained, and to promote social progress and better standards of life in larger freedom. (United Nations 1945, emphasis added)

As shown by this iconic example, a rather broad understanding of human dignity is invoked in preambles, mission statements, and other expressions of the purposes and values of international law. A more precise use of human dignity can be found, for example, in the war crimes provisions of international tribunals where "committing outrages upon personal dignity" are listed as a violation of the laws of armed conflict. This chapter looks at yet a more concrete reference to human dignity as something to be guaranteed as part of the trial proceedings. As stated in the Rome Statute, the founding document of the International Criminal Court (ICC), the Court "shall take appropriate measures to protect the safety, physical and psychological well-being, dignity and privacy of victims and witnesses ... These measures shall not be prejudicial to or inconsistent with the rights of the accused and a fair and impartial trial" (International Criminal Court 2011, 33). What these measures entail is not made explicit. And it is far from clear whether these measures include courthouse design. In this chapter, however, I argue that it does, or it should. Because, as I will outline in what follows, the design of an (international)

FIGURE 17.1. Permanent premises of the International Criminal Court.
(Photo credit: Sofia Stolk.)

courthouse significantly impacts a trial participant's dignity in multiple ways. Moreover, the experience of *all* individuals on the ICC's grounds is affected by its design. This matters to the court because other participants, visitors, and audiences, beyond witnesses and victims, play a significant role in the ICC's appeal to legitimacy (Schwöbel-Patel 2021).

In the following sections, I will explore the design of the ICC's permanent premises in The Hague with a focus on human dignity (Figure 17.1). I will start by situating my argument in the critical international criminal law (ICL) literature. Within this literature, there is a focus on ICL's biases and the exclusionary practices of its institutions. I connect this critical ICL approach to international law's "material turn" and the growing appreciation for the importance of studying international law's physical objects. Specifically, I discuss how the design of courthouses has been analyzed as an embodiment of international law's values but also its biases. In the next section, I examine the architecture of the ICC's courthouse through the lens of human dignity and design. Here I develop the argument that the ICC's practices of inclusion and exclusion are echoed, (re)produced, and enforced by the material design of its courthouse. Finally, I contemplate the opportunities and challenges of using human dignity–based legal design to respond to the structural inequality (re) produced by international criminal law. International (criminal) law has up until now not picked up on the rise of legal design. This chapter closes with some thoughts on the potential of legal design in this area.

17.2 CRITICAL INTERNATIONAL CRIMINAL LAW AND INTERNATIONAL LAW'S MATERIAL TURN

The origins of international criminal law are often traced back to Nuremberg, where the allied powers set up the International Military Tribunal in 1945 to try those who were deemed most responsible for Nazi crimes during World War II. Some decades later, two regional UN-mandated tribunals were established to prosecute war crimes, crimes against humanity, and genocide committed in the 1990s in the Balkans (the International Criminal Tribunal for the former Yugoslavia) and Rwanda (the International Criminal Tribunal for Rwanda). Different types of international and regional criminal courts and tribunals have been established since: for example, the hybrid courts in Cambodia and Sierra Leone and the Special Tribunal for Lebanon. In 2002, the permanent ICC began its operation in The Hague. As the first and only permanent international criminal court, it consolidated the place of ICL in the international legal landscape, which was also physically affirmed by the opening of its newly designed and built permanent premises in 2015.

Although international criminal law is often presented as an inclusive, universal endeavor benefiting humanity as a whole, all ICL institutions have faced criticism of bias, exclusion, selectivity, and stigmatization (Mégret 2013; Nouwen and Werner 2013; Schwöbel 2014, 2018; Clarke 2018; Stolk 2018; DeFalco 2022). Most prominently, Third World Approaches to International Law (TWAIL) scholars have identified the Eurocentric, Western, colonial foundations of international law in general and international criminal law specifically (Anghie and Chimni 2003; Kiyani 2015; Reynolds and Xavier 2016). Inequality is deeply anchored in the foundational structures of ICL institutions and reproduced by its practices. The ICC, for example, has been accused of an "African bias," prosecuting only African nationals, reproducing racial stereotypes, and reflecting a problematic North–South division in which the "civilized" North saves the "savage" South (Branch 2017; Schwöbel-Patel 2018; Clarke 2019). These practices of selectivity and exclusion have affected how the justice done by these institutions has been experienced by trial participants and how it is perceived by the general public. Structural bias, stereotyping, and exclusion in ICL institutions can undermine the protection of human dignity both in its more general understanding as well as the very concrete protection of the dignity of lawyers, judges, victims, witnesses, defendants, and the general audience alike. A deeper understanding of human dignity in ICL therefore warrants a closer look at exclusionary practices at a macro level, but also, as pursued by this chapter, at the more micro level of everyday trial proceedings.

In international law scholarship, there is a growing interest in legal materiality, zoning in on "the artefacts, practices, formats and settings in and through which law acts and is enacted" (Kendall and Kang 2019, 3). Studies in this area shed light on international law's very concrete world-making power and the often very material ways in which it "disciplines its subjects" through physical objects (Hohmann and Joyce 2018, 2). Typically, this approach entails reflexivity and attention to our own positionality, in a theoretical, social, political, and physical sense. In a similar vein, international lawyers have become interested in the physical spaces where international law operates and the way in which it becomes visible and tangible to its subjects or constituencies. The increasing demands of enhanced legitimacy, transparency, and accessibility affect the way in which international courts present themselves, but also what is deemed worthy of scholarly attention (Bianchi and Peters 2013; Hayashi and Bailliet 2017; Stolk and Vos 2020; Schwöbel-Patel 2021; Dobson, forthcoming). In this way, this scholarly "turn to materiality" in international law enables a shift in focus to the reproduction of exclusion and bias in ICL on the micro level, the everyday life of courts and tribunals. Studying the operations of the ICC through this lens of materiality naturally entails a thorough evaluation of the institution's architectural design.

Moreover, not only law's materiality but also its visuality and aesthetics are increasingly appreciated as features that play a crucial role in the (trans)formation of international law. As argued by Miriam Bak McKenna, "[international law is] dependent upon aesthetics and spatial dynamics to elicit faith in its ideals and principles, and to project international legal discourse to the outside" (Bak McKenna 2021, 6). This has sparked an emerging interest in the architecture of the buildings in which international institutions reside (Stolk and Vos 2020; Aalberts and Stolk, 2020, 2022; Bak McKenna 2021; Charlesworth 2022). Buildings are powerful vessels to materialize and communicate ideals and principles (Gieryn 2002). Ideas about transparency, security, and inclusion fostered by democratic institutions such as courthouses transpire not only through their proceedings but also through the aesthetic and functional choices in their architectural design (Resnik and Curtis 2011; Mulcahy and Rowden 2019). The emphasis on the public nature of democratic courthouses affects the requirements of the courthouse design (e.g., it needs to include a public gallery) and its access and security. As mentioned above, ICL institutions, including the ICC, constantly struggle to defend their universal legitimacy. Courthouse design is part of this battle for legitimacy, both as a materialization of democratic values and as a symbolic, communicative device.

Therefore, exploring the architecture of international legal institutions is a great starting point for gaining insight into the material ways in which international courts communicate with their constituencies. Beyond that, studying the spatial arrangements of courthouses gives insight into the everyday practices of movement, access, and inclusion and exclusion of legal institutions. Feminist studies in courtroom geography have drawn attention to the deep entanglement between movement, space, politics, and emotion in courthouses. As Faria et al. (2020, 1104) note,

> The courtroom is a space where global political and economic systems infused with dominant legal discourse manifest materially and where legal subjects are enlivened, forced to navigate the personal and intimate felt experience.

The architectural design of a courthouse is of crucial importance to the sensation of power, justice, emotion, and dignity experienced by trial participants and courtroom visitors. The next section discusses how this plays out at the premises of the International Criminal Court.

17.3 THE ARCHITECTURAL DESIGN OF THE ICC: ACCESS AND EXCLUSION

17.3.1 *A Design Competition for the ICC*

In 2008, the ICC launched an international architectural design competition for the construction of its permanent premises. After an anonymous open round of applications for candidacy, twenty proposals were selected to partake in the design context. Next to the technical specifications, the ICC provided the competitors with a set of key values to be reflected in the design: justice, human dignity, openness, credibility, safety, global, and iconic. Three winning designs were chosen from nineteen entries that were selected by a jury on the basis of criteria such as incorporation into the urban fabric and surrounding landscape, architecture, safety, and sustainability. The ICC consulted with architects, and finally the Danish firm Schmidt Hammer Lassen was commissioned to realize the design.

The ICC and actors around it were very aware of the impact of the design. The Coalition for the ICC (CICC), an international network of NGOs advocating for the Court and monitoring its work, wrote a statement to the jury of the competition:

> Organizations and institutions are often defined by the structures in which they are housed, as these can express the history, power, and virtues of the institutions that occupy them. Critically, they can give organizations an identity that can shape public opinion for the better, or in some cases, for the worse. We must not therefore be waylaid by the iconic intentions of the designers nor of those that have commissioned this project. The new ICC premises must be an icon in a truly potent sense; it mustn't simply exist, it must engage. It should embody cultural and social meaning, placing us in the historical and cultural context of this new system of international justice and reflecting the importance of the International Criminal Court – an authority to help end impunity, powerful and inspiring in its actions, yet welcoming and sensitive to those involved in its proceedings. (CICC 2008)

Also, the CICC was very keen on a design that harnessed the human dignity of all people entering the premises:

> The architectural candidates have had the responsibility to deliver designs that not only satisfy all of the functional requirements of the Court and its staff, but that also positively address the needs and concerns of the various communities that interact with the Court, in particular, victims, witnesses, and defendants. Justice is a very emotive experience for these participants; how the architecture "feels" to them will be particularly significant. (CICC 2008)

This statement echoes insights from research into democratic architecture and principles of legal design. Inclusivity was put forward as a central feature to be integrated into the design. In the words of the architect, "It is important that a formal institution like the ICC does not constitute barriers for people. On the contrary, it expresses the very essence of democratic architecture" (ICC 2010).

As stated on the ICC Permanent Premises website, human dignity was one of the seven key phrases used by the architects to capture the essence of the ICC and its institutional values. The main design feature that corresponds with human dignity and openness is transparency, a value that has been of importance to the design of courthouses for decades (Fischer Taylor 1999). One of the ways to establish a feeling of transparency in the ICC building is the "playful façade" that mainly consists of a pattern of forward- and backward-tilting windows (Oskomera Group 2015). The design includes a wide public plaza "as a natural way of approaching the building." Security features are hidden in the landscape: "The perimeter security concept offers both a high level of security and an unobstructed view to the ICC building. The surrounding landscape is designed to support the security level of the building and in addition it offers beautiful scenery" (Oskomera Group 2015). Natural elements and gardens in and outside of the premises are a central feature in the design (Figure 17.2). According to the architect, "Gardens have always existed as part of all cultures and all religions. The parterre gardens rise up as a green landmark and a symbol of unity, regardless of nationality and culture" (ICC 2010).

In sum, the design idea is to have an open, transparent, accessible building. The architects proposed a building "that conveys the eminence and authority of the ICC, while at the same time relating on a human scale" (ICC 2010). The elements of human dignity and inclusivity feature prominently in the design. However, the ambition to combine human-centeredness with a reflection of eminence and authority is a challenging one. Especially in light of the criticism regarding ICL identified, the authority of the court arguably arises from a system that is structurally unequal. Patterns of exclusion are also a key feature of the design, as can be observed when actually moving through the premises.

FIGURE 17.2. Security entrance to the International Criminal Court.
(Photo credit: Sofia Stolk.)

17.3.2 *Access and Exclusion at the ICC's Permanent Premises*

The dynamics of access and exclusion are significant for the experiences of justice and human dignity in the context of the ICC's design. On a meta level, the choice for The Hague as home for the ICC necessarily implies exclusion. All current situations and cases that are investigated or prosecuted before the ICC focus on areas outside of the Netherlands, most of them even from outside of Europe. The debate on local justice versus international justice and the problematic distance between the ICC and the affected communities over which it rules has been heavily debated since its inception (Branch, 1984; De Vos 2013; McMillan 2020). Traveling to The Hague is out of reach for many; it requires time, money, and a passport that is accepted (on the exclusionary power of passports, see Keshavarz 2015). This also puts into question the accessibility of the court and its trials, particularly for affected communities (January 2009).

Even when trial participants or audiences manage to travel to The Hague, the premises of the Court provide many obstacles. On one hand, the Court is not located centrally in The Hague; it is placed on the outskirts of the city. Although on paper it is part of The Hague's "international zone," this zone stretches out over a wide area, and the ICC is located on its very border. It is rather isolated from the city and not well connected to the public transportation network. As I wrote elsewhere,

> Although the building means to connect the cityscape with the natural landscape, it also sharply marks the transition. It is surrounded by nature, and as such is not really integrated within the urban environment. At the same time, it is clearly an urban building, and thus not wholly integrated within the natural environment either. When approaching the building from the city, its isolation stands out, but it also appears out of place, severed from its international institutional counterparts through lack of proximity. (Vos and Stolk 2020, 77)

The embeddedness of a courthouse within the city affects its physical and its psychological accessibility. As Haldar notes, "law has at once been designated a separate, formal and distinct site and has been located within reach of an urban environment" (Haldar 1994, 193). The ICC building is removed from that urban environment, enhancing its image of being a "distanced" court.

On the other hand, the location of the building on the shore enabled the architects to play with an enhanced ecological connection between the courthouse and the dune landscape. While this too enhances the ambition to bring the court back to a human scale and to emphasize its peaceful atmosphere, this can also be delusional. As artist Lodovica Guarnieri signals in her *(UN)just Peace Tour*, "the dune landscape is used as a defense mechanism and camouflages the policing function of the space and conceal the military rationale of the panorama" (Guarnieri, 2018). Hidden security does not mean that it is not there and not felt. More visibly, before entering the main court building, visitors and trial participants alike must pass through a little building that houses the first security check. Again, a valid ID is required, and all persons and their belongings are scanned. This seemingly formal scene of entering the courthouse security check is loaded with sociotechnical arrangements that interfere with privacy and may produce inequalities and affect experiences of human dignity (Amicelle, Aradau, and Jeandesboz 2015; Valkenburg and van der Ploeg 2015; de Goede 2018). Despite the architect's ambition to conceal security by "ingenious" use of the landscape, the tension between security and accessibility is present everywhere.

After passing the security check, the route to the main entrance leads over a small bridge. The courthouse is surrounded by water, which connotes yet another layer of security. Murray compares it to a medieval castle, with "a gatehouse, castle keep and a moat," and dunes as "hilltop fortifications" (Murray 2016). The building itself is transparent and opaque at the same time. Its façade of trapezoidal windows is intended "to create a feeling of movement and reflection, but also designed to defeat sniper targeting" (Murray 2016). The tilted windows deflect light, and one cannot look inside. The inside of the building itself clearly separates public space from areas with authorized access (Gaakeer et al. 2018). This reflects a key challenge of courtroom design to find "the most efficient way to move bodies round a succession of parallel private and public zones" (Mulcahy 2011, 49–50). Through a carefully constructed network of corridors, different parties – staff, audience, judges, and defendants – will never coincidently run into each other. Staff and visitors can meet in a cafeteria or in the hall that features an exhibition about the ICC's work, but other doors are secured and only accessible with a pass (Figure 17.3).

One of the features of a "democratic" courthouse is the public gallery. But although the galleries are indeed open to the public that manage to enter the courthouse in the first place, the movement and behavior of visitors inside the space is restricted, monitored, and policed. All belongings, including mobile phones, must

FIGURE 17.3. Public gallery of courtroom in the International Criminal Court (ICC) Den Haag, Den Haag, Netherlands. Architect: Schmidt Hammer & Lassen Ltd, 2015. (Photo credit: Anthony Coleman.)

be stored in lockers in the basement. Before entering the public gallery, visitors must pass through another security check. In the gallery, visitors are supervised by guards who strictly follow the Rules of Decorum: visitors are requested to be silent, pay attention, and dress suitably (ICC Rules of Decorum). Security guards observe the behavior of visitors, emphasizing strict hierarchies and institutional control. The gallery is separated from the courtroom by a thick glass wall, which is yet another example of aesthetic transparency yet physical inaccessibility. The message of inclusion and exclusion at the same time communicated by the design is similar to the tension between the rhetoric of universality and the practice of exclusion signaled in critical international criminal law studies. As Mulcahy (2011, 48) notes, this sophisticated "segmentation and segregation" is common to modern courthouses. This segregation is intentional and one of the intrinsic features of courthouse architecture (Hanson 1996): an implicit exercise of power that affects trial participants and visitors alike.

> If soothing daylit spaces are intended to psychologically strengthen the witness, the dark grey holding cell complete with steel table and chair bolted to the floor, a slab for a bed, seatless stainless-steel prison toilet and sink are surely intended to bring the accused down a notch. This is no different from any other court, but it does say something about the idiom, "innocent until proven guilty." Certainly the architecture has already chosen sides. One can't really imagine a Western leader being held here. (Murray 2016)

This striking contrast echoes issues of stereotyping and stigmatization by ICL and its courts discussed in Section 17.2. A human dignity–based legal system should, at the very least, avoid prejudice, exclusion, and abuse of power. This contrast seems to be an unresolved challenge in the legal and architectural design of the ICC alike.

17.4 HUMAN DIGNITY, LEGAL DESIGN, AND ICL: CONCLUDING REMARKS

A central concern of the human dignity, legal design, and ICL nexus is whether the courthouse architecture (re)produces structural inequality. The choice of geographic location, aesthetics, functional design, and security policies all affect the accessibility of a courthouse and, more fundamentally, the distribution of access to justice. For any democratic institution, but especially in a field of law that prides itself for its universal character, access is a key issue. On the other hand, segregation as an intrinsic feature of courthouse architecture signals the deeply exclusive foundations of the legal system itself. If law is an exclusionary mechanism, and functions because of exclusion, one can wonder if this can be "fixed" with more inclusive design. What would human dignity–based design mean in this context?

The ICC's courthouse design presents a complex interplay between consideration of inclusion, safety, privacy, and security. In this constellation, one of the crucial enactments of human dignity in the design for the ICC indeed revolves around access. However, access does not have to equal guaranteeing *full* access for everyone, but it does entail considering the safeguarding of physical and psychological inclusion of a wide range of actors on different levels. From a pragmatic perspective, it is unrealistic to expect that a more inclusive courthouse design can tackle problems of global access and deep systemic issues of asymmetrical power relations. But, as shown above, even enhancing the experience of dignity of the people who managed to travel to the premises is quite challenging in an institution that is exclusionary in its very fabric and operates in a heavily securitized playing field.

Evidently, the current ICC design is not void of human dignity consideration. The designers explicitly mention a choice for light and comforting design to support the psychological well-being of victims and witnesses. However, contrary to Article 33 of the Rome Statute, it is hard to sustain that this design choice is not prejudicial to the accused if we consider the contrast with the somber spaces designated for the defendants. The tendency of ICL to stigmatize and vilify the defendant in its legal proceedings (Mégret 2014; Stolk 2018) is mirrored by the architecture of the ICC building. Another clear gesture toward safeguarding human dignity is the concealing of security features to ensure a more friendly passage from outside to inside the ICC. However, the heavy security check at both the entrance of the courthouse and the courtrooms makes security visible and tangible again. These security demands are difficult to conceal with architectural design. They lay bare the securitization of law, how ICL operates as a control mechanism, and how it is deeply entangled with other security regimes such as border control and counterterrorism.

The design of the ICC clearly communicates its aspirations, as well as its biases and structural mechanisms of exclusion. The design is, like the institution itself, a top-down imposition of "universality" that has no real participatory or emancipatory base among its presumed constituency. The choice of The Hague as its physical location in combination with the Court's selection of cases that are all situated far away from the court create and reinforce deep running local and global anxieties. The complex interplay between legal, spatial, political, and social arrangements impacts the experience of human dignity and accounts for high thresholds between inside and outside, private and public space on the ICC's premises. Thinking through the lens of human dignity–based design may not directly resolve these issues, but it effectively exposes how the distribution of physical, virtual, and psychological access to the Court is highly differentiated, laying bare how the challenge for the ICC to safeguard the human dignity of all individuals involved in its practices is fundamentally embedded in the institution's entangled legal and physical design.

REFERENCES

Aalberts, Tanja, and Sofia Stolk. 2020. "The Peace Palace: Building (of) the International Community." *AJIL Unbound* 114 (Winter): 117–22. https://doi.org/10.1017/aju.2020.25.

2022. "Building (of) the International Community: A History of the Peace Palace through Transnational Gifts and Local Bureaucracy." *London Review of International Law* 10, no. 2 (July): 169–202. https://doi.org/10.1093/lril/lrac013.

Amicelle, Anthony, Claudia Aradau, and Julien Jeandesboz. 2015. "Questioning Security Devices: Performativity, Resistance, Politics." *Security Dialogue* 46, no. 4 (August): 293–306. https://doi.org/10.1177/0967010615586964.

Anghie, Antony, and Bhupinder S. Chimni. 2003. "Third World Approaches to International Law and Individual Responsibility in Internal Conflicts." *Chinese Journal of International Law* 2, no 1 (March): 77–103. https://doi.org/10.1093/oxfordjournals.cjilaw.a000480.

Bak McKenna, Miriam. 2021. "Designing for International Law: The Architecture of International Organizations 1922–1952." *Leiden Journal of International Law* 34, no. 1 (Winter): 1–22. https://doi.org/10.1017/S092215652000059X.

Bianchi, Andrea, and Anne Peters. 2013. *Transparency in International Law*. Cambridge: Cambridge University Press.

Branch, Adam. 1984. "International Justice, Local Injustice – The International Criminal Court in Northern Uganda." *Dissent Magazine*, Fall. www.dissentmagazine.org/article/international-justice-local-injustice/.

2017. "Dominic Ongwen on Trial: The ICC's African Dilemmas," *International Journal of Transitional Justice* 11, no. 1 (March): 30–49. https://doi.org/10.1093/ijtj/ijw027.

Charlesworth, Hilary. 2022. "The Art of International Law: 24th Annual Grotius Lecture to Mark Start of ASIL Annual Meeting." Accessed January 15, 2023. www.wcl.american.edu/impact/initiatives-programs/international/24th-grotius-lecture/.

Clarke, Kamari Maxine. 2018. "Refiguring the Perpetrator: Culpability, History and International Criminal Law's Impunity Gap." In *Interrogating the Perpetrator: Violation, Culpability, and Human Rights*, edited by Cathy J Schlund-Vials and Samuel Martínez, 56–78. New York: Routledge.

2019. *Affective Justice: The International Criminal Court and the Pan-Africanist Pushback*. Durham, NC: Duke University Press.

Coalition for the ICC (CICC). 2008. "Architectural Design Competition for the Permanent Premises of the ICC: Statement to Jury." October 30–31, 2008. On file with author.

DeFalco, Randle C. 2022. *Invisible Atrocities: The Aesthetic Biases of International Criminal Justice*. Cambridge: Cambridge University Press.

de Goede, Marieke. 2018. "The Chain of Security." *Review of International Studies* 44, no. 1 (August): 24–42. https://doi.org/10.1017/S0260210517000353.

de Vos, Christian. 2013. "Investigating from Afar: The ICC's Evidence Problem." *Leiden Journal of International Law* 26, no. 4 (December): 1009–24. https://doi.org/10.1017/S0922156513000526.

Dobson, Jillian. forthcoming. "Mapping the Transparency Turn at the International Criminal Court." PhD diss., VU Amsterdam. On file with author.

Faria, Caroline, Sarah Klosterkamp, Rebecca Maria Torres, and Jayme Walenta. 2020. "Embodied Exhibits: Toward a Feminist Geographic Courtroom Ethnography." *Annals of the American Association of Geographers* 110, no. 4 (December): 1095–113. https://doi.org/10.1080/24694452.2019.1680233.

Fischer Taylor, Katherine. 1999. "The Festival of Justice: Paris, 1849." In *Law and the Image*, edited by Costas Douzinas and Lynda Nead, 137–77. Chicago: University of Chicago Press.

Gaakeer, Jeanne, Ruth Herz, Joan Kee, Linda Mulcahy, Jeremy Pilcher, Gary Watt, and Carey Young. 2018. "Carey Young's Palais de Justice." *Law and Humanities* 12, no. 2 (October): 278–310. https://doi.org/10.1080/17521483.2018.1525863.

Gieryn, Thomas F. 2002. "What Buildings Do." *Theory and Society* 31, no. 1 (February): 35–74. https://doi.org/10.1023/A:1014404201290.

Guarnieri, Lodovica. 2018. "(UN)just Peace Tour." Accessed October 21, 2022. www.unjustpeace.eu/.

Haldar, Piyel. 1994. "In and Out of Court: On Topographies of Law and the Architecture of Court Buildings: A Study of the Supreme Court of the State of Israel." *International Journal for the Semiotics of Law* 7, no. 2 (June): 185–200. https://doi.org/10.1007/BF01816606.

Hanson, Julienne. 1996. "The Architecture of Justice: Iconography and Space Configuration in the English Law Court Building." *Architectural Research Quarterly* 1, no. 4 (Summer): 50–59. https://doi.org/10.1017/S1359135500003079.

Hayashi, Nobuo, and Cecilia Bailliet. 2017. *The Legitimacy of International Criminal Tribunals*. Cambridge: Cambridge University Press.

Hohmann, Jessie, and Daniel Joyce, eds. 2018. *International Law's Objects*. Oxford: Oxford University Press.

ICC Permanent Premises. n.d. "The Building." Archived Page. Accessed January 15, 2023. https://web.archive.org/web/20150104182836/http://www.icc-permanentpremises.org/building.

International Criminal Court (ICC). 2010. "The Permanent Premises of ICC by Schmidt Hammer Lassen Architects." Uploaded December 7, 2010. YouTube video, 3:40 min. www.youtube.com/watch?v=Uu60ZZQ8vzU.

2011. "Rome Statute of the International Criminal Court." www.icc-cpi.int/sites/default/files/RS-Eng.pdf.

n.d. "Permanent Premises of the ICC." Accessed January 15, 2023. www.icc-cpi.int/sites/default/files/itemsDocuments/pr898/Permanent-Premises-factsheet-for-groundbreaking-ceremony.pdf.

January, Sativa. 2009. "Tribunal Verité: Documenting Transitional Justice in Sierra Leone." *International Journal of Transitional Justice* 3, no. 2 (July): 207–28. https://doi.org/10.1093/ijtj/ijp003.

Kang, Hyo Yoon, and Sara Kendall. 2019. "Contents, Introduction & Contributors, Law Text Culture, volume 23." *Law Text Culture* 23, no. 1 (2019): 1–15. https://ro.uow.edu.au/ltc/vol23/iss1/1.

Keshavarz, Mahmoud. 2015. "Material Practices of Power – Part I: Passports and Passporting." *Design Philosophy Papers* 13, no. 2 (April): 97–113. https://doi.org/10.1080/14487136.2015.1133130.

Kiyani, Asad. 2015. "Third World Approaches to International Criminal Law." *AJIL Unbound* 109 (January): 255–59. https://doi.org/10.1017/S2398772300001550.

Manirakiza, Pacifique. 2018. "A Twail Perspective on the African Union's Project to Withdraw from the International Criminal Court." *African Yearbook of International Law* 23, no. 1 (November): 391–424. https://doi.org/10.1163/22116176-02301016.

McMillan, Nesam. 2020. *Imagining the International: Crime, Justice, and the Promise of Community*. Redwood City, CA: Stanford University Press.

Mégret, Frédéric. 2013. "Practices of Stigmatization." *Law & Contemporary Problems* 76, no. 3–4: 287–318. JSTOR.

Mulcahy, Linda. 2011. *Legal Architecture: Justice, Due Process and the Place of Law*. New York: Routledge.

Mulcahy, Linda, and Emma Rowden. 2019. *The Democratic Courthouse: A Modern History of Design, Due Process and Dignity*. New York: Routledge.

Murray, Christine. 2016. "Transparency, Democracy, High-security: Schmidt Hammer Lassen's International Criminal Court." *The Architectural Review*, February 5. www.architectural-review.com/buildings/transparency-democracy-high-security-schmidt-hammer-lassens-international-criminal-court.

Nouwen, Sarah, and Wouter Werner. 2013. "Doing Justice to the Political: The International Criminal Court in Uganda and Sudan." *European Journal of International Law* 21, no. 4 (November): 941–65. https://doi.org/10.1093/ejil/chq064.

Oskomera Group. "International Criminal Court The Hague." Uploaded January 7, 2015, 1:27 min. www.youtube.com/watch?v=TBfdsvf-uxg.

Resnik, Judith, and Dennis Curtis. 2011. *Representing Justice: Invention, Controversy, and Rights in City-States and Democratic Courtrooms*. New Haven, CT: Yale University Press.

Reynolds, John, and Sujith Xavier. 2016. "The Dark Corners of the World, TWAIL and International Criminal Justice." *Journal of International Criminal Justice* 14, no. 4 (September): 959–83. https://doi.org/10.1093/jicj/mqw053.

Schwöbel, Christine. 2014. *Critical Approaches to International Criminal Law*. New York: Routledge.

Schwöbel-Patel, Christine. 2018. "The 'Ideal' Victim of International Criminal Law." *European Journal of International Law* 29, no. 3 (August): 703–24. https://doi.org/10.1093/ejil/chy056.

2021. *Marketing Global Justice: The Political Economy of International Criminal Law*. Cambridge: Cambridge University Press.

Stolk, Sofia. 2018. "A Sophisticated Beast? On the Construction of an 'Ideal' Perpetrator in the Opening Statements of International Criminal Trials." *European Journal of International Law* 29, no. 3 (August): 677–701. https://doi.org/10.1093/ejil/chy041.

Stolk, Sofia, and Renske Vos. 2020. "Law in Concrete: Institutional Architecture in Brussels and The Hague." *Law and Humanities* 14, no. 1 (February): 57–82. https://doi.org/10.1080/17521483.2020.1724407.

The United Nations International Court of Justice. 1945. "United Nations Charter." www.un.org/en/about-us/un-charter.

Valkenburg, Govert, and Irma van der Ploeg. 2015. "Materialities between Security and Privacy: A Constructivist Account of Airport Security Scanners." *Security Dialogue* 46, no. 4 (Summer): 326–44. https://doi.org/10.1177/0967010615577855.

18

James v Birnmann

The Potential of Critical Design for Examining Legal Issues

Phoebe Walton

18.1 INTRODUCTION

There is a lot of energy surrounding the emerging field of legal design. Descending from design thinking, it sees "designerly ways" (Perry-Kessaris 2019, 1) applied to legal problems and is increasingly fixed as its own discipline with standard methodologies, cultural norms, and defined modes of operation and procurement. With the emphasis on the legal, there has been insufficient examination into the design part of legal design. From a designer's perspective, indeed a critical designer's perspective, this examination looks at the design thinking approach to the law, exposing its limitations in addressing systemic issues within legal systems, and in some cases worsening such issues.

Countering the design thinking approach, critical design has the capacity to expose injustices and inequalities within legal systems. This potential is explored in the critical design project James v Birnmann, which was developed within Architectural Design Studio 4 (ADS4) at the Royal College of Art (RCA). By creating a speculative future scenario, James v Birnmann examines injustices propagated through the performance of law, its growing mediatization, and the rising use of artificial intelligence (AI). James v Birnmann demonstrates the utility of critical design engaging with legal issues within a design school context, to widen the discourse around these issues, gain public traction, disrupt acceptance in the current system, and recognize the interdependence of legal issues with wider social concerns. While destabilizing the public's perception of the legal system is vital unto itself, as a key step in legal reform, critical design also has the potential to work alongside a more traditional legal design, to inform (and reform) its practice.

It is important to note that the critical designer lens frames this research, in the recognition of "legal design" itself as a design project, in the decisively outsider perspective and in the illustration of ideas through a design project. As the research points out, cultural context significantly informs how an issue is approached; it is worth considering both the limits and opportunities of the critical design context in exploring the relationship between law and design.

18.2 LEGAL DESIGN VERSUS CRITICAL DESIGN CONCERNED WITH LEGAL PROBLEMS

18.2.1 *Legal Design*

According to Margaret Hagan, founder of the Legal Design Lab within Stanford's d.school, legal design is "the application of human-centered design to the world of law, to make legal systems and services more human-centered, usable, and satisfying" (Hagan n.d.). A relatively new discipline, legal design involves lawyers implementing design projects by working with legal designers within the growing number of practices and laboratories (most of which are located in the United States and the United Kingdom). Considered as an approach, legal design has several applications including, but by no means limited to, improving the communication and clarity of legal information, developing and advancing legal products and services, and building a culture of innovation in organizations (Hagan n.d.).

The application of design to the legal profession emerged from the more general trend of "design thinking" in the twentieth century (Buchanan 1992, 3). Design thinking adopts a designerly approach for use by nondesigners in a range of disciplines such as management, business, and policy (Hagan n.d.). Emerging from a corporate context, design thinking is used to inform innovation and improve practices, making them more aligned to customer's wishes and therefore more competitive. The appropriation of a designer's approach takes the form of a series of defined steps. While these vary slightly within different institutions, the overarching approach remains similar – using a linear design methodology that is solution driven.

Legal design follows a similar logic, which often focuses on making existing systems more efficient. However, what happens when such systems are neither fair nor good? Applying design thinking in this solution-based method fails to address the system's flaws and inequalities; indeed, sometimes it makes them more entrenched. ProPublica examined legal tech software that was developed to predict future criminality as a factor when determining sentencing and bail bonds across the United States. Such software was found to be not only unreliable in predicting future criminality but systematically racist (Perry-Kessaris 2019, 13). As Amanda Perry-Kessaris, Professor of Law at Kent University, points out, "Neither design nor law is ever neutral—politically, economically, culturally or otherwise" (Perry-Kessaris 2019, 12). Considering the significance of the law, it is imperative to consider the kinds of design used in connection with it.

18.2.2 *The Capacity for a More Critical Legal Design*

Critical design opposes the affirmative design found in legal design and design thinking. Instead of "problem solving," critical design is "problem finding" (Dunne and Raby 2013, vii). Considered an attitude (Dunne and Raby n.d.) rather than a method (in contrast to the clear methodological steps of design thinking), critical design uses speculative design proposals to probe complex issues of contemporary life and challenge the status quo (MoMa n.d.). From this perspective, design is a medium for discussion and debate involving different disciplines and social groups. The term was first used by Anthony Dunne in his book *Hertzian Tales* (1999). Dunne and Fiona Raby are widely considered the most prominent critical designers with their practice Dunne and Raby and Designed Realities Studio at The New School. Though critical design is relatively new, its genealogy can be traced to critical theory, the social and political philosophy movement that advocated the importance of questioning and critiquing society to examine and challenge structures of power (Britannica n.d.). What's more, critical design's systematic approach has roots in anthropological studies.

While the critical design attitude seems at odds with the essentially conservative, solution-led approach of legal design, perhaps legal design can embrace a more critical stance? Indeed, it has been argued that design thinking should be more critical generally. In "Wicked Problems in Design Thinking," Richard Buchanan, Professor of Design at Case Western Reserve University, advocates for the "wicked problems approach," first set out by Horst Rittel in the 1960s (Buchanan 1992, 15). This asserts the "fundamental interdeterminancy" of all design problems (Buchanan 1992, 16) and seeks to examine problems at a deeper level, recognizing their interdependence with wider societal concerns. Opposing "quick fix" solutions, the wicked problems approach advocates an expanded conception of what is possible (Buchanan 1992, 21).

This illustrates how the design thinking methodologies within legal design could become more critical. Rather than offering immediate solutions, the ambition would be to generate more nuanced, varied, longer-term, and systemic solutions. However, within the current procurement methods of legal design, with its emphasis on providing solutions as a product to the legal field, the "wickedness" of this approach would no doubt be limited by the context within which legal design currently operates.

18.2.3 *Legal Issues Considered within a Critical Design Context*

Applying a more critical design stance to existing legal design frameworks will be curtailed by the structures defining those frameworks. These contradict critical design, as they are solution focused, methodologically driven, affirmative, and located within the power structures they are attempting to critique. To meaningfully consider how legal systems can be reformed and restructured, it is important that this is considered outside of the system itself and untethered to its stakeholders; critical design studios are well placed to contend with such issues.

Producing critical design projects that focus on legal issues inverts the current relationship of legal design whereby "designerly ways" are applied to legal problems (Perry-Kassaris 2019). Instead, having critical design as the driver rather than the appliqué facilitates work that can probe legal problems, expose the more fundamental issues and how they intersect with broader societal conditions, and engage wider audiences in the discussion. Michael Doherty, Professor of Law at Lancaster University, examines the cultural differences between the legal and design professions, which inform the divergent ways in which lawyers and designers conceptualize and approach a problem (Doherty 2021). Capitalizing on the critical design culture applied to legal issues offers perspectives on such issues not available from legal, and indeed legal design, settings.

18.3 ADS4: A CRITICAL DESIGN STUDIO USING LEGAL FICTIONS AS A METHODOLOGY FOR SPECULATING THE "IMPOSSIBLE"

18.3.1 *Architectural Design Studio 4*

Exploring the work of ADS4 illustrates how a critical design context is able to contend with legal issues. Since 2001, ADS4 has operated within the School of Architecture at the RCA in London. The studio uses design as a critical tool, imagining near-futures and alternative presents that examine and probe complex social, technological, and environmental issues (Greenall, Koller and Mastrandrea n.d.a). ADS4's approach is tied to that established by Dunne and Raby, set out in their A/B manifesto, "Speculative Everything," in which they acknowledge the work of ADS4, with whom they were working at the RCA during their Design Interactions program that ran from 2005 to 2015 (Dunne and Raby 2013, viii).

Dunne and Raby identify architecture as particularly well placed to embrace a critical design methodology because of its ability to construct future visions:

> Of all the design disciplines it is probably architecture that has the richest, most diverse tradition for exploring ideas. From paper architecture to visionary design, its long history is full of exciting and inspiring examples. (Dunne and Raby 2013, 23)

Rather than seeking to emulate or presuppose the real, as with most architectural studios, ADS4 is guided by the fictional nature of the work within this context. The studio advocates the need to democratize processes of speculation, which are usually kept within the remits of powerful individuals and corporations who, through controlling the capacity to speculate on the future, are able to shape it into their own agendas.

18.3.2 *Legal Fictions: The Brief*

The project James v Birnmann responds to ADS4's brief "Legal Fictions," which borrows from legal practices to frame an approach to speculative and critical design. Defined as "an assertion that is accepted as true for legal purposes, even though it may be untrue" (Fuller 1967), the legal fiction provides critical design with a useful mechanism for imagining and speculating alternative realities that exist outside of the current social, cultural, and physical context.

Through designing new legal fictions, ADS4 sought to explore "plausible impossible scenarios" (Disney 1956), a term coined by Walt Disney to explain how Disney's animations made worlds that were impossible seem plausible. Developing these "plausible impossible" worlds, ADS4 acknowledged the provisional distinction between "possible" and "impossible" and how this etymological divide is often established by the powerful to maintain the status quo and social hierarchies.

Delving into the realm of "impossible," ADS4 explored what French philosopher Quentin Meillassoux terms "Extro-Science Fiction" (XSF). As opposed to science fiction that projects future scenarios that expand existing structures of science and knowledge, XSF creates worlds in which "experimental science is impossible and not unknown in fact," whereby "experimental science cannot deploy its theories or constitute its objects within them" (Meillassoux 2015, 5). For Meillassoux, XSF represents the question of induction. First set out by philosopher David Hume, this asks what convinces us "that physical laws will still be valid in the next moment, since neither experience nor logic can give us such assurances" (Meillassoux 2015, 9). Meillassoux essentially claims that there are no assurances for the future: anything is possible, even that which is culturally accepted as impossible.

For ADS4, XSF provided a useful lens for attempting to conceive scenarios outside current social frameworks and conceptual bounds of the "possible," realizing the unstable nature of this term. Designing impossible (yet plausible) scenarios widens dialogue into how to shape reality, as Fiona Raby explains:

> Perhaps, as designers, unreality is the only thing we have left—a tool for loosening the grip on the reality we find ourselves within, to help think beyond known frameworks, and to shift our thinking. In this way, design might begin to contribute to a proliferation of multiple alternative worlds existing in our collective imagination, enlarging it to provide a richer conceptual space of imagining for everyone. (Raby 2018)

Designing these unrealities, using the legal fiction tool as a driver for speculation, facilitates and democratizes valuable discussion in how to shape and reshape the real.

Responding to ADS4's Legal Fiction Brief, James v Birnmann is a critical design project that examines the biases and injustices that arise from the performance of law, the mediatization of legal proceedings, and the rise of AI within legal processes. Through considering the "legal fiction" that the law is maintained by AI, James v Birnmann designs a "plausible impossible" future scenario. Performance, animation, and film are used to communicate the project, widening the discussion around the issues with which the project is concerned to those that are usually obscured from public scrutiny.

18.4 JAMES V BIRNMANN: A NEVER-ENDING LEGAL DRAMA IN A WORLD WHERE JUDGES ARE NO LONGER HUMAN

18.4.1 *Introduction*

James v Birnmann designs a never-ending legal drama situated in a future where law is controlled and maintained by AI. The continual trial acts as a sinister mixture of entertainment and social pacifier for a legal system increasingly detached from human control. As purely symbolic vestiture, the performance is separated from the functioning of the legal system. Following common law tradition, the legal trial is based on precedent of past "real" trials and "fictional" legal dramas; it is an amalgamation of our perception of law.

18.4.2 *The Performative Nature of the Law*

Law is a continual performance. Legal systems are human-made constructs that establish collective values to govern and control society. We perform these systems daily, following their rules and logic. Through this constant performance law appears objective, fixed, and factual – illusions that maintain the system's power and hierarchies. Courtrooms are the epicenter of this charade, where legal structures are promoted through procedure and performance, with rituals and symbolism exerting the law's authority over both the case at hand and the system at large.

A study into existing legal systems, venturing into the domain of comparative law, reveals how each system is represented and amplified through its courtroom trials (Figures 18.1–18.4). In the United Kingdom, these have highly choreographed procedures, costumes, scripts, stage sets, and caricatured character archetypes. The superfluous and heavily prescribed proceedings mirror the rigid complexity of the UK legal system. Azande trials are also ritualistic and tightly orchestrated. For Azande people, supernatural forces are tied to everyday life (Chase 2005, 16); within Azande legal trials, oracles that can access such forces (objects or animals) are consulted. This intertwining of legal and mystical systems promotes "public affirmation of the Azande metaphysical world" (Chase 2005, 22) while also reflecting and strengthening their centralized governance structure, which is dependent on the relationship between these two systems.

FIGURE 18.1. Props, stage sets, and performance in a US courtroom (Walton 2021).

FIGURE 18.2. Props, stage sets, and performance in a UK courtroom (Walton 2021).

18.4.3 *The Media's Representation of Courtroom Trials*

Fundamentally performative, it is no surprise that the law provides popular content for western TV and films. The media's presence in courtroom trials is expanding; the United States televises real cases, with the national network Court TV streaming

FIGURE 18.3. Props, stage sets, and performance in an Azande Benge ceremony (Walton 2021).

FIGURE 18.4. Props, stage sets, and performance in a Medieval Icelandic Althing (Walton 2021).

live court cases from around the country. Similarly, fictional legal dramas and true crime dramas increasingly make for popular watching. These pop culture trials frame the common perception of law, demonstrating an idealistic, biased representation of the legal system. As David Ray Papke, professor of Law at Marquette University, explains,

> The pop cultural trial serves as a symbol of law. The symbol obfuscates inequalities of race and class. It assures us that legal representation is available and effective. It probes facts and uses objectivity to reach fair decisions. (Papke 1999, 931)

Pop cultural trials portray legal proceedings in a way that misrepresents the legal system. This symbolization of law pacifies the public, acts as propaganda for the legal system, and obscures its inherent injustices.

18.4.4 *Are Judges Human?*

Performance and ritual within the courtroom are used to make the proceedings appear objective; characters involved follow established rules that seemingly do not allow their personal subjectivity to influence the outcomes. Exploring this phenomenon, legal realist philosopher Jerome Frank posed the question, "Are Judges Human?" (1931). Frank considers the consequences of the denial of subjectivity and personal prejudice within legal process in terms of typical lawyers and judges:

> He will ignore the immense importance, the inescapable operation, of the personal element in court justice. As a practitioner he will be needlessly baffled by coping with it. He will think it absent, or all but absent. When it appears he will resent it, treat it as improper, as abnormal, as avoidable. Or he will accept it with caution with distaste; cynically, as something poisonous, debasing, bordering on the corrupt. If he becomes a judge, he will try to think as Dickinson portrays the judge thinking; he will pretend to think in that artificial way, pretend to others - and worst of all pretend to himself. (Frank 1931, 23–24)

This artificial objectivity bolsters the validity of law and conceals the constructed, fictitious nature of the system – one that can actually be changed. The denial of human subjectivity within the legal system avoids scrutiny over personal prejudices within legal disputes and the system itself.

18.4.5 *A Future Where Judges Are No Longer Human*

However, what would happen if judges really were not human, but instead Artificial Intelligences? Law is considered a natural sector for the expansion of AI for its ability to process massive amounts of precedent data, its application of legal rules, and its perceived objectivity. The increasing use of AI within Western legal systems is seen in the growing industry of law tech in the United States, with state courts devolving decisions such as sentencing and bail to these private technology companies. Within this algorithmic legal decision-making, biases – usually along racial and socioeconomic lines – proliferate unchecked under the pretense of AI objectivity.

FIGURE 18.5. In this future where the law is maintained by AI, courthouses will be replaced by data centers. This new legal-architectural typology demonstrates the huge quantities of precedent data and processing power used to maintain the legal system (Walton 2021).

Extrapolating this growing trend within legal systems, is there a future where the legal system is maintained entirely by AI? In this future, courtroom trials will no longer be necessary, decisions will be made instantaneously through algorithms, the mechanisms of law will be invisible, and the subjective biases acknowledged but hidden. In this scenario, the performance of law will have to remain to foster trust and legitimize the system.

In this future, current modes of symbolically demonstrating the legal system will be hyperbolized. Courthouses will be replaced by data centers – their public presence giving authority to the law (Figure 18.5). The massive amounts of data being processed to maintain the law will foster a sense of impartiality and emphasize the heightened role of precedent and rules. Symbolism will be intensified, with AI creating its own versions of legalese and architectural forms to reinforce the authority of the legal system (Figures 18.6–18.7).

18.4.6 *James v Birnmann: The Courtroom Drama*

In this future, the courtroom drama, critical in framing the popular perception of law, becomes a key instrument for symbolizing the AI legal system. James v Birnmann is a never-ending courtroom drama that represents the law while being detached from the functioning of the AI-maintained system (Figure 18.8). Considered the Ur trial, it combines past real trials and fictional legal dramas, creating a hyperbolic symbol of law. While the location of the drama is somewhat

FIGURE 18.6. In this future, symbolic representations of the law will be amplified. AI will create their own versions of legalese, the legal language indecipherable to those not in the profession. This language was created through training the AI GPT-2 on existing legalese (Walton 2021).

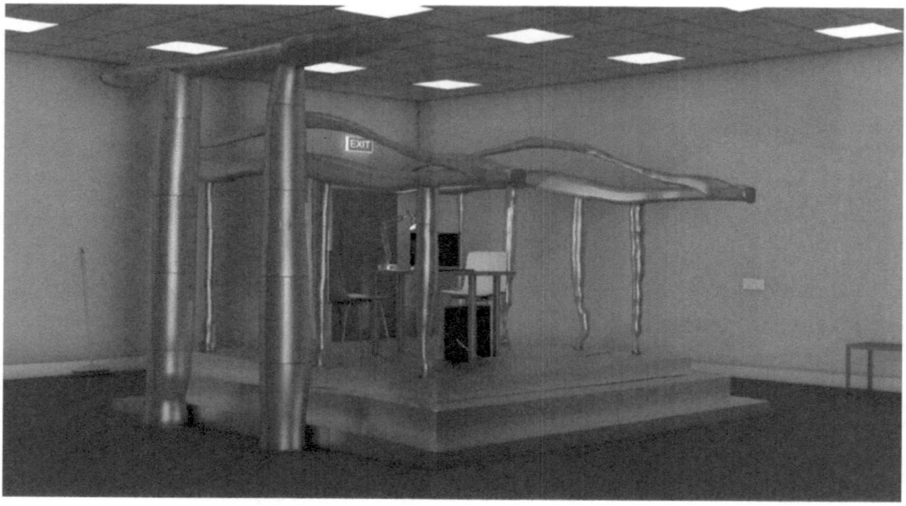

FIGURE 18.7. In this future, the symbolism of courthouse architecture will be reappropriated to validate the algorithmic legal processes hidden within a computer. The Machine Learning AI StyleGAN2 assisted the design of this form, trained on hundreds of images of courthouse architecture (Walton 2021).

FIGURE 18.8. The rotating gavel is an icon for the James v Birnmann TV show. The prop, a key symbol of law, becomes increasingly abstracted by AI processes, mirroring the legal system itself (Walton 2021).

irrelevant, America's presence is pronounced, which, through the mediatization of its legal system, already frames the Western perception of law.

The trial can be viewed in two ways. First, through watching it in person; as with courtroom trials, the performance is open to the public who may watch for entertainment, intrigue, or a desire for a closer connection to the opaque legal system. Second, the trial is televised, on a 24-hour dedicated channel. This performance is mediated by animation, akin to the courtroom sketch, and the trial is transferred into the animated landscape, which makes explicit the representational, symbolic nature of the performance (Figure 18.9).

18.4.7 *Methodology of Precedent*

Following common law tradition, the trial is designed through a methodology of precedent. Props, choreography, stage sets, and camera angles are extracted from the contentious and surreal cases that make it to court. This data is then fed into the design of the legal drama, mirroring the processes of AI learning from precedent data.

The O. J. Simpson trial is significant for its relationship to the media and popular perception of law. For eleven months, the world watched this trial – which grew beyond the case into a wider discussion over racial prejudice in the legal system. The courtroom is recreated as a computer model from footage of the trial. Key moments are restaged from the hundreds of hours of television footage (Figures 18.10–18.15).

FIGURE 18.9. An actor in a chromakey green suit has their motion captured, to be transferred into the animated landscape of the televised James v Birnmann (Walton 2021).

FIGURE 18.10. Restaging the key camera angles of the O. J. Simpson trial within a computer model. The wide shot frames key characters during sidebar discussions (Walton 2021).

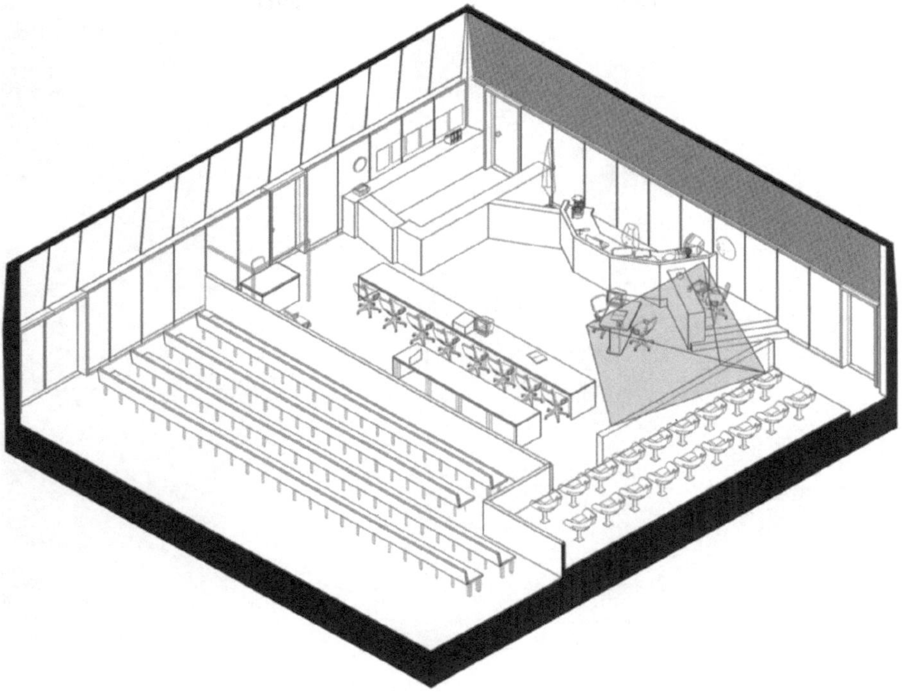

FIGURE 18.11. Extracting the camera angle of the wide shot as precedent data for the design of James v Birnmann (Walton 2021).

Legal dramas also shape the common perception of law. From analyzing prominent legal dramas, shared tropes emerge that inform the design of James v Birnmann (Figure 18.16). These include walking and talking shots, emphasizing the necessity for swift justice, rooms having windows framing the city, demonstrating the law's prominence with society, and the abundance of props including gavels, books, flags, junk food, and clocks, which are frequently used to signify the status, swiftness, and authority of the law.

18.4.8 *Designing the Drama*

AI collaborators assist in the design of the legal drama. AI GPT-2 writes the script; trained on thousands of legal transcripts and prompted by legal dramas, it continues in the indecipherable language of legalese. Jukebox OpenAI collaborates with Mike Post to design the theme music, while Attngan and Vision AI assist in prop design. Framing the AI as collaborators recognizes them as subjects with their own biases and predilections.

FIGURE 18.12. Restaging the key camera angles of the O. J. Simpson trial within a computer model. This famous shot frames O. J. Simpson as he tries on the gloves (Walton 2021).

The infrastructure needed to support the show is immense. It requires a whole world of backlot, stage set, and supporting spaces. Both the stage sets and assisting infrastructure embody the data extracted from past trials and popular legal dramas, collaging the symbols, tropes, props, and spatial layouts. These are fused with the surreal implications of a never-ending performance – of people falling asleep in the vast prop room and corridors doubling up as backdrops for walking and talking sequences. Authoritarian and pop aesthetics bring these spaces together, emphasizing the sites' tension between entertainment and pacification.

Designing the extended title sequence of the show enables one to travel through the animated sites of the legal drama. Opening on a live action scene in a living room, the film situates the show within the wider implications of an AI-maintained legal system: one that is automated and impersonal (Figures 18.17–18.18). The film then enters the animation sequence, journeying through the sites of the legal drama. Within these spaces, the boundary between what is and is not performance space is blurred. Actors, crew, cleaners, and visitors are absorbed in this continual performance of law, and the overtly symbolic architecture participates in the charade (Figures 18.19–18.27). The ambiguity of the animated landscape emphasizes the

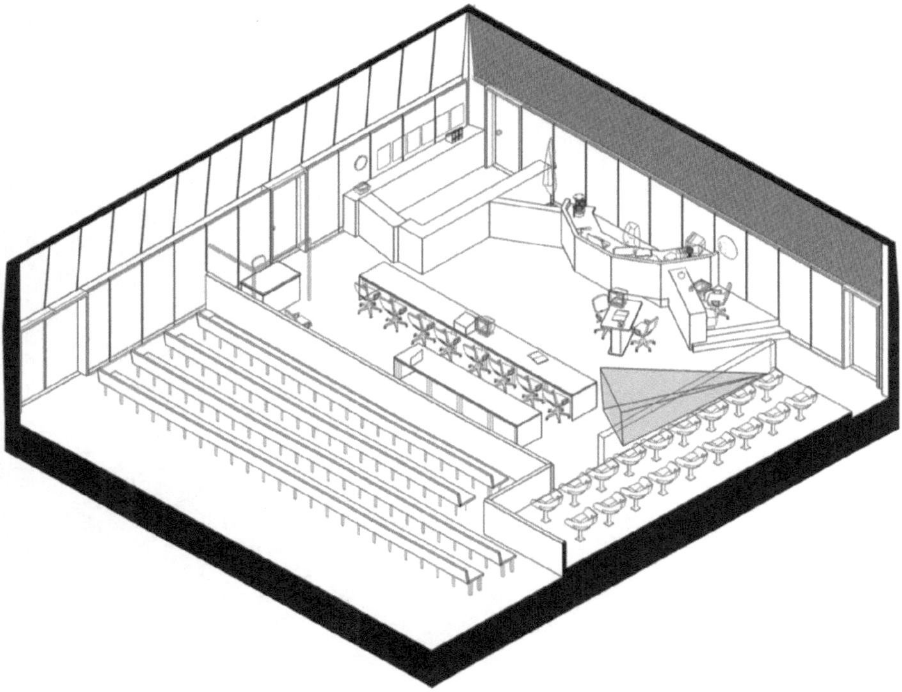

FIGURE 18.13. Extracting the camera angle of the glove shot as precedent data for the design of James v Birnmann (Walton, 2021).

representational nature of the legal performance – are the spaces depicted representations of the physical site or virtual spaces in and of themselves?

18.5 REFLECTIONS ON THE PROJECT: PRECEDENT FOR THE FUTURE

18.5.1 *Implications of the Project*

James v Birnmann explores problems within Western legal systems, including the desire for an objective jurisprudence and the subsequent concealment of the inherent subjectivities, how the performative nature of law maintains the system's power and hierarchies, how the growing media presence of real and fictional courtroom trials exacerbates the biases promoted through courtroom performances, and finally how the increasing use of AI within legal processes deepens the inequalities and biases through concealing the subjectivity within the technology.

James v Birnmann examines how the public's perception of law is critical for sustaining the legal system. Currently, the performance of law, both in "real" legal

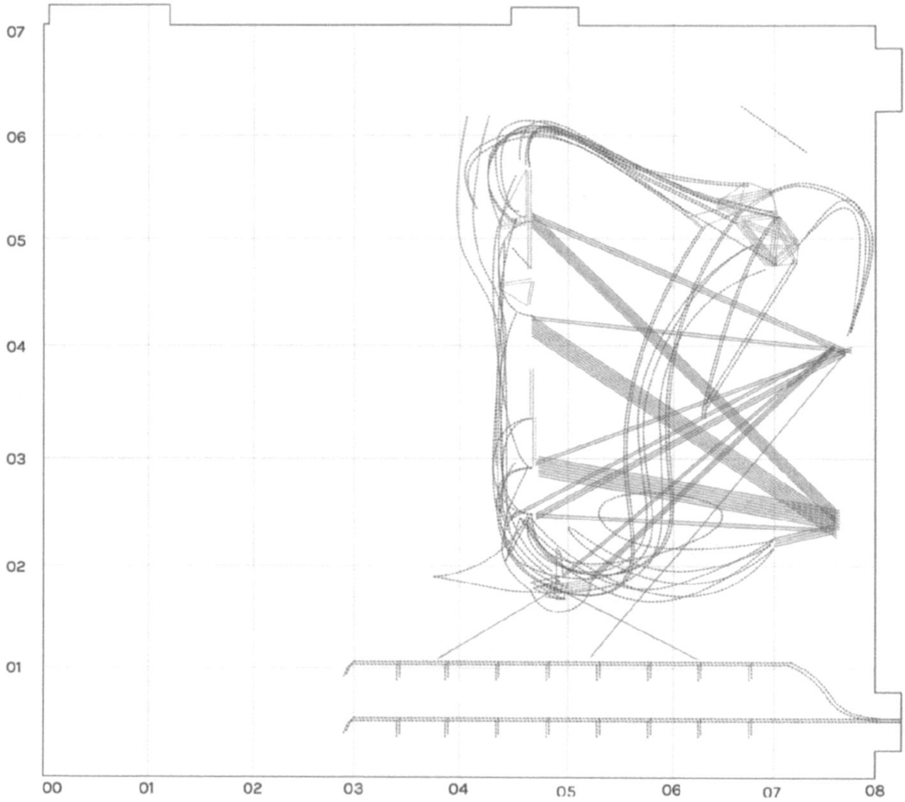

FIGURE 18.14. Extracting choreography of the O. J. Simpson trial through the hundreds of hours of television footage. This choreography sequence depicts the scene of O. J. Simpson trying on the gloves (Walton 2021).

processes and "fictional" portrayals, provides a biased representation of the legal system, masking inherent subjectivities, inequalities, and flaws. The output film seeks to reveal this, utilizing tensions between entertainment and unease, pop culture and authoritarianism. Yet, the film also exploits the importance of the popular perception of law; through adopting popular narratives and aesthetics, it seeks to engage the public with defects within the legal system. In this way, it inverts the usual apparatus that validates and stabilizes the public's perception of law to disrupt their relationship to it.

18.5.2 *Implications for Critical Design Dealing with Legal Concerns*

James v Birnmann demonstrates fundamental issues within western legal systems, emphasizing the need for more widespread reform that cannot be met by current

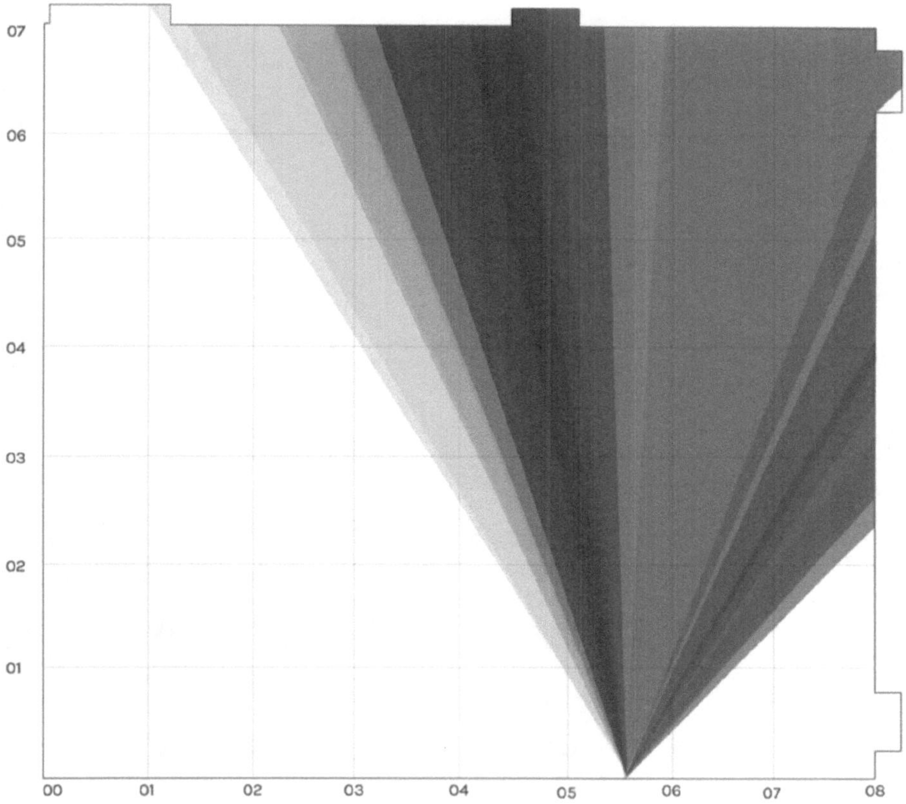

FIGURE 18.15. Extracting camera angles of the O. J. Simpson trial through the hundreds of hours of television footage. This camera sequence depicts the scene of O. J. Simpson trying on the gloves (Walton 2021).

legal design practices. While critical design projects, such as James v Birnmann, do not offer practical solutions to imminent issues within legal practices, they are able to expand upon and define such issues, contextualizing them within much larger systems of problems, or "wicked problems" (Buchanan 1992). In opposition to the affirmative, "design thinking" approach, which seeks to improve yet maintain legal systems, critical design engaging with legal issues has the capacity to destabilize such systems by demonstrating contradictions to the status quo. The objective is to facilitate and widen discussion surrounding alternatives and encourage shifts in perspectives.

Important for James v Birnmann, and perhaps future critical design projects engaging with legal issues, is its development within a design school context by a critical designer, separate from the legal profession itself. A lawyerly approach, as

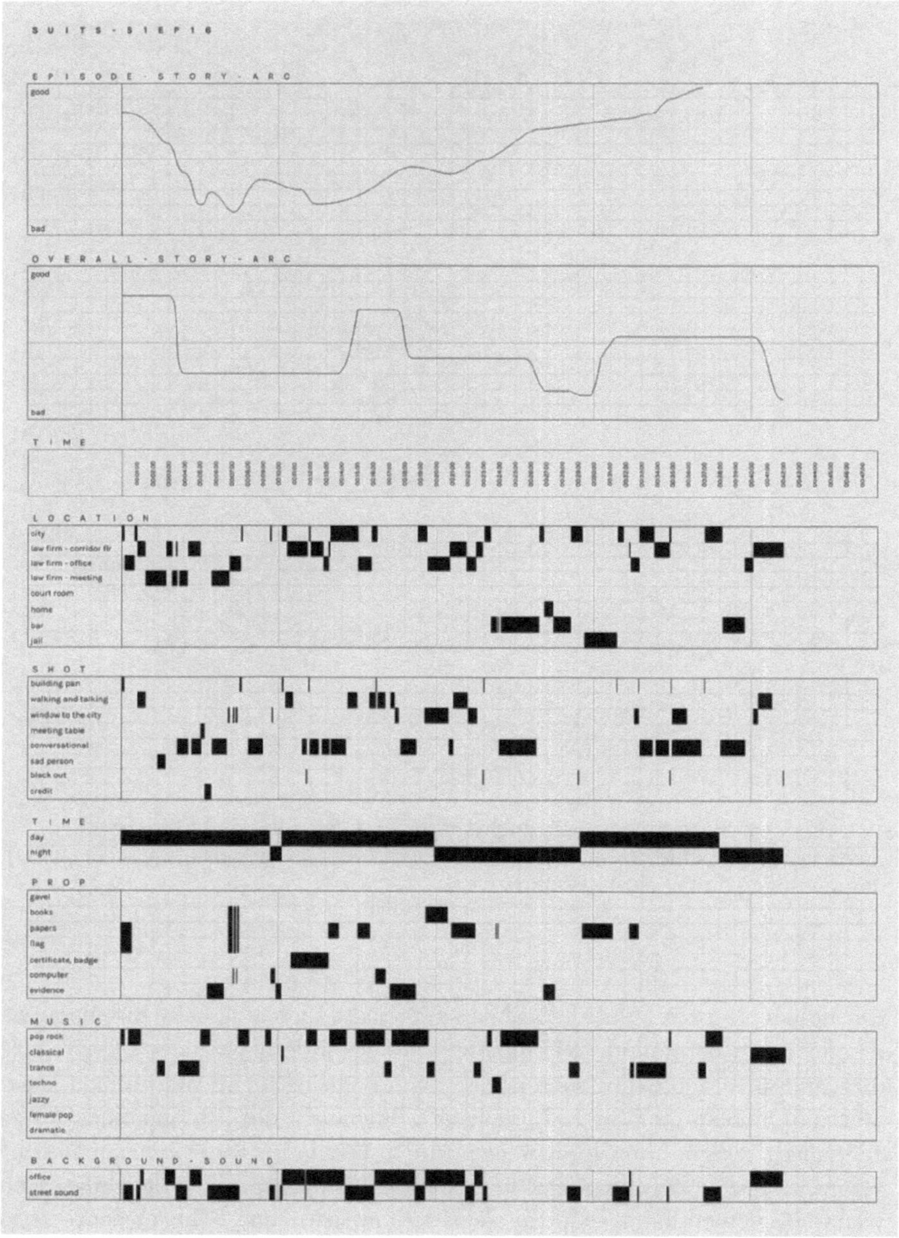

FIGURE 18.16. Harvesting precedent data of legal drama tropes, to inform the design of James v Birnmann. The drawing dissects a scene from the popular legal drama Suits, separating it into its narrative arc, location, shot, time of day, props, music, and background sound (Walton 2021).

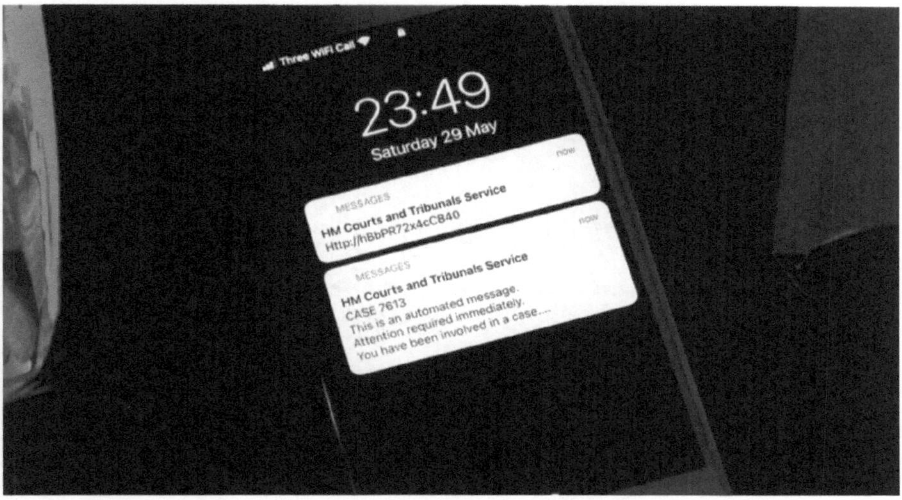

FIGURE 18.17. Film still from James v Birnmann opening title sequence. The opening live action shot shows the implications of a legal system maintained by AI, where legal verdicts are instantaneous, delivered by automated messaging (Walton 2021).

FIGURE 18.18. Film still from James v Birnmann opening title sequence. The film journeys from the reality of someone dealing with this AI-maintained legal system into the fictional representation of the legal system with the James v Birnmann TV show (Walton 2021).

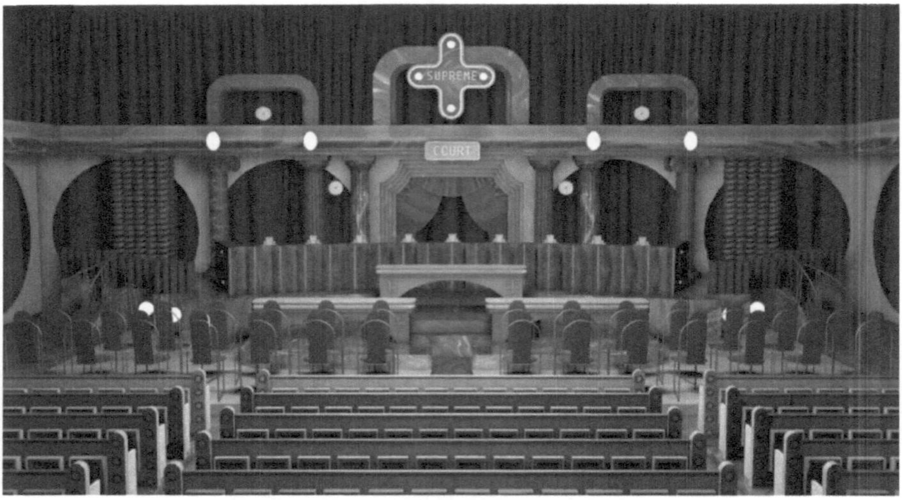

FIGURE 18.19. Film still from James v Birnmann opening title sequence. The film enters the animated landscape of the James v Birnmann set. The Supreme Court pop stage set synthesizes the architecture of the US Supreme Court with pop aesthetics of reality arbitration shows (Walton 2021).

FIGURE 18.20. Film still from James v Birnmann opening title sequence. The scene depicts 5:13 a.m. in the rehearsal room, where actors have been practicing for a scene based on data from the O. J. Simpson trial (Walton 2021).

FIGURE 18.21. Film still from James v Birnmann opening title sequence. The entrance hallway draws on the grandeur of courthouses and combines tropes from legal dramas. More than just functional, it is a space for performance (Walton 2021).

FIGURE 18.22. Film still from James v Birnmann opening title sequence. From the entrance hallway, the scale of the site demonstrates the enormity of the show, necessary for validating and symbolizing the legal system. This panopticon emphasizes the importance of performance throughout the site (Walton 2021).

FIGURE 18.23. Film still from James v Birnmann opening title sequence. The screen room is central to the site of the legal drama, which is based on performance and being watched (Walton, 2021).

FIGURE 18.24. Film still from James v Birnmann opening title sequence. The prop room contains objects that are critical for the performance of law. Alongside O. J. Simpson's gloves and American flags are bottles of ginger beer and snails for the Donoghue v Stevenson case. New props are created, with the assistance of AI, such as the "blue moving sculpture" from GPT-2's script, which has been designed in collaboration with the AI AttnGan (Walton 2021).

FIGURE 18.25. Film still from James v Birnmann opening title sequence. The prop room is infinitely large, continually expanding as more props are generated, emphasizing their importance with the performance of law (Walton 2021).

FIGURE 18.26. Film still from James v Birnmann opening title sequence. Courthouse square is a backlot of courthouse facades. The architecture embodies symbolism from the law and legal dramas with classical style, clocks, gavels, and flags. The square demonstrates the tension between performance and reality within the set, with the space also functioning on a logistical level, fronting warehouses and providing circulation for the site (Walton 2021).

FIGURE 18.27. Film still from James v Birnmann opening title sequence. The O. J. motorway connects the site of the legal drama while also hosting the restaging of the O. J. Simpson car chase. This performance recreates a historic moment that frames the public perception of law, transferring it into popular entertainment (Walton 2021).

Doherty explains, is led by "knowledge characteristics of precedent and hierarchy, and logical and sequential thinking" (Buchanan 1992, 8). In this sense, the legal culture is challenged in imagining, or indeed facilitating, drastic change. In contrast, James v Birnmann illustrates the culture of critical design is able to examine issues in a more radical way. Critical designers are able to utilize an outsider's perspective to criticize existing systems; this proves useful in regard to the law, which is often considered monolithic. James v Birnmann employs a useful naivety to the law, unburdened by the "reality" or "possibilities" of legal systems. Here, impossibility becomes a vital tool, fostering a project that destabilizes preconceived conceptions of what is possible within legal systems.

Finally, James v Birnmann highlights the capacity for critical design to engage legal issues with wider cultural and social concerns. Critical design culture, and the culture fostered within ADS4 at the RCA, recognizes the importance of considering issues in an interdisciplinary manner. James v Birnmann demonstrates the relationship between the law and AI, architecture, pop culture, and the media. This interdisciplinary approach is important for considering legal issues due to the law's expansive nature and relationship with all aspects of society. As the ex–Supreme Court Justice Lord Sumption explains, "law does not occupy a world of its own. It is part of a larger system of public decision making" (Sumption 2019). While existing methods within legal design tend to treat legal issues as somewhat discrete, critical design culture can interrogate the intersectionality of legal concerns.

Considering the overarching significance of law in governing society, it is a ripe topic for critical design projects. After all, the legal system is a design question; the system itself is a designed thing, while it also designs, orchestrating social interaction and connections. Greater critical design projects engaging with legal concerns would prove an important exercise for opening a dialogue into how legal systems can change on a more fundamental level, in contrast to current legal design practices.

18.6 CONCLUSION

Legal design projects can and do improve legal systems and issues. However, their approach is limited – through applying designer thinking to legal issues, design is reduced to a methodology. The affirmative designs offer granular solutions, making the existing system more efficient. While this maintains current systems, it also continues, and in some cases worsens, its existing injustices, inequalities, and biases.

For a more equitable legal system, there is a need for more radical, systemic reform. This needs to widen the discussion outside of the existing system and include a broader range of voices. Critical design practice dealing with legal concerns inverts legal design's relationship between law and design, whereby design becomes the driver and legal issues are applied. Essential for this transposition is investigating such issues within a design school context, inside the cultural framework of a critical design practice that is detached from that of the law. Rather than offering solutions, critical design seeks out and expands the issues within legal systems. As with James v Birnmann, this can be done through designing fictional scenarios of alternative presents or possible (or even impossible) futures. These scenarios, and indeed critical design more generally, have the capacity to destabilize the audience's relationship with systems such as law, shifting their perspectives.

James v Birnmann emphasizes the importance of the public's perception of law for maintaining and validating the system. Disrupting the public's attitude to the legal system is a necessary step to reform on a more fundamental level. This, as James v Birnmann highlights, is needed to tackle the inequalities and biases, such as those exacerbated by AI's and the media's growing influence on legal systems.

As Dunne and Raby explain, critical design is not a replacement for affirmative design (Dunne and Raby 2013, vi). Critical design projects looking at legal issues have the potential to enrich legal design. Their capacity to examine current issues, destabilize current systems, and challenge the limits of "possibility" and "impossibility" can perhaps prompt legal design to be a bit more inquisitive and cautious of the systems in which they operate. As design is political, legal design needs to recognize its complicity and role within systems of hierarchy and power. Having critical design dealing with legal issues, alongside a more traditional legal design practice, has the capacity to affect change more significantly within legal systems.

REFERENCES

Britannica, T. Editors of Encyclopaedia (2019, August 22). Critical Theory. *Encyclopedia Britannica*. www.britannica.com/topic/critical-theory.

Brown, Tim. 2008. "Design Thinking." *Harvard Business Review*, June. https://hbr.org/2008/06/design-thinking.

Buchanan, Richard. 1992. "Wicked Problems in Design Thinking." *Design Issues* 8, no. 2 (Spring): 5–21. https://doi.org/10.2307/1511637.

Chase, O. G. 2005. *Law, Culture, and Ritual: Disputing Systems in Cross-Cultural Context*. New York: New York University Press.

Disneyland. 1956. Season 3, Episode 8, "The Plausible Impossible." Directed by William Beaudine and Wilfred Jackson. Aired October 31, 1956, on Disney.

Doherty, M. 2021. "The Relationship Between Legal and Design Cultures: Tension and Resolution." In *Legal Design: Integrating Business, Design, & Legal Thinking with Technology*, edited by M. Corrales, H. Haapio, M. Hagan, and M. Doherty, 32–55. Cheltenham, UK: Edward Elgar Publishing.

Dunne, Anthonny. 1999. *Hertzian Tales: Electronic Products, Aesthetic Experience and Critical Design*. London: Royal College of Art Computer Related Design Research Studio.

Dunne, A., and Fiona Raby. 2013. *Speculative Everything: Design, Fiction, and Social Dreaming*. Cambridge, MA: The MIT Press.

n.d. "Critical Design FAQ. Dunne and Raby." Accessed November 18, 2021. http://dunneandraby.co.uk/content/bydandr/13/0.

Frank, J. 1931. "Are Judges Human? Part One: The Effect on Legal Thinking on the Assumption That Judges Behave Like Human Beings." *University of Pennsylvania Law Review* 80, no. 17 (November): 17–53. https://scholarship.law.upenn.edu/cgi/viewcontent.cgi?article=8493&context=penn_law_review.

Fuller, L. L. 1967. *Legal Fictions*. Palo Alto, CA: Stanford University Press.

Greenall, T., N. Koller, and M. Mastrandrea. n.d.a. "About ADS4. ADS4." Accessed November 18, 2021. https://ads4.co/about.

n.d.b. "ADS4: Legal Fictions. Royal College of Art." Accessed November 18, 2021. www.rca.ac.uk/study/schools/school-of-architecture/architecture/ads-themes-2020-21/ads4-legal-fictions/.

Hagan, Margaret. n.d. "Legal Design." *Law By Design*. Accessed August 5, 2023. https://lawbydesign.co/legal-design.

Meillassoux, Q. [2013] 2015. *Science Fiction and Extro-Science Fiction*, translated by A. Edlebi. Minneapolis, MN: Univocal.

MoMa. n.d. "Critical Design." Accessed November 18, 2021. www.moma.org/collection/terms/critical-design.

Papke, D. R. 1999. "The American Courtroom Trial: Pop Culture, Courthouse Realities, and the Dream World of Justice." *South Texas Law Review* 40, Paper 537: 919–32. https://scholarship.law.marquette.edu/facpub/537/.

2007. "The Impact of Popular Culture on American Perceptions of the Courts." *Indiana Law Journal* 82, no. 5 (July): 1225–34. www.repository.law.indiana.edu/ilj/vol82/iss5/5/.

Perry-Kassaris, A. 2019. "Legal Design for Practice, Activism, Policy and Research." *Journal of Law and Society* 46, no. 2 (June): 185–210. http://doi.org/10.1111/jols.12154.

Raby, Fiona. 2018. "Foreword: Stitching Worlds, Building Walls, Designing Drones." In *Stitching Worlds: Exploring Textiles and Electronics*, edited by Ebru Kurbak, 8–11. Berlin, Germany: Revolver Publishing.

Sumption, J. 2019. "Lecture 1: Law's Expanding Empire, podcast lecture. In The Reith Lectures." Lecture recorded at BBC Radio 4 on May 21, 2019, 57 min. www.bbc.co.uk/programmes/m00057m8.

Walton, P. 2021. "James v Birnmann." Accessed November 18, 2021. https://phoebewalton.com/James-v-Birnmann.

19

The ReInvent Law Archive*

Renee Knake Jefferson

The best way to predict the future is to [re]invent it.

—Alan Kay (TED 2008)

19.1 INTRODUCTION

On February 7, 2014, the trending hashtags on Twitter included: #SeahawksFront7, #JayLeno, #Starbucks, #Russia, and #ReInventLaw. It's not an overstatement to say that most people can easily identify the first four topics. But ReInventLaw? Few, if anyone other than those of you reading this book, can likely define that one. And this was not the only time ReInventLaw surfaced as a trending topic. It first claimed that mantle on March 8, 2013 (Scutt 2013). Nor would it be the last. It appeared among the top trending Twitter hashtags again on June 14, 2013, and June 26, 2014, competing with the World Cup (Dewald 2013; Goodman 2014).

Why was the hashtag ReInventLaw trending on Twitter multiple times in 2013 and 2014? Those dates coincide with gatherings held around the globe, bringing together academics, design architects, entrepreneurs, innovators, law students, lawyers, technologists, and others to explore better ways of providing legal help to those who need it. The messages heralded inside the room reverberated well beyond it, with just as many if not more following the live-tweeting from the comfort of their individual homes or offices as numerous attendees shared insights and wisdom from the event venue in 140 characters or less.

The ReInvent Law Laboratory, a one-of-a-kind partnership between the acclaimed entrepreneurship-fueling powerhouse Ewing Marion Kauffman

* Portions of this chapter are reproduced here with permission from RENEE KNAKE JEFFERSON, LAW DEMOCRATIZED: A BLUEPRINT FOR SOLVING THE JUSTICE CRISIS (2024); Renee Newman Knake, *Democratizing Legal Education*, 45 CONN. L. REV. 1281 (2013); and Renee Newman Knake, *Cultivating Learners Who Will Invent the Future of Law: Some Thoughts on Educating Entrepreneurial and Innovative Lawyers*, 38 OHIO. N. L. REV. 1 (2012).

Foundation and the Big Ten research institution Michigan State University, helped launch and legitimize a new discipline in law practice and legal education. It did so at a time of resistance from the legal academy and profession. Ahead of itself by at least a decade, the principles and teaching espoused by the ReInvent Law faculty, students, and affiliates are now widely accepted by most bar associations and law schools and even actively pursued by many.

ReInvent Law quickly received national and international attention, garnering numerous awards and landing Michigan State's previously unranked law school on "top ten" lists like the American Bar Association (ABA) Standing Committee on the Delivery of Legal Services Task Force on eLawyering in 2014. The "InnovAction Award" from the College of Law Practice Management was bestowed in 2013, honoring "lawyers, law firms, and other deliverers of legal services who are currently engaged in some extraordinary innovative efforts." The Wolters Kluwer Leading Edge Report recognized ReInvent Law as one of "Three Programs to Watch in Building a Faculty Culture of Innovation" in 2015.

As one of the cofounders, I had a front-row seat to witness the force of ReInvent Law, heralded as a "very, very important development in legal pedagogy" (Blackman 2014). I found myself on the cover of the *ABA Journal* honored as a "Legal Rebel," an "annual honors program for the change leaders of the legal profession" in 2013 (Carter, Francis Ward, and Zahorsky 2013), and I was named to the Fastcase 50, an award that "recognizes 50 of the smartest, most courageous innovators, techies, visionaries, and leaders in the law" that same year (Fastcase 2013).

This chapter draws from my experience along with that of many others who chronicled their own encounters with the concepts and community of ReInvent Law during its few years of existence from 2012 to 2015. There are many lessons to draw from the ReInvent Law story. A few are recounted here, in the hope that this framework might be recreated when the legal profession faces the next crisis or when the next wave of entrepreneurship and innovation needs fuel. But first, let me explain how, as an untenured law professor, I found myself launching a start-up designed to revolutionize the legal profession.

19.2 THE STORY BEHIND REINVENT LAW

Admittedly, lawyers have always been entrepreneurial in some ways (particularly those setting out to hang their own shingles), so one might question why it was necessary for legal education and the profession to take up the endeavor of cultivating an innovative atmosphere. Even if economic pressures were not at play, the fundamental ReInvent Law tenet that the delivery of legal services should embrace a culture and curriculum of entrepreneurialism and innovation was imperative a decade ago and remains relevant today for at least three reasons.

First, an enormous need exists for legal services, a demand that has gone largely ignored by the legal profession. Traditional models – whether hourly billing or legal aid – have failed to address this need, leaving a market ripe for entry. Most Americans lack access to meaningful legal advice and advocacy. Unless one qualifies for legal aid or can afford the three-figure-an-hour rate, it is incredibly burdensome if not impossible to obtain a lawyer for even basic life necessities such as divorce, custody, housing issues, and estate planning, let alone assistance for small property disputes, contracts, and business development. This is not because lawyers are unavailable – law schools are graduating new attorneys at unprecedented rates (Sloan 2021). Part of the problem is lawyer regulation – the existing structure of self-regulation has stifled if not strangled attorneys' ability to reach significant, untapped markets for legal services. Equally problematic, however, is the way lawyers (and lawyers-to-be) conceptualize and create their vision of legal services delivery. And this is where cultivating an entrepreneurial lawyer becomes key, which leads to my next point.

Second, law schools are filled with creative, bright individuals who, given the right atmosphere, will be inventors of new models for legal services delivery in addition to practitioners of law. While it may be unlikely that the next Steve Jobs or Mark Zuckerberg will take up the study of law any time soon, law schools are filled with *potential inventors for the future of law practice*. And *invention* is crucial to addressing the vast unmet need for legal services discussed above. A number of law scholars and economists have offered a compelling case for removing many of the barriers to entry and restrictions upon law practice, a step that would facilitate innovation (Ribstein 2010). Yet the ABA and state regulators continue to resist this reform, except for a handful of jurisdictions like Arizona and Utah that in 2020 eliminated the ban on nonlawyer ownership and investment for law firms and encouraged innovation with tools like Utah's creation of a regulatory sandbox.

Third, developing the qualities of an entrepreneur and innovator can benefit any lawyer in their own career development, whether or not they decide to become an inventor or open a new business. Resourcefulness, risk-taking/managing, creativity, and networking are learned behaviors. Moreover, a difficult job market and a desire for work–life balance also have led lawyers to become entrepreneurs rather than pursue the traditional path to partnership. They struggle, however, with time management, client development, billing, and leveraging start-up costs/overhead – all issues that can and should be covered in the law school curriculum and continuing legal education (Bill4Time 2023).

Legal education in the twenty-first century must do more than prepare practice-ready graduates; we must equip students *to deliver legal services in ways that we cannot predict or even imagine*, ways that technological innovation, economic realities, and cultural shifts will inspire and demand. To thrive, lawyers must have a minimum competence in technology, not only for law practice but also self-promotion. Lawyers must also learn to harness the power of networks, both in-person and digitally. We need curriculum change that involves more than just exposure to existing law practice and tools for setting up a traditional law office. For true innovation, students need courses that involve cross-institution and cross-sector collaboration as well as creative communities – physical and virtual spaces designed to nurture new ideas.

The unmet need for legal services still requires (re)inventing the practice of law in ways that cannot yet be predicted or even imagined – the ReInvent Law Laboratory was designed to fill this void, which had gone largely ignored by the legal profession and the legal academy. The mission of ReInvent Law was to cultivate a creative community through partnerships with other university departments, academic institutions, industry, nonprofit organizations, government, and students. The primary purposes of ReInvent Law were (1) to provide a new element of education through research and experimentation on endeavors designed to solve problems faced by the legal profession, including access-to-justice concerns, and (2) to create new vehicles for the delivery of legal services (College of Law Practice Management n.d.). We wanted to build new tools for delivering legal services and to equip students with training for the technology-infused law jobs of the future. Students in our ReInvent Law courses learned to be "trusted curators" of legal information, in addition to being trusted advisors for their clients. Through our curriculum, collaborators from the fields of law, technology, engineering, design, retail, computer science, and beyond came together in a creative community to engage in conversation and actively construct solutions. ReInvent Law harnessed collaborative energies and expertise for inventing new solutions to problems faced in twenty-first-century law practice while simultaneously encouraging and equipping students to embrace innovative approaches in the practice of law. We were always in start-up mode ourselves as we applied an entrepreneurial approach to legal education, or, as some might say, an *intra*preneurial approach, working as entrepreneurs within an academic institution.

This brings me to lessons from ReInvent Law, which can serve as a blueprint for the future pursuit of entrepreneurship and innovation in legal services.

19.3 LESSON #1: TURN A CRISIS INTO A CATALYST

ReInvent Law was born in reaction to a massive upheaval in the legal profession, taking to heart Winston Churchill's advice to "never let a good crisis go to waste." In the immediate aftermath of the 2008 Great Recession, US law schools saw precipitous drops in applications and enrollment. This was due in part to a significant contraction of the legal industry, with reductions in force sweeping across law firms, hiring freezes being implemented, and fewer and fewer entry-level attorney jobs being posted. At the same time, lawyers and clients, frustrated with the constraints of traditional law practice like the billable hour, began experimenting with new technology and entrepreneurial tools drawn from other professions and service industries (Susskind 2008).

As a law professor teaching the required ethics course Professional Responsibility, I felt compelled to do more than grill my students with Socratic questions about ethics rules. I wanted to prepare them for the economic realities in the early 2000s of a disrupted legal market, a massive tuition-based debt bubble, and disgruntled graduates unable to secure jobs (Lederman 2012). Legal education could not afford to ignore this culmination of forces. Indeed, this is precisely why – contrary to what ran on the front page of the *New York Times* in 2011 – law schools actively pursued reform beginning in the early 2000s and continue to do so (Segal 2011). The *New York Times* author's critique that law schools fail to teach lawyering was not only misguided but ignored the actual problem. Law schools were widely focusing on lawyering skills, incorporating clinical activities, mock simulations, and other efforts designed to provide practical, hands-on experience as well as to encourage collaboration with others (Sloan 2009). However, notably absent in the early 2000s from most law schools was a culture of entrepreneurialism and innovation, let alone a significant curriculum or resources devoted to this pursuit. While this observation is less true in 2023, thanks in part to ReInvent Law, much more work remains on this front.

A handful of law schools began initiatives intended to, among other things, rethink the role and structure of the legal profession, as well as how legal services are delivered. Michigan State's ReInvent Law was one such early effort. A primary motivation for cofounding ReInvent Law was to bring my scholarly work on democratizing legal services through regulatory reform into the classroom for the next generation of lawyers. Michigan State was not the only law school to recognize this need. Other early movers acknowledged the need for this sort of invention in law. Examples include Stanford Law School, with its well-developed partnership in a multidisciplinary laboratory called CodeX, which brings together "organizations from industry, government, and academia" in order "to explore ways in which information technology can be used to enhance the quality and efficiency of our legal system while decreasing its cost" (Stanford University n.d.). Harvard's Berkman Klein Center similarly has an established "multidisciplinary research initiative and collaborative network of university, nonprofit and industry partners. Its mission is to investigate and harness the varied forces—evolutionary, social, psychological, neurological, and economic—that shape the role of law and social norms as they enable cooperation, governance, and entrepreneurial innovation" (Harvard University n. d.). Scholars at the University of Miami Law School founded LawWithoutWalls in 2011, "a part-virtual, collaborative academic model . . . that brings together students, faculty, practitioners, business professionals, and entrepreneurs from around the country and the world to innovate legal education and practice" (LawWithoutWalls n.d.). In 2012, Georgetown Law Center launched the course "Technology, Innovation, and Law Practice," which "exposes students to the varied uses of computer technologies in the practice of law," where teams of students partner "with a legal tech expert to develop a platform, application or system that increases access to justice and/or improves the effectiveness of legal representation" (Skalbeck 2012). The class "culminates in a design competition, The Georgetown Iron Tech Lawyer Contest, which is judged by outside experts in the field" (Skalbeck 2012). The efforts from these schools, and many others, continue to be offered in 2023.

One example of ReInvent Law's work was the creation of Michigan State's 21st Century Law Practice Summer Program, a first-of-its-kind intensive study of technology, innovation, regulation, entrepreneurship, and the international legal marketplace. The program convened in London in partnership with the University of Westminster over the summer for three years from 2012 to 2014, a location selected mindfully in light of the recent deregulation in the wake of the United Kingdom's Legal Services Act of 2007 and the corresponding outgrowth of alternative legal services delivery models. Students were immersed in the study of these new models through a program with three primary educational objectives (Computational Legal Studies 2011):

1. Provide students with a comprehensive understanding of the market for legal services as it transitions to a global legal supply chain in the wake of deregulation, economic pressures, and technological innovation.
2. Prepare students to become practice-ready entrepreneurial lawyers who can leverage information technology to operate more efficiently and thereby attract (and retain) clients.
3. Inspire students to think broadly about future delivery of legal representation and access to justice by exposing them to the innovative legal service delivery models and platforms of the present (and not-too-distant future).

The program covered subjects essential to cultivating a learner who will invent the future of law practice, topics that often are neglected by law schools, including technology, legal informatics, marketing, case studies of new legal business structures, math/statistics, virtual law practice, and digital lawyering. We also encouraged personal reflection on how each student might shape law practice in the future to reach those who currently cannot access a lawyer and to do so in a way that allows for a positive work/life balance. Our partners included industry innovators, government entities, regulators, nonprofit organizations, and international academics, with the program culminating in a capstone "un"conference of panels and presentations. LawTechCamp London in 2012 evolved into ReInvent Law in subsequent years. By creating this new space for students to interact with these cross-institution and cross-sector partners – all of us connecting to consider alternative ways of delivering legal services – the program embodied the very kind of innovative spirit we hoped to infuse in participants.

This is not to say that every law school must create a law laboratory. For some schools, collaborating with other university departments, adding courses on entrepreneurship, or adopting entrepreneurship pedagogy in existing courses may be a more desirable way to expose students to these thoughts and ideas. Erik Brynjolfsson and Andrew McAfee, two professors at the MIT Sloan School of Management at the time, recommend that we "[t]each entrepreneurship as a skill not just in elite business schools but throughout higher education." In this way, they argue that we can "[f]oster a broader class of mid-tech, middle-class entrepreneurs by training them in the fundamentals of business creation and management" (Brynjolfsson and McAfee 2012, ch. 4).

Another example of the ReInvent Law curriculum was "Entrepreneurial Lawyering," a course that employed entrepreneurship as a teaching pedagogy. The class involved "a way of thinking and acting, built on a set of assumptions using a portfolio of techniques to create. It goes beyond understanding, knowing, and talking and requires using, applying, and acting" (Michigan State University College of Law n.d.). This method included "starting businesses as coursework, serious games and simulations, design-based thinking, and reflective practice." Students in the "Entrepreneurial Lawyering" course tackled the delivery challenge facing the legal services industry in start-up mode. Among other endeavors, each student created a business plan and pitched a new legal service delivery model. As a supplement to the traditional job resume, students also left the course with an electronic portfolio of work to provide prospective employers and build their careers. Unlike courses at other law schools focused on teaching lawyers how to *advise* entrepreneurs, we taught lawyers to *be* entrepreneurs. When the *New York Times* visited to cover the course capstone – a pitch competition – the reporter noted: "The Entrepreneurial Lawyering Startup Competition, a showcase of the university's ReInvent Law Laboratory, is not an activity many practicing lawyers would recognize. But it might be the kind of broadened curriculum many of today's students need" (Schwartz 2014).

19.4 LESSON #2: MIND THE GAP

One of the magical aspects of ReInvent Law was how it grew by filling the gaps that typically exist among the academy, industry, and nonprofits. As one commentator noted, "[g]iven *ReInvent Law*'s meteoric rise in just two years, it's easy to see there is an enormous void where legal technology needs to be" (Santoro 2014). The ReInvent Law Laboratory inspired thousands of attendees to gather in Dubai, London, New York City, and Silicon Valley between 2012 to 2014. Hundreds waited over an hour outside the Cooper Union on a cold New York morning in February in the hope of getting a seat in the Great Hall for the free event; the line was so long that it wrapped around the city block (Li 2014). They crowded London's Centre Point-CBI Center leaving standing room only, traveled to the Dubai International Financial Centre, and packed the Computer History Museum's amphitheater in Mountainview, California to hear dozens of Ignite-style six-minute talks from thought leaders, some well-known futurists like Richard Susskind, and others who made a name for themselves in their moment on the ReInvent Law stage, including our Michigan State students (Zahorsky 2013).

But holding successful events does not alone explain the clear resonance of the messages emerging at the time. Dozens of conferences about law happen monthly, if not weekly, without even a tweet. The ReInvent Law events became the catalyst for conversations not only among those in the room but, importantly, among a global community.

The phenomenon was far more than the events themselves. As a journalist covering the Silicon Valley conference reflected, "To my mind, the significance of *ReInvent Law* was not in any single presentation or even the overall event. The significance was that *ReInvent Law* was a manifestation of something larger going on in legal technology during a time of unprecedented innovation and creativity. The speakers and attendees represented a kind of legal technology counterculture that is certain to shape the future of the profession" (Bay 2014). Those who participated in *ReInvent Law* efforts continued to be impacted years later. As Australian consultant George Beaton wrote,

> Seldom if ever, in my life has one day made such a positive difference to my professional career. It may seem self-indulgent to write about this event three years on, but I think it's worth sharing. If only because it involves so many people in the *Remaking Law Firms* community to whom I am grateful and indebted. Some 800 people engaged with 34 speakers and discussants in an electrifying exploration of much that's new and challenging in the legal services supply chain for consumers and businesses ... Not all conferences are equal. On time and dollar investment criteria, *ReInvent Law* massively out-rates any conference I have attended. (Beaton 2017)

Not only did ReInvent Law bring individuals together to create something larger than themselves; it fueled a new approach to the delivery of legal services, bringing dignity to the infusion of entrepreneurship and innovation in law practice, especially through the use of tools like design-thinking and technology.

19.5 LESSON #3: CREATE DIGNITY THROUGH COMMUNITY

The ReInvent Law effort pursued dignity for those who encounter the legal system and simultaneously inspired – and dignified – new approaches for delivering legal services and training for those who do so. One speaker explained the dynamic this way: "Those of us working to change the industry are usually surrounded by lawyers who don't know change is coming or, worse, fervently believe that it's not coming. It's easy for us to feel isolated. *ReInvent Law* presented an opportunity for the tribe to gather, meet in person (many of us for the first time), and realize that the passion and energy for change is greater and more broadly held than we see on a day-to-day basis" (Lear 2013). For the first time, academics and students immersed themselves with "venture capitalists, entrepreneurs, knowledge management experts, and other legal professionals to collaborate and discuss how changes can be made and what kinds of changes those could be" in an effort to spark "innovation in the design and delivery of legal services [to] improve access to justice for underserved populations" (Lear 2013). The ecosystem provided legal designers in particular with early opportunities to promote the potential of design methods in reimagining legal service delivery. This allowed for what one scholar has called a "human-centered approach to innovation that draws from the designer's toolkit to integrate the needs of the people, the possibilities of technology, and the requirements for business success" (Davis 2015, 200). In other words, as she put it, ReInvent Law made "good on its promise to solve problems by developing solutions for the education, practice and regulation of lawyers" (Davis 2015, 203).

19.6 LESSON #4: EMBRACE EVOLUTION, EVEN IF IT MEANS THE END

As with most start-ups, ReInvent Law pivoted. Despite calls for more global events, ReInvent Law London 2014 was the last. Others have built upon that early success to hold similarly styled "un-conferences," including the Clio Cloud Conference, though none offers the same free-of-charge, publicly open format. Many standard legal conferences have incorporated the Ignite-style talks into their format and carved out more networking opportunities, signature hallmarks of the ReInvent Law festivities. A version of the ReInvent Law Laboratory lives on at Michigan State University as under the umbrella of the Center for Law, Technology, and Innovation, primarily focused on student education and faculty research. Most important, the work continues to be done by many of the ReInvent Law students who have gone on to successful careers in jobs that did not exist when they first applied to law school, including a legal solutions architect, a deputy director of the ABA Center for Innovation, a legal project manager, and a manager of client value initiatives, among others.

The end of ReInvent Law, however, marked the beginning of the evolution of the profession continuing to instill entrepreneurialism and innovation. As just one measure of ReInvent Law's influence, consider the impact on regulatory reform and the increased adoption of similar programs by law schools across the country.

In 2012, the ABA House of Delegates voted to make technology competence an explicit ethical obligation in the Model Rules of Professional Conduct. Comment 8 to ABA Model Rule 1.1 now states: "To maintain the requisite knowledge and skill, a lawyer should keep abreast of *changes* in the law and its practice, including the *benefits* and *risks* associated with relevant technology" (American Bar Association n.d.). As of early 2020, thirty-seven American jurisdictions had adopted the revised Comment 8 language verbatim or a provision with similar wording (Lawsitesblog n.d.).

From 2014 to 2016, the ABA Presidential Commission on the Future of Legal Services studied and recommended many of the reforms advocated by ReInvent Law participants (I served as a co-reporter for the Commission). One recommendation from the Commission was the creation of the ABA Center for Innovation, which today continues to engage in work that sounds very much like that of the ReInvent Law Laboratory. Its mission is to "[e]ncourage and accelerate innovations that improve the affordability, effectiveness, efficiency, and accessibility of legal services" (American Bar Association n.d.). The statement of the Center's operating principles provides:

> The Center for Innovation enables the profession, including law firms of all sizes, corporate legal departments, courts, legal services lawyers, lawyers in the criminal justice system, law schools and bar associations, to be creative, daring and powerful forces for change. The Center is entrepreneurial, experimental and agile in its work. Looking beyond traditional collaborators and projects, the Center encourages and supports new kinds of partnerships and initiatives that may succeed, or fail, but will all add to the base of knowledge needed to generate true innovation in the delivery of legal services. (American Bar Association n.d.)

Bar associations throughout North America and beyond launched initiatives devoted to the future of the profession. During 2019, three different states – Arizona, California, and Utah – contemplated regulatory reform that would eliminate the ethical prohibition against outside ownership and investment of law practices (Simons 2020). Both Arizona and Utah ushered in substantial reforms to these rules in 2020, and other states are considering reforms (Strom 2019; Weiss 2019; Ward 2020). As of 2019, more than twenty-five law schools had centers devoted to some combination of access to justice, design-thinking, entrepreneurship, innovation, and technology, and the list is continuing to grow (Legal Innovation n.d., Hagan 2018).

In February 2020, the ABA House of Delegates, with the support of the Conference of Chief Justices, approved a new resolution advocating for "innovative approaches to the access to justice crisis" that "encourages US jurisdictions to consider regulatory innovations that have the potential to improve the accessibility, affordability, and quality of civil legal services" but neglects to even mention, let alone provide for, the ethical concerns associated with innovation other than an acknowledgment of the need for "protections that best serve the public" (American Bar Association n.d.). The Resolution urges jurisdictions "to collect and assess data regarding regulatory innovations both before and after the adoption of any innovations to ensure that changes are effective in increasing access to legal services and are in the public interest" (American Bar Association n.d.).

Across curriculum, practice, and regulation, ReInvent Law made a mark and provided legal designers in particular with early opportunities to promote the potential of design methods in reimagining legal service delivery.

REFERENCES

Ambrogi, Robert. n.d. "Tech Competence." *LawSites*. Accessed August 10, 2022. www.lawnext.com/tech-competence.

American Bar Association. 2020. "Adopted by the House of Delegates." *Americanbar.org*. www.americanbar.org/content/dam/aba/directories/policy/midyear-2020/2020-midyear-115.pdf.

n.d. "About Us." *Center for Innovation*. Accessed July 13, 2023. www.americanbar.org/groups/centers_commissions/center-for-innovation/AboutUs/.

Bay, Monica. 2014. "Tech Circuit: Old, New, Borrowed and Blue at ReInvent Law; Like a Wedding with a Lot of Alcohol, a Joyful Cacophony of Noise, Disharmony and Optimism." *Legal Tech News*, February 11. www.law.com/legaltechnews/almID/1202642313642/.

Beaton, George. 2017. "Reflecting on Reinvent Law NYC, 2014." *Remaking Law Firms*. https://remakinglawfirms.com/2031-2/.

Bill4Time. 2023. "Law Firm Billing: How to Motivate Timely and Full Client Payments." *National Law Review* 19, no. 57. www.natlawreview.com/article/law-firm-billing-how-motivate-timely-and-full-client-payments.

Blackman, Josh. 2014. "ReInvent Law Featured in New York Times." *Josh Blackman Blog* (blog), August 1, 2014. https://joshblackman.com/blog/2014/08/01/reinvent-law-featured-in-new-york-times/.

Brynjolfsson, Erik, and Andrew McAfee. 2012. *Race against the Machine: How the Digital Revolution Is Accelerating Innovation, Driving Productivity, and Irreversibly Transforming Employment and the Economy*. Lexington, MA: Digital Frontier Press.

Carter, Terry, Stephanie Francis Ward, and Rachel Zahorsky. 2013. "Meet Our 2013 Legal Rebels." *ABA Journal*, September 1. www.abajournal.com/magazine/article/2013_legal_rebels_a_banner_year.

College of Law Practice Management. n.d. "Michigan State University College of Law – ReInvent Law Laboratory (2013)." Accessed July 13, 2023. www.collegeoflpm.org/michigan-state-university-college-of-law-reinvent-law-laboratory-2013.

Computational Legal Studies. 2011. "Announcing the 21st Century Law Practice London Summer Program – MSU College of Law – (In Partnership with the University of Westminster)." https://computationallegalstudies.com/2011/11/.

Davis, Martha F. 2015. "Institutionalizing Legal Innovation: The (Re)Emergence of the Law Lab." *Journal of Legal Education* 65, no. 1 (June): 190–206. Social Science Research Network (SSRN).

Dewald, Aaron. 2013. "Five Things I Learned at the Reinvent Law Conference in Silicon Valley." *Center for Innovation in Legal Education Blog* (blog), March 9. www.law.utah.edu/five-things-i-learned-at-the-reinvent-law-conference-in-silicon-valley/.

Fastcase. 2013. "Fastcase 50: 2013 Honorees." Last modified 2023. www.fastcase.com/fastcase50/?class=2013.

Goodman, Joanna. 2014. "Reinventlaw London: One Does Not Simply Start a New Law." *Legal IT Professionals Newswire*, June 26. www.legalitprofessionals.com/legal-it-columns/joanna-goodman/6736-reinventlaw-london-one-does-not-simply-start-a-new-law.

Hagan, Margaret. 2018. "Justice Innovation with Law School Design Labs." *Dialogue, ABA Division for Legal Services*. June 15. www.americanbar.org/groups/legal_services/publications/dialogue/volume/21/spring-2018/iolta-design-labs/.

Harvard University. n.d. "Law Lab." Accessed August 5, 2023. https://cyber.harvard.edu/research/lawlab.

Knake, Renee Newman. 2012. "Cultivating Learners Who Will Invent the Future of Law Practice: Some Thoughts on Educating Entrepreneurial and Innovative Lawyers." *Ohio Northern University Law Review* 38 (May): 1–8. Social Science Research Network (SSRN).

"Law Sites: Tracking Technology for the Legal Profession." n.d. www.lawnext.com.

"Law Without Walls." n.d. https://lawwithoutwalls.org.

Lear, Dan. 2013. "What Is Reinvent Law and Why Should Washington's Young Lawyers Care?" *NWSidebar*, July 16. https://nwsidebar.wsba.org/2013/07/16/reinvent-law/.

Lederman, Doug. 2012. "20 More Law Schools Targeted for Lawsuits Over Placement Rates." *Inside Higher Ed*, March 14. www.insidehighered.com/quicktakes/2012/03/15/20-more-law-schools-targeted-lawsuits-over-placement-rates.

Leichter, Matt. 2011. "Law School Debt Bubble: Aggregate Law School Grad Debt Grew $475 Million between 2008 and 2010." *The AM Law Daily*, November 22. https://amlawdaily.typepad.com/amlawdaily/2011/11/law-school-debt-bubble.html.

Li, Victor. 2014. "Reinvent Law's Message is Change for the Client's Benefit." *ABA Journal*, April 1. www.abajournal.com/magazine/article/reinvent_laws_message_is_change_for_the_clients_benefit.

Michigan State University College of Law. n.d. "Course Descriptions: Michigan State University College of Law." Accessed July 13, 2023. www.law.msu.edu/registrar/courses.php?view=all.

Ribstein, Larry E. 2010. "The Death of Big Law." *Wisconsin Law Review* 2010, no. 3 (August): 749–815. http://dx.doi.org/10.2139/ssrn.1467730.

Safer, Dan. 2006. *Designing for Interaction: Creating Smart Applications and Clever Devices*. Berkeley, CA: New Riders.

Santoro, Victoria. 2014. "Interested in the Future of Legal Tech? So Are These Law Schools." *Law Technology Today*, July 30. www.lawtechnologytoday.org/2014/07/interested-in-the-future-of-legal-tech-so-are-these-law-schools/.

Schwartz, John. 2014. "This Is Law School?" *The New York Times*, August 1. www.nytimes.com/2014/08/03/education/edlife/socrates-takes-a-back-seat-to-business-and-tech.html.

Scutt, Michael. 2013. "Reinvent Law London 2013." *Internet Newsletter for Lawyers*, July 15. www.infolaw.co.uk/newsletter/2013/07/reinvent-law-london-2013/.

Segal, David. 2011. "What They Don't Teach Law Students: Lawyering." *The New York Times*, November 19. www.law.berkeley.edu/php-programs/courses/fileDL.php?fID=8230.

Simmons, Christine. 2020. "Bar Groups Line Up Against 'Dangerous Changes' to Lawyer Regulation." *New York Law Journal*, February 5. www.law.com/newyorklawjournal/2020/02/05/bar-groups-line-up-against-dangerous-changes-to-lawyer-regulation.

Skalbeck, Roger. 2012. "Tech Innovation in the Academy." *AALL/ILTA Digital White Paper*. Oct. 2012. 74-78. https://scholarship.law.georgetown.edu/facpub/1163.

Sloan, Karen. 2009. "Reality's Knocking: The Ivory Tower Gives Way to the Real World's Demands." *National Law Journal & Legal Times*, September 7. https://global-factiva-com.ezproxy.neu.edu/ga/default.aspx?page_driver= (open to subscribers only).

2021. "Law School Applicants Surge 13%, Biggest Increase Since Dot-Com Bubble." *Reuters*, August 3. www.reuters.com/legal/legalindustry/law-school-applicants-surge-13-biggest-increase-since-dot-com-bubble-2021-08-03/.

Stanford Law School. n.d. "Codex." Accessed August 9, 2022. https://law.stanford.edu/codex-the-stanford-center-for-legal-informatics/.

Strom, Roy. 2019. "California Opens Door to More Legal Tech, Non-Lawyer Roles (1)." *Bloomberg Law*. https://news.bloomberglaw.com/us-law-week/california-opens-door-to-more-non-lawyer-roles-tech-solutions.

Susskind, Richard E. 2008. *The End of Lawyers? Rethinking the Nature of Legal Services*. Oxford: Oxford University Press.

TED. 2008. "Alan Kay: Educator and Computing Pioneer." www.ted.com/speakers/alan_kay.

Ward, Stephanie Francis. 2020. "Training for Nonlawyers to Provide Legal Advice Will Start in Arizona in the Fall." *ABA Journal*, February 6. www.abajournal.com/web/article/training-for-nonlawyers-to-provide-legal-advice-starts-in-arizona.

Weiss, Debra Cassens. 2019. "Nonlawyers Could Invest in Law Firms and Own Legal Businesses Under Utah Work Group's Proposal." *ABA Journal*, August 28. www.abajournal.com/news/article/nonlawyers-could-invest-in-law-firms-and-own-legal-businesses-under-utah-work-groups-proposal.

Zahorsky, Rachel M. 2013. "'Law Is Broken.' Will These Legal Tech Gurus Bring About Change?" *ABA Journal*, March 13. www.abajournal.com/lawscribbler/article/Law_is_broken_will_these_legal_tech_gurus-bring_about_change.

Zimmerman, Eilene. 2011. "Skipping the Partner Track for a Shingle of One's Own." *The New York Times*, November 23. www.nytimes.com/2011/11/24/business/smallbusiness/skipping-the-legal-partner-track-for-a-private-shingle.html.

20

The Open Law Lab Blog

Margaret Hagan

20.1 INTRODUCTION

At a lunchtime presentation in my first year of law school, I received one of the best pieces of advice in law school. Andrew McLaughlin (2011) was presenting on his career in technology policy, speaking to a small group of law students who were interested in privacy, AI, the future of the Internet, and starting new legal companies. The students came with questions about how to find a good career path that would not only make a beneficial impact on society but would also be personally satisfying and customized to our specific interests. His answer stuck with me: start a blog.

It took me a few months to actually do it when I started posting up my notes, sketches, and thoughts from all of my law school classes, events, and conferences on a blog I called "Open Law Lab." It took me another year after that to arrive at the point of the blog. My first year of posts embodied my effort to figure out exactly what I cared about, of all the different policies, start-ups, legal areas, and legal career paths being presented to me as a law student. The blog was a way to process and synthesize the firehose of ideas and opportunities that were my law school experience. Did I care about the First Amendment on Internet platforms? Or how to start a legal research start-up to quickly analyze contracts? What about how privacy protections were eroding with increased social media usage? Or how to negotiate with venture capitalists?

All these topics were covered in the classes, student groups, journals, and events I attended on my path in law school that I had carved out around technology and the future of law. I knew I cared about new ways of working in law, responding to how people actually used and interacted with the legal system in the increasingly online world, and figuring out how a new era of big technology companies played into people's lives and well-being. But what exactly did I want to work on in my career? And how could I choose something that would make a positive social impact? I followed Andrew McLaughlin's advice and used this blog to pull out what I liked and cared about during all these "learning experiences" and gradually develop my own point of view.

And that point of view ended up being the nascent idea of "legal design" – looking at the justice system from the point of view of its users, working alongside them to rethink how the system operated, and engaging more institutions in experimentation and adoption of new services, tech, and policies that are human centered. But that idea did not spring forth as a coherent manifesto. Rather, it was a gradual evolution from a mix of blog posts on the growth and regulation of tech companies, the processes of design thinking and entrepreneurship spreading around the Stanford campus in the early 2010s, and the crisis of access to justice, with millions of people unable to effectively use the justice system to resolve key problems around money, housing, family, and employment.

I was taking classes that talked about these various things, and they all interested me. I just didn't know what kind of career I could have that would involve them all, or how to make a positive impact on any of them. What was my position?

I used the Open Law Lab blog posts to test out ideas and put out "radio signals" to different communities to see other people's interests and openness to certain ideas. As I was taking classes at the Stanford Institute of Design about using design to improve civic infrastructure in Kenya, I documented this way of working and the stages of the design process, and started speculating about how this method might be brought to the US justice system. As I was studying legal informatics and tech start-ups, I sketched out notes about how websites and data standards could help organize legal information for people without lawyers. And as I was taking legal ethics classes, I drew out speaker's notes about how hard it is to get a lawyer, the regulations that block innovations, and the effect that legal missteps can have on a person's welfare. As I wrote and drew more, I started to see the links and became more confident in a new opportunity space.

What if we could borrow the mindsets and process of the design school and apply it to the state court system in the United States? The workshops, research, and prototyping that a student team was facilitating in Kenya for "international development" purposes could be adapted to civic challenges right down the road from the university, where people were struggling with eviction notices, debt collection lawsuits, domestic violence, and custody disputes. What if we could borrow the entrepreneurship and tech discussions and redirect them away from a focus on getting venture capital to launch a start-up and toward building innovation capacity in public interest institutions so legal aid lawyers, court leaders, community advocates, and past litigants were empowered to disrupt the legal system with new and innovative ideas?

On Open Law Lab, I started to remix the conversations I was having in these different silos, and gradually found my solid ground two years into the blog: I wanted to work in a field that applied a focus on coming up with new ideas to fix public institutions, that put its end users and front-line workers at the center of this innovation work. I wanted to work in the public interest, but with a mission focused on bringing a service design shift to legal institutions, so that they would be centered on serving people with usability, empowerment, and good social outcomes rather than focus on preserving their institution as it is. Reflecting back, I can see I was a product of my law school time. In the early 2010s, especially at Stanford Law School, there was a strong sense of techno-optimism that new Internet platforms could bring about free speech, transparency, communities, and empowerment. There was also a moment in the US legal community that focused on the future of legal practice, entrepreneurship, and the empowered young lawyer. I inherited much of that optimism for both the promise of innovation and the legal system's disruption.

20.2 A FOCUS ON THE HOW AND THE PRACTICAL

My focus on design methods for improving the justice system was concentrated on questions of "how." I was digging into questions about how lawyers worked, how litigants navigated the system, and how new services or policies might work in the justice system. I realized I cared enormously about practical, even mundane parts of the legal system: how to phrase complicated processes, how to lay out form fields on a page, and how to set up a website about courts. My interests were taking me away from complex, abstract arguments about how to interpret a Constitutional clause or how to build an argument on behalf of a client in litigation. In law school classes, I was building those skills and enjoyed flexing my legal practice muscles. But my passion was steering me to parts of the legal system that were much more concrete, about the "real-life" consequences and the many people who end up in legal aid offices, court hallways, and on courtroom benches.

I began to blog about these mundane things that caught my attention, but all went back to this question of practical strategies to make the legal system more usable. This meant observing how lawyers could hold better meetings by using visual note-taking. Or in photographing how attorneys in self-help centers could lay out walls of forms and process maps in the court to convey complicated legal matters to litigants. Or how judges in family courts converted the design of their room to be more collaborative, friendly, and supportive by setting up different seating arrangements, kids' toys, and visual explainers on the wall. These examples of practical "hacks" of the legal system became something akin to a "literature review." Academic articles were not focused on these improvements in legal communication, services, or system design. But I felt these interventions, many of them scrappy and do-it-yourself, could potentially be quite impactful on people's willingness and ability to engage with the justice system.

I also began to read more design theory and engage with design researchers in this phase of my blog. I sought out others working in government improvements, civic technology, and design for complex systems like health care and finances. I could see so much potential in identifying ways to improve users' experience of the legal system, and I found designers developing the methodologies and research frameworks that could take these case studies to a more rigorous level of analysis. I found the work of service designers[1] and those working on research-through-design to be particularly enlightening.[2] They were laying out a trajectory of rigorous academic work to create new interventions and studying what social and policy outcomes they could have (Zimmerman, Stolterman, and Forlizzi 2010; Hagan and Kim 2017). They might be working in other areas, like data privacy or education. But their methods were generative and practical – creating academic knowledge by creating new design interventions oriented around people's needs, and then studying if and how they worked in pilot studies.

On Open Law Lab, I began collecting and remixing design methods. Many of these were very practical and aimed at people working in corporate settings. What kinds of workshops and activities can you run to come up with new, profitable business offerings? I learned about these kinds of methods in events at the law school, the university, and around the Bay Area as the notion of design-driven innovation proliferated in the mid-2010s. But at the same time, I was interested in adapting these methods to both public institutions (where the goal was not about improving market share or growing profits, but about building trust, dignity, and improved social outcomes) and academic institutions (where the goal was to build knowledge and educational experiences).

20.3 A RADIO SIGNAL OUT TO A LIKE-MINDED COMMUNITY

I continued to publish my collection of ideas about how design methods could be used to reform how lawyers work and how people experience their justice problems. Each post became something of a radio signal, put out on the Internet, and gradually found others who were thinking in similar ways. People began to reach out with ideas and work that resonated with the themes, and curiosity about exactly what a design approach was and how it interacted with more technology-driven approaches to improving the legal system.

There were a few distinct types of stakeholders who were interested in the early versions of legal design. They responded to the Open Law Lab blog posts in different ways.

The first was *legal academics* who wanted to see more law schools focused on empirical research and showed an early interest in design. These professors and

[1] Miso Kim's work on the foundations of service design in human dignity was particularly helpful in my thinking. I worked with her on the bridge between dignity, service design, and the civil justice system in "Design for Dignity and Procedural Justice Advances in Intelligent Systems and Computing" (Hagan and Kim 2017).

[2] For example, I found research through design articles like the following to be helpful in identifying ways to focus on justice interventions in an academic way (Zimmerman, Stolterman, and Forlizzi 2010).

deans were interested in shifting legal academic work away from normative law school articles that prescribed what the legal system should be. Instead, they were intrigued by a design approach's focus on new interventions. This could help academics and their partners create new things and then gather empirical data about how they worked in practice. Design mattered because it could help them make the strongest possible intervention to study and develop better knowledge about what worked. The academics were interested in how design could give them reliable principles and models to guide the development of interventions, in the hope that well-designed interventions would be more likely to get good results in a study. If studies are expensive and time consuming to run, then investing in design work could make it more likely that the intervention they were testing would show a positive result, and the study would be more likely to attract attention and have the intended policy impact.

Clinical law professors and law school center directors were more interested in legal design for the practical skills it could convey to law students. Many of these leaders at law schools were very interested in how lawyers work, and how to train a new generation that was more effective, efficient, and impactful in their work. As such, this type of stakeholder was much more interested in a design approach as applied to the daily tasks of a legal professional. Could clinic teams hold brainstorming sessions using creative methods from the design process? Could a lawyer hold visual mapping sessions with her clients, to better communicate options and get to a decision more promptly? Could a clinic team create business documents using visual design principles so that clients would be more likely to understand and use these legal instruments? In this application of legal design, the goal was not so much the creation of better, more user-friendly "designs" to be tested out. Rather, it was about mixing the design process with legal work to improve the lawyer's process of creating traditional legal work products (e.g., memos, contracts, presentations, meetings, business documents, etc.). These stakeholders wouldn't necessarily describe themselves as entrepreneurial or innovative, but they were interested in creative new ways to do legal work better.

Corporate law firm and legal department lawyers also reached out with interest. There were two themes of interest from this group of stakeholders. The first theme was about developing new services that their firm could offer to clients, or that their department could offer to their business colleagues. Many of them were interested in how a design process could help identify new websites, digitalization of processes, predictive analysis, and other solutions that could improve the uptake of legal services. They were thinking like legal tech start-ups: Where are there inefficiencies, frustrations, and bad user experiences? They wanted to develop an internal start-up culture to "self-disrupt" using a human-centered design process that would help them understand users' needs, spot breakdowns and opportunities, and then develop new innovative solutions that would get clients to use more legal services and be more satisfied with them. Along with this, these internal start-ups were interested in identifying new kinds of services or business models that could complement the more traditional ones. Could they use design methods to find other things their clients wanted or other ways that clients would be willing to pay for them?

The second theme from corporate legal stakeholders was around design for changing management. They wanted to develop better organizational cultures that were innovative, flexible, and collaborative inside their legal groups. They saw design methods as a way to shift the mindsets of their colleagues to be more experimental, focused on users, and open to new ideas. They were excited about the potential of design workshops and sprints to change the perspectives of lawyers who had been trained to be focused on precedent, hierarchy, and conservatism. Especially for corporate leaders who had been trying to get more employee buy-in for new technology and data initiatives, new product and service offerings to clients, and other big changes, there was excitement about the design process to switch people away from being naysayers to all things new. Design methods were exciting because it was not about technology at the heart of innovation, which often alienated legal professionals, who doubted technology's ability to deal with complex legal work and client services. Rather, design methods still put legal people (not engineers) in charge of innovation but shifted mindsets to see existing services from new perspectives, and helped groups make strategic decisions about where to focus new innovation efforts. Many corporate leaders were excited to run legal design sessions with their team, or their entire organization, to find who among their colleagues might be innovation leaders, might have promising ideas for their organization, and might be part of a larger organizational shift.

A final group of interested stakeholders was *access-to-justice leaders*. This stakeholder group included directors of court self-help centers, legal aid attorneys, consultants working on civil justice issues, and judges in charge of a state court or administrative proceeding. This group was already equipped with a focus on the practical mundanities of the justice system. They cared about the "end-user" of the system and were working to figure out ways to help find these people, get them helpful information, and empower them to navigate the system. They had already gone through the "design mindshift" from a focus on the professional or the institution as the center toward placing the user at the center. They didn't necessarily know the terminology or formal methods of design work, but they were already aligned with its values and goals.

When it came to legal design themes, this group was interested in many of the themes already mentioned in my discussion with the other stakeholders. They wanted to create new interventions that could improve people's outcomes (like appearance rates at court hearings, favorable settlement agreements, and housing and financial stability), as the academic empiricists did. They were open to a deliberate, human-centered process (like the design one) to create these new, better interventions that would bring a new crop of ideas to justice institutions about how they could reform in very practical, low-cost, procedural ways.

The access-to-justice leaders were also interested in the transformation of their institutions like the corporate leaders were. They were also struggling with the change of management issues, including employees who were resistant to change, wary of tech-driven innovation, and concerned about new ways of working. The leaders were similarly excited to get more court staff, legal aid lawyers, justice navigators, and foundations to go through design cycles to adopt a user-centered mindset, be open to criticism about current services, and identify opportunities for new services and technologies that could help them better reach outcomes. They wanted to see more public interest professionals trained in design skill sets, and more organizations integrating design work into their strategic sessions.

Finally, these leaders also wanted to rethink how lawyers could communicate with their clients using a design approach. Could courts map out complicated housing court or debt collection processes using timelines and flowcharts? Could legal clinics have placemats of options and legal cartoons that could help a person make sense of the new legal information they were learning? Could nonprofits set up better websites and social media accounts to attract more people to use legal services? Like the law school clinicians, justice leaders were eager to rethink the day-to-day practice of legal professionals by bringing in discrete design methods such as empathy interviews, visualizations, brainstorming, journey mapping, and collaborative workshops.

20.4 SOLIDIFYING A LEGAL DESIGN PRACTICE

From this disparate interest in my posts about what legal design could be, I started to build an actual practice. In the years after I graduated from law school, I began to develop a set of workshops, methods, and research that engaged these stakeholders with design. This included classes on how to change management in law firms and how to design new contracting technologies with legal departments. It also involved conferences, workshops, and brainstorming sessions with academics and clinicians about how we might collaborate to integrate design methods and cycles into their pedagogical and research work.

And it led me to the most dominant, ongoing part of my design practice: justice innovation. I had found my passion was in making the lived experience of the justice system more dignified, empowering, and stabilizing for people. I built my own skills in communication, service, and policy design to develop new interventions and partnerships that could make the justice system less institution-centered and more people-centered. The justice leaders who initially reached out to me, as a third-year law student, are now my colleagues a decade on. They helped me launch pilots, academic studies, and communities of practice around design methods that build greater access to justice. My work continues, as an ever-evolving set of partnerships, skills, insights, strategies, and projects that aim to make a dent in this wicked problem – to shift the huge US justice system to be about human dignity rather than institutional preservation. It will be the work of my lifetime.

REFERENCES

Hagan, Margaret, and Miso Kim. 2017. "Design for Dignity and Procedural Justice." *Proceedings of the Applied Human Factors and Ergonomics International Conference, 2017*. New York: Springer Press.

McLaughlin, Andrew. 2011. "How to Get a Job in Tech Policy." Presented at *CIS Speaker Series, Center for Internet and Society, Stanford Law School, Stanford, CA, February 10, 2011*. https://law.stanford.edu/event/cis-speaker-series-andrew-mclaughlin-how-to-get-a-job-in-tech-policy/.

Zimmerman, John, Erik Stolterman, and Jodi Forlizzi. 2010. "An Analysis and Critique of Research through Design: Towards a Formalization of a Research Approach." *Proceedings of the 8th ACM Conference on Designing Interactive Systems, Aarhus Denmark, August 16–20, 2010*. New York: Association for Computing Machinery.

21

Disciplinarity and the Modes of Legal Design

Michael Doherty

21.1 INTRODUCTION

Is legal design an academic discipline? Academic disciplines can be understood in various ways, including from sociological (the institutionalisation and organisation of knowledge production) (Bourdieu 1988) and anthropological perspectives (academic disciplines as "tribes" with a shared culture and values) (Becher and Trowler 2001). This chapter briefly measures the current state of legal design against the checklist of characteristics of a discipline as proposed by Krishnan (2009) and concludes that legal design does have the characteristics of an emerging discipline. It explores some of the potential negative consequences of erecting disciplinary boundaries and norms but argues that recognition of legal design as a subdiscipline is broadly positive. The chapter concludes that legal design academics (together with their collaborative partners) have a timely opportunity to intentionally design the methods and modalities of their nascent discipline. We can, and should, consciously build an academic discipline that works for its users, be they academic practitioners, students or wider professional communities. The idea that a discipline can "work for its users" in this sense means that it can try to protect their well-being and their freedom to explore intellectual and practical possibilities. It can provide a platform for those in the discipline to tackle the systemic inequities that undermine dignity for those societal groups that they work with and for. It can be an environment, a mode of working and living, in which people can have self-respect and respect for others.

21.2 LEGAL DESIGN

There is a high degree of consensus as to the aims, meaning, and method of legal design. Margaret Hagan (n.d.) defines it as "the application of human-centered design to the world of law, to make legal systems and services more human-centered, usable, and satisfying." For the Legal Design Alliance (n.d.), "Legal Design is an interdisciplinary approach to apply human-centred design to prevent or solve legal problems."

There are variances in the central methodology of legal design. NuLawLab early on used a four-stage approach derived from Kelley and Kelley (2013; Jackson 2016) of (a) inspiration, (b) synthesis, (c) ideation and experimentation, and (d) implementation. The influential work of Stickdorn et al. (2018; Design Council n.d.) on service design methods adopts the British Design Council model of discover, define, develop and deliver, visualised as a "double-diamond" process. The Stanford d. school model has five stages: empathise, define, ideate, prototype, test. Yet even a cursory examination shows that these are slightly different ways of demarcating and labelling a substantially similar multi-step process. They all also agree on the need to apply these models in non-mechanistic and flexible ways.

This harmony should not, perhaps, be so surprising. The core methodology of design thinking was already well developed before its purposeful application to legal systems and services. There have been, very broadly speaking, different points of focus in the different geographical incubators of the discipline: on contracts and visualisations in Europe, particularly Finland and Germany, and on access to justice and the design of dispute resolution procedures from the "law labs" of the United States. Yet, this has not resulted in significant conflicts as to the core aims and methods of legal design.

21.3 THE NATURE OF ACADEMIC DISCIPLINES

An initial question is: Should legal designers even want their work to be organised within the structure of an academic discipline? Trowler (2012, 24) has pointed out that, "Some have argued that disciplines are dead or dying, replaced by interdisciplinary forms of organisation as higher education becomes more oriented to solving pressing real-world problems through multidisciplinary task-oriented formations that draw in expertise from beyond universities." One conception of this relatively new mode of knowledge generation and problem solving is called "Mode 2." Proposed by Gibbons et al. (1994), it contrasts with a traditional Mode 1 where the focus of scientific research is new knowledge created within strict disciplinary boundaries and university institutional structures. Mode 2 is concerned with real-world problem solving in fluid multi-disciplinary teams, using action research, co-operative enquiry, grounded theory and clinical methods (MacLean, MacIntosh and Grant 2002). This structure will have an immediate resonance for legal design.

The descriptive accuracy of the Mode 2 concept, though, has itself been criticised (Fuller 2000), and attacks on the conceptual value as "simplistic" have been recognised even by some of its proponents (Nowotny, Scott and Gibbons 2003). The element of Mode 2 most relevant to this chapter is the critique of disciplinarity that it associates with Mode 1, which developed within a paradigm of pure scientific research, and which seems to have limited applicability to legal scholarship.

A persistent and older model of legal scholarship involves scholars acting as, or closely with, legal practitioners in the practical application of law, that is, in a real-world problem-oriented way (Cownie 2012). Crucially, a key feature of Mode 2, its multi-disciplinarity, presupposes the existence of disciplinary boundaries. The leading modern study on academic disciplinarity by Krishnan concludes that "It is certainly too soon to declare the end of disciplines and there is the strong likelihood that disciplines and disciplinarity can survive in the long-term ... [and] it is unlikely that a single post-disciplinary science could be possible or successful or even desirable" (Krishnan 2009, 55).

As outlined below, there are benefits for academics to have their field recognised as an "academic discipline" in terms of developing academic identities, effective infrastructures and organisational independence. Trowler (2012, 24) acknowledges this "continued salience of disciplinary forms of organization." An interim conclusion is that Mode 2 is an interesting perspective on the economic and social organisation of knowledge production and sketches out many features that legal design ought to be happy to embrace, but does not strike a serious blow to the continuing relevance of academic disciplines.

We should, though, also address the alleged dark sides of disciplinarity. Krishnan identifies criticisms that its "narrow and deep specialization" can foster "insularity and imperialism rooted in partial and ideological thinking" (Krishnan 2009, 4). Exercising a discipline will intrinsically involve policing certain behaviours or ways of thinking (Krishnan 2009, 8). This was the aspect of disciplinarity that Michel Foucault found so distasteful in *Discipline and Punish*. He argued that, "The disciplines characterize, classify, specialize; they distribute along a scale, around a norm, hierarchize individuals in relation to one another and, if necessary, disqualify and invalidate." Followers of disciplines ultimately internalise these rules so that "open repression is no longer needed," and academic disciplines act as a process "limiting the freedom of individuals and as a way of constraining discourses" (Foucault [1975] 1991, 223).

This poses questions to those who want to actively promote the development of legal design as an "academic discipline." If it is a discipline, then it must have boundaries. If it is interdisciplinary – that is, a field of activity traversing academic disciplinary boundaries – then those boundaries must exist and be maintained by the actions of disciplinary practitioners. Lyotard (1984) agrees that academic disciplines are specific practices containing rules that determine which kinds of statements are true or false.

Disciplinarity almost certainly carries with it this "border force," this policing function. Social constructionists such as Biagioli (2002, 16), for example, have argued that peer review is "a means of policing academic discourses and of ensuring their overall coherence." Similar exercises of disciplinary power happen in the selection of research partners, appointments to editorial boards, hiring decisions by faculty committees, and so on. A decision of a legal design editorial board to reject a paper because it did not respect disciplinary traditions (e.g., the Legal Design Alliance ("LeDA") Manifesto) would take us into this realm of Foucaultian discipline. If it decided not to decide, then the editorial board would threaten the intellectual coherence of the subject it is publishing papers on.

Ultimately, it seems that the responsibilities of this function cannot be avoided. Boundaries are necessary. They allow argument to happen. They allow communities of practice to build capacity to generate useful knowledge and go on to do useful things in the world. The answer for legal design may simply be an explicit awareness of this aspect of disciplinarity and a reflexive application of its external facing methodologies to its own practices as a discipline: that is, to be human-centred, to be flexible and to focus on the real-life needs of its practitioners as well as its users. If academic power must be exercised, then let it be in a paradigm upholding quality but that also values equity, inclusivity and (as a particularly radical suggestion) kindness.

The modalities and conventions of a particular discipline can emerge as much from its social practices as from its more formal declarations, organising principles and manifestos. The danger for a nascent discipline is that it can incorporate unspoken assumptions that deserve to be questioned and existing inequities that deserved to be rejected. Legal design has a great and tantalising opportunity to do things differently, and its own rhetoric, if it really means it, should lead it to consciously and positively design its modalities and infrastructure rather than unconsciously follow those of existing disciplines.

21.4 LEGAL DESIGN AS AN ACADEMIC DISCIPLINE

Krishnan, in his wide-ranging survey of the nature of disciplinarity, says that disciplines involve "the organisation of learning and systematic production of new knowledge" (2009, 9). He presents a list of the general characteristics that a discipline ought to have. This section is a short initial proposal of whether and how legal design fulfills these characteristics.

21.4.1 A *Particular Object of Study*

Legal design is a markedly diverse field. As a form of professional practice, it has been most utilised at opposite ends (depending on how one measures these things) of the legal services spectrum. Many ground-breaking projects are in access to justice and "poverty law" fields. There have been innovative developments from Big Law firms, in-house corporate legal services, and legal design agencies. This diversity is reflected in the academic practices of legal design pioneers, from Helena Haapio's work on contracts and proactive law to Margaret Hagan's insistence that the work of the Stanford Legal Design Lab should have a direct positive impact on people facing post-COVID-19 eviction in the United States. The particular object of legal design has encompassed many areas of legal scholarship including intellectual property, privacy, legal technology, judicial administration, legal policymaking, communication of civil rights, and so on. Yet the breadth of this activity should not divert us from the fact that this work has an underlying commonality, an object of study that is the application of design mindsets and methods to legal products and processes.

There are many precedents where the knowledge matrices of existing external disciplines have been brought to bear as a lens to examine very wide parts of the legal field and, as a consequence, to create something new. Legal history and law and economics are just two examples of this disciplinary porosity.

21.4.2 A *Body of Accumulated Specialist Knowledge*

As a nascent discipline, this is necessarily a small but growing body of knowledge. It should be acknowledged that, thus far, the body of accumulated knowledge is rather underdeveloped, but there has been a surge of new monographs and edited collections from 2020 to 2022, plus special editions of journals. A new specialist journal, provisionally titled *Legal Design Journal*, is in development. Yet, the body of academic work on legal design, around a decade after its emergence, remains disparate and only operates in dialogue with other legal design scholarship in limited ways.

A part of this relative disciplinary immaturity is that legal design is very different from other young and new legal disciplines such as environmental law, sports law, and energy law. They, like legal history, law and economics, and feminist legal studies, can review and analyse a huge corpus of existing legal materials. We have no key cases, no body of primary law to pore over. The examples we use will largely be from practice rather than from law reports and the statute book. The case studies available to us are very useful but often limited by commercial confidence considerations.

Theories and concepts can effectively organise specialist knowledge. There are a range of concepts from design, as well as legal classifications, that can organise legal design knowledge, but the golden thread is user-centricity. Other specialist knowledge concepts that are distinct – when viewed from existing legal perspectives – include innovation, prototyping and creativity. Is UX a bit thin as an organising concept? If we think of law not as a system of commands but as a social common good (as much political philosophy, social contract theory and rule of law rhetoric does), then there are important practical, economic, social, and moral reasons why law should work better for people. In other words, human-centricity has the potential to be both revolutionary in its impact on legal systems and services and intellectually coherent with organising theories and concepts with deep roots in legal design's parent disciplines of law and design.

21.4.3 *Specific Terminologies or a Specific Technical Language*

Legal design has lots of specific technical language, mostly derived from mainstream design thinking and service design: UX, journey mapping, ideation, needs analysis, service safari, pain points. Their use in a legal context can seem exotic. As the discipline matures, as it becomes more entangled in the tacit knowledge, the underlying disciplinary matrix, of law, it may become more entwined with legal discourse (e.g., contract design, the A2J gap) and start to appear more integrated into legal vocabularies, and, conversely, to seem more distinct to designers.

21.4.4 *Developed Specific Research Methods*

Again, we have a picture of diversity and some underlying harmony. There is a lot of methods in the method: UX research (qualitative and quantitative), observer and participant research, prototype testing, outcome evaluation. Many of these research methods have been alien or highly marginal to legal scholarship so far.

Legal design scholars also integrate existing methodologies with new design perspectives to evolve new ways of doing legal research, for example, Perry-Kessaris (2021) adding imaginative "designerly" ways to the palette of socio-legal inquiry into economic/legal life.

21.4.5 *Some Institutional Manifestation in the Form of Subjects Taught at Universities or Colleges, Respective Academic Departments and Professional Associations*

There is a persuasive story to tell here that legal design has been successful in starting to carve out institutional manifestations of its work. This is not always easy, as tax law academics in the United Kingdom can attest. There is a competitive market for space in the law curriculum, in support for new programme development and in staffing resource allocation decisions. There are too many legal design course initiatives, clinical legal design programmes and extracurricular activities to list here, but one element of legal design discipline building is worth highlighting: lots of it has happened regardless of institutional support.

Legal design activists have tapped into global networking and collaborations with practitioners to create judicial support programmes, student clinical projects, international conferences and open professional associations. They are not divorced from institutional power and exigencies but hint at new ways to build an academic discipline.

The overall interim conclusion is that the disciplinary conditions have been met. There is a sufficient pattern within the mosaic of activities around law and design to say that something is emerging that can in good conscience be called legal design.

We can characterise this as a process of subject parturition; legal design is developing from the interaction of legal and design disciplines and gradually gaining some independence from them (Metzger 1987). Work remains to be done on what Metzger called subject dignification, an increase in status and acceptability within the academy.

21.5 DISCIPLINARITY CONSTRUCTION AND CHARACTER

Some psychological approaches to discipline classification are based on the beliefs that discipline members hold about themselves (Biglan 1973). This is pertinent to legal design because it implies agency: the ability of discipline practitioners, particularly in the emergent phase, to consciously consider how the modes of the discipline (its operations and structures, the experience of being a legal design academic) can match its ambitions for the delivery of legal services, business contracts, access to justice, and the application of legal tech, among other things. That is, if disciplines are a social construct, let us think about how we want to design our own particular construct.

Anthropology can also provide useful perspectives here, particularly the work of Becher and Trowler (2001) on "academic tribes." According to this analysis, academic disciplines distinguish themselves through "self-created cultural practices and specific values." These tribes speak the same language, participate in the social life of the group and, to a significant degree, share the same beliefs: "[T]he knowledge structures of disciplines (the academic territories) strongly condition or even determine the behaviour and values of academics, who live in disciplinary tribes with common sets of practices" (Trowler 2012, 24).

The language of tribes may be attractive to legal designers involved in carving out new territory and ways of doing their discipline and in presenting cultural practices that may be rather different from their law school colleagues. Krishnan (2009, 24) argues that "academic tribes, especially those with less tradition, strive for developing a strong cultural identity that allows them to prosper."

Yet, there is something further to consider in this academic tribes thesis. As argued earlier in the chapter, the visible culture of an academic tribe is strongly conditioned or even determined by the knowledge structure of the tribe's discipline. That is, physicists are different from engineers in the ways they research, teach, converse, hold conferences and even choose hobbies, because physics is different from engineering. As legal designers, we may accept that the experimental, visual, and practical elements of our methods will influence our culture and behaviour as academics, but we ought not to lose sight of the central tenet that social systems and processes can be intentionally designed. Indeed, Becher and Trowler (2001) stress that their anthropological analysis is only one way of identifying structural factors influencing academics' cultures. Any conditioning of legal design subject matter and methods on our "tribal" behaviour and culture can be critically examined to see if it is fit for its own purposes and consistent with its own rhetoric.

There are a couple of final lines to draw between Krishnan's work and legal design. Historical perspectives on the development of disciplines point to the need for intellectual leadership to define the new discipline, give it a clear agenda and inspire followers. He argues that "founding a new discipline needs adventurous pioneers who are willing to leave their original discipline behind to cover new ground," and that "practically every new discipline starts off necessarily as an interdisciplinary project that combines elements from some parent discipline(s) with original new elements and insights" (Krishnan 2009, 34). Further, he finds that "disciplines are now identified more through the methodology they apply to certain topics or research fields, rather than through the topics or research fields themselves" (Krishnan 2009, 35).

There is therefore scope for legal designers to draw on the best of the epistemological and methodological domains of law and design to influence the social construction of a new subdiscipline. Those inheritances will influence but not determine the direction or nature of legal design, and the "adventurous pioneers" have agency in evolving the modalities of being an academic legal designer.

21.6 WHAT SHOULD THE INTENTIONAL DESIGN OF LEGAL DESIGN AS AN ACADEMIC DISCIPLINE CONSIDER?

Describing a key facet of legal design, Hagan (n.d.) says, "It offers intentionality in the face of a system that has been hacked and patched together haphazardly and without user testing." It would be an irony if legal design were to evolve its own disciplinarity in a haphazard way and without testing for the experience of what we might call the "users" of that disciplinary system, namely its own practitioners, students and those outside academia who want to engage with their work. There are strong signs that this passive approach will not happen, that there is an intention among legal design academics to think deeply about how they want to practice their own particular variant of academia (Doherty 2019).

Service design as applied to customer-facing organisations already acknowledges that its methods can, and should, be used with employees and service providers as well as directly with service users and customers (Stickdorn et al. 2018). Academic practitioners of legal design will still be (largely) working within the academy. They will be seeking career development, research funds, sabbatical leave and research students. This is because they have the same ambitions as other bright hard-working people, but also because they want to go out into the world and use design to make the sorts of differences to legal systems and services that, inter alia, Hagan and Haapio talk about so eloquently. Having the resources and authority of the academy may not always be essential, but they certainly help. No discipline is an island, entire unto itself. If legal design wants to do things a bit differently, it still has to navigate these higher education systems and structures. If it wants, as just one example, to develop different ways of presenting work (apps, posters) which garners academic credibility, then it must do so in a way that acknowledges the existing and overwhelming primacy of text as authority within the legal academy.

21.7 WHAT SHOULD BEING A LEGAL DESIGN ACADEMIC LOOK AND FEEL LIKE?

With that in mind, this chapter concludes with some short position statements or discussion points. These points are about the modalities of legal design as an academic discipline: the particular mode in which being a legal design academic is expressed or experienced. They largely follow aspects of legal design that are extant but seek to develop further discussion of these academic and cultural practices. So, legal design as an academic discipline ought to be:

21.7.1 *Internationalist, Not National*

A large majority of legal academic disciplines have a national focus; this is understandable, as these disciplines are based on the study and teaching of a body of substantive national law (e.g., property, contract and criminal law). This is acknowledged by Becher and Trowler (2001) as one limit on the more extreme visions of globalised higher education, and is further bound up in issues of national legal professional accreditation. Yet, those topics not based on studying specifically national law often also adopt nationally focused structures (to a greater or lesser extent). American law students will use textbooks on international law written by American authors. There is a British Institute of International and Comparative Law.

Similarly, legal education has some specific jurisdictional concerns but is more often concerned with universal questions of pedagogy, yet none of the twelve members of the editorial board of the *Journal of Legal Education* is from outside the United States. UK-based *The Law Teacher* journal is the "international journal of legal education," yet 64% of its editorial board comes from one country – the United Kingdom. In other words, there is scope for legal scholarship to have a more internationalist mode.

As a legal academic discipline emerging in the second and third decades of the twenty-first century, legal design does not have to adopt this infrastructure. The modes of collaborative working and communicating available in a connected world mean that it is easier to write together, to run events together, and to contribute to each other's courses. The dominance of international English, for better or for worse, means that a large majority of practitioners and students have access to a lingua franca. This exposes the need to develop legal design materials in languages accessible to a wide range of language users, and to support the development of legal design centres of excellence that can both take part in global debates and support localised activities.

21.7.2 *Interdisciplinary, Not Mono-Disciplinary*

This follows, of course, from the whole basis of the movement. It involves working with technologists, information designers and visualisation partners. It is part of the DNA of legal design. However, if legal design is the application of design thinking to a social process (a legal system) or a business offering (legal services), why not just bring in a really great service design team? What do law-background legal designers bring to the party?

Hagan (2018) has charted how legal design is a complement to existing legal methodologies such as law in action and empirical legal studies, and Perry-Kessaris (2021) has similarly argued the value of design approaches to socio-legal studies. The drafting and application of general rules to unknown variants of future human behaviour, "doing things with rules," are inherently complex, and there are more obvious constraints on the ability to simplify and visualise legal information than there are in, for example, product design.

That is, the distinctiveness of law as a social phenomenon and of lawyering and lawyerly skills as practices need to be articulated so that this process is not seen as simply the application of one methodology (design) to one knowledge domain (law); to be legal design, not design and the law.

21.7.3 *Democratic and Inclusive, Not Hierarchical*

This a call to the legal design community to try to consciously design working practices during the developmental stage of the discipline so that they avoid some of the callousness and inequity we see in legal practice and academia. It has been argued that the generation of new academic structures can present opportunities "to shed oppressive practices as well as to realise new possibilities" (Winter 1995, 130). How is working in legal design going to be a great experience for early career researchers, students, non-academics, academics who are parents and non-lawyers? Graphic design, certainly in the United Kingdom, is not a great role model here in relation to women, people of color or working-class people. Most of the high-profile innovators in legal design have been women: How can we widen out that positive effect and sustain it?

This is a short question but a difficult one. Its premise – that legal design ought to build so-called progressive values into its cultural practices – ought to be interrogated and discussed. If it is accepted, then its implications will demand certain critical approaches to, as one example, conference organisation. Will they revolve around high-profile keynote speakers? Will participants be invited along "to hear" or to "help create"? How far will organisers go to replace "manels" with balanced panels? What about pricing or even childcare? This is even before we get to issues around project funding, editorial panels, and so on.

As emphasised here, no discipline is an island, and the answers to many of these questions will be conditioned by existing practices within the academy. Yet this is where an awareness of disciplinarity combined with design methods may help the legal design community to build versions of academic life that are more amenable to its practitioners.

21.7.4 *Multi-modal, Not Text-Based*

The legal academy has its traditional structures for research outputs of journals, edited collections and monographs. The core output of a legal design project may be a poster, an app, a diagram, a website, a form, a contract or something even less tangible (e.g., an increase in the number of court staff undertaking concierge-like services). Do we need to translate these into traditional formats (a journal article about a poster), or allow the objects to stand for themselves? This produces a dilemma. To move wholly to a "translation model" undermines the validity of the object as a legal research output. To wholly reject a "translation model" leaves legal designers without a curriculum vitae or a publishing record that would be easily recognised by a funding council or faculty hiring committee. The answer to the dilemma is not obvious or easy, but intentionality about the mode of being an academic within a legal design subdiscipline ought to embolden us to tackle the question directly.

21.8 CONCLUSION

This is an exciting time for legal design. Those who broke ground on this discipline over the last twenty years are seeing an upsurge in interest in what they started to build. More recent arrivals, who may play a role as "consolidators and synthesizers" (Krishnan 2009, 34), are discovering a methodology and a toolkit that open up possibilities for innovation and engagement that were previously a vague itch that they were not quite able to scratch.

The tools and methods for the type of enterprise called for here are already in our hands. Autoethnography is already being used to examine the experiences of clinical legal practitioners in higher education (Campbell 2016). Other forms of participant research could uncover the human-centred needs of early career researchers, of academics who want to get into the field, of consultants and start-ups who want to contribute to more academically focused projects. Personas of these archetypes could be co-created and their onward journeys from first engagement with legal design mapped. Experimental prototypes of conference engagement, or publication models of design objects, or models to generate academic collaboration rather than competition, could be quickly ideated, prioritised, implemented and evaluated.

The outward-looking nature of legal design is one of its most attractive features. It should not exclude careful consideration of what being an "academic discipline" might mean for legal design or internal debate on how its practitioners might intentionally design their own disciplinary culture and working practices to promote equity, autonomy and dignity.

REFERENCES

Becher, Tony, and Paul R. Trowler. 2001. *Academic Tribes and Territories*. Buckingham, UK: Open University Press.

Biagioli, Mario. 2002. "From Book Censorship to Academic Peer Review." *Emergences: Journal for the Study of Media & Composite Cultures* 12, no. 1: 11–45. https://doi.org/10.1080/1045722022000003435.

Biglan, Anthony. 1973. "The Characteristics of Subject Matters in Different Academic Areas." *Journal of Applied Psychology* 57, no. 3: 195–203. https://doi.org/10.1037/h0034701.

Bourdieu, Pierre. 1988. *Homo Academicus*. Stanford, CA: Stanford University Press.

Campbell, Elaine. 2016. "Exploring Autoethnography as a Method and Methodology in Legal Education Research." *Asian Journal of Legal Education* 3, no. 1 (January): 95–105. https://doi.org/10.1177/2322005815607141.

Cownie, Fiona. 2012. "Law, Research and the Academy." In *Tribes and Territories in the 21st Century: Rethinking the Significance of Disciplines in Higher Education*, edited by Paul Trowler, Murray Saunders, and Veronica Bamber, 57–67. London: Routledge.

Design Council. n.d. "The Double Diamond." Accessed May 20, 2023. www.designcouncil.org.uk/our-resources/the-double-diamond/.

Doherty, Michael. 2019. "Is It Time for a Legal Design Journal?" *Legal Design and Innovation* (blog), August 5. https://medium.com/legal-design-and-innovation/is-it-time-for-a-legal-design-journal-63340b92eae.

Foucault, Michel. [1975] 1991. *Discipline and Punish*. London: Penguin Books Ltd.

Fuller, Steve. 2000. *The Governance of Science*. Buckingham, UK: Open University Press.

Gibbons, Michael, Camille Limoges, Helga Nowotny, Simon Schwartzman, Peter Scott, and Martin Trow. 1994. *The New Production of Knowledge: The Dynamics of Science and Research in Contemporary Society*. London: Sage Publications.

Hagan, Margaret. n.d. "Law by Design." Accessed August 5, 2023. www.lawbydesign.co/.

2018. "A Human-Centered Design Approach to Access to Justice: Generating New Prototypes and Hypotheses for Intervention to Make Courts User-Friendly." *Indiana Journal of Law and Social Equality* 6, no. 2 (Spring): 199–239. www.repository.law.indiana.edu/ijlse/vol6/iss2/2.

Jackson, Dan. 2016. "Human-Centered Legal Tech: Integrating Design in Legal Education." *Law Teacher* 50, no. 1 (April): 82–97. https://doi.org/10.1080/03069400.2016.1146468.

Kelley, Tom, and David Kelley. 2013. *Creative Confidence: Unleashing the Creative Potential Within Us All*. New York: Crown Business.

Krishnan, Armin. 2009. "What are Academic Disciplines?" ESRC National Centre for Research Methods Working Paper series 03/09. http://eprints.ncrm.ac.uk/783/.

Legal Design Alliance. n.d. "The Legal Design Manifesto." Accessed May 19, 2023. www.legaldesignalliance.org/.

Lyotard, Jean-François. 1984. *The Postmodern Condition: A Report on Knowledge*. Minneapolis: University of Minnesota Press.

MacLean, Donald, Robert MacIntosh, and S. Grant. 2002. "Mode 2 Management Research." *British Journal of Management* 13, no. 3 (December): 189–207. https://doi.org/10.1111/1467-8551.00237.

Metzger, Walter P. 1987. "The Academic Profession in the United States." In *The Academic Profession: National, Disciplinary and Institutional Settings*, edited by Burton L. Clark, 123–208. Berkeley: University of California Press.

Nowotny, Helga, Peter Scott, and Michael Gibbons. 2003. "Introduction: 'Mode 2' Revisited: The New Production of Knowledge." *Minerva* 41, no. 3 (September): 179–94. https://doi.org/10.1023/A:1025505528250.

Perry-Kessaris, Amanda. 2021. *Doing Sociolegal Research in Design Mode*. New York: Routledge.

Stickdorn, Marc, Adam Lawrence, Markus Hormess, and Jakob Schneider. 2018. *This Is Service Design Doing: Applying Service Design Thinking in the Real World*. Boston, MA: O'Reilly Media.

Susskind, Richard E. 2013. *Tomorrow's Lawyers: An Introduction to Your Future*, 2nd ed. Oxford: Oxford University Press.

Trowler, Paul. 2012. "Disciplines and Academic Practices." In *Tribes and Territories in the 21st Century: Rethinking the Significance of Disciplines in Higher Education*, edited by Paul Trowler, Murray Saunders, and Veronica Bamber, 30–38. London: Routledge.

Trowler, Paul, Murray Saunders, and Veronica Bamber, eds. 2012. *Tribes and Territories in the 21st Century: Rethinking the Significance of Disciplines in Higher Education*. London: Routledge.

Winter, Richard. 1995. "The University of Life plc: The 'Industrialization' of Higher Education?" In *Academic Work: The Changing Labour Process in Higher Education*, edited by John Smyth, 129–43. Buckingham, UK: Open University Press.

IV

Where Legal Design Goes

Building a Field across Disciplines

22

Legal Design Could and Should Be More Sociolegal

Amanda Perry-Kessaris

22.1 INTRODUCTION

Legal design is a rapidly growing field of thinking and practice focused on what design can do for law. There are (at least) three "points of contact" between lawyerly concerns and designerly ways: "a commitment to communication; a need for/ability to create structured freedom; and a need/ability to be at once practical, critical, and imaginative" (Perry-Kessaris 2019, p. 192). Lawyers must make and communicate a sense of legal ideas. If it is to be meaningful, a legal communication must balance structure and freedom: it must nurture the coherence of law, and/but it must accommodate and sustain diverse perceptions, expectations and experiences of law. Lawyers must be simultaneously critical – that is, able to identify opportunities for change; imaginative – that is, able to envisage what the shape of those changes, and their effects, might be; and practical – that is, able to ensure that the change is valuable to those who are implicated in and by it, and to make that change happen. Designerly ways emphasize practical-critical-imaginative mindsets, experimental processes and visual and material communication strategies. By adopting these ways lawyers can generate "structured-yet-free" spaces in which their ability to individually and collaboratively make sense of legal ideas is enhanced, and from which meaningful legal communications are more likely to flow (Perry-Kessaris 2019).

This chapter focuses on legal design and legal designers. While anyone working with law – practitioners, activists, policymakers, researchers and teachers – can attempt to apply designerly ways to their lawyerly concerns, I reserve the term *legal designer* for those who have specific training and/or extensive experience in the field. The core argument of this chapter is that legal design and legal designers could and should be more sociolegal. First, sociolegal research can offer conceptual frameworks, empirical methods and data, and normative direction to legal design. Second, designerly methods can enhance the abilities of sociolegal researchers to make and communicate a sense of things to, with and for themselves, academics in other disciplines, and the wider world. So, if legal designers were to engage more deeply and systematically with sociolegal research and researchers, benefits could flow to legal design, to cross-disciplinary research and to the wider world.

The remainder of this chapter first sets out what it means to take a sociologically informed approach; and then how such an approach might benefit legal design thinking and practice, sociolegal thinking and practice, and cross-disciplinary thinking and practice more generally.

22.2 SOCIOLOGICALLY INFORMED APPROACHES TO LAW, DESIGN AND LEGAL DESIGN

Those who take sociologically informed or "sociolegal" approaches to law are committed to understanding law as a social phenomenon. In contrast to doctrinal scholars, who treat law as an abstract and technical phenomenon, sociolegal researchers pay attention to legal contexts, that is, the social relations that shape and are shaped by legal text, and to subtexts, that is, the moral meaning of text and context, especially how law succeeds and fails in its core tasks of expressing the values and interest that hold us together, coordinating between those values and interests that hold us apart, and ensuring widespread participation in sociolegal life. Sociolegal researchers draw on sociology and social theory to explore legal texts, contexts and subtexts. They conceptualise law at different social levels – such as action, interaction, regime and rationality. They gather empirical evidence of the perceptions, expectations and experiences of actors and groups pursuing different social values and interests – such as emotional, traditional, instrumental or faith-based (Perry-Kessaris 2015). Finally, this socialised vision of law as text, in context and with subtext gives normative direction to sociolegal researchers: they are bound, pragmatically and morally, to work for the "well-being of law" as both "a practical idea" and a "communal resource" (Cotterrell 2018, 31–33).

Design too is a fundamentally social phenomenon – a fact that has always received regular, albeit inconsistent and patchy, attention from design thinkers and practitioners. In the late nineteenth and early twentieth centuries, the leaders of the Arts and Crafts Movement and the Bauhaus school approached design as "a form of social relations," as "playing a role in social relations" and as promoting "certain forms of social relations" (Perry-Kessaris 2020, 1432, 1436). Even as mainstream design thinking and practice have become more commercially attuned and focused on the individual consumer (Julier 2017; Escobar 2018), there have been periodic calls for designers to own and activate their capacity for social impact (Design Manifestos n.d.). Today, design is understood less in terms of atomised actors, ideas, actions and artefacts and more in terms of "dynamic configurations of minds, bodies, objects, discourses, knowledge, structures/processes and agency" (Kimbell 2012, 134–46); whole subfields such as social innovation design are devoted to promoting social change and to doing so in ways that emphasise and activate the social potential of design (Amatullo et al. 2021).

Many legal designers share the sociolegal commitment to interpreting law as a social phenomenon and to working for the well-being of law as a practical idea and communal resource. For example, a desire to make law "work better for people" threads through many of the interviews conducted by Henna Tolvanen and Nina Toivonen for their Legal Design Podcast. It is also reflected in the manifesto of the Legal Design Alliance – "a network of lawyers, designers, technologists, academics, and other professionals who are committed to making the legal system more human-centered and effective, through the use of design" (The Legal Design Alliance n.d.). Some legal designers may be motivated to make law work better for those who make and implement it from above, others to make it better for those who must work with or within it from below. Either way we can say that they share with sociolegal researchers a sense that law is a social phenomenon, and that there is pragmatic and moral value in working for the well-being of law as a practical idea. Indeed, if legal designers were to see themselves as sociolegal designers, and engage with sociolegal researchers – for example, by participating in annual conferences of the Socio-Legal Studies Association or any of the national and global learned societies listed on its website – they might draw comfort from being part of a wider community of experts committed to the well-being of law as a practical, communal, resource.

Because they deal with law as part of real-world legal systems, one might expect legal designers, at least sometimes and in some respects, to be more attuned than other designers to social context and subtext. In fact, legal designers can be limited by their tendency to rely on a user-centred "design thinking" model, and not to draw on the more socialised and systemic approaches such as social innovation design. This point has been made during a Legal Design Podcast episode focusing on Santiago Pardo Rodríguez, Laura Guzman-Abello and Santiago De Francisco Vela, who lead the Lab de Diseño Para la Justicia (Design for Justice Lab) at Universidad de los Andes in Bogotá. It was observed that because designers tend to focus on toolkits and artefacts, they are generally less accustomed to, and less skilled at, wider-ranging contextualised explorations of how systems, such as judiciaries and bureaucracies, shape and are shaped by each other and the wider social world (Willis 2015; Brown 2009; De Francisco Vela, Guzman-Abello and Rodriguez 2021). So, what might a closer engagement with sociolegal approaches do for legal design?

22.3 ENHANCING THE QUALITY AND IMPACT OF LEGAL DESIGN

Sociolegal approaches to law can prompt and facilitate (at least) three enhancements to legal design. First, sociolegal research can offer a conceptual language with which legal designers can prompt and facilitate themselves to identify and move between individualised and socialised perspectives on law. Second, by engaging with sociolegal research, legal designers can prompt and facilitate themselves to deepen, and more effectively action, their commitment to evidence-based design.

Sociolegal research has generated a wealth of specific empirical knowledge about how law is perceived and experienced, used, abused and avoided in particular contexts, as well as insights into how new qualitative and quantitative data might be gathered and analysed. Third, sociolegal research can offer sociologically contextualised reasons for why legal design is important and how it ought to be done. A sociolegal lens can help legal designers to hone and sustain a critical eye on their own practice by emphasising that law, design and legal design all "originate in, derive meaning from, and effect recursive impacts upon human actors, including their actions, interactions, and rationalities." As such they "entail choices." Those choices must be explicit, and their impacts must be critically assessed if legal designers are to play their play in "exposing and remedying biases and inequalities, whether they derive from law, from design or from legal design itself" (Perry-Kessaris 2019, 193).

For evidence of these potential conceptual, empirical and normative enhancements we can look to contract design, where sociolegal ways are already, albeit not explicitly, applied. In less than a decade this most impactful and dynamic branch of legal design has evolved from providing services focused quite narrowly on the clarification of contract provisions through typography and visualisation towards providing wrap-around services in which designerly ways are deployed as early and often as possible to ensure that contractual relationships, and documents that express them, are as meaningful as possible (Passera and Haapio 2013).

To those who see the world through a sociolegal lens it is clear that all contracts are, as a matter of fact, "embedded in complex relations." Indeed, the express provisions of a contract can be understood as "no more than an extremely important part of a dense web of relations" between the contracting parties. Therefore, the drafting and interpretation of contracts, as well as attempts to assess their potential risks and rewards, ought as a matter of logic to combine contextual with textual analysis (Macneil 2003, 208). Furthermore, when we approach contracts as social phenomena, it becomes clear, as a matter of fact, that they shape and are shaped by wider social life. Seen through a designerly lens, contracts are a form of communication. Like all communications, their form and function must be assessed first, in terms of their internal coherence and technical accuracy; second, in terms of how the messages that they are intended to transmit are in fact received; and third, in terms of the "degree to which they enable a good working relationship and cooperation" between the parties, and "effective contract management" by the parties (Waller et al. 2016, 48). Campaigners for the rights of consumers and citizens have long argued that any documents that seek to explain rights and responsibilities ought to be accessible, and that this can be achieved by writing in plain English and applying information design techniques. At the same time there is a growing acceptance that business contracts are too often overly "complicated," even "unintelligible," and, relatedly, that the "process through which they are created remains a mystery to many," including the contracting parties (Tim Cummins, CEO,

International Association for Contract and Commercial Management, quoted in Waller et al. 2016, 48).

One example of how such sociolegal and designerly insights can be deployed to improve contract design emerged from the operations of Nexen Energy ULC (Nexen) in northwestern Canada. Natural resource extraction projects tend to be large scale, long term, high impact and high risk, and lawyers tend to respond with standard contracts that are lengthy, intricate and technical. Furthermore, it is increasingly understood, as it almost never was in colonial times, that it is important – practically, morally and sometimes as a matter of regulatory compliance – to nurture and maintain stable, trusting relations with those who live on and around land affected by extraction (Organisation for Economic Co-operation and Development n.d.). Nexen was keen to "enhance" the engagement of the energy company "with small contractors from local and Aboriginal communities" who might be in a position to supply anything from catering, land clearance and platform construction, to marine and land studies, to medical or guiding services. The local and Aboriginal communities were known to be interested in "working with industry to share in the benefits of resource development taking place on their traditional territories," and Nexen were conscious of the "importance of earning social licence" from project-affected people, and of the need to support them both by "build[ing] their capacity" and by "making allowances" where gaps in capacity were not of material significance (Waller et al. 2016, 50).

A solution emerged from a collaboration between, on the one hand, information designers Robert Waller and Jenny Waller, who specialise in making complex information clear for citizens and customers, and contract design specialist Helena Haapio; and, on the other hand, Nexen contracts and procurement manager Gary Crag and indigenous relations adviser Sandi Morrisseau. Like much sociolegal research, the design process began with interviews. But those interviews were designerly in the sense that they centred on the perceptions, expectations and experiences of specific people as potential users of a specific artefact (contract), as well as in the sense that they systematically generated a practical-critical-imaginative understanding of how things are, how they might be, how we might get there and what might be the risks and rewards. The team also analysed the documents and bidding process already in use by Nexen. By combining insights from these sources they were able to identify four challenges and solutions. To meet the challenge that one complex standard document cannot cover all needs, they proposed the solution of multiple, sometimes overlapping, smaller documents each tailored to different users. To meet the challenge of poor general literacy, they proposed the solution of using core, well-established principles of plain English drafting. To meet the challenge of poor document literacy, and specifically contractual literacy, they suggested using information design techniques to structure and visualise documents in the manner of a user guide. And to meet the challenge of ensuring that documents nurture stable, trusting relationships, they proposed adapting the processes detailed in the documents, and the language in which they were expressed, to align with Aboriginal values and practices (Waller et al. 2016). The article in which this project is reported is especially valuable because it reproduces the prototype documents that emerged from the design process alongside the standard forms that they were intended to replace, as well as detailed analysis of each design decision. It also argues that legal designers can use the architectural device of patterns to achieve a reasonable balance between entirely bespoke and entirely standardised contracts. "Creating design patterns is a naming exercise—identifying a useful, repeatable solution to a common problem, then giving it a name and a description so it can join a designer's repertoire of potential solutions to similar problems" (Waller et al. 2016, 62; see also Haapio and Hagan 2016; World CC Foundation n.d.).

This example showcases how sociolegal ways are already, albeit not explicitly applied by legal designers; and how they could be further applied, in combination with designerly ways, to enhance not only contract design but also the general well-being of contract law as a practical idea. How might a systematic move from legal design to sociolegal design benefit other, especially cross-disciplinary, fields of thinking and practice?

22.4 ENHANCING THE QUALITY AND IMPACT OF CROSS-DISCIPLINARY THINKING AND PRACTICE

The idea that design can enhance cross-disciplinary thinking and practice has a long history. In the 1950s, Max Bill, a Bauhaus graduate working at Ulm School of Design, sought "to make the design process more readily accessible and easy to understand" specifically in order "to facilitate cross-disciplinary work" between designers and, among others, anthropologists and psychologists (Oswald 2012, 68). In 1969, political scientist and cognitive psychologist Herbert A. Simon declared that design ought to be understood as a problem-solving methodology, and that it could act as a "glue" to hold the social sciences together (Bayazit 2004; Huppatz 2015). In 2016, Lucy Kimbell and Guy Julier led the ProtoPublics project, the aim of which was to "clarify how a design-oriented approach complements and is distinct from other kinds of cross-disciplinary, co-produced research in relation to social issues." The core project activity was to bring together five multi-disciplinary teams of social researchers each of which co-designed a social science research project (Julier and Kimbell 2016). In *Doing Sociolegal Research in Design Mode* (2021) I drew on the *ProtoPublics* project and other social and innovation design research, as well as original experimentation, to propose that sociolegal researchers ought to work in "design mode" (Manzini 2015; see also Julier and Kimbell 2016). Specifically, I argued that by adopting a practical-critical-imaginative mindset, experimental processes and visual and material communication strategies, sociolegal researchers can generate "structured-yet-free" ecosystems in which to individually and collaboratively make and communicate sense of legal multiplicity and indeterminacy, and thereby enhance every dimension (conceptual, empirical, normative, relational and processual) and phase (planning, implementation, dissemination and reflection) of their research (Allbon and Perry-Kessaris 2022).

This section focuses on the proposition that if they were to engage more explicitly with sociologically informed approaches to law, legal designers could more readily contribute to cross-disciplinary initiatives and to their wider social impact. Sociolegal research not only enriches the landscape of legal ideas and knowledge but also makes law more accessible and relevant to other disciplines, as well as to public and civil society actors. It is y\\ a meeting point and a source of knowledge and skills, for those who wish to bridge between law and other social sciences and humanities including, for example, history (Sandberg 2021) and archaeology (Threedy 2006; Novkov 2011).

The contribution of legal designers could be especially useful at the intersection of law and economy. Sociolegal researchers have been urgently trying to develop ways of thinking about relationships between legal and economic life that are alternative yet equal to economic and legal approaches (Perry-Kessaris 2014). In so doing they face methodological challenges around indeterminacy and multiplicity. First, sociolegal researchers think not of "the law" on the one hand and "the economy" on the other, but rather of social, including legal and economic, life. So they must think of legal and economic actions, interactions, systems and rationalities as mutually constitutive, shaping and shaped by each other as well as by other forms (instrumental, affective, traditional and spiritual) of social life (Edelman and Stryker 2005; Perry-Kessaris 2015). Second, because they are bound to attend to the well-being of law as a practical idea and a communal resource (Cotterrell 2018), they must focus on empirical realities and try not to predetermine the private/individual or the public/communal to be more worthy or able. For example, they consider how law facilitates, regulates, generates and secures particular economic transactions, or individual wins and losses; and how it facilitates, regulates, generates and secures wealth, including the origins and evolution of sustained economic and legal power and their collective and differential impacts across time, places and peoples (Pistor 2019). Third, they need to take account of multiple perceptions, expectations and experiences in our scholarly community and in the wider world (Darian-Smith 2013).

These challenges can be resistant – anathema even – to the traditional approaches of our core reference disciplines, including sociology, economics and law, which tend to privilege uniformity and determinacy (Law 2004). But they can become more, or differently, visible and accessible when approached through designerly ways. Seen through a designerly lens, interactions between "law" and "economy" generate the kinds of "dynamic, open, complex and networked" problems which designers lovingly term "wicked" (Dorst 2015; Buchanan 1992), and the solving of which designers regard as their specialist concern.

So, it is unsurprising that contemporary economists, especially those who seek to bring questions of justice and sustainability from the periphery to the centre of their discipline, increasingly draw on designerly ways. For example, Mariana Mazzucato (2021) and colleagues at the Institute for Innovation and Public Purpose argue that questions at the intersections of law and economy ought to be treated as "complex design problems," explicitly drawing on the literature and practices of design, especially service-design with its focus on user experience and co-creation. Public authorities ought, they argue, to work in experimental, entrepreneurial spirit, and in collaboration with private and civil society actors, to "co-creat[e]" ambitious, transformative "missions" that prioritise a co-defined sense of public purpose and public value, and then "shap[e]" economic life towards achieving them. They welcome, for example, plans for a "New European Bauhaus" drawing on design and adjacent disciplines to create "a space of encounter" in which to co-"imagine" and then "build" a "beautiful," "sustainable and inclusive future" (Bason et al. 2021).

Furthermore, Kate Raworth (2017) has proposed that economic thinking and practice can and ought to be reframed through the infinitely scalable metaphorical device of a double ring or "doughnut." The inner ring represents the "social foundation of well-being," as manifested in levels of widely recognised human development indicators such as equality and basic physical needs, below which no one should be allowed to fall. The outer ring represents the ceiling of widely recognised ecologically damaging impacts, such as resource depletion and pollution, above which we must not allow ourselves to go. Between the two is the "safe and just space" within which economic thinking and practice ought to take place. Raworth's approach is fundamentally designerly. First, it prompts and facilitates a practical-critical-imaginative mindset by requiring attention to be focused on what is (not) doable and/or desirable. Second, it emphasises the visible and tangible communication of ideas. The doughnut graphic itself accessibly communicates the overall approach to diverse lay and expert audiences. And for every taken-for-granted piece of mainstream economic "graffiti," Raworth proposes an alternative: for Alfred Marshall's diagram of supply and demand curves intersecting to reveal a point of general equilibrium, she proposes a set of feedback loops to better reflect the dynamism and complexity that exist both in reality and in the nuance of mainstream contemporary economic theory. Third, it emphasises experimentation and participation – being open, adaptive and innovative in defining both problems and solutions. The doughnut graphic itself is a structured-yet-free conceptual space, and some civil society users make it material, standing within and around a large-scale version of it as they imagine and engage with possible futures.

How might legal designers collaborate with sociolegal researchers to contribute to these radical economic conversations, and to ensure their wider social impact? One option might be for legal designers to collaborate with sociolegal researchers who are working with futures. A growing number of sociolegal researchers are working with prefiguration – acting as if a desired future were conceptually and/or empirically already present (Cooper 2017; Davies 2018). For example, the Northern/Ireland Feminist Constitutions (FemCon) project aims to "imagine new ways of creating and thinking about constitutional texts" through "practical experiments which can inform future community and political practice," and the Future of Legal Gender (The Future of Legal Gender Project [FLaG] 2022) project asks what if "gender no longer formed part of our legal personhood," including elements of conceptual prefiguration (approaching legal concepts as if they had a desired meaning) and law reform prefiguration (engaging with policy questions not yet posed). By thinking with and through alternative possibilities, we can "disrup[t]" well-used concepts, "surrender" to chance or change and "mov[e] beyond" our here and now (Akama et al. 2018). This is especially true in those relatively rare instances when alternatives are made visible and tangible in (more or less skilfully designed) models. For example, in *Four Legs Good*, artist Jack Tan painstakingly conjured a compelling fictitious Animal Justice Court over three days in the old Victorian courtroom at Leeds Town Hall, within which legal professionals and members of the public were prompted and facilitated to behave as if animals were already equal participants in the legal system (Tan 2018; Perry-Kessaris 2021). In *Facing Facts*, an initiative of non-governmental organisation CEJI-A Jewish Contribution to an Inclusive Europe, paper prototypes were used to prompt and facilitate disparate public- and third-sector stakeholders across Europe to act as if integrated hate crime reporting systems already existed (Perry-Kessaris and Perry 2020; Facing Facts n.d.). And in the *Hands-On Famagusta* project, digital and material architectural models were used to prompt and facilitate Cypriots to behave as if alternative island-wide futures were already present (Perry-Kessaris 2021; Hands-on Famagusta n.d.). In these examples sociolegal researchers are echoing the designerly practice of using prototypes to better see where we have been, where we are and where we might want (or not want) to go (Mazé 2016; Dunne and Raby 2013). If legal designers were more sociologically attuned, they would be well placed to contribute their expertise in law and in prototyping to enhance the quality and impact of these nascent moves.

22.5 CONCLUSION

If legal designers were to engage more deeply and systematically with sociolegal research and researchers, benefits could flow to legal design, to cross-disciplinary research and to the wider world. This proposition raises more questions than it answers. Will legal designers become more sociolegal? If so, how? What kinds of problems/situations will they choose to explore, and what kinds of solutions/approaches will they propose? What conceptual language will they adopt? What empirical facts will they gather and how will they analyse them? What values and interests will they choose to expose, unsettle or prioritise? Time will tell.

REFERENCES

Akama, Yoko, Sarah Pink, and Shanti Sumartojo. 2018. *Uncertainty and Possibility*. New York: Routledge.

Allbon, Emily, and Amanda Perry-Kessaris. 2022. "What Can Design Do for Legal Education?" In *Design in Legal Education*, edited by Emily Allbon and Amanda Perry-Kessaris, 1–15. New York: Routledge.

Amatullo, Mariana, Bryan Boyer, Jennifer May, and Andrew Shea. 2021. *Design for Social Innovation: Case Studies from Around the World*. New York: Routledge.

Bason, Christian, Rowan Conway, Dan Hill, and Mariana Mazzucato. 2021. "A New Bauhaus for a Green Deal." *UCL Institute for Innovation and Public Purpose*. www.ucl.ac.uk/bartlett/public-purpose/publications/2021/jan/new-bauhaus-green-deal.

Bayazit, Nigan. 2004. "Investigating Design: A Review of Forty Years of Design Research." 20:1 *Design Issues* 20, no.1 (Winter): 16–29. JSTOR.

Brown, T. 2009. *Change by Design*. New York: Harper Press.

Buchanan, Richard. 1992. "Wicked Problems in Design Thinking." *Design Issues* 8, no. 2 (Spring): 5–21. https://doi.org/10.2307/1511637.

Cooper, Davina. 2017. "Prefiguring the State." *Antipode* 49, no. 2 (March): 335–56. https://doi.org/10.1111/anti.12277.

Cotterrell, Roger. 2018. *Socio-Legal Jurisprudence: Juristic Thought and Social Inquiry*. New York: Routledge.

Darian-Smith, Eve. 2013. *Laws and Societies in Global Context*. Cambridge: Cambridge University Press.

Davies, Margaret. 2018. *Law Unlimited*. New York: Routledge.

De Francisco Vela, Santiago, Laura Guzman-Abello, and Santiago Pardo Rodriguez. 2021. "Episode 27: Merging Law, Design and Engineering with Lab de Diseño Para la Justicia." Aired on *Legal Design Podcast*, October 28, 46:43 min. http://legaldesignpodcast.com/episode-27-merging-law-design-and-engineering-with-lab-de-diseno-para-la-justicia/.

Design Manifestos. n.d. "Ken Garland: First Things First Manifesto." Accessed August 5, 2023. https://designmanifestos.org/ken-garland-first-things-first/.

Dorst, Kees. 2015. *Frame Innovation*. Cambridge, MA: MIT Press.

Dunne, Anthony, and Fiona Raby. 2013. *Speculative Everything: Design, Fiction, and Social Dreaming*. Cambridge, MA: MIT Press.

Edelman, Lauren B., and Robin Stryker. 2005. "A Sociological Approach to Law and Economy." In *The Handbook of Economic Sociology*, edited by Neil J. Smelser and Richard Swedberg, 2nd ed., 527–51. Princeton, NJ: Princeton University Press.

Escobar, Arturo. 2018. *Designs for the Pluriverse: Radical Interdependence, Autonomy, and the Making of Worlds*. Durham, NC: Duke University Press.

Facing Facts. n.d. "About Facing Facts." Accessed August 5, 2023. www.facingfacts.eu.

The Future of Legal Gender Project (FLaG). 2022. "Homepage." Last modified April 2022. https://futureoflegalgender.kcl.ac.uk/.

Gaiter, Colette. 2018. "Visualising a Black Future: Emory Douglas and the Black Panther Party." *Journal of Visual Culture* 17, no. 3 (December): 299–311. https://doi.org/10.1177/1470412918800007.

Haapio, Helena, and Margaret D. Hagan. 2016. "Design Patterns for Contracts." *Proceedings of the 19th International Legal Informatics Symposium IRIS 2016, February 25, 2016*. Vienna, Austria: Austrian Computer Society.

Hands-on Famagusta. n.d. "Welcome to the Hands-on Famagusta Game Tour." Homepage. Accessed August 5, 2023. www.handsonfamagusta.org.
Huppatz, Daniel J. 2015. "Revisiting Herbert Simon's 'Science of Design'" 31:2 Design Issues 29.
Julier, Guy. 2017. *Economies of Design*. Thousand Oaks, CA: Sage Publishing.
Julier, Guy, and Lucy Kimbell. 2016. *Co-Producing Social Futures Through Design Research*. Brighton, UK: University of Brighton.
Kimbell, Lucy. 2012. "Rethinking Design Thinking: Part II." *Design and Culture* 4, no. 2 (April): 129–48. http://dx.doi.org/10.2752/175470812X13281948975413.
Law, John. 2004. *After Method: Mess in Social Science*. New York: Routledge.
The Legal Design Alliance. n.d. "LeDA: The Legal Design Alliance." Accessed August 5, 2023. www.legaldesignalliance.org/.
Macneil, Ian R. 2003. "Reflections on Relational Contract Theory after a Neoclassical Seminar." In *Implicit Dimensions of Contract: Discrete, Relational, and Network Contracts*, edited by David Campbell, Hugh Collins and John Wightman, 207–18. Oxford: Hart Publishing.
Manzini, Ezio. 2015. *Design, When Everybody Designs*. Cambridge, MA: MIT Press.
Mazé, Ramia. 2016. "Design and the Future: Temporal Politics of 'Making a Difference.'" In *Design Anthropological Futures*, edited by Rachel Charlotte Smith, Kasper Tang Vangklide, Mette Gislev Kjaersgaard, Ton Otto, Joachim Halse, and Thomas Binder, 37–54. London: Bloomsbury Publishing.
Mazzucato, Mariana. 2021. *Mission Economy*. London: Penguin Publishing.
Novkov, Julie. 2011. "Legal Archaeology." *Political Research Quarterly* 64, no. 2: 348–61.
Organisation for Economic Co-operation and Development (OECD). n.d. "Responsible Business Conduct: OECD Guidelines for Multinational Enterprises." Accessed August 5, 2023. http://mneguidelines.oecd.org/.
Oswald, David. 2012. "The Information Department at the Ulm School of Design." Paper presented at *ICHDS 2012, the 8th Conference of the International Committee for Design History & Design Studies, Sao Paulo, Brazil, September 2012*. http://david-oswald.de/downloads/ICDHS2012_oswald.pdf.
Passera, Stefania, and Helena Haapio. 2013. "Transforming Contracts from Legal Rules to User-Centered Communication Tools: A Human-Information Interaction Challenge." *Communication Design Quarterly* 1, no. 3 (April): 38–45. https://doi.org/10.1145/2466489.2466498.
Perry-Kessaris, Amanda. 2014. "The Case for a Visualized Economic Sociology of Legal Development." *Current Legal Problems* 67, no.1 (September): 169–98. https://doi.org/10.1093/clp/cuu016.
2015. "Approaching the Econo-Socio-Legal." *Annual Review of Law & Social Science* 11, no. 16: 1–18.
2019. "Legal Design for Practice, Activism, Policy and Research." *Journal of Law and Society* 46, no. 2 (June): 185–210. http://doi.org/10.1111/jols.12154.
2020. "Making Socio-Legal Research More Social by Design: Anglo-German Roots, Rewards, and Risks." *German Law Journal* 21, no.7 (October): 1427–45. https://doi.org/10.1017/glj.2020.77.
2021. "Could Alternative Econo-Legal Futures Be Made More Possible and Probable through Prefigurative Design? Insights from and for Cyprus." *Northern Ireland Legal Quarterly* 72, no. 4 (Winter): 623–57. https://doi.org/10.53386/nilq.v72i4.936.
Perry-Kessaris, Amanda, and Joanna Perry. 2020. "Enhancing Participatory Strategies with Designerly Ways for Sociolegal Impact: Lessons from Research Aimed at Making Hate

Crime Visible in Europe." *Social and Legal Studies* 29, no. 6 (December): 835–57. https://dx.doi.org/10.2139/ssrn.3387479.

Pistor, Katharina. 2019. *The Code of Capital: How the Law Creates Wealth and Inequality*. Princeton, NJ: Princeton University Press.

Raworth, Kate. 2017. *Doughnut Economics: seven ways to think like a 21st-century economist*. Random House.

Sociolegal Studies Association (SLSA). n.d. "Homepage." Last modified July 2023. https://slsa.ac.uk.

Tan, Jack. 2018. "Four Legs Good." https://jacktan.wordpress.com/art-work/four-legs-good/.

Waller, Robert, Jenny Waller, Helena Haapio, Gary Crag, and Sandi Morrisseau. 2016. "Cooperation through Clarity: Designing Simplified Contracts." *Journal of Strategic Contracting and Negotiation* 2, no. 1–2 (March/June): 48–68. https://doi.org/10.1177/2055563616668893.

Willis, Anne-Marie. 2015. "Transition Design: The Need to Refuse Discipline and Transcend Instrumentalism." *Design Philosophy Papers* 13, no. 1 (January): 69–74. https://doi.org/10.1080/14487136.2015.1085687.

World CC Foundation. n.d. "Contract Design Pattern Library." https://contract-design.worldcc.com.

23

Navigating in a Post-Quantum Legal Design Landscape

Katri Nousiainen and Joonas Keski-Rahkonen

23.1 INTRODUCTION

Modern society is currently facing the dawn of a new quantum era where different quantum innovations, such as quantum computing, are beginning to integrate as part of our life. This quantum evolution will have an influence on many areas, some of which are still unknown. Even though the new quantum technologies are still at the early stages of commercialization, they have already begun to influence the structures of society in a variety of ways. However, it is pivotal that the new technologies are brought into play in an interdisciplinary manner. We can collaborate with other fields to determine the best practice solutions and approaches with the common goal of improving society in general.

Though thought of as rigid, the legal field will also undergo its own quantum reformation from the rise of new technologies. In fact, it is the responsibility of all actors in the legal sphere to ensure that their awareness of current technology applications and implications is up to date. Although only the future will show us the full ramifications of the quantum reformation of society, we will analyze these possibilities from a legal perspective: What will lawyers' job descriptions look like in the post-quantum society? It is also the duty of all actors in the legal sphere to ensure that legislation keeps up with the quantum leap: What kind of new regulatory structures do we need put in place as we head toward the future quantum society? Foreshadowing the integration of new quantum technologies into our society, we set forth a novel road map to assist in navigating through the crosswinds of various incentives. In particular, we want to facilitate conversations on governance structures, institutional design, international relations, regulatory balance, and the functionality of society in the age of quantum technologies.

This chapter is divided into three sections. In Section 23.2, we discuss the general theory of legal design in law and economics framework, namely what is legal design and how design methods – as well as interdisciplinarity – can improve quality in the legal field and what implications it has on dignity. We further discuss how to measure the impact and value of legal design. In Section 23.3, we introduce a novel approach to law and quantum technology in the legal design framework. We discuss some of the incentives for and other implications of employing legal design with quantum technologies. In Section 23.4, we present a novel quantum road map to act as a guide in matters of law, economics, sustainability, and society.

23.2 GENERAL THEORY OF LEGAL DESIGN IN THE LAW AND ECONOMICS FRAMEWORK

Before delving into the consequences of society's quantum leap in the legal arena, we present the general theory of legal design that establishes a foundation for the discussion. In general, the main idea behind legal design is to employ user-centered design to make information, services, products, and processes more comprehensible. The legal design approach aims to create a systemic impact by empowering people with law, fostering more equal standing, reducing information and knowledge asymmetry in society, and enabling better access to law. This approach aims to empower people in using means such as interdisciplinary best practices, plain language, design methods, and technology. The legal design approach provides valuable methodologies and tools to reduce complexity. The legal profession, and society, can benefit from this approach by way of improving the quality of services, processes, and products. The legal design approach provides for improved comprehensibility, reduced transaction costs, decreased complexity, increased quality, fostered competitive business advantage, risk management, and business sustainability. Legal design can be further employed in the legal and economic contexts as described below.

23.2.1 *Innovation and Sustainability*

Leaders around the globe see innovation as one of the fundamental sources for competitive advantage and a way to foster business sustainability (Hoffman 2000; Ireland and Webb 2007; Brown 2008; Cusumano 2010; Amit and Zott 2012; Brem, Maier, and Wimschneider 2016; Dam and Siang 2018).[1] Successful ideas are produced and inspired through a sound understanding of end-users' conditions and the employment of design principles to innovate and create value (Brown 2008; Stanford University 2012; IDEO.org 2015; Hagan 2018). Anyone seeking to earn profits must innovate; profits can be earned by introducing prosperous innovations (Schumpeter 1952; Schumpeter 1961; Schumpeter 1989; Kiessling 2004; Gilbert 2006; Sledzik 2013; Autio et al. 2014; Block, Fisch, and van Praag 2017). The implemented legal design

[1] The following case studies in Brown's (2008) article are particularly poignant: Kaiser Permanente, manufacturer of bicycle components Shimano (89); eyecare provider Aravind Eye Care Systems (90); financial services company Bank of America (92).

approach and practice generate profits and provide for sustainable business development. Comprehensive and transparent practices that are demonstrated in the market signal quality, trustworthiness, and a willingness to comply with one's responsibilities (Erdem and Swait 1998; Jeffries and Reed 2000; Van Slyke 2000).

23.2.2 *Signaling: Profits and Sustainable Business Development*

Trust is generally regarded as valuable for successful relationship building and business practice (Lindenberg 2000; DeSteno et al. 2012). It is considered especially valuable when no efficient judicial enforcement tools are at hand (Cooter and Ulen 2004). Mutual trust and its signaling are the cornerstones for a long-term sustainable cooperation and business practice. Operators who are untrustworthy are suitable solely for one-shot trading, if any. Longitudinal studies have shown that trust will generally provide for more transparency (Larson 1992; Ring and van de Ven 1994; Woolthuis, Hillebrand, and Nooteboom 2005). More deep-rooted cooperation and commitment to obligations will take place when negotiations are conducted transparently and comprehensively (Nousiainen 2021).

23.2.3 *Reducing Transaction and Opportunity Costs*

Transaction costs emerge from making a transaction. They are the total sunk costs from economic trade (Calabresi 1968; Williamson 1979; Williamson and Masten 1999; Young 2013; CFI 2022). Transaction costs are regarded as one the most prominent factors in management and business operations, as they include costs such as the cost of planning, time, designing, coordinating, deciding, and numerous after-trade practices (Young 2013). Information is often regarded as costly (Beales, Craswell, and Salop 1981; Barzel 1982; Merrill and Smith 2001). At the back-end stage, the operators confront ex-post costs that are due to the decisions done at the ex-ante stage (Scott and Triantis 2005; Scott and Triantis 2006). Paying attention to a greater specificity at the front end will reduce the prospect for back-end costs (Nousiainen 2021; Williams 2021).

Ex-ante and ex-post costs can be diminished with the legal design approach (Nousiainen 2022). Adopted from transaction cost theories and economic literature, the legal design approach is capable of decreasing transaction and opportunity costs through comprehensible and transparent practices (Calabresi 1968; Williamson 1979; Williamson and Masten 1999; Young 2013; CFI 2022). Furthermore, legal design decreases transaction costs as information is conveyed in a comprehensible manner. Applying the legal design approach fosters the comprehension of one's rights and obligations and supports conveying information in an understandable manner (Barton, Berger-Walliser, and Haapio 2013; Passera 2018; Hagan 2021; Katz et al. 2021). This reduces transaction costs that could otherwise emerge as ex-ante or ex-post costs. Consequently, transactions will be less likely to see disagreements before a judicial body (Nousiainen 2021).

23.2.4 *Competitive Business Advantage*

The legal design approach signals trustworthiness and supports a good reputation in the market. The implemented and practiced legal design approach is considered a competitive business advantage that facilitates revenue for operators who employ it before it becomes the novel mainstream practice (Nousiainen 2021). Some economic models consider trust as a determinative metric in distinguishing bad from good qualities (Akerlof 1970). Adapted from Akerlof's theory, an operator that practices an implemented legal design approach signals in the market that it is of good quality, not a "lemon" (Akerlof 1970). When an operator demonstrates transparency and comprehensibility in its practice, then others must follow the lead; if not, they are left behind or considered "lemons" and ultimately pushed out of the market. The market is a powerful reflection of its operators. Clients "voting with their feet" and the unpredictability of social media, for instance, can force companies to employ more comprehensibility, transparency, ethics, and human-centered design in their practice. Again, client satisfaction and recommendations are regarded as an influential signal. Trust that is built via comprehensible and transparent practice fosters operators' pursuits to strengthen their market position (Nousiainen 2021).

23.2.5 *Game Theory*

In accordance with the application of the noncooperative game theory approach, even when operators are only pursuing their rational self-interest, it is still in their best interest to employ legal design practice in its operations (Nousiainen 2021). Besides, in most cases, self-interest is not considered being in conflict with cooperation and trust; moreover, the legal design approach is not at variance with lucrative business: actually, quite the opposite (Axelrod 1984). According to the general theory of legal design, the more comprehensible, transparent, ethical, and empowering practices reflect the profits (Nousiainen 2021).

23.2.6 *More Deep-Rooted Commitment*

The legal design approach creates more ingrained commitment, decreases the need for renegotiation, and diminishes unintentional as well as intentional breaches given that operators better understand their rights and obligations. Moreover, negligent behavior decreases, as the operators' relationship is more transparent, established, and empathic because the operators have shared goals (Nousiainen 2021). When the means, objectives, and aims of practices are communicated comprehensively and transparently early on, this creates trust and builds on more ingrained commitment between the operators. The legal design approach leaves less room for ambiguity and hence diminishes earlier existing opportunities for strategic and negligent behavior, namely for the pursuit of self-interest in employing complexity and ambiguousness in one's practice.

23.2.7 *Comprehensibility as a Novel Legal Quality Metric*

Comprehension, a new legal quality metric, is another way of evaluating efficiency and quality in legal products, processes, and services. This legal quality metric should be employed and applied cumulatively with other legal quality metrics such as time, length, usability, use of design methods, clarity, and plain language, as these metrics are the cornerstone of legal quality. Ideally, comprehension should be evaluated on a regular basis, and practices should be developed and improved accordingly. Comprehension can be tested in ways such as writing tests, reading comprehension, and explaining to others via tests, surveys, and interviews (Davis 1944; Keenan, Betjemann, and Olson 2008; Nousiainen 2022).

There are also costs associated with employing the legal design approach. Costs include starting costs to apply the legal design approach, such as the interdisciplinary expertise time spent on implementing and integrating new practices and procedures as part of operator's new approach on a strategic level (Nousiainen 2021). It is anticipated that the benefits from applying the approach will greatly outweigh these costs.

23.3 LEGAL DESIGN FRAMEWORK FOR QUANTUM TECHNOLOGY

As discussed above, the fundamental idea behind legal design is to apply a user-centered approach to judicial information, services, products, and processes to design them to be more comprehensible (Nousiainen 2022). This is of utmost importance when society enters the new era of quantum technologies, and the legal field will also undergo its own quantum leap. In particular, the ambition of the legal design approach is to generate a systemic impact via empowering people with law: in supporting quality and equality, in creating and building value-increasing tools and products, in decreasing knowledge and information asymmetry in society, and in enabling better access to law and legal information. With this approach, people are empowered by employing means such as design methods, interdisciplinary best practices, and technology.

In general, the legal design approach operates in four prominent ways: empowering, improving, supporting, and demonstrating (Table 23.1). It builds on the design thinking process in reaching these functions (Nousiainen 2020; Nousiainen and Perdomo Ortega 2024: 8–13). The design thinking process determines challenges and then executes solutions that account for end-users' needs. These needs are the essence of solutions and concept development. The design thinking process incorporates understanding, thinking, need-finding, creating, and doing (Stanford University 2012).[2]

[2] There exist also various paths regarding the number and content of the design thinking process stages.

TABLE 23.1 *The legal design approach: Prominent functions.*

Empowers	People, communities, entities, and society to decrease, or even fully abolish, knowledge and information asymmetry between parties.
Improves	Quality, efficiency, and ethics whenever the practice or design employs a more user-centered approach.
Support	Ethics and efficiency in policy and decision making by gathering empirical data.
Demonstrates	Law and economics is not just theoretical science; rather, it employs empirical research to offer numerical data to then verify prospective impact and value of a certain legal process, service, or product.

Legal design can contribute to the quantum leap of society by creating a systemic impact on the legal framework. For instance, since legal rules are logical within their structure, they can be defined in a programmatic format (Genesereth 2021).[3] A computable contract lays out obligations and rights in a machine-executable code. It provides a computable specification for the contract terms and clauses. This new angle opens a possibility for contracting to gain from contractual modularity, enabling more feasible customization and contract modification (Smith 2006; Triantis 2013; Williams 2021; Nousiainen 2022b). Nevertheless, further technological advancement and development are required for a prosperous application of quantum technologies to law (Atik and Jeutner 2021). For example, one of the current bottlenecks is the fact that human-language contracts must be translated into a machine-readable form. For further progress, a standard contract language needs to be established. In return, computable contracts will provide incentives and benefits such as increasing process efficiency, improving trust and transparency, enabling more strategic decision-making, and decreasing information asymmetry.

On the legal profession side, the emerging quantum technologies have a potential to substantially improve the quality and efficiency of litigation and contracting practice with reduced transaction costs. In general, the quantum advantage for the legal profession is boosted legal process and contract optimization, as well as the ability to efficiently process enormous datasets, which shortens the pathway to transparent legal solutions. Regarding case law, which builds on legal precedent, quantum-enhanced artificial intelligence can help categorize, track patterns, improve process development, and forecast court or other judicial solutions and results. Quantum algorithms can be applied in contracts to track practices, processes, and the development of patterns useful in foreseeing legal opportunities and risks. In fact, contract management can be used as a risk management tool. However, legal solutions, categories, and patterns should always be evaluated with human consideration in a larger framework, as law is the work of humans.

[3] Definitions of incidents are described employing a set of if-else rules that state divergent incidents, with consequences for those incidents. Employing coded contracts is expected to bring saving in transaction costs.

While the legal profession can benefit from utilizing new quantum resources such as quantum computing to provide for better legal certainty, legal quality, and accessibility to law, safeguards must be put in place to ensure that users are centered. For instance, the legal design approach builds on interdisciplinary best practices, user-centric design, increased comprehensibility, and the fostering of ethical values. The legal design approach helps construct ethically solid datasets and design systems. Subsequently, datasets and design systems for law can be built for training a classical or quantum machine learning algorithm to bring transparency and clarity, to safeguard a more ethical, nondiscriminating, and more user-centric approach to law. Under the complex systems theory of legal design, *where the sum of the contract terms is bigger than its parts*, the system takes the environment into account and guides the quantum data design to be a dynamic system with no closures, and designed in a way that it has ethical standing and user-centricity in its core (Nousiainen 2022b). Combined with employing legally designed language, the quantum-based algorithms can thus become comprehensible and nondiscriminating user-centric tools (Nousiainen 2021). Nevertheless, there exists a real possibility of bias in human-designed data analysis tools (Jeutner 2021). This may lead, albeit often unintentionally, to unequal or even discriminatory practices. The best safety measure against unwanted ramifications is awareness of the possible implications of the new technology.

23.4 ROAD MAP TOWARD POST-QUANTUM LAW, ECONOMICS, SUSTAINABILITY, AND SOCIETY

Besides affecting the work picture inside the legal profession, the emergence of quantum technologies will have a deep impact on legal and societal development, distribution of powers, and international relations generally. However, this interplay is not just unilateral; in fact, it is the duty of different actors in the legal arena, such as lawyers, policymakers, and governmental institutes, to ensure that the needed precautionary measures are taken into account within appropriate and expedient principles. The new quantum era stipulates a new legal order! The first step in this direction is to recognize and acknowledge the possible legal and social ramifications stemming from the integration of the new quantum technologies as a part of our everyday life (Nousiainen et al. (2022); Bertolucci and Jones (2022); Nousiainen and Keski-Rahkonen (2022); Nousiainen and Keski-Rahkonen (2023)).

According to the economic path dependency theories, knowledge is widespread in society, and the learning process is regarded as gradual (von Hayek 1985). It is similar with quantum technologies: We have an opportunity to learn from the past and build on current knowledge. For instance, we can study 1990s policy frameworks related to the internet as an analogous situation. However, it is not enough just to reflect on the past. New information is required, even though its acquisition might come at a cost. In the end, overall knowledge is necessary for prosperous innovation, development, and competition (Nousiainen 2021).

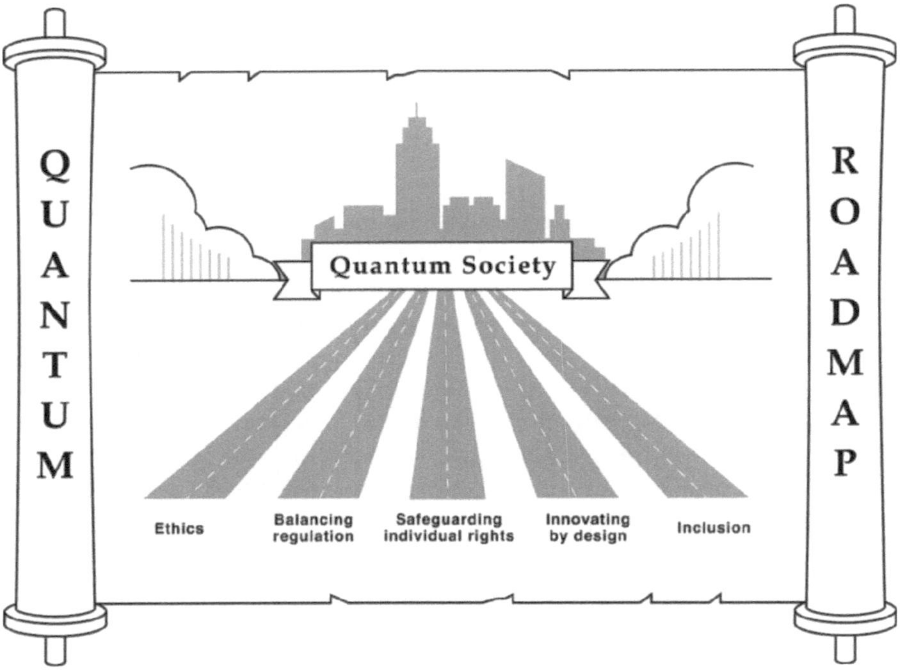

FIGURE 23.1 The quantum road map.
(Image design credit: Sunny Cheng.)

Equipped with this knowledge, we can tackle several open legal and ethical questions brought by the quantum leap of society, some of which are included below. The integration and development of new quantum technologies should be carried out in an interdisciplinary fashion so that we will gain the maximal social benefit. Surprisingly, there has been a minute amount of debate on the regulatory dilemma posed by the rise of new quantum technologies and on the quantum-driven change in the legal environment, both on the national and international levels. Because of the gap, and to stimulate further discussion our quantum road map on law, economics, sustainability, and society is included here (Figure 23.1). This road map for the legal landscape toward the quantum future presents five foundational principles for the social manifestation of quantum technologies: ethics, inclusion, balancing regulatory activities, safeguarding individual rights, and innovating by design.

23.4.1 *Ethics*

The employment or development of new technologies must not aggravate or create inequalities; it should neither create a divergent level of standing through its design nor enable hidden discriminatory practices. Primary calls for the benefit of humankind should be recognized together with commercial incentives. Equal access, public good, and transparency are the guiding ethical principles.

Some open questions for discussion: What ethical risks does quantum technology create, and how can we mitigate those risks? To what extent has quantum technology become a military asset, and what role should international organizations play in governing quantum-based weapon technology?

23.4.2 *Inclusion*

The employment or development of new technologies should be inclusive and provide benefits to be utilized for the good of humankind. Democratic involvement and the sharing of knowledge and resources are the guiding inclusive principles.

Some open questions for discussion: How will quantum technology affect international trade, trade relations, and trade organizations, and what kind of regulatory challenges does it raise? What kind of positive and negative effects will export and import restrictions have on the quantum technology industry from a social, economic, and innovation perspectives? What role should the public and private sectors play, and at which stages? How can, or should, we fund quantum infrastructure?

23.4.3 *Balancing Regulatory Activities*

The employment and development of new technologies must not be hindered through regulatory measures. Regulations should not impede the positive ramifications of the technology but rather minimize the negative ramifications as much as possible. Innovation, common good, effectiveness, and being technology friendly are the guiding regulatory principles.

Some open questions for discussion: What type of institutions and governance structures does the emerging quantum technology require? To what extent can we rely on current and emerging regulatory frameworks, such as those listed below?

- General Data Protection Regulation (GDPR)[4]
- California Consumer Privacy Act (CCPA)[5]
- California Privacy Rights Act (CPRA)[6]
- Regulation of the European parliament and of the council laying down harmonized rules on artificial intelligence (Artificial Intelligence Act)

[4] See Regulation (EU) 2016/679 of the European Parliament and of the Council of 27 April 2016, on the protection of natural persons with regard to the processing of personal data and on the free movement of such data, and repealing Directive 95/46/EC (General Data Protection Regulation), 120, https://eur-lex.europa.eu/legal-content/EN/TXT/PDF/?uri=CELEX:32016R0679; United Nations Security Council, Seventy-second year. "Non-proliferation/Democratic People's Republic of Korea." S/PV.7904. March 23, 2017, 2. https://documents-dds-ny.un.org/doc/UNDOC/PRO/N17/076/47/PDF/N1707647.pdf.

[5] The California Consumer Privacy Act (CCPA), 2018, https://leginfo.legislature.ca.gov/faces/codes_displayText.xhtml?division=3.&part=4.&lawCode=CIV&title=1.81.5

[6] Ibid.

- amending certain union legislative acts (AI Act)[7]
- Digital Markets Act (DMA)[8]
- Digital Services Act (DSA)[9]
- Data Act[10]
- Wassenaar Arrangement (US Department of State 2000).

What can we learn from the history of technological governance and regulatory restrictions?

23.4.4 *Safeguarding Individual Rights and Liberties*

The employment or development of new technologies must not disturb recognized individual rights and liberties, exclude individual access unreasonably without good cause, create or aggravate inequalities between individuals, disturb individual autonomy, create barriers, or obstruct access to justice or other recognized fundamental principles. Prioritizing individual autonomy, fundamental rights and liberties, equality, and fairness are the guiding principles.

Some open questions for discussion: How will quantum technology affect digital surveillance, privacy, fairness, trust, access to information, and human rights? What are recommendations for the private sector to collaborate with the government?

23.4.5 *Innovating by Design*

The employment or development of new technologies must be designed in compliance with equality, ethics, transparency, and human centricity. The design of the technology should foster equal access and support nondiscriminatory practices, transparency, and sustainability. Human centricity, openness, transparency, and sustainability are the guiding design principles.

Some open questions for discussion: What type of innovation should we want? How can and should governments and public entities shape innovation in quantum technology, and what path dependencies might the corresponding actions and inactions create?

In general, the necessary upgrading of the current legislation is a complex, multilateral problem, as illustrated by the exemplary set of issues mentioned earlier. Nevertheless, our quantum road map can assist the various actors to navigate in the

7 Proposal for a Regulation of the European Parliament and of the Council Laying Down Harmonised Rules on Artificial Intelligence (Artificial Intelligence Act) and Amending Certain Union Legislative Acts, April 4, 2021, 2021/0106 (COD). https://eur-lex.europa.eu/legal-content/EN/TXT/?uri=CELEX%3A52021PC0206.

8 European Commission, Digital Markets Act (DMA), https://ec.europa.eu/competition-policy/sectors/ict/dma_en; https://ec.europa.eu/commission/presscorner/detail/en/ip_20_2347.

9 European Commission, The Digital Services Act Package, https://digital-strategy.ec.europa.eu/en/policies/digital-services-act-package.

10 European Commission. 2022. "Data Act: Commission Proposes Measures for a Fair and Innovative Data Economy." February 23, 2022. https://ec.europa.eu/commission/presscorner/detail/en/ip_22_1113.

post-quantum legal landscape of various incentives. Ideally, the aforementioned principles would guide elected representatives, relevant governmental agencies, and institutions, as well as quantum industry members, and would furthermore set a solid foundation for designing the future legal regulation. The common goal is to find the regulatory balance: ensuring the functionality of society while not smothering the evolution and integration of quantum technologies. In the end the future (and current) regulatory framework on quantum technologies should be enforceable and effective. It should be designed in a transparent (understandable) fashion, and the regulatory work should be predictable, with no rapid changes in the regulatory environment.

23.5 CONCLUSION

A bright, new post-quantum world is already upon us. At the same time, the wave of quantum innovations will cause a conundrum in the legal sphere. In this chapter, we attempted to raise general awareness about the impact of the quantum reformation of society. In particular, we discussed the upcoming legal ramifications and presented a novel guide to finding a socially justified legislation path toward the quantum future. Our approach examined the tentative legal future from the point of the legal design framework. Therefore, in the first section following the introduction, we briefly presented the key concepts behind the general theory of legal design in the law and economics framework.

In the section that followed, we introduced the legal design framework for quantum technologies. We addressed the application of legal design and its most prominent functions. This section discussed such quantum resources as quantum computing in the legal design framework and their implications for the legal profession. From the authors' knowledge, this is the first attempt to open an academic discussion on how to foster better-quality legal services with legal design in the quantum technology context. This shortcoming is further enhanced by the lack of greater accessibility of information – such as within case law patterns, prospective decisions, or optimization – that build on quantum application in the legal context. Thus, this section fills in the gap by providing a direction for further discussions. The legal design approach should be applied in the quantum computing context to make law and legal practice more transparent, human-centric, efficient, and comprehensible, as well as to foster better service quality and the values of nondiscrimination. Nonetheless, further research is required to demonstrate and support expectations of benefits derived from this approach on contracts and other legal tools in the quantum computing field.

Besides the work description of an individual legal actor, we must also consider the bigger picture. The whole legal arena, including governmental institutes and commercial operators, must reflect upon the social and legal significance of quantum technologies. Section 23.4 discussed incentives and moral principles, but also challenged that we must be aware of new quantum innovations in different societal settings. We proposed a legal design–based future quantum framework: a guiding quantum road map for law, economics, sustainability, and society. This novel road map sheds light on the ramifications of the emerging quantum technologies relevant to law, economics, sustainability, and society (LESS). Our proposed decalogue comprises five foundational principles for the social manifestation of quantum technologies: ethics, inclusion, balancing regulatory activities, safeguarding individual rights and liberties, and innovating by design. We began our discussion of these five principles with key issues to inspire further conversations on this topic.

Without a doubt, quantum technologies will create a systemic impact on a social level. Thus, it is vital to be aware of and acknowledge the best approaches so the promising new technology will offer the maximum benefit and advantage for humanity. We emphasize that it is paramount to find sustainable moral and ethical standing and regulatory balance, as well as to ascertain the functionality of society, while not suppressing the integration and evolution of quantum technologies.

REFERENCES

Akerlof, George A. 1970. "The Market for 'Lemons': Quality Uncertainty and the Market Mechanism." *The Quarterly Journal of Economics* 84, no. 3 (August): 488–500. https://doi.org/10.2307/1879431.

Amit, Raphael, and Christoph Zott. 2012. "Creating Value through Business Model Innovation." *MIT Sloan Management Review* 53, no. 3 (Spring): 41–49. https://sloanreview.mit.edu/article/creating-value-through-business-model-innovation/.

Atik, Jeffery, and Valentin Jeutner. 2021. "Quantum Computing and Computational Law." *Law, Innovation and Technology* 13, no. 2 (September): 302–24. https://doi.org/10.1080/17579961.2021.1977216.

Autio, Erkko et al. 2014. "Entrepreneurial Innovation: The Importance of Context." *Research Policy* 43, no. 7 (September): 1097–108. https://doi.org/10.1016/j.respol.2014.01.015.

Axelrod, Robert. 1984. *The Evolution of Cooperation*. New York: Basic Books.

Barton, Thomas D., Gerlinde Berger-Walliser, and Helena Haapio. 2013. "Visualization: Seeing Contracts for What They Are and What They Could Become." *Journal of Law, Business & Ethics* 19, no. 47 (January): 47–63. Social Science Research Network (SSRN).

Barzel, Yoram. 1982. "Measurement Cost and the Organization of Markets." *The Journal of Law & Economics* 25, no. 1 (April): 27–48. https://doi.org/10.1086/467005.

Beales, Howard, Richard Craswell, and Steven C. Salop. 1981. "The Efficient Regulation of Consumer Information." *The Journal of Law & Economics* 24, no. 3 (December): 491–539. https://doi.org/10.1086/466997.

Bertolucci, Seth and Isabel Jones, hosts. "Quantum-Computing." *Berkeley Technology Law Journal Podcast*, August 23, 2022. Podcast, website, 38:44, https://btlj.org/2022/08/berkeley-technology-law-journal-podcast-quantum-computing/.

Block, Joern H., Christian O. Fisch, and Mirjam van Praag. 2017. "The Schumpeterian Entrepreneur: a Review of the Empirical Evidence on the Antecedents, Behaviour and Consequences of Innovative Entrepreneurship." *Industry and Innovation* 24, no. 1 (January): 61–95. https://doi.org/10.1080/13662716.2016.1216397.

Brem, Alexander, Maximilian Maier, and Christine Wimschneider. 2016. "Competitive Advantage Through Innovation: The Case of Nespresso." *European Journal of Innovation Management* 19, no. 1 (January): 133–48. https://doi.org/10.1108/EJIM-05-2014-0055.

Brown, Tim. 2008. "Design Thinking." *Harvard Business Review*, June. https://hbr.org/2008/06/design-thinking.

Calabresi, Guido. 1968. "Transaction Costs, Resource Allocation and Liability Rules: A Comment." *The Journal of Law & Economics* 11, no. 1 (April): 67–73. https://doi.org/10.1086/466644.

CFI. 2022. "Transaction Costs." Last modified February 19, 2022. https://corporatefinanceinstitute.com/resources/knowledge/economics/transaction-costs/.

Chen, Janet, Su-I Lu, and Dan Vekhter. n.d. "Axelrod's Tournament." *Stanford University*. Accessed February 17, 2023. https://cs.stanford.edu/people/eroberts/courses/soco/projects/1998-99/game-theory/axelrod.html.

Cooter, Robert, and Thomas Ulen. 2004. *Law and Economics*. 4th ed. Boston, MA: Pearson Addison Wesley.

Cusumano, Michael A. 2010. *Staying Power: Six Enduring Principles for Managing Strategy and Innovation in an Uncertain World*. New York: Oxford University Press.

Dam, Rikke, and Teo Siang. 2018. "What is Design Thinking and Why Is It So Popular?" *Interaction Design Foundation*. www.interaction-design.org/literature/article/what-is-design-thinking-and-why-is-it-so-popular.

Davis, Frederick B. 1944. "Fundamental Factors of Comprehension in Reading." *Psychometrika* 9 (September): 185–97. https://doi.org/10.1007/BF02288722.

DeSteno, David, Cynthia Breazeal, Robert H. Frank, David Pizarro, Jolie Baumann, Leah Dickens, and Jin Joo Lee. 2012. "Detecting the Trustworthiness of Novel Partners in Economic Exchange." *Psychological Science* 23, no. 12 (December): 1549–56. https://doi.org/10.1177/0956797612448793.

Erdem, Tülin, and Joffre Swait. 1998. "Brand Equity as a Signaling Phenomenon." *Journal of Consumer Psychology* 7, no. 2 (January): 131–57. https://doi.org/10.1207/s15327663jcp0702_02.

Genesereth, Michael R. 2021. "Contract Definition Language." *Stanford Law School Blogs: CodeX* (blog), April 7. https://law.stanford.edu/2021/04/07/contract-definition-language/.

Gilbert, Richard. 2006. "Looking for Mr. Schumpeter: Where Are We in the Competition – Innovation Debate?" *Innovation Policy and the Economy* 6, no. 6 (August): 159–215. https://doi.org/10.1086/ipe.6.25056183.

Hagan, Margaret. 2018. "A Human-Centered Design Approach to Access to Justice: Generating New Prototypes and Hypotheses for Interventions to Make Courts User-Friendly." *Indiana Journal of Law and Social Equality* 6, no. 2 (May): 199–239. www.repository.law.indiana.edu/ijlse/vol6/iss2/2?utm_source=www.repository.law.indiana.edu%2Fijlse%2Fvol6%2Fiss2%2F2&utm_medium=PDF&utm_campaign=PDFCoverPages.

2021. "Introduction to Design Thinking for Law." In *Legal Informatics*, edited by Daniel Martin Katz, Ron Dolin, and Michael J. Bommarito, 155–76. Cambridge: Cambridge University Press.

Hoffman, Nicole P. 2000. "An Examination of the 'Sustainable Competitive Advantage' Concept: Past, Present, and Future." *Academy of Marketing Science Review* 2000, no. 4 (January): 1–16. ProQuest.

IDEO.org. 2015. *The Field Guide to Human-Centered Design*. 1st ed. https://design-kit-production.s3.us-west-1.amazonaws.com/Field_Guides/Field+Guide+to+Human-Centered+Design_IDEOorg_English.pdf?utf8=✓&_method=patch&authenticity_token=QZRbnzBBPY3M%2FCd3xeDx424iAXgVkgcTAi74f6cW4pU%3D&resource%5Btitle%5D=&resource%5Bsubtitle%5D=&resource%5Bauthor%5D=&resource%5Babout%5D=.

Ireland, R. Duane, and Justin W. Webb. 2007. "Strategic Entrepreneurship: Creating Competitive Advantage through Streams of Innovation." *Business Horizons* 50, no. 1 (January–February): 49–59. https://doi.org/10.1016/j.bushor.2006.06.002.

Jeffries, F. L., and R. Reed. 2000. "Trust and Adaptation in Relational Contracting." *The Academy of Management Review* 25, no. 4 (October): 873–82. https://doi.org/10.2307/259212.

Jeutner, Valentin. 2021. "The Quantum Imperative: Addressing the Legal Dimension of Quantum Computers." *Morals & Machines* 1, no. 1 (April): 52–59. Social Science Research Network (SSRN).

Katz, Daniel Martin, Ron Dolin, and Michael J. Bommarito, eds. 2021. *Legal Informatics*. Cambridge: Cambridge University Press.

Keenan, Janice M., Rebecca S. Betjemann, and Richard K. Olson. 2008. "Reading Comprehension Tests Vary in the Skills They Assess: Differential Dependence on Decoding and Oral Comprehension." *Scientific Studies of Reading* 12, no. 3 (July): 281–300. https://doi.org/10.1080/10888430802132279.

Kiessling. Timothy S. 2004. "Entrepreneurship and Innovation: Austrian School of Economics to Schumpeter to Drucker to Now." *The Journal of Applied Management and Entrepreneurship* 9, no. 1 (January): 80–91.

Larson, Andrea. 1992. "Network Dyads in Entrepreneurial Settings: A Study of the Governance of Exchange Relationships." *Administrative Science Quarterly* 37, no. 1 (March): 76–104. https://doi.org/10.2307/2393534.

Lindenberg, Siegwart. 2000. "It Takes Both Trust and Lack of Mistrust: The Workings of Cooperation and Relational Signaling in Contractual Relationships." *Journal of Management and Governance* 4, no. 1–2 (March): 11–34. https://doi.org/10.1023/A:1009985720365.

Merrill, Thomas W., and Henry E. Smith. 2001. "What Happened to Property in Law and Economics?" *Yale Law Journal* 111, no. 2 (November): 357–98. https://doi.org/10.2307/797592.

Nousiainen, Katri. (2024). "Legal Design in Negotiation." *Legal Business World* no.3. Last accessed 5/23/2024. https://www.legalbizworld.com/_files/ugd/b30d31_6c2d06eb5db64c40adc3725d3f1bc45b.pdf.

Nousiainen, Katri and Catalina P. Ortega. (2024). "Dark Patterns in Law and Economics Framework." 36 *Loyola. Consumer Law Review*. 90. Available at: https://lawecommons.luc.edu/lclr/vol36/iss1/4.

Nousiainen, Katri. 2020. "What Have I Signed? Do I Really Understand the Contract?" *Contracting Excellence Journal*, September 12. https://journal.iaccm.com/contracting-excellence-journal/what-have-i-signed-do-i-really-understand-the-contract.

2021. "General Theory of Legal Design in Law and Economics Framework of Commercial Contracting." *Journal of Strategic Contracting and Negotiation* 5, no. 4 (December): 247–56. https://doi.org/10.1177/20555636211061611.

2022a. "Legal Design in Commercial Contracting and Business Sustainability: New Legal Quality Metrics Standards." *Journal of Strategic Contracting and Negotiation* 6, no. 2 (June): 137–58. https://doi.org/10.1177/20555636221138972

2022b. "The Application of Legal Design to Complex System Theory on Commercial Contracting within Law and Economics Framework." *Proceedings of the 25th International Legal Informatics Symposium IRIS 2022, February 22–23, 2022*. Vienna, Austria: Austrian Computer Society.

Nousiainen, Katri and Joonas Keski-Rahkonen. (2022). "Legal Business In The Post-Quantum Society." *Legal Business World*. Issue 6. Last accessed 5/23/2024. https://www.legalbizworld.com/post/legal-business-in-the-post-quantum-society.

Nousiainen, Katri and Joonas Keski-Rahkonen. (2023). "Uncharted Legal Design Landscape Towards a Bright Quantum Future." *Harvard Journal of Law and Technology JOLT Digest*. Last accessed 5/23/2024. https://jolt.law.harvard.edu/digest/a-roadmap-for-navigating-the-uncharted-legal-design-landscape-towards-a-bright-quantum-future.

Nousiainen, Katri; Keski-Rahkonen, Joonas; McDonald, Tim; Feldmann, Sascha. (2022) "Towards Society of Quantum Tomorrow" ANZCompuLawJl 6; 94 Computers & Law, Article 6.

Passera, Stefania. 2018. "Flowcharts, Swimlanes, and Timelines: Alternatives to Prose in Communicating Legal–Bureaucratic Instructions to Civil Servants." *Journal of Business and Technical Communication* 32, no. 2 (April): 229–72. https://doi.org/10.1177/1050651917746459.

Ring, Peter Smith, and Andrew H. van de Ven. 1994. "Developmental Processes of Cooperative Interorganizational Relationships." *The Academy of Management Review* 19, no. 1 (January): 90–118. https://doi.org/10.2307/258836.

Schumpeter, Joseph A. 1961. *The Theory of Economic Development: An Inquiry into Profits, Capital, Credit, Interest, and the Business Cycle*. New York: Oxford University Press.

1952. "The General Economist." In *Wesley Clair Mitchell: The Economic Scientist*, 321–40. National Bureau of Economic Research, Inc.

1989. *Essays: On Entrepreneurs, Innovations, Business Cycles, and the Evolution of Capitalism*, edited by Richard V. Clemence. New Brunswick, NJ: Routledge.

2009. *Can Capitalism Survive? Creative Destruction and the Future of the Global Economy*. New York: HarperCollins.

Scott, Robert E. 2006. "Anticipating Litigation in Contract Design." *The Yale Law Journal* 115, no. 4 (January): 814–79. https://doi.org/10.2307/20455639.

Scott, Robert E., and George G. Triantis. 2005. "Incomplete Contracts and the Theory of Contract Design." *Case Western Reserve Law Review* 56, no. 1 (Fall): 187–201.

Sledzik, Karol. 2013. "Knowledge Based Economy in a Neo-Schumpeterian Point of View." *Equilibrium (Toruń)* 8, no. 4 (December): 67–77. https://doi.org/10.12775/EQUIL.2013.027.

Smith, Henrik. 2006. "Modularity in Contracts: Boilerplate and Information Flow." *Michigan Law Review* 104, no. 5 (March): 1175–222.

Stanford University. 2012. "A Design Thinking Process: Mechanical Engineering Design ME113." https://web.stanford.edu/class/me113/d_thinking.html.

Triantis, George G. 2013. "Improving Contract Quality: Modularity, Technology, and Innovation in Contract Design." *Stanford Journal of Law, Business & Finance* 18, no. 2 (June): 177–214. Social Science Research Network (SSRN).

US Department of State. 2000. "Wassenaar Arrangement on Export Controls for Conventional Arms and Dual-Use Goods and Technologies." https://1997-2001.state.gov/global/arms/np/mtcr/000322_wassenaar.html.

Van Slyke, David M. 2000. "Collaboration and Relational Contracting." In *The Collaborative Public Manager*, edited by Rosemary O'Leary and Lisa Blomgren Bingham, 137–56. Washington, DC: Georgetown University Press.

von Hayek, Friedrich A. 1985. *New Studies in Philosophy, Politics, Economics and the History of Ideas*. Chicago: University of Chicago Press.

Williams, Spencer. 2021. "Contracts as Systems." *The Delaware Journal of Corporate Law* 45, no. 2 (March): 219–78. https://dx.doi.org/10.2139/ssrn.3687773.

Williamson, Oliver. 1979. "Transaction-Cost Economics: The Governance of Contractual Relations." *The Journal of Law & Economics* 22, no. 2 (October): 233–61. https://doi.org/10.1086/466942.

Williamson, Oliver, and Scott Masten, eds. 1999. *The Economics of Transaction Costs*. Northampton, MA: Edward Elgar Publishing.

Woolthuis, Rosalinde Klein, Bas Hillebrand, and Bart Nooteboom. 2005. "Trust, Contract and Relationship Development." *Organization Studies* 26, no. 6 (June): 813–40. https://doi.org/10.1177/0170840605054594.

Young, Suzanne. 2013. "Transaction Cost Economics." In *Encyclopedia of Corporate Social Responsibility*, edited by Samuel O. Idowu, Nicholas Capaldi, Liangrong Zu, and Ananda Das Gupta, 2547–52. Berlin, Germany: Springer.

24

Evaluation Capacity Building in Legal Design

Tiana Yom

24.1 THE WHY: INTRODUCTION

As seen throughout the chapters, there are varying definitions of legal design. Margaret Hagan's definition (2020) compliments the definition of evaluation. According to Hagan, "legal design applies human-centered design to the world of law to enable desirable outcomes and prevent the causes of problems from arising and developing into conflict and disputes." Legal designers strive to produce legal products, services, and systems that are useful, accessible, and generalizable (Hagan 2020). The focus of legal design is not only to generate these consumer-centered items but also to understand how legal designers know if these deliverables were used in the way they were intended or if they made an impact on the user. These questions are the starting point of an evaluation, indicating that objective assessment may benefit legal design. Considering how evidence is essential in many legal processes, developing legal design evaluation will strengthen the impact and position of design in the area of law.

Evaluation is a process that critically examines an evaluand, which is the subject of the evaluation (e.g., program, system, intervention). This systematic method assesses the evaluation in order to understand to what extent it achieved its goals. Evaluations fall into one of two broad categories: formative and summative. Formative evaluations (e.g., needs assessment, process, or implementation evaluation) are conducted during program development and implementation. Formative evaluations are useful because they provide guiding information for any changes that need to be made to achieve the desired outcomes. Comparatively, summative evaluations (e.g., outcome evaluation, impact evaluation) should be completed once programs are well established and as they provide information to what extent the program is achieving its goals (Patton 1987; Mertens and Wilson 2019).

Existing literature shows extensive examples of health care design and clinical evaluations as well as evaluations to measure dignity expectations among patients (Johnston, Ostlund, and Brown 2012; Houmann et al. 2014; Oosterveld-Vlug et al.

2014; Ho et al. 2016; Otake et al. 2021). Otake and colleagues (2021) led a cross-sectional study that focused on raising the importance of providing dignified care in various nursing care settings. The research team developed a pilot evaluation instrument, a questionnaire for patients' family members and nurses to evaluate their dignity, expectations, and satisfaction of patients with dementia. The use and findings from this questionnaire developed a better understanding of the expectations of patients with cognitive decline regarding dignity and guidance for the provision of dignified nursing. Similarly, Ho and colleagues (2016) recognized that end-of-life care is a new and growing area in Chinese communities. The research team piloted a Dignity Conserving End of Life Care model in three nursing homes in Hong Kong and developed an evaluation plan that would assess the usefulness and impact of this intervention. Through the information gathered from the evaluation, the research team found this new model to be effective in enhancing dignity and quality of life among terminally ill nursing home residents. Houmann and coworkers (2014) conducted a pretest-posttest evaluation to assess a psychosocial intervention for adult patients with incurable diseases, Dignity Therapy. The research team distributed questionnaires at the start and end of the program to participants. Findings from the evaluation showed that Dignity Therapy is a valuable intervention and its use raised awareness for novel interventions to support advanced cancer patients in palliative care. Oostervald-Vlug and colleagues (2014) developed a novel instrument, the Measurement Instrument for Dignity Amsterdam for Long-Term Care facilities (MIDAM-LTC), which aims to assess factors that influence personal dignity in long-term care facilities. To evaluate the validity, feasibility, and impact of MIDAM-LTC, the research team conducted a pretest-posttest evaluation with ninety-five nursing home residents across six nursing homes in the Netherlands. The results from the evaluation provided suggestive evidence that MIDAM-LTC could be a way to better understand the concept of dignity in long-term care facilities. Johnston, Ostlund, and Brown (2012) understood the difficult task of providing end-of-life care by community nurses and launched the Dignity Care Pathway (DCP). DCP is an intervention that trains nurses to provide dignity-oriented and person-centered care. The research team developed and implemented a pilot evaluation plan that included a mixed-methods, pretest-posttest test design. This evaluation plan kept track of how DCP was performing and provided important information for future DCP iterations.

Additionally, there are well-established frameworks and standards for evaluation in public health (CDC 2017) that are related to legal issues suggesting that Legal design evaluation isn't necessarily new. There have been evaluations assessing the impact of trauma-informed training and practices (Marrow, Kraig, Olafson, and Bucher 2012; Lee, Ostrom, and Kleiman 2014; Katz and Haldar 2016; Roagna 2021). Similarly, there have been evaluations of legal assistance programs, to understand their impact and successes (Grenier and Pattanayak 2012; Felix, Agnich, and Schueths 2017). There is a clear need and a developed interest for evaluation across the legal spectrum. For example, the United Nations (UN) created the Criminal Justice Assessment Tool (2006), and the UN Women and the Council of Europe developed the Framework for Measuring Access to Justice Including Specific Challenges Facing Women (2016). There is also a dedicated Research, Evaluation, and Learning team within the American Bar Association who developed law assessment methodologies, toolkits, and guides (American Bar Association n.d.).

Despite the growing literature on legal design evaluations, the word "evaluation" seems to be interchangeably used with "assessment," "monitoring," "surveys," or "tests." There isn't a common, universal definition of evaluation in legal design. Furthermore, the focus is on the evaluation tools and not so much on evaluation planning including understanding how to develop appropriate evaluation questions; creating a logic model to map out the goals, outputs, and outcomes of the desired evaluation; developing a plan for determining whether the evaluation is effective or not; and so on. To assess whether legal designs made the law more user-friendly, engaging, and easy to understand, legal design evaluations are needed.

24.2 THE HOW: TRAUMA-INFORMED EVALUATION AND CULTURALLY RESPONSIVE EVALUATION

There is an array of evaluation types that can be helpful in legal design, and there is no "right" or "wrong" one. Given the human-centric, community-based, and participatory foundations of legal design, there are two evaluation frameworks that come to mind: Trauma-Informed Evaluation and Culturally Responsive Evaluation (CRE).

According to the Substance Abuse and Mental Health Services (SAMHSA), trauma is defined as an event or circumstance resulting in physical harm, emotional harm, and/or life-threatening harm (SAMHSA 2022). Trauma-informed evaluation is rooted in an understanding of and responsiveness to the impact of trauma (Hopper, Bassuk, and Olivet 2010). This type of evaluation follows a strengths-based framework, where there is an emphasis on physical, psychological, and emotional safety for both evaluators and survivors, and it creates opportunities for survivors to rebuild a sense of control. The grounding principles of this framework include safety; trustworthiness and transparency; peer support; collaboration and mutuality; empowerment, voice, and choice; and cultural, historic, and gender issues (SAMSHA 2014).

Ways to implement trauma-informed evaluations include:

- Place the dignity of participants at the center by placing participants' welfare first in evaluation planning and normalize a range of feelings, emotions, and coping mechanisms.
- Be guided by the participant and provide support, control, choice, and autonomy.

- Implement emotional preparedness strategies for participants and evaluators.
- Identify appropriate, psychologically safe spaces for interviews/data collection.
- Establish safety plans with participants.
- Create opportunities for collaboration with participants to help shape the evaluation process.
- Practice self-awareness of reactions.

The second framework, Culturally Responsive Evaluation (CRE), is rooted in social justice and critical race theory (CRT). This holistic framework gives attention to historically marginalized groups and aims to consider the needs and cultural parameters of those who are served relative to the implementation of the program and its outcomes (Hood, Hopson, and Kirkhart 2015). CRE acknowledges that we all are affected by culture and that we have biases and assumptions that we bring with us when working with participants. Culture and cultural understanding are at the center and connected to all nine stages of CRE. The influence of culture is ever-present, multidimensional, and influences the evaluation process from start (e.g., creating the evaluation questions, developing the evaluation plan) to finish (e.g., analyses, interpretation of findings, dissemination plan).

CRE helps evaluators think differently, particularly helping them move from traditional positions to more culturally appropriate roles and responsibilities. Table 24.1 shows a comparison of traditional evaluation versus CRE, highlighting the role of CRE in enhancing dignity in legal design processes and outcomes. As seen in the emphasis on community connections and relationship building,

TABLE 24.1. *Traditional evaluation versus culturally responsive evaluation (adapted from GMNsight, 2015).*

Traditional Evaluation	Culturally Responsive Evaluation (CRE)
Evaluator: Formally trained evaluators are the experts.	Community members, participants know best regarding the areas of need and strengths.
Role of Evaluator: Leader, judge, expert.	Facilitator, translator, convener.
Design and Planning: Evaluator presents design for funder approval.	Prioritizing rapport and trust building in an inclusive planning process that infuses multiple world views and realities. There is space for narratives and counternarratives. Time is spent to ensure participants feel belonging and ownership of the evaluation.
Data Collection: Conducted by trained evaluator.	Facilitated by evaluator; participants are trained in data collection and implementation.
Analysis: Results are analyzed and interpreted by trained evaluator.	Results and their meaning are derived based on culture and system analyses.

CRE is a periodic approach rather than a single shot at the end. Therefore, this evaluation type can be combined and planned along the design process to create a synergetic impact.

Both trauma-informed evaluation and CRE frameworks follow a unique, chronological sequence, where the dignity of participants is at the core and culture is an integral element.

24.3 THE WHAT: RECOMMENDATIONS

It is exciting to think about where legal design can go, especially with evaluation, as this is a growing space in legal design. There are three areas where it would be particularly interesting to explore evaluations further. The first area is exploring what a multidisciplinary team (MDT) approach in legal design evaluation would look like. The MDT approach is traditionally seen in health care services, where the purpose of the MDT is to gather a diverse group of health care professionals to collectively assess, plan, and manage care for the patient (Taberna et al. 2020). An MDT approach in legal design evaluation would aim to include as many groups involved with the law as possible – judges, lawyers, clients, legal advocates, law school students, administrators, and so on – to comprehensively assess the evaluation. There is a growing interest and advocacy in legal design for multidisciplinary collaboration of all users of the law. This inquiry may be expanded to include MDT in creating an evaluation model for legal designs that can be used as a template for developing robust evaluation plans throughout the legal landscape.

The second area is in the evaluation planning process for legal design evaluations. There are generally three stages of evaluation: planning, implementation, and maintenance. Often, organizations are too eager to go to the implementation stage and disproportionately expend more time and energy on the evaluation design questions (e.g., what's the best way to collect data? Surveys or interviews? In-person or virtual?). To truly yield accurate, intentional, thoughtful evaluation outcomes, all those involved in the evaluation process first need to begin with reflection activities. Milner (2007) proposed two types of exercises for researchers to complete before beginning research and to revisit throughout the study. The first exercise is "Researching the Self," where the goal is to establish self-awareness and acknowledgment of the different experiences, racial and cultural, of the researcher that may influence how they engage in the study.

Adapted from Milner (2007) and Gordon (1990), the following are examples of self-reflection questions recommended for the legal design evaluator:

- What is my racial and cultural heritage? How do I know?
- In what ways do my racial and cultural backgrounds influence how I experience the world, what I emphasize in my evaluation work, and how I assess and interpret others and their experiences? How do I know?

- What racialized and cultural experiences have shaped my evaluation decisions, practices, approaches, epistemologies, and agendas?
- What is my understanding of the evaluation?

The second exercise is "Researching the Self in Relation to Others," where the goal is for researchers – or in this case, evaluators – to reflect on their relation to the participants and/or anyone else involved in the evaluation.

Adapted from Milner (2007) and Gordon (1990), the following recommended questions are added for the legal design evaluator:

- What are the cultural and racial heritages and the historical landscape of the participants in the evaluation? How do I know?
- How do I identify and balance my own interests and evaluation goals with those of the evaluation participants, which may be inconsistent with or diverge from mine? How do I know?
- What are the participants' understanding of the evaluation? How do I know?

The third area is participant engagement, including how to define and connect with participants in legal design evaluations. Participants are asked to devote time to share honest feedback about the evaluation, yet the findings of the evaluation may or may not be shared back with participants. Thus, further work is needed to help answer the following questions: How can legal design evaluation be another tool or avenue for engagement? What does data sharing look like and how can participants have ownership of the narrative and findings? How can legal design evaluation be redefined from a punitive-type checklist of metrics to a continuous quality improvement tool?

24.4 CONCLUSION

Evaluations ought to be seen as an instrumental part of legal design, a part of the beginning stages of legal design planning, and not as an afterthought. Legal design evaluations can help improve program design and implementation with the end goal of meeting the needs of the participants. Subsequently, they can also demonstrate the program's impact. Finally, evaluations aim to generate information for potential new ideas and/or interventions to continue to refine legal design.

REFERENCES

American Bar Association (ABA). n.d. "Monitoring, Evaluation and Learning." Accessed July 25, 2022. www.americanbar.org/advocacy/rule_of_law/about/work_research/.

American Evaluation Association (AEA). 2021. "Trauma-Informed Eval Week: Principles of Trauma-Informed Evaluation by Martha Brown." Accessed August 1, 2022. https://aea365

.org/blog/trauma-informed-eval-week-principles-of-trauma-informed-evaluation-by-martha-brown/.

Centers for Disease Control and Prevention (CDC). 2017. "A Framework for Program Evaluation." Accessed August 1, 2022. www.cdc.gov/evaluation/framework/index.htm.

Felix, Shanna N., Laura E. Agnich, and April Schueths. 2017. "An Evaluation of a Court Appointed Special Advocates (CASA) Program in the Rural South." *Children and Youth Services Review* 83 (December): 48–56. https://doi.org/10.1016/j.childyouth.2017.10.025.

GMNsight. 2015. "Learning with Diverse Communities Through Culturally Responsive Evaluation." Accessed August 1, 2022. www.gmnsight.org/learning-with-diverse-communities-through-culturally-responsive-evaluation/.

Gordon, Beverly M. 1990. "The Necessity of African-American Epistemology for Educational Theory and Practice." *Journal of Education* 172, no. 3 (October): 88–106. https://doi.org/10.1177/002205749017200307.

Grenier, D. James, and Cassandra Wolos Pattanayak. 2012. "Randomized Evaluation in Legal Assistance: What Difference Does Representation (Offer and Actual Use) Make?" *Yale Law Journal* 121, no. 8 (June): 2118–215.

Hagan, Margaret. 2020. "Legal Design as a Thing: A Theory of Change and a Set of Methods to Craft a Human-Centered Legal System." *Design Issues* 36, no. 3 (Summer): 3–15. https://doi.org/10.1162/desi_a_00600.

Ho, Andy H. Y., Annie A. N. Dai, Shu-hang Lam, Sandy W. P. Wong, Amy L. M. Tsui, Jervis C. S. Tang, and Vivian W. Q. Lou. 2016. "Development and Pilot Evaluation of a Novel Dignity-Conserving End-of-Life (EoL) Care Model for Nursing Homes in Chinese Societies." *The Gerontologist* 56, no. 3 (June): 578–89. https://doi.org/10.1093/geront/gnv037.

Hood, Stafford, Rodney K. Hopson, and Karen E. Kirkhart. 2015. "Culturally Responsive Evaluation: Theory, Practice, and Future Implications." In *Handbook on Practical Program Evaluation*, edited by Kathryn E. Newcomer, Harry P. Hatry, and Joseph S. Wholey, 281–317. San Francisco, CA: Jossey-Bass.

Hopper, Elizabeth K., Ellen L. Bassuk, and Jeffrey Olivet. 2010. "Shelter from the Storm: Trauma-Informed Care in Homelessness Services Settings." *The Open Health Services and Policy Journal* 3, no. 1 (April): 80–100. http://dx.doi.org/10.2174/1874924001003020080.

Houmann, Lise J., Harvey M. Chochinov, Linda J. Kristjanson, Morten Aa Petersen, and Mogens Groenvold. 2014. "A Prospective Evaluation of Dignity Therapy in Advanced Cancer Patients Admitted to Palliative Care." *Palliative Medicine* 28, no. 5 (May): 448–58. https://doi.org/10.1177/0269216313514883.

Johnston, Bridget, Ulrika Östlund, and Hilary Brown. 2012. "Evaluation of the Dignity Care Pathway for Community Nurses Caring for People at the End of Life." *International Journal of Palliative Nursing* 18, no. 10 (October): 483–89. https://doi.org/10.12968/ijpn.2012.18.10.483.

Katz, Sarah, and Deeya Haldar. 2016. "The Pedagogy of Trauma-Informed Lawyering." *Clinical Law Review* 22 (Spring): 359–93. Social Science Research Network (SSRN).

Lee, Cynthia G., Brian J. Ostrom, and Matthew Kleiman. 2014. "The Measure of Good Lawyering: Evaluating Holistic Defense in Practice." *Albany Law Review* 78, no. 3 (July): 1215–38.

Marrow, Monique T., Kraig J. Knudsen, Erna Olafson, and Sarah E. Bucher. 2012. "The Value of Implementing TARGET within a Trauma-Informed Juvenile Justice Setting." *Journal of Child & Adolescent Trauma* 5, no. 3 (January): 257–70. https://doi.org/10.1080/19361521.2012.697105.

Mertens, D. M., and A. T. Wilson. 2019. *Program Evaluation Theory and Practice: A Comprehensive Guide*. 2nd ed. New York: Guilford Press.

Milner, H. Richard. 2007. "Race, Culture, and Researcher Positionality: Working Through Dangers Seen, Unseen, and Unforeseen." *Educational Researcher* 36, no. 7 (October): 388–400. https://doi.org/10.3102/0013189X07309471.

Oosterveld-Vlug, Mariska G., H. Roeline W. Pasman, Isis E. van Gennip, Henrica C. W. de Vet, and Bregje D. Onwuteaka-Philipsen. 2014. "Assessing the Validity and Intra-Observer Agreement of the MIDAM-LTC; an Instrument Measuring Factors that Influence Personal Dignity in Long-Term Care Facilities." *Health and Quality of Life Outcomes* 12, no. 1 (February): 1–10. https://doi.org/10.1186/1477-7525-12-17.

Otake, Eriko, Katsumasa Ota, Chikako Ikegami, Yukari Niimi, Satoko Yamada, Jukai Maeda, and Masami Matsuda. 2021. "Proxy Evaluation of Dignity Expectations and Satisfaction of Older Patients with Dementia by Family Members and Nurses." *Nursing Open* 8, no. 6 (November): 3120–34. https://doi.org/10.1002/nop2.1024.

Patton, M. Q. 1987. *Qualitative Research Evaluation Methods*. Thousand Oaks, CA: Sage Publishers.

Roagna, Ivana. 2021. "Assessment of the Existing Systems/Mechanisms for Evaluation and Impact of Human Rights Training: Recommended Methodologies and Tools." *Council of Europe*. https://rm.coe.int/methodology-for-evaluation-of-hr-training-eng-/1680a2732f.

Substance Abuse and Mental Health Services (SAMHSA). 2014. "SAMHSA's Concept of Trauma and Guidance for Trauma-Informed Approach." Accessed August 1, 2022. https://store.samhsa.gov/product/SAMHSA-s-Concept-of-Trauma-and-Guidance-for-a-Trauma-Informed-Approach/SMA14–4884.

2022. "Trauma and Violence." Accessed August 1, 2022. www.samhsa.gov/trauma-violence#:~:text=What%20is%20Trauma%3F,and%2For%20life%2Dthreatening%20harm.

Taberna, Miren, Francisco Gil Moncayo, Enric Jané-Salas, Maite Antonio, Lorena Arribas, Estehr Vilajosana, Elisabet Peralvez Torres, and Ricard Mesía. 2020. "The Multidisciplinary Team (MDT) Approach and Quality of Care." *Frontiers in Oncology* 10 (March): 83–98. https://doi.org/10.3389/fonc.2020.00085.

United Nations (UN). 2006. "Criminal Justice Assessment Toolkit." Accessed July 25, 2022. www.unodc.org/documents/justice-and-prison-reform/cjat_eng/CJAT_Toolkit_full_version23Mar10all.pdf.

UN Women and Council of Europe. 2016. "Framework for Measuring Access to Justice Including Specific Challenges Facing Women." Accessed July 25, 2022. https://rm.coe.int/168069cf4e.

25

The Peril and Promise of Certificates and Degree Programs in Legal Design

Gabriel H. Teninbaum

25.1 INTRODUCTION

There is a scene in the 1984 movie *The Karate Kid* in which the teenage protagonist, Daniel LaRussa, discovers that the mild-mannered maintenance worker at his apartment complex, Mr. Miyagi, is an expert in karate. He learns this after Miyagi thwarts a group of bullies that have cornered Daniel. In the aftermath, Daniel asks, "Hey, what kind of belt do you have?" no doubt imagining a black belt with various stripes emblazoned on it. Miyagi raises his shirt to reveal his belt, answering: "Canvas. JC Penney. Three ninety-eight. You like?" (Tarwater 2022). The joke brings laughs in the theater, but the point it makes is a much deeper one about the dichotomy between a credential and the underlying expertise a credential represents.

It is a dichotomy I think about regularly in my role overseeing the Institute on Legal Innovation and Technology (LIT) at Suffolk University Law School. Among our programs is a LIT Concentration (an optional program akin to an undergraduate major). The program's approach is intended to provide both experiences that enrich and credentials for those willing to put in the work to earn them. The program's guiding focus is on teaching students what they need to succeed in the legal field in the future. This includes more than a dozen courses covering topics like the use of document automation tools to solve access to justice problems, process improvement, and legal project management. We also mix the hands-on with a lot of training on mindset. Among the offerings is a course in legal design as well as a number of courses that bring in elements of legal design training. Outside of classes, we offer various informal experiences, such as participation in the annual Boston Legal Design Challenge where dozens of students from across the nation spend a day with us learning the basics and competing to creatively solve a challenge. The LIT program has been a success: Every year, a handful opt to complete the full concentrations, while more than 100 students take some classes from it (and many more still are members of our LIT Student Association, which meets informally and promotes events).

Rather than being formal about who can learn these topics, our approach is to invite all students to take a nibble of "new law." We start this conversation during new student orientation, where we share data about job trends and market needs. In some years, we have even provided a copy of Richard Susskind's foundational legal tech book, *Tomorrow's Lawyers*, to the entire entering class. Once the upper-level years begin, students can sign up for courses within the LIT Concentration, even if only one course. Additionally, there are upper-level opportunities for legal tech externships, writing projects, independent studies, and participation in our own legal tech research and development lab. Some students go on to complete the entire Concentration while others benefit from engaging with the portion of the program that fits their needs and then move on.

As a result, alumni have changed the way they envision legal work and their role in the field, finding success in ways that are both measurable and immeasurable. Some have graduated and been hired by AmLaw 200 firms (many with job titles that did not even exist a few years ago, like Legal Solutions Architect and Innovation Advisor). Others have used their skills to work in legal aid organizations, at legal tech start-ups, and even as an entrepreneur with the first legal tech product to get funded on the hit TV show *Shark Tank*. Most of them go on to traditional legal roles, but with a better understanding of how innovation and technology can help them do better work.

Convincing students to focus on rich experiences, as opposed to focusing only on credentials, can be a challenge. The culture of law schools is largely a culture of credentials. It is competing for a top 10% class rank, membership in *Law Review*, earning Order of the Coif, completing a Concentration, and graduating *cum laude*. Eventually, the credential-focused graduate defeats the "final boss" by passing the bar exam and joining the guild of lawyers (and a guild it is, one where it is a crime to do the work of a guild member if not licensed). It is credentials all the way down, always with another to reach for (and, of course, it doesn't end with law school and the bar: there's the partner track to contend with after it).

This is not to say that credentials cannot be useful. Completing a course or certificate in legal design offers some evidence to the world that one has studied the philosophies and explored examples of them in application. As an administrator, it is my hope that the credential alone may be a reason to give an applicant an interview when observed as a transcript line among dozens of other applications. It may be a reason for a supervisor to consider a subordinate to lead a challenging project that will require lateral thinking. In short, credentials can open doors. And not only that: in some organizations, pursuing a credential can be a requirement to receive training funds, and it might be seen as desirable to advertise to potential clients that a staff member has trained in the area. Ultimately, though, we cannot confuse proxies for expertise (a credential) with actual expertise (demonstrated over time through performance).

This challenge is uniquely acute in legal design. In legal design, one doesn't get awarded master status. One doesn't arrive at being a legal designer at a given moment any more than a person learning meditation can be certified as "mindful." Instead, it is a process of constant learning and improvement. If taken too far, the drive toward credentials reduces reflection on that which is harder to attach to a resume line: How well did that attorney empathize with their client's needs? How creatively did they approach their office's problem? How effectively did this solution make using the court system more usable?

Not only can credentials distract from the need to learn; they can also affirmatively pose dangers. Awarding credentials in a discipline emphasizing continuous growth is tricky because it suggests to people that you can "arrive." As more people earn the credential, attaining it becomes a de facto gatekeeper leading to excluding those that lack it. Professionalizing legal design may ultimately mean that people who are not of financial means may be dissuaded from learning even the basics, believing that the training will only be of use if a credential is later earned.

So how can an institution square the two? In short, by recognizing the tension and providing not just a credential to those that complete a program but experiences they can share to demonstrate where they are on their own path toward mastery.

25.2 STRIKING THE RIGHT BALANCE

To balance the need to provide substantive training while recognizing the benefits – and, in some cases, needs for credentials – the following principles have helped us strike a balance at Suffolk Law School.

25.2.1 *Give Students the Chance to "Show, Don't Tell"*

One of the joys of learning legal design principles is that it's best done in action. Instead of reading hundreds of pages, one does best by learning a concept and then applying it through a project that solves a problem. In one example, a legal design professor sent his class to the nearby subway station to observe the long lines forming to buy a subway pass. He asked them to interview riders about their experience and gather data about wait times. From there, he asked students to return and work collaboratively to redesign the experience. This process created artifacts: notes, spreadsheets, photos, and, later on, mocked-up diagrams for a new approach. After the project is completed, these artifacts remain as an archive of personal growth. They also form a portfolio of sorts, where a neophyte legal designer can reflect on their growth and their process for achieving a result.

25.2.2 *Downplay Grades When Grades Don't Add Value*

At Suffolk Law, we have offered the Design Thinking course as an ungraded, pass/fail activity. Students are required and expected to attend all the sessions, participate fully, do all the assigned reading, and do their best to communicate with their classmates and instructors . . . but they are not graded. At semester's end, doing one's best to apply the class's lessons merits a "Pass." By avoiding letter grades – particularly for JD students focused on class ranks on the theory that a better rank will improve job prospects – students can focus on the learning as opposed to the grade. Having taught a number of pass/fail courses, I've noticed it changes the dynamic when students know that they are going to pass if they do all they are asked (from a professor's perspective, it also loosens things up).

25.2.3 *Create a Community*

Like Daniel-san, it is helpful to have a Miyagi when learning a complex area of study. Even better to have a whole bunch of other Daniels experiencing the process at the same time. In our programs, we hire a professor for legal design who we know engages with students both inside and outside of class, and will also remain willing to serve as a mentor after the semester ends. We encourage collaboration, conversation, and networking. The idea is to extend the basic explorations encountered during a semester. This takes on a life outside of the classroom with our Legal Innovation & Technology Student Association, which organizes events and maintains an ongoing, informal discussion of relevant topics.

25.2.4 *Build Space for Informal Exploration*

After leaving our day-long Legal Design Challenge, participants are ebullient. Each one of them gives up an entire day – normally a Friday (and anyone who has ever been to law school knows that the law student sabbath begins Thursday at 4 p.m. and runs until noon on Monday) – to learn some basic tenets of design and then work with a group of classmates and solve a problem. From my perspective, it's an exhausting day, with constant high energy and few breaks. Yet, when I see the students at the post-event reception, they are huddled around like athletes who just played a big game, replaying moments of glory. There is no academic credit for taking part. Instead, they have had a fun, energizing, creative experience. They have been given license to flex muscles they rarely use as law students. They leave with smiles, and every year, new participants tell me that a friend told them they had to sign up. This is the ultimate in mixing the opportunity for a credential (winning an award at the event for the team's work) with it being a terrific experience and a rich educational opportunity for everyone.

25.3 CONCLUSION

In the context of increasing legal design, technology, and innovation initiatives, academic institutions are now offering comprehensive programs to equip students with skills in these emerging fields. While this is a welcome trajectory, our experience at Suffolk Law suggests that too rapid a contraction for legal design into a formal profession may inadvertently stifle this budding interdisciplinary movement, leading to fewer practitioners and limited impact in the long term. Instead, a broader definition of a "legal designer," one that includes anyone passionate about enhancing our justice system, should be embraced. While credentials can be beneficial in certain scenarios, the emphasis for law schools should be on a holistic learning approach. The goal should be to foster a community of continuous learners who are passionate about legal innovation and design, rather than focusing too narrowly on the strict requirements that professions and universities require to confer credentials. This approach will better allow for the proliferation of this interdisciplinary movement, leading to more practitioners and a greater impact in both the short and long term.

REFERENCES

Tarwater, Eustace. 2022. "Karate Kid—Mr. Miyagi wears a different kind of martial arts belt." Uploaded on December 14, 2022. YouTube video, 0:18 min. www.youtube.com/watch?v=X2PmColm8b4.

26

Repair and Resistance

Law Students as Leaders of the Legal Design Movement

Antonio M. Coronado

26.1 INTRODUCTION: TRACING A LEGAL HISTORY OF INDIGNITY

This country was born in blood and violence against non-European "others."

—Joe Feagin, *Racist America: Roots, Current Realities, and Future Reparations*

I open this chapter with the words of US sociologist, Joe Feagin ([2000] 2014, 35), for several reasons. The first is a practical one: to ground the sections that follow in the critical scholarships and perspectives from which they emerge.

The second is one of personal reflection and of reminding myself of the visceral reaction I had to seeing this reality (re)centered while in law school. I first read this passage at the end of legal education and – in ways I'm still uncovering – it named, unmasked, and disrupted the prior three years of disorientation upon which law school had insisted. In eleven words, Feagin had slashed through the legal doctrine and neoliberal dogma, reaffirming what I knew to be true before I'd begun the degree. It was a reminder that it is *possible* and, in fact, *necessary* to directly name the violent truths of this settler nation. To past and present law students, it might be unsurprising that I was introduced to this quote in a graduate-level sociology course and not in any of my law school seminars or foundational courses. It took leaving the law to fully locate the harm of its internal logics, and undoubtedly this wound remains.

The third and final purpose of this quote is to situate us – in time, space, body, and self. It is to ask that you join me in reorienting legal education and examining our material, ideological, and temporal relations to legal power across this chapter.

Following Feagin and the countless Black and Indigenous voices of liberatory, decolonial persistence before him, I'll start by naming: US law, in both substance and form, does not promote dignity. Eleven words to remind us in our charting of legal dignity that "dignity" under US settler law is oxymoronic. Universal notions of personal dignity, autonomy, and personhood were not in the legal foundations of this empire, and it is ahistorical to pretend otherwise. But neither is the law neutral as to dignity; the legal profession has and continues to actively facilitate practices of *indignity*.

Substantively, an architecture of *de jure* subordination is one of the few constants in the past 246 years of this settler nation's existence. Returning to the work of Feagin ([2000] 2014, 32), we know these origins to be ones of legally sanctioned and intercontinental genocide:

> While many US founders asserted in the Declaration of Independence and elsewhere that "all men are created equal," they did not mean literally what they said. Their equality and liberty framing was conditional and hypocritical, for it excluded [B]lack Americans, [I]ndigenous peoples, and white women. The real US foundation was crafted to create wealth and privilege for transplanted Europeans and their descendants who stole the lands of [I]ndigenous peoples and enslaved African labor. In this process, Europeans and European Americans came to frame themselves and their society as a virtuous "white" republic.

Critical scholars, movements, and activists beyond academia have named this reality for time immemorial (The Black Panther Party for Self-Defense, 1967; Fenelon and Hall 2008; Neitch 2019). US journalist and author Isabel Wilkerson (2020), for instance, provides a compelling account of this nation's legacy of white supremacist violence and of the entrenched legal mechanisms that perpetuate it. In mapping the horrific logics and laws that connect colonization to Jim Crow and mass incarceration, Wilkerson identifies unequal racist realities as the repeating outcome of our institutions – not aberrations. Naming this systemic configuration is the core project of Critical Race Theory and of more recent efforts, like the 1619 Project, that aim to excavate the racial violence underlying US legal systems (Crenshaw et al. 1995; Hannah-Jones 2021).

But why begin here? Why start this chapter and our discussion of dignity in legal education in the 1700s? I do so because our imagining of a liberatory future is premised on the unimagining of the violent present. I center the past because it is now and all-encompassing. History, as James Baldwin noted, is "literally present in all that we do" and never *not present* in our lives (Baldwin 1995). It is precisely because the US legal profession resides on bloodied foundations that we are the present subjects to bloodied realities. In the words of sitting US Congresswoman and self-proclaimed Christian nationalist Marjorie Taylor Greene, "Today and everyday [sic] is 1776" (@RepMTG, April 23, 2022).

So, when we discuss legal education and its role in advancing notions of dignity, it is imperative we begin with an understanding of the legal histories that bring us to the present moment. By grounding our inquiry in legal history, it becomes direly necessary for us to situate the bar exam, the Law School Admissions Test (LSAT), and all the gatekeeping functions of this profession as living, roaring vestiges of imperial violence and of the law's desire to keep "pure the Anglo-Saxon race" (Roithmayr 1997; Subotnik 2013, 365–66). In doing so, we can make space for the future, unimagine the indignant things our profession protects, and concede that the process of making justice was never meant to include all peoples (*People v. Hall*, 4 Cal. 399 (1854)).

The contours of these histories lock the law in a state of crisis, and they have defined every second of my time in the profession. While preparing for the bar exam, I was disturbed (though not surprised) by a bar prep company's tip on how to approach criminal procedure questions: "If you have no idea what the answer is, choose an answer that sides with the government, against a criminal defendant" (Themis Bar Review 2022). But the worst part is that they were right. Guessing in this way did align with the trend of Supreme Court rulings against criminal defendants. But how depraved – *how malignant-hearted, how wanton, and how reckless* – of a profession do we have to be to uphold a world premised on harm and to bet against the rights, the lives, and the dignity of people?

This chapter proceeds in three parts. First, I look to the ways that a doctrine of indignity organizes the US practice of law at an institutional level, with a particular focus on legal education as a site of lawyer socialization. Next, I identify lessons of indignity that are normatively embedded within traditional legal pedagogy. These lessons, I argue, function to justify the imperial ideologies that underlie substantive US settler law and seek to produce legal workers who are loyal to revisionism. Finally, I turn us to the promise of critical legal design and the need to engage law students in the movement toward human-centered methodologies. Only through practices of resistance, responsiveness, and repair within legal education can we realize a human-centered legal profession and a future predicated on the intrinsic dignity of all.

26.2 US LAW SCHOOLS AND OUR PROBLEM WITH PEOPLE

A recent study from researchers at American University Washington College of Law confirmed what almost every member of the legal profession already knew: Law students are not okay (Jaffe, Bender, and Organ 2022). In a survey of 39 US law schools and 5,400 JD students, researchers found that there had been a "near doubling" in diagnoses of depression and anxiety among law students when compared to the last survey of this kind conducted in 2014 (Jaffe, Bender, and Organ 2022). Similarly, they concluded that there had been an increase in respondents' need for help with their emotional or mental health (up from 42% to 70%) and a significant increase in respondents' suicidal thoughts within the past year (up from 6% to 11%) (Jaffe, Bender, and Organ 2022). These numbers and the experiences that inform them matter if we are to understand how the law conceptualizes dignity.

In this section, I argue that US law schools act as a primary site of socialization for the legal profession in normatively establishing for *whom* and *how* dignity is deserved. By beginning with an analysis of the pervasively adverse experiences of US law students, I insist that our profession facilitates the social reproduction of indignity, replicating the patterns of material and ideological violence that belie substantive US settler law. That is: We harm law students to teach them how to harm; we deny dignity and ask that they do the same.

Here, we might define dignity in a variety of ways. The Dignity Law Institute at Widener University, for example, defines dignity as recognizing "the equal, inherent, and inalienable value of every person" (Widener University n.d.). This definition speaks to the philosophical, legal, and moral considerations at play in both identifying and upholding dignity. But what of community and the value of relations that go beyond the discrete value of the individual? As Kim (2021) demonstrates, dignity as a concept of personhood has come to be associated with increasingly expansive and contrasting definitions, which include both individualistic and collectivist valuations. This, Kim contends, has broad implications for the movement toward human-centered design.

In this chapter and in my work as a legal educator, I aim to disrupt prior pedagogies and literatures by centering a pluralistic understanding of dignity so as to capture the many violent realities that US settler law produces. By employing the four-prong conceptual framework of Kim (2021, 91–93), we might theoretically situate legal dignity in terms of *merit* (or our comparative, earned value), *autonomy* (or the individual capacity to exercise free will and reason), *universal rights* (or "a system that equally distributes resources for all humans and protects them from threats to the basic conditions"), and *interpersonal care* (or respectful treatment at the interpersonal level). In situating dignity across individual-collective and utilitarian-humanistic perspectives, Kim (2021) proposes a shared language for the development of critical service design models. This necessarily includes the delivery of legal education as a service of our profession and a mode of lawyer socialization.

Following from the above discussion of dignity and design methodologies, I turn our attention to the movement toward legal design for an initial discussion of people and power. At a global level, the movement toward legal design has sought to realize human-centered justice by bridging inclusion and equity gaps in both the practice and curriculum of law (Jackson 2016; Hagan and Kim 2017; Hagan 2020). As US legal scholars have previously noted, criticisms of traditional legal pedagogy and of the shortcomings of clinical education have driven this interdisciplinary movement (Davis 2015; Jackson 2016).

While Section 26.3 more thoroughly discusses legal design and the mark that it's had pedagogically in US law schools, I start us with an exploration of its core foundations to highlight a key point: US settler law is not human-centered. Why, then, would we expect legal education to be human-centered or immune from the very problems that legal design aims to remedy beyond the classroom? Take, for instance, the following excerpt from US legal designer, an editor of this collection, and my dear mentor Dan Jackson:

> If lawyers are a portal to the law, people (and organizations made up of people) stand on one side of the portal, and the law stands on the other. Lawyers are very good at existing within the law side; we are trained to inhabit that space. As law teachers, when we include human-centered design instruction in our technology efforts, we increase the likelihood that our future legal technologists will better understand, and be able to address, the actual needs of the people (and organizations) on the human side of the spectrum. (Jackson 2016, 97)

I share this section of *Human-Centered Legal Tech* not because I disagree with Dan – on the contrary, I believe this accurately describes legal education's approach to lawyer socialization and the time hopping that is expected of those who interpret centuries-old settler law. Instead, I share these words to disrupt the notion that lawyers are anything but human. What I believe the movement toward legal design and legal education continue to get wrong is our reluctance to admit that our words have an impact on the social and ideological realities of the profession. So, when we say that lawyers – and law students as the future of our profession – function in *nonhuman* and *time-bending* ways, they are then trained to expect the nonhuman, the surreal, and the inhumane conditions of this profession. Violence begets violence.

Critical theorists underscore the gravity of this point and draw our focus to the ways that education, more broadly, operates as a site of reproduction for the social and political ideologies of the state (Althusser 1971; hooks 2004). Such a contention is of great relevance to our inquiry into legal education and the socialization of lawyers, given the violent legal realities from which US settler law was forged. While prior scholars have examined the process of lawyer socialization in the areas of *legal hierarchy* (Kennedy, 1983), *well-being* (Chlap and Rhonda Brown 2022; Jaffe, Bender, and Organ 2022), *orientation toward the public interest* (Erlanger and Klegon 1978), *technology* (Jackson 2016; Tejani 2019), and *inclusion* (Garth and Sterling 2017), these efforts have tended to be siloed in nature. Moreover, there is a notable absence across these literatures concerning the ways that processes of lawyer socialization normatively reproduce conceptualizations of dignity.

But how many more accounts of the "hazing ritual" and "literal hell" (Hess 2020) that is the bar exam do we need before we advance meaningful change? In the most real and physical of terms: What rate of suicidal ideation (Jaffe, Bender, and Organ 2022) will break US legal education and its methods? How many decades and forms of gatekeeping must the profession engage in (Roithmayr 1997; Subotnik 2013; Ward 2022; Zaretsky 2022) before we can even name the harm as one of *indignity*?

US settler law was not built for people. It was built for the dispossession and displacement of the self, of nature (or the "more-than-human world" [Pellow 2016]), and of the forever "other" (Feagin [2000] 2014, 35). Legal education institutionally reproduces this reality, and so the harm continues. Through practices of exclusion, toxic individualism under white supremacy, and systemic subordination, US law students are taught that dignity is not inherent; it is earned.

We see this across students' journey through legal education. Law students are told that they are credentialed enough to run law review journals – scholarly publications that are cited by the nation's highest court (Feldman 2019) – but not enough to be full-fledged authors in the very same journals. Law students are told that they are credentialed enough to receive the JD but not enough to practice without the procedural (and the taxing, expensive) stamp of the bar exam. Students are expected to understand that people are more than cases or judicial decisions but that their entrance to the profession is tied to grueling exams that are atypical of real-world application – that if they memorize harder or simply highlight more words, they might be able to pull themselves up by their doctrinal bootstraps.

In exclusively prioritizing what Kim (2021) articulates as the *meritocracy* base of dignity, legal education fosters a culture of indignity and selective autonomy. Erased from this reality is any attention to the basic material conditions of students, the relations that should otherwise make up this profession, and the capacity to exercise one's own autonomy. In the law's Lockean and one-directional view of dignity, the paternalism and indignities of legal education serve as schematics from which violent jurisprudence is replicated. US law students are acculturated to believe that they, as voyagers of the nonhuman realm of settler law, are missionaries of dignity and that *only they* may bestow the power to access legal self-determination.

And, in this way, every day remains 1776.

Thus, legal design cannot merely be a movement toward procedural justice. It, like the movements before it, is an iteration of change-making that will either be responsive to its place and power or fail to realize its ultimate goal of human-centered justice. This must include a disruption of the role that legal education and innovation have in the socialization of law students. Our calculus of "human-centered" must be recalibrated to include the inherent biases, institutional positions, intertemporal wounds, and dignity of law students.

As Section 26.3 will explore in greater detail, law students are socialized at a curricular level to deprioritize notions of dignity. This is achieved through a shared curriculum of imperial violence and white supremacy. As graduates and practitioners report, this is in turn mirrored within the profession.

26.3 THE DIGNITY CRISIS OF LEGAL PEDAGOGY

On the second day of the bar exam, I remember sitting next to a law student from Canada. Their frantic typing the previous day had left me feeling unprepared – scattered even – in my attempt to trudge through the twelve-hour exam.

They'd said hello right before our lunch break, breaking some of the tension that had taken hold of the convention center floor since the start of the exam. I returned the pleasantry, nervous and more unsure of myself than at any other point in my life and (very truthfully) uninterested in talking to anyone (let alone another law student).

We got to talking, inevitably making our way to a discussion of the bar's abolition and of the unreal emotions that we were experiencing, and they shared about the difficulties they'd faced in trying to comprehend US constitutional law.

"Why do we even have different levels of scrutiny?" they'd asked, with a bewildered look on their face. "What's really the point of them all being different?"

I don't remember how I responded. Maybe I laughed in return and joked about the mess that is US settler law. Maybe I sighed and gave a half smile, too consumed with the nerves that had undoubtedly returned.

In any case, the real answer to their question was that our settler nation didn't know how to talk about harm. We don't know what repair or response someone is owed when they've been harmed. So, we've quelled our uncertainty with settler logics – time travel, even – and routines of justice in the place of true intention. After all, what really is "rational basis with teeth?" And what is so rational about declaring classism nonexistent (*San Antonio Independent School District v. Rodriguez*, 411 U.S. 1 (1973))?

I open with this story because as a recent law graduate and now legal educator, I continue to grapple with these questions. The ways we teach what settler law is (and isn't) are conscious acts of storytelling. Critical race scholars have maintained this perspective for decades and emphasize the power of countering the harmful narratives that predominate over our institutions (Matsuda 1987; Solórzano and Yosso 2002). This chapter joins the work of numerous critical voices before me in subverting the dominant narrative of how US settler law produces justice. Legal education, I argue, advances a curriculum of indignity that is both known and embraced by our profession.

This is done ideologically by legal education's detachment from the very systems and people it purports to serve. The law is inaccessible. It is incomprehensible (most of the time) and illegible (a lot of the time). Our pedagogical focus on doctrine, legalese, and Latin obscures the real-world implications of what we might otherwise understand as a dangerous endeavor. As has never been clearer to me, the instruction and training of law students is tantamount to the growth of the military, or the promotion of the police force, or any other branch of the repressive state apparatus – because lawsuits and bills can be bullets too. Such a conclusion makes critical analysis and the reimagining of power relations direly necessary for our profession.

But legal education refuses to incorporate critical analysis because doing so would destabilize its very existence. Legal scholars such as Kennedy (2002) and others have investigated this proposition from a lens of "losing faith" in the law and the indeterminacy of legal reasoning. As a law student, I had similarly felt as though I'd lost a sense of self in traversing the nonhuman and inhumane realm of the law. But fighting the disorientation, I found, often felt in vain. Each term, we were told our doctrinal courses didn't have time for in-depth critique or reflection because of the far-off fear that was the bar exam. There was simply *too* much doctrine and *so* little time.

With each class, I watched (and heard) as students who'd been forever insulated from the realities of the legal system were coddled by our curriculum. The bondage and death and cages and terror were just an intellectual exercise to them, a footnote or case note on their path to making $200,000 annually in three years' time and to helping someone else cage and bring terror. But even this – a conditioned and wildly compensated form of labor – came at the price of their mental health, their boundaries, and their very sense of self. As I experienced firsthand, US legal education's lack of institutional focus on critical analysis or reparative methodologies placed a burden on historically marginalized and minoritized communities, requiring that we speak up, show up, and name the harms that legal education wouldn't.

At this intersection of doctrine and student resistance, I see two promising opportunities for critical legal design to interrupt our indignant legal pedagogy. The first is for legal design to join fellow innovators in embracing critical pedagogies and finally acknowledging law students as equal co-educators in the classroom (SpearIt 2012; SpearIt and Ledesma 2014). The second is for legal design itself to be reflective and for critical methodologies to be embedded within the fabric of legal education. While the history of legal design in the United States has been fragmented and at times diverging, the future of critical legal pedagogies rests in the collective and unifying power of naming harm (Hayat 2021). This, I know, can only be realized through the deliberate and intentional inclusion of law students in the movement toward critical legal design.

What might this look like? Adapting the work of Hagan (2020) in *Legal Design as a Thing: A Theory of Change and a Set of Methods to Craft a Human-Centered Legal System*, we might begin with a set of critical legal design testing metrics, such as:

- *Usability* (whether legal education improves students' ability to use transformative legal and nonlegal tools and whether they have a positive experience in doing so);
- *Procedural Justice* (whether students' sense of individual and participatory fairness in their education is enhanced);
- *Engagement* (whether students are more willing to resolve problems of justice-making and to join in the law's reimagining);
- *Legal Autonomy* (whether the knowledge and resources needed to understand complex legal information and to disrupt or reimagine harmful systems are improved for students);
- *Resolution* (whether legal education helps students resolve a problem of justice-making, advance reparative individual and collective interests, and achieve an outcome grounded in notions of dignity); and
- *Administrative Burden* (whether legal education significantly reduces the amount of time, labor, harm, and money needed to achieve the work of justice-making).

Student responses to these types of questions would likely give us the answer our profession has long avoided: Law schools, in their current manifestation, don't work. By reflecting the goals of legal design back toward the legal academy from where they developed and by centering law students' sense of dignity in the process, we might hope to improve this profession while working to bring about its reimagining.

As I hope is clear, a practice of critical legal design in education requires intention-setting, it requires our affirmation of students' inherent dignity, and it will take active forms of reflection – goals that the legal design movement has sought to foster within the practice of law. It is disgraceful (though, as always, unsurprising) that in 2023 legal education is *only now beginning* to embrace courses concerning lawyer well-being and mindfulness (Baker 2016; Buchanan 2018; Duke Law n.d.; Northeastern University School of Law n.d.). It is abhorrent that *only after* several years of heightened, national harm have US law schools begun to address issues of Diversity, Equity, Inclusion, and Belonging ("DEI&B") (Ofori-Ampofo 2022) and structural inaccessibility (Charnosky 2022). These developments must be viewed as linked struggles, threads of the same history of legal indignity, if a critical manifestation of legal design is to be truly liberatory and transformative. Our methodologies must examine the ways that law students' well-being, DEI&B, experiences of discrimination, and navigation of systematic harm are all interwoven, co-perpetuated by traditional legal education.

We must be prepared to revise, recast, and reimagine what legal education can look like and what the pedagogies of tomorrow will encompass. In resisting the urge to re-enshrine perfection, urgency, paternalism, and power – what Jones and Okun (2001) refer to as "characteristics of white supremacy culture" – critical legal design must upend patterns of lawyer burnout, law student harm, and our shared practices of indignity. Applying the above six metrics to students' journeys through law school, traditional US legal education might be viewed in its truest form: as outdated storytelling that does not serve us.

26.4 LESSONS ON DIGNITY FROM LAW STUDENT MOVEMENT WORK

I'm still learning how and when to talk about my organizing efforts as a law student. Not because I don't remember them or because I'm unsure of what to say. But because it's draining and interrupts my rest from one of the most disorienting times of my life.

Right there, for instance – how many times can I repeat my *disorientation* in this chapter before we're both annoyed? How many times can I find other words to describe what felt like being lost with no end and upside down without hope? Were there other words for time, time travel, or dignity? I'm still working through it, so for now I'll borrow from Feagin: Let's start from a place of history.

In 2019, I served on my law school's committee against institutional racism alongside fellow representatives from our school's Black, Indigenous, and people of color (BIPOC)-serving affinity groups. As we grew increasingly frustrated with the bureaucracy and white feelings of the committee, we worked to hold a law student forum, hoping to capture the lived experiences and state of BIPOC students at our school. This forum resulted in a set of takeaways that were then memorialized in a report on behalf of the committee. Among these findings were shared experiences of racist microaggressions, of institutional neglect, and of a lack of doctrinal intention from every aspect of our legal education.

But the neoliberal malaise of legal academia had limited the potential of this work from its very beginning – faculty on the committee may not have anticipated anything to amount from our work together other than the usual anti-bias training or memo. It was our persistence that resulted in the twenty-five-page report and pages of concrete recommendations for change. It was our resistance over Zoom and over email that retained the experiences and original language of student respondents, that affirmed our lived realities. And it was our energies that were depleted along the way.

In Fall 2020, the report went out to the law school community. The following spring (and after a wave of prodding emails from student leaders), the law school's administration responded, providing a list of administrative actions corresponding to the items identified by the report. Among these was the decision to hire an Assistant Dean for Diversity, Equity, and Inclusion (DEI).

We returned to campus the next fall with no news of the new Assistant Dean or of any of the school's proposed actions to bring about change. Two key incidents that semester returned us to a place of resistance. First, BIPOC student leaders were asked by a senior administrator to serve in uncompensated committee roles to develop the very change we had demanded from the institution. Second, the school hired an educational consulting group to lead its strategic planning process, which would also include collecting student experiences and conducting focus groups that would lead to a new set of recommendations for change.

In October 2021, the leaders of the school's BIPOC-serving affinity groups held a weekend meeting, fed up with what we saw as the administration's lack of urgency in the face of our continuing experiences of pedagogical harm. I attended to share where some of this work had begun in 2019 and to help in the development of any student actions. In the meeting, I shared that we had once joked about "serving" the school, so to speak. After that meeting, I drafted and shared a five-page mock complaint against the law school that framed our experiences through the causes of action of fraud, negligence, breach of contract, and unjust enrichment. Accompanying this complaint was a call to action, calling on students to boycott the planned focus groups and school-sponsored events until change had been realized.

The call to action received over 200 signatures of support from current and former students, and we convened over 100 law students to serve the law school administration with our mock complaint. On Friday, October 15, we held space for our peers as we read aloud these counts, named the harms we'd navigated within legal education, and participated in a grounding exercise. I invited all students in attendance to join me in completing a sentence that had been preprinted into half-sheets: "I wish our law school cared about BIPOC students as much as it cares about _____." We shared our responses, some of us crying and others reflecting on three years of pedagogical indifference. After this, we marched one by one to the dean's suite, armed with the pages of our experiences and the half-sheets of our hurt, and we delivered our complaints to the dean's office. Returning to the outdoor convening space, we led students in a closing action of visualizing our dream law school and imagining what it would look like for us to reclaim our legal education.

Amid the commotion and classes of the days leading up to the convening, the administration released an update to all students that the hiring of the DEI dean would commence immediately. Around the same time, I received outreach from faculty on the school's committee against institutional racism, asking how we'd "gotten here." I remember how invalid I'd felt then and how exhausting it felt to remind myself that we hadn't just "gotten here" out of nowhere, that our organizing wasn't random but, instead, *necessary*.

Within a week of this student convening and an instance of anti-Black university policing that had taken place the day after it, the previously mentioned senior administrator had resigned, the consulting group had scrapped the planned focus groups, and we were more unsure than ever who was there to support us. Had the organizing accomplished anything or was the DEI dean hiring update merely a coincidence? What was my role in continuing to apply pressure to the administration when I felt unable to rest or repair from the work? Regardless, I remember thinking that a moment of being heard and collectively affirmed meant more to me than any staff position's hiring.

By late November, I had developed back pain that flared up from day to day. By December, it would hurt to sit, and by January I'd developed a herniated disc that made walking impossible without a cane, plenty of medication, and the help of others. By the end of the month, physical therapy would help me walk again, just in time for my final semester of law school. But by February, my depletion had pushed me beyond the limit of self-preservation. In February, I started medication for my recently diagnosed anxiety and depression. And, in May, I finally graduated.

Both vacant dean positions were eventually filled, and the coalitional work continues.

It's now been over a year since these events took place, and each time I think about organizing or reimagining and people power, I think of the things it cost my body and mind to resist settler logics. I think of the things it took my grandmother to resist settler borders and of the things that we bargain away in order to hold onto ourselves.

26.5 PRACTICING RESISTANCE, REPAIR, AND RESPONSIVENESS

I share this collection of stories from the unreal and unhuman to frame the lessons of this chapter: Resistance, Repair, and Responsiveness. In this final section, I draw upon the many lessons that US law students have brought to the fore in our ongoing work to center dignity in the reimagination of the law.

The first of these lessons from law students is *the need to resist settler violence and to embody a practice of inherent dignity*. In looking to the movement toward Critical Race, we can identify the practice of reclaiming legal education as one that is rooted in a tradition of student activism and law student organizing (The HLS Conference Organizers 2022). In the absence of formalized and institutionally supported critical pedagogy, law students at Harvard Law School and UC Berkeley organized to cocreate the legal education they equally craved and deserved. Both of these student movements were flashpoints in the formation of Critical Race Theory and mapped onto civil rights organizing efforts beyond the academy (Delgado 2009).

Honoring this radical tradition of student activism means embodying a practice of solidarity and of resisting the legal indignities that define both practice and pedagogy. The participants in a future of critical legal design must resist harm by affirming the inherent dignity of one another as equal participant-subjects to the law's reimagining.

Second, our notions of legal dignity must be *pluralistic, intersectional, and subjective* in order to facilitate repair. As increased student-organizing efforts in the past few years have demonstrated, we can and must hold space for the many different law student experiences in our reimagining of the profession (Law Students for Black Lives n,d.; NDLSA 2022). In 2020, the Yale Law School Rebellious Lawyering Conference or "RebLaw" sought to "build a community of law students, practitioners, and activists seeking to work in the service of social change movements and to challenge hierarchies of race, wealth, gender, and expertise within legal practice and education" (Yale University n.d.). In attending this conference as a first-year law student, I was reminded that the work of change-making could never be siloed and that our work intersects with countless interrelated struggles for liberation.

This truth is honored in the solidarity work and intracommunity efforts taking place across law student organizations. Student-organizing efforts, like Law Students for Black Lives, incorporate "advocacy, community-based activism, and educational campaigns" into their work to eradicate racial disparities in the law (Law Students for Black Lives 2022). Other organizations, such as Law Students for a Free Palestine (LSFP) and the National Disabled Law Students Association (NDLSA), know that the work to disrupt harm in our profession cuts across time, lived experiences, and institutions. This is seen in NDLSA's work to support disabled legal professionals "before, during, and after their legal education" (National Disabled Law Students Association n.d.), as well as LSFP's recognition of the interconnectedness of all global struggles for liberation (Law Students for a Free Palestine, 2023).

These student resistance movements affirm law students' collectivity while emphasizing the need for identity- and experience-conscious social change. Extending the four-prong framework of Kim (2021), we can see dignity in legal design as including a conscious and subjective examination of what types of dignity are prioritized in a given space or context. Critical legal designers must investigate legal education as a site of social reproduction and a source of socialization with regard to indignity.

Third, our work to build a movement of critical legal design must be *responsive, accountable, and adaptive* to the lived realities of all peoples, as both participants and subjects to justice-making. In the past few years, a critical mass of law students have organized to demand accountability for the "reprehensible" and violent (in)actions of their law faculty (Barnes 2021; NUSL Call to Action 2021; Patrice 2022; Planas 2022). This has manifested in protests, sit-ins, town halls, resignations, and – in one noteworthy instance – the decision to forego teaching at an institution by US Supreme Court Justice Clarence Thomas (Barnes 2021; NUSL Call to Action 2021; Archie 2022; @GeorgetownBLSA, February 1, 2022; Planas 2022). I focus on these actions of student resistance to demonstrate the lopsided landscape of dignity in our law schools. In making meritocracy primary to our delivery of legal education, students are left with no option but to create, to reimagine, and to forge new ways of honoring an individual and humanistic sense of dignity. Their collective and shared rights to institutional accountability, their individual need to be heard, and their relational needs to be fully understood and responded to are delegitimized by legal education in its current form.

Critical legal design must join in the work of *disordering* US law schools' dedication to indignity. Legal educators, administrators, advocates, leaders, and practitioners alike must work across coalitions to advance dignity within the profession, starting before admission or the LSAT and extending forward into our collective future.

26.6 CONCLUSION: TOWARD A FUTURE OF COLLECTIVE POWER IN LEGAL EDUCATION

As this chapter has demonstrated, law students are indispensable to the futures of critical legal design. Engaging students – from inside and beyond the academy – with the broader legal design movement is necessary for realizing a truly human-centered legal profession. Through continued practices of resistance, repair, and responsiveness, law students have charted a road map for the work of disrupting and unimagining our shared doctrine of indignity.

Student movements have repeatedly shown us that collective resistance is a form of community care from both within and outside legal education. In recognition of this lived reality, a methodology of critical legal design requires that we reflect: How are legal designers and the innovators of our collective future in solidarity with the students, communities, and movements that they claim to serve? Are our relationships and partnerships with students ones that are grounded in pluralistic and subjective notions of dignity? How are legal designers resisting the sociolegal indignities that inhere in settler law?

Moreover, law students remind us that repairing the legal impact of this profession remains linked to our repair of the past-present wounds of legal education. To do so, we must ask whether we are disrupting indignity in both substance and form: Do the student funding and staffing of our legal innovation spaces align with the principles of dignity that we seek to employ in our projects? Are student participants in legal innovation spaces onboarded to the practices of care that we've set for our work? Do we have such practices at all? Above all, are we working to advance a methodology of critical legal design across all of legal education and every area of the law?

Lastly, student-organizing efforts underscore our need to be responsive to the people, places, and realities among which law schools are situated: Does our work serve students in affirming multiple forms of dignity? Are legal innovation spaces attentive to the material needs and conditions of the students of their institution? Do students and community members serve on advisory boards to innovation spaces and are they compensated for their labor and expertise? Finally, who are we accountable to in our work to reimagine?

The conscious political decision of developing a paradigm of critical legal design requires more than creating new structures or courses; we must engage in the dismantling and unimagining of harmful methods and ideologies within our profession. This *must* include legal education. It is only by disrupting law schools' process of socialization and its dispensing of indignity that critical legal design can realize its full transformative power. Only together and with a shared politic of inherent dignity can we achieve a future of human-centered design and a true end to all the many wounds of justice-making.

REFERENCES

Althusser, Louis. 1971. "Ideology and Ideological State Apparatuses (Notes Towards an Investigation." In *Lenin and Philosophy and Other Essays*, translated by B. Brewster, 79–87. New York: Monthly Review Press.

Archie, Ayana. 2022. "Clarence Thomas Drops Out of Teaching a Law Class After Students Protested." *NPR*, July 28. www.npr.org/2022/07/28/1114285261/clarence-thomas-george-washington-university-law.

Baker, R. Lisle. 2016. "Designing a Positive Psychology Course for Lawyers." *Suffolk University Law Review* 51 (October): 207–88. Social Science Research Network (SSRN).

Baldwin, James. 1995. "The White Man's Guilt." In *James Baldwin: Collected Essays*, 722–27. New York: Library of America.

Barnes, Dustin. 2021. "Georgetown Law Professor Fired After Complaining about Black Students' Grades on Zoom Call." *USA Today*, March 12. www.usatoday.com/story/

news/education/2021/03/12/georgetown-professor-fired-over-remarks-black-students-zoom/4662569001/.

The Black Panther Party for Self-Defense. 1967. "Huey Original 1967: The First Appearance of Huey P. Newton in a Rattan Chair." http://post-what.com/1967/05/hueys-re-mix-1967-the-first-appearance/.

Buchanan, Heather. 2018. "Denver Law Course Highlights Lawyer Well-Being and Foundations for Practice." *University of Denver IAALS* (blog), September 27. https://iaals.du.edu/blog/denver-law-course-highlights-lawyer-well-being-and-foundations-practice.

Charnosky, Christine. 2022. "The Pandemic 'Opened the Door to a Better Environment' for Many Disabled Law Students. They Don't Want to Go Back." *Law.com*, June 3. www.law.com/2022/06/03/the-pandemic-opened-the-door-to-a-better-environment-for-many-disabled-law-students-they-dont-want-to-go-back/.

Chlap, Nora, and Rhonda Brown. 2022. "Relationships Between Workplace Characteristics, Psychological Stress, Affective Distress, Burnout and Empathy in Lawyers." *International Journal of the Legal Profession* 29, no. 2 (February): 159–80. https://doi.org/10.1080/09695958.2022.2032082.

Crenshaw, Kimberle, Neil Gotanda, Gary Peller, and Kendall Thomas. 1995. *Critical Race Theory: The Key Writings That Formed the Movement*. New York: The New Press.

Davis, Martha F. 2015. "Institutionalizing Legal Innovation: The (Re)Emergence of the Law Lab." *Journal of Legal Education* 65, no. 1 (June): 190–206. Social Science Research Network (SSRN).

Delgado, Richard. 2009. "Liberal McCarthyism and the Origins of Critical Race Theory." *Iowa Law Review* 94, no. 5 (January): 1505–46. Social Science Research Network (SSRN).

Duke Law. n.d. "779 Well-Being and the Practice of Law." Accessed August 14, 2022. https://law.duke.edu/academics/course/779.

Erlanger, Howard S., and Douglas Klegon. 1978. "Socialization Effects of Professional School: The Law School Experience and Students' Orientation to Public Interest Concerns." *Law & Society Review* 13, no. 11 (September): 11–35. Social Science Research Network (SSRN).

Feagin, Joe R. 1991. "The Continuing Significance of Race: Antiblack Discrimination in Public Places." *American Sociological Review* 56, no. 1 (February): 101–16. https://doi.org/10.2307/2095676.

[2000] 2014. *Racist America: Roots, Current Realities, and Future Reparations*. Milton Park, UK: Routledge Press.

Feldman, Adam. 2019. "Empirical SCOTUS: What the Justices Cited in OT 2018." *SCOTUS Blog* (blog), July 24. www.scotusblog.com/2019/07/empirical-scotus-what-the-justices-cited-in-ot-2018/.

Fenelon, James V., and Thomas D. Hall. 2008. "Revitalization and Indigenous Resistance to Globalization and Neoliberalism." *American Behavioral Scientist* 51, no. 12 (August): 1867–1901. https://doi:10.1177/0002764208318938.

Garth, Bryant, and Joyce S. Sterling. 2017. "Diversity, Hierarchy, and Fit in Legal Careers: Insights from Fifteen Years of Qualitative Interviews." *The Georgetown Journal of Legal Ethics* 31 (October): 123–74. Social Science Research Network (SSRN).

Hannah-Jones, Nikole. 2021. *The 1619 Project*. London: Oneworld Publications.

Hayat, Norrinda Brown. 2021. "Freedom Pedagogy: Toward Teaching Antiracist Clinics." *Clinical Law Review* 28, no. 1 (October): 149–68.

Hess, Abigail J. 2020. "'Literal Hell'—How the Pandemic Made the Bar Exam Even More Excruciating for Future Lawyers." *CNBC*, August 19. www.cnbc.com/2020/08/19/literal-hellthe-pandemic-has-made-the-bar-exam-more-excruciating.html.

The HLS Conference Organizers. 2022. "Critical Race Theory: Inside and Beyond the Ivory Tower." *UCLA Law Review Discourse* 69 (March): 118–48.

hooks, bell. 2004. "Understanding Patriarchy." In *The Will to Change: Men, Masculinity, and Love*, 17-34. New York: Simon & Schuster.

Jackson, Dan. 2016. "Human-Centered Legal Tech: Integrating Design in Legal Education." *The Law Teacher* 50, no. 1 (April): 82–97. https://doi.org/10.1080/03069400.2016.1146468.

Jaffe, David, Katherine Bender, and Jerome M. Organ. 2022. "'It Is Okay to Not Be Okay': The 2021 Survey of Law Student Well-Being." *University of Louisville Law Review* 60 (Spring): 441–96. Social Science Research Network (SSRN).

Jones, Kenneth, and Tema Okun. 2001. "Dismantling Racism: A Workbook for Social Change Groups." www.thc.texas.gov/public/upload/preserve/museums/files/White_Supremacy_Culture.pdf.

Kennedy, Duncan. 1983. *Legal Education and the Reproduction of Hierarchy: A Polemic Against the System*, ii–125. MA: Afar.

2002. "The Critique of Rights in Critical Legal Studies." In *Left Legalism/Left Critique*, edited by Wendy Brown, Janet Halley, and Duncan Kennedy, 178–228. Durham, NC: Duke University Press.

Kim, Miso. 2021. "A Study of Dignity as a Principle of Service Design." *International Journal of Design* 15, no. 3 (December): 87–100.

Law Students for a Free Palestine. (2023). "Students from Over 30 Law Schools Announce Day of Action, Call on Legal Community to Stop the Genocide in Gaza and Occupied Palestine and Demand Ceasefire." Press Release. November 15, 2023. https://ugc.production.linktr.ee/c908724b-aa16–4cef-a3dc-3b8d22150b46_LSFP-Press-Release-11.15.2023.pdf.

Law Students for Black Lives. n.d. "Law Students for Black Lives." Accessed August 15, 2022. www.ls4blacklives.org/.

Matsuda, Mari J. 1987. "Looking to the Bottom: Critical Legal Studies and Reparations." *Harvard Civil Rights – Civil Liberties Law Review* 22, no. 2 (October): 323–99.

National Disabled Law Students Association. n.d. "Our Story." Accessed August 15, 2022. https://ndlsa.org/about-ndlsa/.

Neitch, Kenna. 2019. "Indigenous Persistence: Challenging the Rhetoric of Anti-colonial Resistance." *Feminist Studies* 45, no. 2 (January): 426–54. https://doi.org/10.15767/feministstudies.45.2-3.0426.

Northeastern University School of Law. n.d. "New Course for Fall 2022." Accessed August 14, 2022. www.northeastern.edu/lawstudentaffairs/wp-content/uploads/2022/07/NewCourseMindfulness.pdf.

NUSL. 2021. "Calling All Students Past, Present, and Future: Join in Demanding Change at Northeastern University School of Law." https://bit.ly/DemandingNUSLChange.

Ofori-Ampofo, Lovia. 2022. "Law Schools Incorporate More DEI Work into Their Curricula." *What Great Law Schools Do*. Last modified June 9, 2020. www.whatgreatlawschoolsdo.com/2022/06/law-schools-incorporate-more-dei-work-into-their-curricula/.

Patrice, Joe. 2022. "Yale Law Professor Suggests Punishing Students for Following the Rules." *Above the Law*. Last modified April 4, 2022. https://abovethelaw.com/2022/04/yale-law-professor-suggests-punishing-students-for-following-the-rules/.

Pellow, David N. 2016. "Toward a Critical Environmental Justice Studies: Black Lives Matter as an Environmental Justice Challenge." *Du Bois Review: Social Science Research on Race* 13, no. 2: 221–36. https://doi:10.1017/S1742058X1600014X.

People v. Hall, 4 Cal. 399 (1854).

Planas, Antonio. 2022. "Georgetown Law Administrator Resigns After Probe into Tweet About 'Lesser Black Woman' on Supreme Court." *NBC News*, June 7. www.nbcnews.com/news/us-news/georgetown-law-administrator-resigns-probe-controversial-scotus-tweet-rcna32361.

Roithmayr, Daria. 1997. "Deconstructing the Distinction between Bias and Merit." *California Law Review* 85, no. 5 (October): 1449–507. https://doi.org/10.2307/3481064.

San Antonio Independent School District v. Rodriguez, 411 U.S. 1 (1973).

Solórzano, Daniel G., and Tara J. Yosso. 2002. "Critical Race Methodology: Counter-Storytelling as an Analytical Framework for Education Research." *Qualitative Inquiry* 8, no. 1 (February): 23–44. https://doi.org/10.1177/107780040200800103.

SpearIt. 2012. "Priorities of Pedagogy: Classroom Justice in the Law School Setting." *California Western Law Review* 48, no. 2 (June): 467–79. Social Science Research Network (SSRN).

SpearIt and Stephanie Ledesma. 2014. "Experiential Education as Critical Pedagogy: Enhancing the Law School Experience." *Nova Law Review* 38, no. 2 (September): 249–76.

Subotnik, Dan. 2013. "Does Testing = Race Discrimination? Ricci, the Bar Exam, the LSAT, and the Challenge to Learning." *University of Massachusetts Law Review* 8 (May): 332–402. Social Science Research Network (SSRN).

Tejani, Riaz. 2019. "Chapter 9: The Socialization of Lawyers." In *Law and Society Today*, 171–90. Berkeley: University of California Press.

Themis Bar Review. 2022 (on file with author)

Ward, Stephanie Francis. 2022. "Bar Examinees Have Little Success with Accommodation Requests and Say the Process Is Stressful." *ABA Journal*, June 30. www.abajournal.com/web/article/bar-examinees-have-little-success-with-accommodation-requests-and-say-the-process-is-stressful.

Widener University. n.d. "About Dignity Law." Accessed August 14, 2022. https://delawarelaw.widener.edu/current-students/jd-academics/signature-programs/dignity-rights-institute/dignity-rights/.

Wilkerson, Isabel 2020. *Caste: The Origins of Our Discontents*. New York: Random House.

Yale University. n.d. "Rebellious Lawyering Conference 2020." Accessed August 15, 2022. https://reblaw.yale.edu/.

Zaretsky, Staci. 2022. "The Bar Exam's Motherhood Penalty Is a Barrier to Entry for the Legal Profession." *Above the Law*, June 26. https://abovethelaw.com/2022/07/the-bar-exams-motherhood-penalty-is-a-barrier-to-entry-for-the-legal-profession/.

Conclusion

Building a Future World of Dignity, Equity, and Justice for All

Jules Rochielle Sievert, Dan Jackson, and Miso Kim

For those who have made it all the way through this book, we commend you! Because we know that few people read the entirety of such a book as ours, we offer this concluding chapter as both an executive summary of the insights we ourselves have gleaned from all our contributing authors and a road map for how we think this new field can both accelerate the pace of change in law and society and guide that change toward a future of greater dignity, equity, and justice.

C.1 NAVIGATING THE CHALLENGES: HARNESSING THE POWER OF LEGAL DESIGN

In this moment for the world, as at any point in history where society faced remarkable changes and worked collectively to overcome them, there is tension between the radical change needed for a just and equitable society for all, and the inherent conservatism and slow pace of change in the law, which we have argued is a fundamental architecture of society (Chapter 1 in this volume).

The world today is an intricate tapestry of problems woven from the threads of decisions, discoveries, and developments accumulated over millennia. The current landscape that we face, marked by rapid technological growth, major environmental concerns, and a heightened degree of global interconnectedness, is a direct consequence of past actions. The past inventions led to the present where rapidly evolving digital technology is an essential infrastructure of our societies, but at the same time with an increasing technology gap that further excludes those without the means to access it. Parallelly, the destructive path back to the Industrial Revolution led to our problematic relationship with the environment. Histories also have woven nations closer, leading to an intricately interconnected global community. For the sake of this conclusion, we'll focus on three key challenges of this moment in time that are built on these accumulated decisions, as a prelude to some final musings on how legal design can address them. It's crucial in this regard to acknowledge that these are only a few examples in an extensive list of unique contemporary issues.

The first factor hinges on the unprecedented global interconnectedness that characterizes our society and economy today. Our livelihoods, and even our sustenance, are now intrinsically linked to an intricate global supply chain, a fact brought into sharp relief by the recent pandemic-related supply chain disruptions. Additionally, this global interdependence can be exploited by malicious actors to sow chaos and exert pressure on a worldwide stage. Take for example the significant geopolitical impact that Russia has through its control of energy resources and grain exports. This control acts as a powerful form of economic sway, which some critics may describe as a form of coercion or manipulation.

Second, we are now confronting the stark reality of climate change more urgently than ever before, a crisis demanding a truly global response. Climate harms disproportionately impact marginalized communities, developing countries, future generations, and biodiversity. These groups bear the brunt of climate change impacts due to limited resources, reduced access to decision-making, inadequate infrastructure, intergenerational consequences, and threats to ecosystems and natural resources. One irony of this lies in the fact that the economies and societies best equipped to mitigate the effects of climate change are the very ones causing the most harm. The regions most severely affected by climate change currently lack the resources to implement effective countermeasures. These regions also contribute far less to carbon emissions, making them less responsible for both historical and current climate damage.

Finally, the rapid pace and sweeping impact of digital technological innovation are accelerating exponentially. As digital circuits are miniaturized and computer scientists continue to innovate, we can expect this pace to only quicken. A striking demonstration of this is the recent advancements in quantum computing and the rapid proliferation of advanced generative AI technologies, including ChatGPT. These innovations stand to revolutionize our understanding of, and impact on, the world and quickly reshape the societal landscape.[1]

To address these challenges, it is essential to bring together a design approach that considers the interconnected nature of these factors in the planning, and a legal landscape that fosters collaboration for lasting impact. We need interdisciplinary approaches to breaking down silos and engaging stakeholders from diverse fields and experiences in order to solve these complex problems. And we must do so quickly.

In the realm of law, each factor presents both challenges and opportunities when considered individually. When these factors are combined, they can greatly frustrate

[1] It's intriguing how a paradox emerges from the intertwining of technological progression and environmental impact. The advancement of technology and AI, while contributing to climate change via increased energy consumption, e-waste production, and resource extraction, paradoxically also provides tools to combat this very crisis. These technologies have the potential to increase energy efficiency and foster the development of greener solutions. Thus, we find ourselves in a paradox where the very agents exacerbating environmental damage also offer the means to mitigate it.

and demotivate even the most innovative and persistent legal problem-solvers. The convergence of these challenges underscores the inherent tension between the urgency demanded by the problems we face and the traditional approach to law development and implementation that has prevailed until now. Navigating this complexity requires careful consideration from the legal field, proposing suitable responses, and effectively implementing and enforcing solutions that lead to resolution.

The critical engagement in dialogue, deliberation, and collaboration that legal design offers is crucial to navigating such complexity. This is because legal design can depart from conventional thinking and practices and embrace transformative approaches that address the complexity and urgency of our current era. In this process, we can draw upon lessons learned from past experiences and critically examine the systems and structures that have brought us to this point. By understanding the root causes and interconnected nature of these challenges, we can develop innovative and effective strategies that meet the demands of our time. Critical thinking, collective action, and a commitment to radical care are essential in navigating the complexities of our era and shaping a legal landscape that addresses pressing issues while building a more just and sustainable society.

So many of the strengths of legal design are perfectly matched to the challenges of this moment. As a process or method, legal design offers a structured, creative, and intentional approach that aims to define and achieve specific goals. It utilizes tested methods to evaluate potential solutions, allowing for adaptability and reimagining. Legal design combines diverse knowledge, experience, capacity, and power to tackle complex interconnected challenges. It can be customized and methodized to address the unique needs of each problem and has the capacity to evolve rapidly within its own principles, perspectives, and methods. In particular, it should be highlighted as a foundational principle that legal design is committed to involving and prioritizing the needs, interests, and experiences of those most impacted by the problem being addressed. This inclusive approach ensures a more honest and effective problem-solving process, and the outcomes of which are more likely to have the support of the broader public than solutions developed in the traditional models of task forces, committees, and legislatures.

While legal design holds immense promise, it is important to acknowledge that it is not a cure-all solution and must confront its own challenges before fully realizing its transformative potential. Before it can effectively address external challenges, legal design must address its internal hurdles and refine its methodologies. By doing so, it can iteratively scale and rise to meet the ongoing demands of contemporary problems and contribute to positive change.

One significant challenge faced by the assertion of legal design as a practice or field is the inherent conservatism of law and legal professionals. The nature of the legal institution is designed to resist change, as it has successfully served as the foundational architecture of society. This inherent resistance to change has attracted individuals with high levels of skepticism to the legal profession. Consequently, introducing new ways of doing things becomes challenging when established practices have been in place for decades or even centuries. This resistance to change poses difficulties in gathering institutional stakeholders and players to advance individual legal design projects and create new methods or models. This challenge is amplified by the fact that the relatively new field of legal design still needs development and standardization of its own methodologies, process, practice, and evaluation. Best practices and industry standards are just beginning to be explored. Given the importance and durability of law in society, as well as the advantages it provides to those with power and wealth, significant changes must be carefully considered, rigorously studied, and cautiously embraced.

Ethical and privacy standards pose another early obstacle for legal design. Existing legal norms, such as legal ethics, govern the conduct of lawyers and legal professionals. These norms are shaped by common law, which evolves over time through judicial decisions and through ethical codes established by professional organizations like the American Bar Association. Some legal design approaches can conflict with these rules, particularly when the involvement of diverse end-users as codesigners may clash with lawyers' duty of confidentiality.

Overcoming these challenges requires navigating the resistance to change within the legal profession, developing standardized methodologies, and addressing ethical and privacy considerations. The principle of dignity can guide through these developments. For example, there needs to be more disability justice or applied principles of universal design within the field of legal design. In the realm of legal design, it is also crucial to have a deep understanding and appreciation for cultural differences, incorporating them into the process of designing legal services and information. Because culture plays a fundamental role in shaping individuals' identities, values, and their interactions with the legal system, legal designers must recognize and respect these cultural variations to ensure the solutions they develop are relevant, inclusive, and effective for diverse populations.

Legal design is already beginning to successfully contribute to transformative advancements in the field of law and improve access to justice for many. For example, an early zone of success for legal design exists with the automation of certain tasks, improved documents, visualizing law, and simplifying contracts in the commercial context. Within the social legal spaces and in the zone of legal empowerment, we regularly see project outcomes that increase legal accessibility and inclusivity. We think greater efforts can be made in legal education and within the developing field of legal design to think critically about how we are approaching legal design to ensure future successes are fully representative of the communities being engaged.

C.2 CREATING SHARED SPACES TO ENRICH COLLABORATIVE EDUCATION

We think this volume helps demonstrate that the intersection of the disciplines of law and design holds immense promise for addressing pressing challenges and fostering societal repair. To get there, one priority is to educate the talented legal designers of tomorrow. However, the current siloed approach in education has limited exploration in this interdisciplinary intervention. To unlock the power of this intersection, it is crucial to advocate for robust dialogue and integration of law and design within educational curricula. Here we share some thoughts on legal content in design education, and vice versa.

Design, the art of plan and action, profoundly influences how we interact with the world, shaping societal norms and infrastructure. By incorporating law into design education, students can understand the legal implications of their work to people's lives, assess risks in the system, ensure compliance in the application, and consider the social justice impacts of their design choices from human-centered perspectives. This integration empowers students to challenge and reshape existing legal structures, fostering inclusive and responsible design.

To effectively incorporate law into design education, pedagogical approaches need to shift. Design curricula can begin doing this by including modules that introduce legal concepts relevant to design, such as intellectual property rights, consumer protection laws, accessibility regulations, and ethical considerations. Legal considerations are especially critical as the discipline of design continues to expand its boundary and interdisciplinary collaboration in diverse areas. However, the pedagogy should fundamentally promote understanding about how legal design is a design of information, experience, service, and system that operates with the productive arts of rhetoric, poetics, and dialectic that designers have always been working with, regardless of medium. However, law guides how the collective human action emerges from these productive arts. Therefore, it is essential for designers to understand the conditions posed by law and how to impact its transformation. Collaborations between design students and legal professionals can provide practical experience in navigating legal frameworks and understanding how their design choices can impact the world.

Conversely, integrating design principles into legal education brings significant advantages. Design thinking, with its emphasis on empathy, ideation, prototyping, and testing, can transform the legal landscape. Lawyers with design acumen can create user-centric solutions, making laws, policies, and legal services more accessible and understandable. This integration stimulates innovative solutions for systemic issues, driving much-needed reform and adaptive laws. To embed design principles into legal education, legal curricula should incorporate design methodologies, human-centered research, and a production-oriented attitude that seeks to find possibilities and transform the future. This empowers legal professionals to understand the needs and experiences of the people they serve, creating more accessible and user-friendly legal solutions and systematic changes that work continuously in everyday lives of people who use the legal system. Additionally, incorporating design training allows legal professionals to reimagine legal processes, documentation, and communication and, more profoundly, continue to be reminded that dignity is a foundational principle of the law.

Multidisciplinary collaboration is the cornerstone for bridging the gap between law and design. Effective collaboration among designers, lawyers, and other professionals is essential to leverage the potential of this cross-disciplinary approach. By bringing together legal scholars, designers, and researchers, interdisciplinary projects can explore emerging topics such as legal technology, access to justice, data privacy, and human-centered legal services, fostering innovative solutions for complex legal and societal issues. Workshops, training programs, and interdisciplinary projects encourage dialogue, mutual respect, and learning from different perspectives. Collaboration should extend beyond education into professional practice. Establishing cross-disciplinary teams in law firms, design agencies, and other organizations brings together legal and design expertise, fostering innovative problem-solving.

The principle of dignity is a foundation that is shared between law and design. Centering it as a guiding principle for legal design will promote the positive development of collaborative approaches, methods, and tools for constructive direction, ensuring legal design collaborations are geared toward promoting the autonomy and inclusion of all people.

C.3 THE TRANSFORMATIVE POWER OF LEGAL DESIGN: INNOVATING THE DISCIPLINE OF LAW

As we hope this volume has shown, legal design is a burgeoning field that offers multiple opportunities for continued improvement and innovation in the law and how people access it. It encompasses a range of practices, methodologies, and principles aimed at revolutionizing how legal processes are approached and executed.

One of the key contributions of legal design is its ability to enhance human-centeredness in the legal field. By incorporating user-centric approaches, legal design improves the experience of stakeholders in legal services and information. By making legal processes more understandable, accessible, and engaging, legal design fosters citizen engagement and empowers individuals to actively participate in the legal system. More profoundly, legal design serves as a beacon highlighting law's history as a collective human construction aimed at improving society and people's lives.

Legal design is not only about increasing the accessibility of legal documents or digital interfaces. By simplifying complex legal language and processes, legal design fundamentally bridges the gap between legal professionals and the wider community. To be sure, design approaches make legal information more digestible and the system more understandable, all of which empowers individuals to have the full benefit of their rights and obligations as citizens. In this sense, legal design has had a significant impact on access to justice and public engagement already. By making legal services more accessible to everyone, regardless of their literacy levels or disabilities, legal design has promoted inclusivity and empowered marginalized individuals to navigate the legal system. And by increasing accessibility, legal design has fostered public engagement, enabling citizens to understand their rights, make informed decisions, and actively participate in legal processes.

Of course, legal design also desires to bring innovation to legal education by making complex legal concepts and processes more accessible to students and legal professionals for the future development of the field. By incorporating design methods principles and skills, legal education becomes more interactive, practical, engaging, and, above all, human-centered and forward looking. Legal design empowers learners to think creatively, problem-solve, and understand the real-world implications of legal principles with a focus on the citizens. This transformative approach to legal education can equip future legal professionals with the skills and mindset necessary to navigate the evolving legal landscape.

By introducing new thinking paradigms, employing cutting-edge technologies, and embracing humanistic principles, legal design fundamentally transforms the legal field. It enhances human-centeredness, improves access to legal information, enhances efficiency, promotes access to justice, and brings innovation to legal education. As the field of legal design continues to evolve, it holds immense potential to reshape the legal profession, making it more accessible, inclusive, and responsive to the needs of individuals and communities.

C.4 CONCLUSION

As we envision the future and endeavor to rectify and mend the wounds of the past, legal design emerges as a compelling approach to foster dignity, equality, and empowerment within the realm of law. By integrating design principles and methodologies, legal systems can undergo a profound transformation, operating on a foundation of consistent principles that guarantee fairness, equality, and the absence of discrimination in laws and policies. Access to justice assumes a central role, with legal procedures and processes deliberately crafted to be user-friendly, readily comprehensible, and more accessible.

Respecting human rights is a fundamental principle in the realm of legal design. It requires aligning laws and policies with internationally recognized human rights standards, carefully navigating the ethical and legal considerations of AI design, and emphasizing transparency, accountability, and fairness in decision-making processes. By proactively mitigating potential harms and safeguarding individual rights, legal design ensures that technology is utilized responsibly and ethically.

Furthermore, legal design empowers individuals to actively participate in society and exercise their autonomy. Through the creation of transparent and accessible legal procedures and processes, legal professionals enable individuals to navigate the complexities of the legal system with confidence. This fosters inclusivity and ensures that legal mechanisms are not only comprehensive but also user-centric, amplifying the voices and agency of all individuals. Legal design also influences how people treat each other in everyday interactions, promoting respect for individual and cultural diversity in legal systems.

In sum, legal design serves as a transformative force within the legal landscape. By embracing design thinking and human-centered approaches, legal professionals have the ability to reshape legal systems. The field of legal design thrives on collaboration and encourages participation from diverse disciplines and perspectives. Together, we can co-create systems and tools that redefine emerging problems, dismantle barriers, and foster a more inclusive and equitable society. Recognizing that the effectiveness of our solutions is intricately tied to the individuals who design them, we wholeheartedly embrace the potential of legal design as a collective process. Our goal is to shape a future where justice transcends privilege, becoming a right accessible to all. This pursuit demands an unwavering commitment to both safeguarding and improving the legal system. It is a transformative journey that requires time, persistence, and collective effort.

Through the fusion of our diverse expertise and collaborative endeavors, people actually possess the power to ignite change and mold a legal landscape that truly serves the diverse needs of individuals and communities. In order to achieve this, we must forge a path toward a society built and guided by human rights, autonomy, and respect – visions that are well within our reach and deserving of our unwavering dedication. As we embark on this extraordinary journey, we recognize our agency and tap into the wellspring of our imagination, actively working together to co-create a future where fairness prevails.

The time to act is now. Let us unite in our renewed and continuous commitment to reimagining the legal landscape with unwavering integrity, fully aware that the true power lies in our collective action. Together, we have the capacity to bring about meaningful change and foster a society where justice is not just an ideal but a living reality for all.

Index